With best wishes!

Martha Sue Stroud

For Love of Country
The price of freedom

For Love of Country
The price of freedom

Martha Sue Stroud

NORTEX PRESS ❖ Austin, Texas

FIRST EDITION

Copyright © 2000
By Martha Sue Stroud

Manufactured in the United States of America
By Nortex Press
A Division of Sunbelt Media
Austin, Texas

ALL RIGHTS RESERVED.

Contents

Preface v
Early Beginnings 1
Gray and Blue - Some Who Served 21
World War I - The War to End All Wars 42
Hard Times 88
Day of Infamy - December 7, 1941 105
The War Years in Europe 122
The War Years in the Pacific 137
News of Our Men and Women in Service 160
The Forties 179
In the Line of Duty 204
Lest We Forget 220
Summary 539
Endnotes 541
Index 545

Preface

After writing *Gateway to Texas—History of Red River County* three years ago, I knew that I wanted to write another book to continue on through the time of World War II. When I realized that 1,000 veterans were dying each day in our country, I knew the book had to be written to preserve their stories, along with memories of those who served before. I greatly regret that space would not allow me to continue on through the Korean War, Viet Nam War, Desert Storm and other peace keeping missions.

Many people came forward with family histories, and the first chapter is about those early beginnings. Then more was brought to my attention about the Civil War; hence, the next chapter about those men who wore the gray and blue. It was so interesting to discover that there was a Confederate Hospital here in our little town of Clarksville, Texas.

World War I played a big part in our history. I found no veteran still living from that war and doubted that I would be able to gather much information about those who fought in "the war to end all wars". As it turned out, I have written about one hundred men who answered the call to defend our nation. Some photographs were even shared with me. I was amazed to learn of the statistics about the flu epidemic that killed more of our servicemen than the war.

Those who lived through the Great Depression have never forgotten the hard times. Many people shared their remembrances and emphasized that they were stronger people after living through those difficult times when there were no jobs, no money and very little to eat.

FDR called December 7, 1941, the day Pearl Harbor was attacked, a day of infamy. It will never be forgotten as our nation was plunged into war. Our men and women were called upon to give of themselves in the service of their country as never before. Many made the supreme sacrifice, and many returned from the war with wounds or illness or devastating memories, not ever to be the same again. When President Truman made the decision to drop the atomic bombs on Japan after Germany had surrendered, peace finally came.

During those war years many people kept scrapbooks, and from some of these I was able to tell of news of our men and women in service. The "forties" was a decade different to any before or after it. I researched and found much information in regard to "in the line of duty".

Interviewing veterans of World War II for the last chapter was an awesome experience. They are older men now, and it has been hard to visualize them as young men, some just boys, fighting intensive battles to defend our nation. The families of those no longer living provided invaluable information. All in all, there are interviews or information about five hundred veterans. There is humor and there is sadness, but mostly there is heroism over and over again.

I consider this endeavor an opportunity to reveal how great it is to be an American. There are not enough ways for us to show our appreciation for the sacrifices made from the early days of our beginning as a nation to the present time. Our freedom, the right of enjoying all the privileges of citizenship, was secured at a heavy cost.

CHAPTER 1
Early Beginnings

A book entitled *A Pioneer's Daughter of Red River Valley Northeast Texas* was written in 1950 by Emma Guest Bourne. Parts of this delightful account of her life are quoted below:

"This book has been written because the author thinks it will help the present generation to realize and appreciate more fully the hardships and dangers our forefathers experienced as the foundation for civilization in the Red River Valley of Northeast Texas was laid.

Early in 1800 when my people found homes in Red River Valley of Northeast Texas, the country westward from the Mississippi River to the Gulf of Mexico and Pacific Ocean was a vast wilderness inhabited by ferocious Indians and wild animals. As yet the white man had not entered this choice section of God's creation, save a few scattered Spanish settlements along the southern portion of Texas. This indeed was the Indian's happy hunting grounds. How long he had reigned supremely over this section, no one has been able to tell, but we do know it was a long, long time. Many had lived here all their lives, and many had come here in recent years from the states east of the Mississippi because the white people had driven them from their former homes. The Indian was very content in this section of the country, but this contentment was not to last for long. The white men who had come to America to make homes were soon following the red man across the great river; so early in 1800 the Indian caught his first glimpse of his pale face brother pushing his way up the many tributaries of the Mississippi and making settlements along their bends. As the white settlements grew, the Indians, after dealing monstrous misery by treacherous deeds to the white people, were given homes in the Indian Territory now Oklahoma, north of the Red River Valley of Northeast Texas.

Red River became the gateway to its valleys as early as 1800. Before the invention of steamboats, the navigators of the Red and other rivers used flat boats and canoes, and became expert river navigators and made regular trips up these streams. . . . Besides a few adventurous spirits who were always longing to see the wild west, we see the boat loaded with such things as the white man had long since learned to know were dear to the Red men's hearts. . . . Soon the navigators had an addition to their cargoes in the way of Anglo-American home seekers along the bends of Red River. Early in 1800 we find a few permanent settlers along the river from what is now called Texarkana to the present location of Old Jonesboro. . . . . Navigation of the Red continued until railroads were built through this area which afforded a better and cheaper mode of transportation. . . .

Jonesboro near Red River in Northeast Texas was a well established Anglo-American settlement as early as 1817 and can be truthfully called the mother town of many who in all walks of life went to other sections of Northeast Texas and other sections of the state and helped establish other towns. . . .

After the first year of its establishment and for many years after, Clarksville became the mecca for all immigrants from the states. It naturally became the capital of Red River County which was organized as one of the original counties of Texas. . . . .The part that the citizens of Clarksville and vicinities had in civilizing this grand old state is of such a stupendous nature as to be beyond an attempt to state. It is enough to say though that the citizens of this whole district who had a share in blazing the trails and making livable homes for the generations who have followed, left monuments of love, fidelity to God, honesty, bravery, industry, and perseverance that are as lasting as time. . . .

The foundation had been laid and civilization was peeping over the horizon when I was born that bright December morning in 1862. . . . .My great-grandfather, Isaac Guest, came to Texas with his family long before Texas became a Republic. He built the first log cabin on what is known as Guest's Prairie. His son, my grandfather, John Martin Guest, built the first log cabin on the edge of Blossom Prairie more than one hundred years ago. . . . .This is no other than the home of John Nance Garner's mother for which a Texas Centennial Marker has been placed as John's birthplace. . . . .

Life was sometimes made sad for us at home when we would hear of some great disaster or some of our dear people would die. It was September 1900 when the whole world was grieved at the awful destructive storm that struck Galveston, killing thousands of people and destroying millions of dollars worth of property. . . . . It was another sad time for the nation when our dear beloved President, William McKinley, was assassinated, September 1901. And there was the sinking of the Titanic, with many of its passengers, April 14, 1912, that caused grief throughout the world. In 1906 we read with horror about that awful earthquake that brought death and destruction to San Francisco, California. . . .

Influenza is a new disease to the people of America, especially the younger generations. Yet in the winter of 1918, we all became very well acquainted with it. The epidemic which was sweeping the warring nations of Europe came with the wind across the oceans to America. Such an awful experience we had never had was thrust upon the people here. Our American boys had been sent across the seas to fight in that awful thing they call the World War. We thought it was a sad time when we saw those dear boys, just budding into manhood, take the train to leave for foreign fields, some to never return, and some to return invalids for life and others with such horrible thoughts as to never care to talk about the horrible experiences. Then the news came that Armistice was signed. People were sick and many dying with the influenza, yet the well who could were rejoicing everywhere, and preparations were made to welcome the boys home and programs given to honor their return. . . . ."[1]

★★★

In the early part of the last century, thousands of Americans pulled up stakes, carved "GTT" (Gone to Texas) on the nearest tree and headed for the promised land of East Texas. Many of the settlers had a lasting impact on their newly adopted land. Among them were the remarkable Latimers.

Patriarch James Latimer had led his family from Tennessee, crossing the Red River during the winter of 1833 and settling on land just east of present day Clarksville. They brought with them 50 slaves, necessary tools for farming, equipment for setting up a blacksmith shop, some furniture for their new homes. One of the very first things the Latimers did after arriving in Texas was to help establish a worship center, the Shiloh Presbyterian Church. . . . .

James Latimer, called 'Jimmy' by his friends, soon got into politics. At the time, that portion of Northeast Texas actually was claimed by both the U. S. and Mexico. In 1834 Jimmy was elected to the Arkansas Territorial Legislature. However, Jimmy's three sons, Albert, James Wellington and Henry Russell, became involved in Texas politics, eventually enlisting in the army to fight Mexican Dictator, Santa Anna. Albert rode his mule all the way to Washington-on-the-Brazos to help draw up and sign the Texas Declaration of Independence in 1836.

James Wellington studied law and was admitted to the bar at the age of 19, setting up a practice at Paris in Lamar County. He fought in the Mexican War, returned to Paris and accepted the editor's position of the local newspaper. One day he came home and announced to his wife, Lucy, that they were moving to a tiny burg on the banks of the Trinity River, a community called Dallas. He and Lucy loaded their belongings and printing press onto an ox cart and began the weeks-long trip to Dallas, which at the time boasted a population of 200 people. He wanted to call his paper the Cedar Snag, but Lucy convinced him to name it the Dallas Herald. It was to be Dallas' first newspaper (complete with a motto across the front page that read, 'Our Country, May She Always Be Right, but Right or Wrong, Our Country'). . . . .

Politics always played an important role in the life of the Latimers. James Wellington became Chief Justice (County Judge) of Dallas County. Brother Henry R. held the same post in Lamar County. Both held leadership roles in the Democratic Party. However, third sibling, Albert, became something rare in early day Texas—a card-carrying Republican. He served in the Republic of Texas Congress, the Legislature after statehood, and was a State Supreme Court Justice. He also was a Union sympathizer during the Civil War.

There were few families who did as much as the Latimers to shape the history of East Texas and the great Lone Star State.[2]

★★★

    In 1838 Jacob Blanton received 640 acres as a second class headright grant in Red River County, Republic of Texas (Certificate #79). In 1885 he received an additional 1,280 acres as his veteran's donation for having served as a private under Captain William Becknell during the Texas Revolution. Jacob's headright land was situated on the south fork of Pecan Bayou in an area now known as Blanton Creek and lying about 10 miles north of the Bagwell Community. Jacob stated in his application for a Republic of Texas pension, "I served in Capt. Wm. Becknell's company, the first company he ever raised in 1835, served in every call for said Becknell's company up to the year 1842, received honorable discharge".... Jacob was a contemporary of many well known figures of the Republic era. His name is included in the Republic claims applications of George W. Wright, Henry Stout, John K. Rogers, James Hefflefinger, Isham Farris, and William Cole. There is an interesting footnote to Jacob Blanton's military career in that he not only served the Republic of Texas, but he was also quite briefly enlisted in the Confederate Army. In the muster roll of Company F, Whitfield's Legion of Texas Cavalry, is the following notation: "Jacob Blanton was discharged by reason of overage at the reorganization of the army in May 1862." Jacob and his first wife, Jane McAnear, were parents to nine children born and reared in Red River County. After Jane died in 1870, Jacob married Mary Ann Bellar, but no children were born to this union. On October 7, 1886 Jacob and Mary donated one acre of land to be the site of the first Blanton Creek School and nondenominational church. The first trustees of Blanton Creek School were W. A. Ellett, James Richardson, and William H. Hastings. Jacob died in Red River County on February 17, 1891 at the age of 85 and was buried at the Fobbs (Forbes) Cemetery south of Bagwell. He was a pioneer, soldier, and philanthropist. He signed every recorded document with an X.[3]

★★★

    Edna Howison had a gift. She wasn't a fortune teller. She couldn't tell your future, but she could tell your past. The first time she saw me, she pulled a book from the shelf and pointed to a passage. She had me read about my grandfather six generations back, who was a sheriff in Tennessee and married a girl from Virginia. In her time, Miss Howison could do that with almost anyone living in Red River County. Edna Howison was a historian. She also told me the story of how Bogata got its name. It is true that it was named after Bogota, Columbia. The postmaster spelled it correctly. But, when the paper was folded, the ink ran down the crease leaving a stain down the right side of the second 'o', making it look like an 'a'. During that time period, a small 'a' looked like an 'o' with a leg connected to the right side of it. So, when the paper was delivered and opened, the name was recorded as it appeared, Bogata, Texas. No wonder we pronounce it so badly. But you might say that is how Bogata came into the "fold".[4]

★★★

At a meeting of the Red River County Genealogical Society, we were given documentation about the Manchester (Red River County), Texas Branch of the Northeast Texas and Choctaw Nation District of the Reorganized Church of Jesus Christ of Latter Day Saints. This information was taken by Sharon Stephens Black from handwritten records on L.D.S. microfilm #1955788, Manchester, Texas Membership Records, Blessing of Children, and Marriages, 1879-1919. (There were approximately 250 names with birth dates, places of birth, when baptized and where baptized. There were 33 names under "Blessing of Children" with the date of blessing, place of blessing and parents' names. Under "Marriages" there were 15 couples' names with date of marriage, place of marriage and the Minister's name. Only a very few death dates are noted although many persons have the word "died" at the end of their record.) Prior to 1880, the community of Manchester was called Taylor, Texas.

★★★

The founder and first teacher of the school at Mabry was William L. Mabry. He served in the Texas Legislature during the Reconstruction Period after the Civil War. Quoted here is a letter he wrote from Austin, Texas on March 17, 1873: "Dear Wife, Children and Friends, Not having received anything from you for some time past, I concluded I would spend an hour or two in penning you a few lines informing you that I am in tolerable health at this time and hope when they reach you, they may find you all in the enjoyment of good health. I have nothing to write that I know of at this time that I suppose would interest you; therefore, will be somewhat brief, as I wrote you a few days since by Mr. Young, which will reach you, I suppose before you get this with two hundred and fifty dollars currency. I also sent fifty dollars by Mr. Fleming a day or two before Mr. Young left here. I want you to let Sampson have thirty dollars currency if he wants it, and let Mr. Shannahan have twenty dollars currency, and I will settle the balance with them when I get home. Fleming said also that he would pay over to you as soon as he returned the amount the County was due me. I want you to be as saving of money as you can, but you must not let yourselves nor the children suffer for something to eat. Try to procure corn enough to feed on during plow time, if to be had in that country. I will now present you with two or three pictures that I had taken in this place, but would much prefer presenting the original in person if it could be so. There is some talk now of the Legislature adjourning on the fifteenth next month, but think it doubtful. Whenever that time arrives, I will not tarry long here, but will fly with all speed to the bosoms of my love and family. May the God of love bless you all, and may we soon see each other. Your loving husband, father and friend, now and ever, Wm. L. Mabry".[5]

★★★

The following was compiled by Frank Dickson during the 1930's. He died in 1941, and his cousin, Iva Lassiter Hooker, typed this from his notes written in longhand and on tablet paper. Thomas Allen of Paris, Texas, whose mother was Bonnie Dickson Allen, shared this with me. (Rev. Dickson's wife, Clyde Johnson Dickson, did an oil painting of the Jordan River which hung above the baptistery in the old First Baptist Church in Clarksville, Texas before it was torn down in 1959. Also, she was my Sunday School teacher when I was saved in 1942, and I have several small oil paintings that she did for me then.) In part, this reads:

"My father, John B. Dickson, was the baby in grandmother Dickson's family, born June 7, 1826. He left home as a young man and entered the U.S. Army in the war with Mexico and served under Gen. Zacharia Taylor. He enlisted in the 16th U. S. Infantry at Murray, Calloway County, Kentucky in June, 1845 and served through the entire Mexican War. He was in the engagements of Monterey and Mexico City.

After the war he returned to Murray and helped in building the old County Court House which was constructed with square bricks. Perhaps while working in Murray my father met my mother, Emily Jane Lassister (born August 21, 1834) who was then a young lady in her teens, and their courtship began. When father and mother were ready to marry, she was too young to marry under the Kentucky laws; so they, with a group of young people, got into a boat, crossed the Tennessee River to the Tennessee side. They landed and upon the bank of the river under a beautiful elm tree, they were married April 10, 1851.

Years before, a number of my father's people had come to Texas and settled on what is known as Guest's Prairie. By the close of 1853 father had his plans made to try the wilds of the wilderness of the West. So when my little brother was but three weeks old, they started with all their possessions to the far away Texas. Travel was slow and made with great difficulty in those days. Their possessions consisted of their household goods and the unsold tobacco crop which was boxed and shipped. The move almost broke Mother's heart to leave her people and all she had ever known and come so far, and among a people she absolutely knew nothing about. There were no railroads or good roads in that day. They went by water to New Orleans, then back up the Mississippi River to Shreveport, and from there up the Red River to Jefferson, Texas. By private conveyance they came on to Red River County and lived the first year east of Detroit. From this place they moved out to the edge of the prairie near Old Starksville where they lived for three or four years. While living here, they lost their home and most of its contents by fire. This was a great loss to a young couple in a new country among strangers and just starting out in life. Don't know how long they lived here in their little house on the prairie at the edge of the big woods.

Uncle Bill was a tanner by trade and wanted to live where he could have access to the timber and get bark for tanning purposes. Casting about for a suitable location, they decided to settle on tracts of land about one mile south of the Cuthand Creek and ten miles south from Clarksville. This brought the two families down to the Pine Branch Community where they located and built their homes. Here father and mother lived for many years and reared a large family. This was prior to the Civil War. The country was unsettled and few families lived in the big woods.

Father with his ax felled the trees and hewed his house and farm from the wilderness-like country. The woods were full of wild turkey, squirrels, deer and other animals. The streams of water were full of fish. Hogs fattened and the range was fine for the stock. They did not have much money, but at that time, it did not require so much.

During the early years of this pioneer home, the cruel War Between the States broke out in 1861. The South called for men. March 10, 1862 father enlisted in Capt. John M. Bivin's Company H, Whitfield's Legion, serving some time in Whitfield's command. He was transferred to Gould's 23rd Texas Cavalry, Capt. M. L. Sims' Company where he served until the end of the war. For four years he endured the hardships of a Confederate soldier. He engaged in some of the fierce battles of the war. He was neither captured or wounded. A bullet passed through his cap and grained the skin on the top of his head.

Only those who passed through those trying years know anything of the trials, hardships and sorrows of those awful days. When father went away to the war, Mother was left with the little children and no protection. A Negro lad had been working some for Father. When Father was ready to go to war, he said to this boy, 'Dan, I want you to take care of Miss Jane and the little children while I'm gone; don't let anything harm them.' The boy promised, and Mother said he would have fought to defend her.

The days and experiences of the terrible Civil War can never all be told. Only our mothers who skimped and struggled through those dark days know what it all means. They drank of the cup to its bitter dregs. My mother's lot was hard and lonely during those trying years—four small children when father was called away, and the twins, Mary Ester and Lemuel Jackson, born after he left for the war. The wonder is how she did get along and keep the children and home together. How I wish I could hear and write down from her own lips the story of the four years of experience with the problems of life and her little family—what courage, what persistence, what patience only God knows.

She had to get the cotton and wool, card and spin the rolls to get the thread out of which to weave the cloth for their clothes. The South could not clothe her soldiers, and Mother had to make father's clothes and send them to him. God bless the memory of the women of the South, and may their noble deeds be an inspiration to generations yet unborn.

The war over, Father returned to his little family and all but destroyed home, with courage to face disaster on every hand and undertake the rebuilding of his home. Time marches on and the family went forward in clearing the land and building the home under the trying privations of those early days.

Volumes could be written of the happenings of those happy days. Time moved on, and we all grew older, and many changes and experiences were noted in the Dickson family. When father was not able to care for the farm, they decided to move to Clarksville. On December 21, 1900, they moved into the home here. It was hard for them to adjust themselves to the change, and father was never reconciled to the ways of town life. It was too confining. He worked and made a fine garden, kept his horse and buggy and made many trips back to the farm and to church."

★★★

Mary Jane DeBerry Lowry of Blossom, Texas shared the following about her family. Clarence Charles and Genevieve Moseley DeBerry were her parents. Mr. DeBerry was engaged in the brokerage and cotton businesses for many years and then was a cattle trader and rancher. Mrs. DeBerry was a teacher for several years. They also had a son, Dick. Their lives were spent in Bogata, Texas except for about a year when they lived in Littlefield in West Texas because of Mrs. DeBerry's health problems.

"The Coffman family immigrated to Germany from Sicily, then to England, and later to America with William Penn and the Quakers. The name was originally spelled Kougphmann. David Micheal Coffman was a German wagon maker who was born in Pennsylvania in 1750. He and his wife, Elizabeth Lovell, had twelve children. He was issued a land grant near Russellville, Tennessee in 1785. The rambling two-story log house he built was still standing in 1978. The family spread from there to Madison and Limestone Counties in Alabama.

David's second son, Jacob, was born February 23, 1777 and was a Primitive Baptist preacher. Jacob was married in 1799, and they had ten children, the first of whom was named Lovell. He was my great-great grandfather.

Lovell Coffman was born near Russellville, Tennessee on August 22, 1800. He was married to Cathryn Howard, who was Holland Dutch, on November 16, 1820. They had eleven children. He and at least one brother, James, and their families came to Texas about 1838 when my great-grandmother, Martha Jane, was eight years old. Lovell's team consisted of oxen and a lead horse. When they arrived at Antwine River in Akansas, it was too swollen to cross. A man by the name of Bill Bagwell, who lived there and operated a shop, let them camp in the shop. They made a raft of logs and rafted people across the river for several days, charging them for the service. While they waited, an Election Day came, and after the Election, Martha Jane found a ten dollar bill which helped them on their journey to Texas.

They crossed Red River at old Jonesborough on the north side of what later became Red River County and stopped at old Robinsville with John Robins and lived there several years. They operated a shop where Lovell and his son, James, built a wagon and traded it for 300 acres of land from John Robins; also bought 300 adjoining acres from Ice Farris. This was located about two and a half miles from the present town of Bagwell, ten miles west of Clarksville, which was the nearest post office.

Lovell Coffman was a wagon maker, and since there was fine white oak timber in that section, he bought 600 more acres on the headwaters of Scatter Creek, which became known as Ward's Creek. Lovell was also a blacksmith, Justice of the Peace, and a surveyor. He helped to establish the county lines of Bowie, Red River, Lamar and Fannin Counties. He was a tanner of leather, owned some slaves, and cleared a farm on his land. A deed to this land had never been made to anyone until 1916 when the heirs of his son, Seaborn Coffman, sold the old homestead to Dr. S. W. Wilson of Paris, Texas.

Lovell was a Major in the Texas War with Mexico. When he returned home, there were only a few towns started and no railroads. The wagon and stage coach were the only means of transportation. Lovell hauled freight from Jefferson to Bonham,

Sherman, and other points west. It took about three weeks to make the round trip in a wagon pulled by four fine horses. It was a long, lonesome journey so on one of these trips he took little Johnny Robertson, a distant relative, along for company. There was a camping place near Jefferson on Caddo Lake where he met the boat to get his freight. When they arrived there, he unhitched the horses, got on one of his saddle horses and told Johnny that he was going to see if the boat had come and for him to wait there. He had not been gone long when two men came up to the camp, and one of them was riding Lovell's horse. They had robbed him of his watch and what money he had on him and had thrown his body in the lake. As was the custom, Lovell had a box nailed on the side of his wagon where he kept the money and valuable papers that belonged to the men for whom he hauled freight. These two men broke the lock, took what was in the box, and also got the other saddle horse. They left their ponies and rode off. Later a man who knew Lovell came along in a wagon and after he was told what had happened, he went down to the boat landing. Finding no trace of Lovell, he went back and took Johnny, the wagon and horses to his home and cared for them until he could give out an alarm. Parties searched and fished Caddo Lake for ten days and nights. On the tenth day they found the body of Lovell Coffman in the lake near Jefferson."

"My great-grandfather, Henry Drew DeBerry, rode a thoroughbred horse from Tennessee to Texas about 1848 or 1849, having been told to seek a healthier climate. He crossed Red River in the vicinity of the Coffman farm and stopped to ask to work for a night's lodging. Lovell asked him to stay on and work for him for a while. He did and married Lovell's daughter, Martha Jane, on March 15, 1850. They settled near Woodland where their first son, Martin Luther, my grandfather, was born December 26, 1850. They later bought land north of Bogata. They had nine children. My grandfather married Alice Jane Gaines on November 28, 1978. She had come to Clarksville with her family from Illinois. Her father, Col. Thomas W. Gaines, was a successfully transplanted 'southern yankee'. Martin Luther and Allie had eleven children, ten boys and a girl, and Allie never weighed over eighty-five pounds in her life except when she was pregnant. They had a large farm north of Bogata and were charter members of the Bogata Methodist Church."

★★★

An article by Jack Dodd of the Rosalie Community which was printed in the *Bogata News* on April 4, 1996 is quoted in part below:

"The year was 1885, five years after H.C.F. Dodd (1856-1914) had married Belle Smiley (1858-1932). There were a total of eleven children born to this couple residing in Rosalie. H.C.F. had arrived in Texas from Spartansburg, N.C. when he was only one year old. H.C.F. married one Smiley girl, and his brother, Herschel (1856-1906) had married her sister, Mary Smiley. . . . . .H.C.F. was nicknamed 'Jack'. If you had a name like Hiram Cornelius Franklin Dodd, wouldn't you need a more simple name? I am also nicknamed 'Jack'. With a name like Henry Clay Dodd, Jr., I changed my name when I started the first grade in Rosalie. No problem, just started signing my name 'Jack' on all my papers.

The first child born to H.C.F. and Belle was Martha (Dutch) Dodd who later married Dr. Jones in Rosalie. They were the parents of Lucy Bell Holder. Then came Cora Dodd. She moved to New Mexico and reared her family there. My father, H. C., Sr., was the last child born in the old log cabin homestead about one and a half miles from Rosalie Store. . . . It was time to expand so in 1885 Jack Dodd started a one-story house down by the main road. Main road being Bogata to Clarksville. Jack's father had bought 150 acres on the road years before for seventy-five cents an acre. A classic home site was chosen, a well dug, and foundation started. Planks were from six inches to forty-one inches wide, at least those that were cut locally. Many loads came out of Paris, and Grandpa would take two team wagons to Paris one day and return the next.

On one lumber trip a strange thing happened. Grandma Belle told Jack to take that old stray dog with him to Paris and lose him because she didn't want him around. So on this trip Jack took the stray with him. Dogs were smarter because they could walk or trot under the wagon for miles in the shade and never get run over. Grandpa Jack left out with two teams of mules and a big wagon and the stray dog. The trip to Paris went well, got loaded up about dark. No sign of the old stray dog so Jack took off out of town toward home with his load of lumber. He planned to go about three miles and stop for the night.

About 'dark thirty' Grandpa Jack pulled the wagon off the

road, tied the mules, spread his quilts under a big pecan tree, and lay down. He looked up and saw two boot soles hanging above him. There had been a hanging. He got up, hitched up the team, drove about two miles, and tried it again. He was sound asleep when something woke him up. He was a tall man, and as most men were then, pretty scrappy. In the moonlight he saw two men over by the wagon. Well, Grandpa kept a revolver under his pillow at all times. He let the men get closer and closer, and about the time he was going to pull the pistol, shoot in the air, and holler to scare the would be robbers off, out of nowhere came that old stray dog. That dog bit, chewed and chased those two men for thirty minutes. You could hear that old dog in the woods still biting and barking for a long time. Needless to say, the next day when Grandpa Jack rode into the yard of their new home place, the old stray dog was on the seat with him. My Daddy told me that Grandpa said to Belle, 'Belle, the dog stays'. Nothing else was ever said about losing that stray dog. She stayed."

★★★

During a visit with Bessie Whiteman Strickland at her home in Clarksville, Texas, she told me the following:

She was born October 28, 1913 in Red River County. Her parents, both from pioneer families, were Raymond (Bud) and Emmie Rebecca Allen Whiteman. They were married January 31, 1901 in the Shiloh Cumberland Presbyterian Church at Madras by Rev. S. W. Templeton. The couple went by train from the local station in Clarksville to Honey Grove on their honeymoon. While there, the young bride purchased two cut glass vases, one for her mother and one for her husband's mother. (One of these vases sits proudly on a shelf in the home of her only daughter, Bessie.)

Bud Whiteman was a farmer and rancher, and for several years he was a cattle buyer. The cattle were driven from out in the country to the local railroad depot, penned, loaded into boxcars and shipped to the Ft. Worth stockyards to be sold. He was just going into World War I when it ended, not having been in before because of his large family and the fact that he was a farmer. Later in the 1920's he was a cattle inspector supervising the dipping of animals when ticks and other diseases were prevalent. His cattle brand was the 'Rafter-T' which was registered in 1916.

A part of his life was spent in law enforcement. When he was Deputy Sheriff under Sheriff Will Weaver, he and his wife and small sons lived in the old Red River County Jail. He served as Constable of Precinct No. 1 from 1928 until his death in 1932.

Bud and Emmie Whiteman had seven sons and one daughter. The sons were Raymond Howard, William Allen (Doc), Charles Davis (Pete), Mackey Donnelly (Joe), Forest Dickson (Dick), Otic and Johnny who both died in infancy. Their only daughter was Bessie Maye. Four of these sons are buried along with their parents in the Madras Cemetery. Their mother died November 25, 1951.

Bessie Whiteman and James Allen (Tobe) Strickland were married during the Depression on May 31, 1931. They had three children, James Allen, Jr., Wayne Dickson, and Frances Ann. For the first three years of their marriage, Tobe farmed. Then he went to work at the Ford Place in Clarksville where he worked for eleven years. During this time he worked on cars at night for people in the county. He then worked at the Red River Arsenal in Texarkana for twenty-four years. Tobe died October 5, 1977, and just a few short months later, their oldest son, James Allen, Jr., died on March 28, 1978. This was devastating to Bessie, and she told me that finally she just had to ask God to release her from thinking about her loss all of the time.

During the Depression years on the farm they raised hogs, cows for milk and butter, and always had a big garden. Bessie remembers the 'hog killing days' when the sausage would be fried down and then put into a crock with grease over it. There was a smoke house where the cured meat was kept. She recalls the hams hanging there and how good it was to have ham and eggs and homemade biscuits for breakfast. These were hard times, but folks in the country fared better than those in town because there was always plenty to eat.

Two of her brothers served in World War II. Pete enlisted in the U.S. Navy in 1927. He served in China and Alaska and was a Metal Smith First Class when he died in the U.S. Naval Hospital in San Diego in 1941. Dick Whiteman guarded prisoners of war at McAlester, Oklahoma.

Bessie worked only a short time at the Telephone Office, quitting when she married. After raising her family, she served as Correspondent for the *Paris News* for six years and for the

Texarkana Gazette for three years. She was Director of the Hospital Auxiliary for eight years. She has been a member of the Presbyterian Church since she was thirteen years old and moved her membership from the country to the First Presbyterian Church of Clarksville in 1948. She is one of twenty charter members of the Ruth McCulloch Guild, a ladies' group of the church. The Madras Cemetery Society is the oldest society in the County, and Bessie's mother was a charter member. Bessie served twenty-two years as Secretary-Treasurer of the Society.

In 1946 the Stricklands purchased the W. L. Nunnely home at 507 South Locust Street in Clarksville where they had lived for two years. The house was built in 1868 by W. L. Nunnely, and it served as a Baptist Parsonage from 1912-1927 where it was the scene of hundreds of weddings. The Stricklands restored the house, and on June 6, 1970 a dedication was held when the State of Texas Certificate identifying the house as a Recorded Texas Historical Landmark, was presented by the Red River County Historical Society. The official marker which is next to the front door was approved by the Texas State Historical Survey Committee. Bessie remains in her home which is filled with beautiful antiques. She has traveled extensively with her son, Wayne Dickson, and his family and enjoys visits from them and also her daughter, Frances Ann Axline, her family, and the family of James Allen, Jr.

The American Legion Auxiliary presented Awards of Appreciation to Bessie Strickland and the late Lela Mae Beadle for flying the U.S. Flag at their homes for the years 1983-1984 on the designated Flag Day. Presentation was made by Mrs. Mary Modesta Smith, Chairperson of the John T. Felts, Jr. Auxiliary #45. (When Mrs. Smith was asked how she knew this, she replied that she drove over the entire town of Clarksville each designated day.)

★★★

Beth Raulston, daughter of Aubrey and Rozelle Denton Raulston, wrote a short story about Bagwell in her English Class at Clarksville High School in 1975. Parts of this story are quoted here:

"If you pass through Bagwell, you wouldn't realize that at one time it was quite a town. Among the several businesses of downtown Bagwell was Denton Hardware which was owned by my grandfather, John Carlton Woodson Denton. In about 1912 he and his wife, Sarah Elizabeth (Perry) and two boys, Lynn and Ray, moved to Bagwell from Roxton. The hardware store was purchased from his uncle, John Rush. Among the items sold in the store through his thirty-five years in business were furniture, cookware, animal hides, toys, guns and even caskets. Their labors in this store enabled my grandparents to raise six children, four boys and two girls. They are Calvin, Mason, Laura Mae, Rozelle, Lynn, and Ray who was killed in a hunting accident at Blanton Creek when he was only nineteen years old. The five remaining children all became teachers and spent many years in the education field.

Bagwell had two drug stores. Reese's was the most modern because it had a soda fountain. Dr. Brook's office was there. Vida Cagle had a beauty shop in the back of the store where she fixed hair for an outrageous price of ten cents. She used curling irons heated by sticking them in the chimney of a kerosene lamp. This drug store was the Sunday afternoon meeting place of the teenagers of Bagwell. The other drug store was owned by W. W. Stephens & Son who were both doctors.

There were three dry goods stores, Strickland's, Parker's owned by Newt Parker, and Brooks'. The men of Bagwell had the choice of two barber shops. One was Davis' where some gathered during the day to play musical instruments, usually guitars and fiddles. The other was owned by Charley McCoy and his son, Worth, and his daughter, Molly, worked with him. Moore's Variety Store, owned by Charley Moore, was a rare thing for a town the size of Bagwell. It was small but well stocked. Will Love's grocery store had a machine that would test or grade milk and also a coffee grinder. Jim Paradise had a very large grocery store. J. W. Turk had a meat market. There was Hastings' Service Station and Garage owned by Gilbert Hastings, and C. L. Deakons also ran the same kind of business. A. L. Cruce's Feed and Grocery Store had the first electric refrigeration in town. Ballard Cruce also had a grocery store as did J. W. Simmons, whose store also served as the bus station. The local blacksmith shop was owned by Emmett Young.

The Telephone Office was in the home of Scott McKinney who was also the Constable in Bagwell and owned a grist mill where corn was ground into meal. The telephone operator was Edna Mann. There was a bank, the Bagwell State Bank, and the President was V. D. Jones. Mrs. Joe Davis operated the Davis Hotel which was a two-story building with about twenty rooms. She did all the cooking for the tenants and also the cleaning. Those men who operated the trains that came through Bagwell regularly stayed there. A large building served as the Texas & Pacific Railroad Depot. The main things shipped by train from Bagwell were lumber and cross ties. There were several sawmills around Bagwell, and even one right in town. It was owned by Doc Dill. The County Poor Farm which provided a home for those who were unable to take care of themselves was in Bagwell.

The Bagwell School was a two-story building that housed grades from primer through the eleventh. When it burned, school was held in a church until a new school was built. The faculty consisted of only five teachers. Mrs. Effie Henry taught the first three grades and was my mother's first grade teacher. There have always been three churches in Bagwell, the Baptist, Methodist and Church of Christ.

Old times died out, and young people didn't even consider staying in Bagwell because there was no way of making a living there. Because of this, Bagwell slowly but surely became what it is today."

★★★

The first telephone exchange in Avery was built by M. T. Goodman in the early 1900's. His brother, Fred Goodman, came to Avery in 1908 to serve as a night operator. In the early 1900's Mrs. Ima Edrington's father, Matt Davis, had a store in Ima. He purchased line and two telephones and ran the line from his store in Ima to the Douglas Mercantile. He did this so that when salesmen came, they could call him to place his order since the roads sometimes were impassable. A. R. Poss moved from Texarkana to Avery in 1913, built up the telephone exchange, and stayed till 1920.

Everything centered around the telephone office in those days. The early switchboard was equipped with a hand crank that the operator cranked with one hand while pulling a switch with the other hand to make all sorts of rings of different lengths. A long rural line would have several parties on it; so the operator had to be careful to make a clear difference between the rings. The office was called the Central Office, and it was just that, with a town friendliness and people helping people.[6]

★★★

Shenandoah Passes Over Clarksville—Great Dirigible viewed by several hundreds of Clarksville people on Friday afternoon, October 28, 1924, at 3:00. The ship gracefully glided over the southern portion of the town en route from the Pacific Coast to New Jersey. A few minutes before the vessel was visible in Clarksville, H. C. Dodd, Cashier of First National Bank of Bogata, telephoned the *Clarksville Times* that the ship was passing over Bogata. Within a very few minutes, what very much resembled an immense silver fish, appeared in the southwest and passed on to the northeast. The ship was visible for fully thirty minutes from the time its outline became clearly discernible until it faded from view.[7]

★★★

Much has been said through the years about the bank robbery that took place in Clarksville in 1926. The picture shown here was in the Dallas Morning News, Saturday, September 11, 1926 with caption that reads:

"The scene of the fatal shooting of two bank robbers at Clarksville Thursday, shortly after they had looted the Red River National Bank of $33,125, is shown in this picture, taken shortly after the killings. The spot where one of the bandits was shot down is marked by an 'X', and nearby where his companion was killed is marked with an 'O'. The four men in the center of the picture are left to right, E. Q. Ivy, Constable; S. B. Stanley, Stewart Stanley, his son, and Ranger Captain Tom Hickman. (E. Q. Ivy was my maternal grandfather and did not come upon the scene until the shooting had taken place.)

★★★

There remain so many stories to be told of the historic events that took place in old Red River County. The sad thing is that so many who could have told us so much are gone now. If only we had thought to ask!

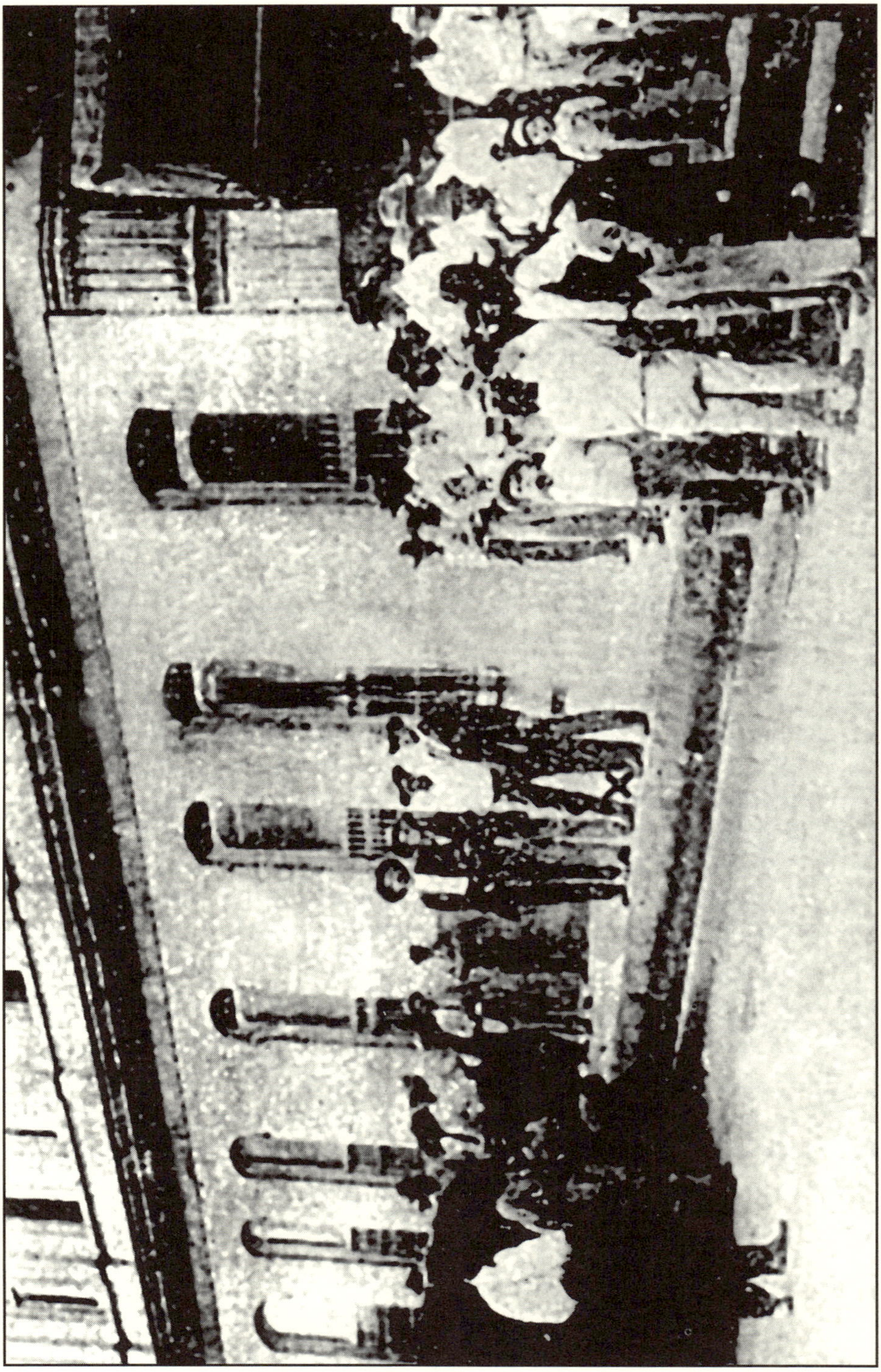

CHAPTER 2
Gray and Blue
Some Who Served

The Republican Party's Candidate, Abraham Lincoln, won the election in 1860 and became President of the United States. Before he took office in March 1861, seven Southern States had seceded from the Union. Texas was one of them. The war was already in force, and many Texans answered the call of the Confederate President, Jefferson Davis, to build an army.

Texas has furnished to the Confederate military service thirty-three regiments, thirteen battalions, two squadrons, six detached companies, and one legion of twelve companies of cavalry . . . making 62,000 men, which with the state troops in actual service, 6,500 men, form an aggregate of 68,500 Texans in military service. . . an excess of 4,773 more than her highest popular vote, which was 63,727. From the best information within reach . . . of the men now remaining in the state between the ages of sixteen and sixty years. . . the number will not exceed 27,000. Governor Francis R. Lubbock, February 5, 1863.

The one great contribution of Texas to the Southern cause was men. Tradition was both made and fulfilled, but at appalling human damage. Whatever their motivation, and whatever their faults, no group of men ever more bravely sustained a forlorn cause. They gave it a certain haunted holiness few Texans ever completely forgot. The Civil War was the bloodiest conflict in modern history, in terms of populations and forces engaged.[1]

★★★

Red River County Texas Genealogical Society Quarterly Fall 1999-Volume XVI had an interesting article about a Confederate Hospital at Clarksville, Texas. Sharon Black, Editor, made the following note: "The document described as follows was obtained from the University of Missouri/State Historical Society of Missouri after Patrick Dolan of Colorado informed me of its existence. It is the diary of a physician from Missouri who was stationed at a Confederate Hospital in Clarksville. The diary is handwritten and will take a long time to transcribe, but I am printing selected excerpts from it along with the introductory information. A copy of the diary has been placed on file at the Red River County Genealogical Society Library."

Baker, J.H.P., (-1913), Civil War Diary, 1864-1865 1 Volume

Baker, an army doctor with General Joseph O. Shelby, was in charge of a Confederate Hospital in Clarksville, Texas, November 1864–May 1865. Diary, October 16, 1864–June 17, 1865, mentions battles of Boonville, Lexington, Big Blue, Independence, and Westport; conscription; retreat of Price from Missouri; medicine; fellow doctors, patients and soldiers; Southern cause; Lee, Johnston, Beauregard, Price, Shelby, Slayback, Sherman; bushwhackers and guerrillas; Lee's surrender, Lincoln's assassination, Johnson's inauguration; Clarksville townspeople; and the parole of Shelby's men, Shreveport, 1865. (28 Sept 1915—Mrs. J. H. P. Baker through T. P. Schooler)

Selected Excerpts:

November 2nd: Our trail is literally strewn with broken down horses, mules, ___, and men. Rations awful short. Nothing but beef & half rations of that ___ & have been in an awful critical situation.

November 3rd: Forage and even grazing situations are very scarce. This road reminds me of the children of Israel traveling through the wilderness. But alas! We have no Moses to lead us. No cloud by day nor pillar of fire by night. What is to be the result of this campaign? No one can see.

November 7th: Crossed Arkansas River and bivouacked 2 ½ miles this side in Choctaw Nation. Grazing fine. Cane excellent. Had a little corn—ground it on hand mill. Enjoyed an excellent supper.

November 8th: Marched about ten miles and bivouacked. A disagreeable night ____ Snowed about day. No forage or rations except wild beef.

November 9th: Marched ten or twelve miles and bivouacked on Post Oak ridge. Quite cool today. Rations short, only beef, no incidents of importance.

November 21st: Traveled 15 miles & bivouacked at the mouth of the Kimiech River or (River of the Dead). Had a cool march today. Plenty of rations for men & horses.

November 22nd: Started at sun up & came on the bank of Red River. I succeeded in crossing early. Command has been all day crossing. Camped near Red River. Had a ____ feast of grapes.

November 24th: Arrived at Clarksville. Established a hospital. Had no ____ unpleasantness connected with it. Formed several acquaintances.

December 3rd: Went out to Dr. Elliot's. Also to see Isaac Lee at friend Baker's. Remained all night at Dr. Elliot's. Had nice piano music & pleasant time.

December 5th: No incidents of particular importance. All my patients are convalescent. Rec a visit from Dr. Morgan. He was delighted with my prospects. Health not good.

December 10th: Returned from Mr. Baker's this morning. Called at Dr. Elliot's to see Mr. Atkinson. He is sharply complaining. Was buffeted by my ride in the country. There are some excellent people in Texas & others who have no sympathy.

December 11th: Went to church but no preacher. Also S.D. Gor__'s. Had a feast of music but didn't enjoy myself a great deal. A man murdered in town this eve. A specimen of Texas civility.

April 4th: Spent a pleasant night at Parson Dysart's. An agreeable ____ even with the old lady. Nothing like spicy conversation but in some instances one might add a little more pepper than spice.

April 5th: ____ Baker very low. His case is surely one of time. Whether or not one can be impressed with presentiments it seems he has foreseen the fatal issue Transferred or rather consolidated my ____ buildings into one.

April 6th: One of the ___est ____ that ever was in Clarksville. Tom and Towie (Tomie?) eloquent as well as salubrious. In fact it was a general thing. 1gal 3 pts pine top.

April 11th: Bushwhackers in town yesterday. They created

quite a sensation. Enrolling officers treat them with profound respect. The reserve corps is small potatoes anyway.

April 24th: Gloomy prospects. News of Lee's surrender. It is generally believed the source is unquestionable ___ be true. Kirby's appeals will amount to but little.

April 25th: Another batch of sensation. Three extras announcing the assassination of Pres. Lincoln & Seward. It won't do for one to believe half they hear. There has been an excited & divided opinion today.

April 27th: Confirmation of Mr. Lincoln's death.

April 29th: The president of the U States has been assassinated also the secretary of state. We disapprove of such deeds it so plainly manifests a degenerate people. It seems we are fast drifting back to the age of the Caesars.

May 4th: Started my outfit to the command under Tho. Grubbs. They left with many regrets but best of all friends have to part. Thus the hospital is closed.

The remainder of the diary describes Dr. Baker's trip home via Paris, Ladonia, Dallas, Rockwall, etc.

★★★

Green D. Dalby was the second child born to Warren K. Dalby and wife, Lucinda (Davis) Dalby. He was born December 22, 1832 in Bedford County Tennessee and died December 28, 1884 at Dalby Springs, Texas. All five of Warren K. Dalby's oldest sons attended McKenzie Institute at Clarksville, Red River County, Texas and later Green D. Dalby became an instructor there. He was a Mathematician and Surveyor. All five Dalby sons served in the army during the Civil War. Green D. spent four years in the army; he was in Medical unit of Company into which his brother was Captain Benjamin Bullock Dalby. He was stationed most of the time while in service at Shelbyville, Tennessee. He received his discharge May 1865. Green D. Dalby was appointed Postmaster of Dalby Springs, Texas July 5, 1877. He married Tirza Quintilla Lumpkin September 19, 1860.[2]

★★★

The following names of Civil War Veterans were given to me by Sharon Stephens Black with the note that all of these men except Robert Nicks are buried at Blanton Creek Cemetery.

William Henry Hastings (her great-grandfather) born Apr. 11, 1845 in Maury Co. TN, son of Cassandra Raulston and her first husband. Came to Red River Co. with mother and stepfather, Robert Anderson Nicks, in late 1850's. Enlisted in CSA at Clarksville, TX about March 15, 1862 and served to the end of the war. Enlisted in Co. H, 27th Regt. of TX Cavalry (also known as Whitfield's lst TX Legion). Stated in pension application that he enlisted in Cavalry but "served most of the time as Infantry". In another document states that he served with Captain Jamison's Regt. of Infantry from 1862 to 1865. Men who attested to his service and said they served with him were J.K.P. Jamison and A. H. Teenor. Married Julia Ann Blanton May 9, 1869 in Red River Co. Died Oct. 13, 1924 in Bagwell, TX and buried at Blanton Creek Cemetery. References: Pension applications of William Henry Hastings, TX (#38772), widow's pension of Julia Ann Hastings, TX, and widow's pension of Nancy A. Nicks (#5350) filed in OK.

Robert Anderson (R. A.) Nicks born May 18, 1830 in TN. Married Mrs. Cassandra (Raulston) Hastings (her great-great grandmother) in early 1850's probably in TN. To Red River Co. TX in late 1850's. Married 2nd wife, Nancy Ann Puckett in 1871. First enlisted in 1861 in the Rosalie Guards, Red River Co. 8th Brigade (a home defense guard). Later enlisted in CSA at Clarksville, TX Feb. 24, 1864 in Co C, Allison's 23rd Tex. Cavalry. Served as a teamster. The person attesting to Nicks' service was his step-son, William H. Hastings. R. A. Nicks died Dec. 11, 1909 in Paden, Okfuskee Co, OK and buried Oakdale Cemetery there. Reference: Texas State Archives record of home guard service and widow's pension application #5350 of Nancy Nicks filed in OK in 1923 (Accepted).

Matthew Payne (Grandfather of Dr. Ross Payne) born Apr. 7, 1841. Enlisted in CSA in Poinsett Co. Arkansas (now Cross Co) in 1861 and served to the end of the war as a private in Co A, 5th Arkansas Infantry. Married Margaret Marks in January 1865. Died Red River County TX March 7, 1897 and buried at Blanton Creek Cemetery north of Bagwell. Reference: Widow's pension application #12012 filed in Lamar Co in 1906. Margaret died 1910 and buried at Blanton Creek.

Willis Commodore Stephens (Dr. W. C. Stephens) (her great-grandfather) born Nov. 14, 1841 in Marshall County Alabama, the son of Nicholas and Mary Stephens. Married a distant cousin, Scynthia C. Stephens in 1860 in Marshall Co. Willis' father was a staunch Union sympathizer, and some of his brothers went to the Union Army, and others to the Confederacy. Against his father's wishes, he was mustered into the CSA, Alabama 49th Infantry Regiment on Jan 4, 1862 for a one year enlistment. After his unit participated in the battle of Shiloh, TN, retreat to Corinth, MS, and battle of Vicksburg, MS, he was captured at Port Hudson, near Baton Rouge, LA on July 9, 1863. Three months later a prisoner exchange sent him home with instructions to go back in the Rebel Army. However, he did not return to the CSA but instead joined John Dickey's Company of Scouts which were in service of the Union but were not enlisted soldiers. Following the war, he deputized and led posses of men (black and white) who fought the Ku Klux Klan which in that area were pillaging and terrorizing both Confederate and Union sympathizers. Willis had a brother who died while a prisoner at Andersonville.

Willis Stephens and family came to Red River County, TX about 1895, and he received his medical degree from Gate City Medical College in Texarkana in 1906. He had been a prosperous farmer & gin operator in Alabama. He practiced medicine and operated a drug store in Bagwell for many years. His son, Dr. Willis Walter Stephens, also practiced medicine there. He died April 26, 1923 and is buried at Blanton Creek Cemetery north of Bagwell beside his second wife, Lucy Ringwall. References: Confederate military record from AL Archives; application for Union Pension for service with Dickey's Scouts (denied); Southern Claims Commission records of Nicholas Stephens; local history of Scottsboro, Alabama. (There is a Confederate Marker at Willis' grave placed there by a relative who knew that he served bravely for the Confederacy but did not know that he had a change of heart before the end of the war.)

Augustus Columbus (A. C.) Tate
born Sept. 30, 1849 in Holmes County, Mississippi. Married Francis Ann Owens in Leake Co MS on Feb 4, 1869. Served as a private in Co D, lst MS Artillery, CSA. Came to Red River Co TX about 1884. Married second time to a widow, Mrs. Batson on March 12, 1905 in Red River Co. Died Jan 30, 1939 & buried at Blanton Creek

Cemetery north of Bagwell in Red River Co TX. Reference: Pension Application #45116 and widow's application #51903 filed in Red River Co.

William Franklin Terry
born Sept. 22, 1846 in Limestone County Alabama. Married Lucinda C. Morgan on Oct. 31, 1866 in Giles Co. TN. Served the CSA as a private in Co B, Escort Cavalry for Gen. Roddy's Army, Col. Johnson's Alabama Cavalry. Died June 18, 1919 and buried at Blanton Creek Cemetery in Red River Co. TX. Reference: Pension Application #23666 & widow's application #36204 filed in Red River Co.

Thomas John Castleman
born March 29, 1839 in Rutherford Co. TN, son of William and Martha Tennison Castleman. Served the Union as a private in Co E, 3rd East Tennessee Cavalry. Married Martha Elizabeth Waggoner. Died March 5, 1908 and buried in Blanton Creek Cemetery in Red River Co TX. Reference: Genealogy done by Janice Mauldin Castleman.

★★★

Joe Ford of Bogata, Texas furnished information about his grandfather, G. W. Ford, who was born in Tennessee in 1834. He served in the Civil War as a part of the Clarksville Mounted Reserves which was organized July 13, 1861 under the leadership of George B. Brem, Captain, and L. D. Vandyke, lst Lt. He served from 1863-1865 in South Texas. While he was gone, his wife, Martha Ramage Ford, born in South Carolina in 1839, and her two children stayed in a log house about a mile and a half from Bogata. William Humphries, founder of Bogata, checked on them once a month. After returning from the war, G. W. Ford served as a Trustee of the Bogata School from 1878-1880.

★★★

War and Political Record of Thomas W. Gaines: Born in Virginia, March 1827. At age 19 he enlisted in Captain James P. Preston's Company of Grenadiers, lst Virginia Regiment and served 19 months in the Mexican War. Moved to Adams County, Illinois in 1855 where in 1857 he married Eliza Fulton. When war was declared between the states, he raised a company and was elected its captain;

then was assigned to the 50th Illinois Volunteers Infantry. At the Battle of Corinth he was placed in command of the regiment and for distinguished bravery was personally complimented by General Grant on the field of battle. In 1862 he was promoted to Major and in 1863 he was commissioned Lieutenant Colonel. After the war he was elected Treasurer of Adams County, Illinois for 4 years under Harrison's administration. He moved to Texas in December 1871 and served 4 years as postmaster in Clarksville, Texas. He remained in Clarksville until he died.[3]

★★★

An article entitled "Descendants Pay Tribute to Lt. Col. Thomas W. Gaines" written by Mary Jane (DeBerry) Lowry was printed in the *Clarksville Times* (no date). It is quoted in part below:

"Times were troubled, just as they had been troubled for so long. A man could hardly remember a time when there had been crows feet of laughter at the corners of his eyes rather than two tiny lines of worry between them. It was a time of disturbances and turbulence; a time of uprooting and planting again, sometimes in unfamiliar soil. Such was the case of Lt. Col. Thomas W. Gaines and his family. Col. Gaines had served in Co. D of the 50th Illinois Infantry Volunteers. He was a good soldier, serving his country as she called him and as he believed. He loved his country, loved her so much that he was willing to tear himself and his family away from familiar territory and serve her in a place completely unknown to him.

A comparatively new frontier then was the state of Texas, so far removed from Illinois as to seem to be at the end of the earth. This was a place of beginning for many, a place of refuge for some. For the Gaines family it was to be a place of change and perhaps of challenge. Loved ones were doubtful if the venture would be either successful or happy, but Eliza and Thomas Gaines were made of sterner stuff than would allow for failure or unhappiness.

They set forth with undaunted faith in God, in each other, and in the great and troubled country they served and loved. Parting from loved ones is always sad, but when the separation is for so long and such a great distance, it is doubly so. There is always the knowledge that there are dear, familiar faces that won't be there when they return. Tom and Liza had been born and reared in the general vicinity of Culpepper County, Virginia and Adams County, Illinois. Home was dear to them, and family even dearer. It was hard to say goodbye. This was a day when disease was prevalent and medical science undeveloped. People died tragically young and babies were heartbreakingly hard to rear, even to childhood.

So the day came when Thomas, Eliza and their three children, Alice Jane, Thomas, Jr., and Artie said goodbye and took a look long enough to last many months, maybe even years. Excitement, too, was in the air, and even tears could not drown it. . . . The pioneer spirit was still strong in the land, and the war had made heroism and courage a thing to be greatly admired. So with the good wishes and warm farewells still lingering in the air, the long trip was begun.

Thomas had also served his country in the Mexican War and perhaps had seen enough of Texas then to whet his appetite for this new adventure. . . . Long days followed, and because it was December, 1871, the trip was anything but pleasant. However, there was still expectancy of a new home with new interest and the hope of a better way of life than they had left behind. . . .

There are places that seem to call to the innermost being and say, 'This is home'. Such must have been the feeling when this little family reached Clarksville, Texas. Here they settled; here they had another son; here they reared their family; and here they were buried after a long and fruitful life. . . . Thomas served as Postmaster for four years. . . . He was a man who could move south after the 'war between brothers' and find a warm place in the hearts of strangers. A man who proved the war was over in more ways than one, and whose descendants are proud of him and doubly glad that he chose Red River County as a 'home' to leave to us. . . . This story is written in loving memory of my great-grandparents." (Thomas W. Gaines is buried in the historic Clarksville Cemetery in Clarksville, Texas, a Union Solider among some twenty-nine Confederate graves.)

★★★

The following article, "Proud of Civil War Heritage" by Margie Williams Mayes was printed in the *Bogata News* in November 1999:

"My grandfather was the son of the first settlers of the Ripley Community in Titus County. They were Christopher and Elizabeth

Rebecca Evans Williams. The homestead is still owned by some of the Williams' descendants.

John E. was born into the family in 1843. He served along with his brother, I. N. Williams, Sr., in the Civil War. He enlisted at Daingerfield, Texas at the age of 19 on October 1, 1861. On December 1, 1861 he was mustered into the Confederate Army under Col. Sam Bell Maxey and Capt. William E. Beeson. The 9th Regiment had the distinction of having served in the Army of Mississippi and Tennessee longer than any other Texas regiment.

Measles and pneumonia broke out in the regiment. . . .They had to move from Paris to Camp Benjamin in Fannin County, and despite their sickness, no pain had been spared to drill and discipline the regiment. On January 1 they took up the line to march to Memphis. By January 25 they had arrived in Little Rock, and the long march had taken its toll on the soldiers. On February 18 they arrived at Iuka and were all beginning to feel better. . . .

Lt. Col. Beeson received his much needed supplies of 788 knapsacks, 500 haversacks, and 450 canteens. . . The stay there was short, and on March 19, 1862 they left by rail and arrived at Corinth. There they found bad water, low and swampy land. They all became sick and lost about two soldiers a day. . . .Sick, poorly drilled, and without reliable weapons, they were about to face the dreaded enemy for the first time.

Lt. Col. Miles Dillard wrote to the *Clarksville Standard* about the 9th Regiment: 'The boys of the old 9th of Texas can never be too highly appreciated for their bravery on the bloody field of Murfreesboro, for never did the soldiers adjust themselves with more honor than they did on that day.'

Then came the battle of Chickamauga. The troops were small and all worn out, but the battle went on. With the number now down to about 1,000, they were forced from the field of battle. They had to leave their wounded and dead, and it was here that my grandfather was captured and taken to Chickamauga on September 9, 1863.

On September 19 he was taken to Louisville, Kentucky. . . Their days in prison were bad; they didn't have coats or shoes, and not much to eat. They were forced to eat raw meat and bugs to survive. When he was released from prison, he and six of his friends started back to Texas. . . .They would stop and work for food. . . .in fact, Granddad stayed with one northern family for over a year.

After returning to Titus County. . . he met and married my grandmother. To this marriage were born four children. My daddy, Nathan Avant Evans Williams was the second son born to this soldier of the Civil War.

During his time in prison camp, my granddad contacted tuberculosis. Being an educated man, he worked as a bookkeeper and raised horses. I am very proud of this heritage that he left. It must have been very hard to fight in this war that put brothers against brothers."

★★★

Two great-great-uncles of Virginia Rose Bowers of Clarksville served in the Civil War. Their father, Garrison Chaney owned land at Avery, and their mother's name was Elizabeth. William H. Chaney was a Private in Co E, 15th Regiment, 32nd Cavalry from Texas. His death certificate dated 1863 shows that he died at Camp Hospitality, probably in Georgia. James M. Chaney was also a Private in the same company. He volunteered at Boston, Texas on January 25, 1862. After being wounded, he was discharged April 23, 1863. Both Chaney brothers were born in Union County, North Carolina.

★★★

Venita Jo Gibbs Oldfield provided a copy of an article about her great-grandfather, John Malcolm Culpepper, father of her maternal grandmother, Nancy (Nannie) Culpepper Bradford, wife of James Cope Bradford. This was published in the *Hopkins County Echo* about 1914. It was later submitted by her cousin, Lavyn Wright Sisco and published in the *Pioneers of Hopkins County, Texas*, Volume II. It reads as follows:

"I (J. M. Culpepper, Saltillo, Texas) was born November 13, 1835 in Upson County Georgia; was married to Sarah E. Stephens in 1856. We raised eight children, five boys and three girls; all married and have families. I have sixty grandchildren and twenty-six great-grandchildren. Am pretty much of a Methodist of the old stripe, having been for sixty years.

I enlisted as a Confederate soldier in 1862. My regiment, Thirty-seventh Alabama was organized at Orbon. James F. Dowdal (Dowdell), Colonel, and Alec Green, Lieutenant Colonel, of Lafayette, Alabama. Was in the forty eight days siege of Vicksburg,

Miss. and surrendered July 6, 1863. After we were exchanged, our company was reorganized at Demopolila, Ala.; then went to North Georgia and went into winter quarters.

Our brigade went on Lookout Mountain, November 24, engaged in that fight, which was in and above the clouds. The next day we formed a line of battle on Missionary Ridge, had a hot fight on the Ridge. Two of my comrades were killed, Ervin Black and John Radney. We had to retreat on; we just left the two lying there.

I went to the reunion at Chattanooga in May, so that I could take an inventory of the mountain and Missionary Ridge, also Chickamauga Park. I found quite a change wrought indeed, but the cannon which I was on detail to help draw upon the mountain by means of a cable rope, is still there on exhibit. Chattanooga treated the Confederates fine; gave us good tents, bunks, water and plenty to eat. There were only two of my comrades there out of 153; all gone to their home. The rest will soon follow.

I have been invited to the reunion at Jacksonville, Fla. by a nephew who lives at that place. If I can save up the means, I will go. If any of the members of my company see, will be glad to hear from them."

Another article was printed in the *Hopkins County Echo* in January 1927. It was also submitted by Lavyn Wright Sisco for publication in *Pioneers of Hopkins County, Texas*, Volume II. Venita Jo Gibbs Oldfield shared this with me, and I quote in part as follows:

"John M. Culpepper was born in Upson County Georgia November 13, 1835 and was married to Miss Sarah Stephenson (should be Stephens) December 18, 1856. To this union were born nine children, six of whom are still living. He was a soldier in the Civil War, fighting for the South.

In the year 1892 he, with his family, moved to Texas, locating in the eastern part of Hopkins County where he remained till the time of his death, his wife having died several years ago. After her death he made his home among his children and grandchildren. Early in life he professed religion and became a member of the Methodist Church and ever remained true to the cause of Christianity.

'Uncle Johnnie', as so many called him, held a wonderful health record. In all his long life, a physician had never attended his bedside until some three months ago when his health became impaired, and even from then on his vitality was very remarkable; he not being confined to his bed much of the time. But all things of an earthly nature must perish, and the old temple of clay had to crumble. On the morning of January 10, 1927, at the home of his grandson, Thomas Culpepper, after everything had been done that earthly hands could do to prolong his life, his spirit took flight and the following day at 2 p.m. his remains were interred in Pine Forest Cemetery. Rev. J. S. Hughes of Saltillo conducted the funeral service followed by the rites of the Masonic fraternity.

The following children survive him: Billy and Dan Culpepper, Mrs. J. C. Bradford, Mrs. Ed Minter of Pine Forest community, Mrs. G. F. Hill of Seagraves, Texas, and C. C. Culpepper of Pine Bluff, Arkansas, besides a host of grandchildren, great-grandchildren, etc. . . . He was a friend to everyone who came in touch with his life, and if he ever had an enemy this writer has never heard of it. No pen of ours can portray the beautiful life he lived. . . The Christian religion was a reality to him, affording him unbounded peace in life and solid comfort in death. . .

Uncle Johnnie attended several of the Confederate reunions, and it was always a treat to him to meet the 'boys in gray'. . . But now this old soldier, the earth-worn pilgrim, has left the ranks of his fellow men to attend a never-ending reunion in the home where the eye never grows dim, nor the ear dull of hearing, nor the body old and bent. Yes, indeed, he 'rests from his labors, and his works do follow him.' May God's blessings be upon the friends and loved ones he has left behind is the prayer of ONE WHO KNEW HIM WELL."

On April 30, 2000 a Confederate Veteran's Memorial Marker was placed at the grave of Pvt. John M. Culpepper in the Pine Forest Cemetery, Hopkins County, Texas. Two hundred fifty family members and friends attended. The program read "Nothing Is Gone Until It Is Forgotten—Lest We Forget". Biographical information about the three years John M. Culpepper spent in the service of the 37th Alabama Regiment of Volunteer Infantry was given by Capos Conley "Chip" Culpepper, a great-grandson, and I quote parts of it below:

"Before going off to war, a popular saying of the time was that a young man was 'going to see the elephant'. Perhaps it was an attempt to describe something you'd never seen before. . . something exciting, exotic, maybe even terrifying—something you had to see for yourself to fully comprehend... Before the war was over, John Malcolm Culpepper saw the elephant more than thirty times. He became very familiar with the strange beast of war.

Today is April 30, 2000—138 years and 2 days ago, on April 28, 1862, John Malcolm Culpepper, then age 26, enlisted in the Confederate Army. Every male member of his family served in the Civil War. John Malcolm, along with two of his brothers, Francis Marion and William Araspes Culpepper served together in Company B of the 37th Alabama. Their oldest brother, Elias Daniel, with the 2nd Arkansas Infantry, was wounded back on April 6th at the Battle of Shiloh in Tennessee—his left arm was paralyzed for the rest of his life, and he sat out the rest of the war at his Pine Bluff, Arkansas home. Their youngest brother, 19 year old Lewis Washington Culpepper, with the 14th Alabama Infantry, died at Evansport, Virginia back in December of the measles. In fact, his regiment was almost wiped out by the disease before it ever saw combat. Even their father, 51 year old William Henry Culpepper, later served as 4th Corporal in the Alabama Home Guard State Militia just before the war ended.

The 37th Alabama eventually contained 1,275 men. Colonel James Dowdell was elected to lead the regiment... The three Culpepper brothers, John, Will, and Frank were joined in the ranks of Company B by their first cousins, Robert Jefferson Culpepper and William Washington Culpepper, both sons of their uncle, John Jefferson Culpepper.

Whenever large groups of men were gathered into camps, disease was never far behind during the Civil War. Epidemics of measles, mumps, dysentery, malaria, typhus and even small pox ran rampant in the camps... By mid-June only 200 men from the 37th Alabama were fit enough to stand at attention on the parade grounds.

On July 25, 1862 John Malcolm's brother, Private Francis Marion Culpepper, died at Columbus... Like his little brother, Lewis, Francis Marion died of measles. He was 28 and left a widow, Elizabeth Haralson, and a 2 year old son, Charles Capers Culpepper.

In September the unit was in its first fight. John Malcolm saw his elephant. It was big and it was angry. The Battle of Iuka, Mississippi on the Tennessee state line was brutal. There were only

304 men fit to go into battle with the 37th Alabama. Twenty-two of them died there, and ninety-five others were wounded. John Malcolm's brother, Private William Araspes Culpepper, was among the wounded. He was sent to the hospital for a month where he turned 23 years old. . .

John Malcolm and his cousins, William Washington and Robert Jefferson Culpepper, were among the survivors from the 37th Alabama at Vicksburg—his surviving brother, Wiliam Araspes was back in the hospital from March until December 1863 and missed the carnage of Vicksburg. . .

In the early months of 1864 the 37th Alabama was involved in many skirmishes and intense fighting in locations in northern Georgia. . . By early March John Malcolm Culpepper and the rest of what remained of the 37th Alabama made it to North Carolina. . . The Union force in the area of Bentonville, North Carolina numbered 26,000 men against only 5,400 Confederates. . .

Today is April 30, 2000—135 years and 4 days ago—on April 26, 1865—General Joseph E. Johnston formally surrendered his once mighty Army to General William Tecumseh Sherman at Durham Station, North Carolina. . . Once again the tattered, bullet riddled 37th Alabama regimental battle flag escaped capture. It was smuggled out at night under a shirt. How it found its way to Auburn University is another story in itself. . . Remember the number of men who formed the 37th Alabama? Out of the 1,275 men who once served, only about 75 officers and men were left in the regiment at the end. John Malcolm Culpepper was one of them. Back on April 9th at Appomattox Court House, Virginia, Robert E. Lee had already surrendered his Army of Northern Virginia to Ulysses S. Grant.

Eight months after the end of hostilities, Joseph Henry Harris of Oakbowery, Alabama, once a member of the 37th Alabama, wrote in his diary on that New Year's Eve 1865 . . .

'I pray God that our land may never be visited by another civil war . . . and the people of the South and North as far as possible forget the past and look with encouragement to the future, relying upon our omnipotent one to shield, protect and love us to the end.'[4]

I'm sure that is a sentiment John Malcolm Culpepper shared because he'd seen his elephant. He lived with the beast for nearly three years, and like it, he would not forget."

★★★

William Washington Coffman, Jacob Warren Coffman, and Andrew Jackson Coffman, all sons of Lovell Coffman, served in the Civil War in the Confederacy.

Andrew Jackson Coffman was in Co. B, 9th Texas Infantry. The 9th, under Col. W. A. Stanley, was at Shiloh and lost 67 men of 226, or 30%. A very bloody battle as you well know and a very high loss for any regiment. The 9th was in Brig. Gen. Patton Anderson's Brigade composed of troops from Louisiana, Texas, and Florida. They lost 434 out of 1,634, or 26.6%.

Jacob Warren Coffman was in Co E, 9th Texas Cavalry. He died of sickness and has a grave and a marker, #24, in the Confederate Section of Elmwood Cemetery in Memphis, Tennessee.

William Washington Coffman's surgeon's excuse from active duty in the Confederate Army reads as follows. He was run over by a wagon and received injuries to his foot and back.

"Headquarters lst Regt
8th Brigade Texas Troops
Clarksville Feby 23

I, C. S. Look, Surgeon of lst Regt, 8th Brigade, do hereby certify that William Kaufman, a member of Capt Yates company is incapacitated for the performance of military duty on account of injuries received on the spine and foot.

C.S. Look

Surgeon lst Regt 8th Brig" (I am wondering if this might not be Dr. E. S. Look, who was a Confederate Army Surgeon from Clarksville.)

A letter from Warren Coffman to his brother, William Coffman, at Lochards Mission, Creek Nation, dated the 7th of December, 1861 reads in part: "I take the present spare moments of writing you. I am well and hope this will find you all the same, good & this is more than a great many of our Regiment can say. One death last night. We went north last Saturday the 30th leaving about 100 men sick with the measles here. We went into the Cherokee Nation & more of our men taken sick & the train turned back here. . . . We are now out of provisions 114 days without bread. Well, I think we will go to winter quarters soon. Young's Regiment have gone. Warren Coffman"

Another letter to William Coffman dated March 29, 1862 from his brother, A. J. Coffman, reads in part: "Dear Brother: These lines leaves me and friends well except our good friend S. Ward he has been sick for 10 days talked all night about his parents and brothers and sisters, not sensible of anything. Now there is new cases of the pnemonia. diahiarrea & flux. Although we have some few days of beautiful spring weather, everything beginning to look like lovely spring. I received your letter which was gladly received. There is some preparations making to fight, the entrenchments only 50 or 60 yards from our camps on the brink of a hill and the enemy is some 15 or 25 miles, also entrenching. . I expect we will stay here some time. Maxey was appointed Brigadier General. Went up in Tennessee. We are left to shift for ourselves in Anderson's Brigade. So I will close hoping these lines may find you in good health and may God deliver us from the increased horrors of this life but at last may we receive that which is for the final faithful. Give my respects to all inquiring friends. I remain your affectionate brother. A. J. Coffman"[5]

★★★

The following was handwritten on the back of the photograph of Confederate veterans which was taken in 1902 at the depot in Clarksville, Texas where they were awaiting departure to attend a Confederate Reunion: "As long as you live, stand by the principles that these old men spilt their blood and offered their lives for—state rights—individual liberty—a complete separation of state and church—a just code that will make citizens of each state love and respect the laws." Mrs. Bessie W. Strickland visited with Mr. Eugene Bowers to determine the names of the men in the picture. Those identified are as follows: (left to right) First Row: (2) Guy Hale, (4) John Sivley, (5) J. K. P. Jamison (6) William C. Allen (7) Big Dan Latimer—Second Row: (3) Bob Gaines (4) William Burkhead (5) Russ Moore (6) J. M. Hubbard (7) William Fulton (8) (?) Adams—Third Row: (1) Matt Aubrey (2) Justus Whiteman (5) Preacher Graham (6) John Criner (7) Thomas Jefferson Fryar (8) W. A. Gaines (9) Mack Deaver

★★★

A picture of Red River County Confederate Army veterans probably taken at the 1921 reunion was printed in the *Clarksville*

A group of Red River County Confederate Army Veterans as they waited to board a train at the Depot in Clarksville, Texas to attend a Confederate Reunion.

A picture of Red River County Confederate Army Veterans probably taken at the 1912 reunion of the John C. Burks Camp, United Confederate Veterans, at the reunion park northeast of Clarksville, Texas (picture from The Clarksville Times, Monday, March 28, 1977)

Times on March 28, 1977 to see if anyone could identify them. This was taken at the John C. Burks Camp which was established in the summer of 1890 in honor of Colonel John C. Burks, a young lawyer of Clarksville, who was killed while leading a regiment at the Battle of Murfreesboro. On July 1, 1893 ten acres of ground about one mile northeast of Clarksville was purchased. A dance pavilion and speakers' stand were erected with a band stand adjoining. Reunions were held each year, generally in August. The 1930 affair was well attended, but only six of the charter members were alive at that time. After the last veteran had died, the reunion grounds were sold on June 23, 1942.

★★★

The Confederate Monument in the center of Clarksville's town square was erected in the 1920's. The lone Confederate soldier faces northeast. The old train depot was north of town, and when travelers got off the train and started toward the square, they were greeted by this solemn reminder of the War Between the States. The inscription on the monument reads:

CSA
(Rebel Flag)
In memory of.
Our Confederate Soldiers
1861-1865
In Memoriam
John C. Burks Camp
No. 656
United Confederate Veterans
1890-1937

True Story of Taps

It all began in 1862 during the Civil War, when Union Army Captain Robert Ellicombe was with his men near Harrison's Landing in Virginia. The Confederate Army was on the other side of the narrow strip of land. During the night, Captain Ellicombe heard the moan of a soldier who lay mortally wounded on the field. Not knowing if it was a Union or Confederate soldier, the captain decided to risk his life and bring the stricken man back for medical attention. Crawling on his stomach through the gunfire, the captain reached the stricken soldier and began pulling him toward his encampment. When the captain finally reached his own lines, he discovered it was actually a Confederate soldier, but the soldier was dead. The captain lit a lantern. Suddenly, he caught his breath and went numb with shock. In the dim light, he saw the face of the soldier. It was his son. The boy had been studying music in the South when the war broke out. Without telling his father, he enlisted in the Confederate Army. The following morning, heartbroken, the father asked permission of his superiors to give his son a full military burial despite his enemy status. His request was partially granted. The captain had asked if he could have a group of Army band members play a funeral dirge for the son at the funeral. That request was turned down since the soldier was a Confederate. Out of respect for the father, they did say that they could give him only one musician. The captain chose a bugler. He asked the bugler to play a series of musical notes he had found on a piece of paper in the pocket of his dead son's uniform. This wish was granted. This music was the haunting melody we now know as "Taps" that is used at all military funerals. In case you are interested, these are the words to "Taps": Day is done, Gone the sun, From the lakes, From the hills, From the sky. All is well, Safely rest. God is nigh.

Chapter 3
World War I The War to End All Wars

In view of the numerous sinkings of American Merchant Vessels in which American Citizens lost their lives, culminating in the shocking attack and sinking of the Steamship Lusitania in which 1,154 lives were lost, including 114 Americans, President Woodrow Wilson, on April 18, 1916, served notice on the Imperial German Government that the sinking of American Merchant Vessels on the high seas, engaged in peaceful commerce must cease under pain of severance of all diplomatic relations. To this notice the German Government replied on April 25, 1916, complying in effect with the demands of the President and stated further that orders had been issued to all German Naval Officers to respect the rights of neutrals engaged in peaceful pursuits on the high seas. On January 31, 1917, without previous warning or apparent reason, the German Government issued notice to all neutrals and particularly to the United States Government that on and after February 1, 1917, all vessels neutral or otherwise and regardless of their employment in commerce, found within a zone entirely surrounding England, the French Coast and Italy, and in the Mediterranean would be sunk on sight. The American reply to this notice was an immediate severance of diplomatic relations, and the German Ambassador at Washington was handed his passports. On February 26, 1917 the President addressed Congress advising the placing of an armed guard on all American Merchant Vessels as a protection against attack by German Submarines. Congress at once passed the necessary law empowering the Naval Forces of the United States to take whatever steps might be necessary to protect American shipping from attack. The German answer to this step was to issue a declaration that all armed guards on merchant ships would be treated as outlaws and pirates and dealt with accordingly. The continued sinking of American ships forced the President on April 2, 1917 to ask Congress for authority to take all necessary steps in the protection of American Citizens on high seas. On April 6, 1917 Congress passed a joint resolution of both houses declaring that a state of war existed between this Government and the Government of Germany, and on the same date the President issued a proclamation to the people and the nations of the earth giving public notice that such state of war was officially declared. The American Troops began landing in France on June 24th.

Of the many unlawful and brutal acts inspired by the German Government, there was none more horrifying to the people of the earth, outside of Germany, than the sinking of the Steamship Lusitania with its human freight consisting of 1,918 non-combatant men, women and children, of whom 1,154 were drowned. . . . This act, more than any of the many despicable acts performed by the Germans caused the United States to take up arms in defense of the peaceful inhabitants of the earth. . . . The vessel was torpedoed on May 7th, 1915 about ten miles from the Irish coast and sank in 20 minutes after being hit; the helpless passengers going to their death in circumstances unparalleled in modern warfare.

The huge German Armies in their onward rush through Belgium and Northern France were within 12 miles of Paris on the morning of September 5, 1914. . . . The Marne Battle began on September 6, 1914. . . . On September 9th the combined French and British Armies took the offensive and rushed the Germans back 75 miles, stopping only on the Aisne River where the Germans began trench warfare which continued until the last few months of the war. Paris was saved by the Battle of the Marne, and it might be said, it also prolonged the war from a matter of a few months which the Germans thought would be sufficient for them to win it, to four years and three months, which it took the Allies to beat them.

The bloodiest and by far the longest sustained battle in the world was that of Verdun, the battle that shattered the hopes of Imperial Germany. . . . The battle opened on February 21, 1916. . . .

Attack followed attack, the French fighting desperately and exacting a fearful price, but gradually being forced back to sheer weight of numbers. Throughout the spring and summer the Germans forced their way towards the city. . . .The word went around among the hard-pressed and tired French soldiers, "Ne passeront pas!" (They shall not pass.), which was an inspiration and a rallying cry. . . . The Germans reached the climax of their achievements towards Verdun in July, 1916. Soon after that the French took the offensive and beat them back step by step until on November 2, 1916 the Germans were forced out of Fort Vaux which they had captured 8 months and 13 days before. Thus ended Verdun, the longest and most determined struggle and the most glorious victory for the French in the history of the world.

No battle in all history more thoroughly and conclusively proved the mettle of the American fighter than the operation in the Argonne Woods. . . . These woods were filled to the limit by the enemy with machine gun nests, hidden artillery, snipers and infantry, yet the American forces with superb dash threw themselves on the enemy with an impetuosity that would not be denied. First over the top and into "No Man's Land" on the morning of September 26, 1918, went the brave boys of the Middle West. The boys of Missouri, Kansas and Oklahoma. They drove through barbed wire entanglements, shell craters, capturing enemy trenches, prisoners and guns. . . . They were soon far ahead of their artillery and compelled to attack a maze of machine gun nests with the rifle. Here the initiative of the individual soldier showed at its best. Many units were without officers, without maps, without food, and short of ammunition. Still they drove on for five days of chill rain, mud and sleepless nights, to a point seven miles from their starting point before tired nature compelled them to dig in and rest, with a net bag of 10,000 prisoners, 14 towns and villages, and 600 guns. The Argonne broke the heart of the German Common Soldier. His faith in himself and his officers was wholly lost, and the beginning of the end was seen by all.[1]

★★★

On November 11, 1918 Germany signed an armistice ending World War I. Out of 2,000,000 American soldiers who served "over there", 100,000 were killed.

WORLD WAR I—THE WAR TO END ALL WARS ★ 45

★★★

"*Songs of the Soldiers and Sailors US*" contained seventy-two songs which were popular during World War I. Printed on the inside cover is "I See America Go Singing to Her Destiny." (Walt Whitman) The most popular songs were: *Keep the Home Fires Burning, Over There, Pack Up Your Troubles in Your Old Kit Bag, There's A Long, Long Trail, and When Johnny Comes Marching Home.*[2]

★★★

In the *Clarksville Times* dated August 20, 1918, the following report of World War I activities involving Red River County people appeared:

"Recent advices from Germany through the War Department, indicate that First Lieutenant **John A. White**, who was reported in a German prison several weeks ago, is now stationed at Camp Limburg, one of the German prison camps. **Leslie Floyd**, who has been stationed at Jacksonville, Fla, was recently transferred to Mobile, Ala. He expects to be on his way to France shortly. **Nelson Walker** returned last week to his post in the Navy after a visit with relatives in Red River County. **Lee Aikin** arrived home Friday from the Army. **Chas. Murrie**, former County Surveyor of Red River County has volunteered for service in the Army. **Will Presley** arrived this week from the Navy. **Louis Counts** who has been taking a course in mechanical training at the A&M College, was transferred to Jacksonville, Fla. **Howard Roberts** has arrived safely in France. **Roy Nance** is supposed to have arrived in France. **Bruce Bland**, who has been critically ill with pneumonia at Mare Island is reported to be out of danger. **Elwin Shackelford** is now stationed at San Diego. **Fulton Latimer** has safely arrived in France. **Ellis Goodman** of the American Expeditionary Forces, writes that he has been sixty miles beyond the German lines in observation flights. **Leonard Emery** has been transferred to an Eastern Camp. **Bryan Shoffner**, cashier of the Russell Exchange Bank of Annona, will enter training camp in the near future."

★★★

From the *Clarksville Times* dated September 1918 the following activities were listed:

46 ★ FOR LOVE OF COUNTRY THE PRICE OF FREEDOM

A group of World War I soldiers as shown in "Songs of the Soldiers and Sailors US"

"**Dr. Clifford McCain**, the Bogata Dentist, was summoned to Camp Cody, N. M. to enter Army Service in the dental department. **Moorman Sivley** who has been in the Navy several years, will spend several days with his parents, Mr. & Mrs. B. S. Sivley. **Elmer Medford** and **Pat Rhodes** of Avery have arrived safely overseas. W. J. Roberts of Bogata has received a message from the War Department stating that his son, **Ethel Roberts**, the first River County boy to be killed in France, met death on July 18. He was thirty-one years old. **Carl Wright Johnson** has been transferred to an officers' training camp. Wm. M. Grady has arrived in France. **George B. Cook** of Clarksville has arrived safely across. **Ben Marable** has been promoted to Captain. Marable was one of the first volunteers to leave Clarksville. **Chas. Ward** has been home on furlough. **Cpl. James Parker** is here visiting his folks. **Ballard Dinwiddie** is now a Captain. **Peyton West** is a Captain. **Jack Patterson** is in the Marines at Washington, D.C.

Thirty-five Negroes were sent to Camp Bowie from Red River County: **Gus Wood**, Bogata; **Ben Coleman**, Annona; **Samp Bridges**, Vesey; **Essien Fowler**, Vandalia; **Jess Austin**, Annona; **Thos. Mason**, Sherry; **Anzett Brown**, Clarksville; **Frank Sims**, Davenport; **Floyd McCrary**, Annona; **Scott Middleton**, Bagwell; **Hubert Frederick**, Clarksville; **Frank Steward**, Bogata; **Cap Houston**, Vesey; **Charles Baker**, Annona; **Mose Gray**, Annona; **Fred Harris**, Detroit; **Jess Stilwell**, Madras; **Floyd Guarke**, Vandalia; **Robt. Gray**, Clarksville; **Luther Booker**, Annona; **Ray Moore**, Clarksville; **Robt. Mims**, Annona; **Will Jones**, Kanawha; **Walton Thomas**, Sherry; **Wm. Adkins**, Riverview; **Steve Wright**, Riverview; **Caraway Sterling**, Vesey; **Joe Noels**, Scrap; **Jake Bratton**, Annona; **McKinley Walker**, Clarksville; **Dan Wilson**, Avery, **Jerome Kirby**, Ft. Worth; **Will Jackson**, Blakeney; **Dot Martin**, Annona; **Ulestus Logan**, Manchester; **Henry Jone**s, Clarksville."

★★★

Casualty reports added a grim note to war news as revealed in the *Clarksville Times* in 1918:

"Latest casualty list contained the name of another Red River County boy who has been buried on French soil—**George W. Garner**, twenty-five years of age, who registered in Clarksville on

June 5, 1917, and who left with the young men of the first calls for Camp Travis. Young Garner leaves a father and four sisters living five miles south of Clarksville. He is reported to have died of disease.

A message was received announcing that **Clarence W. Coleman** was killed in action on the battlefields of France on September 18. Coleman was twenty-five years of age and lived near Detroit. Clarence Coleman was the brother of Miss Cleffie Coleman, one of the operators in the Clarksville Telephone Exchange.

The following have been killed in action: **Ethel Roberts**, Bogata, **Ab Pirtle**, Bogata, **Willie Darnell**, Avery, **Fred Bachman**, Clarksville, **Clarence Coleman**. **Grant Bodwell** of Bogata is missing in action.

R. B. Hollingsworth has arrived safely in France. **Harley D. Roach** of Bogata has been promoted to First Lieutenant in the medical corps. **Ed Allen**, who is stationed on a submarine chaser, formerly a torpedo boat destroyer, expects to leave in a few days to resume his duties.

Another casualty list contained the name of another Red River County boy—**Albert Roy Thames** of Clarksville—who was reported missing in action. Thames was twenty-two years of age and lived southwest of Clarksville. A telegram was received notifying relatives here of the death of **Fred Bachman** who was killed in action. He was the son of Henry Bachman who lives a short distance west of Clarksville.

Alex Griffin, who is at Camp Travis, and **Ben Warren**, at Camp Mabry, are influenza victims. They live at Rugby. **Stephen Dodd** is reported seriously ill from influenza at Camp Travis. He was here during the last Liberty Bond campaign and made several Liberty Bond speeches.

Anzett Brown died at Camp Bowie. He was twenty-two years of age and was employed as a laborer on John Ward's farm before leaving Red River County.

Elbert M. Cook, who volunteered for service in the Army three days after war was declared, was one of the first American soldiers to reach France. **Odis W. Caviness**, son of F. P. Caviness, was injured in battle. He was in the thick of the recent fighting and while chasing huns toward Germany was struck on the knee by a piece of bursting shell. He was taken to a hospital in France.

★★★

The influenza epidemic of 1918 took the lives of a half million Americans. Forty million worldwide died. Thousands of soldiers died of influenza in World War I, more from the disease than in combat. They developed sniffles one day and died the next in many instances. The most susceptible to influenza were children under fifteen years of age and adults between the ages of twenty and forty. Many entire families were stricken, and many children were orphaned when both parents died. Influenza was the century's greatest pandemic, an epidemic over an especially wide geographic area.

★★★

Many years have passed since World War I, and I wondered if information would be available about those who served their country during that time. So many relatives have come forward with their memories, and I am indebted to them for telling me about those in their families who gave so much to the war effort that our nation would be victorious.

Joseph *Melvin* **Gibbs** was born October 6, 1889 in Josephine, Texas. His parents were Moses Calvin and Fannie Miller Thompson Gibbs. He had two brothers, Paul and Silas, three sisters, Rosa, Margie and Nora, a half-brother, Eli Thompson and a half-sister, Mendia Thompson.

On August 24, 1930 he and Argent Bradford from Hopkins County were married. They had three sons, James Preston who died as a small boy, Jakie and Delma and two daughters, Venita Jo and Lovice.

The *Detroit News* printed a story entitled "Life-saving Pocket Watch" in its Special Veterans Day Edition in 1999 that reads as follows:

"Joseph Melvin Gibbs, son of Moses Calvin and Fannie Miller Thompson Gibbs was teaching school in Red River County when World War I began. He taught in Lone Star, Birmingham and Blanton Creek Schools and was under contract with Mt. Era School when his country called.

He, along with four other men, Forrest Milton Scott, William M. Carsee, George A. Birge and Berry Terry from Red River County were the first of the regular calls for men from the county

THE FLAG IN THE WINDOW.

I am lying out here in the mud and the rain
   In a trench with a damp, earthy smell,
"Somewhere in France"—the particular place
   The censor forbids me to tell.
But I think of a little brown cottage that stands
   In a village far over the sea,
Where between the white curtains of muslin and lace
   There's a flag in the window for me.

There's a single blue star on the emblem—some day
   The blue may be changed into gold.
The people in passing say: "Billy has gone
   To France as a soldier boy bold.
A bad egg was Bill; he was shiftless and wild;
   With other folks' money too free,
But we're proud of him now," and so that's what it means,
   That flag in the window, to me.

When we charge on the Boche through the mire and the wire
   At dawn I'll go over the top
By the light of that star and sling steel like a fiend
   And fight to the finish or drop.
It is more than a war cross, all shiny and new,
   Or the best little medal could be,
To know that away in the old U. S. A.
   There's a flag in the window for me.
                      —By Minna Irving, in Leslie's

for the month of August 1918. They were in the 134th Infantry and entrained at Camp Cody, New Mexico for boot camp. Joe was a Private in Company M.

Later, after arriving in France, Pfc. Gibbs was on guard duty when a sniper's bullet hit him. Luckily, he was wearing his gold pocket watch which saved his life. As his children and grandchildren look at the dented watch, they are reminded that none of his forty descendants would be here today had he not been wearing this famous watch.

He had not been in France long when the Armistice was

signed. Since Joe was a teacher, he was assigned the job of teaching the troops who had no schooling. They learned how to write their names so that they could sign their discharge papers.

Viewing the Statue of Liberty gradually coming into view over the horizon as the ship got closer to the home soil of the United States of America was a most unforgettable sight for the returning homesick soldiers!" (Joe Gibbs was discharged July 18, 1919.)

The highlight of the 5th annual Joe and Argent Bradford Gibbs family reunion held September 3-5, 1999 at the Oldfield home in the Midway Community was when Scott Gonzales modeled his grandfather's World War I Amy uniform, complete with cap and leggings. Joe Gibbs died September 29, 1984.[7]

★★★

John Harvey Pratt and James Earl Pratt, brothers, both served in World War I. Their parents were John Leonard "Len" and Sarah Incy "Sally" McWilliams Pratt. Their brothers and sisters were Ella Mae, Zelma Lee, Acha, Joseph Crosley, Emmitt Noel, Eva Onella, Allie Balma and Louise Elizabeth.

John Harvey Pratt was born February 19, 1893 in Cass County, Texas. He and Mirty Mae Swint were married and had four children: Sidney John Harvey, Arlen Leroy, Dorothy Marie, and Nellie Ruth.

He was drafted in 1918 at Red River County Texas and served as a Private in Companies I and K of the 44th Regiment as a Medic and Bugler in France. He was discharged in 1918. He died January 30, 1982.

James Earl Pratt was born December 23, 1895 in Cass County, Texas. His wife's name was Eva and they had two children, L. T. and Angella. Very little is known of his service in World War I. He died in June 1975.[4]

★★★

Guy Even Day was the eldest son of John Wesley and Murta Day. (Her maiden name was also Day.) This was a large family who moved from Wood County, Texas in 1914 to the Bogata area. There were ten other children, now deceased, in the Day family. They were: Caroline, William Steven, Callie, Ruby, Oma, Jessie H., Eddie M., Opal, Ora V., and Mary Frances. Guy was born September 23,

From One Generation to the Next—Pictured on the left is Joseph Melvin Gibbs as he posed in his World War I uniform in 1918. To the right is his great-grandson, Scott Gonzales, as he models the same uniform during the Gibbs family reunion in the Detroit, Texas area in September 1999 (from the *Detroit News*)

1891, died in 1940, and is buried in Laurel Land Cemetery in Dallas. He married Hattie Goings in 1924, and they had three children, Lester G., Anna, and Margie.

Pvt. Guy E. Day was in Co K, 359th Infantry Division, and served in France and Germany. When he left for World War I, his family walked him down a hill, and then he went on alone to the train depot. He wouldn't let them go all the way with him because he knew how hard it would be for them to see him leave. On March 6, 1919 he sent a post card from Germany to his sister, Oma. He said the front of the card represented the Texas and Oklahoma boys and the names of the fronts where they were in battle.[5]

★★★

Robert Jessie Hill was born March 31, 1887 in Simpsonville, Texas. He was the son of Confederate War Veteran, Jessie P., and Martha A. Fletcher Hill. He enlisted in the U.S. Army on January 3, 1917 and was stationed at Laredo and Fort Sam Houston, Texas. He was a Private in the 13th Machine Gun Battalion, Co C. Later this was divided, and he served in the 14th Machine Gun Battalion, Co D. It was with this unit that he was sent to France April 13, 1918. He returned to the U.S. on December 14, 1918.

Robert Jessie Hill and Leola Yancey were married September 26, 1920 at Deport, Texas and had seven children: Wilma Earl, Verdun, Billy Bob, Neva Jo, Martha Jane, Audrey Lee, and George Eugene. (Their second daughter, Verdun, was named for the Battle of Verdun that her father took part in.) He died September 6, 1974.

Some forty-four letters to his mother and sisters were written during this time. The family is thankful that Mrs. Hill kept and preserved the letters in a trunk. I only wish I had the time and space to quote from all of the letters, but below are excerpts from one.

"On Active Service with the American Expeditionary Force, November 26, 1918

Dear Mama,

. . . . I have been with my company since the 26th of September. I was 3 months in the front line trenches up around Verdun and Toue Sector. Went over the top at Saint Michael and never got a scratch but got slightly gassed but not enough to hurt me. I am now in a casual camp at Blais, France. Have been here 2 weeks. I think I will be back in the States by Xmas. I will be sent

Post Card with writing below (St. Miheil Meuse-Argonne)

Trier time. Germany
March 6-1919
Miss Oma Day
    Dear Sister
will send you a S.O.
Post Card. This is
what we wore at to
represent the Texas
& Oklahoma boys +
the names of the
prints that we
fought on. this leaves
me O.K. and hope you
are well. Yours truly

Soldier Mail

Miss Oma Day

Bogata

Texas

American E.F.
U.S.

back to New Orleans and from there home. I would give anything if I could eat Xmas dinner with you, but I'm afraid I won't get to do it. I am afraid I am going to get down sick before I get away from here. I feel bad all the time and have a bad cold all the time and my heart bothers me ever since I came from the front.

Well dear Mama, I must close. Don't write me any more until you hear from me, and I hope the next time you hear from me I will be somewhere in the USA. So good-bye and a big kiss for you from your loving son."[6]

★★★

Bruce Bland, Sr. of Clarksville joined the Navy when he was only seventeen years old and stayed in the service two years. He was a Coxswain, and the ship he was on went through the Panama Canal to the Atlantic Ocean. His parents were J. N. and Annie Laurie Moore Bland, and he had one sister, Marguerite. In 1922 he married Dollie Roberson from Acworth, and they had two children, Bruce, Jr. and Marguerite. He and his friend, Bill Taylor, operated the City Market for many years, and he continued as a butcher and rancher until his retirement. The Blands were long time members of the First Baptist Church in Clarksville. Both are deceased.

★★★

Born June 24, 1894, **R. W. Stidham, Sr.** served in World War I but did not spend any of his service time overseas. His parents were Dr. Joseph and Anna Lee Motes Stidham who are buried at Boxelder Cemetery. He had one sister, Pearl, and two brothers, Gaylord and Reese. He married Susan Maxine (Mackie Mae) Ford, and their graves are in the Garland Cemetery. They had four sons, R. W. Jr., Joe, Dean and Horace. (R. W. Jr. is one of the veterans who served in World War II whom I interviewed.)

★★★

Luther White was a twenty-six year old farmer in Bogata when he enlisted in the Army during World War I. He was a Private assigned to the 5th Engineers. His discharge which hangs on the wall of the home of his son, Bill White of Bogata, states that he had brown eyes, black hair, fair complexion, 5 feet ten inches in height—inducted 2-27-1918 served in the Argonne Forest Battle in

R. W. Stidham, Sr. and a group of his World War I buddies in an old Army vehicle.

France from 10-10 to 11-09-1918. After he was discharged at Camp Bowie, Texas on 3-28-1919, he came back to his Bogata farm and married Bertie Rowden. They had two children, Billy G. and Shirley. (I interviewed Bill, a veteran of World War II.)

★★★

"Veteran Gets Purple Heart 77 Years Late—Los Alamitos, Calif.

Snapping out a salute, 99 year old **Fred Roberts** received his Purple Heart almost eight decades after he was gassed in a bloody World War I battle. 'I feel great. It's great to be an American', Roberts said at a ceremony attended by nearly 250 friends, relatives and soldiers.

As a band played 'Stars and Stripes Forever', Major General Stephen Bisset, Commander of the 63rd U.S. Army Reserve Command, pinned the prestigious decoration to Roberts' chest. . . . The trim, 5-foot-9 Roberts stood stiffly at attention in his garrison cap and neatly ironed brown suit. . . .

The ceremony was delayed by decades because of a mix-up in his Army records. . . 'I am grateful, and if I had to do it all over again, I would', he said. Roberts was wounded in 1918 as his unit—Company D, 151st Machine Gun Battalion, 42nd Rainbow Division—was advancing from Champagne Feront into the Belleau Woods during the second Battle of the Marne in France. His unit was caught in an artillery barrage that included mustard gas. Roberts was treated for gas inhalation and shell shock. He recovered, then spent the rest of his tour of duty guarding prisoners of war near Kripp, Germany.

President Woodrow Wilson awarded Roberts a congratulatory accolade for wounds in honorable service after his discharge in 1919, but he never received the promised Purple Heart."[7]

★★★

Walter Lane Rice was a veteran of World War I and served in France. He was in a company that flew Observation Balloons. He went into the Army in 1917 and was discharged in late 1918. He was married to Ora Mae Nowell, and they raised three sons, Robert Lane, Walter Samuel and William C. (Billy). He lived in Red River County all his life, was a farmer, rancher, and merchant. He died in 1978.

★★★

Walter Lee Reeves, father of Mozelle Reeves Rice, was a veteran of World War I. He served in France in the 141st Battalion of the 36th Division. He was a machine gunner and served on the front lines. He lived in Dallas most of his life, working for the Dallas Railway. He died in 1959.

★★★

Albert S. DeBerry, Paul H. DeBerry, Marvin W. DeBerry, and Thomas A. DeBerry, brothers, all served in the Army during World War I. Albert served in France; Paul was a 1st Sgt., a truck driver, in France, Marvin was a Major, a Surgeon, in France, and Thomas was a Pvt. in the 27th Co, 165th Depot Brigade in France. After the war Marvin was a doctor in the Cuthand area; Paul was a carpenter; and Albert was in the cattle business.

Their parents were Martin Luther and Alice Jane Gaines DeBerry who made their home in Bogata. Other children in the family were Minnie, Luther, Henry, Alan, Clarence, Dick and Gordon.

On November 11th, a year after the Armistice was signed,

Major Marvin Wade DeBerry, a Surgeon who served in France during World War I.

Albert S. DeBerry, Paul H. DeBerry, and Thomas A DeBerry who served in France during World War I.

Thomas Arthur DeBerry was injured by a dynamite explosion during an Armistice Day celebration in Bogata. There was a long string of sticks of dynamite, one for each returned veteran of World War I, strung along the backs of the stores down town. At a signal each veteran was to light a stick so that they would all go off at the same time. Tom's stick did not go off, and when he went to jerk it down, it exploded. He lost his left hand; only two fingers were left on his right hand; his right eye was lost; and only about 15% vision remained in his left eye.

Tom DeBerry went to the House of Representatives in Austin for his first state office in 1923. He was a member of the House for six years and then moved over to the Senate for an eight year sojourn, representing the 8th District which comprised Red River, Lamar, Delta and Hopkins Counties. When his term in the Senate ended, he was appointed by Governor James V. Allred to the State Board of Control. He retired voluntarily on January 1, 1937.

As Senator, he created the fictional characters, "the Splivens Boys", and he gave his colleagues the benefit of an unvarnished version of how a sweating, debt-ridden farmer, living on sowbelly, blackeyed peas and corn pone, and paying taxes, reacted to some of the highfalutin' prospects of special privilege legislation trotted out in the Senate. On December 3, 1936, while Acting Governor, Tom DeBerry proclaimed the week of December 13th to be Texas Turkey Week and urged the cooperation of citizens, cafes, hotels and dining rooms in the use of Texas turkeys during the holiday season and to the end of the year so that the "Splivens Boys" might obtain at least a fair wage for their labor.[8]

★★★

Gibson F. Sims was a Signalman in World War I and served from 1917-1918. He married Mary Bennet, and they had two sons, Leland A and Robert Earl.

★★★

Ollen Ellis Goodman was in World War I and served in France. He was with the Air Service. Three other Goodman brothers, **Robert Ervin, Charles Leslie, and Fred Lee**, also served their country. Their parents were John Robert and Lucina Evaline

Barmore Goodman. Other children in the family were William Jesse, Martin T., Sena Etta, John Purvie, and James Dale.

Ellis Goodman married Josephine Collins, and they had three children, James Ellis, Mary Evelyn and Bonnie Jo. Their grandmother's flag with four stars for her four sons in World War I hangs in James Ellis' insurance office in Clarksville.

★★★

Hiram Chessie Simmons of Annona, Texas served as a Cpl. in the U.S. Army from 1917-1918. He was assigned to the 464th Motor Transportation Company, QMC, and served in France as a Truck Driver. His son, Gene, recalls his father saying the supplies were delivered at night to avoid light, and that during the daytime he slept in a hay stack. (Later in my book, the fact will be brought out that Mr. Simmons lived to have seven sons and a son-in-law in the military service.)

★★★

A local newspaper clipping with a picture of a very young soldier in a World War I uniform reads as follows: "Red River Soldier Killed in Last Days of War—**Cpl. Edward F. Hunt**, Annona, Texas—S. H. Hunt received notice from the War Department notifying him of the death of his son, Cpl. Edward F. Hunt, Company I, 359th Infantry, 90th Division, who died in November (1918) from wounds received in action. Cpl. Hunt was trained at Camp Travis, Texas and was one of the first contingent to leave from Red River County for the training camps. He had been over the top four times previous in November. His division was thrown in action about Nov. l, and it was in the fighting around Sedan that he received the wounds from which he died. The people of Red River County have started a subscription to raise funds to erect a monument in the memory of her sons who gave their lives for the cause of freedom." The Dallas News said, "Young Hunt died the death of a hero, fighting for the universal cause of humanity. Long will his memory live in the hearts of the people of Red River County."

His Father, Mother, Brothers and Sisters had the following published in the paper:

"In Memory of Edward F. Hunt
Born October 3rd, 1891, died Nov. lst, 1918

Dear Child and Brother: Since thy comrades have returned from the horrible fields of battle and have left thee in the silent tomb and have borne us the last message from thee on earth that seems possible to get, and as they bring us the message that you did not fear death and that you had just bowed your head in voluntary prayer to the great Jehovah just a few moments before you received the murderous wound of the Huns' shell, we want to commemorate thy memory with these words from our hearts. Oh dear Edward, words lose their power when we try to express our grief, but we submit to God's will for He knows best.

Eight months and more dear child and brother in France by sorrow driven—Your spirit left this world of pain and went to live in Heaven. We are lonely, oh so lonely now, so sadly we are bereft, but still we would not have you know how sorely we are distressed.

Would not have you know, darling, how fondest hopes decay. For death with its doleful cup dashed them all away. To win our hearts from care and guile, our darling Edward was given. He lived with us on earth a while, but now he's gone to Heaven. Our prayers, dear one, will be while on this earth we are living that God keep us in the faith that leads to our darling ones in Heaven. Your worth on earth dear child and brother had never yet been proven. But God knew best and took you home to live with Him in Heaven.

Farewell dear Ed, a few more days until the ties we had woven are reunited, and we can go to live with you in Heaven. Asleep in Jesus, blessed sleep, from which you'll never wake to weep. A calm and undisturbed repose unbroken by all earthly foes.

Dear Ed, we know God knows best, and with almost unbearable grief we submit to His will and pray that He will give us strength to pray as Christ did for His murderers. 'Father, forgive them for they know not what they do.' Dear child and brother, your sweet life will ever be fresh in our memory although your body now rests in France. Our hearts will be there with you, for we know greater love hath no man than this—that a man lay down his life for his friends. His loving Father and Mother, Brothers and Sisters"

Edward Hunt's parents were Samuel Hinson and Susan Caroline McLeroy Hunt. His siblings were: Annie Malinda, Oliver Randall, Henry Dudley, Cleophas Daniel, Lela Ethel, Samuel Buford, Sudie Florence, Jesse May, Thomas George and John Vasco.[9]

★★★

    A. C. (Blue) Underwood served in World War I in the U.S. Army. He was a Corporal in the Supply Corps and did not go overseas. Wright Patman was his Lieutenant. After being discharged, Mr. Underwood and Nora Mauldin were married and had two sons, Tommy and Billy. The Underwoods made their home in the Cherry Community north of Clarksville, Texas on land that had been in their family for many years.

    Of interest is the fact that A. C. (Allen Clark) Underwood, Sr., father of Blue Underwood, was a twelve year old boy in Tennessee during the Civil War. Their home was in Murfressboro where such a great battle took place. The Yankees took their livestock, crops, food supplies—anything they could pick up and carry—and then burned their home to the ground. The young boy hid in the potato shed out back of the house. He said that he was never able to say "Yankee" from that time on without putting "Damn" in front of it. After the war, the Underwood family came to Texas. They walked part of the way, rode a train, and rode on wagons. A. C. married Nancy Jane Carpenter, and his brother, Oscar (Oss) Underwood married Doshie Carpenter, sister of Nancy Jane. A. C. and Nancy Jane had five children. There were two sons, Frank and Blue (A. C., Jr.), and three daughters, Mae (Grant) and Cecil (Aubrey), and Uta who died at age twelve from the measles.

★★★

    Mac Grady Rudolph (Ruda) Wallace was born June 21, 1894 in Arkansas. His parents were Joshua Bartley and Louella F. Goodman Wallace. He was one of five children, the others being Zelma, William S. (Dump), Glenna, and Harold S.

    Ruda served in Hq Co, 345th Mg Bn, after being called into service from Clarksville in Red River County. He was a PFC and served in France and Germany. He was discharged in San Antonio.

    He was first married to May Rosson, and they raised her two nieces, Ahmoy and Mary Rosson. After May's death, he married Myrtle Cornett and helped raise her daughter, Jayne Cornett. He died October 25, 1965.

★★★

A. C. (Blue) Underwood in his World War I uniform.

Hoyt Bowers served in World War I and was a victim of the poison gas that was used against our soldiers. He was married to Frances Proctor, and they had one son, James Hoyt Bowers, who lives in Plainview, Texas where he teaches at Wayland Baptist University.

★★★

Willard Mabry Rose was called to serve in World War I and took his training at Camp Mabry in Austin. While there, he was accidentally shot in the leg and then sent home due to his injury. He and Anna Virginia Rice were married and had five children: Kenneth, Virginia, Leonard, Dora, and Dan. Mr. and Mrs. Rose are buried in the New Shamrock Cemetery.

★★★

Furman Lee Wolf was born Mach 3, 1897 in Lampasas, Texas and it was there that he enlisted to serve his country in World War I. His parents were Elvis Newman and Lula Virginia Stone Wolf. He took his training at Camp Travis, Texas and was a Regimental Sergeant-Major in the 165th Depot Brigade.

He married Barbara Cunningham, and they had one son, Cab Newman. Mr. Wolf died in August 1950, and he and his wife are buried at Fairview Cemetery in Clarksville. They came to Clarksville in 1930 after purchasing the Colonial and Mission Theaters. In 1938 Mr. Wolf built the Avalon Theater.

★★★

Roscoe Alonzo Martin enlisted in the Army on February 28, 1918 in Wichita Falls, Texas. He was a Wagoner in the Supply Company of the 113th Infantry. He was discharged on May 29, 1919. The date of his death was October 12, 1968.

His parents were Charles Proctor and Amanda F. Morris Martin. He was born January 31, 1894 in Locksburg, Sevier County, Arkansas. He had three brothers, Jullian Russell, Charlie, and William Allen and five sisters, Ida, Helen, Grace, Louise, and Edna. Mr. Martin married Effie Lillian Hastings, and they had three children, Herman Lee, Reba Aileen, and William Weldon.

★★★

Clarence Coleman, uncle of Paul Coleman of Detroit, Texas, was killed in World War I, but I was unable to find any information about him.

★★★

Mrs. Effie Thompson of Clarksville had two brothers who served in World War I. **Ed King Love** was born in 1878 and volunteered for the service. **Sam Love** was born in 1891 and was drafted. She remembers the family going to see the two boys off at the train depot, how sad they all were, and how they cried. Miss Effie was eighteen years old at the time. Her mother, Hannah Tippin Trimble, hated to see her sons go to war, but she said that she knew what had to be done had to be done, and she accepted it. Both sons went to France and made it back home safely.

★★★

James Millican Adams was born November 15, 1893 at Manchester, Texas. His parents were James Monroe and Grace Coker Adams. He had three brothers, Charles, Allen and Joe and five sisters, Ella, Bess, Norah, Sallie and Beulah.

He enlisted in the Army in the summer of 1918 and left from Clarksville. He was a Corporal in the 143rd Infantry, Headquarters Company, of the 36th Division. He served in France in the Battle of the Argonne Forest, and was discharged in 1919.

Mr. Adams married Mary Gladys Davis, and they had two daughters, Doris Lucille and Mary Jim. He died March 17, 1961. Both Mr. and Mrs. Adams are buried at the Manchester Cemetery north of Clarksville.

(I must make note that I remember Mr. Adams in the early 1940's as a Deputy Sheriff and also the Jailer of Red River County while my father was Justice of the Peace. My family lived on North Walnut Street in front of the Norris House which was just a short distance from the old jail. Their youngest daughter, Mary Jim, and I were good little friends, attending the old Grammar School and the First Baptist Church together. We really loved the Court House and spent many an hour playing there. On one occasion Oma Puckett, the local Game Warden, took us up to the Clock Tower, and while we were there, the clock began to strike. It's a wonder we didn't lose our hearing. The living quarters at the jail were very comfortable then, and the cook, whose name was Nell, fed the inmates, as well as the family very well. Mary Jim and I also remember that many times we were walked back and forth from our playtimes by a Trustee (an inmate who could be trusted). What happy times for two little girls when children could be children and really enjoy growing up in a world not so complicated as ours today! It was not long before the Adams' family moved to Houston, and I remember well the day they left and how sad we were. Here we are now though, both in Clarksville and both in First Baptist Church.)

★★★

Geoffrey Winfred Bartlett was the first cousin of Joe Ford of Bogata. A copy of his Honorable Discharge from the United States Army dated July 15, 1919 at Camp Bowie, Texas gives the following information:

He was a Pvt. in the M.T.C. #491. He was born in Red River County, Texas and was 24 years of age when he enlisted on June 14, 1918. He had been a salesman, had gray eyes, black hair, fair complexion, and was 6 feet tall. Pvt. Bartlett received a Bronze Victory Button and a French Pamphlet issued March 9, 1920. He fought in the Argonne Forest from September 15, 1918 to July 2, 1919 and was issued 1 overcoat, 1 pr gloves and 1 bag barrack. As to his character, it was "excellent" with no AWOL or absence under G.O. 31/12 or 45/14.

★★★

The Clarksville Times, July 22, 1999, had a write-up about the Brem Family Reunion which had been held June 19th at Crystal Lake with 54 people attending. In part it read: "In new business a vote was taken and approved to donate $50 each year from the Reunion Fund for the Boxelder and Gilliam Cemeteries. They also voted to purchase a memorial marker for **James Albert Brem**, oldest son of Carey and Ellen Ballard Brem, who served in World War I and died from the effects of being gassed during the war. The marker is to be put in the Carey Brem plot at the Gilliam Cemetery."

★★★

I quote below, in part, from *The Letters of William Henry*

Thompson: Lifeline of Love. This was submitted as An Independent Study for Dr. Rosemary Begemann, Fall Quarter 1990 by Jo Ann McDonald Foster.

"William Henry Thompson was the youngest of eight children born to Fynus and Mary Jane Ward Geer Thompson in the village of Manchester in Red River County, Texas. His birth on February 16, 1891, was in the same small wooden house where his seven siblings had been born, a log house in the pine woods later referred to as 'The Old Place'.

This writer, his great-niece, knew and talked with him often during his old age. He lived into his nineties...

Thirty miles north of Clarksville toward the river, Will Thompson's village of Manchester was a bustling Red River Valley farming community. Many of the Manchester folk were tenant farmers, but the Thompson family were always landowners...

William Henry Thompson left his cohesive, supportive, homogenous, pastoral culture in July of 1918 on a train he boarded in Clarksville, a journey which would eventually lead to France and service with the American Expeditionary Force in France in the Great War.

In a series of letters between July 18, 1918 and June 7, 1919, Will expressed his thoughts on his journey, his experiences, and his loneliness to his two nieces, Mary Gladys and Pearl Estella Davis, and to his brother-in-law, their father, John D. Davis, who remained in Manchester. Will was twenty-seven years old at the time; Mary Gladys was sixteen, and Pearl was fourteen. He had become engaged to Cora before he left; his mother had died in 1916.

Will's first letter is dated July 18, 1918 and is posted from Camp Mills, New York. He would usually write to both nieces on the same day and send both letters in the same envelope. Letters written and posted in New York were on blue-lined tablet paper, approximately six by eight inches, with the American flag in color in the left upper corner and the Y.M.C.A. emblem in the right upper corner. At the bottom in blue was printed the message: 'To the Writer: Save by Writing on Both Sides of this Paper. To the Folks at Home: Save Food, Buy Liberty Bonds and War Savings Stamps.' His letters indicate the journey from Clarksville to New York was long; but he was impressed by New York...

On July 28 he was still in New York and had been to town...

In this letter and others he refers to his wife; however, he did not marry until after he returned to Texas in 1919... By the next letter Will was in France..

Will was in the 142nd Infantry, 36th Division. According to the memoirs of General John J. Pershing, Commander-in-Chief of the American Expeditionary Forces, total strength of the AEF on July 31, 1918 was 54,224 officers and 1,114,838 enlisted men. The 36th Division arrived in France in July, and it was composed of National Guard units from Texas and Oklahoma under the command of Major General William R. Smith. The 36th was originally billeted in the French infantry barracks at Pontanezen, and General Pershing, visiting the newly arrived troops reported: 'The new arrivals were impatient when they could not be promptly moved to the front, which was often the case, and these men were no exception.'

The 36th Division was to serve as a replacement unit in the Meuse-Argonne operation in early October, 1918, to breach the Hindenburg Line, Germany's main position of defense on the Western Front. An order issued October 1, 1918 by German General von der Marwitz reflects the vital importance of the Hindenburg Line to German defense: 'The fate of a large portion of the Western Front, perhaps of our nation, depends on the firm holding of the Verdun front. The Fatherland believes that every commander and every soldier realizes the greatness of his task, and that every one will fulfill his duties to the utmost.'

Through the first days of October the fighting raged in the raw cold and gray rain of the French autumn. The AEF and the French Fourth Army advanced together against German machine gun fire hidden in deep woods, where the fighting was severe, often hand-to-hand, with equal losses on both sides.

However, when the French Fourth Army was stopped at Blanc Mont Ridge, General Pershing sent the 2nd and the 36th Divisions in response to Marshal Foch's plea for assistance. On October 8 the 2nd helped secure St. Etienne, which enabled the entire Fourth Army to advance; but during the night of October 10 the enemy tried to withdraw. The 36th Divison charged after them, reaching the Aisne River on the thirteenth, where it held its line for sixteen days, when it was relieved by the French.

The 36th Division was also designated to take part in the joint Franco-American offensive in the direction of Chateau-Salins, scheduled to begin November 14 with twenty French divisions and six American divisions. However, at 6 o'clock a.m. on November 11, it was announced that hostilities would cease at 11 o'clock a.m. on that date, and word was sent immediately to halt the advancing American troops, scheduled to depart for battle on the day the Armistice was signed...

Will's letters in December of 1918 and February 1919 do not mention his combat experience, but they do reflect a promotion in rank to Corporal. They are all postmarked from LaChapelle, France... about seventy-five miles northwest of Paris. The letters dated December 22, 1918 hint at loneliness, but their tone is cheerful and informative...

Will's boredom reflected the tedium of waiting to go home and get out of the Army after the Armistice was signed in November of 1919... In a letter to Pearl dated March 21, 1919, Will finally discussed his combat experiences... *It may be wrong to kill tho when you are forst to I don't think the Lord will blame you for it. And that was what I had to do, get killed are kill the bosh and it dident bother me to shoot them it was like shooting rabbits runing. After we got them out of the ditches...*

By June 7 Will was back in the United States at Camp Merritt, New Jersey, and looking forward to coming home... Will Thompson did not re-enlist; he came back to Manchester and married Cora, the woman to whom he had referred to as his wife in his letters on June 25, 1919.

True to his written word, Will never discussed his war experiences after he came home, at least not with his nieces, with whom he remained close until his death on March 9, 1987 at age 96. Gladys Adams recalls that Will and her husband, who had served in the battle of the Argonne Forest, would talk together about the war, but if she came within hearing, they would change the subject. Will never told war stories or regaled his family with memories of France... William Henry Thompson responded to life much as his letters reflect his responses to war—with courage, dignity, discipline, faith, and honor."

★★★

Furd Love served in the Artillery as Chief Mechanic on a battery of French 75mm cannons during World War I. He went to France but did not take part in any fighting because the Armistice was signed. He remembered that it was really cold there with lots of snow. Furd had started a cotton crop before he went into service and sold the crop in the fall for a high price and built a house on Peter's Prairie east of Clarksville with the money. He was married to Pearl Reed Love, and they had three children, Furd Hinton, Jr., Alan and Linda.

Also serving in the same outfit as Furd Love were **Lewis Reed**, an attorney, and **Will Anderson** from Avery.

★★★

Oscar Cheyne was born November 1, 1888 in Bonham, Texas. His parents were Josiah S. and Athalanda Furr Cheyne. His siblings were Lonie, Mollie, Will, Effie, Dee, Clyde, Louise, Johny and Hattie. He married Lydia Bolch and their children were Amos Dean, O. T., John Ray, and Joe Don.

Oscar enlisted on Mary 24, 1918 at Clarksville, Texas and was in the 64th Infantry, 7th Division. His training was at Camp Travis, Texas and Camp Mills, New York. He was a Private and served in France and Germany. He was discharged Jun 30, 1919 at Camp Bowie, Texas. He died March 6, 1958.

★★★

Henery Gaddis was born January 9, 1893 at Boxelder in Red River County, Texas. His parents were John and Bell Peek Gaddis. He had two brothers, Austin and Cary, and one sister, Eula. His wife was Willie Mae Baryms, and their children were Doris, John Henery, Billy, Raymond, E. G., and Patsy.

Henery entered the Army soon after World War I began and was a part of Battery E, 77th Field Artillery Regiment. He was a Private who served as a gunner on heavy artillery. The big gun was horse drawn, and he told his brother that his horses were shot down more than one time while they were in battle. Being so close to the big gun was very hard and caused him to be shell shocked, and because of this, he was a disabled veteran. His group fought in the Argonne Forest in France. He died March 15, 1935.

★★★

E. G. Lum, Sr. was drafted in World War I. He caught a train, got as far as Paris, Texas, learned the Armistice had been signed, and came back home.

★★★

Clyde Weatherly, husband of Brenos Lum, served in World War I in what was called the 40th and 8th. Forty men rode with eight mules to a boxcar where guns and equipment were unloaded. The mules then pulled the supplies back to where they were needed. Clyde was one of the forty men. The Weatherlys lost a son, **Charles Edwin Weatherly**, in the crash of a B-24 over Germany in World War II.

★★★

Paul and Winfred Gilbert, brothers, both served in World War I. They were from Tennessee, and their parents were Rev. & Mrs. William Gilbert. They had one sister, Leiron Gilbert. After the war, Paul married Margaret Walker in Pine Bluff, Arkansas. Before their only child, Margaret Pauline, was born, he was killed in a hotel fire. His widow was married three years later to Johnnie Glenn, who adopted her daughter. (The Glenns were our neighbors for many of my "growing up" years, and Pauline remains a good friend.)

Winfred Gilbert married Ruby Wilson, and they had one daughter, Anne Gilbert. Anne married Thomas C. Fisher, and they have three sons, Tommy, Allen, and Bill, and seven grandchildren.

The following letter was written by Winfred Gilbert to his father, Rev. William Gilbert, a Methodist pastor. The Gilbert brothers enlisted and served together during World War I. They were gunners who operated one of the big guns. Winfred's hearing was permanently impaired as a result of this.

"On the Front (Bat. E, 114th, U.S.F.U., U.E.F. France)
November 12, 1918
Dad Dear,

Yesterday (Nov. 11, 1918), at 11:00 A.M. every gun along the whole line of battle ceased firing, and not a shot has been fired by either side since that moment. And all the air a solemn stillness holds. That is the most wonderful incident I have ever experienced. What does it mean? It means 'Home Sweet Home' and loved ones. Isn't it just too good to be true?

Papa, Paul and I are both safe and sound, not a scratch of any

Brothers Winfred and Paul Gilbert who enlisted and served together as gunners during World War I.

description. And oh, how thankful we are that God has spared us our lives and is going to permit us to again be united with the folks at home. It is just marvelous and wonderful. There are many millions of happy hearts tonight—and, of course, there are many aching hearts too. For many have fallen in this awful war.

Papa, the silence is so strange to us. It seems impossible for the stillness to be so profound. For nearly three months, there has hardly been a moment that one couldn't hear the report of a gun and the unearthly scream of a shell as it plunged through the air on its journey of death and destruction. It is such a relief to feel no longer the burden and strain of that feeling, 'It may be my time next'. . . Yesterday was the greatest day of my life and one that I shall never forget. . .This war has taught me the greatest lesson of my life. And I feel that I will return home a better and truer man in every respect than I was when I entered the army. Thank God for this wonderful peace!

Last night the German infantry invited our infantry over to their lines and gave them souvenirs and a big feed. Rockets of all colors went up all night. It is hard to tell which side is the most happy. The Germans are withdrawing as fast as possible. . .

I am seated in a little dugout with an automobile cushion for a seat which is resting on my side of the bed. 'Said bed' consists of a lot of straw spread on the earthen floor, on top of which is a lot of blankets. Paul has retired on the other side of our bed. . . I am on guard at the telephone. For a light I melted a lot of bacon grease that I found in an old bacon can near an infantry kitchen. In this grease I placed an old rag and set 'her off'. It makes a dandy little light.

We are guards on one of our guns, and our positions are right even with the front line trenches, but Fritz is well out of range now, for the rest of the Germans withdrew today. There isn't the slightest doubt in the world but what this old war is over. . . . The Kaiser has abdicated and fled to Holland, and the Crown Prince has signed away his rights to the throne—the situation now rests in the hands of the Socialists. . .

I have lived almost a lifetime in the three months I have been on the front. I hope it won't be that long now until we start back to the old U.S.A. We have just been most fortunate, all of us have, and we are truly thankful. . .

Your loving son,

Winfred Gilbert[10]

★★★

Bert H. Carlton, son of Thomas and Emma Martin Rains Carlton, was born in Arkansas on April 2, 1890. Other children in the family were Claude, Cora, Nola and Ben. Bert married Lettie Crenshaw, and they had two daughters, Frances and Mary Jane. He enlisted in the Navy in 1918 at Paris, Texas and took his training at Great Lakes Training Station, Illinois. He was a cook and was discharged in 1920 in Illinois. His death occurred July 8, 1934 at the Veterans Hospital in Legion, Texas.

★★★

Thomas Crenshaw was born March 25, 1895 at Monroe, Union County, North Carolina. His parents were John William and Mary Jane Stevens Crenshaw. His siblings were Mark, Gertrude, Seaborn, Leatha, Henry, Lettie, Etta, Patria, and Willie. He was married to Clara Bartley and they had no children. Very little is known about his service during World War I except that he was in the Army and served in France. He died in May 1982 at Clarksville, Texas.

★★★

Sergeant Felix Stalls was the son of Mr. & Mrs. W. D. Stalls. He married Dixie Warner who was Alvin Glenn Ballard's first grade teacher. They had no children. When Mr. Stalls was in the nursing home, Sue Gibbs' father let him store things in his corn crib. After Mr. Stalls' death, among the things he had stored was some information about his service in World War I. He served with the 359th in France. Quoted below are excerpts from some of the letters he wrote to his parents.

"Don't get excited when I tell you I'm in the hospital. We went over the top yesterday, September 12, and while I was not wounded, I got some gas—enough to put me out for three or four days. My hands were also scratched by barbed wire which caused them to swell some, but I will be back with my company in a few days. A few were killed in the drive, but we went after them the harder. The worst of all, they shot my lieutenant, and he fell at my side. . . We didn't get close enough to use our bayonets. They ran before we got within 500 yards of them. Snipers shot the most of the men we lost.

Since yesterday morning we have captured 1,500 prisoners. Some were old men and others very young. I will be all right in three or four days and will write again."

"Christmas Eve night finds us on the Moselle River in Germany. We ate supper with a Dutchman. We went over the top in the St. Mihiel drive September 12 and remained on the front until Sept. 20. Went over the top on the Verdun front on November 1; held the line that night and fought all the next day. On the morning of the 11th we were preparing to go over again, but the captain said to wait until he received other orders. At 11 o'clock we heard the German bugles blow for the men to stop firing. We were one happy bunch. Germany is a pretty country, but I have seen all of it I care to. Take me back to Texas where the cotton blossoms bloom."

"Wittlich, Germany, Feb. 22, 1919

Brother, I have a copy of the talk that our Major made to us and I'm going to copy it so you can see what a good one it was.

Speech of Major Tom G. Woolen to 2nd Bn., 359th Inf., morning of Nov. 11th, 1918: 'Boys, before we leave this field I want to try, if I can find words to express to you my deep feeling of appreciation and great debt of gratitude toward you for your work in recent operation, and to tell you that deep and high is my feeling of admiration, honor and respect for your actions on the field of battle. I want each and every one of you to know and feel that deep down in my heart, seared into my soul is a spot that shall always be dear to me, for it shall forever be occupied by you boys, you and your officers. There are none better. You have shown and proved yourselves to be willing to fight and if need be to die for your country. Some of our comrades have fallen, some of our boys made the supreme sacrifice, but you know and I know that they have not died in vain, that their names, their deeds, their actions are immortal, and just as surely as the sun will rise tomorrow to proclaim to the world that God still rules, just as surely are those boys now sitting on the right hand of God, for they died that the ideals, beliefs, and the religion taught to us by Jesus Christ, the son of God, might rule the world. Could God do otherwise than love them and bedeck their crowns with stars? You covered yourselves with glory, you have received high praise from General Pershing, General Allen, General Liggett, General McAlexander, and you are the idol of your colonel, your battalion, and your company officers. Your real satisfaction, your real glory comes from within in that of a clear conscience and clean soul. You know that you have played a man's part and played it well, and when you return to the folks at home with a high head and clear eye, you can receive the well deserved praise and love of mothers, wives and sweethearts. Soldiers of America, I salute you!'

Brother, you ought to have saw that bunch of men. We could not keep the tears back. We was a happy bunch of men. Your bud, Sgt. Felix G. Stalls"

★★★

Joe Lowery, who lived with his wife, Nettie, in the Sherry Community south of Clarksville, Texas, served in World War I. He was exposed to gas while serving in France, and this left him with some physical limitations. The Lowerys lived in a house at the crossroads near the church at Sherry. He owned a small country store and quite a bit of land and was a successful farmer and rancher. He died during the 1950's, and none of his relatives live in the area at this time.

★★★

Louis Humphrey was born December 15, 1896 and was raised in the Sherry Community south of Clarksville. He enlisted in the army during World War I and after receiving basic training was on a ship in the New York harbor awaiting orders to sail for Europe when the announcement of a cease fire was made. The ship sailed anyway but was ordered to return to port after about a day or two at sea.

After this he was a Texas Ranger for a short time. He later married Effie Rains and they lived in the Mabry Community where he farmed. When World War II broke out, he worked as a carpenter helping to build Red River Arsenal in Texarkana, Texas, Camp Wolters in Mineral Wells, Texas, and also a facility in McAllister, Oklahoma. When these were all completed, he came home and worked as a carpenter in and around Clarksville and Paris. In his later years, he was no stranger to those at Allen Lumber Company. He died July 1, 1974.

★★★

John M. Howison of Bogata wrote the following:

WE THINK OF YOU

I hope the censor
            won't refuse
To let me send
        this bit of news,
The folks who watched
        you march away.
Are thinking of you
            every day.

The United States War Risk Insurance is the best in the world.   KEEP IT UP!

AMERICAN RED CROSS
INFORMATION SERVICE
TELEPHONE 1789
Newport News, Va.,

JUN 7 1919

Have just arrived at this port safely and am feeling well. My stay here will be too short (probably two or three days) for you to try to see me. Our program is to go quickly to camps near home for discharge. If, however, anything develops that necessitates your communicating with me, telegraph or telephone the Information Service of the American Red Cross at this port, giving number of my regiment. They will do their best to locate me or forward a message to the demobilization camp. Love.

FELIX

N. B. This information obtained from the U. S. Army.

Post Card (We think of you) and the writing on the card.

WORLD WAR I—THE WAR TO END ALL WARS ★ 79

Louis Humphrey as a Texas Raanger after serving in the World War I.

"My father, **William Clatterbuck "Buck" Howison** (1891-1948) was drafted in 1917 and sent to Corpus Christi, Texas for training. During his stay there, Sam Hughston, Superintendent of Schools hailing originally from Clarksville, and his wife did their bit for the war effort by entertaining him and other doughboys (with priority to those from their home area). This included Sunday dinners and automobile tours of the city. Shortly before his departure for Newport News, Virginia and embarkation for France, Buck's father and at least one sister (Virginia, later Mrs. Rom Bishop) went by train to Corpus for what they feared would be a last sight of son and sibling.

During the visit the senior Howison (Neil M.) gave his only son fifty dollars—a substantial sum in those days. The gift, which detracted from support of other family needs, clearly reflected a father's rather desperate effort to share in his offspring's potential sacrifice.

For both the doughboy and his family, memories of the Civil War conditioned their expectations about World War I. Neil Howison's two eldest brothers died at Gettysburg and Petersburg, and a third had suffered as a prisoner of war. Neither of the deaths had been 'neat'. The folk memory of the Civil War had not involved a merely abstract fear of death, but a personal awareness that military service involved loneliness and the prospect of disease and convalescence without benefit of loving attendance.

Buck was also aware that military training discipline (later known euphemistically as 'chicken') was a severe challenge. He wrote home that he believed 'he could stand it if others could'. When his call to the colors seemed imminent, he wrote to suggest that no family members attend his departure, for he had noticed that the presence of loved ones made departure harder.

In France with Company E, Fifth Engineers, Sixth Division, he did not see combat until the final weeks of war. He spoke only impersonally of his experience, except to express his horror at the memory of an enemy bombardment of a troop of draft animals. The terrified screams of mules and horses apparently shocked him more than any human suffering he may have observed. For a boy reared as he had been in a small farming community, man's inhumanity to man was not a total surprise, but the terrorization of dumb beasts was incomprehensibly evil.

In the post-armistice weeks, Buck was billeted with a French farm family in the province of Yonne in lower Burgundy. In March he shipped home on the America, on which President Wilson returned from the Versailles peace conference. He expressed some slight resentment at having to participate in a victory parade in Manhattan, and for the remainder of his life was intolerant of patriotic 'show'."

★★★

Oscar Smith of Bogata was only twenty-two years old when he entered the service during World War I. He was in the Infantry, a foot soldier in the Remount Cavalry. He served overseas, was not wounded, but did suffer from the effects of the gas used by the Germans. After the war he and Norie Patton were married and had ten children. His son, J. C. Smith, remembers his father telling him about different German towns he went through.

★★★

Sam H. Grimes and Charlie T. Grimes, brothers, both served their country during World War I and were in France and Germany. Their parents were James Augustus and Tennessee Lucille Fisher Grimes.

★★★

Charles O. (Oscar) Glenn was born November 3, 1885. His parents were David H. and Abigile Ellen Tillory Glenn. He graduated from Mayo's College (later to become East Texas State Teacher's College) in 1914 and taught several years.

He enlisted in the Army on May 24, 1918 at Ft. Worth and was discharged January 13, 1919 at Camp Logan, Texas. He was a Private in the Medical Department. On June 1, 1920 he married Eunice Dawson and they had two daughters, Mary Elizabeth and Geraldine. Mr. Glenn died December 23, 1970 in Clarksville.

★★★

William Claude Smith was born June 6, 1891 in Chapel Hill, Sevier County, Arkansas. His parents were William Morgan and Nora Henson Smith, and he had two brothers, Guy Smith and Van Smith. Guy Smith was also in the service during World War I.

William Claude Smith entered the service in Idabel, Oklahoma and was in the 23rd Engineers. He served in France, was field promoted, and discharged as a Sergeant.

He and Gertrude Ross were married in 1920 and had two daughters, Mary Lynn, who died at birth, and Virginia Ruth. They lived in Red River County from the early 1930's where he was a lumberman and had a great interest in oil exploration in the county. He served Detroit, Texas as Mayor and also Justice of the Peace. His death was on May 25, 1979.

★★★

Sam H. and Orlean Glazner Carpenter had two sons who served in World War I. **Sam H. Carpenter** was born December 22, 1894 and **Homer Roy Carpenter** was born November 21, 1896, both in Red River County, Texas. They had three sisters, Belle, Kate and Ola.

Sam served in Company G of the 144th Infantry in Europe and was a PFC. He enlisted a couple of years before his brother did and was involved in some serious action in Europe. Sam never told any details about the fighting but always told of how glad he was to be home after the war. He married Sue McCracken and they had two children, Oran Gerald and John Franklin. Sam died November 26, 1970.

Roy served in the 34th Company of the 165th Depot Brigade as a Pvt. He was discharged December 19, 1918 at Camp Travis, Texas. Roy married Verna Carter, and they had one daughter, Cynthia Carpenter. He died January 30, 1962. His daughter told me that she remembers that his "war story" was about the flu epidemic and all the people in his unit who died from it.

★★★

Cecil Albert Bearden, son of Napoleon Bonaparte Bearden, was born December 6, 1889 in Arkansas. He had two half-brothers, Clyde Bearden and Kenneth Haskins. He entered the service in Red River County and served in the Infantry in Germany and France. When he was discharged, he spent time at the Army Hospital in Wadsworth, Kansas because of the effects of the poison gas. He was deaf, and remained in bad health until his death in 1961. He married

Ida Mae Reed, and they had three children, Sue Nell, Garland A., and Hobert Albert who died when he was only three years old.

★★★

George Isbell was the son of Robert Carroll, Jr. and Mary Susan Westbrook Isbell. There were five other children in the Isbell family: Jim, John, Sam, Will (killed in a tornado in Deport, Texas in 1908), and Louraine. George served in World War I as a truck driver and went to France. I have no details about this but remember that his health was never good after that. He married Frances Brown, and they adopted their son, Gerald, a three year old who came with his brothers, Lee and Leo, on the Orphan Train to Clarksville in 1926. Frances died soon after that, and when Gerald was grown, George married my half-sister, Mary O'Donnell. (Gerald was killed in World War II.) They lived on Peter's Prairie Road where he was a farmer. George died in 1953. He and Congressman Wright Patman were life long friends after serving in World War I together.

★★★

Ira DeWitt Ussery was born October 30, 1894, and his parents were Joseph Lane and Martha Idella Russell May Ussery. He had two brothers, Reubon Jerome and Paul Wade, and six half-brothers and half-sisters. He served in World War I but did not go overseas. He married Maud Ivy, and they had three children, a son who died at birth, and Ira Dickson (Dick) and Bobbye Jean. DeWitt died July 22, 1945.

★★★

Harrison Lee, from a large family in Clarksville, served in the Army as a cook during World War I. His overseas duty was in France, and after his discharge, he returned to Clarksville. He married Pauline Jones, and they had three sons, two of which did not live to adulthood. The other son was William C. Lee. Harison Lee is well remembered in this area for his delicious barbecue and hot tamales.

★★★

General Stevenson Joyner (General was his given name, not his rank) served in the Army in the 25th Company, 7th Battalion, 165th Depot Brigade during WWI. He was inducted on May 5, 1918 at Clarksville and served in the Expeditionary Forces from August 8, 1918 to November 22, 1919 in Liverpool, England. His job was to assemble aircraft that had been shipped in crates to England. After his return to the States, he was discharged. He is the father of Rev. A. C. Joyner of Clarksville.

★★★

Samuel W. Allen, Sr. was born August 9, 1895 at Madras, Texas. His parents were Johnson William and Ada Fulton Allen, and he had a brother, Seth Dinwiddie, and a sister, Sally. He married Mary Ruth Summers, and they had one son, Samuel W. Allen, Jr. Mr. Allen was inducted into the Army in July 1917 at Clarksville and served as a Corporal in the 344th Field Artillery, Battery F. His training was at Camp Travis in San Antonio; he served overseas in Germany; and he was discharged in 1918 at San Antonio. At that time he returned to Clarksville, and he died March 6, 1974.

★★★

Will E. Anderson was born March 17, 1896 in Grand Saline, Texas. His parents were John E. and Lilly Dunsthun Anderson, and the other children were Oscar, Joe, Dora, Merta, Dolly and Bea. He married Martha J. Dixon, and their children were Willie, Ida, Flossie, Gladys, Melvin and Edd. Mr. Anderson was inducted into the Army in Paris, Texas in 1917 and his training was at Fort Dix, New Jersey. He was a PFC in the 47th Artillery who drove casons pulled by horses and mules. He served in the Arrgonne Forest and was discharged in 1919 at Dallas. He was awarded a European Theater Medal with two Battle Stars. Mr. Anderson died January 8, 1953.

★★★

Lilbon Thomas Moore, the son of James Leroy and Margaret Annie McConville Moore, was born February 23, 1895 at English in Red River County, Texas. He had six brothers and four sisters. He married Sallie Elizabeth Buchanan, and they had six children. Mr. Moore was inducted into the Army on October 1, 1917 and trained at Camp Bowie, Texas. He was a PFC in the Auxiliary Remount Depot #328, 36th Division who handled and trained cavalry horses and was later in charge of the officers' mess. He was discharged February 28, 1919 at Camp Bowie. He died April 22, 1997.

In 1993 Mr. Moore received a WWI Commemorative Medal on the 75th anniversary of WWI with a letter signed by Jesse Brown, Secretary of Veteran's Affairs. The medal was presented by the American Legion Post #0542. On his 100th birthday, he was presented a plaque and pin for being the oldest WWI veteran in this area.

★★★

John T. Felts, Sr. was born July 13, 1890 near Cave City in Sharp County, Arkansas, the son of Thomas Franklin and Almyra Pirkey Felts. After graduating from Cave City High School, he taught at several locations in Arkansas. In 1917 he entered the Army and served in France in the Meuse-Argonne Campaign and in Germany in the Army of Occupation. After being mustered out of the army at Camp Pike, Arkansas, he came to English in Red River County where his family had moved during the war. He and Winifred Clark were married in 1922 and had two children, John Thomas Felts, Jr., who was killed in action in the South Pacific in World War II in 1943, and Marian Patricia Felts. Mr. Felts was commander of the American Legion Post in Clarksville three times. This post now bears the name of his son, John Thomas Felts, Jr., who was the first son of a legionnaire from Clarksville killed in World War II. Mr. Felts died August 15, 1954, and his wife and daughter are also deceased.

★★★

The Lions Club in Detroit, Texas has sponsored the Detroit Homecoming for thirty years. It is held each July, and there is always a parade. For many years there was a float honoring veterans of World War I. Those men who rode on that float were **John Harvey Pratt, Thomas Crittenden, Atha Bivins, Joe Gibbs, and Walter Smith.**

★★★

The poem, *In Flanders Fields*, written by John McCrae is one of the most memorable poems written about war. Many have asked about his reference to poppies, and the answer is that poppies only flower in rooted up soil. Their seeds can lie on the ground for years, and only when the ground is rooted up will they sprout. In World War I the whole Western Front consisted of churned up soil; so in May 1915 when McCrae wrote his poem, around him poppies blossomed like no one had ever seen before. Although he had been a doctor for years and had served in the South African War, it was impossible to get used to the suffering, the screams, and the blood here, and Major John McCrae had seen and heard enough in his dressing station to last him a lifetime. As a surgeon attached to the lst Field Artillery Brigade, he had spent seventeen days treating injured men in the Ypres Salient. He called this "seventeen days of Hades" and wished that he could put on paper some of the sensations of that time. The poem was very nearly not published because dissatisfied with it, he tossed it away. A fellow officer retrieved it and sent it to newspapers in England. The *Punch* published it on December 8, 1915.

Lieutenant Colonel John McCrae was a member of the First Canadian contingent. He died in France on January 28, 1918 after four years of service on the Western Front.

In Flanders Fields

In Flanders fields the poppies blow
Between the crosses, row on row,
That mark our place; and in the sky
The larks, still bravely singing, fly
Scarce heard amid the guns below.
We are the Dead. Short days ago
We lived, felt dawn, saw sunset glow,
Loved and were loved, and now we lie
In Flanders fields.
Take up our quarrel with the foe;
To you from failing hands we throw
The torch; be yours to hold it high.
If ye break faith with us who die
We shall not sleep, though poppies grow
In Flanders fields.[11]

CHAPTER 4
Hard Times

After ten years of postwar prosperity, the Great Depression began in 1929. All of America, and nearly all of the world, were caught in its grip. Conditions grew steadily worse. Prices dropped down, down on everything. Cotton sold for five cents a pound, corn for twenty-five cents a bushel, and wheat for as low as thirty-five cents a bushel. Surplus crops piled up because there were no markets. Poverty and want were widespread. Thousands of business concerns, including many banks, closed their doors; and thousands of men and women lost their jobs and tramped the streets in search of work. Many crowded into bread lines or sought relief from the charity agencies, which were unable to meet their needs. In those dark days of distress and suffering, it became clear that our country was going through a period of great change. This was to bring new problems to the government and to our people.[1]

The Great Depression, which began when stock values in the United States dropped rapidly, was the worst and longest period of high unemployment and low business activity in modern times. Thousands of stockholders lost large sums of money. Banks, factories and stores closed and left millions of Americans jobless and penniless. President Herbert Hoover held office when the depression began.

On March 4, 1933 a great change occurred in the national government when Franklin D. Roosevelt was inaugurated as President of the United States for the first time. The broad program for relief, recovery, and reform, ordinarily termed the New Deal, raised new issues and called for new policies in all states.[2]

The Great Depression ended after nations increased their production of war materials at the start of World War II. This provided jobs and put large sums of money back into circulation. The depression had lasting effects on the United States Government and on many Americans.

Horace Greeley Gilliam had the following to say about the Great Depression:

"I was born June 24, 1919 before the Depression of the 30's started. I was born and raised on a farm near Annona, Texas. There were five children; I had three sisters and a brother. The only source of livelihood we had was farming. We farmed about 80 to 100 acres. We raised corn, cotton, ribbon cane to make ribbon cane syrup for the family to eat and sell, hogs and cattle. We sold milk, and we raised chickens for our own source of eggs. We raised about 75% of what the family ate. So I grew up on the farm, and I started chopping cotton. We'd take a hoe and chop acres and acres of cotton by hand to get the grass out of it. Then when we sold it, we would get five cents a pound for it. That would figure about $5.00 a bale.

We divided food with neighbors to have something to eat. A neighbor might be within a half mile of us and they'd run out of meal so they'd come to our place, and we'd share our meal with them. This also applied to corn for feeding horses. If a farmer's corn wasn't ready to harvest and he needed feed for his horses or mules, he'd borrow corn from a neighbor. The ribbon cane on our place down in the bottoms was cultivated for syrup. 'June Bug' Peek's daddy was the syrup maker. We would make as many as 500 gallons of ribbon cane syrup a year. My daddy had to pay five cents for the bucket to put the syrup in, and the best price he could get for the syrup was seven cents a gallon; so he made two cents a gallon. This was how much money was worth during the Depression. We couldn't make any money so he started buying fifty gallon barrels made out of oak, and we started putting the syrup in them. Then he'd put the syrup in a container that someone brought, maybe a glass jug. There was absolutely no money during that time.

I walked over three miles to school at Boxelder, and I had one pair of pants and really didn't have any shoes till I was 18 years old. I had a pair but I had to save them to wear to Sunday School. I went barefooted. My mother washed my pair of breeches at night so I'd have something to wear the next day.

The feed that we bought for our hogs and horses came in white sacks, and fertilizer would come in white sacks. Our mother used these sacks to make clothes out of. This is where we got our shirts and underwear. It was hard for people to live. If you needed a doctor, he would come from Annona, about eight miles, and the only way doctors had to come for years was by horse and buggy or on horseback. Then the T-Model Ford came in, and sometimes you would see a doctor with a Ford. The difference in medical care then and now is that they would charge you $1.50 for the trip.

We sold our crops to cotton buyers in Annona and Avery. The cotton weigher took care of the baled cotton, and there was a shed at Annona where they kept it. When the buyers bought the cotton on the streets of Annona, you took it to the cotton weigher. He'd store it, and then a train would come and take it to different places. Then the tomato came along and took the place of cotton. We started raising tomatoes in the mid 30's while we were still in the Depression. This became one of the largest tomato producing places in the country because of the soil we have. There would be as many as 250 box car loads of tomatoes shipped per year out of Avery. We sold them for as small amount as fifty cents a hundred. If you could get three cents a pound, that would be $1.50 a bushel. Just think what they sell for now.

We went to town on an average of once a month to get staple groceries like coffee, sugar, flour, soda, salt, and black pepper. This was something we couldn't raise that we actually had to have. You could buy a 48 pound sack of flour for fifty cents.

My daddy had four mules to farm with, and he had to feed a family of seven. The amount of money he could go to the bank in Avery and borrow was $50.00. He had to mortgage the milk cows or the mules or the cattle for the crops he was going to raise. That's all they'd let him have to make a living for one year. Then when he paid that back, he could borrow another $50.00.

Back in 1918 we had what we call the flu epidemic that wiped out almost a generation of young people. I was born after that, but my mother and daddy lost two children. Small children just died by hundreds because the doctors just didn't know what to do for them.

You didn't see any new shops opening up during the Depression. The ones that were in existence when the Depression hit did manage, most of them, to stay open. In Annona there were three grocery stores, a bank, one café, the post office, train station, cotton gin and a drug store. Avery was about the same size. Clarksville, the County Seat, had more stores.

I remember when the stock market fell, but we didn't have any money so it didn't affect us. We didn't even understand the stock market, but we wondered if things would get worse, and they did."

On August 27, 1990 the *Clarksville Times* published the following letter written by Mrs. J. P. (Ruby) Goodman of Clarksville, Texas:
"Dear Editor,

Your recent picture and brief write-up of the Clarksville Cemetery called to mind an incident of the Great Depression. It was many, many years ago, and someone had given our boys a cage of pet squirrels. We fed and petted them, and they were so tame we would leave the cage open and let them live in the tree tops and come back to the cage for food. Gradually, as acorns ripened, they took to other trees, crossing streets and getting farther away. But we carried pecans in the car, and they were still so tame we could throw nuts to them and watch as they grabbed a nut and scurried up a tree. In time their migrations took them to the cemetery on Washington Street, attracted no doubt by the big old trees and other squirrels. We would still go and leave nuts for them, and sometimes Purvie would take them pecans on his way to and from work. But the peace and quiet of that 'silent city of the dead' came to be broken by the sound of gun shots. So one day we went, and not one squirrel could we find, but we did find plenty of shotgun shells. We came away sadder and wiser, and a little more tolerant of the human race. Perhaps any man, with his family hungry and living in poverty, would shoot squirrels in a cemetery.

Do you have space for two more mental pictures from the depression, now that the old brain has back tracked so far?

One happened in Pope's Grocery Store. There was a woman buying canned dog food; the cans were about 15 ounces in size and only ten cents each. A woman came in who had every mark of poverty and hard times about her. Her look of pleasure was something to see when she learned of meat at only ten cents a can. Then it was the look on her face, as though the clerk had struck her a blow, when he told her it was dog food. I'll never forget that look. . . shock, disbelief, sorrow, with her outcry, 'Meat! Meat for a dog! When I can't afford meat for my children!'

The other picture was a little caravan on the way to Dallas—a small homemade cart with two wheels evidently from farm machinery, and a box-like bed piled up with household goods. Behind trudged a woman with a heavy bundle on her bent back. And what team pulled the cart? The man and the milk cow. Yes, with ropes for harness, the man and the milk cow were pulling the cart. If you see such as that, you will remember. Thank you for seeing it with me."

(These handwritten notes were in the margin of the copy Mrs. Goodman sent to her son, Kelsey: "Can't remember if I sent one of these. But I do want you all to know what the Depression was like. Purvie and I were so stricken by the sight of that man and the milk cow, pulling like a team of horses, we couldn't speak a word as we passed.")

On November 12, 1964 the *Clarksville Times* printed an article that had appeared in the Houston Post. It was entitled "Former Pupil Recalls Dedicated Teacher at Jake's Creek School" and was written by John Rainey. It reads as follows:

"Her name was Mary Jo Hardman, and I was in the fourth grade. Each day she rode three miles from Annona, in northeast Texas about 60 miles from Texarkana. She made the ride on horseback to teach 12 of us in seven grades in a ramshackle frame building at Jake's Creek. I doubt that she ever made much money, but she never complained. I remember her clearly, a tall brunette with eyes so pretty and brown, determined but kind.

I only spent one year in that school. Of all my schooling, it is the most memorable, however. The next year we went to Clarksville. Of the 12 pupils—we could not be called students, for they are supposed to study—three were Raineys, for my two brothers, Tommy and Bobby, also went to school. All of us lived on farms, but my father was the only one with a job in town. Those were Depression days, and times were hard.

We all met in the single room of the school, and we all walked to get there. Four of the younger pupils walked about four miles.

They came barefooted, except in the coldest of weather. . . I had a red-boned hound dog named Pal. Where I went, he went. Pal came to school every day. In the summer, fall and late spring he spent the classroom hours chasing rabbits for fun and food. When it was cold or raining, Pal came inside, and he usually slept next to a big pot-bellied stove at the front of the room. . .

There was no daily newspaper in Red River County in those days, and none of our families took any newspaper, except perhaps for *Grit*, a weekly published in the east. But Miss Hardman came from an educated family, one of books, radios and newspapers. She shared these with us. The big day at school became Monday, for she brought the massive *Dallas Morning News*, with all the Sunday comics and pictures from around the world. About six weeks before Christmas Miss Hardman got most of us involved in wood-working projects. We made gifts for Christmas. Perhaps this was another of her ways of making school fun for us. . . We stayed after school in order to finish before Christmas. Naturally, she stayed too, often until 6 p.m. I am sure she had to ride that mare in darkness much of the way home. . .

At the end of the school year she took us to White Rock Lake near Annona. Once there we scattered, each finding a spot to explore. The last I heard, she was still teaching. . ."

Our neighbor, Jerry Conway told the following about his family:

"After his father died at an early age, Daddy Joe Conway, my grandfather, was raised in Rattan, Oklahoma by his mother Amanda Conway, and her two brothers, Willie and Hafford Maynard. Daddy Joe had a younger brother, William, and a sister named Hattie. At one time the family lived next door to a family named Humphrey who had a son. His name was William Humphrey, and he became a noted author who wrote '*Home From the Hill*', '*The Ordways*', and many other books.

As an adult Daddy Joe was good with horses and mules. He lived in Sulphur, Oklahoma and ran a horse and buggy taxi service. His Uncle Tom lived in Nashville, Tennessee and ran a dry goods store for a wealthy family named Prince. The Princes and the Isbells of Red River County were good friends. Eventually Uncle Tom moved to Deport and ran a dry goods store for the Isbells.

Uncle Tom got Daddy Joe to move to the Clarksville area where he became a horse and mule trader. He met Katie Halbrooks who lived on the Hancock place near Turner's Lake, and they married in 1915. They farmed the Westbrook place just west of Deport where my father, J. T. Conway, was born December 20, 1915. Daddy Joe's brother-in-law, John Isbell, who had married Annie Halbrooks, owned land down around Turner's Lake on the lower end of Peter's Prairie. John talked him into moving down there and working that land which was called the Isbell Bottom. This is where twins, Russell and Robert Conway, were born. Robert died of the croup when he was a year old.

Later the Conways moved just northeast of the Sherry Community to the McCurry place. Mr. McCurry had been killed when a horse fell on him. The Conways moved there as sharecroppers on Thanksgiving Day in 1921. In 1976 my Dad and I bought this land, and it has been continuously farmed by the Conways since 1921.

J. T. attended school at Sherry where Mrs. Lucille Kunkel and Mrs. Louise Hutchison were teachers. He always had high regards for both ladies. When my parents, J. T. and Marguerite, celebrated their 50th anniversary, Mrs. Kunkel, then living at Regency Nursing Home, attended the reception. School mates J. T. often mentioned besides the Conway kids were Bernard Varley, Pat Westfall, Arvel Jones, and some Reeds.

Sherry had a good basketball team, and Mrs. Kunkel was their coach. They played Boxelder for the county championship in Avery, which had the only gymnasium in the county. Before the game, they bought some bologna to eat, and probably they ate too much since none of them had ever had any. Unfortunately, it made most of them sick. According to J. T., their team would have won the championship if it hadn't been for that bologna. Arvel Jones was on the team and later went on to play for SMU where he was on the team that won the National Championship in 1939. For him, it must have seemed like a long way from the Lennox Bottom down on Scatter Creek to there.

Baseball, the national pastime, was another activity at Sherry. George Spangler was their coach. He had a mule and a horse he hooked up to a wagon to haul the team to their games. J. T. said one game was played in knee deep water, and they never got the ball wet because they were so good. He was the only player in history (far as we know) who ever made all three outs in one inning (offensively not defensively).

During the Depression years a lot of their relatives from Dallas moved in with them to keep from starving to death. These people had a baby that cried a lot so instead of sleeping on the back porch, the regular bedroom for J. T. and his brother, Russell, that year they slept on a mattress out on top of the chicken house to get some peace and quiet. It must be pointed out that even before the company came, the Conway family consisted of Daddy Joe, Komma (my grandmother), and six kids living in that 3-room box house.

Onus Hoover of the community bought a 'Baby Overland' car with no top for $20.00. He got J. T. and Russell, then teenagers, to go with him to West Texas to pick cotton. When they got to the place they were supposed to work at, the cotton wasn't quite ready to pick so they helped gather the maize crop. They worked 3 or 4 days at this, and when they finished, the man told them 'Much obliged'. Onus told the man 'You take that to the store and see what it will buy!' He made him pay the boys for their work. While there, they stayed in an old one-room shack and spread cotton on the floor to sleep on. All they had to eat the whole time was beans and cornbread.

As they were on their way home, it started sleeting and snowing. Since the car didn't have a top, they covered up with a tarp with only their heads covered by saucer caps sticking out. When they got home, J. T. and Russell had $60.00 each and gave it to Daddy Joe. He in turn let them buy themselves a new suit. He saved their money back for them, and the next year they rented 40 acres of land from the Andersons to plant corn on. J. T. said, 'We made a good crop that year, but prices was real cheap. After workin' all year and pickin' it and sellin' it, we cleared 3 bits a piece.'

J. T. also attended school in Clarksville and though he never played on this particular football team, he told this story. Some of the players he mentioned who were on the team included Harold Wallace, Ted Bolton (also known as 'Big Shorty'), 'Speedy' Bates, and Hugh Lowe. They had won the district championship and had traveled to somewhere near Dallas to play the bi-district game. Just before the first play of the game, an airplane flew over the field. Since none of the Clarksville boys had ever seen an airplane, they all just stood up and began watching it. The Bonham team took advantage of that and scored a touchdown before the Clarksville team knew what was happening. The game ended with Bonham winning

6-0. Ted Bolton always said, 'If that airplane hadn't flew over, they'd still be playin', and the score would still be nothin' to nothin.' The following year J. T. did play on the football team, and that team still holds the dubious record for being beaten worse than any other team, 103-0, by Bonham.

Some of the neighbors J. T. mentioned who lived near them at Sherry included the McClanahans, Cornetts, Exums, Greens, Shirleys, O'Dells, Townes and Dodds."

Jack Dodd of the Rosalie Community wrote two articles about the Great Depression. One of these was published in a newspaper on March 28, 1996 and reads as follows:

"It appears people like to read and hear about the Depression, but few speak of it personally. The Depression was sort of like World War II. When we heard about someone else's problems during the Depression, it seemed to make our problems a little easier and made us realize that maybe we really didn't have it so tough after all.

At the old home place in Rosalie is where we worked during the depression. The times of the depression vary from family to family. No, there is no set date for Depression years. Bill Bell and I had a good thing going at Rosalie Store. Babe Gibson would pay us one cent for chicken eggs. Bill and I did very well until our mothers told us no more eggs for candy. It was about this time we got the bright idea to sell Mr. Babe some setting hen eggs. He started getting complaints so he started candling our eggs and put us clean out of business. When you candle the eggs, you can see the little chick inside. Babe Gibson was one of the smartest men I ever knew.

I remember the day Mr. Babe told me to take Birt (my mother) the first loaf of sliced bread. I wasn't about to take Mother sliced bread when she sliced her bread herself. In about a week we tried some. Then in about six months we started buying it. I thought for a long time Mr. Babe was slicing that bread himself.

Our house was on the old Bogata-Clarksville Highway. In fact, this was the only Bogata- Clarksville road at that time during the Depression. It seems each person crossing the country would come to the back door, hat in hand, asking for something to eat. Mother always kept extra ham, sausage, eggs, biscuits, etc. in the old wood cook stove for such occasions. The request was always the same, 'May I have something to eat?', and the answer was always the same,

'Go to the barn, wash up and sit under the big black walnut tree there with the little table and chair and I'll try to find something.'

Everything always went well until one day. Those of you who knew Birt Dodd know that she was a large, strong woman. She kept a tow sack behind the kitchen stove to wrap around kerosene lamps that had fire burning down in the bowl. She would wrap the tow sack around the lamp, holler for me to open the screen door on the back porch, and she could throw that tow sack and lamp plumb into the middle of the field. After awhile I'd go up and bring the lamp back to the house.

Well, one day this young man asked rather curtly, as Mother would put it, for something to eat. Same thing, barn, wash up, sit under the black walnut tree. Things didn't go quite that way. The young man did go to the well by the barn and wash up, but he marched right into the kitchen, sat at Daddy's place at the table and proclaimed that he was ready to eat. I was on the back porch and knew things were about to happen, even though I wasn't sure what, at the time.

At first Mother was surprised, then confused, but not for long. She used a big broom with heavy silks and double stitching. That thing must have weighed fifteen pounds. She calmly reached behind the wood stove, got her broom and with one swoop hit that young man on the right side of his head, knocking him halfway across the kitchen floor. She tore into him with that broom, and he was on his all fours trying to make it to the back porch door. After about forty licks with that broom, he was standing up in the middle of the back yard looking surprised and scared all at the same time. He tried to apologize in his own way and started toward the road. Mother called after him, 'Your plate is ready when you sit yourself down under the big black walnut tree'. Sit he did, and the likes of eating I never saw before or since. Wonder how he told that story to his grandkids? I hope he had the opportunity."

The other article was written by Jack Dodd just recently and is entitled "All Hat and No Cows". It reads as follows:

"It was the dust bowl summer of 1938. Rosalie, Texas was a wide place in the road, a sand road. James Allred was Governor of Texas with W. Lee O'Daniel to follow. No one ever admitted voting for O'Daniel, but he won by a landslide.

I was the oldest of three children of Henry and Birt Holliway

Dodd, at twelve years old. Sister, Mary Lee, was seven, and brother, David, was four years old. We lived in a big old white house in Rosalie. I'm sure the house was white, sometimes, but I don't remember ever painting it.

The routine on the farm was up at four, build the necessary fires in the fireplace and the cook stove, milk the cows (about twenty of the best Jersey milk cows you ever saw). The cows were divided up between Daddy, Uncle Jim and me. Those durn cows were a troublesome mess, milked morning and night every day. And on top of that, about every week or so I would have to walk one of those cows to Watkins' farm, about four miles away, for a visit to the bull. I had all that figured out by then. I early on thought calves were found in the woods. Roosevelt and the New Deal couldn't change that.

Daddy's family was made up of eight sisters and one brother. Every summer we had Daddy's sisters visiting since they were all school teachers, except the youngest. Cathleen, 'Cat', was visiting, and I had just gotten over the annual malaria fever. All of us kids had high fever and had to take Quinine given to us by Dr. Roach. Some people say you can go blind taking too much Quinine. Mother and Daddy didn't pay any attention. We took that bitter stuff along with 666 Chill Tonic till I can still taste it sixty years later. Another thing was the 'itch'. Every winter we would have the '7 year itch'. Simple solution again, smear yourself with sulphur and get into a flannel gown and go to bed. Smell! It sure cured the 'itch' and anything else you may have had.

Mother wasn't feeling very good that summer of '38. She had a cough she couldn't break up, and she wheezed a lot. She just felt right poorly most of the time. Dr. Roach from Bogata and Dr. Lewis from Paris had treated Mother for over a month with no relief to her. Since 'Cat' was visiting and Mother was ill, she said she would take me and go to Roswell, New Mexico to visit her sisters, my aunts, Aunt Cora, Aunt Mary and Aunt Effie. We left the farm and rode the Interurban from Bogata to Paris and caught the train for Roswell. When we got there, we went to Aunt Cora's house to visit a coupla' days. 'Cat' and I had been there for a day and a half when Aunt Mary came over and told us that Mother was not doing very good, and we needed to return to the farm the next day.

We caught the train the next morning for Paris. Red Peyton

picked us up in Paris and took 'Cat' and me to the farm. Daddy was going to milk as we drove up, and he said to go with him. When we got to the barn, I asked about Mother and said that I wanted to see her. Times were very difficult in the late 30's, and I thought I had seen some bad times, but little did I know of the immediate future. Daddy tried not to look worried, and he finally told me that Mother had a very contagious disease, and we were going to have to break up the family. Then he said she had tuberculosis. I told Daddy they were wrong, but he said Dr. Roach and Dr. Lewis were positive that she had TB. I was to go back to Roswell; sister Mary to Bowie with some of Daddy's other sisters; and brother David was to stay on the farm with Daddy. Mother probably was to go to a sanitarium.

Mother was quarantined from everyone but Daddy and Becky Lowery. She couldn't eat with us, sleep with us, even touch us for fear of us getting TB. TB led to pneumonia which led to death. There was no penicillin in those days. That night was the first time ever that I couldn't go to sleep. The doctors were wrong; my mother couldn't be sick; she worked hard every day; was President of the Methodist Ladies' Aid Society; she was too good to be sick.

The next three days were spent getting Mary's and my clothes together to leave. Things just couldn't get any worse. I was once asked if I ever had any crisis as a child. Yes, three! I nearly died at age five with diphtheria; this one with Mother's illness; and when brother David was run over by Dr. Grayson in front of the house in Rosalie. David jumped out of a pickup in the path of Dr. Grayson's Ford coupe. It knocked him thirty steps down the highway. He was so badly broken up that the men had to roll him up in a quilt to put him in Dixon's Olds to go to Paris. Dr. Lewis pulled him through, but that one was close.

We were ready to go our separate ways. Nothing tasted good; nothing was going right; and it was raining. We were going to Paris at 2 PM that day, but about 8 AM Dr. Lewis called from Paris and said to put everything on hold. He was driving out to the farm from Paris. Everything was going through our minds. What was happening? Dr. Lewis drove up and asked to see Birt, as he called her. We waited in the parlor with Mother in the bedroom adjoining the parlor. We could hear the doctor and Daddy and Mother and Becky Lowery whispering. A little later Daddy came into the parlor and started crying. Daddy didn't cry unless something was bad wrong.

He was also full of surprises. Dr. Lewis had told Mother and Daddy that he was for sure that Mother did not have TB, but had asthma. It was a great day for the entire family.

We all stayed home. Mother got up and went back to canning and cooking and all her chores. We all forgot about the Depression for a while due to the good news. Mother lived to be ninety-two years old. Some people say about a man, 'He's all hat and no cows.' Our Daddy took care of us. Our Daddy had cows."

Alan Love recalled this about Depression times: "My Love grandparents had cows, chickens, a garden, and honey for sugar. My Reed grandparents had a nice cotton crop. The bank told them to wait till spring to sell it so they got five cents instead of sixty-five cents a pound for it. Men worked for a dollar a day, and three or four men would be ready for any job that was available. Food was cheap; a shirt would cost only forty-nine cents. Many caught possums, rabbits and coons to sell their hides, and many people ate them. Those in the country were better off, and those in town looked for their 'country kin' to help them. These were hard times."

Mary Reep Bean (Mrs. Clyde Bean) told me the following that she recalled about the Depression: "The first job I got was working at the Pecan Plant for ten cents an hour. If we worked eight hours, we got eighty cents. We had more fun than people do now making fifty dollars an hour. Sometimes you'd come all the way to town and just get to work four or five hours. Winnie King, Jessie Calhoun, Virgie King, and I worked on the grading table, grading pecans. There were four or five of us that did that. Tom Miller would bring up a box of that peanut stick candy, and that was the best stuff you ever tasted. Black Brothers had the Coca Cola Plant and the Pecan Plant and that helped out a lot of people. There just weren't many jobs during the Depression, and nobody had any money. Clyde was working at Silberberg's Store at that time making $50.00 a month. He worked long hours, six days a week. The store was divided in half with men's clothes on one side and ladies' clothes on the other side. They had wood stoves in the winter, and in the summertime Clyde had to get on a twenty foot ladder and get on a top shelf and take down the pipes. He sold men's all wool suits, two pair of trousers, coat and vest for $22.50.

During that time I won $150.00 at the show, and I bought a set of living room and dining room furniture. I wonder what they sold for then—probably about $25.00. I bought it at McClinton's Furniture Store, and it was really good furniture. I was going around the square that Saturday night. They'd go outside and call the winning number at the show. I heard them say 'Mary Bean', and I was tickled to death. When you went to the show, they tore your ticket in half and kept the stubs to draw the winning name from. Clyde was working that night, dressing the windows at Silberberg's.

My Daddy borrowed $15.00 a month to live on and to make a crop on, but we never did go hungry. Mama had chickens, butter, milk and eggs so all she had to buy was sugar and flour. They took their corn and had it ground into meal.

On Saturday night I'd stay in town while Clyde was working because there were so many people there, and that's the way we visited. We'd go around the square and then turn around and go the other way. We'd park a car so we'd have a place to sit. Clyde had to stay till the store closed and then straighten up. Sometimes it would be twelve or one o'clock in the morning before he'd get off. Straggler customers would come in, and he'd have to wait on them."

Our long time friends, Kelsey and Faye Goodman live in Maryland. Kelsey sent a couple of things about the Depression years, one of which is a letter written by Bagby Lennox a few years after Mr. Purvie Goodman, Kelsey's dad, died. The letter touched on the fact that neither of the Clarksville banks failed when so many others were doing so in the 1930's. Mr. Lennox wrote: "...the remembrance of Mr. J. P.'s tireless efforts in helping us rebuild the bank during 1933 came to mind. He insisted that the job was possible and what I especially remember was the many trips we made over the county to visit and explain our plan to the depositors of the old bank... I thought you both (John and Kelsey, his sons) would be pleased to hear this report of a good deed accomplished without any thought of personal gain."

The other thing Kelsey sent had to do with outhouses, and I quote in part below:

"We had a rent house (usually called a 'shotgun house') on one corner of our property, and its' outhouse desperately needed work. This was the era of the WPA (Works Project Administration), during which the government had taken on lots of people as employees and looked everywhere for things for them to do. The WPA was often held in low esteem, and some people jokingly claimed that

WPA stood for 'We poke along'. In fairness, however, the WPA provided jobs and built some roads and bridges that were very useful, and some may in fact still exist. At that time anyone who had any work that needed to be done could contact the WPA office and they would contract to do the job. Dad contacted them about getting a new outhouse built, and it turned out that not only would they do the work, but they also had official U.S. Government outhouse plans. I was about five years old at the time and watched the construction... The structure had a neatly dug hole, and a nice concrete foundation was poured around it which had bolts stubbed up out of the cement... The outhouse was solidly built, painted white, had a door that closed tightly and could be locked from the inside, had a seat that raised much like commode seats do today, and there was a metal vent out the sloping roof. I doubt if history books acknowledge that the lowly, often maligned WPA did in fact have this touch of craftsmanship."

Pearis C. Abernathy sent the following: "I was born in the White Rock community of Red River County, Texas. My Daddy was a tenant farmer. Needless to say, we moved quite often. He tried construction work for a couple of years, and we moved even more often then, about all over West Central Texas.

In January 1933 we were back in farming and moved to the southwest corner of Red River County. I have been in this part of the county since that time. I now own the place we moved on then. I remember the Depression well. I was small, but that's when I stopped being a 'dyed in the wool Democrat'. I vote for the person I consider the best for the office. I didn't like the President's stand on the Depression. Cattle were killed. The meat was left to rot. There were people hungry, and they needed that meat to eat. The cotton was plowed up and left to rot in the fields. People needed that cotton for clothes to wear. The government started giving out small checks if people would do this or that. That is what started our down fall as a nation. The politicians found out they could buy the peoples' votes with those checks.

The President advocated spending the nation out of the Depression with deficit spending. That's the cause of our nation's debt. It spread to foreign countries. They used our tax dollars to buy foreign friends. You can't buy friendship. If something doesn't change in a hurry, all the people that have fought and died for our country have died in vain. There ought to be a law passed that says that anyone that refuses to fight for our great country should be denied citizenship and all the good things we enjoy and take for granted as citizens of the U.S.A. The greatest country in the world is worth fighting for! I love her very much!"

John D. Ball was born June 22, 1920 and his parents were Johnny W. and Ruby Denison Ball. He was born and raised at Minter, Texas. This is what he had to say: "My family and I were born and raised on a cotton farm. For all farmers in my father's time and my time, it was a very trying time. If not for a garden, chickens, milk cows, hogs, and the things that they produced, we could not have made it. Farm labor at $1.00 per day didn't buy much. I guess the best thing was that we didn't know anything but to be poor."

My parents, Jim and Lee Ivy Claiborne, along with my other relatives who lived then, never forgot the hard times of the Depression. Most of them lived in the country so they had plenty to eat. I remember my Mother saying that many days they ate chicken three times a day. The best time of the day was when she saw their mail carrier, Fred Higgins, coming. Once in a while he brought a block of ice, and they had homemade ice cream. My Daddy managed a farm owned by Harry Trilling. It was at Turner's Lake way down on the Peter's Prairie Road, and the roads were terrible when it rained, black mud. His hardest time was when his team of mules was struck and killed by lightning while seeking shelter under a big tree during a bad storm. These were hard times, but there were some good times when their neighbors came over and they had fun visiting and playing dominoes. Everyone was in the 'same boat'. They just accepted the times and hoped for better days.

"The Soil Soldiers" (reproduced by permission from the newspaper and book series *Texas Lore* by Patrick M. Reynolds)

Chapter 5
Day of Infamy December 7, 1941

December 6, 1941 was a lovely, calm day in the Hawaiian Islands. Ashore, the city people of Honolulu, the small-town people and farmers, the beach-dwellers, and the beach-goers enjoyed a golden day which melded into a blue evening of crystal stars and soft trade winds. On the ships at Pearl Harbor, especially the big dreadnoughts along Battle Row, the sailors were relaxed in the easy ambiance of life aboard a ship in port. The heart of the Pacific Fleet, the eight magnificent battleships, lay in a line along the gentle reach of Ford Island in the center of Pearl Harbor. From a hill overlooking Pearl Harbor, you could see them riding calmly in the water, and see the sailors moving about the decks with easy familiarity. It was a typical warm Saturday on a lush and slow paced island, which also happened to be America's military headquarters in the Pacific. It is likely that no one, afloat or ashore, gave much thought to a rumor which the U.S. Ambassador had picked up in Tokyo almost a year earlier, and which he relayed to the U. S. government. The rumor was that a large and powerful Japanese force would attack Pearl Harbor.[1]

It happened on December 7, 1941. One part of America learned while listening to the broadcast of the Dodger-Giant football game at the Polo Grounds in New York. Ward Cuff had just returned a Brooklyn kick-off to his 27-yard line when at 2:26 P.M.

WOR interrupted with the first flash: the Japanese had attacked Pearl Harbor.

Another part of America learned half an hour later, while tuning in the New York Philharmonic Concert at Carnegie Hall. Artur Rodzinski's musicians were just about to start Shostakovich's Symphony Number 2 when CBS repeated an earlier bulletin announcing the attack. The concert goers themselves learned still later when announcer Warren Sweeney told them at the end of the performance. Then he called for *"The Star Spangled Banner"*. The anthem had already been played at the start of the concert, but the audience had merely hummed along. Now they sang the words.

Others learned in other ways, but no matter how they learned, it was a day they would never forget. Nearly every American alive at the time can describe how he first heard the news. He marked the moment carefully, carving out a sort of mental souvenir, for instinctively he knew how much his life would be changed by what was happening in Hawaii. . .

At this moment it was 12:20 P.M. in Washington, D. C., and ten highly polished black limousines were just entering the Capitol grounds. The first was convoyed by three huge touring cars, nicknamed *Leviathan, Queen Mary, and Normandie*. These were filled with Secret Service men guarding President Franklin D. Roosevelt, who was on his way to ask Congress to declare war on the Japanese Empire. The cars stopped at the south entrance of the Capitol, and the President got out, assisted by his son, Jimmy. Roosevelt wore his familiar Navy cape, Jimmy the uniform of a Marine Captain. Applause rippled from a crowd that stood behind sawhorse barricades in the pale noonday sun. The President paused, smiled, and waved back. It was not his campaign wave—this was no time for that—but it wasn't funereal either. He seemed to be trying to strike a balance between gravity and optimism.

The Presidential party moved into the Capitol, and the crowd lapsed back into silence. Here and there little knots clustered about the portable radios which the more enterprising remembered to bring. All were facing the Capitol, although they couldn't possibly see what was going on inside. They seemed to feel that by studying the building itself, a little history might somehow rub off on them.

Like the President, the people were neither boisterous nor depressed. They had seen movies of the cheering multitudes that are supposed to gather outside chancelleries whenever war is declared, but they didn't feel that way at all... A nation brought up on peace was going to war and didn't know how...

But most people... were sure the United States could defeat Japan with absurd ease. The country at large still regarded the Japanese as ineffectual little brown men who were good at imitating Occidentals but couldn't do much on their own...

But rising above the awkwardness, the naivete, and the overconfidence ran one surging emotion—fury. The day might come when formal declarations of war would seem old-fashioned, when the surprise move would become a stock weapon in any country's arsenal, but not yet. In December, 1941, Americans expected an enemy to announce its intentions before it fought, and Japan's move—coming while her envoys were still negotiating in Washington—outraged the people far beyond the concept of any worldly-wise policy maker in Tokyo. Later, Americans would argue bitterly about Pearl Harbor—they would even hurl dark charges of incompetence and conspiracy at one another—but on this day there was no argument whatsoever.

Young Senator Cabot Lodge of Massachusetts had been an ardent 'neutralist' (just a month earlier he had voted against U.S. merchant ships to enter Allied ports), but right after he learned of Pearl Harbor from a filling-station attendant, he was on the air... urging all Americans, no matter how isolationist they might have been, to unite against the attack. Senator Arthur Vandenberg of Michigan, leader of the isolationist bloc, had heard the news in his bedroom, where he was pasting up clippings about his long, hard fight against U.S. involvement in the war. He immediately phoned the White House, assuring President Roosevelt that whatever their differences, he would support the President in his answer to Japan.

It was the same with the press. The isolationist, rabidly anti-Roosevelt *Los Angeles Times* bannered its lead editorial "Death Sentence of a Mad Dog". Some papers tried to prod isolationist leaders into controversial statements, but none were coming. Senator Burton Wheeler of Montana, for instance, snapped back, "The only thing now is to do our best to lick hell out of them".

There was an overwhelming urge to get going, even though no one knew where the road might lead. At Fort Sam Houston, Texas Brigadier General Dwight D. Eisenhower got the word as he tried to catch up on his sleep after weeks of long, tough field maneuvers. He was dead tired, had left orders not to be disturbed, but the phone rang, and his wife heard him say, "Yes?. . . When?. . I'll be right down". As he rushed off to duty, he told Mrs. Eisenhower the news, said he was going to headquarters, and added that he had no idea when he would be back.

The Capitol swelled with the same spirit of angry unity and urgency as the Senators filed into the House Chamber to hear the President's war message. Democratic leader Alben Barkley arrived arm in arm with GOP leader Charles McNary; Democrat Elmer Thomas of Oklahoma linked arms with the old isolationist Senator Hiram Johnson of California.

Next the Supreme Court marched in, wearing their black robes, and then the members of the Cabinet. Down front sat the top military leaders, General Marshall and Admiral Stark. Further back, five Congressmen held children in their laps, lending the curious touch of a family gathering. In the gallery Mrs. Roosevelt, wearing black with a silver fox fur, peeked from behind a girder—she had one of the worst seats in the House. Not far away sat an important link with the past—Mrs. Woodrow Wilson.

At 12:29 P.M. President Roosevelt entered, still on Jimmy's arm. There was applause . . . a brief introduction by Speaker Sam Rayburn . . . and the President, dressed in formal morning attire, stood alone at the rostrum. He opened a black loose leaf notebook—the sort a child uses at school—and the Chamber gave him a resounding ovation. For the first time in nine years Republicans joined in, and Roosevelt seemed to sense the electric anger that swept the country, as he grasped the rostrum and began:

"Yesterday, December 7, 1941—a date which will live in infamy—the United States of America was suddenly and deliberately attacked . . ."

The speech was over in six minutes and war voted in less than an hour, but the real job was done in the first ten seconds. "Infamy" was the note that struck home, the word that welded the country together, until the war was won.[2]

FDR received the news at 1:47 P.M., Washington time. The attack had been in progress for 25 minutes. The 32,600 ton battleship Arizona was hit with 1,100 men killed on this one vessel alone. The battleship Oklahoma was hit, and 400 men died. Ship after ship received direct hits. The terrible cost: 5 battleships, 3 destroyers, a minelayer, and almost 200 aircraft. More then 2,000 American Sailors, 109 Marines, 218 Soldiers, and 68 civilians had died, or would do so as a result of their ghastly wounds . . .

If Pearl Harbor had boosted Japanese ego, the attack had also thrown Americans into black and violent rage. If the Emperor's flowery words summed up the typical Japanese attitude, American feelings were typified by this down-to-earth comment from Admiral Halsey, who returned to Pearl Harbor with the Carrier Enterprise on December 8th: "Before we're through with them, the Japanese language will be spoken only in Hell."

Never before had a nation started a war with such colossal victories. Yet in August, 1945 this same nation would suffer the most shattering defeat in the history of men, when the first atomic bombs exploded upon Hiroshima and Nagasaki. This was to be the terrible price of Pearl Harbor.[3]

Sailing undetected across thousands of miles of ocean, the Japanese armada prowls like a wolf-pack north of Hawaii, readying to execute a well planned surprise attack. . . Commander Mitsuo Fuchida prepared to lead the first wave from the carrier *Akagi*. In Japan it was December 8, but on the decks of the task force 230 miles north of Oahu it was December 7, 1941, and it was exactly 6 A.M. . .

Crewmen cheer as aircraft begin taking off for the attack on Pearl Harbor from the pitching decks of carriers. Japanese aviators regarded the attack as a "divine mission" and vowed to make it a crushing blow. . . . As the attacking force turns due south, launch operations begin in the face of a heavy overcast and a stiff northwest wind. More than 180 aircraft made up the first wave to be hurled against U. S. ships, planes, and men on that warm Sunday in December. . .

An hour and forty minutes after screaming from the carriers' decks, Fuchida's aircraft had deployed over the northern coastline of Oahu, the first of 360 aircraft to be thrown against the sleeping giants waiting just ahead. Fuchida led a group of 49 bombers carrying 1,600-pound armor-piercing bombs. On his right were 40 Nakajima torpedo-bombers and on his left, each carrying a 500-pound bomb, were more than 50 Aichi dive-bombers. . .

Could it be the surprise was going to be as complete as the spies planted on Oahu had promised it would be? The fact that there were no carriers in the harbor was a disappointment, but the latest reports confirmed that the battleships were there, and the battleships were the nucleus of the Pacific Fleet. . .Ten thousand feet below the formation, Oahu came out of the sea green and glistening, an incredibly beautiful sight in the soft light of the great yellow sun. . . No smoke came from the ships in the harbor, so none of them had managed to get underway. Even from that great height it was easy to see the surprise was total, and fatal. It was going to be a glorious victory. . .The dive-bombers climbed to 15,000 feet and split into two graceful, arching groups. One group headed for Ford Island in the center of Pearl Harbor, the other shot like an arrow at Wheeler Field northwest of the harbor. . .

In the harbor along the southwest side of Ford Island the mammoth gray ships lay in the calm of a sun-drenched Sunday. There was the battleship *California*, moored alone; the battleships *Maryland* and *Oklahoma*, with the *Maryland* moored inboard; the battleships *Tennessee* and *West Virginia*, with the *West Virginia* outboard; the battleship *Arizona*, moored inboard of the repair ship *Vestal*; and directly behind the *Arizona*, the battleship *Nevada*. Eight of the nine battleships in the Pacific Fleet were enjoying a quiet day of rest. The eighth, the *Pennsylvania*, was across the harbor from Battleship Row, resting easily in Dry Dock One at the Navy Yard.

In the repair basin were two 10,000-ton cruisers, the *New Orleans* and *San Francisco*. Also in the harbor were four 10,000-ton cruisers; the *Phoenix* was moored north of Ford Island, and the *St. Louis*, *Honolulu*, and *Helena* were in docks at the Navy Yard. Two 7,000-ton cruisers, the *Raleigh* and the *Detroit*, were moored northwest of Ford Island To the north and west of the island were 29 destroyers, considered new. Twenty-six of them had been built since 1933. In various slots around the harbor were five submarines, a gunboat, 11 minesweepers, 23 auxiliary ships, nine minelayers, and a scattering of smaller craft—a total of 96 ships. . .

The morning was so quiet the sound of church bells echoed gently, signaling the 8 o'clock mass. . . Then the harbor rocked with explosions and smoke roiled into the clear morning air. . . The battleships suddenly were blazing and the dense smoke spiraled up and up, dark banners that signaled the death of the ships.

The *Oklahoma* took three torpedoes and began to list, smoke pouring out of her. The *Arizona* shuddered and heaved with the devastation of a bomb in the forward powder magazine. A sudden and intense fire boiled out of the heart of the ship, and her decks were hidden by great, roiling clouds of choking smoke. The *West Virginia* took torpedoes and two heavy bombs, igniting a fire amidships. A torpedo passed beneath the minelayer *Oglala* and slammed into the cruiser *Helena* and exploded. Then a bomb fell between the two ships and went off with a roar. A torpedo smashed into the cruiser *Raleigh* and two others streaked into the side of the *Utah*, formerly a battleship and now an American target vessel. The *Utah* began an ominous list to port, and men leaped from her decks, only to be strafed in the water by passing Japanese aircraft.

Still the planes kept coming. The *Arizona* took five torpedoes and a number of aerial bombs, the armor-piercing bomb which detonated in the forward magazine also set off the *Arizona's* main forward battery and dropped two gun turrets and the ship's conning tower 20 feet below their natural positions. There was a tremendous amount of oil in the water around the ship, and it burned for hours.

Two more torpedoes hammered the *Oklahoma*, even as she capsized. Men were running along the canting hull. In dry dock, the *Pennsylvania* jolted from a bomb blast. The *West Virginia* buckled under the force of two bombs, then lurched from the tearing impact of six torpedoes. She began to settle in the water, her main deck just above the harbor's surface. The *Tennessee*, moored inboard and escaping the torpedoes, was hit by bombs that threw debris at dangerous random about her decks...

The *West Virginia* was sinking. The *California* was settling at the stern. The *Oklahoma* was capsizing, and the *Arizona* was in ruins... Simultaneous with the attack on Battleship Row, bombers and fighters were screaming over Oahu's airfields, scattering death. At Schofield Barracks in north-central Oahu, fighters tore through the mountain pass and raked the compounds and the drill fields with deadly fire. At Hickam Field, near Pearl Harbor, men leaped for cover as bombs tore into shops and buildings, and into the aircraft drawn up in neat rows.

At Wheeler Field the fifty-odd U.S. fighter planes were grouped neatly in front of their hangars. The P-36's and P-40's glinted in the morning sunlight, immobile with surprise as the dive-bombers curved downward and began their runs, with a group of

Zeros close behind. The fighters on the ground wrenched apart with the impact of the bombs, sending fiery pieces of debris into the air. Some airplanes simply vanished in the force of the explosions. Men crossing the runways were caught and killed by the spinning debris and by Japanese strafing planes which came hard out of the sun. Hangars burst apart in the fury of the attack. More than 40 of the combat planes on the ground flamed and burned; others were badly damaged and never got into the air.

At Kaneohe, on the windward side of Oahu, the Naval Air Station was strafed twice, then bombed. Of the 33 planes on the ground, 27 were smashed and burned, some bent beyond recognition. Smoke from burning planes reached high over the sleepy windward side and disappeared in wisps, like black cirrus (clouds) against the morning light.

Around Ford Island, the scene was one of havoc. Men swam about in the water, trying to escape the holocaust. Burning oil covered the surface, a malevolent film with flames licking from it. The air was heavy and hard to breathe. Staccato gunfire mingled with the sounds of screams and curses.

A wave of dive-bombers came in low and fast and struck at the *Maryland* and the *Nevada* and various light cruisers and destroyers. One destroyer, the *Monaghan*, got underway and headed for the harbor entrance. But west of Ford Island the ship spotted a Japanese submarine under attack by the Curtiss and Tangier. The Curtiss had hit the submarine's conning tower but the *Monaghan's* actions were quick and direct—she rammed the submarine, then crossed it with depth charges, and saw the water turn dark with oil. Finally, followed now by the destroyer *Henley*, the *Monaghan* sped toward the relative safety of the open ocean.

Overhead, eight groups of high-altitude bombers began weaving a cruel pattern, crossing the harbor in precise checkerboard formations. The battleship *Nevada* managed to get underway, the only ship of her class to do so that morning. Hit in the forward section by a torpedo, she plowed uncertainly into the channel waters and headed for sea. At the southwestern point of Ford Island the ship rocked with the sudden and brutal smash of bombs. Her deck was dotted with gaping holes and her superstructure was flaming. Could she reach the channel entrance and make it through to safety, or would she sink at the mouth and block the entrance for the other ships? Fourteenth Naval District officers decided not to risk it and the *Nevada* was ordered aground. She turned shoreward and ran her proud hull onto the point of land near the channel mouth.

Alongside the dying *Arizona*, the repair ship *Vestal* managed to get free and anchor again northeast of Ford Island. The *Oglala*, moved by tugs to a more secure position, suddenly capsized. The *Neosho*, filled with high-octane aviation gas, managed to clear herself and stand away from the flames.

Agony twisted the faces of the men in the water. Oil-smeared, some more dead than alive, sailors from the stricken *Oklahoma* clambered onto the hull of the overturned battleship while others slid off into the grimy waters alongside. From the *California*, blazing furiously, crewmen slipped into small boats or risked the water itself, even as more oil from the *Arizona* began to engulf the *California's* stern.

Small boats converged on the burning ships, but in their wake came the Aichi bombers, stitching the water in deadly strafing runs that shattered boats and bodies. More than two dozen of them in taut formation bore down on the hapless men in the water, and flung themselves against the return fire of the working guns on the crippled ships. . .

On the *Raleigh* a small miracle was taking place. None of the cruiser's crew was dead and only a few wounded. An armor-piercing bomb passed through the ship, ripping up the deck in front of a startled engineer, and blew up in the mud beneath the cruiser. Hit in the port side by a torpedo, the ship managed to stay afloat and her gunners poured round after round into the attacking Aichis. When one of them came apart in a violent explosion, the *Raleigh's* gun crews cheered.

In the drydocks the destroyers *Cassin* and *Downes* exploded like roman candles while firefighters fought the flames in spite of the strafing runs and the danger of ricocheting bullets. The destroyer *Shaw*, hit forward by a heavy bomb, blew up with a spectacular burst that flung bodies into the water and scattered debris in all directions. The bomb had exploded all the magazines and tore away the ship's bow.

On the windward side of the island, at Bellows Field, one of the five midget submarines ran aground and the lone survivor struggled ashore, to be captured almost immediately. With midget subs sunk by the *Ward* and *Monaghan* and two others lost at sea, the beached submarine was the last of the five launched long before the Japanese aircraft began their attack. . .

The *Arizona* went down, writhing in death, dying with more than 1,100 men trapped in her hull. The *Oklahoma* died on her side, sinking with more than 400 men entombed below her decks. The *California* sank like a wounded mammoth, going down at the stern. The *West Virginia* settled into the mud of the harbor bottom, her main deck awash in the oil-shrouded water. The *Nevada* lay aground, smouldering and shaken with explosions. Blazing like a gigantic candle, the *Utah* slipped beneath the surface and disappeared. The *Pennsylvania*, *Maryland* and *Tennessee* hunched like great wounded beasts, fighting the destruction that threatened them all.

At Wheeler Field, at Hickam, at Kaneohe and Ewa and Ford Island airstrips, the crumpled forms of shattered airplanes were consumed in the flames that leaped from aircraft to aircraft. Everywhere, there was the shape of death and the scent of murder. Bodies lay on aprons and taxiways and runways of the airfields, or rolled in the disturbed waters of the once-sheltering lochs. Huge fires sucked oxygen out of the morning.

And still the Japanese aircraft poured out of the sky, too numerous to count, bringing death to the already dying. The plaintive wail of the sirens, echoing as the church bells had echoed an hour before, came steadily across the water and died in the thunder of detonations and the churning, crackling sound of the killing flames. . .

In a brief lull—hardly more than a decrease in intensity between waves of attackers—a few American aircraft got into the air and shot down several Japanese planes. Meanwhile, the B-17's, expected earlier, finally arrived in Hawaii to be greeted by a scene of chaos and confusion—and by a swarm of Zeros. In one of the miracles of the day, all 18 of them managed to land safely at one airfield or another. Eighteen dive-bombers from the carrier Enterprise also arrived over Pearl Harbor at the height of the attack and started drawing fire from friend and enemy alike. A commander landed his plane on Ford Island with smoke billowing upward from a hangar, and American bullet holes in both wings. Thirteen of the 18 Enterprise aircraft landed at Kaneohe Naval Air Station, but only nine were undamaged. Those nine refueled, took on 500-pound bombs, and went searching for the Japanese Fleet...

In December 1941, American naval strategy still placed the battleship at the center of the task forces. The aircraft carriers and their ranging airplanes, though in existence, were considered secondary to the battleships in the minds of most naval strategists. Thus, on December 7, the heart of the Pacific Fleet was nine battleships and three aircraft carriers. Eight of the battleships were in Pearl Harbor that Sunday morning; the ninth, the *Colorado*, was undergoing work in the Navy Yard at Bremerton, Washington. All of the dreadnoughts were in the 29,000 to 33,000-ton class.

Of the three aircraft carriers assigned to Pearl Harbor, the Saratoga was being repaired on the West Coast. The carrier *Enterprise* was returning from Wake Island, 2,300 miles to the west (and had sent some aircraft ahead just in time to get caught up in the attack). The carrier *Lexington* was returning to Pearl Harbor from ferrying aircraft to Midway Island, more than 1,000 miles to the northwest. Thus, all three escaped attack on that day. Of the 96 ships in the harbor on December 7, 18 were sunk or heavily damaged...

Ninety-two Navy aircraft were destroyed and 31 damaged. The Army Air Corps lost 96 planes and had 128 damaged. The Navy lost 2,008 officers and men killed, 710 wounded. The Army had 218 killed, 364 wounded. The Marines lost 109 killed, with 69 wounded. There were 68 civilians killed, and 35 wounded. Total casualties for the day: 2,403 dead, 1,178 wounded... Total Japanese casualties: 185 killed, one captured.

But as the task force steamed toward a triumphant welcome in Japan after that terrible morning, the Japanese forces had scored less of a victory than they knew. They had failed to destroy any American aircraft carriers, which became the heart of the rebuilt task forces and turned America rapidly toward new naval strategies. They had failed to destroy the repair facilities on Oahu. With those facilities in operation, America was able to salvage and repair vessels and aircraft which appeared at first to be destroyed. As part of the United States' industrial capability, the repair shops helped put the U.S. forces into the war within days of the Sunday morning disaster. The Japanese attack also failed to destroy the U.S. submarine base or the vengeful U-boats that soon were at sea in search of Japanese shipping. In a serious, even fatal, lapse of Intelligence and pre-strike planning, the Japanese failed to destroy the highly visible oil storage tanks. Those tanks soon supplied the fuel for counter attacking U.S. ships and aircraft. For all the carnage of that bloody Sunday, the Japanese attack was a near-triumph, an incomplete victory.[4]

As a child, I did not really understand what had happened on December 7, 1941. I was with a friend at the Avalon Theater that Sunday afternoon when the movie stopped and Mr. Wolf made the announcement that the Japanese had attacked Pearl Harbor. When I got home, nearly everyone in our family was there. Aunts, uncles, cousins! Our family gatherings were always happy times, but that day was different. I knew something bad had happened because of their somber moods.

Patriotism and love of country were such a part of our lives then. As school began the next morning, our teachers tried to explain more to us about what had happened. The Pledge of Allegiance seemed especially meaningful, as did our flag. We sang patriotic songs. The world map was used to show us just where Pearl Harbor and Japan were. It was not long before we were buying U.S. Savings Stamps each Friday which were used to buy a U.S. Savings Bond when we had accumulated enough. We learned about rationing and the scarcity of many items that had been plentiful. My family kept up with the news in the papers and over the radio. My half-brother, Pat O'Donnell, and my cousin, Jack O'Donnell, were soon in the service, and later another cousin, Dick Ussery, would be drafted. Thankfully, the three returned safely from the war.

Flags with blue stars hung in the windows of homes in our little town to show that the family had someone in the war. Sad to say, many of the flags were turned to show a gold star, meaning that a loved one had been killed. There were many war movies and always a "short subject" that had to do with the war. The U.S.O. in Clarksville was on the north side of the square, and many servicemen came down from Camp Maxey in Paris, Texas. On the weekends some came and attended church and went home with families for Sunday dinner. We lived on North Walnut Street near the Court House and across from the Louie Norris home. Miss Louie rented out apartments to families of service men, and I especially remember a young couple with a small baby who were from Detroit, Michigan. He was at Camp Maxey and came in on most week-ends to be with his family. I enjoyed visiting with them and when he was shipped overseas and she and the baby returned home to Michigan, I missed them. There were drives to sell Savings Bonds, and I remember when movie stars, Bill Elliott, Ann Jefferies and Gabby Hays came to boost the sale of bonds. Those years and what happened are still vivid in my memory.

In the December 1983 issue of *Texas Monthly* an article written by Ann Marable Sparks (Priest) entitled "Pearl Harbor Christmas" was printed. It is quoted in part below:

"That infamous December of 1941, in a small East Texas town, we needed tidings of comfort more than ever before.

I guess the news came to Clarksville in lots of different ways, but for me it came at the Avalon Theater on the square when I was twelve years old. I was at the Sunday picture show with some of my seventh-grade girlfriends. Right in the middle of the best part the sound went off and the lights came up and Mr. Wolf walked out on the stage. He said that he hated to tell us, but the Japanese had bombed Pearl Harbor.

My friends and I blinked at one another, partly because of the sudden light and partly because Mr. Wolf looked so solemn. Everyone began filing out of the theater onto the square, where the store windows were already decorated with red and green Christmas garlands and artificial snow writing that said things like 'We have your Christmas needs'. I passed some workmen who were stringing up the colored lights around the Confederate Monument as I walked home, wondering where in the world Pearl Harbor was and why it had stopped the picture show.

Mother and Daddy sat up all night listening to WFAA from Dallas, more than a hundred miles away. They talked to each other in low voices about people getting killed. Then I heard them talking about my two big brothers, who were down in Austin at the university. I finally fell asleep thinking about whether we would have school the next day.

We did, but it was strange. We pulled down the big map that hung over the blackboard and pointed out Hawaii and Japan. Japan looked smaller than Texas, and Hawaii was just a speck in the ocean. We couldn't even find Pearl Harbor. Then President Roosevelt's voice came over the radio. I'd never listened to a radio in school before. There was a lot of static and President Roosevelt sounded far away, but when he finished speaking, we all knew we were at war.

Our teacher told us to bow our heads and say a silent prayer. I bowed my head, but I didn't know what I should pray about. Mostly, I felt confused. Finally, we said 'amen' and faced the front of the room, where the American flag and the Texas flag stood on either side of the pictures of George Washington and Stephen F. Austin. We put our hands over our hearts and said the Pledge of Allegiance. It seemed, somehow, to make everything official.

We were at war and Christmas was coming, and no one knew exactly what to do about it. We were having Christmas at Grandmother's like we did every year. Her house was directly across Main Street from ours, on a big lot with tall elms and sycamores and pecan trees. I loved it better than any house in the world. I had spent so much time there that I felt as though it belonged to me. . .I was worried that things would be different this year because of Pearl Harbor. So when Aunt Susie had finished decorating, I ran over to Grandmother's and searched through the house for all the familiar things. . .

The decorations were the same as always, but somehow the house felt different. The grown-ups were worrying about things being appropriate. They talked and talked about whether we would go caroling on Christmas Eve and what people would think if we had the fireworks on the front lawn on Christmas night like we always did. Finally they decided to carry on as usual. They said the reason was that this might be the last one, the last time everyone would be together. I guess it made them feel better to have a reason, but it sounded as though there would be no more Christmases after this year.

I couldn't imagine not having Christmas at Grandmother's house, but then I'd never been through a war before. I'd seen lots of pictures of war in the RKO Pathe newsreels at the Avalon, but mostly I'd giggled at the funny-looking soldiers doing goose steps. The closest I'd ever come to war was watching the National Guard drill down on the square on Tuesday nights.

Lots of people went to watch the guard drill. Mr. Erwin and Peyton West and Mr. Roy Dinwiddie looked like real soldiers in their uniforms instead of just friends and neighbors. They barked out orders and called out cadences and made sharp, square turns all around the Confederate Monument. Their boots' striking the red brick streets frightened the purple martins that roosted in the eaves of the buildings and made them chatter and swoop wildly around the square.

School let out the week before Christmas and my brothers, Paul Davis and Bubba, came home from the university with big appetites and lots of laundry. They talked to Mother and Daddy about Pearl Harbor, but they didn't seem too worried. I felt a little better because I'd always trusted my brothers. They went duck hunting at the North Lake, but the weather was balmy and they didn't get many ducks.

Things were beginning to seem normal again, except that the radios were on everywhere, interrupting *Ma Perkins and Stella Dallas* and even *One Man's Family* with war bulletins. Grandmother made everyone in the kitchen stop what they were doing and listen, but somehow by Christmas Eve, she had seen to it that all the preparations had been made...

On Christmas morning I woke up with scratchy eyes, still feeling sleepy from the late night caroling. It was daylight. I rubbed a little peephole in the frosted windowpane by my bed and touched the cold water to my eyelids. It almost never snowed in Texas on Christmas, but there was such a heavy frost on everything that I pretended it had. Through the peephole I could see Grandmother's house, with the wreaths in the windows and smoke coming from the three chimneys. It looked like the house in the picture for December on the Gulf calendar that hung in our kitchen, only prettier...

Daddy and Uncle Ben and Cousin Charlie were talking about the war. They were standing in front of the fireplace, saying things about President Roosevelt and Mr. Churchill and the Pacific and Germany and how there was only one front to fight in 1917. I didn't understand it all, but they looked so serious that I inched my way closer to hear better.

Uncle Ben put his hand on Daddy's shoulder and said, 'Paul, it's going to be a different year for us. I have daughters, but you have sons. It's the sons, the men of this family, that we have to rely on to get this job done. Have you thought that some of the men standing in here right now may not be here next year?' Daddy lowered his head and said under his breath, 'Yes, I've thought about it.' So I started thinking about it too.

I was afraid that Uncle Ben meant my brothers, and I tried to imagine what Paul Davis and Bubba would look like in uniforms and how far away from Clarksville they would have to go. Maybe some of my uncles and cousins would have to go away too. I wasn't certain which ones would be chosen. I only knew that I didn't want any of them to go.

Then Aunt Ruth came to the door and announced that dinner was ready, and it was time for the gentlemen to join the ladies in the dining room. We found our names on the place cards that Aunt Susie had made out of pine cones. The grownups were in the big dining room, and the younger ones at the tables in the front hall. There was a discussion about who should say grace, and when no one could decided, Aunt Ruth said we would sing 'Silent Night' instead. So Aunt Mary played the piano and everyone sang. Practically everyone cried, even some of the men. It made me feel uneasy to see men crying, and when I saw tears in my daddy's eyes, I turned my head away.

I was awfully glad when we sat down to eat because it got noisy again. Glasses and silverware clinked and rattled, and for a long time everyone told everyone else how delicious everything was. Then Mary Deavers and Bessie began clearing the tables and bringing in the desserts, and loud groans went up in unison. We chose from fresh coconut cake, boiled custard, chess pie, date loaf, and Nesselrode pudding. Some took two because they couldn't make up their minds. . .

In spite of how hard everyone tried, Christmas was different this year. When people started laughing too much, others looked at them until they stopped, like people who get caught laughing in church. I knew it must be because of Pearl Harbor.

When dark finally came, everyone got coats and sweaters from the pile on the bed in the middle room and went outside. The men went into the yard to get the fireworks started, and the women stood on the front gallery shivering and calling out to them to be careful. The skyrockets went off first. They zoomed up into the night, exploding in a shower of color over the black sky. Pinwheels whirled down the long front walk, and firecrackers went off in the yard. I set off ladyfingers and listened to the quick, dainty pop-pops. Then some of us stood in a line and shot Roman candles over West Main Street. . . The skyrocket with the little toy man in a parachute was last. Up, up, up it went in a shower of sparks until the final burst of color. Everyone clapped as the parachute floated down slowly, barely missing the roof. Then everything was quiet.

It was over. Christmas was over. But maybe more than Christmas. Something else was over too, but I wasn't sure just what it was. I was cold and a little afraid. I wanted things to stay the same, but I could feel them changing. . ."

REMEMBER PEARL HARBOR!

Chapter 6
The War Years in Europe

On November 5, 1937 Adolf Hitler, chancellor and supreme dictator of Nazi Germany, held a secret meeting in the Reichstag. There, behind locked doors, he confided in his foreign ministers and his top military commanders that he was preparing to go to war. He said that Germany was not large enough for its growing population, and that the country needed Lebensraum (living space). Since none of Germany's neighbors was likely to give up land without a struggle, the problem of living space for Germany, said Hitler, could be solved only by the use of force...

Germany's first objectives would be the conquest of two small neighboring countries, Austria and Czechoslovakia... Then it would be easier to absorb the larger and less densely populated regions of Poland and Russia. "It is my unalterable resolve to solve Germany's problem of space at the latest by 1943-45", said Hitler...

Hitler's generals were astonished by these statements... They all remembered clearly how Germany had suffered after 1918, when it was defeated by the terrible four-year struggle of World War I. They urged Hitler not to risk another war like that... Hitler was sure that Britain, France and the United States would be so anxious to avoid war that they would not interfere with his plans...

Four months later—March 1938—Hitler began his conquests by sending the German army into Austria and proclaiming that country a part of Germany. There was no opposition. . . . Then, six months later, in September 1938, Hitler won such a great diplomatic triumph that his generals were convinced his plans would work.

On September 29, 1938, four men met at Munich, Germany to decide whether Europe was to have war or peace. The men were Adolf Hitler and Prime Minister Benito Mussolini of Italy—dictators who controlled their countries by ruthless police methods—and Prime Minister Neville Chamberlain of England and Premier Edouard Daladier of France—leaders of democratic nations. The purpose of the meeting was to settle a dispute between Germany and Czechoslovakia (over a long strip of mountainous country known as the Sudetenland). . . Hitler claimed that the Czechoslovak government was mistreating the Sudeten Germans and threatened to invade the country if the territory was not ceded to Germany at once. . . Hitler's charges were false.

Meanwhile the Italian dictator, Mussolini, had dreamed of making Italy as strong as the old Roman Empire. He had increased his country's armed forces and begun to expand his power beyond the borders of his country. In 1935-36, despite the protests of the League of Nations, his armies invaded and conquered the small, primitive, African country of Ethiopia.

In 1936 Hitler and Mussolini had signed a treaty promising to help each other in case either was attacked. The real purpose . . . was to provide mutual aid in the exploitation of small countries as a means of expanding and growing stronger. The two dictators had called their alliance the Rome-Berlin Axis. . . Soon afterwards, Hitler and Mussolini had signed a treaty with the militaristic government of Japan, which was trying to expand its power in Asia. This larger alliance was called the Rome-Berlin-Tokyo Axis.

The growing power of Germany and Italy had alarmed England and France, but the two democracies had not been able to agree on joint action, and neither was willing to do anything that might start a war. . . Chamberlain and Daladier were frightened men when they met the German dictator at Munich. . . Without even consulting the Czechoslovak leaders, they agreed that Hitler could have the Sudetenland. . .

Some Englishmen—led by Winston Churchill—were dismayed by what had happened. They were right. Six months after Munich, a defenseless Czechoslovakia surrendered to Hitler. . . . A month later Mussolini seized the little country of Albania, and Hitler began to threaten Poland... He was certain England and France would back down, just as they had at Munich, but even if they did decide to fight, they were too far away to help Poland. Hitler was now ready to start World War II...

Shortly after midnight on September 1, 1939, fleets of German airplanes began to bomb Polish cities. Just before dawn, five great German armies swept over the Polish frontiers. The Poles were hardy and they fought bravely, but except for the air force, their equipment was neither as good nor as modern as that of the Germans... The surrender of the last organized Polish unit took place at Kock on October 5... The Germans rightly compared their fighting method to the speed and power of lightning. They called it Blitzkrieg—"lightning war"... England and France declared war against Germany on September 3...

Despite the fact that they had signed a treaty dividing Poland between their two countries, Hitler and Stalin continued to distrust each other. Stalin... was quite certain that Hitler was planning to attack Russia... so Stalin decided he had better do whatever he could to strengthen his own country... He first demanded that Estonia, Latvia and Lithuania permit Russian troops to occupy army and naval bases in their countries... They agreed to let the Russians come in without fighting... Stalin then demanded that Finland give up some important military bases... Finland was prepared and fought but knew they could not win, and so they made peace with the Russians...

Hitler was preparing for a second Blitzkrieg. The victims this time were to be Norway and Denmark... The British and French reacted quickly to Germany's invasion of Norway... But the Germans were much better prepared than the Allies... The Allied effort in Norway had been "too little and too late". The Germans had captured two more countries...

Hitler felt sure that his army was strong enough now to win a great victory and force the Allies to make peace. He had decided to attack the French and British armies in France... Belgium and Holland were neutral countries, and they were most eager to avoid being forced into war... The Germans planned to make their first heavy attacks against Holland and northern Belgium... The Dutch army surrendered on May 14... By May 11 the entire Belgian defense plan had been ruined. The discouraged Belgian soldiers fell back to the Dyle River to join the Allies... By May 27 King Leopold surrendered the entire Belgian army to the Germans... There was no hope of holding any part of Flanders. The British troops were pressed back almost to the sea near Dunkirk, and the British Royal Navy was preparing to take them off the Continent...

The British and French hurriedly tried to get ready for further attacks, but there was little hope that they could stop the victorious German army. Most of the French and probably more than half of the British were sure they would be completely defeated by the Germans. There was one Englishman, however, who refused to think of defeat. On May 10 the British nation had called on Winston Churchill to replace Neville Chamberlain as prime minister... He told the people, "I have nothing to offer but blood, toil, tears, and sweat."... He was determined that England—and France, too, if possible—win the war.

June of 1940... The Germans gave the French no time to prepare any extensive field fortifications or entrenchments. On June 5 they renewed the attack... The main German attack swept through and around Paris. The French government and army had evacuated their capital on June 13, declaring it an open city to keep it from being destroyed...

Meanwhile, on June 10, Italy had declared war on France. Mussolini had wanted to be sure to get into the war in time to claim some of the French and English colonies. But the French defenders of the Alps, even though they were outnumbered, were able to hold off the Italian attacks... In central France, however, it was clear that nothing could stop the Germans... On June 1 the French signed an armistice in the same railroad car that had witnessed the German surrender at the close of World War I. On June 25, just after midnight, the fighting stopped.

The Germans now occupied most of France, but they allowed the French government to stay in existence in the small city of Vichy. From there Petain went through the motions of governing the French colonies and part of southern France. Actually he was little more than a figurehead in a government completely dominated by Hitler... The German dictator had gained another one of his objectives—control of the French colonies...

Hitler was planning to invade England, which lay just across the Strait of Dover. While his soldiers rested from their battles, his air force prepared to sweep the British Royal Air Force from the skies. The German attack on England was expected at any moment, and hardly anyone outside of England thought that the British could hold out more than a few weeks. But Churchill had spoken for the British people when, just before the collapse of France, he had said: "We shall not flag or fail. We shall fight in France, we shall fight on the seas and oceans, we shall fight with growing confidence and growing strength in the air, we shall defend our island, whatever the cost may be, we shall fight on the beaches, we shall fight on the landing grounds, we shall fight in the fields and in the streets, we shall fight in the hills; we shall never surrender." Now when Britain stood completely alone, he told his people and the world: "Let us therefore brace ourselves to our duties and so bear ourselves that, if the British Empire and its Commonwealth last for a thousand years, men will say: 'This was their finest hour.'" . . .

Mussolini thought he would do a little conquering on his own. He decided to start with Greece. . . On October 28, 1940, an Italian army of 162,000 men advanced from Albania into Greece. . By early December the Greeks had not only driven the Italians out of Greece, but were actually invading Italian-held Albania. . . Hitler had no desire to help Mussolini out of his troubles in Greece and Albania, but he was worried about the British air bases in Greece. . . Early in 1941, Hitler prepared to invade Greece. He began by putting pressure on the governments of Yugoslavia, Hungary, Romania, and Bulgaria. He promised them that they would get parts of Greece or Russia if they would join him—he also promised to destroy them if they failed to cooperate. . . The government leaders of the four Balkan countries were so frightened that they signed the treaties Hitler put in front of them. The German dictator could force them to do whatever he wanted. . .

The German attack on Greece was scheduled for April 6. Then suddenly the Balkan situation changed. The Yugoslav people rose and threw out the government which had signed the treaty with Germany. . . In less than a week the Germans were ready to attack both Greece and Yugoslavia at the same time. . . Though the Yugoslavs fought bravely, they were quickly overwhelmed. By April 15 the fighting was almost over. The last remaining portion of the Yugoslav army surrendered two days later. . . German troops had begun the invasion of northeastern Greece on April 6. The British there held the Germans off without difficulty, but they had to fall back again when the Germans smashed through the Greek positions in central Greece. . . The entire British army was in danger of being cut off and destroyed. General Papagos offered to hold out for as long as he could while the British Royal Navy attempted to take the British troops off the peninsula. The evacuation began at Athens on April 22. The next day the Greeks were forced to surrender. . .During the night of April 28-29 the last British soldiers were evacuated. . .

The Germans knew that if they were to take full advantage of the conquest of Greece, they must control the Greek Island of Crete. . . The attack took the form of an airborne assault that struck four points on the island at once. By the night of May 31, the Battle of Crete was over. . . In accomplishing this feat the Germans had fought with bravery as great as that of the exhausted, poorly supplied British troops. . .

Hitler never carried out his plan to invade Britain. When he sent his Luftwaffee on repeated bombing runs to soften the little island for invasion, the Royal Air Force defeated it so badly in the Battle of Britain that the Nazi dictator decided to attack Russia instead. . . Early in 1941 Hitler began to assemble an army of nearly 3,000,000 men near the frontiers of Russia. . . The Soviet armies defending Russia's frontiers totaled a little over 3,000,000 men. . . Hitler had been so sure that the war would be a quick one that he had not bothered to gather any equipment or supplies for winter fighting. . . Now the cruel Russian winter closed in. The Germans were actually in the suburbs of Moscow when the Russians struck on December 6. After being so close to victory, they were now faced with disaster. . .They spent the rest of the winter deep in Russia. . . By spring 1942 both armies were in better shape. . . By November the Germans were halted everywhere. They had almost, but not quite, reached the Baku oil fields. They had almost, but not quite, captured Stalingrad. . . The improvement in the Russian fighting qualities in the eighteen months since midsummer 1941 had been tremendous. . . During the spring of 1943 the Russians kept up the pressure against the Germans, and pushed them steadily back in central and south Russia. . . There seemed little prospect of any real German victory over Russia. . .

Shortly after the attack on Pearl Harbor, Churchill and his military advisers met with President Roosevelt and the senior American military men in Washington. At this meeting a number of decisions were made that shaped the course of the remainder of the war... The American Army, Navy and Air Force must be built up, and American industry must have time to turn out the equipment needed for American fighting men... The United States and British leaders agreed that Germany was the most dangerous enemy. They therefore decided that Hitler must be defeated before the full might of the Allies was turned against Japan... A powerful navy was necessary for an attack on Japan, and the U.S. Navy had been gravely crippled by the Pearl Harbor attack. There was a danger that if the Allies did not put immediate pressure on Germany, Russia might be completely knocked out of the war...

The next decision that Roosevelt and Churchill and their military advisors reached was to create a command organization to run a war that had spread over the entire globe. This organization was called the Combined Chiefs of Staff and included the top military men of Britain and the United States... The American members were called the Joint Chiefs of Staff...

By the end of 1943 things looked better. The Germans had been pushed back in Russia. The Americans and British had driven Rommel out of Africa, had captured Sicily, had knocked Italy out of the war, and were fighting the Germans in southern Italy. In the Pacific, the Americans had driven the Japanese from most of the Solomon Islands and from their Aleutian Island strongholds on Kiska and Attu. American and Chinese troops had started an invasion in north Burma...

It was true that the Allies had halted or slowed down the wave of Axis conquest. But could they defeat the Axis? If Germany and Japan could hold on to even half the areas they had conquered, history's judgment might be that the Allies had lost the war.[1]

By January 1, 1944 the Allies of World War II had stopped every important Axis attack in Europe, Asia and the Pacific. The Allied invasion of Italy in September, 1943, had caused the immediate downfall of the Italian dictator, Mussolini. There was no longer any chance that Germany or Japan could defeat the Allied "Big Three", the United States, Great Britain, and Soviet Russia. But the Allies could see no prospect of an early victory...

All in all, the war had just about reached a stalemate. The rulers of Germany and Japan had good reason to hope that the punishing losses they had already inflicted on the Allies would cause Americans, Britons, and Russians to make peace rather than fight on indefinitely with no clear prospect of victory...

While American, British and other Allied troops were engaged in a grim, bloody struggle to keep the Germans occupied along the "Winter Line" in southern Italy, Allied leaders in the British Isles were preparing for the most gigantic military operation in all history.

In 1943 President Roosevelt and Prime Minister Churchill had approved the plan of the Combined Chiefs of Staff for a mighty land, sea, and air invasion of western Europe. This plan was given the name of Operation OVERLORD, and was scheduled to take place in May or June 1944. To carry out OVERLORD, nearly 3,000,000 men would have to be equipped, trained, and furnished with supplies...

The Allied military planners had carefully studied the coastline of German-held western Europe to find the best place to land an invading army... High tide was important. Then the landing craft could come closest to shore, and the attackers would not have to wade through so many of the underwater obstacles and mines the Germans had placed along the waterline. At the same time, the attackers would have less open beach to cross. They would be exposed for the least possible time to fire from German fortifications...

Finally the Allied staff officers decided that the best place to make a landing would be the coast of Normandy in northern France... To command all of the Allied forces that would make this great invasion, Roosevelt and Churchill had selected American General Dwight D. Eisenhower, who had been commanding Allied troops in North Africa, Sicily, and Southern Italy... By May, 1944 General Eisenhower reported to the Combined Chiefs of Staff that his soldiers, sailors, and airman were ready for their dangerous invasion... in June.

At the beginning of June, 1944, there were 58 German divisions occupying France, Belgium and Holland. . These forces totaled about three-quarters of a million ground soldiers, many of them tough veterans of earlier German victories, and they were led by excellent officers...

General Eisenhower's forces were getting ready for Operation

OVERLORD, which was now scheduled to take place during the first week of June, 1944. British General Sir Bernard L. Montgomery commanded the Allied ground forces. Under him Lieutenant General Omar Bradley commanded the American First Army, and General Sir Miles Dempsey commanded the British Second Army. Forty-five divisions stood ready to take part in the invasion—nearly two thirds of them American, the remainder British. With additional artillery, tank and engineer units, they totaled about 1,000,000 fighting men. Nearly 1,000,000 more soldiers were ready to provide supplies and ammunition, to take care of the sick and wounded, to drive trucks, to repair equipment, to operate radios and telephones, and to do other important tasks. Without these "support elements", the front-line soldiers could not keep fighting even for a day. Almost another million men comprised the naval and air forces taking part in Operation OVERLORD...

Trouble began even before the assault got under way. D-Day—the day scheduled for the landing—was to be June 5. Troops were loading on their vessels when a storm sprang up on the English Channel. The weather experts forecasted several days of bad weather, but said that there would be one relatively calm day—June 6.

General Eisenhower took a chance and ordered the attack to go ahead, one day later than scheduled. D-Day was now set for June 6, 1944.[2]

Operation OVERLORD, the Allied invasion of Europe, began at precisely fifteen minutes after midnight on June 6, 1944—in the first hour of a day that would be forever known as D-Day. At that moment a few specially chosen men of the American 101st and 82nd airborne divisions stepped out of their planes into the moonlit night over Normandy. Five minutes later and fifty miles away, a small group of men from the British 6th Airborne Division plunged out of their planes. These were the pathfinders, the men who were to light the dropping zones for the paratroopers and glider-borne infantry that were soon to follow.

The Allied airborne armies clearly marked the extreme limits of the Normandy battlefield. Between them and along the French coastline lay five invasion beaches: Utah, Omaha, Gold, Juno, and Sword. Through the predawn hours as paratroopers fought in the dark hedgerows of Normandy, the greatest armada the world had ever known began to assemble off those beaches—almost five thousand ships carrying more than two hundred thousand soldiers, sailors and coastguardmen. Beginning at 6:30 A.M. and preceded by a massive naval and air bombardment, a few thousand of these man waded ashore in the first wave of the invasion. . . The day the battle began that ended Hitler's insane gamble to dominate the world.

Field Marshal Erwin Rommel to his aide, April 22, 1944—"Believe me, Lang, the first twenty-four hours of the invasion will be decisive . . . the fate of Germany depends on the outcome . . . for the Allies, as well as Germany, it will be the longest day."[3]

British and American losses were terribly heavy. It seemed impossible for men to survive and fight under the appalling conditions that now existed on the beaches. . . By nightfall of June 6 the British attackers on the east had established a beachhead nearly 20 miles long and about five miles deep; they had pushed to the outskirts of the city of Caen. On the west, at "Utah" Beach, the American VII Corps held an area almost ten miles wide, with spearheads more than four miles inland. Only in the center, at the American "Omaha" Beach had there been really serious trouble. . .

By June 12 the build-up in Normandy had reached the point where both sides realized that the Allies could no longer be driven back into the sea. . .OVERLORD had succeeded, but would the Allies be able to push their way out of Normandy? . . .

Meanwhile, the Allies were working up a plan that they hoped would smash through the German lines. It was called Operation COBRA. It was a good name, because the build-up of Allied troops in the beachhead was just like the coiling of a snake as it prepares to strike. . .

The Allies soon had trouble setting the stage for Operation COBRA. The Germans were making such good use of the "hedgerows" of Normany that it was almost impossible for the Allies to advance. The Normandy hedgerows . . . are long mounds of earth, several yards thick and usually about six feet high, filled with the thick, gnarled roots of the tangled thickets of ancient trees and shrubs that grow on top of the mounds. These surrounded every little field and lined all the roads. They were ready-made fortresses for the Germans. . .

The first stage went slowly. But as the Allies built up their strength, they found ways to deal with the hedgerows. One of the best devices—invented by a bright young American tank soldier—

was a steel horn bolted to the front of a tank. This would dig into a hedgerow like a bulldozer, while bullets glanced harmlessly off the tank's armor. . .

Now came General Bradley's great attack. . . By July 31, after an advance of 40 miles, the Americans had passed the town of Avranches at the base of the Cotentin Peninsula. It was time for the "cobra" to strike. . . On August 1, the newly created American Third Army swept through the narrow gap at Avranches. . . With magnificent air support, and under the driving, brilliant leadership of Patton, the troops swept ahead. By August 6 they had reached the Atlantic Ocean north of St. Nazaire. By August 13, they held the entire line of the Loire River from St. Nazaire to Angers.

But the Germans . . . did not intend to give up so easily. Rommel had been seriously wounded by an American air attack, but his place had been taken by Field Marshal Gunther von Kluge. . . He mounted an intensive attack on August 6. . . For two days the situation was desperate. . . Then General Bradley . . . threw additional divisions into the line. . . They slowed, then stopped the attack. . . Suddenly the picture changed. . .

It is really doubtful if the Allied success could have been much more complete. In the fighting in Normandy the Germans had lost more than 500,000 men. Two German armies had for all practical purposes ceased to exist. Allies losses had been less than half as great. . .

As the demoralized Germans fled east, the Allies pursued them. . . On August 26 Patton's Third Army led the way across the Seine on the right flank of the Allied armies. Just to his left the American First Army, now under Lieutenant General Courtney H. Hodges, crossed the river on both sides of Paris. The French 2nd Armored Division, attached to Hodges' army, was given the honor of reoccupying the French capital. . .

Patton's American Third Army—racing across east-central France—had to get along with the small amounts of food, fuel, and ammunition they carried with them. Hitler and his generals realized that the Allies had limited supplies in Normandy, and that these would soon be used up. It would be impossible to bring enough supplies over the Normandy beaches and through Cherbourg to furnish the great Allied armies. . . Hitler felt that if the Allied armies failed to receive supplies through these ports, they must stop their advance. And stop they did. Patton's army ground to a halt on August 30 just east of the Meuse River. The other three armies were forced to stop early in September, when they ran out of fuel for tanks and trucks. By this time the Allies had reached the German border. . . General Patton was sure that he could have pushed right on through the Siegfried Line if he had had enough gasoline, and he thought the war could have been over before the end of 1944. . .

When the Allies finally got started again, the Germans fought bitterly and bravely to defend their country. It is doubtful if the war could have ended in 1944 under any circumstances. But that it would end in an Allied victory, no one could now doubt. The question was, when would it end, and how?

The German collapse in northern France had been hastened and assisted by a dramatic Allied blow to the south. On August 15 the American Seventh Army, commanded by Lieutenant General Alexander M. Patch, carried out Operation ANVIL, an amphibious landing on the coast of the French Riviera, about midway between the cities of Nice and Toulon. This army had been convoyed through the Mediterranean to the French coast by an Allied naval task force commanded by American Vice-Admiral Henry K. Hewitt. . . The actual assault landing was made by the American VI Corps, commanded by Major General Lucian K. Truscott. . . The Germans were caught completely by surprise. They had thought the invasion convoy was heading for northern Italy . . . The dawn landing on August 15 was a success. . .

The shattered Germans were retreating as fast as they could to the Rhone Valley, knowing this was their only way of escape to northern France and to Germany. . . For six days the Americans and Germans struggled for control of the Rhone Valley near Montelimar. . . The Americans. . . were constantly short of ammunition, gasoline, food and all other kinds of supplies. The Germans were in headlong retreat; their spirits were low, they were unprepared for battle and too disorganized to fight efficiently. They too were short of supplies, but they were better off for ammunition and gasoline than the Americans.

Finally, by August 28, all three American divisions had concentrated near Montelimar, and in a determined effort they completely closed the Rhone Valley. The battle was over. About 15,000 Germans surrendered near Montelimar; nearly 50,000 more were captured at Marseille, Toulon, and in the valley south of the American roadblock. . . Truscott and his men pursued the fleeing Germans without a pause for rest. On September 11 the leading elements of the south France invasion force made contact with the right flank of Patton's Third Army near Dijon. The Allied front now extended unbroken from Switzerland to the North Sea. . .

By Mid-September 1944 the Western Allies had liberated most of the German-occupied areas of western Europe except the Netherlands and scattered regions in Belgium and France. . . General Eisenhower knew he could not start another big offensive until he could get more supplies to his front-line troops. . . He decided that the most important thing for Allied forces to do, therefore, was to repair the great damaged port of Antwerp, in Belgium, so that he could bring most of his supplies in through that city. . .

Finally, in early November, after both sides had suffered great losses, the British gained complete control of the territory on both sides of the lower Scheldt River, but even then their work was not finished. German mines had to be swept from the channel of the river. It was November 28 before Allied ships were able to bring supplies into the port of Antwerp. . .

By November the Americans had built up enough reserves of gasoline and ammunition to start some more attacks. . . By early December General Patton's men had reached the border of Germany north and east of Metz. . . The American Seventh Army reached the German frontier along the Rhine River and further west. They captured Strasbourg on November 23. . . It was now clear that there could be no Allied victory in 1944. . .

Before D-Day Hitler had warned the Allies that if they did not make peace, he would use a "secret weapon" against them. On June 12 a secret weapon really did come zooming across the English Channel. It was the so-called "buzz bomb", which was actually a sort of pilotless jet plane. . . Three days later they sent 300 of them across the Channel. Most of them struck London where they caused great damage. . . Meanwhile Hitler was boasting of an even more terrible "secret weapon". . . The first of these new secret weapons, the V-2 rocket, struck England on September 8, 1944. . . The blows delivered by great numbers of these fearsome weapons soon began to shake even the stout spirits of the hardy British people. . .

In the foggy dawn of December 16, the German attack swept

forward on a 40-mile front. . . By December 21 no one was quite sure where or when the Germans could be stopped. Operations maps showed the German penetration as a huge bulge in the Allied lines. That is why some newspaper correspondents called this the "Battle of the Bulge". . . By January 16, after a month of terribly bloody fighting, the Germans were almost back where they had started; the Bulge had disappeared. . .

The first great Allied offensive of 1945 began on February 8 with a concerted drive against the Siegfried Line. . . The Germans resisted fiercely, but the Allies pushed steadily ahead. . . On March 6 the armored divisions of General Bradley's two armies smashed their way through the northern Rhineland to the Rhine and Moselle rivers. So rapid was their advance that the Germans did not have time to blow up the railroad bridge over the Rhine at Remagen before it was seized on March 7 by the American 9th Armored Division.[4]

Of all the factors leading to the defeat of Germany, probably no single exploit was more important than the capture—on March 7, 1945—of the Ludendorff Bridge across the Rhine at Remagen. By seizing the span and establishing a bridgehead on the east bank of the river, a handful of officers and men of the Ninth Armored Division created one of the war's true turning points. Here, save for the first sharp minutes on the Normandy beaches, was the Army's greatest quarter hour. Here, a few infantrymen and engineers produced a strategic surprise of staggering proportions. For once the Rhine was crossed, victory was ours. . . The last German barrier is broken. Tanks rumble across over hastily patched gaps. After dark, more tanks and infantrymen pour over—and by dawn several tank companies and two infantry battalions are across. Tanks, half-tracks, trucks and jeeps then cross by the thousands. And off at headquarters, General Eisenhower quickly changes his battle plans to seize an opportunity created by the heroism of a handful of men.[5]

In the last days of March, 1945 the Western Allies gained momentum as they fanned out over the area east of the Rhine River. . . They were now almost as close to Berlin as were the Russians. . . General Eisenhower . . . believed that there were military tasks more important than beating the Russians to Berlin. . . During the night of April 16-17, the Russians struck. Not even the most fanatical Nazi—not even Hitler himself—had any hope of stopping the massive Russian offensive... So it was that it took the Russians six days to smash their way 30 miles to the outskirts of Berlin.[6]

Berlin, greatest city of the European Continent, fell Wednesday afternoon to the Russians, who quoted a high prisoner as declaring that Adolf Hitler had committed suicide along with Propaganda Minister Paul Josef Goebbels as the capital of the blood-drenched Nazi empire tumbled around them... In the surrender that Hitler had said never would come, 70,000 German troops laid down their arms... Nearly 1,000,000 German and Italian Fascist troops made the first unconditional surrender of the war in Europe Wednesday.[7]

Official Statement by President Truman—"Surrender of all German forces took place Monday, May 7, 1945, at a little red school house which is General Eisenhower's headquarters in Reims, France... Germany, which began the war with a ruthless attack on Poland, followed by successive aggressions and brutality in interment camps, surrendered with an appeal to the victors for mercy toward the German people and armed forces." The news for which the world has been waiting for days—that Germany had surrendered unconditionally and that Allied victory had come in Europe—came in an Associated Press dispatch from Reims, France at 8:15 A.M. Central War Time Monday.[8]

VE Day—victory in Europe—was celebrated with great rejoicing in every Allied country, but there was little time for rejoicing by Allied forces in the Pacific and Asia. They were still fighting a war against Japan.

Chapter 7
The War Years in the Pacific

The Japanese Imperial General Staff carefully prepared a war plan to take full advantage of Japan's overwhelming military superiority in the Far East... The Japanese knew that the United States Pacific Fleet, based in Hawaii, would be the only military force that could seriously interfere with their offenses. Therefore the first and most important single operation of the entire initial phase of their war plan was an attack to destroy or neutralize the striking power of the American fleet at Pearl Harbor...

The initial Japanese operations went exactly according to plan. The blow of Japan's First Air Fleet against Pearl Harbor and other military installations on Oahu was one of the most successful surprise attacks in the long history of warfare. All eight battleships of the American Pacific Fleet were sunk or put out of action for many months. Within a few hours, many thousands of miles further west, other Japanese planes began to strike Malaya, Hong Kong, the Philippines, Guam, and Wake...

Lonely Wake Island ... was an important line in the chain of American airfields connecting Hawaii with Guam and the Philippines. The capture of Wake, therefore, would isolate the Philippines, while providing the Japanese with a valuable outpost in their Central Pacific perimeter...

In December 1941, the garrison of Wake consisted of a

detachment of 450 Marines and 12 Marine fighter airplanes. Commanding the Marine detachment on the island was Major James P. S. Deveraux.

During the morning of December 8, Japanese airplanes based on the Marshall Islands began a long-range bombardment of Wake Island that continued for fifteen days. That same day a Japanese naval task force of three light cruisers, six destroyers, and two small troop transports sailed from Kwajelein to capture Wake. On December 11, Japanese marines attempted to land on Wake under the cover of intense naval gunfire support from the nine warships. But equally intense and accurate fire from the United States Marine defenders sank two Japanese destroyers and repulsed the attackers. The badly damaged Japanese task force limped back to reorganize, while the aerial bombardment continued. Greatly reinforced, the Japanese returned to Wake on December 23. This time they had air support from two of the carriers that had attacked Pearl Harbor.

The continuing Japanese air assault had severely damaged installations on Wake, and had exhausted the American Marines. Though they had fought bravely, they could not halt the overwhelming Japanese forces that poured across the beaches. Major Devereaux and his men were forced to surrender.

Meanwhile, on December 8, Japanese planes had begun to bombard Guam, the largest island in the Pacific between the Philippines and Hawaii. Guam was garrisoned by five hundred Marines and sailors, but in accordance with the terms of the Washington Treaty, there were no fortifications, no coast defense guns, no antiaircraft guns. On December 10, covered by intense naval gunfire, five thousand Japanese troops stormed onto Guam before dawn. For several hours the lightly armed Americans fought desperately, but they were overwhelmed soon after daybreak.

Probably the only serious mistake the Japanese made at the outset of the war was their failure to capture the American outpost of Midway Island, only eleven hundred miles northwest of Oahu. . . Things remained quiet at Midway for nearly six months. . .

In 1934 the United States had promised that on July 4, 1946, it would grant complete independence to the Philippine Islands. Meanwhile, it had established the self-governing Philippine Commonwealth to administer the islands while the Filipinos, with American help, prepared for independence. A small military garrison remained in the Philippines while the United States assisted the Commonwealth government to establish its own new army. In 1935 the retired American General Douglas MacArthur was invited by the Commonwealth government to organize and train this army.

In 1941 as war clouds gathered over the Far East, President Roosevelt called General MacArthur back to active duty in the American Army. MacArthur was placed in command of the American garrison in the Philippines, as well as of the army of the Philippine Commonwealth. The Filipino people, under the leadership of their president, Manuel Quezon, were completely loyal to the United States... They had learned that America was a staunch friend.

In December 1941 MacArthur's force consisted of 13,000 American troops, plus 12,000 excellent Filipino soldiers in the Philippine Scouts of the United States Army... The Philippine Commonwealth Army consisted of about 100,000 men, but these were only partially trained, and they had very little equipment. Air support was provided by the United States Army Air Force, with about 140 first-line aircraft.

The Japanese Fourteenth Army, under Lieutenant General Masaharu Homma... was assigned responsibility for invading the Philippines. With nearly 60,000 combat troops, supported by the powerful Japanese Third Fleet.. their first objective was to capture Luzon, the principal island of the Philippines. The Japanese high command expected that this would take about a month and a half...

In late November, because of the threat of war against Japan, a large convoy of American reinforcements, as well as weapons and equipment for the Philippine Army, had sailed from the west coast of the United States. Several more B-17 "Flying Fortress" bombers were scheduled to arrive in December to join the thirty-five B-17's already in the Philippines. With more reinforcement and supplies promised, MacArthur believed that by mid-1942 he could repulse a Japanese invasion. Unfortunately, he would not have that much time...

Air force and antiaircraft units drove off Japanese patrol planes which appeared over the Philippines early on December 8. But about noon... most of the American planes were on the ground at their airfields when they were surprised by a massive Japanese bombing attack. About half of the planes were destroyed, and most of the rest were damaged...

As MacArthur had expected, the principal Japanese landing was made at Lingayen Gulf on the western shore of Luzon... They were met at the beaches by MacArthur's Northern Luzon Force, commanded by Major General Jonathan M. Wainwright... MacArthur had hoped to drive the Japanese back into the sea, but he soon discovered that his inexperienced Filipinos could not stand up against the veteran Japanese. All that saved Wainwright's troops from complete disaster was the effectiveness of the Philippine Scouts 26th Cavalry Regiment and other regular American and Philippine Scout units. Assisted by the heroic defensive efforts of these troops, Wainwright rallied most of his Philippine Army units and began a withdrawal southward to Bataan, as ordered by General MacArthur.

Meanwhile, incessant Japanese bombardments of Manila were causing terrible loss of life and creating panic in the civilian population. For the sake of humanity, therefore, on December 26, MacArthur declared Manila an open city and moved his headquarters to the island of Corregidor...

The most difficult part of the withdrawal to Bataan was to get the South Luzon Force, commanded by Major General Albert M. Jones, past Manila and across the broad and marshy Pampanga River Valley before Wainwright's command was driven back to the shores of Manila Bay... The withdrawal was accomplished successfully. The main credit must go to the courage and determination of the terribly outnumbered, scattered detachments of Wainwright's regular American and Philippine Scout units, who responded magnificently to superb leadership...

On February 8... the Battle of Bataan settled down to a long period of trench warfare, siege operations. The defenders of Bataan were completely isolated from the outside world... Early in January, General MacArthur had been forced to order half-rations for everyone except the sick and wounded. There were no Allied forces available to break the blockade or to send reinforcements to MacArthur. Only small quantities of a few special supplies reached Corregidor and Bataan by submarine. The American government in Washington and General MacArthur on Corregidor knew that defeat in the Philippines was inevitable...

In February, General MacArthur was instructed by the American War Department to leave the Philippines and go to Australia. His experience and ability were needed to command Allied forces in that area. At first he refused to go, but on February

23 President Roosevelt personally repeated the order. On the night of March 12, MacArthur reluctantly left Corregidor with his family and a few staff officers on some American PT (motor-torpedo) boats. He appointed General Wainwright in command in the Philippines. Wainwright moved to Corregidor, leaving Major General Edward P. King to command on Bataan.

Meanwhile, MacArthus's party arrived at Mindanao and transferred to B-17 bombers which flew them to Port Darwin in Australia. Upon his arrival there on March 16, General MacArthur broadcast a promise to the Filipino people, to his troops still holding the line at Bataan—and to the Japanese: "I shall return."

General Homma now began to increase pressure against the American-Filipino defense lines. He knew that the defenders had been on half-rations for almost three months, and were now seriously weakened by shortage of food. On April 1 this reduced ration was again cut in half as Wainwright tried to preserve his dwindling supplies.

The Japanese launched their final attack on April 3, under the cover of overwhelming air and artillery bombardment. The well-trained, well-fed Japanese quickly broke through the defending lines. Though the exhausted, starving Filipinos and Americans fought bravely, they were unable to stem the Japanese advance. On April 9 General King and the remnants of the defenders of Bataan were forced to surrender.

Then occurred one of the greatest tragedies of the war. The Japanese had only contempt for their own soldiers who surrendered, and so they were equally contemptuous of captured enemies, and generally treated them badly. Brutally and ruthlessly they forced the exhausted Allied survivors of the Battle of Bataan to march in blazing heat to prisons in Manila. Hundreds died on this "Death March", and thousands more died as a result of this and later mistreatment. . .

During the remainder of April and the early days of May, Japanese airplanes rained bombs incessantly on Corregidor and on the small forts in the mouth of Manila Bay. . . One by one the American batteries were knocked out by the overwhelmingly superior Japanese air and artillery units. Soon after dark on the night of May 5, Japanese troops landed on the northeastern tip of Corregidor. . . The American artillery had been knocked out; all

American and Filipino troops were now engaged in the fighting, so there were no reserves to meet new assault forces coming across the bay. By noon General Wainwright realized that he could do no more damage to the Japanese, and so, in order to save further loss of life, he surrendered his command to General Homma...

The Japanese had expected to conquer the Philippines in fifty days. It took them three times that long... The few American units in the islands fought with a gallantry never exceeded in American military history. American artillery was particularly efficient. Starvation, disease, and sheer physical exhaustion had reduced the stamina of the defending troops to the vanishing point before they were defeated...

Early in 1942 President Roosevelt and Prime Minister Churchill established a military command organization to direct the wars against Germany and Japan... Supervision of all military operations in the Pacific Ocean areas was assigned the American Joint Chiefs of Staff. Allied naval operations in the Indian Ocean and land operations in Burma, Malaya, and Sumatra were to be supervised by the British Chiefs of Staff...

The Southwest Pacific area, commanded by General MacArthur, included Australia, New Guinea, most of the Netherlands East Indies, and the Philippines... All other Pacific regions were included in the Pacific Ocean areas, commanded by American Admiral Chester W. Nimitz... His area of responsibility was divided into three portions. That north of the 42nd parallel was called the North Pacific area. The region east of Australia, and south of the equator—including the eastern Solomon Islands and New Caledonia—was called the South Pacific area; this was controlled by Vice Admiral Robert L. Ghormley, under the overall command of Admiral Nimitz. The remaining islands, including the Hawaiian Islands and most of the Japanese island groups, made up the Central Pacific area, under Nimitz' direct command...

Between January 11 and February 28 the Japanese had made numerous amphibious and airborne landings on the major islands of the Netherlands East Indies, and had forced the Dutch to surrender on March 9... They decided to seize outposts in the Aleutian Islands and to capture the island of Midway, in the Central Pacific, as well as Papua (southeastern New Guinea), and the Solomon Islands in the Southwest Pacific.

The first step in this new Japanese plan was to send amphibious task forces to seize bases in the southeastern Solomon Islands and in the Louisiade Archipelago, and to capture Port Moresby in southern Papua. American naval forces attacked these convoys, and this led to the air and naval Battle of the Coral Sea on May 7 and 8, 1942. . . The Japanese convoys turned back. They did, however, establish an outpost on Tulagi Ialand.

Less than a month later, Admiral Isoroku Yamamoto led the main Japanese fleet and a large convoy of troop transports toward Midway. At the same time a smaller Japanese amphibious force sailed for the Aleutian Islands. The naval Battle of Midway began on June 3. . . By June 6 the Japanese had suffered a crushing defeat at the hands of the small American fleet, and the expedition to Midway was abandoned. The Japanese succeeded, however, in establishing footholds on the Aleutian Islands of Attu and Kiska. . .

In Papua, the Japanese immediately sent an expedition overland from Buna across the Owen Stanley Mountains to seize Port Moresby. Thus, before General MacArthur could start his planned limited offensives, he was forced to fight a desperate defensive battle for Port Moresby. . . Slowly, in bitter fighting the Japanese were pushed back across the mountains. . . By mid-November the Japanese had been forced to withdraw to strongly fortified coastal positions between Gona and Buna. . . The Allied troops gradually surrounded this powerful stronghold, but the Australians were exhausted. . . and the Americans were entirely inexperienced in jungle warfare. The Allies were also short of rations and ammunition. After six weeks of inconclusive fighting, the Japanese still held all their main positions, while disease and casualties had cut the attacking force almost in half.

General MacArthur then sent Lieutenant General Robert L. Eichelberger to take command of Allied forces near Buna and Gona. By personal initiative and leadership Eichelberger rallied the demoralized Allied troops. When reinforcements finally arrived, he began a slow but steady advance that drove the Japanese back into an ever shrinking perimeter. The Japanese fiercely contested every foot of ground, and losses were high on both sides. The Allied forces captured Gona on December 9. In January they stormed Buna. By January 22, 1943, they had wiped out all Japanese resistance in the area. . .

Admiral Ghormley had been ordered to seize the southeastern

Solomons even before anyone knew that the Japanese were building up a stronghold on Guadalcanal. When the Joint Chiefs of Staff realized what the Japanese were doing, they ordered Ghormley to rush preparations for his offensive. His first objective was now to be the seizure of the newly established Japanese airfield on the northern shore of Guadalcanal.

The principal ground force element . . . was the lst Marine Division, commanded by Major General Alexander A. Vandegrift. Though they had seen no previous combat action in the war, these were tough, veteran troops, trained for amphibious operations and jungle warfare.

On August 7, 1942, Marine landing forces went ashore on the northern coast of Guadalcanal and on the nearby islands of Florida and Tulagi. . . By the evening of August 7, the Marines had driven the surprised Japanese from the airfield and had established a defensive perimeter against the expected Japanese counterattack. . .

Undetected by the Americans, a Japanese naval squadron slipped past Savo Island during the night of August 8-9. It sank four Allied cruisers in a few minutes, then escaped unharmed. The Allied defeat at the Battle of Savo Island, combined with intensive Japanese aerial attacks from Rabaul, persuaded Admiral Ghormley to withdraw the naval covering forces and supply transports from the waters near Guadalcanal. The lst Marine Divison suddenly found itself isolated in its small perimeter around newly named Henderson Field.

Japanese planes now began a series of bombing and strafing attacks which would continue for many weeks to come. . . As their strength built up, veteran Japanese jungle fighters began to harass the Marines' defensive perimeter. The first organized Japanese ground attacks on Guadalcanal began on August 17, but the Marines repulsed them easily. . . During the following weeks the Japanese continued to rush soldiers there by single ship and by convoy. . . By the middle of October, the strength of each side had been built up to over twenty thousand men. On October 23 the Japanese launched a two-division attack against the American position. . . For forty-eight hours the land battle raged before the Japanese finally admitted failure. By the end of January 1943 the Japanese had been completely defeated, and gave up all further efforts to hold the island. Japanese destroyers slipped in at night and evacuated about 13,000 survivors between February 6 and 9. Approximately 25,000 more had been killed in battle, or had been drowned trying to reach the island, while at least 15,000 died of disease or starved. American losses were 1,700 killed and almost 5,000 wounded; most of these casualties were among the Marines. . .

Admiral Nimitz was ordered by the Joint Chiefs of Staff to strike west from Hawaii through the Japanese island chains of the Marshalls, Carolines, and the Marianas. . . In May 1943 an amphibious task force under Admiral Thomas C. Kinkaid assaulted Attu. The principal element of this force was the 7th Infantry Division. After an eighteen-day battle, 2,500 Japanese were killed, and 29 prisoners were taken. American casualties were 561 killed and 1,136 wounded. . . The Japanese now realized that Kiska was next on the American timetable. On July 29, 1943 a small Japanese naval force secretly embarked the 5,400 troops on Kiska and took them back to Japan. . . When American and Canadian troops landed on the island on August 15, they were surprised to find the island deserted. . .

Admiral Nimitz decided to start his advance by invading the Gilbert Islands, on the islands of Tarawa and Makin. . . The landing began on November 21. By the evening of the 23rd, the Army regiment attacking Makin overwhelmed the last Japanese resistance and captured the island. . . The 2nd Marine Division encountered much more serious Japanese resistance at Tarawa. . . For twenty-four hours the issue was in doubt. The Marines suffered terrible losses. . . Finally, after four days of the most intensive fighting, they wiped out all organized resistance. Only about 150 prisoners, almost all laborers, were taken. The remaining 4,650 Japanese were killed. The Marines lost almost 1,000 killed and over 2,000 wounded. Tarawa had been a very costly fight. . .

Admiral Nimitz and his forces now began to prepare for an advance through the Marshall Islands. Kwajalein was their first objective. General Smith's V Marine Amphibious Corps was given the mission of making the landing. This time the assault troops were the 4th Marine Division, and the Army's 7th Infantry Division, veterans of Attu. The total strength of the assault force was 42,000; the Japanese defenders numbered more than 8,000.

On January 29, 1944, Nimitz' forces began an intensive aerial and naval bombardment against the small group of coral islands which made up Kwajalein Atoll. . . The Japanese did not give up easily; the fighting raged for over a week on the islands of the atoll. But by February 8 all resistance had ceased, the fanatical defenders having been killed almost to a man. The Americans lost 1,500 men killed and wounded...

Admiral Nimitz' next objective was the atoll of Eniwetok... defended by a garrison of 3,400 men. A combined landing force of Army and Marine units, totaling nearly 8,000 men, landed there on February 19. The defenders were overwhelmed in four days of vicious fighting... The important islands of the Marshall group were now under American control...

Nimitz decided to "leapfrog" over Truk to the Marianas Islands... Overall responsibility for the invasion was given to Vice Admiral Raymond A. Spruance who commanded the powerful Fifth Fleet. The Amphibious force was commanded by Admiral Turner. Under him, the assault force was again commanded by newly promoted Lieutenant General H. M. Smith. This force of three and a half Marine divisions and two Army divisions was divided between Smith's V Marine Amphibious Corps and the III Amphibious Corps under Major General Roy S. Geiger...

On June 15 the 2nd and 4th Marine divisions of the V Corps landed on the south shores of Saipan. Next day the Army 27th Division also went ashore. As had been expected, they met the most determined resistance yet encountered in the Central Pacific fighting.

While the Battle of Saipan was raging, Admiral Geiger's III Corps was approaching Guam, where it was scheduled to land on June 18. Suddenly, Admiral Spruance ordered the convoy to turn eastward, away from the Marianas. Patrol planes had sighted the Japanese fleet steaming eastward through the Philippine Sea. Spruance felt that it would be a mistake to make the landing in the middle of a great naval battle.

The Battle of Philippine Sea lasted from June 19 to 21... Spruance won a decisive victory, destroying most of the Japanese carrier planes and sinking many of the enemy ships. The Japanese had failed in their effort to interfere with the landings in the Marianas...

Saipan was finally captured on July 9. The Japanese lost 27,000 killed and 2,000 captured. American casualties were about 3,500 killed and 1,300 wounded...

On July 21 the Army's 77th Infantry Division, the 3rd Marine

Division, and a Marine brigade assaulted Guam. Japanese resistance was almost as strong as on Saipan. But the island was finally captured by August 10. Meanwhile Marine units landed on Tinian on July 24 and captured it after nine days of intense combat. The principal islands of the Marianas were now firmly under American control. . .

The next important step in General MacArthur's plans was a proposed landing in the Admiralty Islands, lying west of New Britain. The Admiralties were important because of their airfields and harbors and because the capture of these bases would complete the American ring around Rabaul. The invasion was scheduled for April 1944. In late February MacArthur decided that a bold attack on the Admiralties might catch the enemy by surprise and also advance the Allied timetable by two months. His staff was dismayed because they did not think such an attack could be successful without more troops and longer preparation. Despite almost unanimous advice against such a daring operation, MacArthur nonetheless ordered one division to make an . . . exploratory probe of Los Negros Island. Because his staff considered this operation so dangerous, MacArthur announced that he would personally accompany the leading unit ashore. He would then decide whether the attack should be continued, or whether to withdraw and wait to carry out the invasion in April.

The surprise assault was successful. His troops seized the vital airfield on Los Negros Island before the enemy realized what was happening. MacArthur, standing on the beach with the division commander, decided that the attack should continue. "Hold what you have taken," he said, "no matter what the odds. Don't let go!"

Returning to his headquarters, MacArthur rushed reinforcements to Los Negros. The Japanese counterattacked violently, but the American troops repulsed them and forged ahead. By April, the entire Admiralty group was securely in American hands.

During March and early April Australian troops on New Guinea pushed steadily westward from Saidor. They captured Madang on April 25. At this point, however, the reinforced Japanese 18th Army stopped all Allied advance. . . They had established a large supply and maintenance base at Hollandia. . . beyond reach of MacArthur's fighter aircraft. Here they began to construct several airfields for future air operations. . .

MacArthur solved this problem by planning to have two

American regiments land at Aitape, about 125 miles east of Hollandia, at the same time the Navy carriers were supporting the main landing of two divisions near Hollandia. . . . MacArthur and his engineers were sure that the Aitape airfield could be made ready for use before the carriers had to withdraw. Then land-based air cover from Aitape would replace carrier air support at Hollandia. The plan worked perfectly. . . . On April 22 the American 24th and 41st divisions, landed on beaches 25 miles apart, west and east of Hollandia. With excellent carrier air support they converged inland against the Japanese airfields. In five days they had seized the entire Hollandia region, losing less than 100 men killed and about 1,000 wounded. The Japanese left about 5,000 dead behind them, while the survivors dispersed into the jungles. The landing at Aitape was equally successful; the airstrip was ready by April 24, two days ahead of schedule. Japanese resistance was stiffer than at Hollandia. The Americans lost 450 killed and 2,500 wounded. More than 9,000 Japanese were killed. . . The Hollandia operation was one of the most brilliant actions of World War II. . . This was typical of the tactics and strategy of General MacArthur's campaigns.

Without pause or hesitation, MacArthur's troops continued their leapfrog advance westward along the New Guinea coast. On May 17, they seized Wake Island. Ten days later, a division landed on the powerful Japanese fortress of Biak Island . . . and captured the island only after a month of bitter fighting. . . . Another landing was made on July 2 on neighboring Noemfoor Island. On July 30, Allied troops made their final amphibious operation in New Guinea by landing at Sansapor. . . against little opposition.

By the end of July 1944 General MacArthur had effectively conquered the entire northern coast of New Guinea. . . In the New Guinea campaign, MacArthur's troops killed 35,000 Japanese. Their own losses had been less than 2,500 killed and about 16,000 wounded. In all of military history there is no instance of comparable results in territory gained and losses inflicted, at such a small cost in life. . .

The Army Chief of Staff, General George C. Marshall, believed that the next logical step would be for General MacArthur to advance from New Guinea to the Philippines, which would then become the base for a joint Army-Navy assault on Japan. He and his staff saw no need to become involved in lengthy operations either on Formosa or in China. . .

At a conference at Pearl Harbor in late July, President Roosevelt decided in favor of the Army plan. General MacArthur attended the conference, and his . . . presentation persuaded Roosevelt that attacks against Formosa and China would be far more costly of American lives. MacArthur also pointed out that the United States had a moral obligation to liberate the loyal people of the Philippine Islands as soon as possible. . .

There was close cooperation between Admiral Nimitz and General MacArthur in preparing for the advance to the Philippines. They planned a landing on Mindanao in November, to be followed by an attack on Leyte in late December. . . Admiral Halsey's Third Fleet, covering these preliminary operations, had been striking powerful carrier blows at Yap, Mindanao and the central Philippines. . . Halsey radioed Admiral Nimitz recommending an early move against Leyte, without bothering with Mindanao. . .

Within twenty-four hours MacArthur informed Nimitz . . . that he would be ready to attack Leyte on October 20 instead of December 20. . .On October 19 two tremendous amphibious assault forces approached the east coast of Leyte. . . Totaling about 100,000 combat troops, they were loaded on 350 transports and cargo ships, plus 400 other smaller amphibious craft. Admiral Thomas C. Kinkaid's Seventh Fleet was assigned to cover the landing. . . Further out to sea lay Admiral Halsey's mighty Third Fleet, the most powerful naval force ever assembled. . .

At 10:00 A.M. on October 20, 1944, under the cover of a terrific naval gunfire bombardment, the assault waves of the X and XXIV Corps swept toward the beaches on a front eighteen miles long. While the leading elements were still fighting to secure the beaches, General MacArthur, accompanied by President Sergio Osmena of the Philippine Commonwealth (former President Quezon had died), splashed ashore from an assault landing craft. Speaking into the microphone of a portable radio transmitter, MacArthur broadcast a message to the 17 million loyal people of the Philippines, who had been waiting for him for two and a half years: "I have returned. By the grace of Almighty God our forces stand again on Philippine soil. Rally to me! Rise and strike!"

Even before the American landings, the Japanese had been preparing for a major naval counterblow. All of the remaining combat elements of the Japanese fleet. . . converged toward the

Philippines... This brought on the greatest naval battle in the history of the world... The final result of the battle for Leyte Gulf was a tremendous American victory, and the effective elimination of the Japanese navy as an obstacle to further American operations in the Western Pacific... While this gigantic naval struggle was taking place between October 23 and 26, General Krueger's Sixth Army was establishing itself firmly ashore. But the American soldiers were encountering the fiercest kind of opposition... The Japanese had 260,000 troops in the Philippines... They rushed reinforcements to the island... Japanese army and navy planes violently attacked the American carriers in an effort to gain control of the air over the beaches. Here, for the first time, the Japanese used Kamikaze (suicide plane) tactics.

The aerial struggle was the most intense of the Pacific war, but Navy planes, assisted by Army Air Force fighters on hastily created landing strips near the beaches, finally gained control of the air. Below them the soldiers forged ahead... Finally the pressure was too much for the Japanese. On December 21 the exhausted remnants of their veteran 1st Division broke and fled... Although fighting would continue in the mountains of western Leyte for several weeks, for all practical purposes the Battle of Leyte was over.

General MacArthur's next objective was the island of Luzon... Krueger's objective was Lingayen Gulf, where Homma and his army had landed three years and one month earlier... They hit the beaches at the head of Lingayen Gulf on the morning of January 9, 1945. By night 68,000 troops had been landed and controlled a beachhead 15 miles long and 6,000 yards deep...

The Sixth Army's advance toward Manila was rapid... On January 30 a small force of American Rangers and Filipino guerrillas made a daring raid behind the Japanese lines to rescue several hundred Allied war prisoners at Cabanatuan... For two weeks the Japanese struggled bitterly to hold the island. The battle ended only when the defenders, surrounded in tunnels that the Americans had built before the war, blew themselves up. Later, a total of 4,215 dead Japanese were counted; nobody knows how many died in the tunnels. Of the 3,000 Americans who took part in the Battle of Corregidor, 140 were killed and 550 wounded.

In February and March, Eighth Army troops landed in other areas of the Philippines, rapidly extending American control over most of the islands. . . By June the Japanese troops had been driven into the inaccessible jungle regions of the high Philippine mountains. Here they remained . . . until Japan surrendered. . . .

During the summer and early fall of 1944, American engineers were busy building tremendous airfields and supply installations on the Marianas Islands of Saipan, Guam and Tinian. As the construction work approached completion, vast quantities of supplies, gasoline, and bombs began to arrive in Navy cargo ships. Then squadrons of new B-29 Superfortress bombers began to fly into the fields.

On November 24, 1944, the B-29 squadrons made their first attack on Tokyo. This was a round-trip flight of three thousand miles. . . Many damaged planes and their crews went down in the ocean as they tried to make the long trip back to the Marianas. Almost midway between Tokyo and the Marianas bases lay the rocky, heavily fortified island of Iwo Jima. . . In late 1944, Admiral Nimitz was ordered to seize the island. . which would be extremely useful in American hands. . .

Iwo Jima is only eight square miles of waterless volcanic rock and sand. It is honeycombed with caves and interconnecting tunnels. In 1944 these led to well-concealed and strongly protected Japanese pillboxes and covered gun positions scattered throughout the island. . . Minefields had been laid not only on the beaches but also completely across the island. . . Iwo Jima was probably the strongest single fortification assaulted by any troops during World War II.

Beginning in December and continuing through January and most of February, the Americans attacked Iwo Jima every day by land-based bombers from the Marianas, or by carrier planes, or both. American naval forces frequently hammered it with long-range fire. . . By dawn of February 19, Iwo Jima had sustained the most intensive bombardment ever placed on a target of that size. . .

The V Marine Amphibious Corps, 75,000 men strong, comprising the 3rd, 4th and 5th Divisions, swept ashore on the southeastern beaches of the island at 9:00 A.M. on February 19. . . During the bombardment the Japanese had taken refuge in their deep, underground shelters, while a few lookouts . . . watched for the arrival of the attackers. . . The Japanese jumped out of their shelters and at once laid heavy fire against the Marines arriving on the beaches, and against the waves of landing craft still approaching from the transports off-shore.

The Marines began to suffer heavy casualties, and for a while the advance was held up... Despite their casualties, and despite the fearful danger, the Marines began to move forward. By nightfall they had driven all the way across the southwestern portion of the island. The defenders of strongly fortified Mount Suribachi, on the southwestern tip of Iwo, were isolated.

For four days a vicious hand-to-hand battle raged around Mount Suribachi before the position was finally taken on February 23. Though still under heavy fire from the main Japanese positions, a group of Marines raised an American flag on the summit of the hill...

During these days high winds and heavy seas interfered greatly with sending supplies and reinforcements ashore... On February 25, however, the weather cleared, permitting more ammunition and supplies to be rushed to the beaches... The crisis of the Battle of Iwo Jima was over, though three weeks more of desperate fighting lay ahead. Inch by inch, yard by yard, gun position by gun position, the Marines fought their way north and east across the island. Finally, on March 17, General Smith was able to announce officially that organized resistance had been overcome. Individual Japanese, still taking refuge in hidden caves, nevertheless continued to fight for many days more.

Over 21,000 Japanese were killed on Iwo Jima, and more than 200 were taken prisoner. But the exact number of Japanese dead will never be known, since many were sealed up in their underground shelters. The battle had been a costly one for the Americans, who suffered almost 25,000 casualties, nearly 7,000 being killed... Before the end of the war more than 2,250 B-29's, carrying about 25,000 crewmen, made emergency landings on the airfields of Iwo Jima. Most of these planes and men would probably have been lost if the Marines had not sacrificed themselves to capture the island...

Late in 1944 the Joint Chiefs of Staff ordered Admiral Nimitz to invade the Ryukyu Islands as soon as possible after the capture of Iwo Jima. These islands would be used for air and naval bases to support landings on the main Japanese islands... Okinawa is sixty-five miles long and varies in width from two to eighteen miles... This was the first time that American forces had been required to fight in a large area inhabited by a hostile Japanese local population...

The most difficult problems were those caused by Okinawa's distance from any large American supporting and supply bases...

A tremendous invasion force would be necessary to capture such a large and well defended island, therefore many supply ships would be required to make the long round trips from Okinawa to Hawaii or San Francisco. All of the initial air support would have to be supplied by naval carriers, and much bomber support would be required from the carriers throughout the operation. . . Since Okinawa was within easy striking range of air bases in Japan, the Navy would have to provide protection against expected air attacks. These things contributed to make this the most difficult planning problem which any American staff had encountered so far during the war.

To carry out the invasion, Admiral Nimitz established a unified amphibious force, under Admiral Raymond Spruance, commanding the Fifth Fleet. The actual amphibious operations were to be directed, as before in the Central Pacific area, by Vice Admiral Turner. The expeditionary force was the Tenth Army, commanded by Lieutenant General Simon B. Buckner, Jr. His army consisted of five Army and three Marine divisions, numbering about 225,000 combat troops, plus an equal number of support and garrison troops. After a careful study. . . it was decided that the best landing beaches were those on the west coast of Okinawa, near the town of Hagushi. . .

The Japanese realized that Okinawa was a likely target for an American invasion. The island was garrisoned by the Thirty-Second Army, totaling about 140,000 men. . . Most of Japan's trained airplane pilots had been killed in the disastrous battles of 1943 and 1944. And most of Japan's combat vessels had been sunk.

But the Japanese navy and air force had many brave, untrained men who were willing to sacrifice their lives for their country. So the Japanese secretly moved 350 motor-torpedo boats to the Kerama Islands off the southwestern coast of Okinawa, and concealed them there. These boats, loaded with high explosives, were really large, manned torpedoes. The volunteer suicide crews were to ram and sink American warships and transports gathered for the landing near Hagushi Bay. At the same time a force of Kamikaze suicide airplane pilots were to fly their explosive-laden planes into other vessels of the American fleet. . . Their plan was to attack the troops who had come ashore while the suicide boats and planes were smashing the invasion fleet.

On March 26, the 77th Infantry Division made a sudden, surprise landing in the Kerama Islands. Five days later it captured the nearby Keise Islands... The Japanese had not foreseen these moves. The seizure of the Kerama Islands resulted in the capture of all the suicide motor-torpedo boats they had hidden there. This ruined an important part of the Japanese defensive plan.

During the early hours of April 1 the great amphibious armada approached Okinawa. Hundreds of naval vessels . . . joined swarms of carrier bombers and fighters in placing on the Hagushi beaches the heaviest assault bombardments yet undertaken. Shortly after dawn, the 2nd Marine Division pretended to land at several places along the southeastern coast of the island, attracting Japanese attention there.

At 8:30 A.M. an eight-mile-long line of landing craft swept onto the Hagushi beaches. On the north were the 1st and 6th Marine divisions of the III Marine Amphibious Corps, under General Geiger. The right-hand part of the line was made up of units from the 7th and 96th Infantry divisions of General John R. Hodge's XXIV Army Corps...

More than fifty thousand American troops, including supporting artillery, landed in the first eight hours of the invasion. . . The first important Kamikaze attacks came on April 6 and caused much damage to American transports and warships. That same day a naval task force of ten vessels sped from Japan toward Okinawa to join in the attack. One of these was the giant battleship Yamato, largest warship in the world at the time. But on April 7 American carrier planes sank the Yamato and five other vessels; the four remaining escaped back to Japan, seriously damaged. There was no further Japanese naval interference with the invasion.

The Kamikaze attacks continued, however. But once they had learned the Japanese suicide tactics, the Americans were able to prevent the suicide planes from doing serious harm. . .Meanwhile land operations were continuing. . . The 77th Division was able to seize nearby Ie Island, after a hard fight of five days.

On May 11, the III and XXIV corps began Buckner's planned offensive. . . They fought their way into and through the flanks of the Japanese positions. The advance was slow and costly, but the battlewise American troops could not be stopped by even the most fanatical Japanese resistance. . .

During the early days of June the Japanese organized a last-ditch defense in the mountainous southern tip of Okinawa. . . . The Americans began an assault of this rocky position on June 12. . . . On June 20 all organized defense now collapsed as Japanese troops for the first time in the war began surrendering in large numbers.

But General Buckner did not see this final victory he had planned. On June 18, two days before the end of the battle, he was at a Marine battalion forward observation post, peering at Japanese positions less than three hundred yards away. One of the few remaining Japanese artillery pieces scored a direct hit on the observation post, killing General Buckner immediately.

About 130,000 Japanese were killed in the campaign, and 7,400 prisoners were taken. American losses, including those on the war ships providing naval and air cover, totaled over 13,000 killed and about 36,000 wounded. The Navy, in fact, suffered its heaviest losses of the entire war. Thirty-six vessels were sunk, and 368 warships, transports and other vessels were damaged. Nearly 8,000 Japanese aircraft were destroyed; the Americans lost 763. Now with an outpost and a major base only 350 miles from Japan itself, the Americans were ready to start planning for their final invasion.

During the summer of 1945, the tremendous armed might of the United States got ready to bring about the final destruction of the Japanese Empire. General MacArthur, Admiral Nimitz, and their staffs began coordinated planning for invading Japan. . . . Landings were to be made on the island of Kyushu in November, and on Honshu in March. Troops from Germany were being brought to the Pacific to take part in this last great battle. . . .

Japan had at least two million well-trained, well-equipped ground troops on the four main islands. She had at least as many more in Manchuria and China. Therefore, although they hoped that the Japanese would realize that further resistance was senseless and would only result in the loss of the lives of millions of soldiers and civilians, Allied leaders felt they had no choice but to continue their invasion plans. Meanwhile, in the Potsdam Declaration of early July, they promised Japan a just and honorable peace if she would surrender. They threatened the nation with complete destruction, however, if she continued the war.

It was clear to the Japanese government that their nation had been defeated, but the idea of surrender was very distasteful to them.

. . America now decided to prove to the Japanese that she was serious. . . . The hope was that Japan could be shocked into making peace before both sides suffered terrible casualties in land battles. . . . On August 6, 1945, therefore, an American B-29 dropped the first atomic bomb on the military base city of Hiroshima. About sixty thousand civilians and soldiers were killed by the bomb, more were injured, and over half of the city was wrecked. Three days later a second bomb dropped on Nagasaki, where Japanese losses were almost as great. . .

On August 10 the Japanese government decided that it must make peace at once, and sent a message through Switzerland offering to surrender on the basis of the terms of the Potsdam Proclamation. The Allied governments accepted this surrender offer, and on August 14 (August 15 in the Far East) the fighting stopped.

On September 2, 1945, General MacArthur, as Supreme Commander for the Allied Powers, accepted the formal surrender of the Japanese nation on the deck of the United States battleship Missouri in Tokyo Bay. After nearly four years, the Pacific war with Japan was ended.[1]

CHAPTER 8
News of our Men and Women in Service

Scrapbooks belonging to Mrs. Lindsay McAllister, Ben Bowers, Clyde Bean, Bessie W. Strickland and Lawrence Wood (kept by his sister, Elsie Wood Alsobrook during World War II) proved invaluable in securing information about those who were in the service. There were clippings from the *Clarksville Times*, *Deport News*, *Bogata News*, and the *Drug Store News* which was printed by different people in Red River County and mailed to those away from home in the service of their country. Unfortunately, very few articles were dated, but shown below are some of the many pieces of news found in those scrapbooks.

"*Drug Store News*—Published every two weeks by the young people of the Churches of Clarksville, Texas and sent free to Red River County men now in the armed services of the United States—Haywood Antone, Editor—Isobel Farrier, Business Manager—Vol. I, June 12, 1942, No. 5—Special acknowledgment should be made to the *Clarksville Times* from which we have taken several of the news stories. Typing and mimeographing were done by Billy Barton and Rev. Carroll B. Ray. Jimmie Stiles and Patricia Felts helped with writing the stories and addressing the envelopes. The expenses of this issue of the Drug Store News were paid by the Clarksville Pharmacy. The owners, T. H. Tanner and F. M. Morehead, want to use this method of sending their best wishes to the many men from this county who will receive this issue of the paper.

News of the Town—Stiles Drug. Co. began filling its windows with pictures of servicemen from this county about three weeks ago. Now, those pictures take up practically all of the window space and the store has given up the idea of displaying any of its merchandise in the windows. The pictures are all handsome, familiar faces of boys from Clarksville and the county. A complete list of those whose pictures adorn the windows is as follows: **Thomas Dwight Hoald, Lt. Wilson Ralston, Franklin Eiler, Wendel Benningfield, Ray Cagle, Sgt. A. N. Griffin, Morris Soward, Deward Dale, Sgt. Morris Dycus, Cpl. Lewis Bartlett, Ben Bowers, Cpl. Stanley G. Tyndell, John E. Bledsoe, LeRoy Hamilton, Malcolm McGuire, Roy A. Abernathy, Cpl. Nowlin Green, Otis King, Jr., Bobbie M. Taylor, Wallace Abernathy, M. T. Coffman, Sgt. Charles Wharton, Cecil Phillips, Durwood Joyner, Howard P. Barnett, Sgt. Joe P. Soward, Forrest West, Sidney Cagle, Travis Henry, Pete Wright, Jim Anderson, Luther L. Gray, Donald Rains Bynum, Charlie F. Hale, Jr., A. J. Meets, Norman Hemingway, Harry Igo, Lloyd Lewis, Fred Johnson, Homer A. Giddens, Lt. Miss Jewell Derryberry, Lt. Travis L. Mauldin, Gerald D. Higgins, Haskell Peek, James T. Benningfield, Allen B. Proctor, Bill Nance, Sgt. Darcus W. Emery, Charles M. Thompson, Dee Thompson, Wendell Thompson.**

The month of May saw a nation-wide drive by the druggists of America to sell war bonds and stamps. All of the Clarksville drug stores helped in the drive. Bullington's Drug Store led in sales in Clarksville. Total sales by the store, according to W. W. Bullington, amounted to about $15,000, a sum which was almost half the county's quota for May which was $42,000.

At a meeting of the Directors of the Red River County Rodeo Association last week, a proposal to eliminate the 1942 show was unanimously supported... Decision to cancel this year's rodeo was due entirely to the national emergency and because of the necessity of giving first consideration to the country's war effort.

Clarksville had a test air raid last Wednesday night, June 3. The alert was sounded by the fire siren. There had been no advertisement of the blackout previously, and a number of citizens did not realize it was in progress. For the most part the lights of the city were dimmed. The all clear signal was sounded ten minutes later. From now on, a blackout will be called by continuous blasts of the whistle at the mill. The fire whistle will be turned on, but the mill whistle will confirm an impending air raid.

More than $2,000 has been raised in Red River County for the U.S.O., according to County Chairman, Ross Hughston. This report did not include several of the larger communities which have not completed their drives. All but approximately $500 of the county's donations to this fund came from Clarksville, where a city-wide campaign was conducted under the supervision of F. L. Wolf.

The second annual flower show sponsored by the Elysian Garden Club of Clarksville was held Friday, June 12, in the high school gymnasium. No admission was charged, but a free-will offering was made with the proceeds going to the Red Cross. Highlighting the show were two exhibits by the local florists, Shackelford's Greenhouse and McCulloch Greenhouse, both displays following the patriotic theme. Just inside the door was the Shackelford display, a large 'V' composed of several hundred pot plants with an American flag and red cross to one side. Following the red, white and blue motif was the display of the McCulloch Greenhouse, a formal dinner table with a white damask tablecloth, a red carnation certerpiece, and blue dishes.

The following men have been in Clarksville on furloughs during the past two weeks: **Cpl. Ona H. Moore, Cpl. Floyd Green, Pvt. Henderson Coffman, Pvt. Bill Bettes, Ernest Sutton Collins, Capt. Max Witmer, and Lt. Willard McCoy.**

Dr. J. L. Wright has been commissioned a Captain in the U. S. Army and will report for active duty soon. **Frank Milan**, formerly of Clarksville, is now stationed at Long Island, New York. Frank has been living in Hollywood for the past few years. In a recent letter to Ann Sothern of the movies, he asked her to send him some wire coat hangers and an autographed picture of Hedy Lamarr. Frank and Miss Sothern have been friends for many years.

Four Red Cross workers who have established records in Clarksville are Mrs. John Weaver and daughters, Misses Elizabeth and Ellis, who have knitted 44 sweaters for soldiers and sailors, and Mrs. M. A. Holland who has knitted ten. Mrs. Holland did her sweaters while in bed, recovering from a broken limb."

★★★

"BOGATA BOY PINNED IN ICY CREEK BY HEAVY GERMAN FIRE by Pvt. Carroll L. Walton, Fifth Army Field Correspondent, with the Fifth Army, Italy—Having German machine gun fire fall on you so heavy you're unable to move is an experience one remembers for quite some time. But when you have to lie in a cold mountain stream during the ordeal—how could you forget it? That was the sentiment of **Pfc. Norvill Pettit** of Bogata, Rt.1, after undergoing the test on the Fifth Army front in Italy.

The patrol had almost reached the little mountain town it was to investigate when German machine gun fire opened up from two hills. The only thing resembling cover was a stream several hundred yards away. They dived in without giving it a second thought. Nazis set up a few flares and started laying mortar fire on them. They were unable to move out of the ditch and fight, as the Germans had the upper hand, Pettit recalled.

After staying in the icy mountain stream for about an hour with the situation unchanged, the patrol leader decided to call for artillery fire on the position and pull the patrol back out of range. Successfully done, the patrol was able to get back unscathed to the Fifth Army lines."

★★★

"**Sgt. Haskell R. Lassister,** son of Mr. and Mrs. Bryan Lassiter of Caddo, Oklahoma, former Fulbright residents, and grandson of Mr. and Mrs. R. H. Bryson of Deport, who was with the 9th Army in France, has been killed in action on Dec. 8, according to a message received by his grandparents. Sgt. Lassiter had been in the army for two years and received his training in Kentucky and at Camp Barkeley, Abilene. He had been overseas since October."

"**S/Sgt. James Wallace Thomas,** son of Mrs. Lula Thomas and the late W. I. Thomas of Bogata, was killed in a plane crash Monday morning at March Field, Calif., according to a telegram received by his mother from the War Department. He was 19 years of age, had been in the service 14 months and was first engineer on a B-26. He was born in Bogata March 24, 1924, and after graduating from Bogata High School in 1941, attended Paris Junior College. Surviving besides his mother are one sister, Mrs. John Lee Bell of

Bogata, and two brothers, Julian Thomas, aviation cadet at Deming, N.M., and Donald Thomas, student at the University of Texas in Austin. The accident occurred when the four-engined Liberator bomber from Blythe, Calif. Air Base crashed into a parked plane on the runway at March Field. "

"A very interesting letter has been received by Mr. and Mrs. Luther White from their son, **Pfc. Billy Gene White**, who is in the Marines and on the island of Saipan. It says in part: 'We landed here the 13th and I can tell you I have had some pretty close calls. We have been here a month. We had to eat K-rations for twenty days—ate them and liked them. The battle on the Marshalls was play compared to Saipan. Don't worry about the crops being bad and cattle being cheap. We have something to be thankful for and that is being alive. Thanks for the pictures. My little sis seems to have grown up since I left. You and Dad look just about the same, and my dog, Wimpy, is looking good. I will go to church tomorrow; being in these battles has taught us to believe in prayer.'"

"With Fifth Army, Italy—Doubling as a jeep driver, **S/Sgt. Roy L. Hutson** of Deport, took a fresh supply of 81-millimeter mortar ammunition through a mined area to within a few yards of his gun section while serving on the Fifth Army front in northern Italy. Returning to the rear to guide vehicles taking shells to his 350th Regiment unit of the 88th 'Blue Devil' Infantry Division, Hutson found portions of the road mined. Taking the wheel of the lead vehicle, he conducted the column safely to the unloading point. His parents, Mr. and Mrs. John T. Hutson, reside in Deport."

"**Sgt. J. R. Stroud**, son of Mr. and Mrs. Lonnie Stroud, is spending a 30 day furlough at home in Clarksville after over a year overseas. He was wounded in the fighting in Belgium and has received the Purple Heart. He was a member of Co. I, 144th Infantry Local National Guard Company." (He also received a Combat Infantry Badge ETO with 2 Battle Stars and a Good Conduct Medal. He died in Clarksville in 1945 as a result of his war injury. He was my husband's uncle.)

"Code of the Corps—Above the deafening thunder of the guns... in the thick of the battle... in driving storm or blackest night... men in the Signal Corps hear four words ever ringing through their minds... 'Get the Message Through!' These four words form a guiding code that will live forever... in countless deeds of heroic action . . . in the tremendous technical achievements it has inspired . . . and in the proud traditions of the Corps. " (Lindsay McAllister of Clarksville served in the Signal Corps.)

"Mr. and Mrs. Joe Thornton of Bogata have been notified by the War Department that their son, **Pfc. Vernon A. Thornton**, had been killed in action at Manila on Feb. 15, 1945. He entered the service in August 1940, receiving his first training at Ft. Clark as a member of the Fifth Cavalry. He later went to Ft. Bliss and was sent from there overseas in May 1943. Sgt. Thornton's company had been in three major battles on Admiralty Island, Leyte in the Philippines, and Manila, where he lost his life. He was married to Margaret Barton on Oct. 15, 1942, who with his parents and two brothers, Paul and Kenneth survive. He was 23 years old."

"Mrs. John B. Long received a V-Mail letter April 19 from her husband, **Pfc. John B. Long**, saying he was liberated from a German prison when the Yanks took Stalag 9B Prison Camp at Badorb, Germany, and would be home in about five weeks. Pfc. Long was reported missing Jan. 25, and no news had been received of him since, until his letter came last week-end. Mrs. Long is making her home with her parents, Mr. and Mrs. Ed Proctor, east of Detroit. Pfc. Long is the son of Mrs. Stella Long of Garland and is 24 years old. He was attached to the 102nd Infantry Division and has been overseas since Oct. 1944."

"**Charles Tanner Allen**, Yeoman 2c, son of Mr. and Mrs. Charles Allen of Dallas, former residents of Bogata, has been reported missing in action by the War Department. He was graduated from Bogata High School in 1941 and was a student at Oklahoma A&M College when the Japs attacked Pearl Harbor, at which time he enlisted in the Navy. He was aboard the ship Hoel in the South Pacific waters for the past 16 months. His ship was one of the six lost at the time the Princeton was lost, during the invasion of Leyte in the Philippines." (Charles Tanner Allen was reported missing in action in 1944 and declared officially deceased in 1945.)

★★★

This is the story of Seaman Lewis **Yeley**, who was aboard the U.S.S. Princeton, a light aircraft carrier, which was sunk in battle with the Jap fleet. He boarded the *U.S.S. Princeton* Aug. 5, 1944 in the Marshall Islands and 24 days later sailed out of the Marshalls with a number of ships:

"The task force headed for Palau, a Jap-held island. Our TBM bombers and F6F Hellcat fighters were sent over the island and unloaded tons of bombs and made strafing attacks. They hit the island two days and then moved onto the Philippine Islands. We bombed the island three days. The first morning enemy planes followed our planes back from the raid, and in a short time we were knocking down Jap planes all around us. We were in a rain storm that morning, and the Jap planes were hard to see. If anyone asks me if I was scared, I will just say 'yes', because I sure was. At the end of the second day we headed toward Japan and bombed Formosa Island and sank several ships in the harbor. The next day I was down in the mess hall, four decks below and before I knew it, nine Jap torpedo bombers were coming in low on the water for a torpedo run on us. Just as soon as we saw them, the captain gave the word to sound 'general quarters'. Before I could get half way to my G.Q. station, the boys on my ship had shot down three Jap planes. One of the Jap pilots tried to suicide our ship, but failed to make it. His plane blew up before he got close enough. He had already dropped his torpedo at us, but missed. We had quite a bit of action while we were there. We left and went back to the Philippine Islands, and there is where it all happened.

The first morning we sent our planes over the island and they dropped their bombs. They had just begun to return to the ship when a Jap dive bomber sneaked out of a rain cloud on us and dropped a 500-pound bomb which hit about midship. I saw the Jap plane coming out of the sky at us, but I didn't take time to see him drop his bomb. A few minutes later the captain gave the word to leave the ship. I went over the side on a line, while some of the boys jumped over. I was in the water about four hours before I was picked up by a destroyer. It don't give you such a good feeling to be surrounded by sharks, which got some of the boys.

After we were picked up, we were taken to Ulippy, which is a little island in the Pacific that is held by our forces. There we were put on a troop ship and brought to Pearl Harbor and then placed on a troop ship headed for the good old U.S.A, and given 30 days survivors' leave. Now I am at home once more and very proud to be here. If I go back to sea, just give me the new *Princeton*, and I can still fight Japs."

★★★

"Mrs. H. D. Roach has received a War Department certificate announcing posthumous award of the Purple Heart to her son, **Lt. (jg) Thomas Donald Roach**, U. S. Naval Reserve, on the 26th of August 1944, for military merit and for wounds received in action, resulting in his death. Lt. Roach had won the Air Medal, and his mother received the Star denoting the second Air Medal award for operations in the South Pacific August 3, 1943. Lt. Roach was the son of the late Dr. H. D. Roach and Mrs. Florence Roach of Bogata."

"**Pvt. Curtis E. Maroney**, son of Mr. and Mrs. O. M. Maroney of Boxelder, and **Pvt. Leo L. Parker, Jr.**, son of Mrs. L. L. Parker, Route 3, Clarksville, have won the right to wear 'Boots and Wings' of the U. S. Army Paratroopers. They have completed four weeks of jump training, during which time they made five jumps, the last a tactical jump at night, involving a combat problem on landing."

"**Pfc. William D. Moore**, son of Mrs. Margaret Moore of Bagwell, has been wounded in action in the European Theater."

"**Pvt. Bobby D. Jones**, son of Mrs. Clara M. Jones of Bogata, is a prisoner of the Germans."

"Two Clarksville men are receiving their initial Naval indoctrination at the U.S. Naval Training Center, Great Lakes, Illinois. They are **Isaac F. Conway**, son of Mr. and Mrs. Joe Thomas Conway, and **Clovis T. VanDeaver**, son of Mr. and Mrs. T. M. VanDeaver."

"Mrs. Lee Quarles received a telegram this week, bearing January 19 date, announcing that her brother, **Sgt. Joe Buchannan**, who was previously reported on January 16 as missing in action, had been killed in action on December 25, 1944 in Belgium."

"**Ensign Vivian Mauldin** (NC) USNR, left Thursday morning to report for active duty at the Naval Hospital in San Diego. Ens. Mauldin is the daughter of Mr. and Mrs. W. E. Mauldin of Cuthand."

"The *Times* has received a copy of the Netherlands, East Indies *Ramp*, official weekly newspaper of the Third Engineers Special Brigade, containing the following references to **Lindsay McAllister** of Clarksville: 'Outstanding is the work of T-4 James L. McAllister, who was war radio operator for a group that pioneered sounding and charting of dangerous water off the tip of New Guinea. McAllister's boat went down in a heavy sea off the northern reaches of New Guinea, and though he and the rest of the crew survived, they lost all their personal belongings and had an unpleasant half hour in the angry sea."

"**Charles Calvin Brannan**, Clarksville, recently graduated from the Aviation Electrician's Mate School at Jacksonville, Fla. and was promoted to Seaman First Class (AEM) in the U. S. Navy. Brannan is now a qualified Aviation Electrician Mate and will probably see service with a Naval Air Unit."

"**Sgt. William H. (Bill) Forester**, 25, son of Mr. and Mrs. John Forester of Marris Chapel, was killed in action in Northern Italy on April 29, 1945, according to a message from the War Department received by his parents on May 15. He entered the Army March 19, 1941 at Ft. Sill, Oklahoma. He landed in Africa in September 1943 and also fought in Sicily and Italy. He was born June 9, 1919 and was a member of the Bogata Graduating Class of 1938. Survivors include his parents, two sisters, Mrs. Robert Blair of Dallas and Mrs. Alvin Barnes of Bogata, three nephews and one niece, his grandfather, Robert Forester of Halesboro and a host of relatives and friends to mourn his untimely death." (He was shot in the back by a sniper and died April 29, 1945. Burial was made in the Bogata Cemetery December 15, 1948.)

★★★

"May 10, 1945—After 31 months overseas and two battle wounds in as many major Pacific campaigns, Sgt. **Eugene M. White** describes the Infantry this way: 'That's where they separate the men from the boys.' The husky Texas veteran, who fought with the 43rd Infantry Division on New Georgia and Luzon as assistant squad leader in a rifle company, is back in the U.S. for treatment of his second wound. He is the son of Mr. and Mrs. Rufus White who live on Rt. 1, Bogata. He has earned the Combat Infantryman Badge for exemplary conduct in action against the enemy. He was first wounded on New Georgia by Japs who sneaked into his company's perimeter one night to drop hand grenades into foxholes. 'One grenade exploded right on the rim of my foxhole and fragments of it struck me on the back and left hand. Nobody dared move above ground in the dark so I lay in there until morning and got first aid then. My wound wasn't serious.'

The next time, however, was a different story. It happened on Luzon. 'We were on the way back to our own lines after a scouting patrol when we ran into Jap mortar fire. The Japs had spotted us moving along a trail and called in mortars on us. Fragments of one mortar shell caught me in both legs. Fortunately, a medical aid man was along on the patrol, so he bandaged me right away. Then my buddies had to carry me six miles on an improvised litter, part of the time still under fire.'

Sgt. White received the Purple Heart with an Oak Leaf Cluster for these wounds and also is entitled to wear the Philippine Liberation Campaign Ribbon authorized by the government of the Philippine Commonwealth. His Asiatic-Pacific Theater Ribbon carries two battle stars for the campaigns in which he saw action."

★★★

"Mr. and Mrs. Paul D. Marable have been officially notified by the War Department that their son, Lt. Paul **D. Marable, Jr.**, is a prisoner of war in Germany. "

"Three sons of Mr. and Mrs. J. B. Brooks are in the Navy in the Pacific area. **James Howard Brooks** has recently been promoted to Electrician's Mate Second Class. He has been in the Navy two years and has had nineteen months' service with the Pacific Fleet. **Seaman First Class Billy Eugene Brooks** with the Coast Guard has been in service since October, 1942. **Coxswain Raymond Benjamin Brooks** who entered the service in December 1942, is with the Naval Armed Guard and participated in the New Guinea and Marshall Island campaigns and is now engaged in the action in the Marianas."

★★★

"**Cpl. Martin (Buddy) Johnson**, son of Mrs. Emmons Abernathy of McCrury, who lost his life aboard a Japanese transport ship on December 15, 1944, entered the service in February 1934 and surrendered at Corregidor May 7, 1942. He was among the prisoners who were in the Bataan Death March.

Following is part of the letter from the Major General confirming the telegram informing his mother of his death: 'From available information it appears that 1,619 prisoners of war were embarked on December 14 at Manila on a Japanese vessel, presumably for transport to Japan. The ship was bombed and sunk in Subic Bay, Luzon, Philippine Islands, on December 15. After considerable delay there has been received from the Japanese government a confirmatory report of that sinking, with partial official lists of those lost and of the survivors. 942 prisoners of war are officially reported by the Japanese to have lost their lives at the time. Of the survivors remaining in the hands of the Japanese, forty-nine are reported to have died and others to have been later transferred to Japan. Only two of the prisoners of war aboard are known to have evaded recapture."

★★★

"**Lt. Paul E. Horne, 23**, who was reported missing in action over Italy on Feb. 10, 1944, is now listed as killed in action according to a report received by his parents, Mr. and Mrs. Will C. Horne of Paris, from the War Department. At the time he was reported missing, Lt. Horne, pilot of a Flying Fortress, participated in a mission to Albano, Italy, 12 miles southeast of Rome. In a report, it was stated that his plane was damaged by enemy antiaircraft fire and fell into the sea.

Lt. Horne's parents recently received word that the Air Medal and one Oak Leaf Cluster were to be awarded to him for meritorious achievement in aerial flight while participating in sustained operational activities against the enemy from Jan. 16 to Jan. 27 and Jan. 28 to Feb. 10.

A graduate of Paris High School and Paris Junior College, he entered the service December 28, 1941. He left the U. S. in December 1943. Lt. Horne's twin brother, **S/Sgt. Frank F. Horne**, is in England. Besides his parents, his twin brother, and another brother, **Lawrence Horne** in the Army, he is survived by a third brother, James Horne of Paris and two sisters, Ruth Horne and Mary Alice Horne. The family formerly resided in Bogata."

★★★

T/Sgt. James Curlee Bailey has received a discharge having a credit of 146 points. He completed 72 missions with the 9th Air Force. He has been in the Army over 3 years with 16 months overseas. He has received 15 decorations and is said to be the first Red River County man discharged on the point system." (He was the son of Mr. & Mrs. J. B. Bailey, Clarksville. He entered the Army Air Corps in 1942. He was awarded the Air Medal with fourteen Oak Leaf Clusters, Distinguished Flying Cross and Purple Heart. He was wounded on a mission over France in 1944. At one time he was reported missing in action, and Sammy Humphrey remembers delivering the telegram informing his parents about it.)

"**Sgt. Edgar R. Cornett**, son of Mr. and Mrs. A. J. Cornett of Clarksville, was wounded on Luzon April 7th. He was recently visited in the hospital by his brother, Pvt. Travis Cornett."

"**Pvt. Bernard Rains**, son of Bailey Rains of Clarksville, has been returned to the hospital in the Philippines for further treatment of his wounds."

"**Thomas Hutchison** of Clarksville, who has been serving with the crew of a landing craft in the Pacific, is home for an 18 day visit. He was wounded at Iwo Jima but is recovering."

"**Lt. Ben F. Edwards**, son of Mr. and Mrs. Frank Edwards of Clarksville, is visiting at home. Ben was badly injured when his bomber was shot down on Luzon last March. He is making good progress toward recovery."

★★★

"**Capt. Jack Howison**, Hq. 17th Tank Bn., U. S. Army, now somewhere in Holland, is the youngest son Mr. and Mrs. J. W. Howison of Bogata. He went into the armed service in July 1941 and received his first basic training at San Antonio and after Pearl Harbor at Camp Polk, La. He went to Officers Candidate School at Ft. Knox, Ky. and was commissioned Lt. in 1942 and then Captain in January 1944. His tank division went overseas in July 1944 and after 30 days in England, he has been in combat duty in France and Holland.

Capt. Howison has and is taking part in the tank battles around the city of Metz, one of which will go down in history for its strategy and destructive power against great odds—the first one being the one that started west across Deurne Canal two weeks ago. Their headquarters was established at a point near the main Deurne-Meijel highway, north of the village of Heitrack, right in the main line of German attack. Instead of an infantry patrol as was thought to be, the Germans employed two panzer divisions supporting infantry and the heaviest column of artillery and air support they have been known to use on the Western Front. The group of American tanks greatly outnumbered in men, and equipped with light tanks, held for two days against repeated attacks of German panzer units of Tiger tanks. They were finally forced to give ground, and this withdrawal placed them with the small canal at their backs, along which all bridges were destroyed by German artillery. This was the most precarious situation they had had to deal with in the three day battle. They solved it by building a bridge across the canal with rocks, logs, and a few jeeps. Though they killed hundreds of the attacking Germans, they had only one man killed out of the entire battalion. Some of the escapes from wrecked and burning tanks were miraculous."

★★★

"August 11, 1945—Bogata Officer is Awarded Silver Star—For gallantry in action on April 26, **2nd Lt. Louis V. Sawyer** was presented the Army's third highest award—the Silver Star Medal—by Col. William P. Withers at Camp Detroit near Laon, France in the Assembly Area Command. He is the son of Mr. and Mrs. G. A. Sawyer of Bogata. His wife, the former Betty Warrick, lives in Opelousas, La.

Lt. Sawyer was a platoon leader with the 76th Infantry Division's 304th Regiment. The citation accompanying the award noted that Lt. Sawyer distinguished himself when he organized a motorized rescue party and led it through constant artillery and mortar fire to regain an outpost captured by an enemy patrol. It continued in part: 'Discovering that the enemy were holding four prisoners, Lt. Sawyer led his men in the attack against the position. The enemy fiercely defended their position with fire from automatic weapons. Undaunted, Lt. Sawyer boldly continued the advance, killing three of the enemy and forcing the remainder to surrender quickly. He thus effected the daring rescue of the captured American soldiers.'

Lt. Sawyer presently is motor vehicle maintenance officer at Camp Detroit, assisting in the re-deployment of Air Force personnel to the Pacific. He entered the armed forces in April 1942 and went overseas in January 1943 to join the 76th Division in

Luxembourg. He participated in their smash through the Siegfried Line, crossing of the Moselle and Rhine Rivers, and the drive across Germany as part of a task force with the Third Army's 6th Armored Division. Besides the Silver Star, Lt. Sawyer also has been awarded the Purple Heart for wounds received in action last February near Meckel, Germany."

★★★

"Mr. and Mrs. J. N. Philley of Dallas received a letter from their son, Pvt. Larry E. Philley, written in a prisoner of war camp in Germany. It is the first news they have had from him since a message from the War Department informed them that he was missing in action in Germany on December 6, 1944. He stated that he was still improving every day and that he did not receive any of his Christmas packages. He is the only grandson of Mrs. J. E. Philley of Deport.

An air mail letter dated April 28 from Pvt. Larry E. Philley to his parents told them that he could not tell where he was, but that he had been liberated and that his wounds were improving under the care of an American doctor. This is the first definite news that he was still alive, as the letter written from the German prison camp, M-Stammlager PID, Dortmund Westfalen, was undated, account of which was in last week's paper. The Red Cross reports the above camp has been liberated.

Larry enlisted in the Air Corps in September 1942 and was transferred to the Infantry in 1944. He went overseas in September 1944, landing first in England and then Holland in November. He was in the 84th Division with the Ninth Army. This is the division the Germans called the 'Hatchet Men' from their insignia and the ferocity of their fighting. As the Ninth Army has been shrouded in secrecy until recently, little could be learned of what happened, but newspapers report this division's first battle was at Geelenkerchen. They also saw heavy fighting around Aachen, and it is presumed that this is where Larry was wounded and captured."

★★★

"**Gerald Warren Isbell,** son of George Isbell of Clarksville, was among 1,770 American prisoners killed when a submarine torpedoed the Japanese ship on which they were being transported to Japan

October 24, 1944, according to a communication received from the War Department Wednesday. The report stated the casualty list had been confirmed June 16. Only nine Americans survived the torpedoing which took place approximately 200 miles off the coast.

Young Isbell was a graduate of Clarksville High School, class of 1940. He voluntarily enlisted in the Army August 27, 1941; was sent to the Philippines, arriving September 26, and was stationed at Ft. William McKinley when the Japanese attacked on December 7, 1941. First reported missing, he was later listed as a Japanese prisoner. He was a part of the Bataan Death March. The last letter received from Gerald was in November 1941. During the past three years several cards were received."

Gerald was the youngest of three brothers who were placed in an orphanage by their father after the death of their mother from complications in childbirth. This was in Watertown, New York; their parents were Ezra and Julia Clement; there were seven children in the family. The other brothers placed in the orphanage were Lee Nailling and Leo Rodgers. In 1926 the boys, the youngest three and the oldest only nine, became a part of the Orphan Train Movement in our country when their father took them from the orphanage and put them on one of the trains. In the spring of 1926 the Orphan Train stopped in Clarksville, Texas for the first and only time, and all three brothers were adopted by local families, George and Frances Isbell, Ben and Ollie Nailling, and Joe and Othelo Arnold Rodgers. (Gerald's adopted mother died only three years after he was adopted, and he was raised by his father, George Isbell. After Gerald was grown, George married my half-sister, Mary O'Donnell. Just a short time ago we found among some of her things Gerald's Purple Heart that was awarded to him posthumously. We were privileged to give it to his brother, Lee Nailling.)

Lee Nailling was drafted into the Army in 1944 and served in Europe. In 1945 he was assigned to help guard a German prisoner of war camp. It was during this time that he heard that Gerald had been killed. Lee was awarded the ETO Ribbon with one Battle Star and the Army of Occupation Medal. He was discharged in 1946. He and his wife, Novelle, reside in Atlanta, Texas.

Leo Rodgers served in the Army from 1937 until 1945. During World War II he served in the South Pacific. He received a Philippine Liberation Medal, Victory Medal, Asiatic-Pacific Theater

Medal, and American Defense Medal. Leo and his wife, Dorothy, resided in Paris where he died January 4, 2000.

★★★

"Fight on Iwo Jima Just Plain Hell", says Sgt. Thedford—Huge Japanese mortars were the worst hazards encountered on Iwo Jima, in the opinion of **Marine Sgt. Vernon Thedford, Jr.**, recently convalescing at Santa Margarita Naval Hospital at Oceanside, Calif.

Sgt. Thedford took part in the terrific struggle for that Jap-held volcanic island for seven days before he became a casualty. During that time the big enemy mortars cut down fellow leathernecks all around him by the score.

Thedford was in a reserve battalion when the Fifth Amphibious Corps' assault forces struck the island, and he watched the first few hours of combat from a Higgins boat off shore. But by mid-afternoon of D-day, he was up on the front lines in the thick of battle. As the Higgins boat dashed in to land its cargo of men, a Marine and a Sailor were wounded by machine gun fire. From then on, 'It was just plain hell', Thedford reported. 'We could see the big, black flashes of mortar shells flying in every direction, and the Japs seemed to have every shell hole on the beach spotted.'

Sgt. Thedford served in the Marine Corps from 1937–1941 and then re-enlisted soon after the war broke out. He went overseas in January 1944 and saw action at Kwajalein in the Marshall Islands and at Saipan and Tinian in the Marianas before the battle of Iwo Jima."

★★★

Bogata Boy Has Close Call Off Iwo Jima—Thanks to the action of the craft's tail gunner, the 7th AAF Liberator bomber aboard which **T/Sgt. Leon Mayes** flew as engineer-left waist gunner, was saved from crashing into the ocean off Iwo Jima.

After being hit by flak during its bomb run over an Iwo Jima airfield, the Liberator started a gradual drop toward the sea. The flak fragments had severed a rubber gasoline hose, flooding the bomb bay with fuel and filling the bomber's interior and oxygen system with fumes. Two members of the crew were knocked out from the effects of the fumes, and all the others, with the exception of the tail gunner, were overcome almost beyond control of their senses.

They descended for forty minutes, entirely oblivious to their plight. They dropped from more than 18,000 feet to within 700 feet of the ocean before the tail gunner made his way into the bomb bay, opened its door and allowed the gas fumes to escape. The pilot then regained his senses and leveled off the plane. During the glide, they were attacked by ten enemy fighter planes, but four of the squadron mates came to their rescue and helped fight off the Japs. The lost gasoline robbed the plane of use of one motor, and they flew back to an alternate base with the other Liberators acting as escorts.

Luckily, the tail gunner wasn't affected. However, he had been cut off from contact with the others in the crew because the flak had also severed the intercom wires. The tail gunner, who had teamed up with the top turret gunner to shoot down a Jap fighter during the bomb run, finally realized that a serious situation existed and, equipped with a portable oxygen bottle, went into the bomb bay and opened the doors.

Sgt. Mayes' parents, Mr. and Mrs. Archie Mayes, resided at Bogata. His wife, Dorothy, resided at Pueblo."

★★★

"**Lt. John D. Latimer**, USNR, a Navy fighter pilot from Bogata, has just returned to the U.S. Naval Air Station, Alameda, Calif., after more than 300 air hours of combat against the Japanese and a score of two Zeros down in strikes against Iwo Jima, less than 500 miles from Tokyo. He flew with Fighting Two, one of the Navy's crack Hellcat squadrons which in eight months rolled up a record score of 506 enemy planes destroyed.

A son of Mrs. R. L. Tyer of Bogata, Lt. Latimer has been awarded two Air Medals for his seven months of combat during which time he participated in numerous strikes against Japanese-held island fortresses sprawled over the Pacific.

On June 24, 1944 he shot down a Zero and thus added to Fighting Two's score of 67 planes downed in the second carrier assault against Iwo Jima. On July 3, Fighting Two made a single sweep over Iwo Jima again, and this time shot down 33 enemy fighters, one of which was by Lt. Latimer. His squadron had its baptism of fire in the invasion of the Gilbert Islands, and from then on conducted a succession of raids from Makin to Manila, often penetrating deep into enemy controlled air for strikes on targets hit for the first time since Pearl Harbor. Squadron VF-2 hit the Japanese on four different occasions on the Philippine Islands in a prelude to the battle which landed U.S. troops there. Besides knocking enemy planes from the sky like clay pigeons, VG-2 sent 50,000 tons of Japanese shipping to the bottom with 500 and 1,000 pound bombs rigged to their F6F's designed primarily for aerial dog fighting.

Nearly a year after Lt. Latimer won his Navy wings, he joined the famous Fighting Two squadron, commissioned on June 1, 1943. A few months later, they left the West Coast for the Pacific where they destroyed a total of 506 planes, 261 of them airborne, participated in a total of 2,050 sorties, 1,841 strikes and tallied 14,090 combat hours in the air."

★★★

"Bogata Boy Drops Bombs Over Normandy Seven Minutes Before D-Day Landing—Dropping bombs over Normandy and France seven minutes before the first Allied troops landed there on D-day was quite an experience for **T/Sgt. James Cecil Rogers**, radio operator on a B-17, Flying Fortress.

Sgt. Rogers is back in the States after completing 31 missions over Germany and France, including several raids over Berlin and Hamburg. He has been in England the past 11 months and reported to Santa Monica, Calif. for reassignment on September 1. He ha been visiting his sister and her husband, Mr. and Mrs. M. N. Simmons in Paris. His mother, Mrs. J. H. Lawson, recently moved to San Antonio.

Describing the bombing trip on D-day, Sgt. Rogers says: 'It was really interesting to note the number of ships we had crossing the Channel that morning. There were a few times when it began to get rough, and all I can say is that I am very lucky.' He made his last mission on June 20, making six of his missions after D-day. On his 18th raid to central Germany, their Flying Fortress came back with 68 flak holes, the record for their group. It was a good record though because with the 68 flak holes, not an engine was lost. They were losing gas all the time, but lost no altitude and were able to make it back to their base right along with the others.

Sgt. Rogers is holder of the Air Medal with three Oak Leaf Clusters and the Distinguished Flying Cross which he received for excellent work as lead radio operator on several missions. He entered the service July 2, 1942."

NEWS OF OUR MEN AND WOMEN IN SERVICE ★ 175

Heading used on each issue of the 'Drug Store News' which was published and sent to the servicemen in World War II.

Chapter 9

The Forties

The *Clarksville Times* dated January 1, 1943 had an article entitled "High Points of 1942 Briefly Reviewed" which is quoted below:

"A momentous war year for the nation has been just another twelve months for Red River County. A review of 1942 reveals nothing big started, nothing outstanding accomplished in this immediate area. Local citizens have shared in the country's war effort unreservedly. Hundreds have gone to war projects, more than 1,000 left during the year to serve in the armed forces, hundreds of thousands of dollars were invested in stamps and bonds. Restrictions imposed by the war economy were met and abided by willingly. Thus passed a year for this section of Northeast Texas. High points in the activities of the last twelve months were chronicled by the *Times* and are herewith presented briefly.

January—On the eighth of the month Clarksville staged a blackout. It was a purely local affair, organized and directed by the civilian defense group. Success was almost 100 per cent. A stamp and bond quota of $509,000 was set for Red River County in 1942. A Red Cross war fund drive was launched, with $4,000 as the goal. It was reached before the drive ended.

February—More than 1,600 Red River County men twenty to forty-five years of age registered for selective service in February. A civilian defense registration was conducted in Clarksville with 1,346 persons listed in one day. The Delaware improvement project was suspended because of a shortage of laborers. At the approximate date of suspension the WPA approved a supplemental allotment of $18,560 to be used for paying workers when and if the project reopened. It will not be reopened. The disposition of the $18,560 awaits future development.

March—Construction was begun on the Dingee packing plant at Clarksville. Two of the heaviest snows recorded at Clarksville in more than fifty years fell on the first and eighth of March. Each snow exceeded six inches in depth.

April—Clarksville bank deposits rose to a thirteen year high, as revealed by statements published early in the month. There was another selective service registration involving men forty-five to sixty-five years of age, and a total of 2,567 were registered. A registration was held for retailers of sugar, preliminary to the setting up of a rationing system for this item. Rainfall at Clarksville in April amounted to 11.23 inches, highest figure of record for this month.

May—Sugar ration books were issued to about 27,000 Red River County citizens, who found themselves doing what all Europe had long since been doing in the case of all items of food. The Dingee packing plant opened. The CCC Camp at Bogata was liquidated. Clarksville closed half a day to permit several hundred local citizens to go to nearby fields and pull peas in an effort to save the crop, normal harvest of which had been rendered impossible by continued heavy rains. Approximately twenty per cent of the 500 acre crop was saved.

June—Selective Service registration involved approximately 600 young men eighteen to twenty-five years old. A county wide drive for scrap rubber was launched. Final reports on this campaign revealed 122,000 pounds collected.

July—Record tomato season with 174 cars green wrap fruit shipped form Avery, a number of cars from Bagwell, and more than 1,000,000 pounds of ripe tomatoes sold to Dingee cannery at Clarksville. Annual July fourth rodeo called off on account of war. No holiday observed in Clarksville. July primary brought 4,846 voters to polls in Red River County, a larger number than anticipated under existing conditions.

August—Clarksville school authorities announced the elimi-

178 ★ For Love of Country The Price of Freedom

Envelope that held a War Ration Book used during World War II (from the personal files of Mr. and Mrs. Charles Shelton)

nation of football for the duration. The Times noted the 100th anniversary of the first newspaper to be established in Clarksville, the Northern Standard, launched August 18, 1842, by Col. Charles DeMorse. First bale of 1942 cotton arrived on August 18, sold for twenty cents a pound, highest opening price in more than ten years.

September—Summer routed early with an all time temperature

Ration Calendar (from the personal files of Mr. and Mrs. Charles. Shelton) reading of forty degrees recorded. No previous September minimum had been reported at this level. A county wide drive undertaken for the collection of scrap metal, with schools, various organizations, and thousands of individuals cooperating. Response was widespread and the drive very successful.

October—A gasoline rationing panel was named, preliminary to the setting up of system in the county for restricting use of this product. Big fall bean canning season under way. Nearly half million pounds processed at Clarksville. Record prices paid.

November—Highlighted by war bond jamboree on eleventh, sponsored by the Rotary Club. Month's sale of bonds nearly $75,000, helping overcome poor showing made in a few previous months. Gasoline and coffee rationing became effective.

December—No Christmas lights over the business district. Many of the usual pre-holiday activities absent. Scarcities in merchandise lines usually in demand for giving, but ample stocks of hundreds of other items. Nearly everybody well supplied with money. Big holiday trade. Destitute families fewer than any time in twelve to fifteen years. Quiet Christmas. Landlords getting ready to register rent property December 30. Everybody wishing everybody a happy new year but wondering what will really happen before it passes."

In 1936 the Yellow Cab Company from Paris had a few cabs here, but it didn't work out. In 1940 George Gamble, who had been operating a café, purchased a blue and gray 1940 Ford and charged ten cents for a ride in his City Cab. Then he bought out the Yellow Cab Company and in 1941 sold his café and had five cabs. Two women were hired to answer the phone, and the fare went up to fifteen cents. When FDR put a freeze on the making of autos and tires in 1942, Gamble moved his business to 201 East Broadway and raised the fare to twenty-five cents. Though gas was rationed during the war, the Yellow Cab was deemed to be essential public transportation so they could operate. He wound up with fifteen cabs, and business was great—ran day and night from 1942-1945. Saturday was the biggest day around 2:00 P.M. when people in Red River County came to town to shop, visit and go to the show. Fares finally reached thirty-five cents. After the war, when people were able to buy their own cars, business slowed down.[1]

Songs of 1940—"All the Things You Are", "I'll Never Smile Again", "Blueberry Hill", "Fools Rush In", "In the Mood", "When You Wish Upon a Star"
Songs of 1941—"Chattanooga Choo Choo", "Amapola", "Maria Elena", "White Cliffs of Dover"
Songs of 1942—"White Christmas", "I Don't Want to Walk Without You", "Deep in the Heart of Texas", "I've Got a Gal in Kalamazoo", "Don't Sit Under the Apple Tree", "Praise the Lord and Pass the Ammunition", "When the Lights Go On Again"
Songs of 1943—"You'll Never Know", "Comin' In On a Wing and a Prayer", "As Time Goes By", "People Will Say We're In Love", "Moonlight Becomes You", "You'd Be So Nice To Come Home To", "They're Either Too Young or Too Old", "That Old Black Magic", "Oh What a Beautiful Morning"
Songs of 1944—"I'll Be Seeing You", "Long Ago and Far Away", "I'll Walk Alone", "I'll Be Home for Christmas", "Together", "It Had To Be You"
Songs of 1945—"Dream", "Sentimental Journey", "If I Loved You", "It's Been a Long, Long Time", "Till the End of Time", "The More I See You", "I Can't Begin to Tell You"
Songs of 1946—"The Gypsy", "To Each His Own", "Laura", "The Old Lamplighter"

"I'll Be Home For Christmas"

I'll be home for Christmas,
You can plan on me.
Please have snow and mistletoe
And presents on the tree.
Christmas Eve will find me
Where the love light gleams.
I'll be home for Christmas,
If only in my dreams."

The *Bogata News* printed the following (date unknown):
"If you're a heartsick wife, mother or sweetheart, you'd do a lot to give that boy a better chance to get back safe. Well then, DO IT! Someone's life is in your hands! Round up your scrap metal— it's needed to make steel. Steel for armor plate to protect him from bombs and bullets. Steel for weapons to help him do the job that must be done before he can come home again. You don't want pro-

duction figures. It's enough to know that 50 per cent of all new steel is made of scrap—that our steel mills now have only enough scrap in sight to last another 30 days at the most! What happens after that, depends on all of us. If production falls, and you've not done your part, will you rest easy?"

A post card dated October 16, 1943 addressed to Miss Dean Holloway, Clarksville, Texas reads as follows:

"Sometime ago you made application with us for work in our pecan plant. You are requested to report at the plant at 2 o'clock in the afternoon, October 20th, 1943. The plant will not open for a few days, but we would like to explain the details of the work you will be expected to do and assign each of you to the place you will work. Other details will also be worked out. We shall appreciate you being on hand promptly at 2 o'clock. Thank you. Black Brothers Co."[2]

"Silk Hosiery Gathered in Red River County—Thirty-eight hundred pairs of used silk and nylon hosiery were gathered in Red River County during a recent campaign staged by J. Haskell Johnson, Clarksville, Joseph B. McAdams, Dallas, associate executive secretary of the Texas Salvage Committee said. Miss Nancy Jamison, Clarksville, was leader among the girls, bringing in 1,300 pairs of stockings. Miss Binney Moore, Avery, was second. John Crater and Buddy Connell, Clarksville, were boys' winners in the county wide contest." (Name and date of paper unknown)

Information about the Red River Army Depot, Texarkana, Texas was received from the Public Information Office on the Depot. It reads as follows:

"This depot was built in 1941-42. Purchase of a site in Bowie County, approximately 17 miles west of Texarkana, Texas was authorized 21 June 41. Advantages of this location other than proximity to Texarkana, Ark-Tex, a transportation center, were plentiful unskilled labor; good water supply; inland location, comparatively safe from air attack; thin population; good for establishment of explosives safety distances; and availability of land cheap. The 15,000 acres were purchased for $389,000. Red River Ordnance Depot was so officially named and designated a permanent installation by WD General Orders 8, 9 Aug 41. An Ordnance Officer (Major G. S. Dingee) took command 26 Jan 42; the first ammunition was received 25 Apr 42. The 702 igloos had been completed in less than seven months, a world record. The original construction completed in 1942 for about $35 million consisted of 930 permanent buildings and structures and hundreds of miles of roads, railroads, and utilities lines.

Planned as a reserve ammunition depot only, Red River was given three other missions as war needs demanded: tank repair in Oct 41; general supply storage in Feb 42; and Ordnance unit training in Aug 42. Related functions—armament, transport vehicles, tire and track rebuild, fabrication, demilitarization, renovation, etc. have been added. Storage of strategic material was assigned in 1946; and in 1948-49 Red River was made the distribution depot for the Fourth Army Area and overseas through OSANO. Approximately 12,000 Ordnance troops were trained here during World War II, and 3,000 more for the Korean fighting.

Functions of six other installations have been absorbed by this depot. Certain storage and shop functions were transferred from Normoyle and Little Rock Ordnance Depots in 1943; armament rebuild functions from San Antonio Arsenal in 1947. Camp Stanley has been a storage activity of this depot since Jul 49, even though given a DCSLOG mission in 1958. . . Lone Star Ordnance Plant and this depot were loosely joined as the Texarkana Ordnance Center 1943-44 under the Red River Commander, and Lone Star was totally under this command from Nov 45 until May 51. Without any changes in mission except of assumption of command of Lone Star, this depot was re-designated Red River Arsenal 1 Jan 46. It was changed back to Red River Ordnance Depot 1 Nov 61. As a result of the reorganization of the Army, the depot became an Army Supply Depot under the Supply and Maintenance Command effective 1 Aug 62 and was re-designated Red River Army Depot. . .

Notable records have been made by the depot. The most vehicles ever at one CONUS depot, almost 58,000, were amassed in 1945-46. Later 35,000 of them were moved from shoulders on Lone Star roads to the Red River area in six months, without a disabling accident. . . Since 1946 more than 70,000 vehicles have been rebuilt here, and other material in proportion. . . "

Many, many men and women from our area have been employed at Red River Army Depot and Lone Star Ordnance Depot since their beginnings. Choosing to live in Red River County, these people car pooled, and for a long period of time during the war, buses took employees back and forth to work.

An interesting article written by Mary Jane DeBerry Lowry of Blossom, Texas reads as follows:

"I was in high school when World War II started. There was an army camp in Paris, about 25 miles from where I lived in Bogata. During those years there were many soldiers in and out of our little community. We had regular groups of women and girls who met together and rolled bandages for the Red Cross. Some of us took knitting lessons, and we knit socks, sweaters, and scarves to be sent to servicemen who were in cold areas of the war.

During the time the camp was active in Paris, there were many soldiers who came to Bogata on the week-ends. The townspeople began to ask them to their homes for a home cooked meal, and sometimes for an overnight stay. Many times my father would bring home a soldier or two with him for Sunday dinner. Many of them attended church services in the local churches, and someone always took them home for dinner. Many times they were just picked up off the street, as my father did, and they were always so nice and polite and so thankful to be able to be in a home again and to have a home cooked meal.

Of course, so many things were rationed, among them being sugar, lard, tires and gasoline. We had ration books with stamps in them, but sometimes if you had the stamps and the money, all the commodities would be gone before you got to the store, and neither the stamps nor the money did any good. The soldiers also had ration stamps, and if you brought home a soldier several weeks in a row, he would bring part of his sugar with him and give it to the family who had him for lunch. Sometimes they would bring it in their sock, and we always laughed and said that our tea tasted like a soldier's dirty socks.

There were good times and bad times. Of course, there were so many sad times—so many boys from our community didn't come home. There was always great rejoicing when one did. I remember my mother standing at the sink or the cabinet making biscuits in a big bowl. She mixed the dough with her hands. She would see a convoy going by, and our biscuits would be salted with tears because I had a brother in the service. He was in the Navy, far away then, and she remembered other women who had sons passing our house at that particular time. Sometimes when a convoy passed by our high school, which was right on the highway, the teachers would turn out classes and let us all go down to the highway and stand and wave and shout words of encouragement to the men in the trucks. Sometimes they would throw out pieces of paper with their names and addresses on them, and boys and girls would pick them up and write to them. Some really close relationships were made between these pen pals.

I remember the end of the war when the armistice was signed. I was in Paris Junior College by then, and it was announced over all the loud speakers. Not much else but rejoicing went on after that during the day. The First Methodist Church in Paris (the oldest church there) sent out word that day that they would be having Holy Communion. Anyone was welcome to come, take communion at the altar, and give thanks for peace which had been prayed for so long. When we got there, the communion cups had been made from melted down brass shell casings. It was a most impressive service, one I have never forgotten."

A newspaper clipping, newspaper name and date of publication unknown, reads as follows:

"A Japanese submarine, resuming undersea warfare against American shipping off the Pacific coast for the first time since 1942, torpedoed and sank the Liberty ship *John A. Johnson* between California and Honolulu in November 1944 and machine gunned and rammed the survivors, the Navy announced.

Crewmen of the *Johnson*, brought to San Francisco, described the sinking and subsequent Japanese atrocities in a Navy sponsored interview. Ten of the 70 merchant and naval crewmen were killed and six wounded. All were victims of enemy atrocities after their ship was attacked.

Torpedoing of the *Johnson* was believed to be the first official reported enemy submarine operation near the Pacific coast since a tanker was attacked 25 miles off Oregon October 4, 1942. It sank while under tow. Tokyo radio twice announced Japanese submarines were operating off the west coast during the last weeks of 1944.

After attacking the *Johnson*, the submarine surfaced on the moonlit waters and crisscrossed through the oil smeared sea in search of surviving sailors who hid and prayed beneath bobbing sacks of flour. Gleeful, shouting Japanese seamen sprayed the struggling American seamen with machine gun fire and rammed a loaded lifeboat in a deliberate charge that maimed some of the victims."

History of Camp Maxey—Camp Maxey is located about eight miles north of Paris, Texas. It was activated July 15th, 1942 with Lieut. Col. C. H. Palmer as Camp Commander. The 102nd Infantry Division was the first division to be organized here and was activated on September 15th, 1942 with Gen. John B. Anderson as the Commander General. Col. Robert O. Annin became the second Camp Commander on March 25th, 1943. Since its activation, thousands of soldiers have been trained here for combat and other active duties overseas.

Camp Maxey was named in honor of General Sam Bell Maxey who served in a distinguished manner during the Civil War and later served as U. S. Senator for the State of Texas. He was a resident of Paris. . .

The Army Ground Forces, Army Service Forces and Army Air Forces have had an integral part in the development of Camp Maxey activities. The great variety found in northern Texas terrain provides this Camp with ideal facilities for working out infantry problems. The installations include many features of training for modern battle conditions. The Artillery has its own range along with those furnished for the smaller caliber guns. The obstacle course presents stiff problems while the infiltration course along with the "German Village" provide a reality to the problems which are outstanding in such maneuvers. . .[3]

An article dated January 21, 1944 in the Paris News told of a prisoner of war who was buried at Camp Maxey with full military honors. It reads as follows:

"The first and only grave in the prisoner of war cemetery at Camp Maxey appeared early in December when Richard Winninger, German prisoner of war, was buried with full military honors by his comrades and American Military Police. Winninger, a one time member of the well known Afrika Korps, died in a Camp Maxey hospital.

In the procession to the grave, former German soldiers in their uniforms marched behind the hearse, ranking non-commissioned officers first. Next came a group bearing flowers followed by other prisoners of war. Black hand painted crosses decorated the red ribbons trailing from the flowers, while one ribbon bore a Nazi swastika.

MP's snapped their rifles to present arms and the German soldiers raised their hands to their caps in a military salute as the casket was taken from the hearse. At the grave, Chaplain Cotter of the 96th General Hospital read the rites of the Catholic Church, and one of the ranking non-commissioned officers delivered the eulogy. As the Chaplain read the graveside service in Latin, Military Police again presented arms; the choir of prisoners in the background sang hymns, and the casket which was covered by a Nazi flag, was lowered. . ."

The *Paris News* dated October 10, 1945 ran the following article entitled "Taps Sound for IARTC at Maxey After Years' Service":

"A great war weapon is now silenced, for Wednesday the Infantry Advancement Replacement Training Center at Camp Maxey is officially inactivated and closes.

More than 68,000 doughboys trained for fighting duty in the IARTC, and Wednesday the last of the Infantry ship from this city. The training center at Maxey has been one of Paris' major contributions to victory, and since the opening day on October 17, 1944, a total of 70,497 men have passed through as either instructors or trainees. . .

Infantrymen from Maxey fought in both European and Pacific battles. Now some IARTC graduates will head toward Tokyo to insure permanent peace. These doughboys—wherever they've been or wherever they're going—will long remember Camp Maxey. . . Scores of Infantrymen married local girls.

Troop trains have carried thousands of soldiers from Paris each day for the past several weeks. Infantry Center barracks are now empty, and only a skeleton force of administrative officers and enlisted men remain. Whole areas appear like a 'ghost town'. The IARTC at Camp Maxey is gone—but never to be forgotten."

An issue of the *Paris News* dated October 19, 1987 had an article entitled "Former German POW Pays Return Visit to Camp Maxey". It reads in part:

"Henry Casten of Hamburg, Germany, returned Thursday to Camp Maxey north of Paris where he was held as a prisoner of war during World War II. Caster found weeds and brush grown up and covering the decaying walls of rock buildings that housed himself and other German prisoners of war. The German said the return to Paris and Camp Maxey was a trip he was compelled to make.

Though he never had a great deal of outside contact with Texans while at the camp, he said he had fond memories of the place in Texas where he was a prisoner. He brought with him his son,

Werner Casten, because he wanted his son to share a look at the place that was once home to him for over a year...

Casten was an explorer or parachutist in Hermann Goering's regiment. He was wounded in Italy, south of Rome, in 1944 and was captured and placed on a hospital ship to go to Africa. Interred in Libya, he escaped but was later recaptured in Spanish Morocco and turned over to the Americans. He came to America and was placed in a camp near Baltimore... He was sent to Camp Gruber at McAllister, Oklahoma and next arrived at a small railway depot next to Camp Maxey, parallel to the highway north of Paris.

His emotions as he got off that train rushed back to him in memories Thursday afternoon as he found the gate to Camp Maxey and recalled getting off the train. He still has camp money coupons that he used at Camp Maxey where he was stationed with about 500 other prisoners while he stayed in Lamar County from October 26, 1944 to October 5, 1945...

Casten is 61 years old now... He works as a customs officers in Hamburg... He said he was treated fairly in Paris and that was why he wanted to come back... For Casten, it was one fleeting look at what came to be his home away from home when he was 18, a long time ago. "[4]

All guts for Old Glory, one person's choice for Woman of the Century is Rosie the Riveter. The World War II propaganda poster paints a portrait of the icon who gets my vote for Woman of the Century: Bandana wrapped around her head (with a singular feminine curl peeking out), muscular arms, blue work shirt. With her jaw set and chin held high, she proclaims, "We Can Do It".

Rosie the Riveter was true to her word. Some 20 million women went to work and war in shipyards, refineries, aircraft plants, train yard, offices, stores, shops. Not all of them were Rosies, but Rosie the Riveter became the symbol of women's ability and willingness to do their part. Their mettle held the homefront together while brothers, husbands, sons and fathers were shipped overseas...

With the bombing of Pearl Harbor in 1941, Rosie traded her stylish dress, nylons and heels for workmanlike overalls, sock, shoes. By 1944 some 3.5 million women had joined labor unions. Rosie could weld, wire electricity, repair a forklift, drive a truck in the oil fields and light a Bunsen burner, all while growing a victory garden in the back yard and helping out at the USO canteen...

By 1946 millions of women were laid off as soldiers returned to their old jobs. Rosie had met the challenge in what for many was a first job. She changed our consciousness about women working outside of the home. She had earned her independence and a sense of self-realization. She never forgot what she did and who she was. . . Rosie's legacy is one of courage and grace. When she stepped aside after the war, she did so with chin up. She never was in it for herself. . ."[5]

These statistics were found in the *Clarksville Times* dated June 29, 1943: "U. S. casualties of war total 90,860 so far. Sam Rayburn, Czar of North Texas, creates little enthusiasm in demand for solid backing of New Deal. Seventy servicemen from Texas were killed in 1942. The U.S. is expected to produce 115,000 planes next year."

Kelsey Goodman sent a few remembrances about the 1940's which I quote below:

"After WWII broke out, most people had something called a 'Victory Garden'. We always had some vegetables, but we also usually raised corn to feed the chickens, cows and hogs. Some years we had cotton. In the late 30's Dad bought the old Confederate Reunion grounds (17 acres). It still had the original timber on at least part of it, so Dad had it cleared so we could farm it. We raised corn there at least two years. . .

By the late 1920's Dad had become part owner of a 'Travelaire' light plane. I have heard two other names associated with flying during that era: John Thomas McKenzie and Gene Lee. . . Dad disposed of his interest in that plane, but by the late 1930's he owned his own Piper Cub. When WWII broke out, the government asked owners of private aircraft to sell them their aircraft for use in training men who were in line to go into regular pilot training. The program was called Civilian Pilot Training. Our plane went to a training site in Texarkana, and we went there at least once to 'visit' it. Some of the old timers will remember the Piper Cub operating off the strip behind our house. Others will remember in the late 1940's a Luscombe that Dad bought after WWII. . .

During WWII Dad was over fifty years of age so did not go into the service. The city formed an Air Raid Patrol, and he was one of the inspectors. Several night drills were held, and he would go out on the street looking for homes where light shown out a window. When he encountered this, he would knock on the door and advise the people about it.

Living just one street away from Highway 82 led to other experiences. From time to time a military convoy would pass through Clarksville, and it didn't take long for the word to spread. The convoys would sometimes stretch for miles and miles. Lots of Clarksville people would come out and stand beside the highway

This photo from July 1942, shows downtown Clarksville bustling wtih activity. Townspeople, businessmen, school children and office workers, numbering at least 500, gathered to head for the pea patch where they harvested a food crop valuable to the nation's armed forces. They helped establish a pattern for the entire country to copy in the war effort during World War II. While the county's regular work force was in other counties working in munitions plants or in the armed services, civilians went to work to save the crops. Paul Creager, then President of the Clarksville Chamber of Commerece, was the originator of the idea.

(Taken from A Pictoral History of Red River Conty)

and wave to the 'boys' as they passed. Some of us watched with anticipation hoping one would throw out a folded slip of paper with his name and address on it. I found some of them and would write a letter to them. The feeling in most families, especially ours, was that we should do all we could for servicemen. We somewhat 'adopted' two or three from Camp Maxey, and they were welcome in our home any week-end they wanted to come. One's name was Lindo Hollingsworth, and he enjoyed playing our piano. Another was named Alexander Barnoth. After I joined the Navy I visited 'Barney' in his home just outside Boston. . .

From time to time there would be War Bond Rallies, usually held on the square. The featured movie star for one of them was a western hero named 'Wild Bill Elliott'. . .When the rallies were held, various things were done to get people to buy bonds. Chocolate candy was practically impossible to get during the war, and on at least one occasion a box of Hershey Bars was auctioned off. Efforts were made to sell bonds and stamps in the schools, and students were encouraged to sign up to buy a 10 or 25 cent stamp each week. We pasted the stamps in our book, and when the book was full, it was worth $18.75, and we could trade it in at the Post Office for a $25.00 bond. . .

As things became unavailable, there was an expression that they had 'gone to war'. Sugar, meat, gasoline and tires were just a few of the things that were in short supply. Some cars were set up on blocks 'for the duration' when parts became unavailable. . .

When the war ended, I was a soda jerk at Stiles Drug Store (later Blackmon Pharmacy). Many of the men who returned did not find a job right away. Some took advantage of the GI Bill and went to school. Others spent much of their time there at the soda fountain swapping stories. They joked about being in the 'Fifty Two— Twenty Club'. If unemployed, a veteran was given $20.00 a week for 52 weeks. I listened as best I could to every tale they told. Gradually their numbers thinned as they drifted to larger cities, found a job, or went back to school. Clarksville, no doubt, seemed tame after what some of them had experienced."

An advertisement in the *Clarksville Times* dated June 22, 1945 reads:

"War Bond Premiere, Monday, June 25th, starting at 9:30 P.M.—'The Valley of Decision' starring Greer Garson and Gregory

Peck and 'To the Shores of Iwo Jima' photographed by the Combat Cameramen of the Navy, Marine Corps and Coast Guard—Admission by purchase of War Bonds only—Men are still dying; America must keep trying; Here is your opportunity to put the mighty 7th War Loan over the top!—Avalon Theater, Your Friendly Theater—Phone 104"

In the *Clarksville Times* dated July 11, 1999 is a Letter to the Editor written by Ed Pryor. He and his wife, Helen, live north of Clarksville. The letter, entitled "Fond Memories" reads in part:

"I started school at Bagwell in 1948. My kids always tell me they are tired of hearing this story, but I walked three and a half miles to school and three and a half miles home every day. But this was not the longest walk for students in the Bagwell school.

When I started school in the fall of 1948, there were six of us in the first grade. Mrs. Effie Henry taught first, second, and third grades all in one room. By the time a kid got in the second grade, he already knew most of it because he had heard it the year before. And by the time you got in the third grade, you had better know it because you had already heard it for two years. Mrs. Henry was a very good teacher and made a big impression on a lot of young lives. Mrs. Witmer was the other teacher, and Mr. Cass was the Principal and also taught classes. There was, of course, no air-conditioning at the school. The water fountains were outside in front of the school, and the outhouses were about a hundred yards to the west of the school. . .

One of my favorite things to do on Saturday mornings was to go and watch Chuck Murphy shoe horses. I know this doesn't sound like fun to many kids in this day and time, but I have always loved horses, and for me, this was an adventure. Chuck was a legend in his own time and shod horses all over the country. He shod everything from race horses to farm horses and was a pretty good vet also. He used the hot-shoe method of shoeing horses. Very few people go to this trouble now. Most horses are now cold-shod. Chuck would generally stop shoeing just in time to go to his café and start cooking hamburgers for lunch. . . I have wondered many times in later years how well Chuck washed up between shoeing horses and cooking hamburgers. Back then it didn't make any difference.

During this period of time I remember four grocery stores in Bagwell; Chuck Murphy's café; a barber shop; a garage that was operated by Chester Linton (who later taught shop for many years in the Clarksville Schools); the old bank building (long since closed by my time); and a movie theater. We had movies every Thursday night, and it cost nine cents to get in. A man came and set up a screen, and the seats mostly consisted of 1x12 boards laid across saw horses. The movie was always a serial. The reason for this, of course, was so you had to come every Thursday if you wanted to see all of the movie. Each movie lasted at least two weeks and sometimes longer. . .

And this also reminds me of another story. I know everyone has heard the story of the man who was big enough to go bear hunting with a switch. Well, I saw Big Henry Barton whip a bear, and he didn't even have a switch. And this is the way it happened (at least this is the way I recollect it.) This happened in the late 40's or early 50's because I was still just a small boy, and Big Henry was still a teenager or maybe in his early 20's. A man came to town with a tent and a trained bear. This bear was trained to wrestle, and he was a very good wrestler because he beat all comers. That is, until some of the locals (who wouldn't wrestle the bear themselves) pushed Big Henry into the ring. (I think Slim Hulen was one of the pushers.) Now Henry didn't really want to wrestle the bear because even though he was as big as the bear, he was a shy boy. However, when Henry was pushed into the ring, the bear made his first mistake of the night. He slapped Big Henry. And then the fur flew. Henry picked the bear up over his head and slammed him to the ground; jumped on top of him and you could hear the air whoosh out of the bear's lungs. The man who owned the bear was screaming, 'You've hurt my bear! Get off of my bear!'. When Henry released the bear, the man quickly caged him, took down his tent, loaded everything up and fled into the night. We never saw him in Bagwell, Texas again. I could write several other tales about Bagwell. I know space is limited. Maybe now someone else will write more."

On July 4, 1946 my half-sister, Pauline O'Donnell Means, and her four children, Doris, Jimmie, Don and Jerry, moved from Hugo, Oklahoma to Clarksville to make their home with my parents, Jim and Lee Claiborne and me. Seeing three young boys grow up in a small town during those years leaves many memories of how our nation used to be, before things changed so drastically in such a short period of time.

Don Means died suddenly on June 5, 1990 as he walked down the road in front of his land at English. He had served for seventeen years as Pastor of the Bagwell Baptist Church. I interviewed Jimmie and Jerry on July 5, 1996 and will quote some of what they had to say. Jerry died on July 1, 1999 after an unsuccessful double lung transplant operation.

Jimmie began by remembering that it had been fifty years since they had moved to Clarksville from Hugo. We lived on East Madison Street then. They both remembered the Hunt family who lived across the street from us. John Paul Hunt, their son, was still in the service, and there were two girls, Cynthia and Betty Ann. Later the Glenn family lived in that house. The neighborhood kids were Jim and David Burgess and John Wayne and Jerry West. He recalled his friends in Hugo, Wallace Palmer, Letha Jo Fly, and Watha Jo Henderson (Stroud).

Jerry said, "My first two years in school were during the war, and I remember drives in school, like metal drives, and also rationing like at the little store where you'd line up to buy five pieces of bubble gum. Everything was rationed. I remember Saturday nights in Hugo—the soldiers going up and down the streets. We kids would salute them. Sometimes they'd give you a dime. There were just droves of servicemen. The trips we made to Clarksville back in those days seemed like an awfully long trip—going to Paris on the old Jordan or Nance Bus Lines, standing up in the aisles because there were so many soldiers riding the buses. We'd change buses in Paris and then ride on to Clarksville. We learned a lot in those days. We made the heck out of kites and bird traps and model airplanes that you could buy for a nickel. We didn't have television to entertain us, but I do remember us having a radio that we listened to all the time."

Then Jimmie said, "Some of my earliest memories of doing things in Clarksville centered around the Court House—those bars at the front and sides, but primarily the ones on the east side were the ones we played on, 'skinning the cat'. When you went into those big front doors and turned to the right, you went into Jim Claiborne's office. He was Justice of the Peace for many years. There were just a lot of things about that Court House that I remember. It had a certain smell to it. They kept it wide open. The doors and windows were open and they didn't have any air conditioning units in the windows. In fact, now I don't like the way it looks with those units in the windows."

"You know, Jim, there seemed to be an air of authority about the Court House back then—Jim Geer and Taylor McCoy and those people back then. There was always a great mystique about that courtroom. It just looked like law was going to be dispensed up there. There was ornate woodwork, the high backed judge's chair, and the high backed chairs the jury sat on. I've served on jury duty up there myself, and they've lowered the ceiling, and there's not much left except where the judge sits. It seems to have lost all the old by being modernized."

"You're right, Jerry. There's another thing I remember. There was a water fountain and you drank out of those flat paper cups. Sometimes we'd get to go up to the bell tower, and we took paper airplanes to sail in the air. You know, we'd stray across the street to the Post Office and play on those steps. They had a couple of slanted things on each side that we'd try to either walk down or slide down on. Of course, it's changed now too. There was a lot of fun around the Court House and the Post Office back then."

"We lived in a good neighborhood. The summers were really nice. We'd sit around under a bois d'arc tree out in the front yard to keep cool. Everybody seemed to enjoy it. I remember laying out there in the swing right after eating and going to sleep. The sound the locusts made would lull you to sleep. We didn't have any air conditioning so it was lots more comfortable out under the tree. I know you remember that, Jim."

"Yes, and talking about that, I remember the oscillating fan we used at night and the sound it made when it changed directions. After that first summer when school started, it was a hard time for me. I went to the gym; the schools were a lot different; everything was different—the kids and the teachers. It was hard getting started. You and Don had each other—just a year apart, and Susie and Doris were in the same grade so I was the one in the middle with no one else in the family there."

"That's true, Jim. The summer before we started to school, the Hunts across the street gave us grave warnings about school. They painted a picture of Miss Ella Watson being really strict, and they told us about Miss Addie Dinwiddie, Miss Vera Rogers, and Mrs. Esther Varley. We started in the old Grammar School, and it made the Hugo school look like SMU. It was so old and drafty, and it leaked. It had a lot of character but was in a pretty sad state of repair. I started the third grade there, and most of the kids I started with, I graduated with. There were a few exceptions, but by and large, we went all the way through together."

"You know, Jerry, I started the seventh grade over on the third floor of the high school and then moved over to the new Elementary School. Then in the eighth grade I was back in the gym again. I remember that you could look out the back windows at the Band Hall. I can still hear a particular song that the band played over and over again."

"Speaking of the band, Jim, the Drum Major then was Tommy Allen. I remember both Walker Hays and his son, Billy Hays, who were great Band Directors. They put on field marches and skits at the football games, and I remember the Coltharp twins being in them. The summers were what I liked growing up when all the guys would come over to our house. Henry Hooser in his Model-A Ford and Robert in his; Wayne Smith, who had the first motorcycle I knew of; Clinton and Curtis Evetts who would come up on a tractor sometimes. Then Sonny Washington had an old Packard. All those guys just tolerated us. I remember the music—Susie had a record player and all those 78's—Perry Como and Tommy Dorsey."

"That reminds me, Jerry, of an Andre Kostelantez album with Jerome Kern songs which was really good. When the old needles would get worn, we'd put a nickel on top of the stylus to weight it down so it would still keep playing. I still remember a lot of those old songs—*"To Each His Own"*, *"The Old Lamplighter"*, *"The Gypsy"*. There were songs by the Ink Spots. After we grew up, we started adding a lot of music, show songs. We probably had all of Mario Lanza's records.

"Jim, people had a different respect and attitude for the law then. We knew Curtis Lemon and all those guys, and they knew us because Jim Claiborne was Justice of the Peace all those years. I remember one time that Curtis Lemon took me and Don down to the jail and showed us that box of stuff they took off prisoners—knives and things like that. We saw where the prisoners had to stay, and it was grim looking. Then, if a policeman wanted to see you, he didn't go looking for you; he sort of asked for you and word got around to you pretty fast, and you went looking for him. J. C.

Beville was another lawman. It seemed like a more innocent time. We'd go to football games, and you didn't have to worry about fighting. Doris and Susie and their friends would go to the midnight show on Saturday night, and it might be 1:30 in the morning when it would be over. They'd just walk home and never think a thing about it. Things have really changed."

"I agree, Jerry. In my opinion television is probably the most single thing that has influenced not only Clarksville, but society as a whole in the last forty years. The first TV I saw was over at Mr. Bailey Rains' house across the street from us. People were sitting around with the picture so snowy you couldn't see it. They thought it was pretty good that night. It would take a couple of people to get one tuned in. One person would be outside turning the antenna, and another would be inside telling them when the picture got good enough to watch."

"The whole thing, Jim, is that we were neighborhood oriented, small town oriented, but look at the town we moved into. Just look at Clarksville as a whole. It was a pretty complete town. We had two different movie theaters, mostly westerns at the State or Texan as it was later called, and the better movies at the Avalon. We had clothing stores galore, two nickel stores, drug stores with soda fountains, lots of cafes, three hotels, a taxi service. Not everyone had a car, and going to Paris was a big thing."

"I was the first of the three of us to deliver papers. Don started next and then you, Jerry. Remember how we used to put those circulars in the papers, and Cab Wolf would give us a pass where we had to pay twelve cents to get in? We saw lots of shows that way. I started delivering papers the next summer after we moved here. I got $2.00 a week, and I did this almost eight years. The most I ever made was $5.00 a week. The customers would range up to probably 140 on a big route. That was seven days, 365 days a year."

"Well, Jim, I got $1.00 a week for the town route under B. Farrier. I had 81 customers and serviced the news racks and cafes and sold to the guys riding the Red River Arsenal bus each morning. When Mr. McMahan took over, he raised me to $2.00 a week. It was an education. Those bicycles had special made baskets, heavy ones. I also helped deliver milk five days a week for fifty cents a morning. I met the Dinwiddies at the old Bonham house. I took the milk from the car to the porches and brought the empty bottles back."

"Do you remember, Jerry, when we'd caddy on the golf course at North Lake? They paid us fifty cents a round. Those little canvas bags with a few clubs were good, but some guys had those big leather bags with every club there was. Leonard Johnson, who lived up the street from us, and I decided to mow yards one summer. We'd mow and trim and get to split a dollar. I know you remember when Doris won that Talent Contest and got to sing on the Early Birds Radio Show in Dallas. When I started to high school, Miss Ruth Marable asked me if I was Doris' brother and then asked me to sing. I sang in the Choral Club, solos in the Assembly Programs and then in the Kiwanis Minstrels and really liked it. I remember Miss Ruth's Speech courses also, that she taught us to always have a firm handshake."

"Yes, Jim, Clarksville was a good town to grow up in. It was a slower time, more innocent. Remember the telephone system we had? If you called someone and they weren't home, the operator might tell you where they were. Saturdays were so much fun. Old man Carl Roberts was dear to my heart. He used to let us boys hang around his store down there on East Main. There'd be me and Don and Mack Humphrey and the Webb boy we called "Spider" Mr. Roberts would always pack his old car up with all us kids and take us to the Bogata Rodeo. In 1957 I was in the Navy and going overseas. I was riding a bus from Clarksville to Norfolk, Virginia and there was Carl Roberts in his rocking chair, wearing that old straw hat, a fly swatter in his hand, sitting under the overhang of his old station. Thirty eight months later after being overseas all that time, I came back into town in September 1960 and looked and there was Carl still sitting in that chair."

"Jerry, some people talk about the good old days, but some things weren't all that good. The medical situation wasn't all that good. I had my tonsils out when I was in the seventh grade, and I think I was sicker from the ether than from the operation itself. We had Drs. Wright, Reed, Payne and Marx and a hospital. The doctors made house calls."

"Of course, Jim, I'll never forget Dr. Marx because he patched up my hand when I had my hunting accident. His experience as an Army Doctor helped him so that he didn't have to amputate my hand. We boys hunted a lot, and this day Curtis Evetts had taken Don and Bobby Morris and me rabbit hunting down at Aikin

Grove. It seems like yesterday, but it was in 1951. The Lord had a hand in that."

"Jerry, I heard someone say that people in our age group are a unique group because we're the last ones who grew up without television. I was in high school when I saw my first TV and in college when we finally got a set at our house. You can't say that television is good or bad, but a combination of both. I think people were ahead with radio because the writing for radio had to be descriptive writing. Really, it was the theater of the mind. Even now I sometimes get tapes of old radio shows and really enjoy them. Times were surely different then, and overall, I guess it was about as good as it could be. When I come in now and drive around Clarksville and see a house that I remember, it brings back a nice feeling."

"Yes, Jim, I know what you mean. On my paper route, I went from the old Fire Station by the Clarksville Pharmacy to the Alps Café owned by Forrest and Elaine Burgess, on to Blackmon's Drug Store, Main Hotel, Eric Bollman's store, by the DeMorse house, on by Dr. Payne's office and then across the square to the Brewer Hotel. Then to the Corner Café on Market Square, by the old *Clarksville Times* Office on North Walnut, by Red River National Bank and Bullington's and First National Bank. After my hunting accident, I went to National Guard a lot with Robert, and it got me to thinking about a military career. Of course, I liked to travel because of the Dallas News trips I had won. (Jerry spent twenty years in the Navy as a Photographer.) When I stopped at the Alps Café, I remember Mr. Glenn Coltharp, Allie Crow, Chester McDaniel and Homer Sargent being there. Tom Exum and Aubrey Quarles also had cafes in town. You and Don and I hung out around the old blacksmith shop owned by Donald Fryar. He had two strong, burly black men, Charlie Mathis and Ballard Owens, who beat out plow shares and cycle blades for mowers. They were all so good to us, sending us to get snacks for them and then sharing with us. One thing I remember about being in the hospital after my accident was that Miss Addie Dinwiddie walked up there to see me and brought me some apples. I remember in her room at the old Grammar School, the slogan on her wall was 'Let nothing discourage you. Never give up!' I don't have any complaints or regrets." (I wish I could quote the whole interview between my two nephews. It has brought back many happy memories of my family, and sad ones as well when I think of those who are no longer with us.)

This is a picture of East Ward School which had been a part of St. Joseph's Academy owned by St. Joseph's Catholic Church. (We attended this school during World War II years.)

Chapter 10
In the Line of Duty

The first and most honored combat decoration in America's military history is the Purple Heart. General George Washington established the award in 1782 as a simple piece of cloth cut into the shape of a heart. The distinctive medal we know today was authorized 150 years later, in 1932, on the 200th anniversary of Washington's birth.

Considered to be the most beautiful of all U.S. decorations, the heart-shaped medal bears the silhouette of George Washington and the Washington family coat of arms. It is recognized around the world.

Today, the Purple Heart is awarded to all branches of the military as well as to civilian nationals of the United States, "for military merit as a result of wounds received in action against a hostile foreign force", including international terrorism or military operations while serving as a part of a peacekeeping force. Many Purple Hearts are awarded posthumously. Some attest to lifelong scars and lasting pain. All are worn with pride.

It is with enormous gratitude for the personal sacrifice of America's Armed Forces that the Purple Heart Tribute has been created. There has never been a finer tribute to those deserving men and women of the U.S. Armed Forces who sacrificed life and limb for their country and the cause of freedom.[1]

★★★

The Medal of Honor is the highest award for valor in action against an enemy force which can be bestowed upon an individual serving in the Armed Services of the United States. Generally presented to its recipient by the President of the United States of America in the name of Congress, it is often called the *Congressional Medal of Honor.*

The origin of this decoration goes back to the Civil War. Before that time, medals and decorations were considered to be too like the titles and awards given in England, and fighting for one's country was considered a duty. It soon became clear that there were those who were believed to have gone "above and beyond" this call, and on December 21, 1861, the Chairman of the Senate Naval Committee, Senator James W. Grimes, introduced a bill to promote the efficiency of the Navy. Navy Secretary Gideon Wells was looking for a way to inspire sailors to improve their work. This bill was approved by President Abraham Lincoln which provided for the preparation of 200 Medals of Honor to be awarded upon such petty officers, seamen, landsmen, and marines as shall most distinguish themselves by their gallantry in action and other seamen like qualities during the present war. Thus the Medal of Honor was created.

USA: Assistant Surgeon Bernard Irwin is credited with the earliest MOH action (13-14 Feb 1861), but Jacob Parrott was the first man to actually receive the Army Medal of Honor. Parrott's medal was given for actions during "The Great Locomotive Chase" in April 1862 and was presented on March 25, 1863.

USN: The first Navy Medal of Honor action was performed by John Williams on June 26, 1861, although Robert Williams was the first to be presented the actual medal.

USAF: Although it had been a separate service since 1947, Air Force Medal of Honor recipients during the Korean War still received the Army Medal of Honor for their actions. The actual Air Force Medal was adopted in 1965, and was first awarded to Bernard Francis Fisher on January 19, 1967 for his action in Vietnam on March 9, 1966.

USMC: The first Marine Corps action and presentation is credited to John Mackie during the Civil War.

USCG: Only one Medal has been awarded to a Coast Guard member, Douglas Munro, who served in World War II.

There has been one woman to receive the Medal, Dr. Mary Walker, while assigned as an Asst. Surgeon during the Civil War. Her Medal was rescinded in 1916 when the Army purged its files to cut down on what they thought were "unwarranted" issues. It was reinstated in 1976.

The Army officially dropped 911 recipients from the rolls in 1916 during the "purge", which had been issued for reasons of re-enlistments and special honor guards, which they felt were not "heroic" deeds...

The Navy medal was the first to be struck, followed quickly by the Army version of this award. There are three different types of Medals of Honor today: the original simple star shape established in 1861 which the Navy, Marine Corps and Coast Guard have retained; a wreath version designed in 1904 for the Army; and an altered wreath version for the Air Force, designed in 1963 and adopted in 1965.

In 1946, the Medal of Honor Society was formed to perpetuate and uphold the integrity of the Medal of Honor and to help the Medal of Honor recipients. On April 12, 1957, the 85th Congress passed legislation incorporating the Medal of Honor Society into the Congressional Medal of Honor Society (CMOHS) and was signed into law by President Eisenhower on August 5, 1958. The objectives and purposes of the Society are as follows:

To form a bond of brotherhood and comradeship among all living recipients of the Medal of Honor.

To remember in reverence and respect those who received the Medal of Honor posthumously and those who are now deceased

To protect, uphold and preserve the dignity and honor of the Medal at all times and on all occasions.

To protect the name of the Medal and the individual recipients of the Medal from exploitation.

To provide appropriate aid to all persons to whom the Medal has been awarded, including their widows and children.

To promote allegiance to the Government of the United States of America and to its Constitution, and to serve our nation in peace or war.

To promote and perpetuate the principles upon which our nation is founded; to foster patriotism and to inspire and stimulate our youth to become worthy citizens of our country.

As of now, 2,363 Medals have been awarded to the Army; 745 to the Navy; 295 to Marines; 16 to the Air Force; 1 to the Coast Guard; and 9 Unknowns. There have been 3,410 total recipients and 3,429 total Medals awarded. Of those, 19 have received the Medal of Honor twice. As of 13 October 1999, there are 150 living recipients.[2]

★★★

On the walls of Brasenose College, Oxford University, England, this letter of the "rail-splitter" President hangs as a model of purest English, rarely, if ever, surpassed:
"Executive Mansion
Washington, Nov. 21, 1864
To Mrs. Bixby, Boston, Mass.
Dear Madam,
    I have been shown in the files of the War Department a statement of the Adjutant General of Massachusetts that you are the mother of five sons who have died gloriously on the field of battle. I feel how weak and fruitless must be any word of mine which should attempt to beguile you from the grief of a loss so overwhelming. But I cannot refrain from tendering you the consolation that may be found in the thanks of the republic they died to save. I pray that our Heavenly Father may assuage the anguish of your bereavement, and leave you only the cherished memory of the loved and lost, and the solemn pride that must be yours to have laid so costly a sacrifice upon the altar of freedom.
    Yours very sincerely and respectfully,
    A. Lincoln[3]

★★★

It is the soldier, not the poet,
Who has given us freedom of speech.
It is the soldier, not the campus organizer,
Who has given us the freedom to demonstrate.
It is the soldier, who salutes the flag,
Who serves beneath the flag,
And whose coffin is draped by the flag,
Who allows the protestor to burn the flag.[4]

★★★

GENERAL MacARTHUR AND THE BIBLE—Before he was graduated from West Point, General Douglas MacArthur had read the Bible through six times. Thus our thorough going American hero has set a splendid example in his reading of the Bible.

★★★

"Army Profanity—The General is sorry to be informed that the foolish and wicked practice of profane cursing and swearing, a vice heretofore little known in an American army, is growing into fashion. He hopes the officers will, by example as well as by influence, endeavor to check it, and that both they and the men will reflect that we can have little hopes of the blessing of heaven on our arms if we insult it by piety and folly. Added to this, it is a vice so mean and low, without any temptation, that every man of sense and character detests and despises it."—George Washington

★★★

Your Chaplain Speaks—"Why Christian Missions—An American soldier who had been cast unconscious upon a wild shore 'over there' came to consciousness to feel himself pinned to the beach by two Aborigines who were holding sharp spears to his chest. 'You Jap?', they inquired menacingly. 'No, I'm an American', the soldier managed to answer as the spears pinned him tighter to the sand. As the American spoke, the native's eyes rested on a little silver cross the soldier wore on a chain around his neck. Immediately, the native spoke to his companion in dialect. Their faces brightened, and the spears were withdrawn as the first pointed to the cross, smiled, and said, 'Jesus Number One Man'. (That soldier certainly ought never to hesitate to give to the work of missionaries.)"

★★★

"Prayer by an Unknown Soldier

Stay with me, God. The night is dark.
The night is cold; my little spark
Of courage dies. The night is long.
Be with me, God, and make me strong.

I love a game. I love a fight.
I hate the dark. I love the light.
I love my child. I love my wife.
I am no coward, but I love life.
Life with its change of mood and shade.
I want to live; I'm not afraid.
But me and mine are hard to part;
Oh, unknown God, lift up my heart.
You stilled the waters at Dunkirk
And saved your servants. All your work
Is wonderful, Dear God. You strode
Before us down that dreadful road.
We were alone, and hope had fled.
We loved our country and our dead.
And could not shame them; so we stayed
The course and were not much afraid.
Dear God, that nightmare road and then
That sea! We got there—we were men.
My eyes were blind; my feet were torn.
My soul sang like a bird at dawn.
I knew that death is but a door.
I knew what we were fighting for.
Peace for the kids, our brothers freed.
A kinder world, a cleaner breed.
I'm but the son my mother bore.
A simple man, and nothing more
But, God of strength and gentleness
Be pleased to make me nothing less.
Help me, O God, when death is near
To mock the haggard face of fear.
That when I fall—if fall I must—
My soul may triumph in the dust.
Amen"[5]

★★★

9th Armored Division -" Father's Day Thoughts

This day the Nation's tribute yield
To Dads of soldiers in the field.
The blows you're striking for the right
Will make the tools with which we fight.
I send with pride to such a one.
This message from a soldier son."

Love,
Your son, Ben (Bowers)

★★★

An unknown author one day penned a poem called "I Am Your Flag". It is the essence of what "Old Glory" should mean to each of us not only on July 4th, but daily.

"I am your flag

I am the flag of the United States of America.
I am called Old Glory.
I am called the Star Spangled Banner.
I am the rockets red glare;
The bombs bursting in air.
I am the omnipotence of patriotism.
I am the trenches in France, Germany,
Belgium, Anzio, Normandy, Omaha Beach, Guadalcanal and Korea.
I am the jungle of Vietnam and the sands of Desert Storm and the streets of Bosnia.
I am One Nation Under God.
I am the names of those who never came back
To keep this republic free.
When you salute me,
You are actually saluting them.
I am the symbol of America,
The Home of the Proud, the Brave, and the Free."

★★★

"It Was a Time of Heroism, Patriotism, and Firm National Purpose. . .

It was also a time in which the citizens of this nation can take great pride. Those six incredible years, 1939 -1945, taught incredible lessons which free people of the world should not forget.

In September 1939, Hitler unleashed Nazi Germany's awesome 'Blitzkrieg', and Nazi hoards swept through Poland, Holland, Belgium, Norway, Denmark, and France in only nine months. By August 1940 the Luftwaffe had begun the London Blitz, and U-Boats were sinking American ships. All this before 1941.

Two full years after Hitler attacked Poland, with half the world involved in full-scale war, America was still asleep. On December 7, 1941, the Empire of Japan destroyed or damaged two-thirds of American sea power at Pearl Harbor. From that day on, America became totally united.

Within a year, the U.S. was equaling the combined Axis war production, and an army of 16,000,000 men and women was being equipped and trained. Within four years the Swastika and Rising Sun had been beaten into unconditional surrender.

We should be proud of that victory. Present and future generations of Americans should be made aware of this nation's accomplishments during that period."[6]

★★★

Fly Your Flag—Today is Veterans Day. Formerly designated as Armistice Day to commemorate the end of World War I, Nov. 11 was set aside in 1954 to honor all the men and women who have served in our nation's armed services. Fly Old Glory in tribute to the members of our military establishment who have fought bravely throughout the world to protect the American way of life from those who would have destroyed it.[7]

★★★

"By Nimitz – and Halsey – and Me

The mellow blue eyes of Admiral Nimitz twinkled and his tanned face creased in grins when he read the following poem to the throng at the Hotel Baker luncheon. It was written in September 1945 by Gordon Beecher, now Captain, USN:

> Patty McCoy—an American boy -
> Left his home in the old One Star State.
> He set out to sea in a shiny DD
> And he wound up in Task Force Three Eight.
> He cruised for a while with a satisfied smile.
> Then he took his pencil in hand.
> And here's what he wrote in a well-censored note
> To the folks back in State-side land.
> Me – and Halsey and Nimitz
> Have sure got the Japs on the run.
> We're drivin' 'em wacky in old Nagasaki.
> We're settin' the damn Rising Sun.

Kyushu and Kobe and Kure
Are wonderful ruins to see.
We've got 'em like gophers a-seekin' a hole.
The way that they burrow is good for the soul
And everything out here is under control
By Nimitz – and Halsey – and me.
Me – and Halsey – and Nimitz
Are havin' a wonderful time.
What we ain't uprootin'
By bombing and shootin'
Would fit on the face of a dime.
They say they're a face-savin' nation,
And that may be as true as can be.
They're taking a pushin' all over the place.
We give 'em the Arsenic minus Old Lace.
They're gettin' a kicking but not in the face
From Nimitz and Halsey – and me.
Me – and Halsey and Nimitz
Are anchored in Tokyo Bay.
The place is just drippin' American shippin',
They stretch for a helluva way.
We hear that the fighting is finished,
And that is the way it should be.
Remember Pearl Harbor – they started it then.
We're warnin' 'em never to start it again,
For we have a country with millions of men
Like Nimitz – and Halsey – and me."

★★★

Jimmy Doolittle is best known, of course, for the daring Tokyo raid from the carrier Hornet that earned him the Congressional Medal of Honor. . . Most know him as a war hero and commander of the 12th Air Force in North Africa, the 15th in Italy, and the 8th in England and Okinawa during World War II. . .

Doolittle enlisted in the Army Air Service in World War I at the age of 21, learned to fly at Rockwell Field, San Diego, served as an instructor and qualified as a pursuit pilot in 1918. He missed combat in Europe during the war, a disappointment that helped spur him to subsequent greatness as a race pilot, stunt flier, engineer, researcher, and commander of enormous air fleets in World War II. . .

In 1930 Doolittle, then a major, resigned from the Air Corps to manage the aviation department of the Shell Petroleum Corp., continuing in this position until he returned to active duty a decade later. . . He returned to active duty with the Air Corps as a major in 1940, became a lieutenant colonel the following year and was promoted to brigadier general, skipping the rank of colonel, after the Tokyo raid of April 18, 1942. . The fast-pace master of the calculated risk retired as lieutenant general after World War II with a score of decorations. . ."[8]

★★★

A post card dated December 10, 1944 from Sgt. Woodrow Bowers to Mrs. Lindsay McAllister had on the front "Merry Christmas" with pictures of a bathing beauty sitting under a palm tree and Christmas bells surrounded by ribbons and holly. This was in Mary's scrapbook and reads:

"From the wide Pacific Ocean
To the great Atlantic shore,
I have seen many things,
And will see many more.
I've seen many a Christmas come and go,
I've seen them with and without snow.
Of all I've seen, 'tis the first for me,
To see coconuts on my Christmas tree."

★★★

An Associated Press article in a Greenville, Texas newspaper dated June 17, 1999 reads as follows:
"Greenville to Celebrate Its War Hero's 75th Birthday

Audie Murphy, who parlayed his World War II heroism and boyish good looks into a long career in the movies, will be honored on the day that would have marked his 75th birthday. Gov. George W. Bush has declared Sunday to be 'Audie Murphy Day'.

'His character and courage represent the best our state has to offer, and he remains a hero and an inspiration to us all', the governor said.

Murphy was born June 20, 1924 near Kingston in Hunt County, the son of tenant farmers. As a boy, he learned to hunt and became an expert shot, a skill that would help him in his military career. Murphy enlisted in the U.S. Army shortly after his 18th birthday. He took part in the invasions of Sicily and Southern France as a member of the Third Infantry Division.

He rose in rank from a Private to Second Lieutenant by the end of 1944. In late January 1945, German infantry and tanks attacked his company near Holtzwihr in northeast France. Murphy ordered his men to fall back while he remained at a forward command post calling in firing instructions to the artillery. As the enemy closed in on him, Murphy climbed aboard a burning tank destroyer and used its 50-caliber machine gun against them. Alone, atop a vehicle that could have exploded at any moment, he continued firing until his ammunition ran out. Ignoring a leg wound, he then made his way to his company, refused medical attention, and organized a counterattack that forced the Germans to withdraw.

Murphy was awarded the Medal of Honor for his heroic actions. In all, he received more than thirty medals, including three Purple Hearts, and the Croix de Guerre of both Belgium and France, making him the most decorated American combat soldier of World War II.

Murphy continued to serve his state and country after the war, rising to the rank of Major in the Texas National Guard and the U.S. Army Reserves. His memoirs, *'To Hell and Back'*, became a best seller. He then went to Hollywood where he made more than forty films, including *'The Red Badge of Courage'* and the film version of *'To Hell and Back'*."

★★★

After the war ended, an album entitled *"The Men and Women in World War II from Red River County"* was published. The album cover is blue and white with a U.S. Flag. The inside has a Dedication Page which reads "To the memory of those men and women who so nobly gave their lives for their country, we dedicate this book. We bow our heads in their memory and offer a silent prayer that they have not died in vain." The album that I have belonged to Lindsay and Mary McAllister and is dated September 17, 1946. It has been such a help in writing this book.

There is a picture of the Red River County Court House and a letter from John T. Felts, Post Commander, John T. Felts, Jr., Post No. 45, American Legion, Clarksville, Texas with pictures of Mr.

Felts and his son who was killed in action in 1943 when he was lost in a plane crash at sea. The letter reads in part as follows:

"The war has been won, as all our wars have been won, because we were in the right, and even our enemies are fortunate in that we have won, because our Nation has never engaged in a selfish war, nor has it exacted an unjust peace from a fallen foe. Now the Peace must be won, and the world put on the right course by our precept and example. We will have to show the same pioneer spirit that cleared the forests and conquered the mountains and the plains, for never in our long and glorious history have courage and fortitude been needed more."

From the page entitled 'In Memoriam', the pictures and write-ups within the book itself, and other information I have received, I list below names of those from Red River County, Texas who were killed in action in World War II. We visited the Veterans' Memorials in Bogata, at the Court House in Clarksville, and at the Boxelder and Gilliam Cemeteries. I am sure this list is not complete, and I am indeed sorry for any name that is omitted, but I did the best I could in securing this information.

Hubert Alford
Vade Allen
Charles Tanner Allen
Walter E. Bellotte
William H. Bishop
J. B. Bowie, Jr.
Grady Austin Branson
George W. Brown
Joe Buchanan
Adelbert R. Cagle
Jasper Clinton Caldwell
Robert Houston Canterbury
M. T. Coffman
John E. Coleman
Stroud R. Coleman
Charles W. Cotton
Buford E. Denny
Willie T. Enox
Arthur B. Ervin
Bennie W. Faucett
John Thomas Felts, Jr.

Woodrow W. Leverett
James Robert Loftin
Johnnie L. Lovell
Herman Lee Martin
George E. Mathis
Lois M. Mauldin
Willie Mays
Ballard D. McCain
Wayne D. Miller
Thomas M. Moore
Carl L. Morris
Robert L. Noe
Willie Oliver
Joe D. Parker
Louis E. Peek
Roy S. Rains
Lawrence Rawleigh
Clifford F. Reid
Thomas Donald Roach
Archie G. Roberts
Theodore R. Riddle

William H. Forester
Oscar M. Fowler
John T. Freeman
Hubert J. Funk
Arthur Gable, Jr.
Leoran Chester Gallender
Rufus E. Garrett
William Albert Giddens
William James Gist
James Paul Gullion
Norris L. Hargus
John M. Henderson
Lloyd L. Holloway
Joe J. Hooser
Cecil C. Howland
John W. Hulen
Gerald W. Isbell
Curtis Jackson
Martin L. Johnson
Charles David Jones
Lomax W. Jones
Charles L. Kennedy
Thomas L. Lawson

Harold S. Ridley
Fred F. Scott
Hugh M. Sharpe
Errel Lee Sheppard
Dowdy Buel Shirley
Elmer Shoulders, Jr.
Pete Slaton
W. E. Stephens
Edward A. Steele
James R. Stroud
Herman G. Thomas
Wallace Thomas
Jessie D. Thompson
Vernon A. Thornton
Jasper Bruce Tull
Sims C. Ward
Lowery C. Warren
Marvin C. Watkins
Forrest R. West
David M. Williams
J. D. Wright

GOD BLESS AMERICA

While the storm clouds gather
Far across the sea,
Let us swear allegiance
To a land that's free.
Let us all be grateful
For a land so fair,
As we raise our voices
In a solemn prayer.

God Bless America
Land that I love
Stand beside her and guide her
Thru the night with a light from above.
From the mountains to the prairies
To the oceans white with foam.
God Bless America
My home sweet home
God Bless America
My home sweet home.

(Could anyone who lived during World War II ever forget hearing Kate Smith sing God Bless America? She introduced this song, written by Irving Berlin, on Armistice Day, 1938, and sang it many, many times during the war years.)

Chapter 11
Lest We Forget

"O beautiful for heroes proved
In liberating strife,
Who more than self their country loved,
And mercy more than life!
America! America! May God thy gold refine,
Till all success be nobleness,
And every gain divine."[1]

My first interview with a veteran of World War II was on June 14, 1999 when my husband and I visited with **R. H. Peek, Jr.** (better known as "June Bug") and his wife, Eudora at their home in the Gilliam Community in Red River County. This is what he had to say:

"Way back yonder when they didn't have any cars or nothing, I had two uncles who lived down back of the graveyard, and one was coming out on foot one morning. My daddy stepped out on the porch and saw him coming, and said, 'Well, I got me a big boy'. My uncle said, 'What'd you name him?', and my daddy said he hadn't named him yet. Well, it was in June so my uncle said, 'Just call him June Bug', and I've had that name ever since. I was born June 29, 1925 right near here in this Gilliam Community. My parents were Rufus Henry, Sr. and Ethyl Peek. A Peek married a Peek. My brothers and sisters were Marvin, Wayne and Otis, the boys, and the girls were Lallie, Johnnie Bell and Geraldine. I married Eudora Rhea in 1952, and we have two children, Carolyn and Billy. First we lived in a log cabin over on the highway, and it's about to fall in now. We call our place here 'Sweet Memories'.

I went in the service in December 1943 after a six month deferment to help my daddy finish his crop. I took my basic training at Camp Fannin south of Dallas. I was only eighteen years old. I was there six months and came home for fourteen days and then went overseas. I loaded on the boat to go overseas the day I was nineteen years old. We were on the water about fifteen days. We landed at Naples, Italy, and we went over as replacements. We joined the 88th Division after we got over there. That was the Infantry, and they called them the 'Blue Devils'. I was overseas about eighteen months.

Our first night up on the line we lost all our officers, the Battalion Commander and Company Commander, all the big shots. Then we come back and got some more men and in about three or four days we went back up on the line. I believe it was the second night we was on the line that we got captured. It got dark, and the Germans had been firing on us all night. They was dug in up on top of this mountain, and we was down in this valley. About daylight we decided we was going to take them. On the right and left sides there was machine guns. They never had fired, and we didn't know they was there so they opened up and started firing, and they had us trapped. There wasn't no way of getting out. We was in a draw on the side of this mountain. Several men tried to get out and go back, but when they got up on this ridge out of this gully, the Germans just mowed 'em down. Me and this other boy seen it, several of them shot, so we just kept running up and down this little old draw. They was dropping hand grenades over on us. They were called 'potato mashers', and if we could get to them soon as they hit, we'd pick 'em up and throw 'em back. About the second or third one that came over hit the butt of my M1 rifle and just busted the stock all to pieces.

We was running back and forth, and this boy that was with me said, 'Let's give up. If we don't, they're going to kill us.' I said, 'All right. You go first, and I'll follow you.' Then he said, 'No, you go first, and I'll follow you.' Well, we was still running up and down this draw dodging them hand grenades and arguing over who'd go first. I'd just about had all of it I could take so I told him I'd go. Then I looked up and saw this German right on top of this hill. He had a P38, and it looked like he had it right between my eyes. He had his other hand motioning for us to come on. Don't think I didn't go! I told this other boy to come on.

We got up there, and my buddy had a hand grenade in his ammunition belt. It was right in front, and this German reached down and pulled the flap up and stuck his finger in that ring and was going to pull it out of his belt. I hit his hand and shook my head. I couldn't talk German so I didn't know what else to do. I pulled the grenade out and handed it to him, and he never did pull the pin on it. They just had a big hole dug out up there with a machine gun in it. We hadn't been there thirty minutes till our boys began shelling the fire out of us. We just all dived in that hole there together. Some of 'em was hit, and some wasn't. I got hit in the leg and hip, and the American with me got hit. A German or two got hit too.

After the shelling stopped, the Germans started carrying us on back as prisoners. We was all hopping along helping each other just like we was all good buddies. It was all we could do. Someone had called in the artillery, not knowing we was there. It was early morning when they captured us, and we walked all day. We finally came to an old house and stayed all night there. The next day we started walking again and finally got back to where their trucks was. They loaded us in them and from there we went on into Germany. We was in one camp for two or three days. We was already in Germany cause we wasn't that far from Germany when they captured us. Then they moved us to Munich, about the third largest city in Germany, and that's where we stayed.

They had a big railroad station, and you never seen such tracks and switches and all that sort of junk like that in all your life. We was right across the street from it in the building where we stayed. The Russians would bomb that thing nearly every night so they'd get us out and carry us to an air raid shelter. There was an old brewery they used for a shelter, and we'd go down a couple of floors under the ground. They slipped in on them one night, and they didn't blow the air raid alarm. They caught us in the building and started dropping the bombs, and they weren't very far from us. We had a man with us who could speak German, and we told him to ask them guards when they heard an air raid alarm if they'd just open the gates and let us go to the shelter, and we'd promise to come back. There wasn't no way to get away. You might get killed. So they did this, and when they heard the alarm, they opened the gate, and we'd take off down there. We had a couple of hundred yards to go. They gave us some new shoes with wooden soles with tacks and things in the bottom of them and just canvas across the top. At night when we was running to the shelter, it looked just like a bunch of lightning bugs. They didn't treat us all that bad, but they worked us, and we didn't have nothing to eat. That was the main thing.

When they called me in, I weighed about 175, and when I got out, I weighed about 135. I lost a lot of weight. For breakfast we had just what we called a ten gallon milk can full of coffee, or what they'd call coffee. I don't know what it was—stump roots boiled, I think. They just set it out there, and we could drink all we wanted or just let it alone. We'd have to go out and work after just having that for breakfast. We'd just go where they'd bombed and clean it up and look for dead people. At dinner they'd bring us a little bowl of soup. We called it grass soup. It had what looked like green onion blades chopped up in it, and I guess mashed potatoes. It was real thin. You wouldn't get a bowl full, and that's all we had for dinner. At night when we got in, we'd get two or three boiled Irish potatoes with the peeling on them.

When we was out working, we could find small pieces of wood—it was in the wintertime—and we'd slip them under our coats and bring them in and put them under our mattress. We'd slip in Irish potatoes. If we had any cigarettes, we could swap that to the German civilians for bread, and we could swap chocolate to them. We got Red Cross packages, one for two people every two weeks. They'd be two or three packages of cigarettes, some crackers and jelly, and stuff like that. We slipped this wood and potatoes in, and I'll never forget '44 on Christmas Day. I went out there in the yard and took my wood and built me a fire. We got a powdered milk can in the Red Cross deal. I took it and filled it about half-way with potatoes and the rest with water and put it on that fire. I boiled them potatoes. I didn't have no bread, salt or pepper, no nothing—just potatoes, but it was good. That was my Christmas dinner in '44.

We finally got where we got mail. I got three or four letters from home. It took a good while to get it started. They censored it all and what they didn't want us to know, they marked it out. We could write, and they checked all our mail, what we wrote. When I was captured, my folks heard over the news or some way that I was missing in action. Then in another week or two they found out I was captured.

One morning when we went out to work, we figured something was wrong. You could hear the big artillery cause it was so close to town. There was white rags hanging out the windows, and we didn't know what they was for. We got out there, and they didn't tell us to go to work or nothing. At dinnertime they marched us back in. The white rags had come down. When they was put out, the people had decided they wouldn't put up a fight for the town. They would just surrender and let 'em come on in. Then they decided they'd put up a fight after all for the town. They took us down to the air raid shelter. You could hear them big guns, the artillery, and directly here come a Major and I believe a Captain—Americans. That was after seven months. You never seen the like of hugging going on. They took us outside and lined us up. They wanted to know how we'd been treated, and if the guards had been good to us. We told 'em they had been good to us. We had one old German man that was a guard, and he told us he was going to take off his uniform and put on civilian clothes. He asked if we'd take care of him, and we told him we would cause he'd been good to us. They told us they didn't have nothing but eggs and bacon. They brought us some cases, and we cooked us some and it was good. They told us to stay near the barracks cause we'd be on our way home.

We came in and got a sixty day furlough. I had to go to Ft. Ord, California to get my discharge and then back home. I came in on a Sunday evening. Then the highway ended up here at CR 1701. I got off the bus there at Clarksville and walked over to the drug store on the south side of the square. I believe it was the Clarksville Pharmacy. Leon Russell was standing there, and he recognized me and asked where I was going. I told him I was trying to get home, and he told me he'd take me. He brought me to the end of the road cause it was really muddy. I cut through and thought I'd come up to the back of the house. Well, my mother had something wrong with her leg, but when I got to the gate, I hollered, and she was the first one out there." ("June Bug" Peek was awarded the Purple Heart, Marksmanship Medal, European Theater Medal with three Battle Stars, and a Good Conduct Medal.)

★★★

A. C. (Blue) and Nora Mauldin Underwood had two sons who were in the service during World War II.

The oldest was **THOMAS ALLEN (TOMMY) UNDERWOOD** who was a Seabee and ran a crash crane to clean out debris on the French Frigate Sound in the Wake Island Group. He was a Motor Machinist, lst Class, and manned a three-inch AA gun. Tommy was discharged before Billy. In November 1949 he was killed in a pipe line accident while operating a bulldozer in Koontz, Texas. His wife, Nora Johnson Underwood, and their daughter, Nora Gail, survived him, but both are now deceased. The two brothers never discussed the war after their service was over.

BILLY UNDERWOOD told me the following: "I entered the U.S. Navy on March 1, 1944 and attended the Central Missouri State Technical College in Warrensburg, Missouri and the Aviation Ordinance in Norman, Oklahoma for eighteen weeks. Next I attended the Gunnery Aviation School in Virginia. I was an Aviation Ordinanceman, Second Class, and shipped out from Norfolk, Virginia on the USS Bogue on the Atlantic Ocean, through the Panama Canal, to North Island at San Diego. Then I went on the USS *Matanikau* to Pearl Harbor and on to the Gilbert Islands which are a part of the Marshall Islands. There we picked up about 1,000 Marines who had seen such fierce fighting that the crew of the ship were not even allowed to go near them. The Marines were taken to Pearl Harbor, and then the ship returned with supplies. My brother, Tommy, was on R&R at Pearl Harbor, and we went sightseeing on a motorcycle with a sidecar. My ship then went back to Roi Island in the Marianas. The torpedo bombers brought the mail, and I well remember receiving forty-four letters and five packages at one time.

While the ship was in operation off Japan, there were many battleships and carriers there. I was on a Jeep Carrier. The Saratoga was the largest ship, and mine was the smallest at Pearl Harbor. We operated behind lines for the main ships when they needed things. The planes were involved in everything, and we loaded them with ammunition. We went west to the north end of Honshu, the main island of Japan, where Tokyo is, and then to Omuta Bay. There were six Jeep carriers and twenty-one LST's loaded with soldiers. When a plane went down, the destroyer would pick the men up. They would be sent over in a bosun chair on a line between the ships. Five gallons of ice cream would be sent back to the rescuers.

This was two weeks before the war ended. Before the official surrender, they put all soldiers ashore, and there was no opposition. There was no one left to fight. I saw only one soldier, and he was running. The men loaded their cameras and took pictures of the prison camps and the prisoners. Some of the camps were empty, and some were still full.

We went then to Tokyo Bay where the peace treaty was signed on the *Missouri*. There were rows of battleships and carriers. The men on my ship couldn't see anything, but at a certain time, we stood at attention and saluted. After we left there we ran into a big storm, and one Jeep Carrier was disabled. It was left in Guam, and we went back to Pearl Harbor. While there, I saw Richard Jackson from Clarksville. We had to count points to be able to come home. We towed targets for ships to practice. I flew in B26's, torpedo bombers, four hours each day. We went early and had the rest of the day off.

As the ship returned to San Francisco, I remember hearing the song, '*California Here I Come*' being played. I was discharged at Norman, Oklahoma on May 10, 1946. I attended college and then went to work for Williams Brothers Construction as a heavy equipment operator." (Billy was awarded the Victory Medal, American Campaign Medal, Asiatic-Pacific Medal, and an Expert Pistol Medal.)

Billy Underwood and Kathryn Huneke were married January 30, 1952 and had two daughters, Kathy and Nancy. Their home is on their ranch north of Clarksville in the Cherry Community where Billy and Tommy Underwood were raised. I am sad to say that Billy died January 17, 2000. Kathryn remains in the new house they had just built on their land.

★★★

My husband and I were privileged to drive to Saratoga, Arkansas to visit with **ALVIN D. (DURWOOD) JOYNER** and his sister, **LENA JOYNER**, who lives next door to him. Both served in World War II. Their parents were Alvin and Betty Crabtree Joyner, and there were six children in their family: Lester, twins Robert Ray and Lena, Durwood, David and Neil. The children were raised on a farm in the community of English, due east of Clarksville, Texas.

Lena said, "In 1944 I was unhappy with my job, but my boss

Brothers Billy and Tommy Underwood during World War II.

Lena Joyner and her brother, Durwood Joyner, showing photos of how they looked while in the service during World War II.

didn't want me to quit. There was a Marine Corps Recruiting Office right down the street from where I worked so I decided to enlist in the U. S. Marine Women's Reserves. My boot training was in North Carolina. From there I went to Oxford, Ohio where I trained in the radio school at the Miami University. My next assignment was at the San Diego Naval Air Station where we had to wait for the barracks to be finished to live in. Then I was stationed at the El Centro Marine Corps Air Force Base in Santa Ana, California. That's where I was discharged from.

I really wanted to go overseas, but my Commanding Officer wouldn't sign the papers because he didn't think it was a good idea to send a woman overseas. So I stayed in the States. I did office work and met some very nice people whom I have kept in touch with over the years. Four in particular because four people were in a cubicle working together. We still exchange Christmas cards, but one recently died.

I was raised at English and attended the Swanville School where my Aunt Myrtle Joyner was my teacher. This was before she married Ernest Witmer, Sr. At that time, teachers had to be single. I went to school there for seven years and then went to school in Clarksville, graduating from Clarksville High School in 1938.

I was discharged from the U.S. Marine Women's Reserves in 1946 after having served two years in the service of my country."

Durwood related this to us about his war experiences: "I went in the Army in May 1935. I was in the Infantry and trained at Ft. Frances E. Warren in Cheyenne, Wyoming. I stayed in the Army three years and got out in '38. Two months later I joined the Marine Corps in San Diego. I didn't have to go through boot training again since I'd already been in the Army. Then I went to the Philippines; left San Francisco on Thanksgiving Day in '39. We got there the first day of January 1940. The Navy Yard there was a submarine base. There were only about ninety Marines there. There were some 4th Marines that came in there from China before the war started. I was packed ready to come home but, of course, didn't get to since no ship could get in there.

I was on duty the night that they hit Pearl Harbor. This man heard about it and came back and told us. The next morning they bombed the Navy Yard. I had been a guard at the Navy Prison and Asst. Warden. Most of us went to Corregidor and stayed there for a while. Then they shipped about thirty of us back to Bataan to guard Wainwright after MacArthur left. The next commander was named King.

I made that Bataan Death March. If there was anything worse than that, I'd hate to be around it. There was one incident that I've always wondered about, just what I'd have done. You didn't dare help anyone or they'd kill you. Well, there was brothers in the Army on that march. One fell, and the other went back to help him. The last time we saw them, they'd left them on the side of the road. We never did know what really happened to them, and I always wondered what I would've done if it had been me and my brother. You never know what you'd do till something happens.

After I made the march, I hadn't been there fifteen minutes till they put me in a truck and sent me back up on a hill where they were firing across Corregidor at the air base they had on Bataan. We stayed there several days. Then they took about fifty of us to work on a bridge crew, rebuilding the bridges they had blowed up. We moved from there to different places, and at one camp I cut wood for a solid year every day. You didn't cut nothing no bigger than you could carry cause you had to carry it out yourself if the weather got bad and they couldn't get a truck in. You might have to carry it over a mile.

They had what they called sweet potatoes to feed us, but all we got was the vine. They got the potatoes. I ended up on a ship going to Japan to the copper mines. I worked in the copper mines for a long time. It was really rough there. There was about 150 of us, fifty Marines, and fifty Americans, and a mix of everything. There was some Dutch Javanese. We didn't have much to eat. We had rice in the Philippines, but in Japan we got maize or crushed barley, and the rice tasted as good as candy, if we ever got any of it.

I stayed there till the war was over. The American that was in charge of us had been MacArthur's aide. After the war was over, they told us not to leave there, but he took off anyway. He went to Tokyo and got hold of MacArthur, and they sent somebody up there right quick, and we got out of there a lot sooner than the rest of them did. Most of them went by ship, but they put us on a plane. I went to San Francisco and stayed there for a few days and then went to Norman, Oklahoma till I was able to go home.

I was a prisoner of the Japanese for forty-four months. It was rough! The Bataan March was terrible, so many killed. I was twenty-five years old when I was captured. Lots of them died along the way, were killed if they tried to help somebody. There's not much that you've heard of about the Japanese that didn't really happen, and it happened to everybody. I saw a lot of it. We was on one of those bridge details, about 150 of us. They'd already told us that if anyone took off, they'd shoot ten around us. Well, this one man took off, and sure enough, they picked out ten and shot them.

If the war hadn't ended when it did, it would have been a massacre. It would have took a long time to take Japan. We saw some of the fortifications they had along the beach, and it would have been something. The bomb being dropped saved our lives.

The Army had a good many people in Bataan, but there just

wasn't enough to do anything about the fighting there. It wasn't King's orders, but he surrendered. There was some nurses there, but the only time I ever saw any of them was when we were being put on a ship to be sent to Japan. I was on the ship just ahead of the ones that were torpedoed. That ship I was on was so crowded that you got to sit down just once in a while. It was a terrible mess there. It's a wonder anybody lived through that. There was a lot of seasickness.

We had some barracks that we stayed in when we was in Japan. Of course, it was up in the mountains, and we stayed right close to some tunnels. Working in those copper mines was something. You'd go down in there, and it'd be so cold. They'd put you in places where they'd already dug out. There'd just be a hole there, and some places they put you in, you couldn't even stand up. You'd just have to crawl. If you moved wrong, you could get caught in that thing. There wasn't a day, I don't guess, that there wasn't earthquake tremors. There was some cave-ins. They didn't shore nothing up unless they really had to. We were really fortunate cause I didn't hear of anyone getting caught in one of those cave-ins.

I was fortunate all the way through in the places I was in. Even in prison camp, I don't know why, when we didn't have much of anything, we was able to get some extra stuff. As far as I know, I wasn't ever sick. We got a few Red Cross packages, but we didn't get any mail. I think my family got a card or two from me with nothing much on them. (Lena spoke here and said that their father's hair turned gray overnight during the time that Durwood was a prisoner of the Japanese.)

You know, there wasn't but fifteen of us in the Navy Yard when I first got there. There was a Commanding Officer that I'd been with in the States. The Navy Yard prison was built on top of a wall the Spaniards had built. Down under it was a prison, a dungeon. Luzon Island was where we were, across the bay from Manila. When they bombed Pearl Harbor, we had nothing whatsoever to fight with. We had some 50-caliber machine guns that we set up after we heard about it. We had one big gun that we'd practiced with, and it was real old. The planes came over the next morning and never even broke formation. They just tore it all up. They had moved all those 4th Marines out of China to the Philippines. It's hard to forget about all that. For a long time I had nightmares. I used to get mad when I came back cause some people didn't believe what had really happened. I guess they thought it was just propaganda.

There was a Captain Short who escaped Bataan. Very few escaped. They tried it, but there was just too many Japs out there. If there was any good Jap guards, I didn't run into them. Sometimes they'd treat you all right, and then the next minute they'd just as soon to beat you or bayonet you.

We knew the war was over cause they quit sending us out in the copper mines. We worked in three shifts, 24-hours a day. Four or five days before the war was over, one morning I was supposed to go to work, but they just put us outside. When our planes came over, they strafed us the first time, but then they came over and dropped us some food. We couldn't eat much of it. All we'd thought about all those months was eating. I had an infection in my gums once. They had a doctor there who lanced that, and it got well. Many died of starvation, fifty or sixty a day, many from dysentery and other diseases. It was rough!"

Durwood was discharged February 12, 1946 and had the rank of Sergeant. He married Valeria Stanton, and their two daughters were Diane and Janet. His home in Saratoga, Arkansas is on his wife's home place. Durwood's parents lived at Hooks, Texas during the war, and both worked at the Defense Plant. Mr. Joyner left the telephone number of his sister, Myrtle Witmer, with everyone, in case he couldn't be reached at home. As it turned out, Myrtle got the message that Durwood had been released from the Japanese. It was nighttime, but she and her sister drove to Hooks to tell the Joyners the good news.

Durwood was awarded the WWII Victory Medal, Army Unit Badge, Philippine Defense Medal, American Defense Badge, Distinguished Unit Citation, Good Conduct Medal, and Prisoner of War Medal for honorable service while a POW.

We felt honored to see his Medals and to talk with a veteran who lived through such horrendous times as he did. In talking about those times, it was brought out that Durwood's hard work on the farm before going into the service probably contributed to the fact that he made it. It is hard to even imagine that he survived the Bataan Death March, besides the years of imprisonment and hard labor in the copper mines.

Photo of Durwood Joyner taken at the time he was liberated from the POW camp in Japan.

★★★

"I am writing this in memory of my brother, **LOIS M. MAULDIN,** to those who remember him in his earlier years of life, living on a small farm in the McCoy Community. He was born

November 26, 1919. His family consisted of his parents, Donnie G. and Myrtle Cagle Mauldin, older brother, T. L., and younger sister, Naomi. In 1930 another brother, Billie, was born; then a little sister, Betty J., was born in 1933.

Lois helped with the family chores that were necessary on a farm. He was a very compassionate, quiet, and easy going person, always helping or trying to help make life a little easier for those around him. After he and T. L. became older, they both sought labor in Clarksville in order to help Mama and Daddy with finances. Since this was during the Depression, money was really scarce.

The only other way to earn a little money was to join the National Guard in Clarksville. When Lois became of age, he enlisted, along with many other boys of Red River County. After mobilization on November 25, 1940, of Company I, Third Battalion, 144th Infantry, 36th Division to Brownwood, Texas, Lois was selected to attend OCS at Ft. Benning, Georgia. He graduated as a 2nd Lieutenant on September 24, 1942. He then went with the 7th Infantry, 30th Infantry Division, into the North Africa Campaign under Maj. Gen. George S. Patton. Plans were made for an amphibious landing on Sicily.

Lois lost his life on August 12, 1943 as they advanced toward Messina, Sicily. Messina surrendered to Maj. Gen. Patton. Later his body was returned to the United States and laid to rest with a full military funeral at Lanes Chapel Cemetery near Clarksville, Texas. He received the Purple Heart posthumously.

I do hope the generations following this war will understand what all the fathers, sons, husbands, and brothers were fighting for. There were many who did not return, but they wanted peace and love on this earth." (written by Naomi Mauldin Davis)

★★★

Tragedies of American Wars—Boone's 7th Infantry, 30th Infantry Division, was in Sicily in August 1943. The Army Center for Military History publication *Sicily and the Surrender of Italy* says that along with two battalions from the 15th Infantry, the 7th was west of San Fratella, near the island's north coast. One battalion of the 30th and a battalion of the 15th were south of San Fratella, and one battalion of the 30th Infantry was southwest of the town. The terrain was hilly; the days hot and dry.

230 ★ For Love of Country The Price of Freedom

The group picture with the American flag of the servicemen on the day of liberation from the Japanese.

Plans for Aug. 8 and 9, 1943 called for 2nd Battalion, 30th Infantry to make an amphibious landing east of San Fratella, move inland and block the coast road, dislodging German forces and allowing the 3rd Division to continue its push toward Messina. After the landing by 2nd Battalion, 30th Infantry, 7th, 15th and the remainder of 30th would push east, driving Germans before them.

Landing began shortly after 3 AM, August 8. By 4:15 AM the landing was complete, but the battalion had been put ashore in the wrong place, west of the specified area. The Battalion Commander decided the 30th would support the 7th Infantry attack, rather than continue moving inland. Later that morning German forces between the 7th and 30th attacked with two Italian tanks and two German tanks. Three tanks were knocked out, and the Germans retreated.

The 7th Infantry attacked east, and by 11:30 AM, August 8, cleared the hills and were in the village of Sant'Agata. By late afternoon the 7th closed to the Rosmarino River. That evening the regiment and the remainder of 3rd Division resumed the advance along the coast road and toward Messina. Sporadic fighting continued along the coast road until August 17 when Messina surrendered to Maj. Gen. George S. Patton.[2]

★★★

On November 25, 1940, Company I, 144th Infantry, a member of the 36th Infantry Division, Texas National Guard, was mobilized into federal service for what was thought to be a training period of no longer than one year. The unit had been based in Clarksville since the National Guard was organized in 1921 following World War I.

The mobilizing and training period was due to the unrest in other parts of the world. The regular services did not have trained personnel and equipment to adequately defend against the obvious intentions of Adolph Hitler. Nazi Germany was gobbling up large chunks of Europe, and the United States was not prepared for what might eventually take place.

The planned one year of training included most of the Guard and Reserve military units in the country. Company I, along with the other units of the 36th, was to be located at Camp Bowie near Brownwood, Texas, but Camp Bowie at the time of mobilization was in the process of construction and could not be occupied for several weeks. Therefore, it was necessary for all units to remain at their home stations until facilities at the new camp would be ready for occupation.

Clarksville had never had an armory that compared to other armories around the state. For years the Company I armory was upstairs on the east side of the square; then in later years moved to the south side. Since space was limited at the armory, a part of the company (including the kitchen) was quartered at the Boy Scout hut near the athletic field in the south part of town.

The local facilities were home based for the citizen soldiers from November 25, 1940, until January 7, 1941. On January 7 the local unit, along with other units of the 36th began the move to Brownwood. The 36th spent most of 1941 at Bowie, with the exception of about two months with the Third Amy maneuvers in Louisiana.

For several weeks rumors had been circulating that, due to the problems in the European countries, the one year would be extended for some time. For most of the Company I men, soldiering was at least a different life than dragging a cotton sack or hauling hay. The regular training routine was continued until December 7 when the Japanese bombed Pearl Harbor.

The bombing altered all plans that might have been; just two days later the 144th Infantry was on troop trains rolling west. The men of Company I would see a much different part of the country for the first time in their lives. Many had never seen the desert or mountainous country. About three days later Ft. Lewis near Tacoma, Washington was the stopping place for the regiment. Units were deployed at strategic points around Puget Sound. Company I was first located at Paine Field with part of the Company sent to Orcas Island near the Canadian border. As the weeks passed, the units were moved from many points in Washington, Oregon, and later down to California.

The personnel of Company I had gone into the service together and stayed together several months more than the one year period. Later, in 1942 the Army began issuing orders for small groups to be transferred to other units; this continued until only a training cadre was all that was left of the original GI's from Clarksville. Company I eventually had men in every theater of operations where American GI's were sent in World War II. . . Several were lost

Part of the Company I, 14th Infantry at the time of mobilization on November 25, 1940 in combat in various parts of the world, and several died in later years due to wounds received from enemy action. . .

At the time of mobilization, the Company was commanded by Captain C. R. Dinwiddie. Other company officers included lst Lieutenant Max O. Witmer, 2nd Lieutenants Howard K. Ray and Kelley Arnold.[3]

Among those Clarksville men who were mobilized with Company I, 144th Infantry, was TRAVIS L. (T. L.) MAULDIN, brother of Lois M. Mauldin. He was born January 15, 1918, and his family history is given along with his brother Lois'. T. L. married Virginia Melton, and their children are Sandra, Peggy, and Travis L.

T. L. was also selected for OCS at Ft. Benning, Georgia and graduated as a 2nd Lieutenant in 1942. After his discharge from the Army in 1945, he remained in the National Guard and retired with the rank of Major. He died February 6, 1996.

★★★

THOMAS S. HUTCHISON was born in Red River County in 1910. He entered the Navy in 1944, trained in San Diego and served on Iwo Jima and the Aleutians. He was awarded the ATO Ribbon, APO Ribbon with one Battle Star, Naval Unit Citation, Purple Heart and Victory Medal. He was wounded on Iwo Jima and discharged in 1946. Thomas was on the second ship that hit the beach at Iwo Jima to unload Marines and Seabees. His ship was shot up, knocking the propeller off, and it was two days and nights before another ship came to tow them away. Through powerful Navy binoculars, Thomas saw the first flag and then the second flag being raised on Iwo Jima. Thomas wrote the following letter on February 19, 1944 to his wife, Louise Ward Hutchison, and their two children, Tommy and Lou:
"Somewhere in the Pacific
My Dearest Wife and Children,

Sweetheart, it has been a good while since I have been able to write, and even now it will be a week before this can be mailed, and now after so long a time, I can tell you all about what has taken place since January, for I realize you must have been worried about where I have been and how I made out.

Your guesses about Iwo Jima were absolutely correct, for we were there on D-Day, on the beach, and if I never see a spot like that again, it will be too soon, for I have been in some awful places, but that was undoubtedly the roughest and the most dangerous spot a person could imagine finding himself in. You probably read numerous accounts of the 'battle of Iwo' and might have seen some newsreels of it, and I want to tell you that none of it was exaggerated in any shape, form or fashion, as to how tough a battle it was or how many of our men lost their lives.

I'm getting ahead of myself, so I'll start at the beginning, which in this case will be February 19th, or D-Day, and that is the only date I can use for military secrecy, but is the actual date we hit there. Neither can I give the names of any of our ships, or numbers, but I believe it was reported in the news that over five hundred of them participated.

En route there we were told our destination and had a fair idea as to what Iwo looked like, but no one aboard realized what we were going into. It was truly a 'Hell on earth'. On the morning of D-Day, bright and early, everyone was on deck trying to get the first glimpse of anything that might be going on. Soon our large and medium bombers came into sight, headed for the target and escorted by swarms of fighters and dive bombers. Just about then, faintly in the distance, Mount Suribachi, the highest point on the island, came into view. In a shorter time than it takes to tell, the first planes started returning to their bases and carriers, and then a steady stream of them were in the air, going and coming.

As the island gradually came into view, we could see what was taking place, and that was my first view of modern warfare in its fully horrible destruction. Surrounding it on all sides were units of our Navy, from the largest battleships to the smallest landing craft. There were every type of ships a person ever heard of—battleships, cruisers, destroyers, mine sweepers, gunboats, and many other types. Even some of our battleships that were raised from the grave after the sneak attack on Pearl Harbor participated in this attack. Some of the big babies were out two or three miles throwing 16-inch shells into Suribachi, while others were not more than one-half mile off shore doing the same.

At that time we were still a good distance off, and we would see a giant mass of flame and smoke and then a good while later would hear a dull boom. As we came closer, we could see and hear the cruisers and destroyers and smaller ships. Overhead, our large and medium bombers, along with dive bombers and fighters, were giving Suribachi and Iwo's two airfields and the beaches a terrific bombardment and strafing. The T.B.F.'s and Hellcats would come over in formation and then peel off and power dive, the T.B.F.'s loosing bombs and rockets, and the Hellcats streams of heavy machine gun fire, until it seemed that Iwo would be blasted out of the ocean and not a Jap would be left alive. But in that thought we were fooled, for they were dug in deep underground and had to be smoked out, one cave and pillbox at a time, and before it was all over, our boys discovered over fifteen thousand pillboxes, all connected with a maize of tunnels and passages. When you thought you had some of them cornered in one spot, they would pop up behind you and shoot you in the back.

We managed to land tanks equipped with flame throwers, and we could see them crawling up the beaches and throwing their deadly flames as they worked over the pillboxes and machine gun nests, trying to establish a beachhead so the Marines could land. And let me stop here to tell you that the Marines are the finest fighting outfit in the world, and I saw many a fine boy go on the beach that day knowing that he stood one chance in a hundred of coming out alive. They had the guts and determination to face certain death in order that we would have two good airfields on Tokyo's doorstep. So the next time you see a Marine and he seems a little 'cocky', just stop and think that he has a good reason to be.

By noon, we were up close and could see the whole action on the beach. The going was mighty tough trying to land, and from our vantage point, we would see wrecked small boats and amphibious tanks on the water's edge. Many of them were put out of action by accurate Jap mortar and machine gun fire, as we later found out, but some of them were broached by the current, leaving the men helpless in the water to face the deadly hail of bullets and shells. At this distance, we could only see the wrecked craft, and not the men themselves, but after dinner when we hit the beach, we were in the middle of the whole thing, and I am telling you this exactly as I saw it, not from someone else's experience, or from their viewpoint.

General quarters sounded, and we knew we were going in. All of the men rushed to their battle stations and the order came in, directing our course and what spot on the beach we would hit. I got to my station, which is gunner on the port, forward heavy caliber machine gun. Everyone was wearing life belts and helmets, and as it later proved, several lives were saved by wearing this equipment. In fact, for three weeks no one dared stick their head up above deck without their helmet on. I personally did everything but sleep with mine on, and if I could have slept in comfort, I wouldn't have pulled it off at all.

So we shoved off, and I know that each and every man aboard wondered what the next few minutes held in store for them. As we neared the beach, we got a clearer view of the wrecked equipment on the beach, and then for the first time could see the men struggling in the water and the men on shore trying to dig a foxhole for protection. Of these men in the water and on the beach, many of them were past struggling, for they were already dead. Mortar fire was dropping on the beach and at the water's edge, and almost every shell that hit threw up a geyser of sand and water, and many of them fell among the men causing deaths and terrible wounds, but those ashore kept on trying to take cover for it was sudden death to the ones who were exposed.

As we got within a couple of hundred yards off shore, we could see the Marines trying to wave us back, but we had our orders to go in, and there was nothing we could do but go as we had things aboard that were badly needed. We hit the beach, and it seemed like a lull came on, and except for an occasional burst of machine gun fire or a mortar shell falling close, everything was quiet.

The Captain gave the order to lower the ramp, and then all Hell broke loose! We had beached almost on top of a Jap pillbox, and the Jap gunner lost no time in lining us up in his sights. As the ramp started down, this damned Jap let us have it. Heavy caliber bullets started at the bow of the ship and started back. It was too late to duck, nothing to do but stand and take it, and it was coming pretty fast. All of the firing was coming from the starboard side of the ship, and in trying to protect my back, and also attempt to get in a few shots, I swung my gun around to that side, a move that undoubtedly saved my life. The first burst of his fire gave him the range, and the second did the damage.

We had some of our men hit, some seriously and some not so bad, and for a few seconds bullets were flying everywhere. One bullet went through the magazine of my gun; another hit a tool box under my foot; a third went through a life-line stanchion about six inches from my hip, and the fourth hit me in my right knee just above the kneecap. Luckily, the one that tagged me had glanced off of something and just the steel jacket struck. The order came over the loud speaker to abandon the guns and get down on the deck where there was some protection. Right then and there, I moved about as fast as I ever did in my life. A few of the men needed assistance to get down, and we helped them to cover.

Then of all times, the damned Japs started lobbing mortar shells in, and they started creeping up on us as they got the range. It was a miserable feeling to hear those heavy shells getting closer, knowing that there was nothing we could do and thinking maybe the next one had your name on it. Realizing it was too hot for us to stay, we got the order to retract from the beach, and we lost no time in doing so. As be backed off, we could see shells hitting where we had just left.

I rolled up my pants leg and there was the bullet sticking out of the flesh. Except for feeling a slight jar when it hit, I hardly knew it had struck. We transferred some of our wounded to hospital ships, but as mine was only minor, I stayed aboard and our pharmacist mate dug it out and patched me up, and I'm as good today as ever.

Overhead our planes were still bombing and strafing, and off shore shells were pouring in over our heads, seeking out Jap positions and gun emplacement. Let me stop here and tell you that our air cover was magnificent. Our carrier based planes kept all Jap planes away with the exception of two that got through several nights later, and they did no damage and were driven off or shot down. We never found out which.

By late that afternoon the Marines had established a beachhead, one that the Japs had no hopes of breaking. From then on, our work was hard, and except for about four or five days after D-Day, not so dangerous. But for a few days, every time we were on the beach, mortar shells fell all around and snipers were constantly trying to pick you off, but as the Marines gradually pushed the Japs back, this type of foolishness came to a halt. Thank God!

After our initial beaching on D-Day, we had no more casualties, although the ship was hit many times, and one day as I was standing on the ramp, a heavy mortar shell fell into a group of Marines about fifty feet from me, wounding a few and tearing one poor boy's leg off and piercing his chest. We brought him aboard, but he was too far gone to do anything with, and he died as he was being transferred to a hospital.

I could go on for hours telling you of incidents that happened, but I realize you must be tired of hearing this, and I know you must have read all about it in the paper so I will shut off for a while. But I will add that I have been recommended for the Unit Citation. That makes a couple more ribbons to wear, which make pretty decorations.

Honey, I am worried about Grannie for I haven't heard from her in some time, but do expect to hear from her in the next couple of days, when we expect to receive a big bunch of mail. It has been almost two weeks since we have gotten mail, and it will be very welcome.

How are Tommy and Little Sis getting along? As time goes on, I miss seeing my darling family more and more, but of everyone I miss, it is particularly you and the children, and I pray and hope that it will only be a short time before I get home. Give my love to everyone and know that always I love you more than life itself.

I love you truly,
Thomas"

★★★

JAMES ROBERT WRIGHT was born January 3, 1922 to Jim and Sallie Johnson Wright. He had two sisters, Ruby and Dimple. He attended Clarksville High School and was drafted into the U.S. Army in January 1943. After basic training he was sent to Camp Howze in Gainesville, Texas and then to Camp Livingston, Louisiana. He was transferred to Fort Ord, California and assigned to the 25th Infantry Division, known as the 'Tropic Lightning Division' because of the design of their shoulder patches. The parent unit of the 25th was the old Hawaiian Division, and the shoulder patch is the outline of a taro leaf with a streak of lightning from top to bottom.

They were sent to the South Pacific, to New Caledonia, where they were readied for the Philippine invasion. In late December 1944 they left New Caledonia and landed on Luzon in the Philippine Islands in January 1945. James Robert's unit spent 150 consecutive days on the front lines. During that time he fell down the side of a mountain with a machine gun tripod strapped to his back. After a few days in a field hospital with a wrenched back, he left and went back to the front. He said, 'The fox holes were better than being in the hospital!'

At one time their unit captured a Japanese payroll officer. They had a great time scattering money off the mountain to the four winds. After they went to Japan in the Army of Occupation, they realized they had probably thrown away a small fortune, as the Japanese currency remained the same. When the war ended, the 25th was sent to Japan as part of the Army of Occupation, stationed in Nagoya.

James Robert was discharged in February 1946 with the rank of Staff Sergeant and was awarded the Good Conduct Medal, American Theater APO Ribbon with one Battle Star and Philippine Liberation Medal with one Bronze Star.

In June 1943 he and Bettye Joyce Tiller were married. They had two sons, Jim Bob and Billy Dale (Frog). James Robert was engaged in the trucking business and was also manager of the Red River Co-op Gin from 1974 until his death in May 1985. (written by Bettye Wright)

★★★

LAWRENCE WOOD was born on December 15, 1918 in Red River County. His parents were Douglas and Emma Grant Wood, and he had four brothers and sisters: Paul, Elsie, Carl and Frances.

He was in the U.S. Army Air Force during World War II and served as an airplane mechanic. In 1947 he and Martha Roberts were married, and they have spent their entire married life on the spot where they live in the Rugby Community. (A scrapbook in his possession which was compiled by his sister, Elsie Wood Alsobrook, during the war has been a great help in writing this book.)

★★★

JAMES LINDSAY McALLISTER was born May 3, 1912, the only child of J. O. (Bud) and Missura Cornett McAllister. He and Mary Lucille Lamb were married August 23, 1937 in Clarksville, Texas.

Lindsay entered the U.S. Army in 1942 and trained at Camp Edwards, Massachusetts, Camp Gordon, Georgia, in Florida, and at Fort Ord, California. He was a part of the Third Engineer Special

Brigade, 288th Signal Company and spent forty-four months in the Army, twenty-six of those in New Guinea, the Philippines and Japan. He received a field promotion from T-4 to 2nd Lieutenant.

On January 19, 1945 while in the Philippine Islands he wrote Mary and said, "I saw General MacArthur the other day. He is a tall, fine looking man and looks exactly as all his pictures do except maybe a little older. He will be sixty-four pretty soon, I think. Things are looking mighty good in this theater."

Lindsay was discharged in 1945 and was awarded the APO Ribbon with four Battle Stars, Philippine Liberation Ribbon, Victory Medal, AD Ribbon, Good Conduct Medal and Meritorious Award. He served for many years as Postmaster in Clarksville where he and Mary made their home. Lindsay died May 30, 1979, and Mary died June 10, 1999. (I was so pleased when Mary's nephew, John Thomas Lamb, and his wife, Lorraine, shared five scrapbooks they had put together from things Mary collected during World War II.)

★★★

JOHN T. (PETE) METTS was born in Red River County, Clarksville, Texas on January 25, 1919. He was the youngest child of John T. and Lizzie Thacker Metts. His half-siblings were Hershel, Haywood, and Hazel. His siblings were Robert H., Pearl, Johnie Margaret, Bonnie, Pauline, and Ethel. Pete Metts married Bonnie Lee Pyles on August 4, 1939 in Clarksville, and they had three daughters, Shirley, Linda, and Betty.

He entered the U.S. Army on December 20, 1944 and served as a PFC in the 491st Replacement Company in the Asiatic-Pacific Theater of Operations. He was a Duty NCO in charge of a group of men escorting them from place to place at a replacement depot during their processing. He saw that the men were issued their bedding and clothing and were properly fed. He was discharged at the Separation Center, Fort Sam Houston, Texas on January 18, 1946 and received the Asiatic Pacific Campaign Medal, Good Conduct Medal, and Victory Ribbon. He died January 4, 1998.

His daughter, Betty Metts Kelsoe, told me this: "In the letters to Aunt Pauline Brantley, he spoke of the days they were on ship, but the military cut out the amount of days. He told of his training in San Antonio, and that he had hit 210 times out of 225 in his rifle training. He spoke in every letter of heavy rains and the cold weather in An Jo Japan, and that he did not see how the Japanese stood it because they did not wear heavy clothing. He was put over his group in the 6th Army Division, and his duty was to tell them what to do. He stated how he hoped to become a Sergeant and if he did, he wanted to tell Mother when he got home so he could surprise her.

Daddy was the youngest of nine in his family and the only boy out of four who served in the military. I could sense the proud feeling he had from being in the Army and serving in World War II. Never once did he speak of not liking what he was doing. This was a real accomplishment for a 25 year old Northeast Texas farm boy to have served with no regrets."

★★★

JOE J. (JODIE) HOOSER was born at Whiterock in Red River County in 1920. His parents were Jesse C. and Mary Williams Hooser. The other children were Ramah, Dan, J. C., Lela, Mable, Omie, Lillie, Helen and Melvin. He was not married.

Jodie joined the U.S. Army before the war and was attached to Company K of the 23rd Infantry. He was a part of the Normandy landing and died June 22, 1944. S/Sgt. Hooser led his men over an area with underground mines. Not many survived and those who did were in a really bad shape, having suffered severe wounds and losing limbs. He is buried at the Normandy American Cemetery & Memorial, St. Laurent, France, Plot 1, Row 11, Grave 8, with a Headstone Cross. He was awarded the Purple Heart posthumously.

★★★

Beal V. Sr. and Ella Mae Proctor Bowers had three sons in the service during World War II. Those sons were Ben F., Beal V. Jr., and Woodrow. Two other sons, Robert and Jack, died when they were young children, and there were two daughters in the family, Veda and Inez.

On August 27, 1999 we visited with Ben and Virginia Bowers here in Clarksville to talk about Ben's experiences. **BEN F. BOWERS** was born March 3, 1920, and he and Virginia Rose married on November 8, 1947 and have two children, David and Deborah.

Ben had this to say: "I was drafted and went into the service on February 22, 1942. I went into the Army at Ft. Sill, Oklahoma and did my basic training at Ft. Knox, Kentucky. From there I went to Ft. Riley, Kansas where the 9th Armored Division was formed. After I left there, I went for desert maneuvers in Needles, California in the hot summertime. Then we came right back for winter maneuvers at Camp Polk, Louisiana. It was quite a drastic change. I can't tell you the exact day I left Camp Polk and went to Camp Kilmer, New Jersey from where I went overseas.

We were on the *Queen Mary* going over, and it took us only eight days, and we landed at Glasgow, Scotland. I did get a little seasick. We left there and went to Tidsworth, England where we camped for a while, and then we went to South Hampton, England and crossed the English Channel into France. The Channel was real rough. They put us on a boat at night, and when we started out, I took a couple of Dramamine so I slept all the way across. I sure didn't want to get seasick if I could help it. There was just water everywhere, and at night it looked like we were way out in the ocean. We stopped, and the next morning the tide had gone out, and we went on dry land. We were in France where all the hedgerows were. The beaches were all cleared, practically all of France was cleared by then. We went right on across France, right through Paris. All the tanks went right through the towns up on the Belgium-Luxembourg Border. We were sitting right there when the Battle of the Bulge broke. We did a lot of chasing and hiding and everything else.

I was a cook, and the cooks were always between the lines. In other words, the artillery and all that was behind us, and the Germans were in front of us. At night we'd sit and you could hear the artillery back in the forest. I was in a tank battalion. We operated out of a 6x6 truck where we kept all the kitchen supplies. Don't think it wasn't rough trying to feed the troops. You'd have to set the field stoves out to cook and then set them back in when you had to move. They ran off a generator, and you had all that stuff to clean up and get the carbon out of the lines before you started another meal. After about one cooking, you had to clean it all up to start over again. We moved with the tanks for our protection and to keep the men fed. In the Battle of the Bulge they got to coming in, and we were in such tight places that we had a big tarp pulled over the 6x6 to stay in the dry. We unrolled the tarp and we were sitting out there with our guns ready because we were a sitting target. This really made it hard on your nerves.

We saw a lot of men hurt and killed. The Battle of the Bulge finally quieted down. One time I went about 36 hours without any sleep at all, trying to protect myself. When we got back to where it was kinda safe, I remember sitting down in the kitchen and falling off dead asleep. I was sitting on a box of GI soap, and when I woke up, I was covered with the soap.

We spent a few nights in the Argonne Forest, and it was so dark. Of course, you couldn't have any lights at night. We had our tent set up; another cook and I did that together. Then he pulled one shift, and I pulled another; it was separate. At night we had to clean up the kitchen so we could cook breakfast the next morning. It was so dark we had to feel our way to the tent.

The outfit I was in was on the Rhine River. We were ahead of the pack when we got to this town where the Remagen Bridge was, and it was still in tact. Our battalion commander ordered troops on across that bridge, and they got all the German demolition cut about ten minutes before it was supposed to blow up. We went on across it even though there were holes all in it from being bombed. I spent one night there in that town, and they wanted us to make coffee for the men. We were out of water in that 6x6, and along beside it we carried cans of water, and all the water we had left was up near the front of the truck. It was my turn to go get the water, and I started after it. They saw me getting the cans, and they started shooting at me so I fell down on the ground. It was raining so I got behind the dual wheels on the truck. That night we slept in a basement that was filled with potatoes.

The next day my group crossed the river. We had a trailer we pulled that carried more supplies, and we had to take turns guarding that trailer. There was a boy named Willie Bedoin, and he was standing there beside it when a round of ammunition hit it. He was hollering for help, and I heard him call my name, but I couldn't get there. He was from up north, and when we were at Camp Polk, he came home and spent a week-end with my folks. Claude Chambers was the preacher at the Christian Church. We lived on East Broadway just beyond the Catholic Church. Willie was Catholic, and when we got up that Sunday morning, I told him he could go to that church, but he said he wanted to go with us. There was a hymn he liked, and Brother Chambers let us sing it.

We traveled on through Germany. We were just about to liberate all of Germany. There was Berlin, and then south of it was a big town named Leipzig. The group I was in went south, and we met the Russians in Czechoslovakia. It was over, and we came back for the occupation of Germany. Another real sad thing happened. About ten minutes before the war was over, there was a boy named Arthur Critchlow from West Texas, and he was in a tank going down a hard top road and a round of ammunition hit the road in front of the tank. It went right up in that tank right through the seat he was in.

We left Germany and came back to Marseilles, France where we got on the boat to come back home. (My brother, B. V., and I met up in Paris, France after the war was over.) It was just a wash tub, just a little boat. We came through the Mediterranean by the Rock of Gibraltor. It took us over twenty days to get back home. I got back in the States on December 19, 1945, and they rushed us down to Tyler, and I was discharged on Christmas Eve day. I got my draft notice on Christmas Eve day of 1941. I came on back to Clarksville. The government would pay you '52-20'—$20.00 a week for 52 weeks until you found a job. I started working for the telephone company on July 1, 1946 to replace Mr. George Brackett. I worked for them over 36 years."

Ben was awarded the ETO Medal, Good Conduct Medal, Victory Medal, and ETO Ribbon with three Battle Stars.

BEAL VINSON BOWERS, JR. was born November 15, 1916 in Clarksville, and his family history is the same as Ben Bowers'. He married Mary Virginia Moore and they had two children, Robert Lawson and Stephen Beal. The family lived in Hugo, Oklahoma at the time of his death on August 31, 1992.

B. V. entered the U.S. Army on April 25, 1944 and was attached to the 68th Armored Division as an AAA AW Creman. He trained at Ft. Bliss, Texas and was in the European Theater in Co 33 and Co 45 in Rhineland, Naples, France and the Battle of the Bulge. After being wounded in France in 1945, he was discharged on January 15, 1946 at Camp Fannin in Tyler, Texas. He was awarded the EAM Campaign Medal with one bronze star, Purple Heart, Victory Medal, and Good Conduct Medal.

WOODROW BOWERS entered the Army Air Corps and trained in Texas, Wisconsin, Florida and Utah. He served in New Guinea, Dutch East Indies, Leyte, Mindoro, Luzon and Okinawa.

Woodrow was awarded the APO Medal and the Philippine Liberation Ribbon with eight Battle Stars. He was discharged in 1945. He married Joyce Patterson, and they lived in Texarkana at the time of his death on January 20, 1985.

★★★

J. C. AIKIN was born March 21, 1927 at English, Texas. His parents were Erbie George, Sr. and Lilous Melton Aikin. Other children in the family were a son, Erbie George, Jr. and daughters, Bobby, Dorthey, and Floy Mae. J. C. married Mary Sue Moore, and they are both retired and live in Clarksville.

J. C. volunteered for the service in Paris, Texas on December 29, 1944, when he was only seventeen years old. He was a Coxswain (CB) V-6 in the U.S. Navy and took his training at the USNTC at Great Lakes, Illinois and USNTC at Davisville, Rhode Island. He was attached to the 28th USN Const. Battalion and 125th Naval Const. Battalion. J. C. served on Okinawa and was discharged June 16, 1944 at Norman, Oklahoma. He received the Victory Medal and Asiatic-Pacific Campaign Medal with one Star.

★★★

John and Maud Bannister Cozort who lived in Red River County, Texas had eight children. They were Coba, James, John, Madeline, William (Maxie), Virginia, Bobby and Tom. (When visiting with Tom Cozort, I commented on the unusual name of Coba and was told that it was a combination of the first two letters of Cozort and Bannister.)

BOBBY COZORT entered the Army in December 1943 at the age of eighteen. He took his basic training at Camp Fannin in Tyler, Texas and then went overseas in the Infantry, Company A 59-TR-BN as a replacement after D-Day. In less than a year, on September 15, 1944, Bobby was killed in action on the edge of Germany.

He received the Purple Heart posthumously, Bronze Star Medal, Distinguished Unit Emblem, European-African-Middle Eastern Campaign Medal with three Bronze Service Stars for the Normandy, Northern France, and Rhineland Campaigns, WWII Victory Medal, and the Combat Infantry Badge.

The Cozort family received the following letter:

"In grateful memory of Pvt. Bobby J. Cozort, AS#38641153, who died in the service of his country in the European Area September 15, 1944. He stands in the unbroken line of patriots who have dared to die that freedom might live, and grow, and increase its blessings. Freedom lives, and through it, he lives in a way that humbles the undertakings of most men.

Franklin D. Roosevelt

President of the United States of America"

Another Cozort son also served during World War II, and Tom showed me a clipping about him that reads as follows:

WILLIAM M. COZORT, MAJ. (RETIRED), born in 1918, died unexpectedly in Alabama in 1988. A native of Clarksville, Texas, after his retirement from the U.S. Army, he was employed with Civil Service at Ft. Rucker from 1961 until 1974 where he served as Purchasing and Contracting Officer at the U.S. Army Aviation Test Board.

Maj. Cozort was a World War II veteran and received the Distinguished Unit Citation, American Defense Service Medal, American Campaign Medal, European-African-Middle East Campaign Medal, the WWII Victory Medal Army of Occupation (Germany), Purple Heart, Air Medal with four Oak Leaf Clusters, Croix De Guerre with Silver Star, National Defense Service Medal, Armed Forces Reserve Medal, and Senior Army Aviator Badge."

Maj. Cozort was shot down three times while serving as a liaison pilot who spotted for artillery in France and Germany. He was wounded once. He made a career of the service.

His brother, Tom, remembers that when Maj. Cozort was stationed at Camp Maxey in Paris, Texas, he flew an army plane near their home in Red River County. He landed the plane either on the highway or in a pasture and took Tom for a ride.

★★★

George M. and Clara Martin Sharpe had two sons in World War II. They also had a daughter, Nancy. **S/SGT. HUGH M. SHARPE** was born May 13, 1919 at Detroit, Texas. He married Louise Fry, and their son, Hugh Michael Sharpe Gunther, was born three weeks after Hugh's death. His widow later remarried, and their son was adopted by her husband whose name was Gunther.

Hugh served in the 734th AAF Bomb Squadron and was killed

January 16, 1944 in a plane crash in British Guyana near Brazil while en route to the European Theater.

JACK M. SHARPE was born October 17, 1917 at Detroit, Texas. He married Dorothy Nell Horn and they had two children, Linda and Jack M., Jr.

He enlisted January 6, 1942 in the U.S. Naval Reserve, Eighth Naval District, Dallas, Texas. His training was at the U.S. Naval Reserve Midshipman School, Columbia University, New York. He attained the rank of Lieutenant and served as Executive Officer, USS LCI (L) 344 and Commanding Officer, USS-LCS-17. Lt. Sharpe was released to inactive duty on January 26, 1946 at San Diego. He was awarded the American Area Service Ribbon; Asiatic-Pacific Area Service Ribbon with four Bronze Stars for operations or engagements in the Eastern New Guinea Operation, Bismarck Archipelago Operation, Western New Guinea Operation, and Okinawa Operation; and the Philippine Liberation Ribbon. He also participated in the assault and occupation of Trobriand Island and in the Aomori-Ominato-Hokkaido Operation.

★★★

LIEUTENANT COMMANDER JOHN H. BAILEY, USNR, was born December 17, 1921. His parents were Benjamin Garvie and Eugie Elizabeth Tomlinson Bailey. His siblings were Tyrus Reginald, B. G., Blanchard S., Herman C., and Anna Marie. He married Elizabeth J. (Betty) McDavid, and they had three children, Sherry, Larry Wayne and John David.

He enlisted in the service at Dallas, Texas in May 1942 and was assigned as a Seaman on the USS Bainbridge, Destroyer #246 and then transferred to Naval Aviation Training. He was awarded his wings and commission at Pensacola Naval Air Station on August 29, 1944. He was a carrier pilot on Petrof Bay, CVE 80.

Lt. Col. Bailey had this to say: "My carrier with the Pacific Fleet was anchored off Saipan in the Marianas Islands when the atomic bombs were dropped.

For naval aviation training I was sent to the following colleges: University of Washington in Seattle; Yakima Junior College (War Training School) in Yakima, Washington; St. Mary's College, San Francisco; University of Oklahoma (Primary Training Base); and Pensacola, Florida Naval Air Station. I joined the fleet in Seattle after qualifying for carrier landings at Glenview Naval Air Station on the Wolverine on Lake Michigan. The training took eighteen months.

In 1943 I took a train from Norfolk, Virginia to Seattle for flight training. This trip took about five days. Before the carrier left for the Pacific Theater, we had night landing training at Hilo, Hawaii."

He received the Naval Aviation Wings-Carrier Pilot; American Campaign Medal, and Asiatic-Pacific Campaign Medal. He served on destroyers on the Atlantic Ocean and Caribbean Sea and on a carrier in the Pacific Theater. He was discharged at Orange, Texas in September 1946 and stayed in ready or organized reserve until 1962.

★★★

HUGH WESLEY O'DONNELL was born January 17, 1925 at Cuthand, Texas. His parents were Hugh Albert (Bill) and Emma Lou Moore O'Donnell. His brothers were Gaston, Billy, Marlin, Donald Ray, and Gordon, and his sisters were Thelma, Betty and Reba. Wesley and Dorris Adams were married June 28, 1947. An infant son born November 29, 1948, died the same day; a daughter, Teresa was born in 1950; another son, Hugh, was born in 1955 and died in 1974.

He entered the service on June 26, 1944 at Clarksville, Texas and took his training at San Diego. He was a Seaman, First Class and served at the NTS Armed Guard Center in San Diego, on the USS Sea Cardinal, and on USS LST #134. He was discharged from the Navy on May 21, 1946 at Norman, Oklahoma and was awarded the Victory Medal, American Campaign Medal, and Asiatic-Pacific Campaign Medal. Wesley died May 30, 1996.

★★★

On September 20, 1999 my husband and I visited with Vernon and Mary Virginia Holley Earley here in Clarksville. They were married July 20, 1947 and have three children, Roger, Steve and Pam. One son, Keith Stanley, lived only one day. **THOMAS VERNON EARLEY** was born October 3, 1923 in Fannin County north of Honey Grove, Texas. His parents were Thomas N. and Winnie Dodd Earley. There were three other sons, Arvelee, who died at eighteen months of age, and Charles and Robert. Vernon remembers his mother having two flags that hung in the window to show that the Earleys had two sons, Vernon and Charles, in the service. Robert was married, had two children, and farmed so he did not have to serve.

CHARLES E. EARLEY entered the U.S. Navy in 1944 and trained at Great Lakes, Illinois. He was stationed in San Francisco and did not go overseas. His wife was Ethyleene Solomon, and they had three children, Carolyn, Larry and Brent.

Vernon had the following to say about his experiences in World War II:

"I was drafted in January 1943 from Red River County. Actually we were connected with I Corps and the 33rd Division. I took my basic training in Cheyenne, Wyoming; then to Stockton, California for special schooling; then to Camp Cook, California for nine months. And then to Ft. Lewis, Washington for about two months—then overseas. We were the first troops to ship out of Portland, Oregon. I was with Ordinance.

We were in Townsville, Australia for two months and then shipped out from there to New Guinea and stayed there nine months. That's where I got malaria fever—both ear drums ruptured, and jungle fungus set up in both ears—really gave me fits and still gives me fits. From there we went in on Luzon in the Philippines. We were in the first wave that went in there, and it was quite a challenge for all us guys who'd really never seen no action. We were just kids, but that's how Uncle Sam wanted us. I turned nineteen overseas. We spent nine months on Luzon, and I guess after the Japs were pushed out, I enjoyed that more than anywhere I was. Well, the Filipinos were gracious people and bent over backwards to make you feel welcome. Of course, I played the guitar, and after all of it settled down, the Special Service issued me a guitar, and I became very popular at funerals, wakes, and weddings. Lots of eating—good food—part of it I didn't recognize, but it was quite a good deal. They served eight and nine course meals and really went overboard for us. We had a Filipino tent boy after we settled down, and I saw this guy coming down the road with eighteen or twenty dogs. I said, 'He go hunt'?, and the tent boy said, 'No, he go peddle'. It was good food, but I imagine in some of those courses I had some dog meat.

I had both ear drums ruptured, and I didn't get a Purple Heart even though they offered it to me. I didn't take it because I knew it would scare my Mother and Daddy to death. I never did get it and lost five points coming home since I didn't take it. I stayed in the hospital back in Australia with that fungus in my ears. My ear lobes nearly dropped off. I had penicillin shot after shot and finally it cleared up. I took malaria—really, my first attack was on Luzon, but I picked it up in New Guinea. I was on the malaria squad in our company. I sprayed all the water and containers where mosquitoes would collect. In New Guinea it was famous for its rain. It rained there every day about 4:00 in the afternoon. You could set your clock by it. Our old clothes could be clean, but they mildewed. They would have a half inch mildew a lot of times, and the only way we could get it off was to step out in the ocean and let the water take it off. Then we'd dry off. We were issued cloth tennis shoes that stayed wet all the time, and your skin absorbed all that. Your feet stayed wet all the time, and your skin just shriveled. I really don't know how we lived through it. If ever there was a hell hole, New Guinea was it. I did make some good friends there and had some buddies though.

Well, I started barbering and became the official company barber. On Luzon I moved up to battalion barber, and I was in 'high cotton'. I even sent money home. I was making actually more than the Lieutenants were making. I was just a Corporal and sent $100 home very month. My dad and brother bought yearling heifer cows from Clark Crader, and when I got home I had 35 head of cattle. I never will forget this. My brother bought this place from Brose Medford and cultivated the land. There was 580 acres of wooded land that joined it, and Robert and my dad had leased that land to run cows on. We had about 100 head of cattle. Brose Medford said to me, 'Vernon, let me sell you that place', and I said, 'Mr. Brose, I can't buy it. I'm fixing to get married, and I'm going to sell my cows and just row crop. He said he would sell me the land for $8.00 an acre, 5% interest, and I could make the payments like I wanted to. I wouldn't take him up on it, and that place still joins the place I ended up with, Robert's place. They cleared all the brush up, and some of that land sold for $400 an acre. I could have bought it for $8.00 an acre.

When I came home the last time on a furlough, Virginia and I had a date, and we wrote each other while I was overseas. I knew she was the girl I was going to marry, if she'd have me.

After Luzon we went into Japan itself, on Honshu Island where Tokyo is. I had the best time there I guess I had the whole time I was in service because I drove a full Colonel around. He had a jeep that I named 'Ginger'. He was a photographer who really went in for it so we drove all over Japan to places not many people got to see. The religious capital, I can't think what it was, but I know Dr. C. B. Reed went over there. We were stationed in Kobe and Osaka. It was the only place where their Buddha religion was, and it was spared—never bombed. We got on a plane and flew over Hiroshima and Nagasaki. There's no way to describe it—block after block after block with nothing left. Some of the really good buildings were hollowed out, but still stood. They were gutted. It was a bad situation. We stayed there for five months before I came home. I was discharged January 1, 1946. I landed in Portland, Oregon, and I never was as proud in my life to see our country. We had turkey and dressing on the ship coming back, but I nearly starved to death going over. I lost 29 pounds on the trip overseas. Stayed on the ship 29 days and lost 29 pounds. We had nothing but dehydrated food, and it was steamed. You talk about homesick boys by the time we got to Australia. I never was seasick. There was one boy who took his steel helmet and strapped it around his neck like an apron. There was some rough waters. I saw a tornado on the water—looked like an hourglass sucking that water up in that funnel. It was about 18 miles from our ship. It was all quite an ordeal.

Going to Luzon there was a Jap plane coming into our ship with the intention of sinking it—you know, one of those kamikaze planes, those suicide planes. They caught him with a three inch shell just about 100 yards out, and he ricocheted on that water and came up on that ship, but he exploded as he ricocheted up. He was a pilot with a wooden leg.

Mail would catch up with you in batches—sometimes 25 or 30 letters after we finished action. Mother wrote every day, and Virginia wrote pretty regular. I wrote at least twice a week. I was on guard duty one night, and I had a tablet with real thin tissue paper, and I sat there and wrote a letter as pretty as you ever saw by moonlight. Biggest old moon you ever saw.

They put me on the machine gun squad when we hit the Philippines. As much excitement as I ever stirred up when I was over there was when we went in this little town on Luzon. I noticed when we unloaded that evening at about 4:30 the Ordinance Boys unloaded some tanks of acetylene and oxygen in big cylinders. This captain said we didn't have nothing to worry about, but to shoot anything that moved. We had machine guns set up on four corners, and I was on guard duty about 8:00 when I heard something drag across the tin on an old house that had burned. It sounded like a man walking so I gave it a burst and then all at once it seemed like the whole world had exploded. I'd shot with armor piercing bullets. They loaded the machine gun with regular, AP and tracers, and I had shot through that with one of those AP and hit an acetylene tank. I'm telling you, I had the whole I Corps out and the captain came running up. I just nearly shot him, and he said, 'Earley, don't shoot me.' I was really excited. Next morning we found a big old water buffalo. I had started at his head and went to his tail and really opened him up. I Corps was probably six or eight miles away so they got on the radio and told them about it. I was glad when it was over. We got married and farmed." (Mary Virginia Holley, daughter of Jim and Rosa Sinclair Holley was working in the office of the Pecan Shelling Plant in Clarksville during this time and remembers that Byron Black, Sr. was in charge of the sale of U. S. Savings Bonds. She remembers the campaigns that were launched to sell bonds. Each county had a quota to meet.)

Charles Earley's youngest son, Brent, gave Vernon a British Enfield Rifle mounted on a board with a plaque inscribed:

"Commemoration of 50th anniversary of VE VJ Victory 1945 -1995

presented to Vernon Earley, U.S. Army, WWII

In appreciation for his efforts and sacrifices on our behalf

The Earley Family 1995"

Vernon Early was awarded the Good Conduct Medal, APO Ribbon, ATO Ribbon with two Bronze Stars and an Arrowhead, and four Overseas Bars. He was discharged in 1946. The Earleys are retired and make their home in Clarksville.

★★★

HENRY CLAY (JACK) DODD, JR. is the son of Henry Clay, Sr. and Birty Lee Holliway Dodd. He was born in Paris, Texas on December 1, 1926. A daughter, Mary Lee, and another son, David Hiram, were also born to this family. Jack married Gloria

Ann French, and they have three children, Kristy Lynn, Danise Ann, and Henry Clay III.

Jack enlisted in the U.S. Navy in July 1944 and was trained at Gulfport, Mississippi. He was stationed in San Diego and served in the South Pacific, Yellow Sea, and Okinawa as F 1/C aboard the USS Minneapolis, a heavy cruiser. He was discharged at Norman, Oklahoma in July 1946 and was awarded the China Liberation Medal and Victory Medal. He and his wife reside on Dodd family land in the community of Rosalie.

★★★

DARWIN FLOYD was born March 26, 1921 at Boxelder, south of Annona, Texas. His parents were John D. and Florence Stout Floyd. There were five sons in the family: Darwin and his brothers, Paul, Mack, John C. and Amos. After his discharge, Darwin returned to Boxelder, and he and Earldene Fogleman were married on January 26, 1946. They have three children, James Dean, Jan and Joan. Darwin said the following when we visited with them at Boxelder where they still reside:

"I volunteered for the Army because I didn't want to pick cotton or work in the sawmills. I entered the service on August 16, 1940 and did my basic training at Ft. Sam Houston in San Antonio. After basic training, I went to Military Police Training but didn't like it so I transferred to the 2nd Quartermaster. After Pearl Harbor the 702nd Ordnance was formed as part of the 2nd Infantry Division. Our job was to maintain equipment—work on tanks, half tracks and weapon carriers. I was a Staff Sergeant over four other soldiers. In November 1942 we were transferred to Camp McCoy, Wisconsin.

On October 18, 1943 the 2nd Infantry Division landed in Belfast, Ireland. The trip going over was really rough with waves that seemed as tall as the ship. We went to Swansea, England and then on to Wales. After crossing the English Channel, we were ferried from the ship by LST's to land on Omaha Beach on June 7, 1944, the second day of the invasion. It was a real bad day. The beach was not secured, and the Germans had moved a new division in. They were in concrete bunkers on top of the hill looking down on the beach where the troops were landing. Everything they had was being fired at us. Americans who had been killed were floating in the water. The Army Air Corps had sent in gliders carrying troops, but when they tried to land, they crashed into poles that the Germans had put up in the fields.

Our troops went about a mile and a half up the hill on to Trevieres Forest and then to St. Lo, fighting hard all the way. The hedgerows were a big problem there so our group designed a blade to go on the front of tanks that would push holes in them. We picked up steel off the beach to make the blades and on the steel was 'Made in USA'. I saw General Eisenhower when he and his staff came over to inspect and approve the use of the blades.

The Germans weren't SS Troops, Hitler's pick and choice, but we ran into them later at Vire. On August 15th we were at Tinchebray, and then we went to Brest, France where we were supposed to be for two or three days. It turned out that we stayed from August 21 to September 18 before going straight into Paris where we went right by the Eiffel Tower. At Brest the SS Troops just wouldn't give up, and if any of their own men tried to surrender, they shot them. The Germans hated Americans.

We stopped at St. Vith, right on the edge of Germany and then crossed the Rhine River on March 29, 1944 to Giessen, Germany. It was a bad winter. Snowed about three months. So cloudy the planes couldn't come in for support. The fighting was hard, and the closer we got to Berlin, the harder it got. Many of the German soldiers were young, maybe just fourteen or fifteen years old. Sometimes my men and I would be as much as fifty miles behind the Division, working on equipment, and then we'd have to catch up with them. We didn't have to worry about the German Air Force because it was already taken care of. Buzz bombs were a big problem and hit a lot of our equipment.

I saw General George Patton toward the end of the war when we were at Merseburg. This was on April 15th, and we were about sixteen miles from Berlin. From that location we watched Berlin burn. Patton wanted to go on into Berlin, but the Russians got to go in first. I liked Patton. He wasn't hard on us soldiers, but he was tough. Always carried his pearl handled pistol with him.

We ate C-Rations the first three months we were in Europe, but we did have Thanksgiving and Christmas dinners. We got mail, but it took quite a while for our letters to get to the U.S.

When the war ended, the 2nd Infantry Division went back

through Plzen, Czechoslovakia across to Le Havre, France. I had enough points so that within five days, I was headed back to the U.S. The trip home was smooth sailing, not like the trip over. I had served three years and two months in the U.S. and one year, nine months and twelve days in foreign service, a total of nearly five years. I was discharged on July 27, 1945 at Ft. Sam Houston in San Antonio after serving in Normandy, Northern France, Rhineland, Ardennes, and Central Europe." (Darwin was awarded the Bronze Star Medal, Company 74, Hq 2nd Infantry Division, July 25, 1944; EAME Campaign Medal with five Bronze Stars; American Defense Service Medal, and a Good Conduct Medal.)

★★★

Frank and Mary Bennett Vancill of Clarksville, Texas had three sons in the service during World War II. They were **LEON M. (JACK) VANCILL, HORACE VANCILL, AND EARL VANCILL.** The Vancills also had four daughters, Martha, Louise, Geraldine and Nellie.

Jack Vancill entered the Army in 1942 and trained at Kerns, Utah. He served in England and France and was discharged in 1947. Jack and Dorthy McGuire were married in 1950, are retired, and make their home in Clarksville. He was an employee of the Texas Highway Department.

Horace Vancill entered the Army in 1944. He trained at Camp Hood, Texas and served in Manila. Horace died January 30, 1988.

Earl Vancill entered the Army in 1940 and trained at Brownwood, Texas. He served in France and was wounded there in 1944. Upon his discharge in 1945, he was awarded the Purple Heart and a Bronze Star. He married Erma Dell Varley, and they had two children, Kenneth and Betty. His grandson, Jonathan Archer, talked with him before his death on November 29, 1995. The following was written for a school project:

"My grandfather, Earl Vancill, was a Staff Sergeant in Company I, the 181st Infantry, which departed from New York harbor, passing the Statue of Liberty. Due to the threat of German U-boats, the voyage took eighteen days to zigzag across the Atlantic to England. From England he was sent to Normandy under the command of General Omar Bradley. He actually landed on Omaha Beach several days after the initial invasion.

After surviving the invasion of Normandy Beach, he was hit in the chest with 88-shrapnel outside St. Lo, France. He remembers the Germans standing on the other side of a barbed wire fence talking and pointing their weapons at him. Trying not to even blink an eye, he thinks they were discussing whether to shoot him again or just to let him die, if he was not already dead. After surgery in France for massive chest wounds, the loss of half a lung, and the loss of several ribs, he was sent to England for two more surgeries. Upon arrival in England, he was informed that he had actually been reported 'dead'.

From England he was sent to South Carolina where he was immediately transported by train to Brooke General Army Hospital in San Antonio. After numerous operations and a thirteen month hospital stay, he was then ordered to Keisser, Arkansas where he served the remainder of his Army duty at one of the German POW camps here in the United States.

Although it has been over fifty years, my grandfather still does not like to discuss the invasion of Normandy. Living with the memories of all the dead and dismembered bodies is a horrifying experience one learns to live with, but never forgets."

★★★

Will and Viola Cowell Abernathy had four sons in service during World War II. They also had two daughters, Thelma and Joyce. The only member of the Abernathy family who is still living is Joyce Abernathy Wisinger who furnished this information.

WALLACE ABERNATHY was the first of the Abernathy sons to be drafted and entered the Army in January 1942. His basic training was at Camp Chaffee, Arkansas. He served in the North African area and then in Italy for a total of three years. Wallace was awarded the EAME Medal with four Bronze Stars and a Good Conduct Medal.

ROY ABERNATHY was drafted six months later and did his basic training at Camp Hood, Texas. Roy spent two or more years in the Asian part of the war. Most of his time was spent on the Burma-China Road. Sometimes his family would not hear from him for as long as three months, and then it would be a photostatic copy. Roy was discharged in 1945 and awarded a Presidential Citation with four Battle Stars, Good Conduct Medal and Infantry Combat Badge.

RALEIGH ABERNATHY was drafted later because he was married. His service time was spent in the state of Washington with no overseas duty.

MUREL ABERNATHY, the youngest son, was given deferments because the Abernathys were farmers and his help was needed to raise the crops. After a couple of deferments, he just couldn't take it any longer and joined the Army. He served in Luzon, Leyte, Mindanao and Japan and was awarded the AP Ribbon, Victory Medal and Good Conduct Medal. Murel stayed in the service for thirty years and served two stints in Thailand during the VC War.

★★★

James Earnest and Jennie Mae Cherry Hayes of Clarksville, Texas had four sons who served in the U.S. Navy during World War II. The Hayes brothers had another brother, Kenneth, and two sisters, Dorothy Jo and Margaret. Mr. Hayes and his first wife, Edna Sewell, had one son, Willie, and four daughters, Muriel, Effie, Louise, and Lucille. There was one other half-sister, Nella Parks. (One night while eating out, we saw Margaret Hayes Smith and her sister and brother-in-law, Winifred and Dorothy Jo Hayes Townes. The Townes reminded me that when they married in 1943 my father, who was Justice of the Peace, performed their marriage ceremony at our home. My mother and I were their witnesses. Many weddings took place during the war in our living room. I thought it was all just too romantic for words.)

S/2 C JAMES MARVIN HAYES entered the Navy in 1943 and trained in San Diego, California. He served on the Escort Carrier Hoggatt Bay in the Pacific. When his ship was torpedoed, he didn't think he would survive and wrote a letter to his wife, Lorene Screws Hayes who was at home with their baby. No one but his wife ever read that letter. He was discharged in 1946.

AMM 3/C BERL SWANCY HAYES entered the Navy in 1942 and trained at Great Lakes, Illinois. He served in the Pacific and was discharged in 1945.

MOMM 2/C GAVIN EDWARD HAYES entered the Navy in 1942 and trained in San Diego, California. He served in Japan and was discharged in 1945. He was the husband of Toby Allbritton.

S 2/C BILLY WAYNE HAYES entered the Navy in 1946 and

trained in San Diego, California. He served in the United States and was discharged in 1948.

★★★

THOMAS C. BLEDSOE was born January 17, 1916 in the Madras Community east of Clarksville in Red River County. He and his wife, Lucy Wood Bledsoe, are retired and still reside in that community. His parents were George and Edna Veach Bledsoe. He had two brothers, Walter and Weldon, and a sister, Magaline. When we visited in their home he said:

"I entered the service soon after World War II began. I was in the Army and served as a Truck Driver in Company C of the Signal Battalion. My training was at Camp Maxey in Paris, Texas and I was at Camp Polk, Louisiana for maneuver training. The Battalion left for overseas from New York and landed in Northern Ireland. While we were going over, I tried to sit in the middle of the ship to keep from getting seasick.

We went to England to get our equipment, returned to Ireland, and then crossed the English Channel to France. We landed the day after D-Day. I was next to the last man to board the LST and the second man off. The truck right in front of me went completely down in the cold water. When I left the LST in the truck I was driving, I kept my foot on the accelerator to be sure to keep the motor running. If the engine had stopped, water would've entered the exhaust, causing the truck to stall. When we landed on the beach, there were many dead all around us.

From France we went to Germany. Our job was to lay the telephone lines to the front line for communication. There were a lot of boys in Company C from Louisiana. Alvin Sauls from Clarksville was a mechanic in Company A, and we saw each other a few times.

Company C was in Austria when the war ended, and we headed back to the States from there." (Tom received the ETO Medal with four Battle Stars.)

★★★

WESLIE GERALDINE BLAIR was born September 19, 1918 in Red River County. His parents were Forrest H. and Cassie Murphy Blair. He had a twin sister, Cassie Estilene who died when she was only two and a half years old. The other children in his family were a brother, Forrest H., Jr. and two sisters, Elizabeth and Juanell. His widow, Mary Blair of Clarksville, visited with us and told the following about her husband:

"Weslie entered the U.S. Army on November 29, 1942 and served in the Infantry Brigade, Mortar Platoon in Field Artillery. He was promoted to Private First Class in 1942 and to Corporal in 1945. He was stationed at Camp Wolters and Camp Barkeley in Texas; Camp Polk Louisiana; India, California; and Ft. Dix, New Jersey. He served overseas in Birmingham, England; Normandy; France and Southern Germany.

The ship that took Weslie and the others in on D-Day at Normandy Beach was continually peppered with shells. After landing, the soldiers walked for thirty-one days before they were captured by the Germans. He had two close calls. A mortar shell landed two inches from his head while he was in a foxhole, but it never went off. Then he was hit with a hand grenade across the face. This left a scar, but even though he was unconscious and laying on the grenade, it didn't explode.

One of his best buddies was an Indian from Oklahoma. When they were landing on the beach, the Indian went off the side of the boat and threw Weslie out with him. They were the only ones who survived when the front dropped. He thought he would never come up out of the water with all the gear he was carrying on his back. They took one hill six times, and the last time, they walked on bodies. No time to pick them up.

Weslie was a prisoner of war from July 6, 1944 to April 15, 1945 at Willie, Germany, Stalag 4B. (A Stalag was a German prisoner of war camp for noncommissioned and enlisted personnel.) Another prisoner told him that he would be better off if he would volunteer to work, and he did. They worked in fields digging potatoes and repaired houses that had been damaged by bombs. He also worked in a razor factory and a sugar factory. They were guarded by civilians, stayed in a stadium and even stayed in some bomb shelters with Germans. Some were friendly and some were not.

Three months before the liberation, several of the prisoners escaped and got within a mile of American lines, but they were captured again. This time they were put in solitary confinement in a basement of a building. The windows were even with the street, and that's how light and air were let in. They ate bread and water, but each day an elderly German lady came by and dropped food through the windows. They ate better there because of her kindness. There was a great deal of sympathy on the part of the Germans for the American prisoners. A Fascist mayor would be elected one day and hanged the next.

The prisoners had a church service in the Stalag on Sundays. Weslie had a New Testament in his pocket but had lost it. There was no Bible or Sunday School Book so they prayed and talked about their lives. His Sunday School Teacher in the Junior Department of the Baptist Church had made him memorize Bible verses. His friend, the Indian, also knew some verses from his childhood so they used seven verses in their service each week.

When they were liberated, a troop of Germans were taken prisoners. Weslie said a captain told them that since they had lost everything when they were captured, they should take what they wanted. He had lost his pocket watch so he took a watch with a fob chain on it from a German Officer. When he went in the service, he weighed 185 pounds. When he was liberated, he weighed only 129 pounds. The kitchen where they took them was kept open 24 hours a day so they could catch up on their eating."

Weslie was discharged October 18, 1945 and was awarded the Purple Heart, Good Conduct Medal, ETO Ribbon, Bronze Star and Infantry Combat Badge. On June 2, 1945 he and Mary Fogleman were married, and they had two sons, Gerry and Melvin, and a daughter, Gail. They lived in Annona, and he was an employee at the Red River Arsenal until his retirement. Weslie died November 19, 1977, and Mary still resides in Clarksville.

★★★

Two O'Donnell double-cousins served in World War II. Their fathers were John and Pat O'Donnell, Sr., and their mothers were Willie and Sarah Lee Ivy. John and Willie also had two daughters, Kathleen and Margaret. Pat and Lee also had two daughters, Mary and Pauline. Lee Ivy O'Donnell was left to raise three small children after her husband died during the flu epidemic. After they were grown, she married Jim Claiborne, and I was born to that union.

JACK O'DONNELL, son of John and Willie, was born July

30, 1913 in Red River County. After graduating from Clarksville High School, he helped his father farm their place on the Peter's Prairie Road. He was drafted into the U.S. Army and mostly did office work, spending time in Oregon and Washington before going overseas to Japan in the Army of Occupation. After his discharge, he returned to the farm and remained there until his death March 11, 1990. (Jack was my first cousin.)

PAT O'DONNELL, son of Pat and Lee, entered the Army Air Force on October 30, 1942 while living in Arizona. He was born June 22, 1914 in Red River County. His basic training was in California, and he was stationed in Utah where the coal dust was very harmful to an asthmatic condition he had. On September 21, 1943 Pat received a medical discharge. He returned to Clarksville and married Virginia Suggs from Bogata in 1944. They had one son, Michael Pat. Pat died July 14, 1960 after suffering for many years with lung problems. Virginia lives in Bogata, and his son is in Dallas. (Pat was my half-brother.)

★★★

THOMAS DONALD ROACH was born November 11, 1918 in Bogata, Texas, the son of Dr. Harley D. and Florence Grant Roach. He had a sister, Frances. When Donald was just a small child, an older friend started calling him "Whistle Britches", which was shortened to "Whis".

While "Whis" played football on the high school Bulldog team, coached by Dixon Hatcher, the team won a District Championship in 1937. On a football scholarship, he played three seasons at Paris Junior College, coached by "Clemo" Clements. While at PJC, his name was changed to "Whizz", and being an outstanding player, he was selected All State Left End. His former coach, Dixon Hatcher, coached many years at PJC and taught there even longer. He gave a "Whizz" Roach Scholarship until he left the college in 1955.

Donald was Vice President of his PJC Freshman Class, President of his Sophomore Class and named Junior Rotarian. An Aviation Club was organized there; Donald joined and was the first to make the cross country solo flight.

He enlisted in the U.S. Navy and was sworn in as Air Cadet May 20, 1941. He received training at Grand Prairie, Texas and at the Naval Air Base at Corpus Christi, Texas. He was commissioned an Ensign and awarded his wings on March 26, 1942. Donald reported for duty at Seattle, Washington on April 18, 1942 and was in service at Dutch Harbor, Alaska from July until November 15, 1942. He then returned to duty in Seattle and sailed from the U.S. on December 9, 1942 for duty in the South Pacific combat zone.

After serving in the Pacific a short time, he received the following Citation: "In the name of the President of the United States, the Commander, South Pacific Area and South Pacific, takes pleasure in awarding the Air Medal to Ensign Thomas D. Roach: For meritorious achievement in aerial flights against the enemy while serving as the pilot of a fighter escort plane attached to a Marine aircraft group in the Solomon Islands area during the period from February 3 to March 6, 1943. Ensign Roach participated in eight attack missions directed against enemy ground installations at Munda Point and Vila Plantation and in one fighter sweep against Munda Point. All of these attacks were carried out in the face of heavy antiaircraft fire, and on February 4 he took part in an attack against a Japanese task force composed of twenty destroyers, protected by twenty to thirty Zero type fighter planes. At this time the enemy planes were dispersed before they could impair the success of the mission. On February 12, 1942 he was the pilot of one of seven fighters escorting a patrol plane on a rescue mission to Rob Roy Island, where the patrol plane remained on the water for fifty-five minutes within easy striking distance of enemy positions. In every instance Ensign Roach displayed initiative and courage in keeping with the highest traditions of the U.S. Naval Service."

On April 1, 1943 Donald was promoted from Ensign to Lieutenant, Junior Grade. Later he received this Citation: "The President of the United States takes pleasure in presenting the Gold Star in lieu of the Second Air Medal to Lieutenant Junior Grade Thomas D. Roach for service as set forth: For meritorious achievement while participating in aerial flight as Leader of a Fighter Division in combat against enemy Japanese forces in the Solomon Islands Area from June 21 to July 17, 1943. Leading his four-plane fighter division on thirty-three combat missions, Lieutenant Junior Grade Roach, during two of these engagements, attacked a group of Japanese aircraft and personally shot down a total of four twin-engined bombers. His courage, skill, and fearless devotion to duty were in keeping with the highest traditions of the U.S. Naval Service."

Donald received another honor: "The President of the United States takes pride in presenting the Distinguished Flying Cross posthumously to Lieutenant, Junior Grade Thomas Donald Roach. Citation: For heroism and extraordinary achievement in aerial flight as Pilot of a Fighter Plane in Fighting Squadron Twenty One during operations against enemy Japanese forces in the Solomon Islands Area on June 30, 1943. Leading his division to intercept an enemy bombing strike against our shipping, he pressed home his attack and, destroying two of the hostile bombers, materially reduced the effectiveness of the enemy strike. His airmanship, courage, and devotion to duty were in keeping with the highest traditions of the U.S. Naval Service."

On July 26, 1943 Donald "Whis" Roach was shot down over the water near Rendova Island which is near New Guinea in the South Pacific. He was reported as Missing in Action by the Navy Department. He was survived by his mother, Mrs. Florence Grant Roach, a sister, Frances, and her husband, William Rozell, and one nephew, Neil Rozell, all of Bogata. His father, Dr. Harley Roach, died the 7th of July 1942. "Whis" was stationed in Dutch Harbor, Alaska at the time and could not come home for the funeral service.

★★★

JAMES HERBERT PERKINS was born November 21, 1911 in Volney, Virginia. His parents were Gordon and Sarah Katherine Jones Perkins, and he had four brothers and two sisters.

Herb was drafted into the U.S. Army in 1942 and received his basic training at Camp Crowder, Missouri. He served in the South Pacific, Australia and New Guinea and was awarded a Bronze Star. His discharge was in 1945 at Camp Fannin in Tyler, Texas. A "blind date" arranged by Lois Dunne of Clarksville got Herb and Mary Gray together, and they married in October 1945. They had one daughter, Ann Katherine (Kitty). Herb died September 12, 1997, and Mary now resides in Paris.

★★★

Alice Vaughan Clark submitted the following information about her father, **VERNON VINCENT VAUGHAN**, and her mother, Alice Jane Vaughan, who was a very good friend of mine. I regret that she did not live to see my first book published because

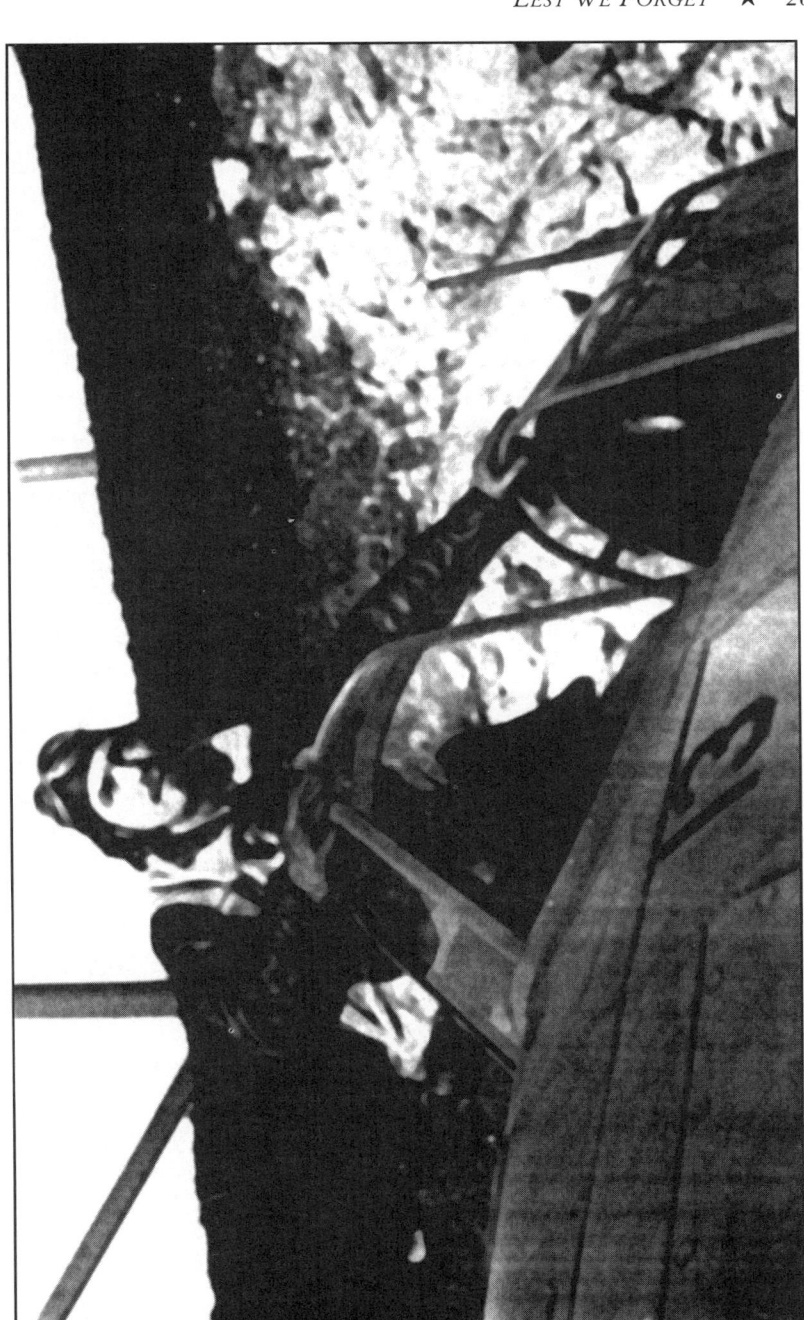

Lieutenant, Junior Grade Thomas Donald Roach

she really enjoyed history and was very well read. Their daughter said:

"Vernon was born in Thief River Falls Minnesota on March 11, 1921, and his parents were William and Adeliade Luella Holden Vaughan. He was the youngest of five children, and had two brothers, William and James and two sisters, Mary and Helen. His dad was a farmer and had a General Mercantile Store in Highlanding, Minnesota. His mother was a teacher, midwife, and Postmaster.

Alice Jane was the only child of Ernest Franklin and Nannie Baker Henry. She was born March 1, 1923 in East Dallas, Texas. Ernest was a law officer and a guard at the Federal Reserve Bank in Dallas. Nannie was a homemaker. Her parents were from Red River County as were Ernest's. His parents were Mattie Jane and Samuel Franklin Henry, and her parents were Alvin Bosley and Mary Alice McLean Baker. Alice was named after both grandmothers.

My Mother and Dad met in 1943 when Vernon was stationed at Red River Army Arsenal as a Mess Sergeant, and Alice was working at Lone Star Ammunition Ordinance during World War II. They met at a dance center in Nash, Texas when Vernon had a week-end pass, and I recall Mother saying that when she saw him, it was 'love at first sight'. They started dating and were married in New Boston on August 24, 1943.

Vernon was sent overseas to France and Germany shortly after they married. Alice took a train to his home in Minnesota to meet her new in-laws. Over the years I have read the letters and telegrams my parents sent to each other, and they were filled with true love for each other.

Vernon received his discharge from the Army on November 14, 1945 at Camp Butner, North Carolina. He was awarded a lapel button and emblem, American Defense Service Medal, and WWII Victory Medal. He returned to Minnesota to his family to which the first of nine children, Patrick Henry, had been born. During the next five years three more children were born, Helen Nan, Alice Verna, and Kathleen Luella.

Alice hated the north and wanted to return to the south. Vernon and his family packed up, and when they reached the Texas state line, Alice made him stop the car, and she got out and knelt down and kissed the ground. Vernon got a job at Red River Arsenal, and they lived in New Boston, but he longed for a job outdoors.

They moved back to Clarksville where he worked for J. B. Cunningham as a welder. Their fifth child, Pamela Rena Ilene was born, and during the next few years they had four more children, Michael Joseph, Vernon Vincent Vaughan II and Victoria (twins), and James Baker. Alice had been an only child and had always longed for brothers and sisters. Each of the Vaughan children was planned and loved, and they had planned to have twelve children; however, their dream was shattered in August 1958 when Vernon was stricken with polio and paralyzed from the waist down. This was a devastation for Alice, one that she never got over, and here their love would be tested over and over again.

Alice had nine children ranging from six months to fourteen years of age, no job, no income, and bills to pay. This is when dear friends and even strangers came in to help. She had pride and was determined to make it work and never once received any type of welfare for her children. Vernon was in St. Michael's Hospital in Texarkana for ninety days, and Alice visited him every day except for one. She got rides and even hitchhiked to see him but never told him about this for many years because she knew it would make him angry. After Vernon went to Houston, the visits were limited because of money problems. Alice got a job at Oriental Laundry and worked from sunup to sundown. She worked then for Kaiser's Cleaners, baby sat, never took lunch breaks. Her children took her a glass of tea and maybe a peanut butter sandwich. Of course, her days were not over when she got home because there was supper to fix, the children's homework to see to, their baths, washing and ironing. She made sure her children went to church, and both parents always stressed the value of education.

When Vernon was dismissed from the hospital in Houston, he returned to Clarksville, bound and determined to make a living for his family. With the help of Mr. Cunningham, he rigged hand controls for their old Plymouth and passed the driving test. At that time people with disabilities were 'left out in the cold'. He was never again able to go uptown because there were no wheelchair ramps. He had a dry cleaning route, paper route, and finally he was asked to do a brick job. He told the man of his limitations, but the man said he would have special scaffolds made so that Vernon could do the job. He had a reputation of doing quality work and had built many a home in Clarksville.

By this time Alice had a job at Lone Star Ammunition Ordinance, and things were looking better. The children were all taught that hard work never hurt anyone, and each one has turned out to be successful in his own way. During the next seventeen years, there were many ups and downs, but the Vaughans worked their way through each of them. They raised their oldest son's son, Shane, until he died at the age of sixteen. They had twenty-four grandchildren and nine great-grandchildren.

Vernon had his third and fatal heart attack in August 1975 while visiting me in Omaha, Nebraska. My Mother, for the sake of her children, again picked up the pieces and continued raising the children and grandson still at home. She had some difficult times, but she was determined that their family would stick together. It was her love for Vernon and her family that allowed this to happen. She died June 1, 1996."

★★★

ELMER JUNIOR SHOULDERS was born in Red River County, Texas on November 25, 1925. His parents were Elmer and Rena Spangler Shoulders, and the other children in the family were Doris, Joyce, Carnell and John.

He was drafted into the Army and left July 20, 1944. After seventeen weeks of basic training at Camp Wolters, Texas, he was sent overseas to Germany in January 1945 and was shot and killed on April 4, 1945. His unit had pulled back from the front, and a group of the men were cleaning their guns. A gun went off, and he was shot in the chest and died the next day. His body was returned and the burial was at Fairview Cemetery in Clarksville.

★★★

As my husband and I were leaving a yard sale in Clarksville one Saturday morning, we noticed a man driving up in a car with the special license plate denoting that he was a recipient of the Purple Heart. I walked up to him and told him that I was in the process of gathering information about World War II for the book I planned to write. I asked him if he would talk with me, and he looked me straight in the eye and said, "I'll tell you one thing about the war—it was Hell!" On September 4, 1999 I talked with **LENARD R. BRUMMETT** who had seen much action in the ETO. He said:

"I was born in Wood County, Texas in 1921 and was inducted into the service in Tyler on July 11, 1942. When I was discharged in Tyler on November 11, 1945, I had served three years, four months and one day.

While I was doing my basic training in California, I was turned down for overseas duty and sent to Camp Carson, Colorado for more training. From there I went to Topeka, Kansas where I was assigned to work in a hospital. I volunteered for the paratroopers, but while I was training, I broke my ankle. They told me they were going to return me to hospital work, which I didn't care for at all, so I volunteered then for the Infantry. I was a machine gunner in the 63rd Division, 2nd Battalion, and when we went overseas we landed at Marseilles, France just after the Normandy Invasion. From there we went through Belgium and then on into Germany through some real tough fighting. I saw lots of Germans taken as POW's. We were right off the autobahn highway near Stuttgart when the war ended. When we heard that news, it really did feel good.

The next day we received orders to go to Japan, but since it took a while for us to leave Germany, the war with Japan ended, and we got to return home to the U.S."

Mr. Brummett received five Battle Stars, a Good Conduct Medal, the Purple Heart, and two Bronze Stars. He told me that he received one of those Bronze Stars because he "acted a fool" and went out into a mine field with toilet paper and M-1 Rifle Clips to make a path for the other men to follow. The other one was received on the Siegfried Line when his company was pinned down in the Dragon Teeth (concrete barriers that came up out of the ground to stop any vehicles from going through). It was his job to get ammunition to the men who were needing it. Barely twenty-one years old when he was inducted into the service, Mr. Brummett went through a lot and was still a young man when he was discharged.

★★★

When we visited with Mr. and Mrs. Gene Simmons in Annona, Texas, the following information was given about the Simmons family:

Seven sons and a daughter were born to Hiram Chessie and Sudie Florence Hunt Simmons of Annona, Texas. All seven sons and a son-in-law, husband of their daughter, Margaret Sue, were in the service of their country. Three sons served during World War II: **JAMES HIRAM SIMMONS**, T/4 U.S. Army, 32nd Quartermaster, 1941-1945, who served in Hawaii; **ROBERT SAMUEL SIMMONS**, T/5 U.S. Army, 1943-1945, who served in Bismarck Archipelago and New Guinea; **DAVID VASCO SIMMONS**, T/4 U.S. Army, 1848 SCU USDB, 1944-1947, who served in CONUS; and **BENJAMIN A. GARRETT**, SFC, U.S. Coast Guard, 1942-1946, who served on the USS General Waggle AP 119 on both the Atlantic and Pacific Oceans while they hauled troops to different destinations.

During World War II, J. T. Jolley, owner of Jolley's Funeral Home in Clarksville, worked through the American Red Cross so that James at Pearl Harbor, David in California, and Robert in the South Pacific, could all be at home on furlough at the same time.

Robert Simmons saw lots of combat duty. He was a gunner on a landing craft that had a seven man crew. Their job was to drop troops off on shore, and they only had 50-caliber machine guns. On one mission, after dropping off the troops, they headed back to the ship and were strafed by a Japanese kamikaze pilot. All on board were killed except Robert. The boat was going wild in the water; the pilot had been cut in two; so Robert took control of the craft and headed toward shore. He went on shore wearing only shorts and stayed in a foxhole for three days before being able to return to his ship.

The other sons who served their country were: **JOHN WILLIAM SIMMONS**, Sgt. U.S. Army, Co C, 15th Infantry Regiment, 3rd Infantry Division, February 1952-November 1953, who served in Korea during the Korean War; **EUGENE CROCKETT SIMMONS**, lst Lt., USAF, Pilot, 561st SFS, 12th SF W SAC, September 1953-September 1956, who served in CONUS during the Cold War; **THOMAS NEWTON SIMMONS**, Colonel, USAF, Pilot, Commander 63rd Military Alft GP, 1955-1982, served in Germany, Norway, Viet Nam and CONUS; **MARVIN NEIL SIMMONS**, AFC USAF Res, 69th Troop Carrier Squad, May 1957-May 1962, served in CONUS during the Cold War.

★★★

THOMAS E. ALLEN was born February 14, 1921 in Clarksville, Texas. His parents were Thomas Early and Bonnie Dickson Allen, and he had a brother, James William, and a sister,

Nell Dickson. He married Frances C. Rosson, and they have two daughters, Linda and Lou Ann.

Thomas was drafted on October 3, 1942 at Clarksville and did his basic training at Kerns, Utah and at Lowry Air Force Base in Denver. He was an Aerial Photographer on a B-17 plane, attained the rank of Sergeant, and served forty-four months state side. He was discharged February 26, 1946 at the Camp Beal army base in Sacramento, California. He and his wife reside in Paris, Texas.

★★★

My husband and I visited with Clyde and Mary Bean at their home north of Clarksville on July 20, 1999. **CLYDE ROBERT BEAN** was born on November 3, 1912 in Red River County. His parents were Cadmus and Eva Blankenship Bean, and he has one sister, Louise. On November 18, 1934 he and Mary Reep were married. They have three daughters, Sheree, Martha Clyde and Mary Beth. Clyde had this to say about his experiences in World War II:

"I entered the service on December 28, 1942 in Red River County at the age of thirty. I was drafted. I got my basic training at Ft. Hood, Texas and Ft. Benning, Georgia and spent thirty-six months in the service. When I was at Ft. Benning, my grandmother died. Mary and I were there, and we got to come home for her funeral. They were just covering her up when we got there. Mary stayed a long time at Ft. Benning with me. She worked for 'Tom's Toasted Peanuts', on a line. She had to work cause I didn't get enough pay to cover my ride into camp after I paid everything else. We did manage to save a little money every month. I wasn't drawing but $50.00 a month, and Mary made $75.00 a month when she made production, and that was a lot of money then. We lived on Rose Hill and rented a room—couldn't find a house.

We landed overseas at Glasgow, Scotland and then went to France. I was with General Patton, and the old saying is that Patton didn't care as much about his men as he did his equipment. I was in the Third Army, 80th Division and was in battle a lot. Getting up and down out of those foxholes finally made me get down with my knee, and they had to split my trousers off me to get me back to the hospital.

We carried an old boy that couldn't walk down to the river, but we couldn't get him in one of those rubber boats so we left him in the bushes where he could holler at somebody. We got in this boat—it was a small river—and we went across in this boat that was almost flat, but it would float. We floated till we got to a big boat out in the river and then got in it and went across. They were shooting at us, but they never did hit us, and when we got across, it was clear just like Red River down here. We made it back till we came to a house, and we spent the night there. The next morning we got out and found our way around. This was just two of us.

One time when we were in battle, we got in this house that had mines all around it. We found out there was a cellar under this house. Over there they had lots of cellars under houses. I don't know how many of us it was, but anyway we stayed in it overnight. We could hear the enemy up in this house walking around, and we could tell it was the Germans. We stayed quiet and they never did find the trap door going down in the cellar. That's where they stored Irish potatoes so that's all we had to eat for the three days we stayed there in that cellar. You could see out of the peep holes, and one morning we looked out and could see one of our officers coming up. We hollered at him, and he wanted to know if we had any ammunition for our guns, and we told him we were loaded with ammunition. Well, we finally got a chance to get out of there. We'd go from one house to the other running cause they'd be shooting at us. We could see them peeping out of windows and doors, you know, but we'd be running behind these houses. I saw a lot of Germans, alive and dead. They'd load them up in trucks. In the fields, we'd see lots of dead Germans.

We went out one morning with the company, and 13 out of 180 was all that was left. That's counting the officers and everyone. We was going over a hill into a little old town, and they were really shooting at us. I can remember how they throwed one of those bazookas right in front of me. Come to find out, I was the only one up there cause the rest of them already went back. Man, I turned around, and I crawled back over this hill. They didn't hit me, and I don't know why. Those Germans were right up ahead of us. That bazooka just didn't come far enough to hit me.

One time we were marching into a town, and it was at night. I was a Sergeant and didn't know it till I got out of service. We was marching up there, and I tried to get them not to put me ahead. I had an officer with me that had never been on the front line before. I never will forget that he said, 'What are we going to do if they attack us?' I told him we were going to fight like hell. They got to shooting at us, and there was a big stack of hay out on a meadow before we got into this town. A bunch of us made it and got behind that bunch of hay. Well, I had my men laying down on the ground. That officer made it behind that stack of hay; so I went out to check my men and made it out to them. He stayed behind cause he was scared to death and didn't know what to do. I got in contact with these men laying on the ground so he hollered: 'Bean, we got to get up and meet this other flank.' There was three, and we were right in the middle. I told him to get up, that I was ready. I got my men and told him to start, and I'd be with him. He had to lead, but he didn't, and I didn't get up. The flanks went up, and we were in the middle.

I got right to the edge of Germany right where their foxholes were, but I stayed in France. We'd get replacements, and I'd tell them what to do, give them orders. Quick as we'd get in battle, they'd stand up just like they were shooting at rabbits. Then the Germans would shoot them down. We got many a one killed.

The first battle I got in was the worst one. When we crossed that river, that's when I got wounded and they reported me missing in action. They took me to the hospital and kept me all day. I was wounded in my face, but it never went in my mouth. Two doctors were waiting on me there, and the reason they kept me so long is cause they were trying to keep me from being scarred. They done a good job. This was a base hospital out on the field, and I stayed there a few days, and then they sent me back to a hospital in England. I stayed there a little over three months before they sent me back on the front line. Going back up to the front line, there was an old doctor that waited on me and checked me out, and he said, 'I'll tell you one thing. You're not going back on the front line if I can do anything about it.' Well, they put me on limited service so I never did have to go back on the front line.

I went to an outfit where ever so often we were pumping gas up to the front line. We had three lines, airplane, and two other kinds, 100 octane and 80 octane. That thing was running day and night. We had a house out there that the cook stayed in, and I forget how many of us was there. We stayed in a little old house. I was with that outfit till I came home. Those Germans would come along and puncture our lines and draw gas out. They'd set their cans under there and steal that gas. We had to walk that line and tighten those couplings to do away with them getting gasoline. We walked them lines every day.

I remember one time after I got in limited service, we put up a big water tank with bolts. We'd go around and tighten all those bolts. We had a sergeant over us, and I remember we got a vacation while I was there. We got one of those weapons carriers and some gas. We went into a town and was going to stay five or six days. One night we had I don't know how many five gallon cans of gas in this weapons carrier, and we got it stolen. The Germans stole it.

During this time we had a cook, and he was a good cook. On the battlefield we ate C-Rations most of the time. I don't remember how many days we'd go sometime without cleaning up or shaving. It was really cold over there. I went in as a replacement in France after the invasion. The Germans planned this fight long years before we got there. They had rows of hedges with foxholes dug between then. They'd shoot at us from there. They still say it was better going to them instead of them coming to us. That was between France and England. We had to cross water getting there. That hedge started close to the river.

One time my mail caught up with me, and I got over 100 letters. I just sat down and sorted them all and read the last date first. I was over there when my Daddy passed away. The war was over then. That's why I don't like the Red Cross. My commanding officer said I could come home just as soon as they heard from the Red Cross, but I didn't get to.

After they told me I was coming home, I could see the boats going out, and I'd think mine would come every day. But anyway, some of them going out in the field to work took me with them. The company commander came out there one day and looked at me and said, 'Bean, aren't you supposed to go home?' I told him I was so he told me not to work but to rest. I had my points, enough to go home."

Clyde Bean received the Purple Heart, Combat Infantry Badge, Good Conduct Medal, American Defense Medal, and the ETO Medal with two Battle Stars.

Clyde had a large map in the scrapbook, and the following information has been taken from that:

"The Blue Ridge Path through France, Luxembourg, Germany and Austria—Compiled by the G-3 Section Hq 80th Infantry Division, 22 May, 1945

The task force formed at Southampton on the English Coast. Troops were loaded on transports and the 80th Infantry Division was assigned to land on Omaha Beach-France on D-Day. This was near the city of Cherbourg.

From Omaha Beach the 80th Infantry Division fought through the cities of St. Jures, Avranches, Laval, Sille le Gillaume, Alencon to Argentan. From here the division turned in its efforts to take a strategic town named LeMans. From LeMans they marched through Orleans, Montargis, Sens, Chalons Sur Marne, Bar LeDuc, St. Mihiel, Commercy, Nancy and St. Avoid where they encountered the Maginot Line and then behind this, the Siegried Line and Germany itself. The Mainot and Siegfried Lines were heavily fortified ground emplacements of concrete and hedgerows and were well defended by the Germans.

Eventually the 80th broke through these barricades and continued on their way to Berlin. They passed through Wendel, Bad Durkheim, Kaiserslautern, Monheim, Worms, Rockenhausen, Mainz, Wiesbaden, and Frankfort. The fighting was house to house with many American soldiers forfeiting their lives. Then on to Lich, Homberg, Kassel, Eisenach, Gotha and Erfurt. At this point the 80th was only 110 miles from Berlin but was not destined to be a part of the taking of the city. The division was ordered south through Bomberg, Nurnberg, Rensburg, and Simbach to Austria."

★★★

PAUL H. BUTTS, son of Dr. T. R. and Lydia Wycough Butts was born December 9, 1919 in Annona, Texas. The other children in his family were, Turner C., Eulalia, Lela, Blaine, and Howell. He married Virginia Roberts, and they have two children, Paul Bradley and Deborah.

Paul enlisted in the Army Air Corps on January 8, 1942 at Paris, Texas. His training was at Sheppard Field, Texas, Tucson, Arizona, Wendover Field, Utah, Colorado and New Mexico. He was a M/Sgt. in Communications. He served in the European Theater—England, France and Germany. He received the ATO Ribbon, EAME Ribbon with two Bronze Stars, Victory Medal, and Good Conduct Medal. He was discharged on December 12, 1945 at Tyler, Texas.

★★★

Christmas Card sent from France in 1944 by Clyde Bean to his wife, Mary.

MILOW HUME of Cunningham was twenty-four years old when he was inducted into the Army. His parents were Leslie Irving and Bessie Burtrude Galbreath Hume. His siblings were Thelma, Lleen, Milan, Nonie, Maurine, Erbert, Frank, Ina and Weldon.

Hume spent 748 days as a prisoner of war of the German Army. The 47th Infantry, 9th Division, E Company, was fighting off German troops in the mountains of El Guettar in Central Tunisia while tanks and Panzer units blasted away in the valley. Casualties were high on both sides as the battle waged for days.

He escaped serious injury when a bullet whizzed through his pack, ruining everything he had. As the battle continued, Pvt. Hume, who had been farming his family's land near Cunningham when his country called him to service in January 1942, was down to his last seven rounds of ammunition. Fighting had been going on for two days and three nights, and that day had begun early when gunfire illuminated the predawn darkness.

Hume recounted the battles in North Africa, his capture, and two years and eighteen days as a prisoner of war. It is not a story he tells often because it is an ordeal that stays with him, even today.

It began that day on a hillside near El Guettar when he and a soldier from another platoon encountered a German machine gunner. Turning to his fellow soldier, a man who would become a friend, Hume said to aim at the trigger and fire. Before a shot could be squeezed off, there were three Germans with sharp bayonets right behind them. They made them give up their guns, and the two men felt lost. At the hands of the Germans, they had new orders to follow. Their captors told them to gather wounded Americans and Germans and move them behind the lines. Hume and his fellow soldiers had fought long and hard during the 600 mile trek from Casablanca to Oran and 250 miles further to Algiers, then on to Sbeitla and El Guettar where the battle, but not the war, ended.

The German soldiers told them they should be glad the war was over for them because prisoners were fed well. That meal of thick meat and vegetable soup was the last good meal they had. About a week later, ten POW's, including Hume, were put on a German plane and taken to Europe. During a refueling stop in Naples, Italy, the sound of Flying Fortresses was heard. The prisoners were rushed back on board, and as the plane took off, the bombs began to fall. From Naples the prisoners were taken to

Capo, Italy where they stayed for a time with few rations and little care. Finally, they were loaded on a train for transport to German prison camps. Hume thought about escape, but there was no way to get out of the locked boxcar. The train carried the men to Moosburg, Germany where thousands of American prisoners were held until liberation by the Third Army in 1945. Six to eight men shared a loaf of bread about eighteen inches long. That was one day's meal, and the next day soup was what they ate. Meals like that over a two year period caused Hume to drop from a solid 165 pounds to a mere 100 pounds. A monthly parcel from the American Red Cross and an occasional one from home helped.

Hume and his friend and a dozen other men stayed at Moosburg for three months before being sent to a farm. He told his fellow prisoners that time would pass more easily if they worked hard for their captors. They did, and for a time the plan worked. Then one day their greatest fears came to pass. The POW's were passing bundles of wheat from the barn loft down the line to a threshing machine when a German guard came in and began screaming at the first in line. Then he struck him with his rifle butt. Hume remained still, knowing he was second in line and might receive the same treatment. Two hours later, he was screamed at, but the guard was then removed.

Working along with the Americans were Polish women and Russian soldiers who had also been taken captive. One of the Polish women was named 'Stasha', and Hume later named his daughter after her.

The war was advancing, and the prisoners were moved as the Germans retreated. The move took 67 days and nights, and there was little food. On the third day there, they heard bombers overhead, and the bombs began to drop. Hours later the POW's were picking up the dead and helping the wounded villagers. The retreat continued, and the travel, cold weather, and lack of food was hard on Hume. His friends put him on a cart they rigged to move him along the trail for five more days, but eventually they had to leave him on the roadside. He was so sick that he thought he would not live much longer and felt that abandonment meant sure death. A group of American soldiers found him and took him to a hospital taken over by the Allied Forces. There two nurses took care of him day and night, and once his strength returned, he was transferred to a French hospital where he received good care and had plenty to eat. Two weeks later the Germans surrendered, and the French had a street dance. He asked if he could go and was told he could if he felt like it, so he did. When he was returned to the U.S. sometime later, he said it was wonderful. (This information is taken from an article in the Paris News written by Sherrie Langston, no date. It was given to me by Milow Hume's brother, Weldon Hume, of Paris, Texas. Milow Hume is a resident in the Deport Nursing Home at this time.)

Some handwritten details written by Hume about the captivity were also given to me by his brother. In part he said: "Big crops of Irish potatoes, carrots, sugar beets, wheat and corn. Used wheat, sugar beets and Irish potatoes in a factory, boiled it down and made it into alcohol for planes. Our cook got a ration every morning to fix a mid-day dinner. Got a piece of meat of some kind to season the stew. After two months we started getting Red Cross parcels. Some time it was two men to one box or it might be four men to one box. Got it every week, but sometime we would skip a week. Helped gather those big crops of potatoes, and they would make big piles on each farm all over Germany putting up all of the food for winter. They would cover those piles of potatoes with the bundles of wheat straw and then pack dirt on top of the wheat straw. They would clean out the barns and put it on the fields where the crops came off of.

In the Red Cross parcel was one can of Prem or it would be a can of corn beef, some little blocks of sugar, one small jar of coffee, two chocolate bars of candy, a can of margarine, two packs of cigarettes, a small can of powdered milk. I'd trade my part of the cigarettes for food. After three months they sent through the Red Cross a big parcel with a change of underwear, shirt and pants.

The way we worked it was doing something every day, no matter what kind of weather. We got off every 3rd Saturday to clean up where we all stayed and to clean our clothes. Then if we had time, we would play ball or some kind of game. For Christmas we got a fruit cake, four of us for one cake. The Germans had a poor old horse they had been working. They killed it and asked us if we wanted any of the horse meat. We all said, 'yes'. I sliced some of it into steak and some of into roast, hacked the steak and fried it. It sure was good. All the men liked it. The Germans paid us. It was about seven cents in our money each day. We bought us a pair of hair clippers and a razor and some blades. One thing about it, we all kept clean."

★★★

Our good friend, Sonja Alexander Hoffman, contributed the following about her father, **J. D. ALEXANDER** of Clarksville:

"At the beginning of the Second World War the United States had a sad lack of trained pilots and other military personnel. J. D. Alexander found that his age and health prohibited his joining the regular armed forces. He was a former athletic director of schools at the college level, and as such could serve in a training capacity at the University of Tennessee. He was well known to the staff of the university since he had served at Lincoln Memorial University for several years and at East Carolina Teachers College (now East Carolina University).

There was a Naval Officers Program established at Knoxville on the campus with the university, providing training in physical endurance and survival. The flight cadets were 18 or 19 year old boys coming from farms, industry, colleges, and the jobless due to the ending of the Depression. For many it was the farthest they had ever been from their homes, and he often told of the homesickness they suffered. Flight instructors did not have the time to deal with this and provide training in planes that was so essential. This fell on the laps of those in other areas of the program. My father often lamented the loss that was inevitable to the nation when these young men were shot down. They were to him the 'cream' of the nation's future. Later he realized that this was the history of war.

I myself remember that I wondered why he could not take us with him as we had resided near Knoxville, and it was to my nine year old mind a much better place than where we were living. My heart has been in that area always, and yet I have lived in Texas most of my life, even when I could choose where I would live. Mother kept the farm going during his absence, and when his contract ended, we then had the dairy and sold milk to Lamar Creamery which then went to Camp Maxey soldiers.

The many convoys which passed our home in the Mabry Community on U.S. Highway 82 on the way to the coasts for deployment to the front will always be a memory of World War II to me. The men seemed, even now, to be very young, and they often threw out slips of paper with their names and addresses on them. I guess they, like warriors throughout time, had a wish for mail or word from home.

These were trying times for all families who had men away from home, and ours was one of them. I am proud now that my father served his country in a way that only he could, using his broad experience and education to further the war effort."

★★★

GEORGE R. (DICK) GULLION was born May 14, 1922 in Detroit, Texas. His parents were Fieldon and Charlie Senter Gullion, and his siblings were Rena, Susie Kate, John and Elic. He married Christine Barnett, and they had two children, James Richard and Tammie Jean. Dick died January 8, 1979.

He entered the Army Air Corps on September 5, 1942 at Dallas, Texas. He was attached to the 3543PD AAFBU SAD AAFPD in San Antonio, Texas. He was an AP Instrument Mechanic 686, and his training was through a General Instruction Course, Bendix Company, Philadelphia, Pennsylvania and a B-29 Maintenance Training in Amarillo, Texas. He was a Corporal and received an American Theater Ribbon, WWII Victory Ribbon and Good Conduct Medal. His discharge was at San Antonio on March 13, 1946.

★★★

R. W. STIDHAM was born January 23, 1920 at Boxelder in Red River County, Texas. His parents were R. W., Sr. and Mackie Ford Stidham. There were three other sons, Joe Willis, Gerald Dean, and Harold Earl. On January 21, 1950 R. W. and Juanita Hall, daughter of Sidney and Edith Emery Hall of Annona, Texas were married. They are the parents of a son, Robert Sidney, and a daughter, Marilyn Ann. R. W. is retired from Southwestern Bell, and the couple has moved from their farm in Mt. Pleasant to Sulphur Springs. When we visited with the Stidhams, R. W. had the following to say about his service during World War II:

"I went in the service in '41 and I liked twenty odd days of serving four years. I was a Staff Sergeant, Technician, 3rd Grade in the 392nd Ordinance Tank Maintenance Company. I want you to read this letter from President Truman. He sent this to me when I got home. To me he was the greatest President we've ever had. You remember he had something on his desk that said: 'The buck stops here'. Here's the letter:

'To you who answered the call of your country and served in its Armed Forces to bring about the total defeat of the enemy, I extend the heartfelt thanks of a grateful Nation. As one of the Nation's finest, you undertook the most severe task one can be called upon to perform. Because you demonstrated the fortitude, resourcefulness and calm judgment necessary to carry out that task, we now look to you for leadership and example in further exalting our country in peace. Harry S. Truman'

I could shoot any gun they had. Heavy machine gun, light machine gun, 50-caliber, tank guns which were 57mm and 105mm. I could drive any vehicle they had. I had a driver's license for all of them. I took amphibious and jungle training in Hawaii back in those God forsaken hills. I went to Aberdeen, Maryland for special training, and then I went to Ft. Lewis, Washington for more special training. My basic was at Ft. Knox. We shipped out from Ft. Lewis and landed in Hawaii after the Japanese attack. In other words, we saw the destruction that had happened. We lived in Schofield Barracks that still had bullet holes in it. After we took amphibious and jungle training, we left there and island hopped.

The major campaign that we made was Okinawa. We lost 4,300 people there. First thing, we cut the island into. By the way, something that made it easy was because we hit one side of the island, and we were maneuvering on the other side of the island. That's where they thought we'd come in. They had machine gun nests; they had everything, but where we came in was behind them. The 96th Division Cemetery was the one the Army used, not the Marines. This little camera I had, I took a picture of it, and it had five crosses in it. When I left and went to Korea later, I took that same camera and set it on the same place I had before. It took a picture, and it run out of crosses. You know what I mean, the distance, the camera couldn't cover it all.

General Buckner was killed there. You know, Buckner Bay. He was in an Artillery outfit down there, and a sniper shot him. So was Ernie Pyle killed. He came and stayed all night with us one night. He said he was going over to a little island off Okinawa. Anyway, our outfit ordered two tanks to go, and I just happened to be one of them. I was about 300 yards from him when he got killed. He was standing up in a Jeep, and a sniper shot him. He was the only correspondent that told the whole truth. Others told a story about something, but they didn't tell the whole thing. They left out parts of it, but Ernie Pyle didn't do that. He came right down where you were, sat there and talked to the men. The captain came in to see if he wanted to go eat with him, but he'd say he'd just eat with the guys. I liked him. He was 'down to earth'.

Something else that comes to mind is when Captain Booth, the Company Commander, told us he wanted us to look back toward Japan. He said there was a big plane coming in with thirteen P-38's. That was the people to sign the Peace Treaty after the atomic bomb was dropped. Then he said for us to get our binoculars so we could see because they were going to sign the Peace Treaty on that ship out there. This was the USS Missouri. You could see them with the binoculars but couldn't really tell much about what they were doing. That plane came in and brought Tojo, the Prime Minister of Japan.

You know, this was Army standard, and the married guys with kids went home first. Then the married guys, and then the single guys. Well, I wasn't married so they sent me down to Korea. By the way, when we were on Okinawa, we had a typhoon. They had to drop us food from the air. Anyway, after we built back up and got straightened out, I went to Korea. On the way there, they said we hit the edge of a typhoon, but I felt like we were right in the middle of it.

In Korea we disassembled munition plants. We used Japanese prisoners for workers. I had fifteen of them, and I saw that they worked cause I knew what had happened. A lot of things they didn't tell, I saw with my own eyes. They sent our men who had been prisoners back to us, and you were assigned to a certain prisoner. I had a sergeant who weighed 175 pounds when he got captured. When we had him, he weighed less than a 100 pounds. Anything he wanted, he got.

They told us we were the first outfit to use flame throwers on tanks. A tank would come in with both guns ruined, and they'd rebuild those guns so they could put a tube in the barrels to let the flame come out the end. They stripped the inside of the tank so that containers of Napalm could be stored. There were five tanks in a company. Four of them were fixed that way, and the fifth one was fixed with a bulldozer blade. This was barbaric, I know that, but it was either live or die, one or the other. The Japs would go in the caves in the daytime, and at night they'd come out and you just wouldn't believe what would happen. General Buckner said we'd try this so the tanks would pull up to the mouth of those caves and blow flame in there. Then they'd take the tank with the blade on it and seal the caves up. In about a week or ten days we could tell the difference in what happened at night.

Something else interesting was about the Death Leap. Maybe not interesting, but that's the way it was. Instead of being captured, these Japanese would go up on this steep mountain and jump off to kill themselves. When they didn't have a chance, they'd do that. What caused part of it was that we had a little reconnaissance plane that would give us information. The Japs shot him down, captured him, and crucified him, just like Jesus was crucified. That's facts. I saw it and know what I'm talking about. That's the reason I liked Ernie Pyle. He told it just like it was. Some of these other correspondents told the truth, but not the whole truth. Ernie Pyle wrote down what you said and what he saw.

We had the greatest country in the world when we came back, but it's not anymore. Morals and ethical standards are zero.

On the way over we had pretty good food. When we got to Okinawa, I carried a ten-pack on my back. In other words, I had ten meals, and it was pretty good food. When they got the mess halls set up, our Company Commander, Captain Booth, took care of us, and we had something good to eat.

There were two airfields on Okinawa. When we were off duty, the Captain asked us to build that airfield. We built the runways out of coral reef. They dug it up, and we hauled it in our trucks. They had one airfield, and we built one. I saw those planes take off, the gull wing Corsairs. They'd put down this metal mesh on top of the coral, and they'd take off with bomb loads.

It was pretty bad! A bad situation! In other words, to me there's no heroes that came back. The heroes stayed over there. They gave it all. Some of the rest of them were in combat a whole lot more than I was. Marines that went north in Okinawa had a time of it. They fought for every inch of that island. I had a friend who had a twin brother on Iwo Jima. He and I hitched a ride on a cargo plane going over there to see him. There were more people lost on Okinawa than any other island.

Me and my buddy, Billy Stafford, bunked together. That first night they told us to hunt something to stay in, and we found a cave. He threw a hand grenade in there to clear it, and we found out the next day that it was an Okinawa cemetery. They had those urns in there with ashes, and we'd done something we shouldn't have done. The captain straightened it out the next day with the help of an interpreter.

When I came to the States, I landed in California and then went to Ft. Sill, Oklahoma. That's where I went in from Red River County, where I got all my shots. I was discharged January 3, 1946 at Ft. Sam Houston, Texas." (R. W. Stidham was awarded the Asiatic-Pacific Campaign Ribbon with One Star, a Marksmanship Medal, American Campaign Ribbon, and Army of Occupation Ribbon.)

★★★

H. C. FLANAGAN was born January 20, 1921. His parents were Hugh and Nettie Smith Flanagan, and he had one sister, Velma. On August 27, 1941 he and Bonnie Whitley were married, and they had two daughters, Patsy and Regenia.

H. C. served in World War II in the Army and was inducted on December 19, 1944. At that time he went to Ft. Sam Houston, Texas, and then on January 14, 1945 to Fort Hood, Texas where he received his basic training. After coming home on leave, he was sent to Fort Ord, California for about one month and then on June 10th was shipped overseas on what he called 'a very slow trip'. While en route overseas, they had a frightening experience when their ship was attacked by a submarine. Some of the men were throwing their things overboard. Finally, because of the ship zigzagging on its course, they lost the sub. The ship made three stops—Pearl Harbor, the Solomon Islands and the Caroline Islands. Their landing was on Luzon in the Philippines, and they served on Leyte Island where their job was to go up in the hills and find the Japanese soldiers who did not know that war had ended. H. C. returned to Wheeler Field at Pearl Harbor on March 28, 1946 and really enjoyed his stay there. He returned to the States July 26, 1946. He died February 15, 1985, and Bonnie resides in Clarksville.

★★★

GAVIN WATSON, JR., the only child of Dr. Gavin and

Emma McClinton Watson, was born in Red River County in 1921. He and Martene Holland were married in 1962. Gavin became the County Judge of Red River County in 1954, serving until 1978, when he resigned to become Editor and then Editor-Publisher of the *Clarksville Times*, assuming the title of Editor-Emeritus in semi-retirement in 1985. They were active members of the McKenzie Memorial United Methodist Church in Clarksville, and Gavin played a big part in civic affairs until his death in 1998. Martene lived only a short time after Gavin's death.

Gavin entered the Army Air Corps in 1942 and trained in Santa Ana, California, Tennessee, and Salt Lake City. He was discharged in 1945 after serving in England and was awarded the Distinguished Flying Cross, Air Medal with three Oak Leaf Clusters, ETO Ribbon with three Battle Stars, and a Presidential Citation.

In the July 2, 1998 edition of the *Clarksville Times* an article was published about Gavin. It is quoted below:

"Former Red River County Judge, former Clarksville Mayor, and World War II veteran Gavin Watson, Jr. died last week. He will be long remembered for his love of Clarksville and Red River County and his untiring efforts for both.

During the annual Fall Bazaar in October 1995 in a special ceremony commemorating the 50th anniversary of the end of World War II, Judge Watson gave a moving speech honoring the veterans of that terrible war who were willing to sacrifice everything to defend this country which they loved above all else.

On this Fourth of July we will once again celebrate the anniversary of America's independence and freedom. Gavin is no longer here in person to celebrate with us, but he is here in spirit. It seems appropriate now to recall his words on that special day two years ago.

'It is a great honor to be asked to be here today with all of you as a representative of the millions of Americans who have served in uniform to protect and defend our America the Beautiful. I am especially pleased to say a few words about World War II because that was my personal war, and the legion of my generation who fought in that great conflict are gradually dwindling down to a precious few.

But today we are especially noting the end of that cataclysmic struggle, inasmuch as this is an important World War II anniversary since it ended a half century ago.

Unfortunately and tragically, the price of freedom throughout the long history of mankind has always been sacrifice, sacrifice, sacrifice, which all too often has meant the ultimate sacrifice, the giving of one's life that others might live in peace and freedom from slavery.

It has always been that way. Only those countries and cultures whose citizens have been willing to lay down a living gauntlet of bodies to stem the enemies have survived. Thank the Lord that Americans have been of that dedicated character to insure my future and your future and the future of these United States. We have survived because of their sacrifices.

And, my friends, especially you young folks, World War II was a conflict of actual survival to determine whether our civilization as we knew it would continue or not. And be assured that at times the issue was closer than many of us realized.

Many of you, perhaps most, were not alive during the dramatic 1940's war years and time has dimmed the memory of those who were. So, the idea is far too prevalent today that World War II was a foreign struggle far removed from our shores and that a defeat would have been nationally embarrassing . . . but of little future consequence.

Not so my friends, let me assure you. If we had lost that European war against the totalitarian governments, it is likely that today the swastika would be flying from this flagpole and that we would be giving the Nazi salute instead of exchanging high-fives. We would have been enslaved as were the citizens of the many countries that our enemies conquered. . .

And what if Japan had perfected the atomic bomb first? Does anyone doubt that this nation of fanatics who totally, without warning, bombed Pearl Harbor on a sunny Sabbath morning while church bells were ringing out for worship services, would not have obliterated our great cities one by one with nuclear holocaust horror? But it didn't happen, did it?

These terrible consequences were blocked because our Allies and our American men and women in uniform threw themselves into the conflict—many, many at the cost of their lives. How many are we talking about? Well, in the three and half years of World War

II almost 300,000 Americans were killed in combat; another 115,000 died of non-combat but service connected ailments or injuries or illnesses. That is a total of over 400,000 Americans who gave all they had to save this world. And still another 670,000 returned home without fingers or toes or arms or legs or eyes or their emotional stability. That's what the word 'sacrifice' means.

We can't thank those heroes—it's far too late—fifty years too late—for what they did, but we can pause on this 50th anniversary year in the midst of these joyous festivities to honor their memory and reaffirm our commitment to maintain the free and glorious America they gave their lives to preserve.

Would you bow your heads for a moment of prayer for these hallowed heroes? Oh, Lord, we ask thy blessing upon this great nation of ours and its citizens. Lead us in the paths of peace and justice that we may bring about a world of friendship and sharing and brotherhood, living together in blessed harmony and without conflict. And, oh Lord, be with all of those American heroes, both living and dead, who have gloriously offered themselves as sacrifices that this nation shall not perish from this earth. Amen'

★★★

MARVIN ELLIAM STEARMAN was born December 28, 1924 at Sulphur Bluff in Hopkins County, Texas. His parents were Willie Jackson and Florene Hare Stearman. He had two brothers, Horace and Willie Lee and three sisters, Marie, Ruby and Glenna. He married Naomi Baird and they have two children, Belinda and Larry E. Marvin entered the service on June 20, 1944 at Camp Wolters, Texas. He was an Armored Tank Driver in the Armored Infantry and did 17 weeks of basic training at Ft. McCullan, Alabama. He was a PFC and served in the Ardennes Campaign, Rhineland Campaign, Central European Campaign, and in Germany for nine months. He was discharged in 1947 at Camp Hood, Texas and was awarded the Combat Infantryman Badge and European-African-Middle Eastern Theater Ribbon.

This is what he had to say about his experiences: "After basic training I was shipped to Germany. While on a ship trying to cross the English Channel, we were off shore for four or five days waiting for the fog to lift. Days and nights were the same—no beds, no plumbing, very little to eat. Landed in France, then tank training, and on to the front lines in Germany. Crossing the Rhine River while they were bombing it and waiting for our engineers to repair it. A lot of suicide missions were taking place. After finally crossing, we drove all night in 'black out'. When daylight came, we were surrounded by Germans. I pray things that I saw happen there never happen in the U.S.A. Five men in my squadron came home uninjured. One interesting thing I did see was Hitler's hideout in the mountains."

★★★

Dave and Jessie Weaver of Clarksville, Texas had two sons in the service during World War II. **DAVID J. WEAVER, JR.** was born October 10, 1922 in Clarksville. He entered the Navy Air Corps on June 14, 1942 and trained at Pensacola and Deland, Florida and San Diego. He was a carrier pilot and dive bomber pilot and later a landing signal officer on a carrier. He served in the Pacific in the Philippines, Truk, Saipan and Guam. He met Mary Kirkland in Jacksonville, Florida, and they were married and had three children, Kirk, Alan and Lisa. David was discharged from the service in 1946. He was awarded the APO Ribbon with three Battle Stars, Philippine Liberation Ribbon with one Star, Fleet Unit Citation, and the Victory Medal. David died in 1965.

BILLY T. WEAVER was born February 9, 1926 in Clarksville. He enlisted in the Army Air Corps in December 1943 and trained at Ft. Sill, Oklahoma, Amarillo, and Albuquerque as an Electrician. Billy married Ann Wright and they have two children, Linda Carol and Keith. The Weavers reside in Clarksville.

★★★

I interviewed **OLLIE STAFFORD** on August 27, 1999 at the Clarksville Nursing Center where he now resides. He was born August 1, 1912 in Lewisville, Arkansas and came to Red River County as a baby. His father died when Ollie was only three years old. Along with his three brothers and two sisters, he was raised by his mother, Ella Stafford. He married Irene Benningfield, and she preceded him in death. They had no children.

Ollie said: "I was drafted in 1942 and took my training in California, Ft. Lewis, Washington, and Camp White, Oregon before I went overseas. I was in the 96th Infantry Division. I went overseas and landed on the Philippine Islands. We went from there to Okinawa and that's where I was wounded. I hit Okinawa on April 1, 1945, and I was wounded on April 21, 1945. On that beach it was all fighting. The Japs were dug in those hills and caves, just everywhere. The Big Joes were just scattered out everywhere. I was in a rifle company. I was Platoon Sgt. over the fourth platoon—two machine guns and three mortars.

We had to kill a woman the first night we was on Okinawa. We had orders to shoot anything that moved in front of us. Way in the night she came down there dressed in white and talking, talking. We didn't know what she was saying. Of course, those boys on the machine guns, two men on each one so that if one got killed the other could take over, were anxious to pull the trigger. I said, 'No, no'. She went on past us so I got on the phone and called the Company Commander and asked him what to do about it. He said, 'If she comes to the hole, shoot her.' When she came back, I told them to let her have it. We went out there the next morning, and she was cut in half. She had a big knife on her. Lots of shooting and stuff like that.

We just had to keep going no matter what—there wasn't no turning back for us. That was the orders. We had to cross a deep, wide draw that was pretty deep, and wide as this room. They was firing machine guns, and we had to cross it one at a time, run across it. I was standing there waiting for my platoon to go across, you know, talking to an old boy, and that's where I got wounded. A mortar shell hit me in the shoulder.

It was all just awful, but we had to do it. We didn't take no prisoners, not that I can remember. We just had to shoot them and go on. That outfit I was in was just a Rifle Company in the Infantry. We was always on the front. If we run into something we couldn't take, the Company Commander would call in the artillery.

We didn't have much to eat—just little old cans of food. Pretty rough! I was on Okinawa about twenty days before I got hurt. Course, we'd already taken the Philippines, and I fought all through that and never got a scratch on me. After I got hurt on Okinawa, they sent me to Saipan to the hospital, and I stayed there till the war was over.

Going overseas on the ship took a long time. It was really slow getting there. Irene and I married before the war. We were married fifty-four years. After the war, I came back to Clarksville in Red River County and farmed.

In the Philippines there wasn't no houses. Those people just lived out in the woods in old shacks made out of coconut leaves. On Okinawa they had concrete things that looked like storm houses. When people died and was cremated, their ashes was put in an urn that was kept in there. All around these they had a concrete like fence just up so high with a gate in front. Me and my men in my platoon stayed in one of them one night. I bet there was five hundred Japs on the other side of it. Course, they didn't know we was in there. There wasn't a lot of them like that one we stayed in, but I guess some of the people had money and had this one. We hid out there that night. I don't know a whole lot to tell you—just shooting going on and keeping moving.

We had a little old Jap boy that stayed with us all the time. We fed him. I don't guess he had no folks. I don't know. Okinawa was a pretty nice clean island, but the Philippines was nasty. They had a whole lot of coconut trees, those short little bananas, and a whole lot of big old water buffaloes. They'd come in at night, and the devil would break loose shooting, thinking it was somebody. The next morning there'd be two or three of them dead.

This was just war—shooting and moving on and fighting, and I never have forgot it. It was really rough! If you got pinned down, you just had to wait for help. Lots of times you'd get pinned down, and you couldn't move cause the bullets would be flying so bad. You'd have to call and get them to bomb them overhead. You'd have to tell them how far and the distance and all. The officers always had something to talk on."

Ollie was discharged in 1946 and returned to River County to farm. He was awarded a Good Conduct Medal, Purple Heart, APO Ribbon with two Battle Star, and a Philippine Liberation Ribbon.

★★★

Margaret (Marty) Davis Wilcox of Annona, Texas sent me the following about a World War II veteran:

"**ALBERT HOUSTON DAVIS** was born September 28, 1921 and was raised in Red River County in the English/Springhill areas. His parents were William Jasper and Vessie Lerner Jones Davis. He had two sisters, Marcell and Alva Mae. The family farmed and ranched.

On July 8, 1942 he entered the U.S. Army and was a PFC in

Company F, 145th Infantry. His training was at Ft. Robinson, Arkansas, and he was a machine gunner for seventeen months, loading, aiming and firing the water-cooled 30-caliber machine guns. He also inspected and replaced all worn or defective parts. His company protected rifleman from enemy fire by laying down a withering fire which kept the enemy pinned down, allowing riflemen to advance upon the enemy.

He served thirty-five months in the Asiatic-Pacific Theater (Northern Solomon Islands and Luzon) and was discharged at the Separation Center in Fort Bliss, Texas on December 22, 1945. He was awarded the Combat Infantry Badge, Asiatic-Pacific Theater Ribbon, Good Conduct Medal, Victory Medal and a Bronze Star.

Upon returning home he met and married my Mom, Frances Marie Stroupe. They had four children, myself (Margaret Marie), James Houston, Carolyn Fay, and Carl Ray. We lost our Dad on Thanksgiving Day, November 28, 1968, in the VA Hospital at Shreveport, Louisiana. He was the best Dad God ever put on earth. Then we lost our Mom on February 20, 1984, and then our brother, Carl, on June 1, 1999. Thank you for the opportunity of others knowing that my Dad served his country proudly."

★★★

A. D. STEPHENSON of Bogata, Texas submitted the following about his military service during World War II:

"I left Bogata after graduation from high school in 1942 with every intention of joining the Navy. While on the bus on the way to Dallas, an elderly man boarded the bus at Greenville and asked me where I was going. I told him I was on my way to Dallas to join the Navy. He said, 'Why don't you fly these airplanes?' I said, 'Do you think they would let me do that?' He said, 'It won't hurt to ask them'. As a result of this conversation, I walked into the recruiting room that had a picture of a pilot standing by an airplane and started my Air Force career on June 25, 1942.

My first duty assignment was in the Glider Pilot Program. I had glider training at Goodland, Kansas, Lamesa and Dalhart, Texas, and Victorville, California. While at Victorville the dry lake bed we were flying from ended up with about three feet of water in it after a very big unexpected rain, and we suspended glider training for several weeks. During this period part of the younger trainees were selected to attend the Aviation Cadet Pilot Training Program. I graduated from Pilot Training on January 7, 1944, and was assigned to Roswell Army Airfield for about a year to instruct and train bombardiers. After this assignment I was selected to go through the B-29 Aircraft Commander Program at Roswell and Alamagardo, New Mexico.

I flew B-29's seven years, RB-36's three years, and B-47's nine years. I served in the Strategic Air Command, Command Post in the 306th and 310th Bomb Wings. I was Alert Force Commander in the 310th Bomb Wing. In my long and varied Air Force career, I feel that God guided my life every step of the way. I retired from a B-52 Strategic Air Command Wing on January 1, 1966 at Sheppard Air Force Base, Texas only to start another career."

A. D. is the only child of Dessie A. and Mabel Bogard Stephenson and was born in Bogata. He and Miriam Grayson were married on March 3, 1950, have two children, Mark and D'Ann, and one grandson, Stephen Zachary. They reside in Bogata.

★★★

Berry (Chut) Thompson and his wife, Effie, of Clarksville had one daughter, Gratie. They also raised his niece's son, **RUFUS STERLING**, from the time he was four years old. Rufus served two years in the service during World War II. He was in France but saw no combat duty because the war was nearly over. Rufus was born April 8, 1918 and died April 23, 1974.

★★★

ANDREW J. BARTLEY, JR. (A. J.) was born July 13, 1921 at Aikin Grove, south of Clarksville. His parents were Andrew Jenkins, Sr. and Myrtle Bartley, and he had two sisters, Deloyce and Marcedis. A. J. and Ana Bel Clack were married in Detroit on June 14, 1942 and had been married nearly fifty-eight years at the time of his death on March 23, 2000. They have two children, Dan and Gayla.

A. J. was inducted into the Army in December 1942 and was a Pvt. in the Infantry. He had only a few weeks training at Fort Wolters, Texas before going overseas where he served for a year on several islands in the South Pacific. Because of injured knees, he was sent to a hospital in New Zealand and then to the Modesto Valley Hospital where he was discharged after treatment. He was awarded a Good Conduct Medal and APO and ATO Ribbons. (Ana Bel stayed with a sister, Bennie Bee, in California and worked in a shipyard while A. J. was in the service. I guess we could call her "Rosie, the Riveter".)

★★★

BILLY G. (BILL) WHITE was born May 14, 1925. His parents were Luther and Bertie Rowden White, and he has one sister, Shirley. He and Noma Jean Bell were married February 16, 1946 and had one son, Ronnie. Both his wife and son are deceased.

When we visited with Bill in his home in Bogata, Texas, he told us the following about his time in the Marines during World War II:

"I enlisted in the Marine Corps in October 1943 when I was just a little over eighteen years old. Once a Marine, always a Marine. I went through boot camp at San Diego, a long way from Bogata. I've lived here ever since I was seven years old. My Daddy was in World War I. He got me an agriculture deferment for six months, and I used about three months of it before I went into the Corps.

I went to San Diego in October and went through six weeks of Boot Camp. Then I went to Camp Pendleton and stayed about six weeks, and then I joined the Fourth Marine Division there at Oceanside. We did a little maneuvering there at Camp Pendleton. We boarded the ship at San Diego and headed for the Marshall Islands for our first campaign. The island we hit was Roi, and it was joined by Namur. It's all one island but has two names.

That was the first time a division had ever left the U.S. and headed for a campaign or battle without stopping. We didn't stop from the time we boarded ship in San Diego till we hit Roi-Namur. That was a long time on the ocean. We were in the Pacific, the Marines and the Navy. The Army and the others were mostly in the European Theater. We just hit island by island. We secured Roi-Namur in about two to three weeks, and then we came back to Honolulu and stopped there.

Maui in the Hawaiian Islands was our home base. There we got replacements and did some more training before we went to our second campaign which was Saipan and Tinian in the Marianas chain of islands. Well, we stayed on Maui where we came back to rest and regroup a couple of months before going to Saipan. We were out there a good while, about a month and a half. We took Saipan first and Tinian was just across the way. That's where the Enola Gay left from that took the atomic bomb to Japan.

Then those of us that were left after this went back to Maui again. Time didn't mean anything to a young guy, but I'd say we stayed there two or three months that time. They'd brief us on different things but never would tell us where we were going until we got on board the ship on the high seas. That's when we were going to Iwo Jima. The Fourth and Fifth Marine Divisons were the assault troops on Iwo, and the Third was held in reserve. I got wounded the second day on Iwo. I went through three other campaigns and didn't get a scratch. We had gone in on the beach, swung around, and was up on the side of a hill and dug in that second night. These planes, our planes, came in strafing. Me and my buddy were eating K-rations, and I saw them coming in from the west. I told him they were too low and raised up to jump in my hole, and when I did, it hit me. My buddy got down, but a lot of other guys up the line got hit. They were strafing the Marines but thought we were Japs.

They operated on me aboard ship. I got the Purple Heart, Presidential Unit Citation, and Asiatic-Pacific Medal with four Battle Stars for the campaigns I made. I was a PFC. They sent me this book that shows all about the islands. It's all about the 4th Marine Divison, and you can use it if you want to.

Those islands were just deep white sand. The Seabees came in after we secured the islands and took their bulldozers and dug big trenches and just pushed the Japs that had been killed into them and buried them. On Saipan our group went in on Charan-Kanoa. There was a sugar mill there. Anyway, we swung around and here on this point there was a cliff up high, and these natives and Jap soldiers were pushed into that point. The Japs were making those natives throw babies out into that coral stuff, and this water would come back in, and the foam would be red with blood from those little kids.

Lots of Japs would go into caves on Saipan, and it was a big island. They'd bring a tank with a flame thrower and shoot that flame in there. Then they'd bring up another tank with a dozer blade and seal the caves off.

I wouldn't take anything for what I went through, but I wouldn't want to do it again. Out of my company which was about 200 men, I don't imagine there was over twenty men that wasn't either wounded or killed through the four campaigns. You know, as a young boy, I never thought about getting wounded, and I sure didn't think about getting killed. My Daddy was in combat in World

War I, and he told me, 'Bill, I know what it is and you can get killed'. I told him I'd go to town at night and all my buddies were gone to the service, and I was ready to go. He told me to go ahead so I went. I was in a little over two years. After I left the hospital ship off Iwo, they took us to Guam where I stayed about ten days. Then they carried me to Honolulu and then back to San Francisco and on down to San Diego. I got a leave and came home and then I went to Florida to a Naval Station on guard duty. I was there about three months, and then I cam up for discharge on the point system."

The history of the Fourth Marine Division that Bill referred to reads in part as follows:

"Every Marine Division has its own personal history—its own kind of esprit, its unique combat experiences, its own section of the vast Pacific which, because so many of its men still lie there in vigilance under the white coral sand, can belong to no other. Guadalcanal, New Georgia, Bougainville, Tarawa, the Marshalls, Saipan, Iwo Jima and Okinawa are all different, and the courage and suffering and glory that went into the taking of them are different too. Thus the memories of the men in the other divisions will be different from those of the Fourth. This history is an attempt to make permanent the record of the men in the Fourth Marine Division who fought so valiantly on islands in the Pacific.

In many ways the Fourth was more fortunate than some of its sister divisions. It was overseas 21 months, whereas a tour of 26 to 30 months was not unusual for the divisions which preceded it. Its zone of action was exclusively in the Central Pacific; jungles, oppressive heat, and tropical disease were not part of its experience. . . It was in combat but a total of 63 days; it was based, between operations, in the next best place to the States—the Island of Maui. Long months of isolation in some rainy jungle or on a barren rock were never part of the Fourth's experiences. It was also the first Marine Division to return to the States and be deactivated after the war.

But in contrast to this, no division participated in more violent combat than did the Fourth. In 63 days it saw more action than did many units during months of jungle fighting, or in long campaigns in Italy and France. Every day was its own bloody battle, and every acre of Roi-Namur, Saipan, Tinian, and Iwo Jima its own battlefield. The Fourth set something of a record in making four beachheads—all of them bitterly opposed—in less than 13 months.

And if men escaped the discomfort of steaming jungles and the plagues of insects and disease, they were not so fortunate where enemy bullets and shells were concerned. Sixty-three days of merciless but futile enemy opposition accounted for probably the highest casualty rate of any Marine division. During the four operations in which the Division was engaged, a total of 81,718 men saw action one or more times. (This is a combined figure of totals of all operations for the Reinforced Division, i.e., some served in all four operations, and thus are included four times.) Out of this total of 81,718, there were 17,722 casualties (some being wounded more than once) in killed, wounded and missing in action—a total of 21.6 per cent. The percentage of the original 17,086 men who left the States with the Fourth and later became casualties would be even higher than this. These figures are not stated boastfully but as solemn facts that testify as no words possibly can to the contribution which the Fourth made to victory in the Pacific.

A division is merely a name until its component parts are joined and integrated into a single fighting unit. This process, for the Fourth, took more than a year. . . On August 16, 1943, the Division was formally activated and was now ready to undergo intensive training as a unit in preparation for combat. . . Early in January 1944 the Division boarded ship at San Diego. . . The Fourth Marine Division set three new records on its first operation. It became the first division to go directly into combat from the U.S.; it was the first to capture Japanese mandated territory in the Pacific; and it secured its objective in a shorter time than that of any other important operation since the attack on Pearl Harbor. . . For weeks the coming battle had been known only by its code name, 'Operation Flintlock'. Not until the big convoy had passed the Hawaiian Islands was its destination revealed to all hands—the twin islands of Roi-Namur in the Kwajalein Atoll of the Marshall Islands. Simultaneously, the U.S. Army's Seventh Infantry Division was to invade the island of Kwajalein in the same atoll. In many ways Operation Flintlock would be the most important of the Pacific War to date; it would constitute the first offensive strike against the enemy to secure a base for operations. . The invasion of the Marshalls was to be the spearhead of this drive, and the Fourth Division shared the responsibility for its initial success. . .

The Division reached Maui during the period from February

21 to 25, but there were some who would not come back. One hundred ninety Marines had been killed and 547 wounded during the brief engagement. Overnight the 'green' Fourth had become veterans. The Japanese could testify to that. We had captured 264 prisoners, while another 3,472 enemy troops lay buried on tiny Roi-Namur. Operation Flintlock was now history!

On May 29, 1944, slightly more than three months after returning from the Marshall Islands, the Fourth Division sailed for Saipan, capital and stronghold of the Marianas Islands. . . Saipan was only 1,485 miles from Tokyo—within B-29 range of all points in the Japanese home islands. American possession of Saipan would also cut the enemy's supply and communication lines from Japan to her armed forces in the Southwest Pacific. . . Saipan was the headquarters for the Japanese Central Pacific Fleet, its 31st Army and Northern Marianas Defense Force. . . D-day was June 15, 1944. . . Although the enemy maintained a stubborn defense for 25 sweltering days, yielding ground only under the combined weight of our infantry, artillery, and air power, it was the first three or four days of fighting that will always be remembered as the toughest. . . The offensive spirit never wavered. Hand-to-hand fighting was not infrequent. To call the honor roll of all heroes is impossible within the limitations of this history. They will be remembered by their comrades, if by no others. . .This was the spirit, and these were the men who made victory possible. . .

And it seemed at times as if Saipan were all hills. Marines captured one only to be confronted with another. These, and other typical terrain features, acquired such names as Radar Hill, Dead Man's Gulch, Poison Ridge, Impostor's Hill, Death Valley, Nameless Crag, and Back-Break Hill. Each was a bitter reminder of the thing for which it was named. . .

American manhood wrote the final chapter of Saipan. . . At 1220, July 9, after 25 days of continuous fighting, Old Glory went up on Marpi Point. . . Altogether, the Fourth sustained 5,981 casualties in killed, wounded, and missing, 27.6 per cent of the Division's strength. But 23,811 Japanese soldiers were known to be dead and 1,810 had been taken prisoner. We had won the most important Pacific base to date. Saipan was more than a mere stepping stone to Tokyo. It was an intersection on the main highway. . Now a new challenge faced the men of the Fourth. It was announced that the Division would make the beachhead on nearby Tinian two weeks later...

It was no secret that we were getting ready to add Tinian to our list of Marianas bases. The enemy had more than a month to strengthen and add to his defensive positions. Jig-day was set for July 24, 1944. To the Fourth Division went the task of making the assault landing... The loss of at least one-fifth of the Japs' effective strength in one night broke the back of the defense of Tinian... Despite the opposition, troops succeeded, with flame throwers, demolitions, and a liberal use of automatic rifles, in wiping out all pockets of resistance and by August 1, had reached the plateau on the other side of the ridge. At 1855 on that same day, Tinian was declared secured. Officially, the battle had lasted nine days... On August 14 the last units of the division boarded ship and began the long trip back to Maui. The blitzkrieg on Tinian had cost the Division 290 men killed, 1,515 wounded, and 24 missing. About 9,000 Japanese Army and Navy personnel were dead, and another 250 were prisoners. The daring strategy of capturing the island through the back door had paid handsome dividends. Guam had been secured on August 10 by the Third Marine Division, the First Provisional Marine Brigade, and the U.S. Army's Seventy-seventh Division. The most important Marianas bases were now in our hands. In recognition of its work on Saipan and Tinian, the Fourth Division was awarded the Presidential Unit Citation. The Division was making history...

The war had entered its final offensive phase, and to carry it to the Japanese home islands we needed nearby bases. Iwo Jima was 758 miles from Tokyo, 727 miles beyond Saipan, and 3,791 miles from Pearl Harbor.. The Fourth Division formed but a small part of the vast assemblage of naval, air, and land power that eventually crushed the enemy stronghold... Marines knew the battle would be tough—how tough was anybody's guess... To seize the island, it was planned to put nearly three times as many men ashore as there were defenders... At dawn on D-day Marines saw Iwo Jima for the first time... They saw an ugly lump of volcanic sand and clay... H-hour was 0900... At that moment it seemed that taking Iwo would be easy... Then the Japs came to life... Nothing but well aimed grenades, flame throwers, and bayonets routed them. At 1700 all units were ordered to dig in and prepare for a night counterattack.

D-day—the most momentous and costliest D-day of the Pacific war—was drawing to a close. More than 1,000 Fourth Division Marines had already been evacuated to hospital ships; an undetermined number lay dead. . . It was not until the next morning, when Marines along the airfield could look back on the beach, that the full extent of our losses were apparent. The wreckage was indescribable. . . It was clear that Iwo would be the Division's toughest battle. By the end of the second day casualties totaled 2,011. . . This was to be the situation for 24 grim days—the time it took for the Division to go from Motoyama Airfield No. 1 to the eastern coast just above Tachiiwa Point, a distance of slightly more than three miles. . . On February 22, the Twenty-first Regiment, still attached to the Fourth Division, passed through the Twenty-third and advanced to the southeastern edge of both airstrips of Airfield No. 2, against continued bitter resistance.

It was on the following day, February 23, that news reached the Division that Old Glory had been raised on Mount Suribachi following its capture by the Twenty-eighth Marines. No one knew then—not even the men who had raised it—what a historic moment it was to become. . . It made Marines feel proud to know that after four days, their flag flew at the island's highest point. . . Slowly the enemy gave way. . . Our tanks, although hampered by mines and loose sand, managed to deliver the coup de grace to many Japs who tried to flee. Casualties for the Division had mounted to 3,163, but our objective had been gained. The Twenty-fourth Marines, after a slow, bloody battle, had taken Charlie-Dog Ridge on February 24. . .

Then began the week-long battle for Hill 382 and Turkey Knob, the bitterest and costliest engagement of the whole battle for Iwo. At some time or another almost every battalion in the Division was committed in this battle. . . To this the enemy had added every weapon which might be used in repelling an attack. . . The easiest way to describe the battle which followed is to say that we took the Hill almost every time we attacked—and that the Japs took it back. . . Many brave men died on Hill 382, in the Amphitheater, and in the storming of Turnkey Knob, and there were many noteworthy acts of bravery. Again, it can be said that no one outfit deserves the credit. All three Infantry regiments were involved. The Engineers furnished demolition teams. Joint Assault Signal Teams and artillery forward observers were at the front with riflemen. Quartermaster personnel brought up food and ammunition under fire. And corpsmen, as always, were to be found wherever a Marine was in distress... At last Capt. Walter J. Ridlon's F Company, and what remained of E Company, aided by a depleted platoon of C Company, reached the summit—and stayed there. Turkey Knob had fallen a short time before and the Amphitheater too was in our hands... On March 3, Hill 382 was officially ours, but it had been taken at a terrible cost. Casualties now totaled 6,591 men... The battle was not over... The Japs still held out in hundreds of caves.. From now on the fight was to be, more than ever, a matter of cave warfare... During the next two days the attack continued to be heartbreakingly slow... Once more Marines discovered what is always being forgotten in modern war: that there are places which bombs and shells cannot reach. Instead, they must be taken by men alone—willing to die. Slowly and relentlessly we pushed the enemy back... On March 10 began the final stage of the battle. Jap defenders fought until they were individually routed out and killed by riflemen, demolition and grenade teams, and flame throwers... At 1800 on March 16, twenty-six days and nine hours after the first troops landed, Iwo was declared secured. The greatest battle in Marine Corps history was over. On March 19 the last units of the Division boarded ship, and on the following day, the convoy sailed for Maui...

The Division had paid a heavy price. Nine thousand and ninety-eight men had become casualties—almost half the division strength. Of these, 1,806 were killed in action. It had been a battle in which no quarter was given. An estimated 22,000 Japs had been killed by the three divisions, 8,982 having been counted in the Fourth's zone alone. Another thousand were believed sealed in caves or buried by the enemy. Only 44 prisoners had been taken by the Division. But our sacrifice had been an incalculable step forward in the progress of war...

IN MEMORIAM

There were many Marines in the Fourth Division who made the supreme contribution to victory. Like so many of their brothers in other divisions, like those who fell before them on the shores of

Tripoli and in the Argonne Forest, they now guard 'the streets of Heaven'. On Roi-Namu, on Saipan and Tinian, and on Iwo Jima, they keep their ceaseless vigil. Of all the monuments to war, none will last as long to us of the Fourth Marine Division as our memory of the white wooden slabs that glisten so brilliantly over their graves.

Many were killed on their first day of battle and on the very beaches where they are now buried. Others fought doggedly for weeks only to fall in the last skirmish which preceded the raising of our flag. There are thousands of graves altogether. The dead are Catholics, Protestants, and Jews. They are boys of 18 and men of 40. There are privates, there are lieutenant colonels. They will not be forgotten. . . .

The ceremony will long be remembered. Colors flew at half mast. The firing squad stood at attention. Reverently the men waited to pay tribute to their fallen comrades as a general rose and went to the altar. 'They are heroes all', he said. 'They have died that we might live. They have written a glorious page in our country's history'.

A slight breeze lifted the tiny flags on the graves for a moment and let them down gently. A Catholic Priest went forward to say Mass. He committed the dead to God's care. 'May choirs of angels receive thee'. . . The Protestant Chaplain took his place at the altar, reciting the burial service for the dead. 'Lord, Thou hast been our dwelling place for generations'. . . . The Jewish Chaplain went forward, read part of the burial service in Hebrew, part in English. In respect to Jewish custom, everyone donned his helmet. 'Let us even in our grief find light in our faith in God'. . .

Many Marines wept silently for buddies who were among the fallen. Because they had come so close to death themselves, they shared, more than the others, the grief of its finality. The rifles of thirty men sounded three volleys over the rows of sand mounds. When they finished, a bugler blew 'Taps'.

The generals rose to leave; it was a signal for others to follow. Some lingered briefly among the graves to whisper a last prayer, to pay one final tribute to those who, out of thousands of Americans in the Pacific, had come to stay. The face of every man who had come here this day reflected the realization that this was an unpayable debt. The suffering of these dead had been our victory. Freedom was their password, death the price they had paid for holding high the torch of Liberty.'

Of the eight men who were awarded the Medal of Honor for 'conspicuous gallantry' while serving with the Fourth Marine Division, five did not live to have the honor bestowed on them personally... Those who live to wear it do so proudly and yet with the spirit of humility befitting true heroes. They share the highest glory of which it is a symbol, yet hold it in solemn trust for comrades less fortunate. Whether they live or whether they died, our Nation is richer for their actions."[4]

★★★

TOM B. (BRUTON) WILLIAMS was born April 2, 1909, and his parents were Will and Gippie Bruton Williams. He had two sisters, Lucille and Carrie Frances, and one brother, Doug. He and Doris Dawson were married July 20, 1968, and Bruton died December 30, 1985. Doris resides in Clarksville.

Bruton entered the Navy in 1943 and trained at Camp Peary, Virginia. He served overseas in New Guinea and the Philippines and was discharged in 1945. He was awarded the Victory Medal, American Theater Ribbon, APO Ribbon and Philippine Liberation Ribbon

★★★

WOODROW WILSON LEVERETT was born at Mabry, Texas on November 5, 1912, the fourth of eleven children born to John Waymon and Rena Bell Holleman Leverett.

Woodrow was born the day Thomas Woodrow Wilson was elected President of the United States. He was a quiet, soft spoken man with dark brown hair, brown eyes and olive complexion, about five feet eleven inches tall and of slender build. Like the children before him, Woody learned how to make a living at an early age. He farmed, cut wood and fence posts, cleared land, and played the guitar with his father and two brothers, Ben and Joe. He was good natured and fun loving, attending all of the dances, box suppers and picnics in the community. He attended various community schools until he completed the seventh grade.

He started trying to enlist in the National Guard at an early age but was not accepted until 1940 when the war in Europe became very threatening. The 36th National Guard Division was mobilized in 1942 after the attack on Pearl Harbor, and he was sent to North

Africa with his fellow Texans. He was wounded in action in St. Malo, France on August 8 and died two weeks later on August 16, 1944. He is buried in the Brittany American Cemetery in St. James, France.[6]

★★★

HERSHEL FARLEY was born in Paris, Texas on February 22, 1907, the son of Bert Tate and Belle Sain Farley. He had two brothers, Wayman and Tom, and six sisters, Mamie, Emma, Rachel, Doris, Florence and Marjorie.

The family moved to Red River County near Detroit in 1918 where Hershel finished his schooling. His father and two older brothers were carpenters so you might say that he was born 'with a hammer in his hand'. Besides building locally and in the surrounding area, he spent three years with the U.S. Engineers in Panama and Alaska. He and Wilson King went to Panama in the fall of 1941 and had been there only a few months when World War II was declared. They worked on a hospital there and then after a little over a year went to Seward, Alaska where they built army barracks. He and Wilson came home at the end of 1943.

Hershel volunteered for military service and was inducted into the U.S. Navy Reserves on March 22, 1944 at Tyler, Texas. His basic training was at San Diego. From there he went to the Southwest Pacific aboard the U.S.S. Cascade which was a Destroyer Tender. (Of course, he worked in the Carpenter Shop.) He spent about 18 months at sea and wound up in Osaca Bay in Japan. He was separated from the service on December 4, 1945 at Norman, Oklahoma after 21 months.

On February 24, 1946 Hershel and Veda Bowers were married in the First Christian Church of Clarksville. He continued in construction and in 1953 bought the Harve Cornett place 3 miles west of Clarksville and for the next 15 years raised and sold registered Hereford cattle. He also bought the Pool place at Birmingham and the John Cagle place at McCoy. He kept only the Cornett place after going out of the cattle business in the late 60's, and they lived there 40 years, moving to town in August 1993. (information furnished by his wife, Veda)

★★★

A newspaper article, "Local Boy Reported Missing In Action

Found To Be Prisoner of Japanese" reads as follows: "Corporal **ORVIL WELCH**, son of Mr. and Mrs. J. W. Welch, who was reported missing in action following the fall of Corregidor in May, is now a prisoner of the Japanese, according to a telegram received Wednesday by his father. At the time the War Department advised that young Welch was missing in action, it had not been determined whether he was a part of the Corregidor garrison missing while serving on Bataan. He was with the Coast Artillery and had been in service about four years when the Japanese attacked Pearl Harbor. Information that he is a prisoner of war brought relief to his relatives here, but their anxiety has not been entirely removed because of the certain knowledge that Japan has not adhered to the rules of international law in the treatment of captured soldiers and sailors."

A hand written note by Jan Welch Richie reads: "Corporal Welch's Commanding Officer was Major General Jonathan Mayhew Wainwright IV who took command of all U.S. forces in the Philippines on March 11, 1942. At Corregidor on May 6, 1942 Wainwright was forced to surrender to the Japanese. From that time until August 1945 Major General Wainwright was a prisoner of war in Formosa and Manchuria. Corporal Welch was taken prisoner at this same time and served his time with his Major General. Wainwright became a good friend to Welch, and they shared many prisoner of war experiences before their release in 1945."

Orvil Welch joined the 2nd U.S. Cavalry Regiment in 1937 and was trained at Ft. Riley, Kansas. He was wounded on Corregidor in 1942, made the Bataan Death March, and was a prisoner of the Japanese for three years and two months. He was awarded the Good Conduct Medal, Purple Heart, four Battle Stars, Victory Medal, American Defense Medal, APO Ribbon, and Philippine Liberation Ribbon with two Oak Leaf Clusters. He died in the early 1990's and was never in good health after what he went through.

★★★

Jim and Blanche Robison Vickers had seven children, James Monroe, John Ray and twin sister Faye, Arthur Lee, Billy Joe, Harold Franklin and Jimmy Glenn. Four of their sons were in the service during World War II. Their sister, Faye Conine of Bogata has furnished the following information:

JAMES MONROE VICKERS was born March 11, 1918 in

Red River County, Texas. Just out of high school, he entered the Army in 1936 and took his basic training at Ft. Warren, Wyoming. He was discharged but called back when the war started. He served in Normandy, Northern France, Rhineland and Ardennes; was wounded in Belgium in 1944; and was a prisoner of war of the Germans for five months.

He told that they rode a train going to the prison camp, and all along the way the train stopped, and the dead were piled up in the snow and ice. He could never eat turnip greens after he came home because they had to pick greens growing in the fields and bale them. They drank the juice just to survive. The turnips were completely frozen in the ground. His feet froze because of the snow and extreme cold.

He was discharged in 1945 and awarded the ETO Medal with five Battle Stars, Bronze Star, Purple Heart, Unit Citation and Good Conduct Medal. He was married to Alice Guthrie, and they had one daughter, Linda Sue. He died August 5, 1970.

JOHN RAY VICKERS was born April 14, 1921 in Red River County. He entered the Army Air Corps in 1942, trained in San Diego and served in the Central Pacific and North Solomons as a Tail Gunner. He was awarded the Air Medal with six Clusters, Distinguished Flying Cross with one Cluster and APO Ribbon. After his discharge he re-enlisted and made a career of the service. After his retirement he and his French wife, Marie, made their home in Tours, France where he died August 2, 1981. He is buried there. His two sons, John Ray, Jr. and Jerry Dale were from his first marriage.

JERREL D. VICKERS was born February 6, 1924 in Red River County. He entered the Army January 18, 1943 and was a Truck Driver in the 446th Antiaircraft Artillery Battalion. His training was at Camp Hann, California and he went overseas in 1944 and was there over a year serving in Normandy, Northern France, Ardennes, Rhineland and Central Europe. He was discharged October 30, 1945 and awarded two overseas service stripes, the American Theater Medal, EAME Medal with five Bronze Stars, a Good Conduct Medal, and a Unit Commendation Star 60, #12 Hqs, 20th Armored Division, dated June 17, 1945. He married Claudia Morgan in 1946, and they had two children, Carolyn and Louis Dean. He died July 21, 1991.

ARTHUR L. VICKERS was born in Red River County on July 12, 1926. He entered the Navy on January 18, 1942 and served on the USS Columbia. He was discharged October 31, 1945 and was awarded the American Defense Ribbon, APO Ribbon, Dutch East Indies Medal and Victory Medal. He married Betty Huddleston, and they had two children, Paula Fay and Arthur Lee, Jr. He died July 25, 1978.

★★★

ROBERT WALKER was born in Detroit, Texas on June 22, 1909 to Will and Annie Edwards Walker. He had one sister, Elizabeth. In 1932 Robert and Nannie Ruth Gullion were married, and they had one son, Thomas Robert. Robert went to the Navy in 1942 and was assigned to the postal service. He spent two years in Hawaii working at the Navy Post Office and then worked in San Francisco in the same capacity until the war was over. He was discharged in December 1945 and returned to Clarksville where he was a rural mail carrier for many years. Robert died March 27, 1965, and Nannie Ruth lives in Clarksville.

★★★

JASPER BRUCE TULL was the son of Robert H. and Florence Wood Tull of the Dimple Community. He was only twenty-two years old when he was killed in action near the Danube River in 1946. The family also had twins, Boyce and Joyce, and another son, Jack, who as a young boy was killed in an accident.

J. B. entered the Army in 1942 and trained in Texas, Louisiana and California. He was a part of the 86th Infantry Division, and a write-up about that division reads in part as follows:

"Last in and first out—that was the unique record of the 'Black Hawk' Division on the Western Front. But the men of the 86th didn't expect to be finished with war when, a few weeks after V-E Day, they were rushed from Austria to the French Coast and then to New York, where they were acclaimed on June 17 as the first division to return from the war. There had been a good reason for their speedy homecoming. They were on their way to Japan. They got there with less trouble than they had originally expected; their Pacific job turned out to be not battle, but occupation.

The Black Hawks fought for only 42 days in Europe. But during that brief spell of action they earned respect from friend and foe alike for their speed, maneuverability, and courage. The 86th served under four armies—the 15th, 1st, 7th, and 3rd—claimed to be the first of all our divisions to cross the Danube River, and fought with distinction in mopping-up operations in the Ruhr pocket."

A letter dated December 29, 1945 from 1st Sgt. Robert W. Sawers to Mr. Tull reads in part as follows:

"I know you will be surprised to hear from me, but I will write a few lines because I am sure your son would have done the same for me. I wanted to come to see you but never got the chance. I want you to know your son was the best friend I ever had in the Army. I was very sorry to know he will not return. I was wounded about two or three minutes before your son was killed. I was heading two platoons in our assault on the enemy. Sgt. Tull with his platoon was on the right of his squad leaders and myself. We were shot at the same time. . . He and I were together all the time. He was a fine boy and a good soldier. I want to say, Mr. Tull, that he loved the Lord very much and was always very truthful. He never drank or cursed. . . I want you to know my sorrow goes with you all, and I sincerely believe your son is in Heaven where there is no war or grief. I pray that God will protect him and someday he and his family will meet to never part again. May God bless all of you."

S/Sgt. Tull was awarded a Good Conduct Medal, Expert Infantryman Badge, Bronze Star, and the Purple Heart posthumously.

★★★

Walter and Ora Mae Nowell Rice had two sons who were in the service during World War II and another son, Walter Samuel, who is a Presbyterian Minister.

ROBERT LANE RICE served for almost three years in the Ninth Air Force and was in the European Theater from November 1943 to November 1945, serving in England, France, Luxembourg and Germany. After the war he was an officer in the Texas National Guard in the 49th Armored Division for five years. He married Mozelle Reeves in 1942 in Dallas. They have four children, Ruth Ann, Cynthia Lane, Nancy and Bill and live in Paris, Texas. Before retirement Robert Lane worked thirty-eight years in the insurance field.

WILLIAM C. (BILLY) RICE served in the Philippines and in the Occupation of Japan. He was in the Signal Corps as a lineman. He was discharged in 1946. He was married to Lou Ella Guinn, and they had a daughter, Guinndolyn Lane. Billy was a farmer and rancher and died in 1958.

★★★

Ernest Morton and Sula Pearl Strout Peek of the Boxelder Community east of Annona, Texas had four sons in the service during World War II. Other children in the family were Dick, E. M., Jr. and a sister, Pearlene.

R. L. (RAYMOND LEON) PEEK was born March 31, 1920. He was working in Tyler, Texas when he was drafted and not accepted. In 1941 he volunteered and enlisted in the Army Air Corps. He received his training at Sheppard Field and in Columbia and Charleston, South Carolina. R. L. served as a Flight Engineer and was in the Aleutians. In 1943 he was in a plane crash where one crewman was killed. He was wounded at Adak and was discharged in 1945. He received three Battle Stars and an APO Ribbon.

While in Greenville, South Carolina R. L. met and married Alice Dudley, whose parents were Reuben and Lucy Ann Haley Dudley. They met in October 1944 and married in February 1945. When R. L. died in 1997, they had been married fifty-two years. They had two children, Dudley and Alicia Kay. Alice resides in Clarksville.

DILLARD PEEK entered the Army in 1943, trained at Ft. Sill, Oklahoma, and served in the European Theater Operation. He was discharged in 1945 and was awarded the ETO Ribbon with three Battle Stars, Good Conduct Medal, Bronze Star, Victory Medal and ATO Ribbon. He married Christine Lawson, and they had one daughter, Suzanne. Both Dillard and Christine are deceased.

DAN M. PEEK entered the Army in 1945. He received his training at Camp Hood, Texas and served in the Pacific and Japan. He was married to Ruby N. Jones, and he died October 13, 1991.

HARROLD B. PEEK entered the Army in 1944. He trained at McCullen, Alabama and served in the European Theater Operation in Central Germany with the Fifth Armored Division in tanks and half-tracks. He served twenty-two months in all, one year being overseas near the end of the war. In talking to him, I was told that he lost one really good buddy when his platoon was taken out. Shortly after the war, several soldiers were eating dinner waiting for the road to be repaired. It was pretty cool and muddy, and they were using a hedge for a table. All of a sudden two German girls walked by singing "You Are My Sunshine". It was a thrill for the men to hear it. He told me that he hated war but wouldn't take anything for his experience.

★★★

M. K. WALLCE, JR. was born May 29, 1918 in Red River County, Texas. His parents were Michael Kelly and Donnie Jane Watkins Wallace. He had three brothers, Ernest, Emmett and Ilie and five sisters, Nellie, Virdie, Lela, Audrey, and Mary Florence.

M. K. served in the Army operating heavy equipment. He was in Pamona, California, Aberdeen, Maryland, Toledo, Ohio and Alaska on Adak Island. He was discharged after the war and returned to Clarksville. He died October 21, 1978.

★★★

This *Country Doctor* story by Lee Somerville was a *Dallas Morning News* Sunday Showcase feature, October 8, 1967.

"If it hadn't been for the Battle of Anzio in 1943, **PAUL GEERS** might never have become a medical doctor. If he hadn't, the town of Whitewright would probably be without a doctor now. Doctors are scarce items in small towns. Young doctors who try semi-rural practice often become bored with the lack of social life, tired from constantly working. They move on to large cities, and they are not replaced.

Dr. Geers doesn't see it that way. 'There aren't any dull moments in country medicine', he says. . . 'We began practice here twelve years ago, and we're still waiting for the excitement to die down.' Dr. Geers has delivered babies while he sat crippled in a wheel chair, has performed minor surgery while standing on crutches.

He's a former Infantry Captain, medically retired due to combat wounds. He's a man whose life was saved by Army surgeons. He's a doctor who makes night calls in freezing weather, a man who built a large rest home because he wanted his older patients to have 24-hour-a-day care. He wears a metal rod inside the femur of his left thigh. That bone was broken during an automobile accident while Dr. Geers was on his way to perform surgery. His right leg is horribly scarred by war wounds, and unhealed sores still drain. . .

His career started with the Battle of Anzio in 1943. Paul Geers was a lieutenant then, on patrol trying to capture German soldiers for Intelligence. Coming back to a semi-safe zone, he heard the shrill, high whine of an incoming artillery shell. He looked up, froze for a millisecond as the sound thinned and silence began. Silence meant that the shell was coming directly at him. When the sound stops, you're in the impact pattern. Dead silence means death. Moving quickly, booted toes digging in soft mud, he tried to get out of the way.

Earlier that morning a weapons carrier had stuck in the Anzio mud. The carrier was gone, but deep ruts and high chunks of mud blocked his path. Paul Geers stumbled, fell, instinctively flattened in the watery ruts. The shell exploded. Shock waves thrust his stocky body into the air, held it weightless for what seemed forever. When he crashed back into the mud, he couldn't move. Warm blood flowed against his skin and his paralyzed body prickled with the numbing, gray sensation of violent injury. He willed himself to remain conscious, called for help. His men found him, began screaming, 'Medic!'. Then there was a calm voice. 'Easy, Lieutenant, easy. You'll be okay.' An American medic had arrived.

Four years of serious illness and eleven operations followed. Army surgeons saved his shredded right leg, restored order within his mangled body. During the sleepless nights when he lay on his hospital cot and stared at the ceiling, Paul Geers decided on a new career. He'd be a medical doctor.

Guidance counselors pointed to his crutches, to the steel braces on his right leg. How could a cripple perform surgery or deliver babies? Besides, he was married and had children. There were easier occupations.

Paul was stubborn. As a kid in Bagwell in Red River County, he had worked hard. He'd picked cotton, plowed corn, worked at any honest job available. When he played football at Clarksville High, he had played to win. He'd joined the Texas National Guard, 36th Division, as a buck private, but he hadn't stayed a private. Now he listened respectfully to guidance counselors but remained stubborn. It was his life, not theirs.

In 1947 Captain Geers asked for and received medical retirement from the Army. Enrolling in college, he fought a dual battle. In addition to good grades, he had to convince medical authorities that he was physically able to practice medicine. He received his medical degree in 1954, interning at El Paso General Hospital. After his internship he deliberately chose to settle in Whitewright, a town of 1,400 people. . .

Paul Geers has a love for medical practice, a love dating back to the Battle of Anzio in 1943."

Dr. Paul Geers died in Whitewright, Texas on October 4, 1986. A full page obituary in the *Whitewright Sun*, the local paper, contained this paragraph: "His humanitarian ideals were an inspiration to all who knew him. He received publicity in national newspapers and magazines as a medical doctor who made house calls and did operations while on crutches, delivered babies from a wheelchair, took payments in chickens, poke salad and long term credit, opening his office any time of the day or night for those who were sick or in need."

Lee Somerville said: "He was a wonderful man. When we were growing up, we picked cotton in the same field. During World War II, after he left college to go with the 36th National Guard Division, he married one of my school teaching younger sisters, Rosalie Somerville. We were not just brothers-in-law; we were friends." Dr. Paul Geers was awarded "Handicapped Person of the Year" for the State of Texas in 1981.

★★★

LEWIS E. BARTLETT was born June 27, 1918 in Red River County. His parents were James F. and Mary Frances Eve Cagle Bartlett, and there were eight other children in the family, William, Annie, Ona, James, Jesse, Beulah, Verna, and Velma. He married Lucy I. Smith who died in July 1979, and then in September 1980 he married Christine Barnett Gullion whose husband, Dick, had died in January 1979.

Lewis joined the Army Air Corps on January 8, 1941 at Tyler, Texas. He was trained at an ACTS Airplane Mechanic's School and became an Airplane Maintenance Technician 750 with the 69th Bomb Squadron, 42nd Bomb Group. He served in the Northern Solomons, New Guinea, Southern Philippines, China and Bismarck-Archipelago. He was discharged September 10, 1945 at Ft. Sam Houston, Texas as a T/Sgt. and was awarded the American Defense Service Medal, Good Conduct Medal, American Theater Campaign Medal with one Bronze Star, Asiatic-Pacific Campaign

Medal with five Bronze Stars, and Philippine Liberation Ribbon with one Bronze Star. He and Christine reside in Clarksville.

★★★

HUBBARD McDUFFIE's parents were Hubbard B. and Janie Maud Lanier McDuffie. There were four girls in the family, Hoyt, Edna, Betty and Dorrace and three other boys, Jack Russell, Willard Bruce and Woodrow. The family moved to Annona in 1937. Hubbard and Doris Rae Geary were married November 2, 1946. Her parents were Raymond and Inis Caviness Geary, born and raised in Annona. Hubbard and Doris are retired and reside between Annona and Boxelder.

Hubbard entered the Army Air Corps on September 1, 1942. After his basic training at Keesler Field in Mississippi, he was shipped to Douglas Air Craft Factory in Santa Monica, California to learn to build planes in that time era. He was then transferred to Continental Airline, a civilian airline, in Denver and stayed at Lowery Field. There he actually worked on the Continental planes that flew passengers from Denver to other destinations. After Denver, Hubbard was asked to be a flight engineer. He took 50 hours of flying training and six weeks of classroom training at a base in St. Joseph, Missouri and was then sent to Love Field at Dallas. This was a part of the Ferry Division of Air Transport Command, and he was a Flight Engineer attached to the 62nd Ferrying Squadron. They ferried B-24's from the factory in Fort Worth to modification centers in Louisville, Kentucky, St. Paul, Minnesota, and Birmingham, Alabama. Then they picked up modified planes and delivered them to all points in the U.S. and Canada and some to the British.

Because of Hubbard's numerous hours of air time and training, he was selected to go to the Army Trans World Airlines at Homestead, Florida for airline training. Then he went to Palm Springs to wait until the base at San Francisco could be prepared to send them on overseas flights. After several months he was sent to Hamilton Air Force Base in the Air Transport Command and flew overseas to all points. As the base grew too large, he was sent to Fairfield Air Force Base.

One of the assignments was to take supplies to the Philippines. On one flight the cargo was listed as having 11,000 pounds of human blood to be delivered to Leyte Island. The plane was then converted to a hospital ship, and they brought wounded servicemen back to the hospital at Hawaii. Hubbard wondered why they placed the amputees all together. He was told it was to help each one see others in the same shape he was in so he would not feel sorry for himself. Most of the time the amputations had been done at field operations, and the odor was the worse he ever smelled, something he never forgot.

The crew members on the plane were very young, and it was hard to understand how they were trained so quickly to be pilots on four-engine planes. On one occasion Hubbard realized he was the oldest on the plane flying out across the ocean, and he was just twenty-three.

There were close calls. One was when the hydraulic pump on the third engine of the plane leaked and died. The pilot wanted to fly another half hour; that didn't work; things got worse; and after passing the point of no return, the plane began to cut out. They had to feather the prop, flying the plane the last six hours with only three engines, making the fuel very low. Then there was the time they were in a typhoon. The plane was thrown from side to side and tossed up and down. Hubbard was in the co-pilot seat and was thrown up to the ceiling, hitting his shoulders and the back of his head. The pilot took the plane off automatic pilot and flew it manually. The waves could be seen from the plane, and the clouds were walled rather than being parallel to the earth. They made it back to Saipan but later heard that some of our ships were sunk during the typhoon.

The third close call was when the plane was flying to Honolulu from San Francisco. They got off course and were headed to Wake Island. The plane carried enough fuel for 12 hours flying time and 3 hours reserve. After flying 12 hours, the island was not in sight. Honolulu shot a beam called IFF (Identification, Friend or Foe) to see where they were and then gave them a new heading to use to fly back. They had to pull the fuel mixture back to thin to burn more air and less fuel so they could make it back to Honolulu. When they landed, they had been in the air 15 hours and didn't have enough fuel left in the plane to wash a pair of coveralls.

While in service Hubbard ran into several men from Red River County. He saw Johnny King on Biak Island; Tom Perkins on Leyte; Jack Sivley in San Francisco; Jeff Bryant on Okinawa; James

Simmons, Ralph Meals and Billy Pat Griffin in Hawaii; and Howard Horn in Minnesota. Everyone was for the war and never complained about anything except the food, saying it was "poison" and that they never got enough to eat.

When the war ended, Hubbard was in Honolulu and got orders to fly to Okinawa. From there he made five trips to Japan, moving the personnel and equipment of the 11th Airborne and the 27th Infantry Divisions. The Japanese still had planes which could not be used due to lack of fuel. From Atsugi Base near Tokyo Bay he watched on September 2, 1945 the B-29's formation as the Japanese signed the surrender on the battleship *Missouri*.

Hubbard was discharged from Barksdale Air Base in Shreveport, Louisiana on December 3, 1945 after three years, three months, and three days service. He was awarded an APO Ribbon with four Battle Stars.

A letter of commendation from Russell W. Munson, Lt. Col Commanding of the Fifth Ferrying Group, Ferrying Division, Air Transport Command at Dallas reads in part as follows:

"To the Entire Personnel, This Command:

Success in any venture depends upon cooperation of individuals working as a group toward a common goal... You were peaceful, law-abiding citizens who have risen to combat enemies seeking to destroy doctrines upon which this country was founded. To protect these, a necessary military machine was established. The change from citizen to soldier disrupted your lives and fortunes. The manner in which all of you subordinated yourselves to the rigors of military life is a glowing tribute to all Americans.

We have overcome the impossible to progress towards our goal of winning the war. It is typical of accomplishments performed in all branches of the U.S. Armed Forces. In a short period, this command has become one of the leading groups in the Ferrying Division of the Air Transport Command. We have surpassed all other groups in fulfilling quotas of pilots and delivery of aircraft. It is an accomplishment which makes every one proud of being a member of the Army Air Forces."

★★★

CLARENCE OTHO GREEN was born February 28, 1918 in Durant, Oklahoma, the son of Hollister S. and Berdie Buena Gregg Green. He had two brothers, Carl and Loyd Ray and a sister, Willa

Mae. In 1940 he and Nellie Marie McClure were married, and they had fifteen children. He enlisted in the Navy in 1943 and took his training in North Carolina. He served on a ship and was discharged in 1944. After returning home he was a logger and sawmill operator. He died May 12, 2000.

★★★

LEWIS BRYANT GRANT was born December 1, 1914 in the little village of Swanville about ten miles east of Clarksville in Red River County. Lewis was his grandfather Grant's name, and Bryant was the maiden name of his mother, May Bryant Grant. His father was Dowdy Grant. Lewis was known by everyone as Bryant. He had an older brother, William, who ran a store in Hooks, Texas until his death in 1980. The boys had a younger sister, Louise, who is now Louise Brown of Annona, Texas. The three went to school at Swanville, close to their home, for their first years of school but had to take a buggy ride of several miles to Annona to attend the higher grades.

While Bryant was still a youth, the family moved to English, a nearby community that was already very important in the Grants' lives because his grandfather was a Methodist preacher, and he and his family were a big part of the Methodist Church there. Bryant decided that working at a store in English would be better than working on a farm, so he began working in the old historic store there. On May 25, 1941 he married Margie Storey of English who taught school at Avery for many years.

In March of 1942 Bryant was called into military service. First he went to Mineral Wells, Texas, the Induction Station at Camp Wolters. Then he was sent to Camp Roberts in California, then to Cape Cod in Massachusetts, and then back to California, this time to Fort Ord on the Pacific Coast. In December 1942 he received a military qualification of Expert Rifleman.

By this time he had become a Staff Sergeant in the Headquarters Company, Boat Battalion, 542nd Engineer Boat and Shore Regiment, working as a supply N.C.O. In January 1943 he and his group were assigned to the Asiatic-Pacific campaign and went first to the Bismarck Archipelago in the South Pacific. From there they went to New Guinea and then to the Southern Philippines. Before returning to the U.S., they went to Japan, arriving there only a few days after the atomic bombs were dropped on that country.

Soon after this, the group returned to the U.S. to Seattle, and after several days Bryant was given a cold train ride to Ft. Sam Houston in San Antonio where he received an honorable discharge from military service on November 17, 1945. It had been almost four years since he had been in Texas. He received a Good Conduct Medal, Asiatic-Pacific Campaign Medal with three Bronze Stars, Philippine Liberation Ribbon with one Bronze Star, Victory Ribbon, one Service Stripe, and five Overseas Service Bars.

Bryant spent the remaining years of his life in English where for many years he owned and operated the old store. He and Margie had one child, a son, Jonathan Bryant Grant. Until his death on November 2, 1997, Bryant played an important role in the life of his community and the surrounding areas and was a concerned, caring neighbor. And, as an article in the *Clarksville Times* once said of him, all people were his neighbors.

★★★

SAMUEL W. ALLEN, JR. was born November 7, 1924 in Clarksville, Texas. He was the only child of Samuel W., Sr. and Mary Ruth Summers Allen. He married Mary Aline Fodge and they had two children, Paula Dianne and Paul F. The Allens make their home in Clarksville.

Billy Sam enlisted in the Army in July 1943 at Clarksville. He was in the 33rd Division (Qartermaster) and did his basic training at Fort McCellon, Alabama, Fort Benning, Georgia, and Fort Hood, Texas. He attained the rank of 2nd Lieutenant and received a Good Conduct Medal and Pacific Area of Operation Medal. He served in the Southwest Pacific (Japan) and the Philippine Islands and was discharged in September 1946 at San Antonio. He served in the Texas National Guard from 1947 to 1967 and was discharged with the rank of Major.

★★★

THURMAN ROBERT (BOB) ISBELL was the son of John and Annie Halbrooks Isbell. He had two brothers, John, Jr. and Gilbert and two sisters, Pauline and Virginia. All three Isbell sons were in the service during World War II. **GILBERT H. ISBELL**

entered the Navy in 1943; trained in Corpus Christi and was discharged in 1946. **JOHN D. ISBELL, JR.** entered the Navy in 1943 and also trained in Corpus Christi. He served on Whidby Island and was discharged in 1946.

Bob and Odessa Solomon and J. T. Conway and Marguerite Gray were married in a double wedding ceremony. The two men were first cousins, their mothers being sisters.

Bob entered the Army Air Corps in 1942 and received his training as an airplane mechanic at Chanute Field, Illinois. He served in China, Burma and India. The airplanes worked on had to be flown to determine that they were repaired properly so Bob did a lot of flying to test engines. These were scary experiences because sometimes they flew with only one engine. After returning to the states, he was stationed at Love Field in Dallas where he and Odessa lived until his discharge in 1945. Bob was awarded the APO Ribbon with one Battle Star, the Presidential Citation, and a Good Conduct Medal. Then they returned to Clarksville. Bob died June 17, 1991, and Odessa resides in a retirement home in Paris.

★★★

LLOYD L. HOLLOWAY was born June 19, 1913 at Fort Towson, Oklahoma. His parents were William Foster and Mary Jane Taylor Holloway. He had two sisters, Willie Mildred and Opal Etheline, and two brothers, Clyde Burett and Hubert Harmon. He and Janie Prentice Banks were married January 17, 1934.

Lloyd entered the Army in 1942 and trained in Texas, California, Arizona and New Jersey. He was a Staff Sergeant and served in the European Theater Operation and was killed in action in France on June 17, 1944. He is buried in the U.S. Military Cemetery, No. 1, St. Mere, Eglise, France. He was awarded posthumously the Purple Heart and Campaign Ribbon Awards.

Janie's niece, Shirley Sloan Hamm, furnished me a copy of a letter received by her Aunt from a friend of Lloyd's. The letter was from "Somewhere in Germany, 3 January 1945" and reads in part as follows:

> "Dear Jane,
> Here it is the 3rd of January and I just received your letter dated the 23rd of Nov. 1944. Our mail service has been terrible the past two months as supplies and ammunitions have the priority. . . I'm sorry I could not write you sooner than I did. . . Please

forgive me, as you know Lloyd was one of my best friends and I miss him very much. I also know that he expected me to write you the details, and Jane, I can tell you in this letter. . . Before I write the details I want you to know that I'm glad you're a proud woman with beautiful memories. Lloyd and I had a lot in common and I feel that the least I can do is help you, should you ever need it.

I hope I do not sound harsh as I write the details. I want to tell you with as little pain as possible so please forgive me if it sounds cruel. . . The day it happened Lloyd went forward of the company with his Captain. The Captain had to return and left Lloyd with another man at the observation post. While there, he was slightly wounded and his buddy was killed. Being ahead of the company, he was captured by the Germans. They dressed his wound and were about to evacuate him to their lines when our tanks opened fire in the woods where he was. They left him there and he was wounded again in the leg by our own guns. That happened early in the evening. The enemy fire was so great that our aid men were unable to cross the open field between us as they had us pinned down. It was several hours later that he was found with a bad leg wound which he kept in a cold stream of water to ease the pain. I talked to the men who carried him in and they said he looked all right. . . It took me two weeks to find out where he was. Then one day they told me he had gone a few days after he was hurt. . . His First Sgt. checked the cemetery and saw his grave and gave it to me. . .

There aren't many of us old 90th Division men left of the original bunch. We're still in the 3rd Army hoping every day we'll see the end of the war. Living under a constant strain and tension is nerve wracking and it has aged us all. We pray every day for the war to end so we may return home and once again try to live a normal life. Jane, I'll close with all my wishes that this year will bring you a ray of sunshine.

Your friend,
Jimmie A."

★★★

WILLIAM J. (DUDE) CORBELL, JR. was born November 18, 1922 in Red River County, Texas. His parents were William J., Sr. and Annie Ruby Stevens Corbell. His brothers and sisters were Christine, Dorthy, Billie, Nina, Tommie, Ray, Peggy and Carol. He had one son, Charles R. Corbell.

Dude was drafted into the Army in 1943 at Clarksville. His training was at Camp Howze in Gainesville, Texas and he was a part of the 88th Rangers at the rank of Pvt. A newspaper clipping reads in part: "Mr. and Mrs. W. J. Corbell of Bogata received word from the War Department saying their son, W. J., Jr. had been missing in action somewhere in Italy since May 12. He had previously been wounded in the Cassino battle but had recovered after three weeks and returned to combat duty. He was serving on the Italian front and was wounded in action and awarded the Purple Heart in the early spring. It is possible that he is a German prisoner and not yet reported. His many friends are hoping this is true and that he is still alive."

Pvt. Corbell was a prisoner of war in Stalag 7A in Germany for thirteen months. After being liberated, he was discharged in 1945 at Seattle. He was awarded the Purple Heart two times, a Bronze Star, Combat Infantry Badge and Campaign Ribbons for serving in North Africa, Sicily and Italy. He died February 14, 1992.

★★★

HERBERT R. (HUB) MILLER was inducted into the U.S. Army during World War II at eighteen years of age. He spent fourteen weeks in basic training at Camp Hood, Texas and then six weeks in Hattiesburg, Mississippi. He was then shipped to the European Theater in the 69th Infantry Division and served in England, France, Belgium and Germany. Hub was fighting through France and Germany on his 19th birthday while politicians and radio announcers were informing the American people that their eighteen years olds were being drafted but not being sent overseas to fight.

His unit, with the First Amy, was cut off for weeks in the Battle of the Bulge behind enemy lines. His feet froze, and from that day forward his feet were never warm. He was thought to be dead because nothing was heard from him for six weeks. Then 32 letters were received by his wife in one day. He had continued to write but, of course, there was no place to mail the letters. The Red Cross followed them constantly, except when they were cut off, and supplied coffee and doughnuts even on the front lines of battle.

Hub saw a lot of death from his buddies to enemy troops and never forgot the misery of war. Probably the death that affected him the most was that of John Hulen from Clarksville. They were inducted the same day, took basic training and fought through the war together. After Hub got home, he visited John's family to express his regrets and to tell his family what a valiant soldier he had been.

Once when Liepzig, Germany was under siege by house-to-house combat, the city ran up a white flag. When U.S. troops started in, the firing started over. The white flag went up three times, and women and children covered the streets with hands up. When American soldiers started in, they fell back and the soldiers were facing large guns and shells everywhere. Many American boys were killed. The Army pulled back once more, and for 24 hours the city was shelled and leveled to the ground. Nothing was left, and the American foot soldiers and tanks marched on, fighting all the way to the Elbe River to meet the Russians.

General Hodges' First Army was to take Berlin, but the order came to halt and let General Patton's Third Army take Berlin. Politics had won once again. Whoever got to Berlin first was to take it, but disappointed soldiers cooled their heels until Patton could get there.

Hub was discharged June 2, 1946 with honor after having served from April 1944 to June 1946 in the 69th Infantry Division of the U.S. Army. He received a Rhineland Central Europe Ribbon; European Theater Campaign Ribbon with two Bronze Stars for heroic achievements during military operation; Meritorious Unit Award; Army of Occupation Ribbon (Germany); Good Conduct Medal; Expert Rifleman Medal; and three Overseas Service Bars. He loved the country he fought for, and nothing upset him more than people who dishonored the flag of this country.

Hub was born January 24, 1926 in Lipan, Texas. He died February 4, 1991, leaving his wife, Beryl Jean Legate Miller; a son, Randy Miller; a daughter, Carla Miller King; their families; two sisters, Margaret Watson and Christine Wilson, and three brothers, Earl, James and Edward Miller. His parents were Rufus E. and Margaret Eva McAnear Miller and are both deceased. (This information was submitted by Hub's wife, Beryl Jean.)

★★★

JAMES BYRON EXUM was born June 24, 1919 in Red River County, the son of Tom and Leon Conine Exum. He had two sisters, Tommie and Carol. He was married to Vivian Nelson and their children were Gail, Nelson, Rickey, Weldon (deceased), Bob and Sharon. James died in December 1999.

James enlisted in the U.S. Navy on September 26, 1944, and his training was at San Diego and Gulfport, Mississippi. He was an Electrician's Mate, 2nd Class and serviced electrical equipment on minesweepers in the Asiatic- Pacific Areas. Through the point system he received an honorable discharge from the Navy on April 7, 1946 at the U.S. Naval Personnel Separation Center in Norman, Oklahoma. He was awarded a Victory Medal, American Campaign Medal and Asiatic-Pacific Campaign Medal.

★★★

THURMAN QUARLES, the son of William Richard (Dick) and Rachel Smith Quarles was born at Acworth in Red River County, Texas on October 7, 1918. He had two sisters, Thelma and Dorothy Blanch, and two brothers, William Richard (Billy) and Garland Eugene. His wife is Tommie Marie Exum Quarles.

Thurman enlisted in the Army on October 2, 1940 at Clarksville and was a Staff Sergeant in Company I, 144th Infantry, 36th Infantry Division. His training was at Camp Bowie in Brownwood, Texas. He was a truck driver, telephone orderly, teletype operator and squad leader in combat and served in France, Luxembourg, Belgium, and Germany. He was discharged at Fort Sam Houston in San Antonio on October 13, 1945 and was awarded a Good Conduct Medal, Combat Infantry Badge, ETO with three Battle Stars and an American Defense Medal. Thurman and Tommie are retired and make their home in LaGrange, Texas.

★★★

Robert L. and Mattie V. Kelley Sauls had two sons, Roy James and Alvin, and three daughters, Frankie Lee, Bill, and Grace. Both sons served in World War II.

ROY JAMES SAULS married Minnie Meeks on January 1, 1939, and they have three children, Paula, Royia and James. He entered the Army in November, 1942 and did his training at Camp Wolters and Camp Howze, Texas; Camp Claiborne, Louisiana, and Camp Kilmer, New Jersey. He remarked that the training in Louisiana wasn't easy and that the rains were awful. You didn't dare touch the top of the pup tents because they'd start leaking.

When I visited with Roy and Minnie in their home in Clarksville on August 23, 1999, he had the following to say: "They intended for us to go to Cherbourg, France, but the fighting was so hot there that they sent us to Glasgow, Scotland. The trip over was very smooth. We were in a convoy of either 47 or 57 ships and didn't even realize it. We caught a train in Glasgow and went to Newberry, England just out of London and waited for our equipment to catch up with us. From there we went to Omaha Beach, and it was already cleared. Then from there we went on into Holland and waited again for equipment to get to us. From there we went on to Polenburg, Germany where there was a lot of fierce fighting. I don't remember how many days we were there. Then we went into the Battle of the Bulge, and actually we were out in the fields most of the time. We went on up to the Elbe River and crossed there and set up kind of a camp there.

I was a Staff Sergeant in Supply. Our truck driver had to go each day and move troops or supplies, and he was captured so that left us across the river. I never will forget it. One of our men told us the bridge would be destroyed and for us to get across the river. We started from there on foot. We were back with the company headquarters, but our troops were in a barn. Someone was smoking one night and carelessly set the barn on fire, and we had a Sergeant to burn up. This was in 1944. We went on into a town up there on the Elbe River, and it was practically blown off the map. I never will forget one occasion when we were going to take the food up on the line. The artillery shelling was so bad that we just had to hit the ground. It stayed so bad that finally the Sergeant in charge told us to pour the food out and go back to camp. The next day the Platoon Sergeant told us that it had been so bad that he wouldn't have asked his men to get out of their foxholes to get the food if we had made it up there with it. That was one of the closest calls, and then I'll never forget standing guard one night in the Battle of the Bulge. Our artillery was behind us, and theirs in front of us. Then we'd be wondering if those buzz bombs were going to run out of gas right over us.

We got through the Battle of the Bulge, and they put us in the Army of Occupation in the town of Lodenberg which was about 25 miles from Heidelberg. While there I got a pass to go to Salzburg, Austria and see Suey (Alvin Sauls, his brother). I caught a plane from Manheim, Germany to Munich. As luck would have it, I was hitchhiking from Munich to Salzburg, and a specialty truck that was hauling films back and forth from Munich picked me up and carried me into Salzburg. Well, I got the same ride to Munich, but when I got there, the weather was foggy and the plane was all socked in so I had to highway it again. I had a Captain and two Lieutenants who picked me up and took me quite a way, but I had to walk quite a way too. I saw Hitler's hideout around Salzburg. I made one trip to Paris, France and then came back to Camp Kilmer, New Jersey.

Coming back we were on a small ship, slipping and sliding, trying to eat, and there were a lot that were seasick. It was terrible. That Statue of Liberty was wonderful to see. It was great to get a good meal and real milk because we'd been used to powdered milk and eggs. We didn't go hungry, but it was Army chow. There they sent us to our closest destination to home and dismantled the 84th Infantry. They were called the 'Rail Splitters". I went on a train from Camp Kilmer to San Antonio. When I got to St. Louis, I called Minnie. She came from Greenville to Clarksville and picked up Mother and was going to meet me in San Antonio. As luck would have it, my train was pulling in, and I looked out the window, and they came driving up. That was about the extent of it. We saw a lot out of the back of a truck. The little children came up to get chewing gum. We got a ration ever so often and they seemed to know when. It was quite an experience, but I was just one of thousands who did it." Roy was awarded the Victory Medal, ETO Ribbon with three Battle Stars, Good Conduct Medal and Expert Rifleman's Badge. He served in Belgium, France and Germany. He was discharged in 1946.

During our visit we talked about the "Medicare Golf Group" who, after retiring, played golf almost every day at the Clarksville Country Club. They were Roy, Paul Marable, J. R. Harcrow, F. M. Morehead, Dr. C. B. Reed, Tobe Strickland, Ellis Goodman, Purvie Goodman, G. W. Geer and Everett Fuller. Roy is the only one of the golfers who is still living.

ALVIN A. SAULS was born January 1, 1909 and married Vella L. (Flaxie) Cain on May 30, 1929. They had two children, Patti and John. He entered the Army in 1942 and trained at Camp Maxey, Texas and Camp Polk, Louisiana. Alvin served overseas in the Battles of Normandy, Northern France, Rhineland and Central

Europe as a Mechanic in Company A of a Signal Battalion. He was discharged in 1945 and awarded the ATO Medal, EAME Ribbon with four Bronze Stars, Good Conduct Medal and Victory Medal.

Alvin and Flaxie were our neighbors for over twenty years, and they were good neighbors. Alvin died May 4, 1990, and Flaxie resides in a retirement home in Tyler, Texas where her son, John, and his wife reside. We have missed them both.

★★★

Both sons, the only children of Rufus and Mary McSwain Waldrep served during World War II. **BURNELL WALDREP** was born June 19, 1911 in Waldo, Arkansas. He married Cherry Price, and they had three children, Neal, Laurie and Norma. He enlisted in 1934 at McDill AFB in Tampa, Florida and was a lst Lieutenant and served in JAG. He received his discharge at Sheppard AFB in Wichita Falls, Texas.

M. E. (MARVIS EDMUND) WALDREP, better known by everyone as "Tump", was born May 22, 1913 in Waldo, Arkansas. He married Mary Frances Benton, and they had two children, Richard E. (Dick) and Joanne. He enlisted in the service in 1941 at March Field, California and was a lst Lieutenant in the Finance Department. After his discharge he and his family made their home in Clarksville. Tump died November 29, 1960, and Mary Frances resides in a retirement home near her daughter and her husband, Thomas Fowler, who live in Sherman, Texas.

★★★

NORRIS L. HARGUS was born July 7, 1917 in Detroit, Texas, the son of Alfred Pete and Jennie C. Toney Hargus, and he had one sister, Doris M. He married Edna Edwards. He was drafted on March 10, 1942 in Red River County and took his training at Ft. Benning, Georgia. A Corporal, he served in the 90th Infantry Division under General George Patton in England, France and Germany. Cpl. Hargus was killed in action on December 6, 1944. He was awarded posthumously the Purple Heart and five Battle Stars.

His sister, Doris M. Parks, provided this information and included a note that reads as follows:

"A serviceman came to see us about two years after we lost him.

He told us they were all crossing the Saar River in Germany. The Germans were getting close, and the Sgt. ordered them to double the load on the barge Norris was on so they could move on faster. The barge was in mid-stream and broke in half because it was overloaded. My brother could not swim, but this soldier told us it would not have made any difference. Their packs were so heavy, and the water so icy, no one on that barge survived. This soldier was on the barge behind the one that broke into, and he saw my brother go down."

★★★

BILL LYNCH (EULIS OREN), the son of Sam and Mae Jewel Lynch, was born February 27, 1911. He had three sisters, Mattie, Pauline, and Lois, and a brother, Aubrey who died in infancy. He and Hasseltine (Tiny) Leavelle were married on December 24, 1941 in Detroit, Texas and had one son, Gary.

Bill entered the Army Air Corps in October 1942 and served as a cook at Perrin Field in Sherman, Texas. On January 1, 1943 Tiny moved to Sherman. Bill's sister, Mattie, and her husband, **H. D. JACKSON**, also a cook at Perrin Field, were already there. The two couples had bedrooms in the same house, and since money was scarce, the wives slept late, ate no breakfast and went downtown to Heston's Drug Store at noon every day to eat a plate lunch that cost only thirty-five cents. This consisted of a meat, two vegetables and homemade pie. Sometimes they bought an apple or a candy bar to eat later. Before the war, Bill had a 1936 Ford that he left in Clarksville for his mother and sister, Lois, to use. Tiny and Mattie walked everywhere they went. At night the two ate a bowl of cereal (borrowed bowls from the landlady), and the milk poured over the cereal was kept between the screen and the window to keep it cool since there was no refrigeration. Later on they moved and shared half a house that had a kitchen and two bedrooms. Those were hard times for the two couples, but they were happy. Bill's name came up on the list to go overseas several times, but some of the Yankees hated being in Texas so much that they volunteered to go overseas rather than stay.

Bill and Tiny saved $70.00 and got a 1932 Model-B Ford and then later sold it and bought a 1936 Ford Coupe with a rumble seat from Ed Wadley. After the war they made their home in Clarksville. Bill died May 21, 1991, and Tiny remains here.

★★★

JAMES L. DEAN was born January 10, 1928 in Red River County. His parents were John A. and Amanda Clem Huddleston Dean, and he had a sister, Melba, and two brothers, Edwin E. who served as Chief Bosun Mate from 1948 to 1969 and John Robert who was a Pvt lst Class killed in Korea in 1951. He married M. Mozelle Bailey, and they had three children, James E., M. Lynette, and Kelley Ruth. He enlisted in the Navy in January 1946 at Lamar County, took his training at San Diego, and served as a Seaman First Class for two years. He was discharged in January 1948 at Alameda, California.

★★★

NEAL GILBERT was born February 21, 1921 in Gilmer, Texas in Upshur County. His parents were Joseph and Hattie Pritchett Gilbert, and he was one of twenty children. His mother had a son when she married his father; they had twelve children; and then after her death Mr. Gilbert married again, and they had seven children. Neal and Frieda Kishner Palmer were married on December 22, 1945 and have four children, John, Susan, Cathy and Betty Jo. In 1953 the Gilberts moved to Clarksville with Magnolia Brush Company. Neal's sister, Olene Schultz, and her family moved here at the same time. Neal is now retired, and he and Frieda reside north of Clarksville. They are members of the Church of Jesus Christ of Latter Day Saints in Paris, Texas.

We visited with the Gilberts, and Neal told the following about his World War II experiences: "I was drafted. I tried to join the Navy but when they went to take my fingerprints, I had this crooked finger so they wouldn't take me. They said I'd get that tangled up in ropes. So I just waited and was drafted into the Army in September of '42. I took my basic training at Ft. Knox, Kentucky. I was in the 2nd Armored Division. My basic training was in the kitchen; I was going to be a cook. After we got out of basic training, they sent a bunch of us to Africa as replacements, and I landed in Casa Blanca. Part of the 2nd Armored was up at the front and part of them wasn't. I joined the part that wasn't. They were stationed in a cork tree forest. I joined them, and they put me in a tank. I never cooked a bit. They put me as assistant gunner to load the big cannons. We didn't ever get up to the front there but went to Sicily and stayed a while. The 2nd Armored Division made the landing in Sicily.

Then we landed in Scotland and rode a train down to England and spent some time there waiting for the Normandy Invasion. We didn't go in on the first day at Normandy, but we went in on day three. We built up again after we landed there and made a drive. It was some real difficult fighting there in that country. Every little section of land was broken up and divided by a hedgerow. Over the years they'd built up real high. On all our tanks they had to weld iron prongs on the front so we could get through the dirt in those hedgerows. There was a lot of close fighting there because you couldn't see. Right across the hedgerow would be the enemy sometime. We had quite a few casualties, and we did quite a bit ourselves to the enemy there.

Anyway, we started fighting there, and we fought all the way through France, Belgium and Holland. We were in Germany, and it was coming up Christmas. We'd pulled back from the front, and we were getting ready to have Christmas there in the rest area. The Belgium Bulge hit, so they loaded us up. We went the same way the enemy was going, and we went and got in front of them. We came back toward them, and when we met them, we drove them back ten miles in one day. I guess they'd lost a lot of their strength. Then we were relieved by the British Army. Then we went back down and started south to cut the Germans off. Patton was coming from the south, and we met them and cut the Germans all off. Once we did that, it wasn't long till it was all over. We fought sometimes at night. We'd come into a town, and it would be dark as we fought the enemy.

The 2nd Armored Division started out at Ft. Benning, Georgia. Patton was the Commander of that division, but as the war went on, he got higher in rank. I never did fight under him. Simpson was the General over the 9th Army that I was with when we went through France. Really, over all of us was the British Field Marshall Montgomery.

Anyway, after the Belgium conflict was over, we went on and fought till it was over. The 2nd Armored Division went to Berlin and did all the parading and stuff like that. There was an autobahn, a big highway they had. We lined our tanks up in a long line, and we'd stand out in front of them. People from different countries came by. Stalin came by once. Winston Churchill came by another day, and Harry Truman was there. We stayed there, and they told me they wanted me to be a Staff Sergeant over the kitchen. I told them 'no', that I was going home.

We lost quite a few men. I was in Company I, and the name of my tank was 'In the Mood'. I was in two tanks that were shot out from under me, and three others that had to be replaced because of damage. From the time the Division started at Ft. Benning, there were eight 'In the Mood' tanks, but I wasn't in all of them. All the tanks in Company I had to have names beginning with 'I'.

One of the tank drivers was here about a month ago. His name is Bruce Riggs, and he was born in Pennsylvania and lives in North Carolina. He's strictly southern now. One day after the war was over, he visited us. We had only one child then, Johnny, and an uncle and aunt and their child living with us. There was a trailer pulling in the yard, and it was Bruce, his wife and little boy. They had just loaded up and moved to Texas, and we didn't even know they were coming. So they lived in our driveway. We go back a long way, and he's the only one that comes by to see us.

I was in some pretty rough battles. I never got hurt. One time a shell went off close to me that just tore my clothes off. I didn't even get a scratch. Two guys were killed in a tank I was in, but I never did get hurt. It was cold in those tanks, just sitting. Sometimes we got out in the snow and slept. During the Belgium breakthrough, for some reason or another, we were held up in an area for a couple of days. This Bruce and another guy went off and killed a pig that belonged to a local farmer. They brought it back and hung it up right by our tank. An artillery shell hit it and blew it all to pieces.

We had K-rations and C-rations. Well, we had a kitchen that followed us, and every time we weren't right on the front, they'd be there. Anyway, I fought in seven different combat commands because I have seven stars. I was the gunner on the tank. I prayed a lot.

I saw a lot of terrible things happen. We had one tank in the company that had a bulldozer blade on it. The tank commander had already had two brothers killed in the war, and he was bitter. We got in a big open field one time with some German soldiers in foxholes. If they came out, he'd shoot them, and if they didn't come out, he buried them alive. Another time the Infantry was dug in holes all around us, and we were in our tanks. It had rained all day. One of the German soldiers was laying out there wounded, and when we moved out the following day, someone could have rescued him, but one of the Infantry just shot him. I just couldn't go for things like that.

We had two guys in our tank that were shot. We were in a wooded area in France after we landed there. There was a ridge up above us, and there was someone with a rifle up there, and we couldn't find him. He'd shoot down at us. There was just a little hole in the top of our tank that you could close, but it wasn't closed. He killed the tank commander so the next in line moved up in his place. I told him not to stick his head up, but he did, and he got shot. This guy was a young man that played drums in the band with Charlie Spivak. His name was Doug Harris, and he was from New York. The tank commander was Frank Farnady from Wisconsin.

We took a lot of prisoners. They'd come in and surrender to us and somebody took them back to the rear. I saw some of our planes hit and knocked down. Sometimes it looked like thousands of planes coming over. When we pulled off after landing in France, we had a bunch of P-47's to help us. Sometimes the enemy would be maybe just a hundred yards from us. Those planes would come in and just scoot over us and drop bombs. The guns on the German tanks were superior to ours. I hit a German tank one time and knocked it out. It burned. Most of the time our shells bounded off their tanks. I didn't like having to kill people, but I didn't want to be killed either. I don't have any idea just how many people I killed. We had a machine gun, and this big 76-mm gun. We'd catch enemy truck convoys moving, and I shot into them and they'd catch on fire.

One time after one battle, our battalion just had six tanks left. I was in the medium tanks, and we had one company of tanks that was real light and could run real fast. We ran onto some kind of a machine gun in a big long open area. They had anti-tank guns. When we'd even get close to them, they'd knock our tanks out. Those light tanks just circled and finally knocked them out. We ran over mines with tanks and got the tracks knocked off.

We were moving another time, and our platoon commander told us to pull up to a corner and take a firing position to the left. We started out there, and I saw a big shot come at our tank. It didn't hit us so we backed up and stayed there quite a while. An anti-tank weapon to knock out the German tank was brought in. Before our men could shoot the Germans, they shot them. The tank caught on fire and when the men tried to get out, they were shot. It was just right in front of me. None of them got out.

I went in in September 1942 and never got a leave till I got out in 1945. When I first went in, I went to Mineral Wells for three or four days. Then on the way to Ft. Knox, Kentucky, the train went by my sister's house in Dallas where I had lived with her and her family. I saw her little girl, Helen, playing in the yard. She was just a little girl. It was tough! By the time I saw Helen again, she was a big girl.

I came out as a Corporal. If I'd taken that job in the kitchen, I'd have come out a Staff Sergeant. I came out with seven Battle Stars, a Good Conduct Medal, and a Marksmanship Medal, even with my crooked finger. One time I was the front tank, and we came to a bridge with the enemy on the other side. They were firing on us all day. Some Lieutenant in a tank was sent in just to 'observe', and they got Silver Stars. Of course, we were doing what we always did. They came up there to 'observe' and stayed about five minutes.

When we were taking Basic Training in the kitchen, they told us to go out and fire a bolt action 03 rifle. I'd shoot and they'd hold up a checkered flag because I was hitting the bulls eye. I didn't know what they were doing. All I did in that kitchen was get up at about three in the morning and work till dark. It never amounted to a 'hill of beans'.

Before the war I joined the CCC and left from Gilmer. There were several people there from Clarksville. Alton Wortham was in the same camp with me. I think that was one of the best things the government ever did for people. We were poor, and I didn't know how to do a thing. That's the reason I wound up in tanks cause I had run bulldozers. We built dams, fences, roads. They taught us how to work. We were building a dam and were blasting away down deep in the rocks. I was running a compressor. I moved a rock, and it twisted around and cut my finger. They sewed it up, but it never straightened out.

General Patton was a controversial kind of person. A lot of people put him down because of the tactics he used and the words he used like when he'd say, 'We'll take it if it takes a two ton truck to haul the dog tags back.' But the way he fought, sometimes he lost less than if he had hung back. One time just before we made the invasion of France, we were standing inspection, and Montgomery inspected us. Before the end of the war, they had streamlined some of those divisions, but the 2nd Armored was still like it was. Montgomery made the statement that the 2nd Armored was the most powerful unit he knew of anywhere. I fought with a good many different Infantry Divisions and also a lot with the 82nd Airborne Division. In Germany the people were nice to us. In Sicily they were nice too, but they were kinda put out cause we were in their country and made them get out of our way. We were totally committed then. We had a cause and a reason to fight." (Neal's son, John Gilbert, served two tours of duty in Viet Nam. He volunteered for the second tour.)

★★★

LELAND A. SIMS, son of Gibson F. and Mary Bennet Sims, was born January 24, 1922 in Jackson, Tennessee. He had one brother, Robert Earl. He married Ruth Suggs (only sixteen when she went to New York to get married) and they had three children, Robert A., Deborah and David L.

He enlisted in the Navy in 1942 at Dallas and was a Signalman III Class. His training was at San Diego; he served aboard the destroyer *John Paul Jones*; then transferred to a mine sweeper in the Pacific and Atlantic. His sea duty was for twenty-seven months. His discharge was in October 1945 at Norman, Oklahoma. He and Ruth are retired and reside in Dallas.

★★★

CHARLES W. WILKINSON was born April 17, 1924 in Bogata, Texas, the son of Charley and Mamie Pearla Wright Wilkinson. Seven children were born to this marriage. Dan Mabry, Stanley and Allie Pearl all died at a young age. The other three were Dora, Margaree, and Thomas Paul, who is deceased. Charles married Geneva Evans, and they have one son, Marvin Lynn Wilkinson.

When I contacted him about my book, he sent an article he had written which was entitled *"A Bogata Farm Boy in the U.S. Army Air Force"*. I quote it in part below:

"Shortly after my eighteenth birthday, Hoyle Dean Bailey and

I decided to join the Air Force. We hitchhiked to Paris and went to the recruiting office. They signed us up and put us on a bus to Dallas. This was on June 5, 1942. The next day they gave us our physicals and then put us on a bus to Ft. Wolters at Mineral Wells. We went then to Sheppard Field at Wichita Falls and were given shots and began our basic training. Also, we were given a battery of tests to decide what type school we were best suited for. I very quickly developed a great dislike for Sheppard Field. My brother, Thomas, who was an instructor in the gunnery school at Harlingen, Texas told me that if I really wanted out of there to volunteer for gunnery school. He said they were needing aerial gunners in the worst way. . . Hoyle Dean and I decided that was for us. . . Hoyle Dean failed the eye test . . . I passed my physical; went to Harlingen; and after about six weeks I graduated from gunnery school. . .

I was shipped to Salt Lake City replacement center. . . They made us drill instructors. . . Then on to Davis Monthan Field at Tuscon, Arizona. Here I was placed on a B-24 crew as a tail gunner. Lt. E. G. Feeley was the pilot. This was in August 1942. The first of September we were shipped to New Biggs Field in El Paso where we flew four hours and went to school four hours each day. . . The first of October we were shipped to Topeka Army Air Base for more flying and ground school. . . Here they finally paid me up to date. . . I sent most of my money home, and my parents came to see me and brought my younger sister, Margaree Glover and her son, Joe. My older sister, Dora Thompson, from Burbank, Oklahoma also came.

On the first of November we were shipped to Smokey Hill Air Base at Salina, Kansas. . . and we were the first combat crews to arrive there. On the first of December our brand new B-24's arrived, and then we did our final month of flight training. During December we did our cross-country flying. On one flight we flew out over the Gulf of Mexico and got to fire our guns. I had flown many hours in my tail turret, tracked clouds and such, but had never had a chance to fire my twin fifties until now. . . Now I got to fire about twenty-five rounds from each gun at the clouds. We also went up about twenty thousand feet altitude so we could try out our oxygen masks. Then back overland to Deridder, La. to spend the night. The next day we flew back over the Gulf where we fired our guns again; then to Orlando, FL to spend the night. We were to spend only one night there, but we lost one plane and crew in the Bermuda Triangle. We flew search for them the next day instead of returning to Kansas. They were never found.

Then back to Kansas. This flight was our preparation for flying overseas. With our navigator now having navigational experience on long trips and over water, our crew having been on oxygen for thirty minutes at a time two different times, and our gunners having fired their guns, we were now ready for combat duty.

We left Smokey Hill Air Base on January 1, 1943 for Morrison Field at West Palm Beach, FL. During landing the nose wheel of our new pink B-24C developed a wobble, and we now faced the rough duty of a ten day lay over. While there I saw another Bogata man when I ran into W. V. Humphrey in the PX. He was a pilot on a B-26 and was headed overseas. We landed at some of the same bases going over. Our last visit was at Khartoum in Central Africa. He went on to North Africa while we went to Egypt.

On January 11, 1943 we left Morrison Field. . . I remember thinking, as I sat in my tail turret watching the receding shoreline, that this would probably be the last time I would see the good old USA. . . (After many different stops) On January 22 we flew to Abu Sueir, Egypt where we joined the 376th Heavy Bombardment Group stationed there. . .

The 376th went overseas in May 1942. The original plan was for them to go to China, but when they got to Cairo it was decided that because of Rommel's push toward Egypt, they were needed there. They were kept in the Middle East Theater and never did go to China.

We flew out of Abu Sueir . . . and then moved to a field in the desert near Tobruk. This was our first experience at desert living, and we experienced our first air raid by the Germans while there. . . Then we moved to an abandoned oasis village, Soluch. . . After a few weeks we moved to an airfield near Benghazi, Libya. . . right on the Mediterranean Sea where we stayed from April 7, 1943 until I finished my combat tour of three hundred combat hours in August 1943.

When I flew my first combat mission was the first time I had been on oxygen for more than thirty minutes at a time. It was the first time I had fired my guns at a target. I think back now how unprepared we were for combat and wonder how any of us survived. We got our training under fire.

The first few missions I flew we would have only six to nine planes available to fly. My last mission had five groups taking part. The 376th was not up to full strength of forty-eight planes, but we did put twenty-eight in the air for this mission. This mission, August 1, 1943 to Polesti, Romania oil refineries was the only mass low-level mission by heavy bombers flown in WWII. One hundred seventy-eight B-24's took off from the Benghazi area. Fifty-four were lost. Forty-one in the target area, eight were interned in Turkey, five crashed for various reasons with five hundred forty men lost. Then another fifty men were returned either killed or wounded. All told, over three hundred were killed on that mission. The five groups and their commanding officers were: 376th with Col. K. K. Compton; Col. Kane 98th; Col. Johnson 44th; Col. Baker 93rd; and Col. Wood 389th. There were five Congressional Medals of Honor won on this mission. This was my last combat mission. On August 3, 1943 I flew to Cairo, Egypt to begin my trip back to the good old USA.

A little history of the 376th: They were the first heavy bomb group to go overseas. They flew their first mission in May 1942. The 376th flew more missions than any other heavy bomb group in WWII. They were the first to bomb Europe. They were the most decorated heavy bomb group in WWII.

A little background of the B-24: The first B-24's were sent to the British Air Force. They were designated the LB-30. The B-24D was followed by several other models. Over eighteen thousand were produced. They flew higher, faster and carried a heavier bomb load than any other bomber until the B-29 came out near the end of the war. They also had the longest range at that time.

I flew two missions that later became well known. Both have several books written about them. The first was on April 4, 1943, to Naples, Italy. My pilot, Lt. E. G. Feeley was leading the second element of Section B with Lt. Bill Hatton flying our right wing in the 'Lady Be Good'. This was the mission from which the 'Lady' did not return. She was found in the desert some four hundred miles south of Benghazi in 1958 by a British oil exploration crew. The guns on the plane would still fire. The water and coffee were still drinkable. The tires were still inflated. The bodies of the crew were found. One man was found one hundred twelve miles away. He had walked that far in heat that reached 130+ in the daytime with very few drops of water. The other mission was the August lst low level Polesti mission previously reported."

S/Sgt. Wilkinson was discharged September 8, 1945 at Ft. Smith, Arkansas. He was awarded the Distinguished Flying Cross, Air Medal with five Oak Leaf Clusters, Presidential Unit Citation with Bronze Oak Leaf Cluster, and three Theater of War Medals.

★★★

GILES E. McCARVER, the only child of James Edward and Pearl Giles McCarver, was born at English in Red River County on July 11, 1918. He married Vera Brandon, and they had one son, Giles Richard (Dick).

Giles went into the service in Dallas on June 13, 1943 and his boot camp was at Main Station, Naval Air Station, Corpus Christi, Texas. He was a Yeoman Second Class Petty Officer and his duties included all types of legal matters, court martial investigations, and recording court martial trials. He spent 24 months in the Legal Office there. He was then transferred to the Personnel Office Carrier Air Service #6 at Alameda, Claifornia, then to the Legal Office at Livermore, California, and then to the Naval Air Station at Shoomaker, California for processing to be discharged from the service on December 7, 1945.

He remarked that he was fortunate that his orders did not take him overseas and that his commanding officer, Lt. L. S. Stemmons from Dallas, was a wonderful person who treated those under him as he would have wanted to be treated and always looked after them.

★★★

JAMES C. PARKS was born November 30, 1921 at Acworth, Texas, the son of Chester and Gladys Hazel Greer Parks. He had two sisters, Christine and Mary Jane. He married Dorrace McDuffie, and they had two children, James Michel and Tommie Joe.

His entry into the service was on July 8, 1942 at Acworth, and his basic training was at Camp Robinson, Arkansas, Camp Hood and Camp Maxey, Texas. A PFC, he was a truck driver in the 629th Tank Destroyer Battalion of the Infantry and he served in Europe. On November 5, 1945 he was discharged at San Antonio and was awarded the Victory Medal, American Theater Operations Medal, EAME Campaign Medal with five Battle Stars and a Good Conduct Medal.

★★★

CLARENCE L. NIX, JR. was born November 5, 1920 in Denton, Texas, the son of Clarence L. and Willie Lee Johnson Nix. He married Claressa J. Cobb; they had one daughter, Joyce Lynne and one grandson, Nikki Jamal Coulter. Coach Nix (the only name we know him by) and Claressa were married forty-nine years when she died on November 24, 1995. He worked in the Clarksville School System for fifty-three years as a Teacher-Coach, which included ten years as a Junior High School Principal from 1956 to 1966 at Cheatham. He coached nineteen years at Cheatham and during this time the boys won four football titles and five basketball titles, and the girls won eight basketball titles. He taught and coached twenty-one years at Clarksville High School before retiring and still works in the Alternative Program. (Our sons were both privileged to be coached by Clarence Nix and both have good memories of him.)

During World War II, after entering the service on June 15, 1942, he served in the U.S. Coast Guard on the *USS Gloucester* as a Steward Third Class and also in the officers supply. His sea duty consisted of twenty-six months, and he was discharged on February 26, 1946 at Seattle, Washington.

★★★

JAMES T. (JAY) PENNY was born June 4, 1920 in Bowie County, Texas. His parents were Floyd and May Godwin Penny, and there was a large family of seven sons and three daughters. On May 12, 1940 Jay and Margaret Bishop were married, and they have four daughters, Judith Ellen, Sharon Kay, Kathy Ann, and Vicky May.

Jay entered the Army in 1945 and served in the 6th Infantry Division. His basic training was at Camp Hood, Texas. The Division was then sent to Luzon in the Philippines. He told of being in a foxhole with two other men when a hand grenade was tossed in. The other two men died, but he was spared. Later he went to Korea as a driver for a general, and when the general came back to the U.S., he brought Jay back with him. He was awarded a Good Conduct Medal, APO Ribbon and Rifleman Badge. After his discharge he lived in Red River County with his family until his death on October 31, 1991. Margaret still resides in Clarksville.

★★★

CAB N. WOLF, the only child of Furman Lee and Barbara Cunningham Wolf, was born May 3, 1922 in Lampasas, Texas. He and Carroll Manly were married and had three children, Laurie Ellen, Dana Jo, and Cab Lee.

Cab enlisted in the Army Air Force on July 11, 1942 at Austin, Texas. He was a Sergeant Major in Squadron A, 350, 2nd Army Air Force Battalion. His training was at the 343rd College Training Detachment where he qualified as a Gunner on a B-17 and B-29. He was discharged on February 22, 1946 at Camp Fannin, Texas and was awarded the American Theater Campaign Medal, Good Conduct Medal, and World War II Victory Medal. He then returned to Clarksville where he lived with his family until his death on September 10, 1999. (The Wolf family is remembered as having built the Avalon Theater as well as owning the State Theater which was later named the Texan) Carroll remains in Clarksville.

★★★

CHARLES T. (SKEET) HOLLEY was born December 9, 1922 in Red River County. His parents were Charles M. and Rosie McGill Holley. There were two other sons, James B. (Ballard) and Hugh (Bud), and a daughter, Dorothy. Bud served during the Korean Conflict. Skeet married Margaret O'Donnell who died in 1974. They had three children, Johnny, Kathy and Charles. He later married Mary Fuller Dillow and they now live on Peter's Prairie Road east of Clarksville.

Skeet entered the Army on February 4, 1943 and was a part of the 332nd Field Artillery, 86th Division. He was trained at Camp Howze in Texas, Louisiana, Oklahoma, and had amphibious training in California. Because he was in the hospital in California, he did not go overseas when his Division went to the Battle of the Bulge. Practically the whole outfit was wiped out by a German Panzer Division who overran them. He had been corresponding with a boy he had gone through training with, and when his last letter was returned undelivered, he knew his friend had been killed in action. Skeet received a medical discharge in August 1945 at Ft. Meade, Maryland.

JAMES B. (BALLARD) HOLLEY was born September 9, 1919 in Clarksville, Texas. He and Margaret Cross were married September 27, 1940 and had two children, Phyllis Carol and Britt Alan. Ballard and Margaret now reside in Clarksville.

Ballard was inducted into the Army in November 1942 at Tyler, Texas. He left Clarksville for Camp Wolters, Texas and from there went by train to Camp Hann in Riverside, California. After training there with the 413rd Antiaircraft Battery Battalion in July 1943, they departed by train for Camp Pickett, Virginia. From there in September 1943 they went to Fort Dix, New Jersey and took extensive training for the coming invasion of France. They traveled on the Chesapeake Bay in Massachusetts, going through New York City, and Boston and then back to Fort Dix with the convoy going through the Holland Tunnel from Brooklyn under the Hudson River to New York City. Then on the first of November they were sent to Camp George Washington on the Hudson River in New York. On November 15, 1942 they boarded the *Queen Mary* along with 21,000 troops. They landed in the Faith O'Clyde Harbor three days and thirteen hours later. The *Queen Mary* traveled at 65 knots, approximately 90 miles an hour and traveled alone. Then they had final training for the invasion on D-Day.

Ballard was a Corporal and served in the motor pool, driving and handling all types of vehicles and machinery. He served in the First Army in the European Theater in England, France, Belgium and Germany. He served overseas for twenty-three months and thirteen days, returning to the U.S. in November 1945. He was awarded the Arrowhead for D-Day Invasion and five Bronze Stars for five major campaign battles and was discharged November 7, 1945 at Kelly Field, Fort Sam Houston in San Antonio.

A Commendation from Brig. Gen. E. W. Timberlake, Headquarters, 49th Antiaircraft Artillery Brigade dated 10 May 1945 in Germany reads in part as follows:

"At the conclusion of our victorious campaign through Europe, I want to express my deep appreciation to you, and through you, to the officers and men of your seasoned Battalion, for the outstanding drive, tenacity of purpose, and aggressiveness with which the 413th AAA Gun Battalion performed all combat missions in the Normandy, Northern France, Ardennes, Rhineland and Central European Campaigns.

The 413th AAA Gun Battalion landed on Omaha Beach, Normandy, France as part of Assault Force 'O' on 6 June 1944 under withering hostile artillery and small arms fire, and fought its way to positions near St. Laurent-sur-Mere. Due to the Battalion being the only artillery ashore for the first few days of the invasion, and with no aerial targets presenting themselves during daylight hours, the 413th AAA Gun Battalion devoted itself to effectively supporting the troops of the 2nd Infantry Division in their attack on Trevieres and smashed two hostile tank and troop concentrations in Cerisy Forest in so doing. . . The experience gained in the first few days on the Beach Head, against tanks, led to the Battalion being attached to the 3rd Armored Division, in a Tank Destroyer role early in July 1944, and remaining in this capacity for two months, participating in the two spearhead thrusts which liberated Avranches and Granville. . . During the Allied race through France, Belgium, Holland into the heart of Germany, the Battalion moved aggressively and progressively forward, participating in the St. Lo Breakthrough, the defeat of the Mortain-Vire German counter offensive, the vital crossings of the Seine, Aisne, Meuse, Roer, Rhine and Weser Rivers. . .The termination of hostilities on 9 May 1945 found the Battalion on the Weser River, well on the road to Berlin, with the record that no objective defended by it, from the initial assault of the Normany Beaches to the Weser River had been damaged by aerial attack. During the European Campaign the 413th AAA Gun Battalion performed all missions in a superior manner; had 427 aerial engagements, destroying 62 hostile planes; had 50 ground engagements, destroying 16 tanks, 160 armored and motor vehicles, as well as innumerable gun positions, bunkers, ammunition and supply dumps, and occupied places. The Battalion delivered 42 concentrations in support of assaulting infantry with excellent results destroying over 600 enemy ground personnel, capturing over 900 prisoners and greatly facilitating the advance of front line Infantry.

The fighting instincts, esprit de corps, and effective aggressiveness of the officers and men of the 413th AAA Gun Battalion during the most critical battles of the European Campaign redounds to the glory of the Battalion as a whole, and reflects the leadership, high degree of personal courage, and tactical and technical skill of Lt. Col. Donald MacGrain, who led the Battalion in the greatest military campaigns of all time."

★★★

NONAR COUCH was born July 22, 1920 in Annona, Texas, the son of Ira and Mattie Couch. He had two brothers, Herman and Arvil Lee, and two sisters, Mildred and Helen. He married Ida Smith and their children are Shirley, Noman, Ruby, Dorothy, Rickey, Kenneth, Herman and Judy.

Nonar was inducted into the Army on August 14, 1942 at Tyler, Texas. His basic training was at Alexandria, Louisiana, and he was a Gun Crewman Artillery (Sharpshooter) in the SV Battery, 666th Field Artillery Battalion. Pvt. Couch served overseas in Central Europe, Ardennes and Rhineland. He was discharged November 26, 1945 at Ft. Sam Houston, Texas and was awarded the American Theater Campaign Medal, EAME Campaign Medal with three Bronze Stars, Good Conduct Medal, two Overseas Service Bars, one Service Stripe, and the Victory Ribbon.

★★★

MOWERY WAYNE VICKERS was born January 22, 1924 in Clarksville, Texas. His parents were Henry Wyatt and Enie Morgan Vickers, and his brothers and sisters were H. W., Thelma, Jonnie, Pat, and Kenneth.

He married Louise Ferguson, and they had two children, Mark and Dane.

Cpl. Vickers volunteered for the Army Air Corps in January 1943 at Corpus Christi. His training was at Ft. Sam Houston, Texas and Chanute Field, Illinois. He was an Aircraft Hydraulic Specialist and processed aircraft to be sent to Russia while stationed at Fairbanks, Alaska. He was discharged in November 1945 at Shreveport, La. and was awarded a Sharpshooter Medal, Alaskan Campaign Ribbon, and Good Conduct Medal.

★★★

DARRELL S. WARD was born July 6, 1918, and his parents were Robert Andrew and Maud Lou Butts Ward. The other children in the family were Arden, Elgin, Jewel, Robert, Jr. and Fay.

When Company I, Third Battalion, 144th Infantry, a part of the National Guard, was mobilized and sent to Camp Bowie in Brownwood, Texas on November 23, 1940, S/Sgt. Ward was the Mess Sergeant. He stayed in the service until he was discharged on September 23, 1945 at Camp Rucker, Alabama and was awarded a Good Conduct Medal, Expert Rifleman Medal, and ETO Medal.

★★★

Robert C. (Bob) and Rena Gladys Moore Hulen had two sons who served in World War II. They also had a daughter, Sally. The family lived on their farm at Aikin Grove, south of Clarksville, and the land still remains in the family.

ROBERT ALLEN HULEN, better known as "Slim", was born March 19, 1920. He and Mary LaNell ("Red") Whiteman were married almost forty-seven years when she died in April 1993. On July 26, 1997 Slim and Ella Mae Todd May were married and reside at Madras, southeast of Clarksville on the land that Slim and Red purchased from her father in 1950. This was her grandfather's place, where her parents had lived, but the house burned during the war. On the wall hangs a Family Land Heritage Certificate of Honor, Rocking H Ranch, 1852, which reads: "For a century or more of continuous ownership and operation as a family agricultural enterprise. To the dedication and perseverance of the founders and heirs of these lands, we owe the basic wealth of Texas." (Signed by John C. White, Commissioner, Texas Department of Agriculture) We visited with Slim and Ella Mae in their home on February 9, 2000 and listened as Slim told about his brother, John Wallace, and himself during World War II.

Slim entered the Army on February 11, 1942 in Red River County. He had this to say: "My basic training was at Camp Polk, Louisiana and then at Camp Coxcomb, California and Ft. Benning, Georgia. While at Camp Polk in February and March there were a good many boys from the Northeast who had a hard time with the weather and had red faces from blistering in the sun. They had never heard of chiggers, and while on maneuvers, they really found out about them.

I was in the service two years before my brother was drafted, and I never really thought that John would be called. While in Europe John and I were lucky enough to see each other two different times. I drove a long way just to visit with my brother for a few minutes. John came over one time and spent the night with me.

On June 4, 1944 my Division sailed on the *Queen Mary*, a troop ship so big that it was like being in a big city where you could easily get lost. There were 17,000 in my Division and even more than that on the ship. It took only five days to cross the Atlantic and land in England where we stayed a month. When we came back after the war, it was on a liberty ship, and it took two weeks. From England we went to France, Holland, Belgium and Germany, where we were when the war in Europe ended.

I served in the Military Police where I directed traffic, transported prisoners and guarded Two Star General Hasbrook. His jeep driver spoke German, which was really a help, and we went where the troops were. There wasn't too much traffic in France, but I stood on a corner and motioned vehicles by while the General was inside a building. I was in the Third Armored Division which later was formed into the Seventh Armored Division.

One time when we were delivering prisoners, it was so dark, we couldn't read our maps because we only had the 'cat eyes' on our vehicle for light. We were stranded because a bridge had been blown up. It took the engineers all night to repair it. We unloaded the prisoners. Low on drinking water. There was a German Sergeant among the prisoners who could speak English because he had lived in Houston at one time. I told him what I wanted done, and he would instruct the prisoners. There was no trouble. On the way back, almost in the Argonne Forest, some Germans gave us a bunch of beef. At this point we met another Jeep with a Major and a Captain in it. I asked the Major to advise us if it was safe to go up to the top of the hill to see if we could go back that way. He said we could go, but the Captain in the back seat shook his head 'no'. We stayed in the forest and shared the meat with others. An Armored Division moved at a fast pace so it took a while to get back to our own Division.

Before the war was over, the Division had contact with German officials who agreed to surrender many troops. The communication lines were down so my crew and I went with the Chief of Staff, a Colonel, to the German camp. There were soldiers everywhere, and the interpreter helped negotiate the surrender. My driver and I went back and forth to radio what was going on and to take messages back to the Colonel. Then the negotiation stopped, no talk at all. It was scary. A General from Tennessee told us not to worry because the U.S. would be on that German camp in a minute if they tried to do anything. Eventually, we were waved on and when we returned, we tied a white flag to the jeep's antenna. The Germans filled the Jeep with their rifles. This surrender was bigger than anticipated, the beginning of the end. A short time later the war was over.

Hearing the war was over was a gradual thing. The first indication was when we were given three day passes. I drew one for Paris, France and came back on a German train that was as uncomfortable as a wagon. I looked out the windows and saw German soldiers giving themselves up to the Allies. There was a big open field, a hay meadow, where people were coming on foot and on bikes to surrender. We sent the prisoners back as fast as we could to a place on the Baltic Sea.

My Division started breaking up and went back to Belgium. The General gave members of his personal staff a watch and shook hands with us. We lived like kings for two weeks while we were waiting for a boat to go home on. We ate and slept and were fed real well. I was sent back to the U.S. with a thirty day furlough. The South Pacific was our next destination, but I kept thinking that I had a good many points and might not have to go. Then the war ended in the South Pacific. I originally left from New York but landed back in Boston. I had looked for this for a lifetime, four years. I was awarded an ETO Ribbon, Good Conduct Medal and Bronze Medal with four Battle Stars." (After returning to Red River County, Slim rodeoed and ranched. In 1947 he became a Deputy Sheriff and was elected Sheriff from 1957 to 1964. He retired April 1, 1988 after serving as a Special Texas Ranger with the Texas and Southwest Cattle Raisers Association. Since then he has continued raising cattle.)

JOHN WALLACE HULEN, son of Robert C. (Bob) and Rena Gladys Moore Hulen, and brother of Robert Allen (Slim) and Sally, was born January 5, 1926.

John was drafted into the Army in 1944 when he was only eighteen years old. He was in the 69th Infantry Battalion and trained at Camp Hood, Texas and Camp Shelby, Mississippi. John and those who trained with him served in England, France, Belgium, Germany and Holland as replacements. They were in big battles, but he only received a scratch on his leg from shrapnel. As mentioned earlier, he and his brother, Slim, met up with each other twice in Europe. John was not bitter or scared about the battles he was in. One of his buddies asked him, 'How can you be so calm?' John replied that he knew he had to do it!

John died on September 27, 1945 in Brelzfield, Germany, after the war was over, when an ammunition dump exploded. His body was returned with a military escort in the latter part of 1947. Burial was at the Aikin Grove Cemetery south of Clarksville in the community where he had been born and raised. A good friend, Jake Holster, brought John's saddled pony, Smokey, to the cemetery. The military escort gave John's mother a United States Flag.

At the time of John's death, his brother, Slim, was on a boat coming home from Europe. He landed in Boston and then went to San Antonio to be discharged there from the Army. He was anxious to get home to Red River County. There was a young man with a car who gave soldiers rides to Dallas for $10.00 each. When Slim arrived at the Dallas Bus Station, he saw Ruby Dycus who had been visiting in Clarksville and was on her way back to San Antonio. She told him how sorry she was to hear of his brother's death, and that was how Slim learned about it. All the way home on that bus he dreaded facing his parents.

The Hulens kept John's '33 Chevrolet in their garage for ten years and then decided to let someone else have it. John was a Calf Roper before going into the service. Slim and his wife, Ella Mae, are trying to find a silhouette of a cowboy roping a calf to put on his grave stone at the Aikin Grove Cemetery. John Wallace Hulen was awarded the Good Conduct Medal, Combat Infantry Badge, ETO Ribbon with two Battle Stars, and the Purple Heart posthumously.

★★★

HUB (HERBERT LOMAN) WHITEMAN, the son of Squire Loman (Babe) and Dora Francis McGill Whiteman, was born in Red River County in 1910. His brothers and sisters were Sis, Kate, Jim, Winfred and Mary LaNell. He married Marie Benningfield, and they had no children.

Hub entered the Army in 1942 and trained at Camp Howze, Texas. He was in the Military Police in Europe and was discharged in 1945. He was awarded the EAME Medal, American Theater

Medal with one Bronze Star, Victory Ribbon and Good Conduct Medal. Hub died in 1977, but his widow, Marie, still lives in Clarksville.

Hub was a well known rodeo participant, having been the World Champion Bull Dogger in 1941. He later rode broncos and became an Amateur Champion Bronco Rider. Through the years he owned several "bull dogging" horses, but his favorite was a little mare named "Ruby". When he went into the Army, he sold her to another cowboy. After coming home from the war, Hub bought a fine young horse from Bill Likins' ranch in Oklahoma. For a while he rode that horse which was really better than "Ruby". Finally, in 1949 he bought "Ruby" back, but then later on when he was coming back into town from a rodeo, he ran off the road, and her neck was broken.

At that time the McKenzie United Memorial Methodist Church in Clarksville had a pastor named Richard Irwin. Richard, as he was called by everyone, served here from 1945 to 1950. A young man, probably in his late 20's or early 30's, the Rev. Irwin was of a new generation, a breed apart. When Hub's horse died, she was buried on the north end of Hub's place in the country. A graveside service was conducted by Richard, and he later remarked that there were more cowboys there than in his church on Sunday.

★★★

ARDELL D. EMERY was born March 8, 1920 in Red River County, the son of Aaron Lewis and Marna Bowman Emery. Ardell was a retired farmer and rancher and died October 26, 1999. He was preceded in death by his wife, Romie Tolison Emery, who died in 1991. They had one son, Bruce, who resides with his family in Clarksville.

Ardell entered the Army in 1943, trained at Camp Wolters, Texas and Fort Chaffee, Arkansas and served in the European Theater. He was a prisoner of war of the Germans for several months. Upon his discharge in 1945, he was awarded the Combat Infantry Badge, ATO Ribbon, EAME Ribbon with three Bronze Stars and the Victory Medal.

★★★

I visited with Billie Bishop, the widow of Robert Bishop, in

Bogata, Texas, and she was very helpful in giving me information about the two Bishop brothers who were in World War II. Romulus and Dixie Horner Bishop had four children, Robert, Roma, Edna, and William Horner (Bill). Mrs. Bishop died in 1923, leaving Mr. Bishop with four small children to raise. He then married Virginia Howison who was a good step-mother to them. There was one child born to that marriage, a daughter, who died at birth.

WILLIAM HORNER (BILL) BISHOP was born May 19, 1921 and married Betty Thomas September 7, 1940.

He entered the Army Air Corps in January 1942, trained in Missouri, Texas and Florida, and was commissioned 2nd Lieutenant at Foster Field in February 1943. A newspaper clipping reads as follows: "W. R. Bishop of Bogata has received word from the War Department that his son, Lieutenant William H. (Bill) Bishop, was killed in action over Italy on January 22, 1944. He served in Africa, Sicily, and Italy. Lt. Bishop was awarded the Air Medal with four Oak Leaf Clusters and the Purple Heart posthumously. He went overseas in May 1943 and served as a Fighter Pilot."

ROBERT BISHOP was born December 31, 1913 in Titus County, Texas. He and Berniece (Billie) Franklin were married December 17, 1943 and had two daughters, Melanie and Pene who spent twenty years in the Air Force and retired in 1988 as a Major.

Robert enlisted in the Army in 1935 at Ft. Sill, Oklahoma and was in the Reserves when war broke out. While at Ft. Sill he was in the horse-drawn artillery. (At some time he was an MP, an expert in 50-caliber machine guns, and was asked to remain in the states as an instructor in machine guns.) He was called back into the service in 1941 and chose to be in the Army Air Corps. He served for 9 years, 9 months and 29 days (his words) in the two branches of service. During the war he was an Aircraft Armament Technician and Aerial Gunner in a B-25 Mitchell medium bombardment group in the Mediterranean Theater. His overseas duty was in Corsica, Italy and France. He wanted to see action because his younger brother, Bill, was a pilot in fighter planes and was missing in action at the time Robert was sent overseas. Robert's father wanted to keep him from going into combat, but Robert did not go for that. He flew on seventy missions and was discharged in 1945. He received a Presidential Unit Citation, ETO Medal with three stars, and an Air Medal with six clusters. (While Robert was in the service, his wife and his sister, Roma, both worked in defense plants to help the war effort. A woman who did that was often referred to as "Rosie the Riveter".)

After the war there was a housing famine in Texas. Real estate people refused to allow children in many of their buildings. The Bishop's daughter, born in December 1945, was the cause of their having to buy a house which a "just returned" veteran found difficult to do while trying to find a job and to put his life back on track.

"*Men of the 57th*", an Official Newspaper published at the time of his death said: "TAPS—Robert Bishop—On September 27, 1988 death released Robert Bishop from the disabilities forced upon him nearly two years ago by a massive stroke. He is survived by his wife, Billie, a daughter, Melanie, who lives in Bogata, and a second daughter, Major Pene Bishop USAF (ret).

Among Robert Bishop's things we found some information about the 57th Bomb Wing which reads as follows: "The 57th Bomb Wing was a medium bomber combat unit with the 12th Air Force during WWII. Operating largely in the Mediterranean Theater, the Wing earned a reputation as 'bridge busters' as a result of its bombing in the Po River Valley and along the Brenner Line in Northern Italy. Long before this, however, the Wing fought over North Africa and Sicily and aided in such invasions as North Africa, Sicily, Salerno, Anzio and Southern France. In fact, no combat wing in the ETO participated in more invasions than the 57th.

The 57th also played a vital role in the advance of General Mark Clark's Fifth Army from Southern Italy to the hills of Lombardy. Two pilots of the 57th, Fred Dyer and George Wells, each flew 102 combat missions, a record for World War II medium bomber pilots. . . . One of the most important roles in the Mediterranean theater campaigns was played in aerial warfare by the 57th Bomb Wing, a command composed of B-25 Mitchell medium bombers, some of which began their combat history as early as the first landing in North Africa in November 1942. Since that time, the B-25's participated in every major campaign from Tunisia to the final drive resulting in the unconditional surrender of all German armies in North Italy. . . During this time the Mitchells flew 165,573 combat flying hours. . . Shortly before the final drive in Italy, the Wing swiftly moved into northern Italy and when D-Day came, it found them preparing to put up the greatest effort ever known on the part of

William Horner (Bill) Bishop with his squadron (He is on the bottom row, fourth from the left)

medium bombers. In April 4,638 sorties were flown in close support of the British 8th and American 5th Army troops with attacks on enemy troop concentrations, supplies, defense area, and communications. It was fitting, indeed, when the B-25's flew their final missions—those of dropping leaflets on the enemy announcing the unconditional surrender of the German armies in Italy."[5]

Bridgebuster I published a story entitled "Ed and I, the Saga of a 487th B-25 named McKinley Junior High". This tale came to the attention of leaders at McKinley Jr. High School in Muncie, Indiana. The following article entitled "Thirty-six Years Later—Saga of McKinley's War Bomber", written for the Muncie School's magazine, brings to a close this exciting story of an important World War II vignette.

"After a diligent search through records and memories, faded and dusty with time, a veteran pilot of World War II has finally written the ending of a story that began thirty-six years ago in the former McKinley Junior High School. The story began in 1942 while the war was raging across Europe and the South Pacific. Allied troops had scored some successes after June's Battle of Midway, and skirmishes across the continent and Africa had turned in their favor.

And back home in Indiana the war effort on the home front went on in earnest in support of the fighting men. Citizens rallied in spite of meat rationing, oil rationing, and the hardships of war. But probably no one had rallied to the cause more than students and faculty at McKinley, who had united themselves in spirit to those on the front by selling war bonds and stamps. The Treasury Department's War Savings Staff, in charge of selling war bonds to finance the costly battles abroad, had come up with a special event called the 'Buy the Bomber Campaign'. Any state, county, city or organization could have a bomber named in its honor by selling a certain quota of war bonds. This special promotion proved to be one of the most successful incentives for bond sales to that date all over the U.S.

McKinley Junior High School decided to meet the challenge. In order to 'buy the bomber', the school had to raise, through bond sales, $75,000 for a pursuit ship plane, $175,000 for a medium bomber, or $300,000 for a heavy bomber within a designated period of time and only for that specific purpose.

Richard Hunt, social science teacher and student council advisor had initiated the correspondence with the War Savings Staff for involvement in the campaign and sponsored the bond selling efforts. Principal Charles G. Hampton and school clerk, Jane Harris, put in a good deal of time for the sales drive and kept county, state and federal offices up to date on the school's progress. Fred McKinley... was only a beginning teacher in 1942. He remembered though that the students worked hard selling bonds to parents, people in the community, indeed to anyone they or the school staff could find who was willing to support their monumental undertaking. He recalled that at the time, McKinley housed 7th, 8th, and 9th grade classes or some 1,100 to 1,200 students.

From September 14, 1942 to April 23, 1943, the school finally raised $219,997.85 in war bonds and stamps—an amount well over the minimum for the two-engine bomber. It meant the name of McKinley Junior High would soon be sent across the continents in honor of the school's dedicated efforts... Not until the summer of 1978, almost forty years later, did the successors to those students and teachers learn of the bomber's fate. Harry D. George, co-pilot of the plane, sent a letter to McKinley Middle School in July, ending at last the tale of the bomber that gave McKinley national recognition...

According to Lt. George's accounts, at 7:35 on June 22, 1944, the McKinley Junior High went down in the mountains between the cities of Bologna and Florence, Italy. Two men went down with the plane. Of the four men who jumped from the burning plane, Radio Gunner Sgt. Ahistrom jumped without a parachute, and Machine Gunner Sgt. Obravatz was captured by the Germans and was a POW. The third, Bombadier Lt. Dombrowski was captured but later escaped and fought for 50 days in Italy. The fourth man, Lt. George, landed about 200 miles behind enemy lines near the Italian town of Barberino di Mugello. The townspeople, in spite of danger to themselves, hid the co-pilot from the Germans for three months until he was able to make contact with American troops and return to the States.

Lt. George's letter went on: 'The plane and crew served in the 487th Squadron of the 340th Bomb Group of the 57th Bomb Wing of the 12th Air Force stationed in 1944 on the island of Corsica for the purpose of the invasion of Italy and France during the last phases of the war... The groups mentioned above served admirably and

487TH BOMB SQUADRON (M)

1942 — 1945

NORTH AFRICA · SICILY · CORSICA · ITALY

A B-25 with "Lady Luck" in a four leaf clover on the side.

well during the conflict and bestowed honor on those connected with them in whatever manner.'

Had the group at McKinley known of the exploits of the bomber they had worked so hard to buy and the victory it had helped to win during World War II, they would certainly have accepted the honor . . . bestowed upon them with pride and satisfaction. Thus the story of the plane that bore the name of McKinley Junior High School high over the troubled skies of Europe is now complete. And yet it is really not ended because the story of McKinley Junior High, its students of the past, their plane and its crew, the students of today and tomorrow, and all their achievements, goes on as always, bringing honor to Muncie itself."

★★★

JIMMIE LEE DICKERSON was born June 28, 1925 in Clarksville, Texas, the son of Louie and Maggie Gray Ricks Dickerson. He had two sisters, Dorothy and Gearldine. He married Eula M. Edwards and they had no children. He entered the Army in October 1943 and took his training at Camp Wolters, Texas and in Columbia, South Carolina. He was a PFC, a truck driver, and went overseas to Germany. He was discharged May 5, 1946 at Ft. Smith, Arkansas.

★★★

IRA D. (DICK) USSERY was born July 21, 1926 in Clarksville, Texas, the son of Dewitt and Maud Ivy Ussery. The first son born in the family died at birth. Dick had one sister, Bobbye Jean. He entered the Army in 1945 and trained at Ft. Hood, Texas. Dick was my cousin, as our mothers were sisters, but I was unable to find many details about his service. His sister and I remember that he did office work and was stationed in Indiana. She and their mother made the trip up there to see him, the adventure of a lifetime for her as a young girl. She recalls that the train was full of sleeping servicemen. After the war Dick married Peggy Cass. Their children are Richard, Barbara and Marian. He died December 2, 1984.

★★★

W. D. (DUB) RHODES was born in Cisco, Texas on May 9, 1919, the son of Walter Harvey and Alma Mae Ray Rhodes, and he has a sister, Alice. He married Carolyn Ruth Wilhite in the Army Chapel in San Luis Obispo, California on May 18, 1942. The Army Chaplain who performed the ceremony, with their families present, was from Mexia, Texas. Their three children are Charles Reynolds, Carole Lynne and Rhonda Lucille.

Dub was in Medical School at Baylor University when the war broke out in December 1941 and volunteered for the service that month, entering at Ft. Sill, Oklahoma. His training was at the Medical Training Centers at Camp Grant, Illinois and Camp San Luis Obispo, California. He was a 1st Lieutenant in charge of laboratory personnel, and when he was preparing to go overseas, he was sent to Camp Barkley in Abilene, Texas instead where he stayed for two years. While there Dub worked with Dr. J. L. Wright who was the head of the hospital. At that time Dr. Wright and Dr. C. B. Reed were partners in a medical clinic in Clarksville. After consulting with Dr. Reed, Dr. Wright offered Dub a job with them as Laboratory Technician when the war ended. The Rhodes moved to Clarksville in 1946 where they remain today after retirement.

★★★

BRUCE M. BLAND, JR. entered the Army Air Corps in 1942 when he was only seventeen years old. At the time, he was a student at Paris Junior College in Paris, Texas. His parents were Bruce M. and Dolly Roberson Bland, and he had a sister, Marguerite.

Bruce's training was at the Air Force Southeastern Training Command in Alabama, Georgia, Tennessee and Mississippi. He graduated as a Fighter Pilot and then was a Bomber Pilot on a B-17. There were eleven crewmen, and Cab Wolf was the Turret Gunner on the plane. Bruce served in the U.S. and was at Lincoln, Nebraska preparing to go overseas when the war ended. He was discharged in 1945 at Maxwell Field, Alabama and was awarded the Victory Medal, ATO Medal and Good Conduct Medal. He remained in the Air Force Reserves for seventeen years after the war. He makes his home in the McCoy Community.

★★★

RICHARD EARL NANCE was born December 7, 1922 in Lamar County. His parents were Sidney R. and Ola Bramlett Nance. He had one brother, Elbert, and three sisters, Eva, Leola, and Audrey. In 1945 he married Helen Hoffman in Port Orchard, Washington, and she preceded him in death in 1992. He married Clara Reeder Storey on April 29, 1994 in Paris, Texas. He had two step-children, Steve Storey and Shelly Storey Field. Richard died March 23, 2000. I had contacted him about my book and enjoyed talking with him over the telephone. He sent me some information which I relate here, along with some things from his obituary that was in the *Bogata News*.

Richard enlisted in the U.S. Coast Guard in October 1942 at Wichita Falls, Texas and was a Gunners Mate, 2nd Class. He was discharged April 1946 but re-enlisted in December 1951 at Seattle, Washington during the Korean Conflict. When he was discharged the second time in December 1954, he was a Gunners Mate, 1st Class. His job in the Coast Guard was to keep the ship's guns operational and to train gun crews. In World War II he served aboard the *USS Patrol Frigate Sandusky* for over three years. He was awarded ribbons for the American Area Campaign, Pacific Area Campaign, Philippine Liberation with two Stars, WWII Victory Medal and Good Conduct Medal. During the Korean Conflict he served three years aboard the Coast Guard Cutter, *USS Klamath*. He received the Korean Service Medal, National Defense Service Medal, United Nations Service Medal and the Expert Rifle and Pistol Medal. He retired in 1982 as a Senior Staff Supervisor Equipment Specialist for the 96th U.S. Army Reserve Command, Ft. Douglas, Utah with thirty years total military service.

Richard wrote an article which was published in the *Bogata News* in November 1999. I quote one part of that article here: "Most history books tell about the battles between the Battle Wagons, Cruisers, and Aircraft Carriers with those of the enemy. Little, however, is told about the smaller ships that provided support against the enemy submarines and aircraft. Small ships had to take only one hit to be sunk, and many were lost in typhoons in the Pacific. The Atlantic waters off the coast of the U.S. were patrolled by cutters, frigates and dirigibles to seek and destroy submarines. The shoreline was patrolled day and night by men on foot, some with dogs. . . The enemy submarines sometimes evaded the patrol ships at sea and got in close to shore to put off spies and saboteurs. Many of them were captured after they reached shore by those on shore patrol duty. At this time, I would like to salute and thank all Veterans and service persons who have served our great country."

★★★

CARL PARRIS, son of N. J. and Lula McDaniels Parris, was born October 20, 1925, in Gainesville, Texas. He had six sisters and one brother. He married Nancy Roberts, and they have three sons, Carl David, Tom and Steve. Carl was drafted into the Army in November 1943 at Dallas and was trained at Camp Hood, Texas. He was a part of the 562nd Amphibious Engineers and drove a landing barge to pick up supplies. He was a PFC and served on Leyte and in the Philippines. He was discharged in August 1946 at San Luis Obispo, California and received a Sharp Shooter Medal. Carl and Nancy are retired and live in Clarksville.

★★★

JAMES HAROLD WATSON, son of Jim and Alice Watson Watson, was born January 25, 1922. He was in the Army in the Infantry during World War II. He was overseas in Germany when the war ended and stayed one year after that to serve as a guard on a supply train. His sisters, Hazel Quick and Ramah Ward, gave me this information, and it is really all they could recall about his service time.

★★★

ODELL RICKS, son of Tom and Malisa Dixon Ricks, was born February 9, 1918. His brothers were Will, Richard, Eddie, A. J., and L.V., and his sisters were Ruby, Maggie, and Cornilia. He married Ora Lee Woodson, and their children are Odessa, William C., Pauline and Dennis K.

Odell entered the Army on January 29, 1944 and trained at Camp Wolters, Camp Swift, Ft. Sill and Ft. Bragg as a Truck Driver. He was a Corporal and served in Okinawa and Korea and was discharged December 16, 1945 at Ft. Sam Houston, Texas. He was awarded the American Theater Campaign Medal, Asiatic-Pacific Medal with one Bronze Star, Good Conduct Medal, Victory Ribbon, and one Overseas Service Bar.

★★★

HAROLD PORTERFIELD was one of eight children born to H. S. and Irene Williams Porterfield. He was born March 7, 1915 in Clarksville, Texas. He married Hazel Bean and they had two children, Michael Ray (Mickey) and Linda Sue. Harold entered the Army on October 12, 1942 at Tyler, Texas and was a Pvt. who served in the Infantry as a Rifleman. After he was discharged at Camp Adair, Oregon, he returned to Clarksville. He died February 24, 1982.

★★★

ALVIN EUGENE SHADID was born October 21, 1923 in Clarksville, Texas. His parents were John and Ethel Straub Shadid, and he had two sisters, Kathryn and Elizabeth. He married Charlene Williams. His children are Glen, Deana and David Shadid and John A. Laster.

He enlisted in the Army in 1943 at Clarksville and took his training at Ellington Air Field. As a Corporal he served in Belgium, the Battle of the Bulge, Normandy, Northern France, Ardennes, Rhineland and Central Europe. He was discharged January 4, 1946 at Ft. Sam Houston, Texas and was awarded the EAME Campaign Medal with five bronze stars, Good Conduct Medal, Victory Ribbon and three Overseas Service Bars. At the time of his death on March 13, 1999, he was retired and living in Clarksville. Charlene preceded him in death. (His sister, Elizabeth Murphy, said this: "I know that anyone who lived through World War II, as we did, was never the same.")

★★★

THOMAS WREN was born in Clarksville, Texas on October 14, 1924. His parents were Mack and Allie Maud Gaines Wren, and he had one brother, Richard Dean (Dick). On December 13, 1975 Thomas and Wilma Tucker Humphrey were married and made their home in Clarksville. He was a mail carrier for thirty-two years before his retirement. Thomas died November 9, 1997, and Wilma remains here.

He volunteered for the Marines at Dallas, Texas, and since he was not quite eighteen years old, his parents had to give written permission for him to join. He was discharged a short time later because of his eyesight. He waited and volunteered on March 29,

1943 for the Army, and his training was at Camp Hood, Texas. He served in France, Austria and Germany in the Combat Infantry. In Austria it snowed all winter and was so cold that they almost froze to the ground. Thomas remarked one time that he would like to visit Austria instead of going through the country like he did on his belly. He was discharged in 1945 and was awarded the Combat Infantry Badge, ETO Medal, Victory Medal with three Battle Stars and a Good Conduct Medal.

★★★

PLES COLLINS was born March 7, 1922 in Bowie County, Texas, the son of William Howard and Ida Bell Collins. He had six brothers and two sisters, James Mick, Howard, Norman, Earnestine, James Lawrence, Amos, Catherine and Henry. Ples and Bennie Jean Moore were married December 21, 1945. He had just returned from WWII; they met one Friday night and married the next Friday night. Their children are Debra Jean, Ples Ricky and Nadra June. Ples died August 27, 1999 and was preceded in death by his wife of 49 years.

An article by John Fooks entitled "WWII Vet Recalls Infamous March" in the Texarkana Gazette dated November 27, 1993 reads in part as follows:

"Some things are just too horrible to talk about! Ask almost any ex-prisoner of war who did time in a Japanese prison camp during World War II. He may talk about general experiences POW's shared, but most won't go into the details.

'There are some things that shouldn't be mentioned,' said Ples Collins of Nash, a survivor of three and a half years in prison camps in the Philippines and Japan. . . As a medical technician for the Army Air Corps, Collins saw more than his share of the atrocities of war. He was stationed at Fort William McKinley in the Philippines when the war started on Dec. 7, 1941. On Dec. 24, Christmas Eve, he and others got on barges destined for Bataan where he was assigned to a general hospital and worked in different units during the next eight months. On April 9, 1942 the commanding officer at the hospital told the hospital employees the island was about to be overrun by Japanese and that they could leave if they wanted to. The commander said he was staying, and his men stayed with him, including Collins.

'We were captured that day', Collins said. 'We stayed there about four months until the patients could be moved. Then we moved to Camp O'Donnell prison camp on Luzon Island.' Collins was a prisoner there for the next year, serving as a medical technician. When he first arrived, there were about 20,000 prisoners of war in the camp, and no running water to speak of. There was only one water hydrant, and men had to stand in line literally three or four days to get a canteen of water. . . Collins was constantly busy. He also had to serve on burial details and once helped bury 375 men in one day. 'We had to crawl under buildings to get some of them out', he said. 'It was really bad, but there were some things that were worse that don't need to be mentioned.'

Collins was one of the last to leave the camp when it was shut down by the Japanese. He was moved to a camp on Luzon where he stayed about three weeks before being transferred to another camp for about six months. Then he was transferred back to the second camp for another six or eight months. In March 1944 he was taken to a camp in northern Japan where he stayed for more than a year.

'It was bad no matter which camp you were in. When I got to that last camp, I didn't work as a medical technician any more. I worked in the ore mines. Sometimes the snow was ten feet deep', he said. Collins labored in the mines until September 1945. Then one day the regular guards simply disappeared and young Japanese boys were brought in to guard the prisoners. The men heard the war was over, and one morning Collins and eighteen others walked out of the camp and climbed on a train headed for Tokyo. . . They stayed on the train until they arrived in Yokohama where they found Americans. Like most POW's, Collins spent the next several weeks in hospitals. . . He returned to his hometown of Texarkana in October 1945. Collins is a member of the Four States Chapter of the American Ex-Prisoners of War, a support group for ex-POW's from any war."

★★★

CECIL BEAN, son of Arley and Velma Blankenship Bean was born February 7, 1918 in Red River County. He had three sisters, Hazel, Pauline and Sarah and two brothers, Bobby and George Mac. He married Johnnie Lee Humphrey and they had two sons, Eddie and Larry. Cecil entered the Army on November 30, 1940, part of

Company I, 144th Infantry Division and went to Brownwood, Texas. He was a PFC, worked in the kitchen, and served in the South Pacific. He was discharged at San Francisco on December 7, 1945 and returned to Clarksville. Cecil died February 15, 1985, and his wife died in February 2000.

★★★

GEORGE R. SMITH was born August 19, 1928 in Bogata, Texas. His parents were George L. and Peral Gray Smith, and he had one sister, Dorothy. He and Wilma J. Cleaver married and had two children, George R., Jr. and Barbara G. He enlisted in the Army Air Corps on November 7, 1945 at Bogata and became an Airborne Radio Operator in Air Traffic Control. He was a CMSGT and served in Italy during the war. He retired from the service on February 1, 1969 at Del Rio, Texas.

★★★

JETT WARD was born January 3, 1899 in Red River County, the son of James Henry and Nola Etta Winders Ward. The other children in his family were Minnie, Edith, Myrtle, Corley, Charley and Elizabeth. He and Ramah Watson were married December 2, 1946, and he had two step-children, Betty and Billy DeShazer. Jett was in the National Guard when the war started and went on active duty June 17, 1942, working in mail distribution. He was discharged at Ft. Ord, California June 25, 1945, and returned to Clarksville where he lived until his death March 17, 1972.

★★★

WILLIAM L. FINLEY, the son of William F. and Oneida Taylor Finley, was born November 1, 1923. He had three brothers, David, James and John and one sister, Imogene. Bill entered the Army in 1943 and trained at Camp Toccoa and Ft. Benning, Georgia and Camp Mackall, North Carolina. He was a paratrooper and served in Italy, France, Belgium and Germany. He was discharged in 1945 and awarded the Expert Combat Infantry Badge, Parachutist Wings, ETO Ribbon with five Battle Stars and a Good Conduct Medal. He was living in Clarksville at the time of his death April 16, 1997.

★★★

ROBERT CAREY WOOLEY entered the Army in 1942 and trained at Camp Wallace, Texas. He served in the South Philippines, West Pacific and Ryukyus. He was discharged in 1946 and awarded a Good Conduct Medal, APO with three Battle Stars, Philippine Liberation Ribbon with one Star, and Victory Medal with one service stripe. His parents were Francis Marion and Bonnie Dixie Gray Wooley, and he had two brothers, Frank Dixon and James Harold, and one sister, Mamie Estelle. He and Imogene Finley married and had one son, William Marion. The Wooleys live on their ranch in Red River County.

★★★

JOHN M. HOWISON said the following about his experiences in World War II:

"In my fourth semester at Kilgore Junior College, I told my draft board that I was ready to go, and on April 9, 1943, aged 18, I was given a bus ticket to Camp Wolters at Mineral Wells and was sworn in. I believe that I was less motivated by patriotism than by a sense that I would be out of step with my generation if I 'missed going to war'. I knew nobody who did not believe that the United States was on the side of right.

At the Camp Wolters reception center we were introduced to military discipline and close-order drill and were given several tests to determine what the Army would do with us. We were allowed to express preferences—mine were for infantry (the real thing), paratroops (manly and exciting), and for the Army Air Corps' aviation cadet program, where you might learn to fly and could become an officer. I became an aviation cadet and in June of 1944, I graduated as a Navigator and Second Lieutenant. After assignment to a B-24 crew and undergoing some training with the crew, we crossed the Atlantic on a 'Liberty Ship' stacked in bunks five deep in a cargo hold, landed in Naples, and went by train to Puglia and the 460th Bomb Group at Spinazzola.

On December 9 my B-24J was shot up over Vienna and tried to make it to the Russian lines some 120 miles to the east. Near the town of Dobra Voda in what is now Slovakia, we were losing altitude and trailing fire, so we were ordered to bail out. Of the crew of ten, five were picked up by Czech partisans and joined their ranks, and five, including me, were made prisoners. After being put through the interrogation center at Uberursel, where I was slightly wounded, we were sent to spend a cold winter at Stalag Luft I at Barth, on the Baltic Sea. When Russian forces approached and the Germans reduced their guard to a minimum, our own chain of command ordered us to stay put and await evacuation. A few of us were foolish and restless enough to risk court martial and swam out of the camp to start walking westward toward allied lines. I was evacuated to a hospital in the English midlands and spent a few weeks in London before taking another 'Liberty Ship' for home and discharge.

Having been informed that I was missing in action, my parents did not learn until several months later that I was not dead, but a prisoner. I believe that worry contributed to my father's death by stroke three years after the end of the war. My mother survived to face the death in Viet Nam ten years later of my brother, Graham, a helicopter gunner." (Graham received an Army commission upon graduation from Texas A&M.)

John M. Howison's parents were William C. "Buck" and Raviah Sullivan Howison. He married Joan Carney in Tehran, Iran in 1954, and they had three children, Martha Lynne, John Neil, and Stephen Carney. Joan died in Bogata in 1989. On January 1, 1997 John and Rachel Clark Braswell were married.

John was awarded the Air Medal, the Purple Heart and campaign ribbons and was authorized to wear a caterpillar with a "ruby" eye. The latter had no official standing but was allowed for anyone who parachuted from a plane on fire.

★★★

ROBERT L. ADAIR was born June 18, 1927 in Clay County, Texas. His parents were John F. and Verna Owens Adair, and he had three brothers and three sisters. Bob came to Red River County in August 1963 and was the Foreman on the Fleming Ranch on the English road for eighteen years and the Foreman on the Chapman Ranch for fourteen years. He and Alice Joyce Fowler Allen were married in February 1964, and there are two children, Gerry and Donna. Bob is a rancher, and he and Alice Joyce live in the Pine Branch Community.

Bob enlisted in the US Navy in January 1945 at Clay County

and did his boot camp training on a floating dry dock. He was a Seaman First Class stationed in San Diego and was discharged there in December 1946.

★★★

JOHN ROBERT SUMMERS, the son of Harold and Carrie Mae King Summers was born December 16, 1918 in Clarksville, Texas. He had one brother, Bill. He married Mildred Beasley, and they had one daughter, Nancy. John Robert went into the service in 1942 and was trained at Camp Crowder, Missouri. His overseas duty was at New Hebrides, Guadalcanal, New Georgia, the Solomons, Admiraltys and the Philippines. He was a Sergeant First Class at the time of his discharge in 1945 and was awarded an APO Ribbon with eight Battle Stars. He died on January 16, 1966.

★★★

JOHN HENRY WEEMES was born September 22, 1914, the son of George Washington and Martha Ann Elizabeth Williams Weemes. He had five sisters, Ora, Lucille, Barbara, and twins, Bessie and Essie. He married Nellie Gertrude Cantrell and they had six children: Henry Curtis, Margaret Joan, John Bernard, Richard Ray, Joseph Rodger and James David. He entered the Army in 1941, was assigned to the Infantry and trained at Camp Bowie, Texas, Camp Blanding, Florida and Camp Edwards, Massachusetts. He served overseas in France, Italy and Africa. At the time of his discharge in 1945 he was awarded the Purple Heart and an Oak Leaf Cluster. He was wounded in Italy in 1943 and 1944. He died March 1, 1997.

★★★

J. D. WRIGHT, son of J. W. and Mary (Lizzie) Grimes Wright, was born in Detroit, Texas on February, 17, 1922. He had a brother, Henry, and two sisters, Seena and Lee. J. D. was killed in action on December 9, 1944 in Italy when a bomb made a direct hit on the army field kitchen he was working in. He was buried in a military cemetery in Pietramo, Italy. He was awarded the Purple Heart posthumously.

★★★

Three sons of Joseph Hugh and Rebekah Mae Near

McLaughlin were in World War II. They had seven other children, Mabel, Florence, Vivian, Effie, Lorena, Laura and Martin. **ALVIN JOSEPH McLAUGHLIN** was born April 9, 1915. He was in the Army and drowned while on a pleasure outing with several of his buddies in 1941. **MYRON DANIEL McLAUGHLIN** was born June 12, 1913 in Plainview, Texas. He married Wilmer Lee Wright and they had two children, Janell and Charlene. He enlisted in the Army on June 24, 1939 at Ft. Logan, Colorado and was a truck driver in the 2nd Infantry, Company A, Engineer Training Battalion. At the time of his discharge at Ft. Belvoir, Virginia, he was a PFC. He died June 29, 1995. **JAMES H. McLAUGHLIN** served from March 11, 1942 to November 21, 1945 in the 90th Infantry Division, 359th Battalion and was inducted in West Texas. Little is known about him because when their house burned, his records were destroyed.

★★★

EARL WATSON VARLEY was born August 11, 1922 in Red River County, the son of Malcom T. and Rebecca Mae Jones Varley. He had four brothers, Edward, Byron, Clarence, and James and one sister, Erma. He married Martha Jane McGill, and they had two daughters, Johnnie and Paula. Both Earl and his wife are deceased. Earl entered the Army in 1942 and trained at Duncan Field, Texas and Albuquerque, New Mexico. He served in the European Theater and was awarded the American Theater Ribbon, EAME Ribbon with four Bronze Stars, a Good Conduct Medal, and a Victory Medal when he was discharged.

(His brothers, Clarence, James and Byron also served in World War II.)

His daughter, Paula, wrote this about her father: "He was in France at some point of the liberation. My sister said he talked about the people throwing flowers to them, and hugging and kissing them, showing their gratitude. I remember him telling a story about an elderly French woman offering him and some of his buddies food. She kept saying something in French. They didn't understand so she stuck her front teeth out and pretended to hop; then they knew she meant rabbit. I remember him saying something about a bank in Germany where money was just all over the floor. I guess he meant it was no longer any good. I'm not sure about that. I know that his going to Europe was very important to him. I know it was for a war, but he was awed by the countries and cities. He knew it wasn't a vacation, but he loved being able to see all of it. He always wished he could go back to see it again during peace time. My sister told me that he mostly drove supply trucks, taking gas to the tanks."

★★★

JOHNNY LORY LOVELL was born September 19, 1918 at Cuthand. His parents were James Delbert and Leta Mae Brotherton Lovell. His brothers and sisters were Myrtle, Mildred Agnes, James Edward, Dorthy Louise, William Albert and Dirl Randolph. He entered the Army in September 1942 at Clarksville and was assigned to Company H of the 143rd Infantry. His training was at Camp Wolters, Texas, and he was a Pvt. He was killed in action on September 24, 1943 in Italy and is buried at Sicily Rome American Cemetery in Nettuno, Italy, Plot F, Row 15, Grave 26. He was awarded the ETO Medal and Purple Heart posthumously. (A relative told me that Johnny's mother died thinking that he was still alive, just missing in action. She held out hope to the end that her son would be all right.)

★★★

RAYMOND ROLAND SCREWS, the son of John Henry and Hellen Esper Nash Screws was born in Ida, Oklahoma on April 29, 1922. Others in the family were Era, William Thad, and Lorraine and Lorene who were twins. He married Madge Catherine Josephine Lovell, and they had three children, Roland, Raynard and Rachael. He was in the CCC from October 11, 1939 to March 31, 1940. He entered the Army in September 1942 in Red River County and was a part of the Black Hawk Division of the Infantry. He trained at Ft. Ord, California and his Division was in the first wave to hit Okinawa. Only six survived, and he was one of them, even though he was wounded in 1943 and missing in action for three years. No news at all about him until his family received a telegram saying he had been located in the Philippines. He was sent back to California and then to Fitzsimmons Hospital in Denver for about three years for treatment. He was discharged in 1945 and awarded the Purple Heart and Oak Leaf Cluster. He died at Lisbon Veterans' Hospital in Dallas on April 28, 1986.

★★★

Kidd and Myrtle Casey Foster had four sons in the service during World War II. Their other children were Carl and Anna. **ELMO KIDD FOSTER** was born March 8, 1919 at Ladonia in Fannin County, Texas. He married June Bunch, and their children were Richard, Kenneth, Ronald, Eddie Dale, Dennis Kevin, Juanita, Virginia and Teresa. He was drafted at Mineral Wells in 1944 and took MP training at Camp Rucker, Alabama. He was attached to Company B, 62nd Infantry Training Battalion. He was discharged in 1946 and received a Marksmanship Badge. He died February 21, 1996. **LUCIEN PAUL FOSTER** was born November 23, 1920 at Detroit, Texas. He married Margaret Smith and they had one daughter, Susan Marie. He was drafted in 1942 at Detroit, trained at Camp Roberts, California, and was attached to the 78th Infantry Training Battalion, Company A, 4th Platoon. He was a Corporal and served as an MP in Security. He took part in the Anzio Beachhead in Italy and was discharged in 1945 at San Francisco. He died April 27, 1958. **DALE FOSTER** was born August 1, 1923 at Detroit. He married Inez Steuben and they had two children, Geary Dale and Vickie. Dale enlisted in June 1944 at Mineral Wells, was trained at McClellan, Alabama as an Electrician and Carpenter and was attached to the 43rd Divison. After serving overseas in the Philippines, he was discharged in May 1946 at Ft. Bliss, Texas and was awarded the Philippine Liberation Medal, Asian Liberation Medal and Infantry Badge. **DONALD CASEY FOSTER** was born October 28, 1925 at Detroit. He married Gene Polland and they had two children, Donna Jean and Bobby Neal. He volunteered for the Amy Air Corps and was trained at Scott Field, Illinois and Sheppard Air Force Base at Wichita Falls, Texas. He was a Staff Sergeant and served as a Radio Operator and Radio Technician in the Electronic Field of Radio Communication in Germany, England and France. He was discharged in April 1944 at Ft. Sam Houston and received the Radio Technician Award and the Electrical Technician Award. He died April 1, 1988.

★★★

DOUGLAS MITCHELL, son of Francis Marion and Ada Bell Douglas Mitchell, was born June 9, 1910, at Fulbright, in Red River

County, Texas. His brothers were Clyde and James, and his sisters were Nola, Maude, Essye, Lilly Mae, Beulah and Opal. He had one half-brother, Albert, and a half-sister, Edith. On November 14, 1944 he and Inez Westbrook were married, and they had one daughter, Sheryl. (They were married while Doug was on furlough by Rev. Claude Martin at the old Baptist Parsonage on South Locust Street in Clarksville, near where they make their home now.) When I visited with Doug and Inez, he had the following to say:

"I volunteered for the Army Air Corps on January 9, 1942 and took my basic training at Sheppard Field in Wichita Falls, Texas. I boarded the *Queen Mary* in Boston on February 18, 1942. They told me the ink hadn't had time to dry on my enlistment papers when I started overseas. This was the first time troops had been hauled on the *Queen Mary*. The luxury liner had been changed into a troop ship, and it was too large to sail through the Panama Canal. We were sailing south to Australia and had been out at sea only about three days when I asked a man, 'Pop, where are we going?' The man replied, 'I don't know about you, mate, but I'm going to Sydney, Australia.' He was an Aussie.

We had stopped at Key West, Florida for fuel and supplies and then went to Rio de Janeiro. The harbor was beautiful, at the foot of Sugar Loaf Mountain. Then we went across to Cape Town, South Africa; across the Indian Ocean to Freemantle, Australia; and around Australia to Sydney Harbor. While there, since we were unassigned, new units were made, and I was assigned to the 455th Service Squadron attached to the 5th Air Force Unit.

We had been overseas several months when a friend of mine from Center, Texas showed me a newspaper clipping that his folks had sent to him. It read in large letters, 'Head of Nazi Spy Ring captured—Plot uncovered to sink *Queen Mary* with 10,000 troops aboard.' A spy was caught operating a short wave system on Sugar Loaf Mountain overlooking the harbor. The *Queen Mary* was warned, and we were able to avoid the submarine attack.

This had been a 19,000 mile 'zigzag' journey—forty days and nights at sea. After a short time there, we went on to Port Moresby, New Guinea. There we turned in our clothing for new outfits that would be cooler to wear since we were only three degrees off the Equator. Also, I had to turn in my new rifle that I had cleaned and assembled many times. I was given a 1917 World War I rifle instead.

We were sent to New Guinea in a 'holding action' until the main line of defense could be set up across northern Australia.

My family or my fiancee, Inez Westbrook, didn't hear from me until May of that year. Inez and I were to have married December 20, 1941, but after the bombing of Pearl Harbor, we had to postpone the wedding.

I landed at New Guinea about the first of April 1942—dodging Jap bombs and shells—for $21.00 a month. We received mail after a while and had to eat a lot of C-Rations, but mostly Australian Rations—lots of rice, dehydrated potatoes, onions, powdered eggs. The unit was sent to Brisbane, Australia where we stayed for eighteen months as a repair depot, and this was a rest from the jungles. Then we were sent back to the southeast end of New Guinea where we stayed until October 1944 when we were sent home on rotation when a ship was available. I spent thirty-two and a half months overseas and then had a twenty-one day delay en route home.

The men stayed in tents, but there was a thatched hut that served as a day room. There we listened to the radio at nights and heard 'Tokyo Rose' say that while the servicemen were having a hard time, their wives and sweethearts were going out with defense workers. We received the 'Drug Store News' from home, and in one issue I saw that Lindsay McAllister was stationed in New Guinea. I hitch hiked to where Lindsay was stationed, only to find that he was to be away two or three days so I didn't get to see him. Another time I heard that a friend was about three miles down the road so I started hitch hiking and thumbed a ride in a jeep and found that the driver was a Brigadier General.

While on leave, Inez and I married, and I went back to Santa Ana, California for replacement. My father was getting old and was sick so I told them I would like to be stationed somewhere in Texas. When I got my orders, I was sent to McCook Air Force Base in Nebraska. I arrived by train on Christmas Eve, and the snow was boot top deep. I stayed there until my discharge on September 10, 1945. H. D. Jackson and his wife, Mattie, were there, and after Inez finished the school year at McCoy, she joined us. Woodard Prentiss was stationed there also at that time. After my discharge, Inez and I settled in Red River County where we still live. I was awarded the AP Ribbon with three Battle Stars, Good Conduct Medal, and the Presidential Citation. In the early days of the war, bombers flew to

New Guinea to be filled up with gas and loaded with bombs. My outfit played a big part in the Coral Sea Battle where about eighteen enemy ships were sunk. My half-brother, Albert, served in the Army Air Corps but didn't go overseas. My brother, Jim, served in the Army of Occupation in Japan. I wouldn't take a million dollars for my experience, but I wouldn't give a dime for it again."

★★★

Sam and Ollie Campbell Westbrook had three sons in the service during World War II. Their eldest grandson, Sammy L. Humphrey, remembers that his grandmother kept a four-star flag in the front window of their home while her sons were away. The fourth star was for her son-in-law, Doug Mitchell, husband of their daughter, Inez. Two of the Westbrook daughters, Berta Mae and Hesta Lee, worked at defense plants in Texarkana during the war. Other children in the family were Gladys and Johnny.

CLYDE W. WESTBROOK entered the Army in 1942, trained at Camp Wolters and Camp Bowie, Texas and Camp Polk, Louisiana. He served in Africa, Italy and the Philippines and was discharged in 1945. Clyde was awarded a Good Conduct Medal, ETO Ribbon with four Battle Stars and APO Ribbon. He married Evelyn Melton and they have one son, Don. Clyde and Evelyn are both retired and make their home in Clarksville.

MAURICE G. WESTBROOK entered the Merchant Marines and then the Navy in 1944 and trained at Great Lakes, Illinois and Shoemaker, California. He served in the APO on the USS BATAAN. At the time of his discharge he was awarded the APO Ribbon with three Battle Stars, the Victory Medal and ATO Ribbon. He married Dorothy Robertson and they live in Longview, Texas. They have two children, Marcia and Sam.

JAMES R. (ROBERT) WESTBROOK was born March 5, 1910 in Deport, Texas. He married Hazel Strain, and they had three children, James Robert (Jimmy), Marleah and Kathy. He entered the Army in 1942 at Tyler, Texas and trained at Camp Adair, Oregon, Ft. Lewis, Washington and Camp Beale, California. He was a PFC in Battery A, 361st Field Artillery and served as an Occupation Specialist, Truck Driver, Light 345. Robert served in the South Philippines, Ryukyus, and Okinawa and was discharged in 1945 at Ft. Sam Houston, Texas. He was awarded the American

Theater Campaign Medal, Asiatic-Pacific Campaign Medal with two Bronze Stars and one Bronze Arrowhead, Philippine Liberation Medal with one Bronze Star, Good Conduct Medal, Victory Ribbon, one Service Stripe and two Overseas Service Bars. He died July 18, 1999, and his wife is also deceased.

This information has been furnished by his two daughters. A personal note is that their son, Jimmy, was born when Robert was overseas and he did not see him until he was fifteen months old. Also, Marleah was named for a friend that Hazel met while she was living in Oregon near where Robert was stationed. Two other women from Clarksville were there. Hazel was in contact for many years with the couple she lived with.

★★★

ELTON M. ROSEBERRY was born July 24, 1920 in Waldron, Arkansas, the son of Charles I. and Susan Octavia Peyton Roseberry. He had three brothers, Charley, Kelly and Bennie, and four sisters, Grace, Cora, Edna and Nora. He married Lorena A. Foster, and they had three sons, James, Larry and Richard, and three daughters, Wanda, Carol and Melba. He died June 23, 1990.

Mr. Rosesberry was a Sergeant in the Army Air Corps, entering the service in June 1942 at Clarksville. He received his training at Sheppard Field, Texas, Sioux City, Iowa and Nebraska. He served as a cook in the 412th Bombardment Squadron and was in the ETO for twenty-eight months with some time in England near London. He was discharged October 15, 1945 at Ft. Sam Houston, Texas. He was awarded the Good Conduct Medal, ETO Ribbon with six Battle Stars, Distinguished Unit Badge and two Oak Leaf Clusters. While he was in London, he fell on a cobblestone street while riding a racing bicycle and had trouble with his elbow swelling the rest of his life. The Roseberry's first son, James, was born December 1, 1943. Sgt. Roseberry received a telegram telling him of his birth but did not see his son for two years. (His daughter, Carol, informed me that their father used to entertain his family by telling stories about D-Day. He set up food service in the back of trucks for the soldiers.)

★★★

Three sons of Oscar C. and Lydia Myrtle Bolch Cheyne were in the service during World War II. There was one other son, Joe Don.

AMOS DEAN CHEYNE was born July 20, 1921 in Annona, Texas. He married Veda Lorene Palmer, and they had three children, Charles Oscar, Bobbie and James Howard. He later married Thelma Lorene Chesshire and their children were Janice, Randy, Melinda, Donna and Kevin. A Sergeant in the Army Air Corps, he enlisted June 17, 1942 at Tyler, Texas and trained at Sheppard and Randolph Fields in Texas. As an Airplane Mechanic, he served in the ATO. Upon his discharge on November 13, 1945 at Randolph Field, he was awarded the ATO Medal, Victory Medal and Good Conduct Medal. He died August 20, 1997.

OSCAR TERRY CHEYNE was born August 27, 1923 in Annona. He married Mureline Minter and they had two children, Bruce and Betty. He entered the Navy on May 12, 1944 at Tyler, Texas and was trained at San Diego and Seattle. His sea duty as a 3rd Class Gunner's Mate was aboard the USS Rockbridge (APA 228) in the South Pacific. He was discharged at Camp Wallace, Texas on February 1, 1946 and received the Philippine Liberation Medal, APO Ribbon, and ATO Ribbon with two Bronze Stars.

JOHN RAY CHEYNE was born March 13, 1927 in Annona. He married Wanda Dudley, and they had four children, Connie Lanelle, Jimmy Ray, Terris Glen, and Brenda Gail. He enlisted in the spring of 1945 at Texarkana and was trained as an Able-bodied Seaman in the United States Maritime Service at Catalina Island, California. This service was under War Shipping Administration (Merchant Marines). He died May 24, 1987.

★★★

BERT T. JOHNSON, son of Buster and Ada Hall Johnson, was born September 14, 1915 and had six brothers and sisters. He married Maudie Mae Chiles on June 30, 1940, and they had four children, Diane, Donald, Kay and Johnny. He entered the Army on December 4, 1942; trained in Michigan and Wisconsin; and served as a Sergeant in the European Theater. He was discharged in 1945 and awarded a Good Conduct Medal and ETO Ribbon with four Battle Stars. He died November 11, 1985.

★★★

Paul Davis, Sr. and Maude Dorothy Cook Marable had two sons in World War II. They also had a daughter, Dorothy Ann.

ALLEN CORLEY MARABLE was born August 26, 1924 in Clarksville, Texas. He married Mildred Alice Wooley, and they had three daughters, Marilyn, Amy Margaret and Cathy Ann. "Bubba", as he was known in most parts of Red River County, entered the service in February 1943 and received his training at Camp Hood and Fort Bliss, Texas and Lake Charles, Louisiana (ASTP). As a T/5 he was a part of the 3228th Ordnance Depot Company whose duty it was to supply automotive and armament to the 101st and 82nd Airborne and 29th Infantry Division. He served overseas in the European Theater in Northwest Germany. He was discharged in March 1946 at Ft. Bliss and awarded a Good Conduct Medal and ETO Medal with two Battle Stars.

PAUL DAVIS MARABLE, JR. entered the Army in 1942 and trained at Camp Roberts, California, Ft. Sill, Oklahoma and Camp Barkeley, Texas. He married Betty Lou Lewis, and they had four children, Betty Sue, Paul D. III, Linda Ruth, and Robert Lewis. I quote below parts of a letter dated August 17, 1999 that I received from him:

> "Red River County had many in service, of course; but imagine my surprise when after completing officer training and reporting to Battery B, 143rd Field Artillery Battalion of the 90th Infantry Division, I found that our sergeant in charge of wire communications was Floyd Green, and that the first sergeant of Battery C of the same battalion was Sidney Cagle, both graduates of Clarksville High School, a couple or so years ahead of me. Then, compounding my surprise while waiting in England for the Channel crossing, I was visited by Sergeant Lloyd Holloway of Clarksville. Lloyd told me that because of his mission of commanding a reconnaissance jeep, and my mission of artillery forward observer, neither of us would return home. Lloyd was right about himself. He was killed in action. And he was close to right in my case. The other two FO's in our battalion were put out of action, one with a leg lost and the other KIA. I just think it amazing that four of us from the same home town were serving in the same division."

In 1971 Paul Davis Marable, Jr. wrote *Two Hundred Fifty-Five Days*, about his experiences as a Prisoner of War of the Germans. I quote in part below:

"I had actually been captured by the enemy! Captured! Now parts of the pre-capture we had received in England came back to me, the lecture nobody had paid much attention to, considering it unthinkable that anybody could be captured...

It was mid-afternoon of June 19, 1944. From then until the morning of January 21, 1945, seven months later, I was to be the unhappy guest of the Third Reich...

There it was on my dog tags: name, serial number, record of tetanus shot and booster, blood type, name and address of person to be notified in case of death or injury, and the 'P' symbol for Protestant. I arranged to get my information turned into the man in civilian clothes (Red Cross). Even so, it was sixty days after being captured that Mother and Dad were notified...

But now, trapped in my solitary cell, I knew a sick fear greater than any combat anxiety I had felt. I had never been this desperately afraid before. The heavy explosions of the 500 or 750-pound bombs kept me from hearing anything else, even if ordinary noises could have penetrated the cell walls. Probably I'm here in this building all alone, I told myself. This is the way I'll go. Nobody else around. Wheeling from my stare at the high window, I charged the heavy door with my shoulder, ran up half the outside wall toward the bars over the frosted glass of the window, ran back to the door and kicked it. I was soon yelling, whimpering, elbowing, kicking in a useless rage and fear. My energy suddenly left me, and I found myself gulping air and trembling, standing in the center of this despised cage.

'The Lord is my Shepherd, I shall not want.' The lines came to me from nowhere. I had not prayed, even inwardly, since being captured. I don't know why. 'He maketh me to lie down in green pastures. He leadeth me beside the still waters. He restoreth my soul.' The lines kept coming to mind, and I forgot the flares and the numbing explosions. 'Yea, even though I walk through the valley of the shadow of death, I fear no evil; for Thou art with me.' Nothing had my attention any longer except the power of the lines of the Twenty-Third Psalm. 'Thy rod and thy staff, They comfort me. Thou preparest a table before me in the presence of mine enemies. Thou anointest my head with oil. My cup runneth over. Surely goodness and mercy shall follow me all the days of my life, And I shall dwell in the House of the Lord forever.'

Still standing in the center of the cell—for how long I didn't know—I found that I was no longer afraid... My transformation from raving, frustrated, fear-ridden puniness to the calm well-being I now felt may be explained in psychological terms to the satisfaction of some, perhaps, but I choose to believe that the mystical presence of Healing Power had come to me. I had no doubt then nor now that the peace was of God. I prayed for a long time, informally, forgetting to use Thee and Thou properly, but pouring out words of my depths. . .

Food was at all times and in all ways a serious matter. . . We ate in groups of eight men each, by cubicle. One of us would measure out into the eight bowls—spoonful by spoonful—every bit of our quota of soup for the meal. . . Occasionally Red Cross parcels arrived and were carefully stored until there were enough parcels for each man to have one. . . In each box were a can of Spam, a can of corned beef, a can of jam, a can of liver paste, a can of oleo margarine, a can of powdered milk, a small box of some type of graham cracker, a chocolate 'D' bar, some lump sugar, a can of powdered soluble coffee, and a few other things. .

Winter was on us now in full force. Heavy snows had set in. . . On Daddy's November 10th birthday, I thought of how he had always admitted being 'cold natured', going into rigorous shakes when winter's first norther whistled through. Here, all of us had the shakes. . . Heat in our barracks could hardly be felt. . . We took turns hugging the furnace for a few minutes at a time. With more need for body heat, food should have been supplied in better quantity. It wasn't. . . Most of us spent all the time we could in our bunks, dressed in all the clothes we had except shoes, and covered with the two blankets each had been given earlier and with our overcoats, trying not to freeze. . . As December came, our plight worsened, as a 19th Century novel might say. Food continued to be the same ersatz coffee for breakfast, the issue of black bread with enough stalk ground in to look like sawdust, the bowl of thin cabbage or sugar beet soup for lunch, the boiled potato for supper with sometimes a spoonful of corned beef. . .

One day, lying in my topside bunk, I thought, 'This could be the way we go.' I knew that before we got too weak we would all join in some sort of final effort to be free. It would be costly, but it would beat freezing to death for all of us. . .

With Christmas approaching, thoughts of feasts at home in other times came out in conversations more and more until finally anyone mentioning home or food was hushed by seriously-meant yells of 'quit', 'cut it out', shut up, damn it', or more profane equivalents. It had been a long time since the last Red Cross food packages, and the meager diet and gripping cold were showing themselves to be adversaries of our tempers and spirit as well as of our bodies. Then, wonder of wonders, we received another shipment of those life-saving boxes... We ushered in the Christmas Season with carols, special worship services and discussions meant to convey that really, we should love our enemies...

Foot troops, presumed to be German, had been passing along the road for about an hour... The troops were not German but Russian, drunk Russians... After much jawing with the chaplain, the drunken troops went on. All they knew to say was 'Berlin', pointing westward... The date was January 21, 1945. From then until February 28, thirty-nine days later, our hardships changed in degree but not much in nature. For a few days our food and warmth were remarkably pleasant; but later, with the Russians in charge of us, the cold and hunger returned. For the full seven weeks with our noble allies, the Russkies, we never knew whether we were still prisoners or somehow liberated. Countless times a day we got no answers to our questions of 'What happens now?', 'Where do we go from here?', or 'Have our people been notified?'"...

We were startled by the appearance of an American Major, fully fleshed and in clean uniform. He was a member of the military attache's staff in our Moscow Embassy, he told us. The American Ambassador had not known until the day before of our existence, he said. The Major had flown from Moscow to check our situation and to learn if we would be able to board a British merchant ship now in the Port of Odessa when it left for Port Said, Egypt. We would be able, he was assured. It was the happiest news we could recall during any of the several months past... Word came that food was coming in from the British ship in the harbor. We ripped open the cartons as soon as they arrived. Mincemeat. Box after box of it...

The big day arrived—February 28, 1945. We had been under Russian control for thirty-eight days. Back through the gates we marched, the last gates and the last fence or wall for us... The old merchant ship in the harbor looked to me like the *Queen Mary*, and I said so... Up the gangplank at last!...

The trip across the Black Sea... was serene. Weather became

warmer by the hour. The ship's crew was attentive. We ate four small, tasty meals every day . . . Exercise around the decks after a good meal . . . Already the good things were beginning to erase and overcome 255 days of something less than a picnic. (first as a war prisoner of Nazi Germany, then as an unwelcome guest of Red Russia).

Details could be told you of our rest camp outside Port Said, Egypt . . . our balmy cruise to Naples, Italy . . . the second Mediterranean cruise and Atlantic crossing in an American ship . . . reunion with Mother and Daddy in the Greyhound bus station in Dallas and home again. These are all well-remembered and treasured events; but all pleasant, every one, and not attached to the 255 days."[7]

★★★

A newspaper article with pictures of five servicemen reads as follows: "Fighting Far From Home—Five sons of Sam H. Westbrook, Deport (Lamar County) farmer, are serving in the United States Army, three in North Africa, one in the Southwest Pacific, and the fifth in a camp in Georgia. Farmer Westbrook's most welcome caller these days is the mail man, and seldom a week passes that letters fail to arrive from some of the boys. The Westbrook soldiers are Boyd, 24, in Africa; Esker, 38, in Africa; Donald, 22, in Africa; Elbert, 36, in the Southwest Pacific area; and Earl H., 26, at Camp Gordon Georgia. (Elbert Westbrook was the father of Ouida Westbrook Humphrey.)

★★★

MARCELL ATLAS CROSS, the son of Albert Atlas and Ida Frances Altom Cross was born January 14th, 1920 in Red River County, Texas. He had six brothers and sisters. He married Mary Christine Bolton and they had two sons, Ronnie Marcell and Rodney Gene. Marcell and his wife are retired and live in Clarksville.

He was drafted September 9, 1943, trained at Camp Fannin, Texas, and became a part of the 358th Infantry Regiment, A.T. Company, Pioneer Platoon. He was a PFC and served as a Rifleman and Mine Sweeper who searched for and destroyed booby traps and laid mines and booby traps to assist our forces. Marcell's overseas duty was in Normandy, Northern France, Ardennes, Rhineland and Central Europe. He was discharged January 5, 1946 at Camp

Fannin and received the Purple Heart and a Bronze Star. He told me, "Most of what I remember would be better to forget. From 1929 to 1941 were hard years, and from 1941-1946 worse."

★★★

WILLIAM J. BONE was born March 6, 1927 at Petty, Texas, the son of William B. and Helen Ethel Coco Bone. He has one brother, Bobby Gene. He married Martha Louise Landers, and they have three daughters, Martha Jo, Elizabeth Claire, and Rachel Leigh. He and his wife reside in Paris, Texas

Bill was drafted in June 1945 at Dallas and was a Sergeant T-4 in the Infantry Antiaircraft working with electronic signal equipment. He was discharged at Ft. Bliss, Texas on November 4, 1946 and received a Rifleman Badge and Good Conduct Medal.

★★★

W. E. (DUB) STEPHENS was born near Bagwell, Texas on October 19, 1907, the third son of Will Ed and Alta Hastings Stephens. Dub became one of five fatherless boys when Will Ed died in 1912. His brothers were Gilbert, Elbert, Rex and William. His mother struggled to raise her sons alone, and they learned very early to help farm the home place, attending school at Blanton Creek whenever possible, and only after the crops were laid by. Their mother died when Dub was only seventeen years old, and the boys were set adrift to make it on their own. He and his older brothers, ages 22 and 20, determined to keep the family together and accepted jobs from an uncle which involved a move to Amber, Oklahoma. During the years at Amber, they worked their uncle's land, lived in a sharecropper's house, and sent their two little brothers to school.

When all the brothers were old enough to make it on their own, all but one of them moved back to Bagwell, some with wives and families by then. Dub never married, and in 1942 he entered the Army. He trained at Camp Cooke, Camp Young and Camp McCoy and served in the European Theater of Operations. He was listed as missing in action on December 19, 1944 while serving with a tank division in Luxembourg, Germany and then reported as being dead. His body was brought back to Red River County after the war and burial was at Blanton Creek Cemetery with military honors. He was awarded the Bronze Star and Purple Heart posthumously. He did not live to tell of his war experiences, but wrote home occasionally, just short letters.

★★★

ARCHIE E. RAINS, the son of Adlia E. and Etta M. Crenshaw Rains was born December 7, 1922 in Steuben County, New York and had one brother, Adam Gathings. He married Vivian L. Tuggle, and they had two daughters, Barbara E. and Teresa A.

Archie was inducted into the Army on February 4, 1943 at Tyler, Texas. He attended Motor Vehicle Operators School at Ft. Frances E. Warren in Cheyenne, Wyoming. He was a Pvt. who served in the 3350th Quartermaster Truck Company. He drove a two and a half ton truck in Alaska for eleven months, hauling ammunition, clothing, food, personnel, medical supplies and engineer equipment. He drove both single and in convoys over improved and unimproved roads in all kinds of weather. There were short trips and very long hauls of up to 1,000 miles round trip. He was trained to make minor repairs to the vehicles. His time in Alaska was one year, seven months and twenty-one days. He was discharged February 17, 1946 at the Separation Center at Camp Chaffee, Arkansas. He died March 23, 1996, and Vivian preceded him in death.

★★★

J. V. BAIRD was born at Boxelder, Texas on July 4, 1923, the son of John and Eula Lumpkin Baird. He had seven brothers and sisters, Ava, Iris, Leon, Burvell, Katherine, Harriet Jean and Virginia. He married Dovie Tucker, and they had three children, Sharon, Rickey and Rodger.

In 1942 J. V. enlisted in the Coast Guard at Key West, Florida. He trained in New Orleans and St. Augustine, Florida and was a 3rd Class Petty Officer in the Motor Pool and Highway Patrol. He was discharged in 1946. The Bairds make their home in Boxelder.

★★★

JAMES R. McCULLOCH, JR., the only child of J. Ritchie and Ruth Ellis Reed McCulloch was born in Clarksville, Texas on August 27, 1915. He married Martha Ann Kunkel, and they had two children, J. Ritchie III and Martha Ann. The McCullochs now make their home in San Antonio.

Prior to the declaration of war, he was in charge of purchasing in Cuba for Nicar O Nickel Company, a US Defense Plant in the Oriente Province. The only other source of nickel was in Europe. He entered the service in December 1943 at Havana, Cuba. His training was at the Supply Corps, U.S. Navy—Harvard Business School. He was a Lieutenant Junior Grade who served as Disbursing Officer aboard the USS Appalachian, AGC 1 from December 1943—May 1946 in the Philippines, Nagasaki, Hiroshima and Hokkaido after the surrender of the Japanese.

His discharge was in May 1946 at New Orleans, and he was awarded the American Theater of War Medal, Asiatic-Pacific Area Medal, World War II Victory Medal, and Philippine Liberation Medal.

★★★

HORACE E. (GENE) HAWKINS, the son of William John and Mary Jane Askins Hawkins, was born April 30, 1919 in Johntown, Texas. The other children in the family were Etta, Mammie, Irene, Cleo, Isabel, Earl and Lilie May. Gene married Lydia M. Baxter, and their children are Eugenia Kay and Roger G.

He entered the Army on December 28, 1942 at Camp Wolters in Mineral Wells, Texas. His training was at Camp Maxey, Texas and Camp Polk, Louisiana, and he served as a Staff Sergeant with Company A, 92nd Signal Battalion, 3rd Amy as a telephone lineman.

Gene told me this about his service: "My company loaded on the boat at Camp Shank, New York on October 28, 1943 to go to Liverpool, England. From there we went to Belfast, Ireland; Holland and south to Oxford, England. From Southhampton we crossed the English Channel, and the water was rough. We landed on Omaha Beach on D+10. The beach had already been cleared. I was wounded in France October 14, 1944. Next we went into Germany. A German gas truck was burning, and I had climbed a telephone pole to repair wires that had been burned. A jeep drove up, and General Patton got out and asked the soldier on the ground where he could find General Anderson with the 5th Armored Division. The soldier told Patton to ask Sgt. Hawkins up on the pole so I came down and handed General Patton a phone so he could talk with General Anderson who was in a tent a little way up in the woods. Patton said, 'Hi, Andy! I've been wondering about you and how you're doing.' It wasn't long after he stopped talking before General Anderson drove up in his jeep and they had a good visit." (I asked Gene what he thought of Patton, and he said, "I liked him".)

Gene's service was in the ETO in France, Germany and Austria, and he was discharged October 24, 1945 at San Antonio. He was awarded the ETO Ribbon, Good Conduct Medal, Bronze Star, five Battle Stars, and the Purple Heart.

★★★

JAMES ELLIS GOODMAN was born February 10, 1923 in Clarksville, Texas. His parents were Ollen Ellis and Josephine Collins Goodman, and they had two daughters, Mary Evelyn and Bonnie Jo. James Ellis has one son, Dick. He and his wife, Mary Payne Goodman, reside in Clarksville.

James Ellis enlisted in the service on June 19, 1942 at New Orleans, Louisiana as a U.S. Navy Reserve Aviation Cadet. His training was in the Pre-Flight School, University of Georgia and U.S. Navy Navigation School in Hollywood, Florida. He was commissioned June 17, 1943 as a 2nd Lieutenant U.S.M.C. Reserves. He served one year in the South Pacific as a Navigator and then returned to Flight School at Ottumba, Iowa and the U.S. Naval Air Station at Corpus Christi, Texas. His overseas time was in the South Pacific—the Solomon Islands.

James Ellis said: "In May or June 1942 I got four of us together to enlist. There were John T. Felts, Jr., David J. Weaver, James W. (Buddy) Vaughan and myself. After we took our test, we then ended up in New Orleans for more tests. All four of us passed. John T. was delayed one day, and we were furnished a railroad ticket home.

We all enlisted as Aviation Cadets in the Navy. Since Buddy already had a pilot's license, he was sent first to report for duty. The other three of us ended up in Texarkana taking civilian pilot training, and then we went by train to Athens, Georgia to the University of Georgia for pre-flight training, arriving there November 11, 1942. On graduation from there, John T. and I volunteered to go to Navigation School in Hollywood, Florida. I remember that if we went there, we would be commissioned earlier, and then in one year we would come back and take pilot training as an officer. We left David there.

On graduation John T. and I took our commission as 2nd Lieutenants in the U.S. Marine Corps Reserve. Each of us then were with our own crew and ferried DC-3 aircraft to the South Pacific. On or about December 27, 1943 John T. went down in a plane full of pilots, and we never found any trace of them. I was on several searches.

Once when I had some time off when I was on New Caledonia, I ran into Sam Hocker at New Herbides. Then another time when I was on Bougainville, I saw a picture that was signed 'E. Petty'. Jake Holster came up about that time, and we had a good visit. Sure enough, the picture was by Earl Petty from Clarksville."

James Ellis was discharged in January 1946 at the U.S. Navy Air Base in Jacksonville, Florida. He was awarded the Presidential Unit Citation and three Battle Stars.

★★★

ROGER MAURICE LOVE, son of Willie Hubbard and Laura Viola Bagwell Love, was born October 23, 1916 in Bagwell, Texas. He married Mary Elizabeth Glenn and they had two daughters, Debra and Melissa. The Loves reside on their land west of Clarksville.

Maurice entered the service at Clarksville and was a Corporal who served as a Teletype Operator in the 44th Heavy Bombardment Group of the 8th Air Force. He was based at Shipdham Air Base, sixty miles south of London from January 1943 to July 1945. Upon his discharge he was awarded the EAME Campaign Medal with nine Bronze Stars and Distinguished Unit Badge with one Oak Leaf Cluster.

In 1984 and 1987 Maurice and Mary Elizabeth traveled to Shipdham, England and visited the old barracks where Maurice stayed during World War II. The flight control tower was still there, but not in use. The grounds were in cultivation, but the old roads still ran through the fields.

★★★

VALTON BYERS was born April 1, 1920 in Springtown in Parker County, Texas. His parents were Dillard and Etta Young

Byers. His brothers and sisters were Frank, Marvin, J. L., Dora, Mae, Ruth, Ruby and Mildred. He and Lawana Wynn were married in San Diego on March 8, 1942. (Their wedding was to have been in December 1941 but had to be postponed.) Their son, Gary Allen Byers was born April 5, 1943 in San Diego.

Valton worked for Consolidated Vultee Aircraft Company in San Diego from October 1941 to May 1944. He supervised a group of six milling, nibbling and drill press operators. He operated the machines himself before becoming a group leader. His duties included checking finished work against blueprints, using precision measuring instruments.

Valton was drafted August 14, 1944 in Dallas, Texas. He had been given a three month deferment because of his father's illness, and his father died in July. He was attached to the 54th Armored Infantry Battalion and took his basic training at Camp Fannin in Tyler, Texas for four months. He then left Dallas on January 1, 1945 to go to Camp Kilmer, New Jersey. From there he went to England, France, Belgium and Germany. He served in the Third Army under General George Patton, had the rank of Sergeant and served as a Squad Leader, leading a squad of twelve men. He also served as Sergeant of the Guard at a prisoner of war camp at Dachau where he supervised the work of prisoners. Many of these prisoners had been SS Troops.

Valton was discharged from the Army on May 6, 1946 at Fort Sam Houston, Texas. He returned to his job at Consolidated Vultee (later to become General Dynamics) and stayed there until 1967 when he and Lawana moved to English, a small community east of Clarksville, where they had bought a place in 1960. From 1970 to 1983 he was the instructor of the Metal Trades Class of Clarksville High School. Valton died June 15, 1992, and Lawana still lives at English in the home they built there.

★★★

WILLIAM C. (BILL) BETTES is the son of W. P. and Della Craigo Bettes. The family had two other sons, Walter L. and Jim, and Walter was also in the service during World War II. Bill and Gloria Smith were married in 1947 and have three children, Billy, Tommy and Betty Lou. The Bettes' are both retired and make their home in Clarksville, Texas.

Bill said this: "I enlisted in the Army Air Corps on January 12, 1942 in Paris in Lamar County. I knew what was coming and decided to go ahead and enter the service at that time. I was in the 8th Air Force, 455th Fighter Group, that flew B-51 Mustangs, as a Staff Sergeant in the Personnel Office. My training was at Sheppard Field in Wichita Falls, Texas.

After completing my training there, I went to Langley Field, Virginia for six or eight months; then to Syracuse, New York for four months; and on to Ft. Dix, New Jersey. My group left Staten Island, New York in March 1943 on the *Queen Elizabeth* heading for Europe. It took only three days for us to cross the Atlantic. We had no escort and zigzagged all the way over to avoid attack by German submarines.

The *Queen Elizabeth* landed at Firth of Clyde, Scotland. The group went by train to the coast of the English Channel and then to Steeple Morden, England where a fighter group was based. While in England, we were only about twenty miles from the front. I remember the V-2 rockets as they came over and that one landed only about a hundred feet from us. At one time I went into Cambridge on a pass, and then two weeks later, the area was leveled by a bomb. There were sirens night and day; no lights—total blackout.

From there we went to San Quentin, France and then to Germany where we stayed until the war was over. I saw Hitler's hideout on the Austrian border and also saw the horrors of the Dachau Concentration Camp where so many Jews were sent to the gas chambers. After the war was over, I went on an eight hour flight in a B-17 over Germany at an altitude of five hundred feet which enabled me to see the destruction of the land.

I spent almost four years in the service and was discharged on December 19, 1945 at Camp Fannin in Tyler, Texas. I was awarded the EAME Medal, Victory Medal, ATO Ribbon, Good Conduct Medal and Sharp Shooter's Medal."

In 1997 Bill, Gloria and their two sons, Billy and Tommy, traveled to Europe to the places where Bill had been during World War II. This was a gift from Tommy to his family, but his sister, Betty Lou, was unable to go at that time. "*Saving Private Ryan*" was being filmed when they were there, and this prevented their visiting the cemetery on Omaha Beach. They did visit Utah and Omaha

Beaches, and we can only wonder at what memories this trip brought back to Bill.

WALTER L. BETTES entered the Army Air Corps in 1941 and trained at Kelly Field, Chanute Field, Gawau Field and Portland AAB. He served overseas in Bismarck Archipelago, the Solomon Islands, New Guinea and China. He was discharged in 1945 and awarded the APO Medal with five Battle Stars, ATO Medal with one Battle Star, and Philippine Liberation Ribbon with one Battle Star. He married Martha Jane Hill and they had two children, Bobby and Patsy. The Bettes' live in Alamagardo, New Mexico.

★★★

John Harvey and Mirty Mae Swint Pratt had two sons and a son-in-law who served in World War II. The other children in their family were Dorothy Marie and Nellie Ruth.

SIDNEY JOHN HARVEY PRATT was born on April 4, 1920 at Blakney in Red River County, Texas. He married Winnie Bee Cross and they had one son, James Leroy. Sidney was drafted in 1942 in Dallas and trained at Ft. Sill, Oklahoma and Camp Campbell, Kentucky. He was a Staff Sergeant in the 12th Armored Division, Company 714 Tank Battalion and served as a mess sergeant and gunner in the tank division. He was discharged in December 1945 at Camp Kilmer, New Jersey after serving overseas in France and Germany and was awarded a Sharp Shooter Medal, two Bronze Stars, WWII Victory Medal and three European, African and Middle East Campaign Ribbons. Sidney died April 15, 1989.

ARDEN LEROY PRATT was born December 5, 1922 at Blakney. He married Christine Stephens. He was drafted; trained at Chicago; and was a Staff Sergeant who served as a radioman and tail gunner in the 9th Air Force. His overseas duty was in France and Germany, and there is no information about the medals he received upon his discharge in 1945. He died September 11, 1987.

JOHN ORVAL ABNEY, the son of Ed and Rosa Lee Crow Abney, was born in Abernathy, Texas on May 17, 1926. There was another son, William Osco Abney. He and Nellie Ruth Pratt married and had three children, Rose Marie, John Edward and Thomas Harvey. On August 9, 1944 he was drafted in Dallas and was attached to the 20th Infantry Division, Company F as a mess sergeant and combat infantryman. His overseas duty was in Luzon, Korea and Leyte. Upon his discharge October 31, 1946 at Fort Sam Houston, Texas he was awarded the Asiatic-Pacific Theater Campaign Ribbon with one Bronze Star, Army of Occupation Ribbon (Japan), three Overseas Service Bars, and a Sharpshooter Medal. He died December 20, 1980.

★★★

LOUIS E. PEEK, son of Wylie Tom and Mellie Knight Peek, was born September 2, 1917 in Red River County, Texas. He had two brothers, Earl and Ervin, and two sisters, Lallie and Margie. At the time of his enlistment in 1942 into the Army Air Corps, he was planning to be married, but the marriage was postponed because of the war.

His training was at Jackson, Mississippi and Tyndall Field, Florida. Louis was a Staff Sergeant and served as a tail gunner on a B-25 bomber. He served at New Guinea in the South Pacific and in Australia. He was wounded on Formosa and died August 21, 1943 after spending several days in the hospital. His body was returned with a military escort and burial was at Savannah Cemetery, west of Avery, Texas. He was awarded the Purple Heart, Gold Medal with Oak Leaf Cluster and Silver Star. When the family home burned, all his medals were lost along with the holder that had held the 45-revolver he always carried.

His nephew, Joe E. Wilburn of Avery, remembered several stories about his uncle. The crew of the B-25 bomber was a close knit group. If the pilot had chosen to, he could have rotated the men who served under him, but he chose to keep the same group for every flight. There was a pact between them that anyone who survived would contact the families of those who did not make it through the war.

After the war ended, Louis' family was visited by the pilot, Phil McCartney of Oklahoma City. He was on his way from Florida to his home and could have easily chosen not to stop in Avery. Because of their pact, he did stop for a visit with the Peeks. This group of men who served together had a great deal of trust and mutual respect for each other. He told Louis' family that it would be hard to know just how many enemy planes had been shot down by Louis, and that he was an expert on any kind of weapon. The following incidents were also talked about that day.

Once they were headed to Brisbane, Australia, and because of a mistake by the navigator, their destination was missed by about two hundred miles. It was the middle of the night; they were low on fuel; they were going to have to bail out, and no one was eager to do it. Louis volunteered to be the first to jump. The Australians were friendly to the American pilots, and after two or three days, the crew got back together after staying in farm houses in the countryside.

There was only one time when the U.S. was strictly alone in an attack around Midway. The whole Japanese Naval Fleet was destroyed that day. Our planes flew close to the water almost all day. They had a nose gunner, top gunner, belly gunner and tail gunner. When the Jap zeros came in, they tried to come in on the tail and belly gunners so the pilot flew close to the water to they couldn't get under the plane.

Louis shot down two zeros on one mission. They were cruising along through a white thunderhead when Louis radioed the pilot to say there were some Japs coming in. He told him what speed and altitude he should use, and then the zeros came out, one on each side of the plane. Their 50-mm machine guns took care of the zeros, and it was a pretty sight to see them tumbling down. If those zeros had come under the belly of the plane, it might have been a different story.

On another mission to a South Pacific Island (either Guam or Wake), the camera showed that they shot down six Jap zeros that day. McCartney said they realized that heavy damage had been inflicted on them and that they were being chased back to New Guinea. The plane was really shot up, but none of the crew was injured. He had minimum control over the plane and knew they were going down. When they came upon an abandoned airstrip in New Guinea, he did a belly landing because their landing gear was not in tact. It would have been a safe landing except for a fuel drum that had been left on the runway. He had to land the best way he could. Louis was injured and taken to the hospital where he died a few days later. The Peeks were told that Joe Murphy who lived south of here was the crew member who got Louis out of the plane. When a serviceman had made twenty-five missions, he was eligible to return to the U.S. The sad thing about this was that this was Louis Peek's twenty-fifth mission.

★★★

WILLIAM RICHARD JACKSON was born January 25, 1924 in Red River County, Texas. His parents were John H. and Corenne Askins Jackson, and he had one sister, Maude Ruth. He and Ida Mae Barton married and had one son, David Richard Jackson. Richard enlisted in the Navy on June 15, 1943 at Dallas and trained at the AMM School NATTC in Norman, Oklahoma and in Ground Crewman Training in V-F NAS Sanford, Florida. He was an Aviation Machinist's Mate, Third Class V-6 and was attached to the Navy V-12 Unit, Louisiana Polytechnic Institute in Ruston, Louisiana; NTS Great Lakes, Illinois; NAS Lake City, Florida, and on the *USS Copahu* (CVE-12). Richard was discharged April 20, 1946 and awarded the Victory Medal, Good Conduct Medal, American Campaitn Medal and Asiatic-Pacific Campaign Medal. He died July 30, 1960.

★★★

HASKELL H. SUMMERS was born July 7, 1924 in Red River County. His parents were W. H. and Vestel Clem Summers, and he had four brothers and sisters, Wilbert, William, Ivy and Ruth. He married Helen Stringer and they had one adopted son, Jimmy R. Summers. In 1943 Haskell enlisted in the Navy at Bogata, trained at San Diego, and attained the rank of Coxswain. He served in the South Pacific Islands and was discharged at Norman, Oklahoma in November 1945. Haskell was awarded five Bronze Stars, APO Ribbon with two Bronze Stars, Philippine Liberation Medal, American Theater Medal and a Victory Medal. He died November 17, 1982.

★★★

CURTIS DOWARD HALL was born September 11, 1918, and his parents were Garlin and Virgie Cox Hall. He entered the Army Air Corps in 1940 and remained in the service until 1970, working in the Accounting Department. He and his wife, Grace, had two daughters, Catherine and Patricia. He died March 24, 1984.

★★★

WILLIAM RALPH MULLINS, the son of W. N. and Emma Estell Kerbow Mullins, was born March 19, 1910 in Detroit, Texas.

He had two sisters, Lala and Ruth. He entered the service in Red River County and was trained at Ft. Ord, California. Very little is known about his service except that he was a Private and served in Patton's Battalion as a truck driver. His relative related hearing him say that at one time in Europe the snow was over knee deep. He heard a blast and was knocked to the ground. When he got up, the only remains of his three buddies were splinters of bone, flesh and drops of blood. He died in 1974.

★★★

WILLIAM C. LEE was born February 26, 1924 in Clarksville, Texas. His parents were Harrison and Pauline Jones Lee. There were two other sons who died before reaching adulthood. William married Ernestine Dickerson, and they had two children William Charles, Jr. and Cornelia Ann. He enlisted in the Army Air Corps in 1943 and took his training at Sheppard Field in Wichita Falls. He was a Private stationed in Louisiana, Oklahoma and Ohio. William was discharged in 1945 and spent many years as a school administrator. He died May 7, 1999.

★★★

MORRIS S. PHILLIPS, the son of Felix G. and Willie A. Stuart Phillips, was born at Woodland on May 23, 1915. His siblings were Floyce, Rubye, Haskell, Earline, Eugene and Edwin. He married Alma Lee Edmonson, and there were two sons, Larry and Stephen and a stepson, James Hemingway.

Morris entered the Army on August 15, 1941 at Dallas and was attached to Troop A of 8th Engineers as a Foreman Constructor and Rifle Marksman. His training was at Ft. Wood, Missouri, Ft. Belvoir, Virginia, Ft. Bliss, Texas and Camp Sutton, North Carolina. He attained the rank of Staff Sergeant and served overseas in Australia, New Guinea, Admiralty Island and the Philippines. He was discharged September 12, 1945 at Ft. Sam Houston, Texas and was awarded a Good Conduct Medal, APO Ribbon with four Bronze Stars, Philippine Liberation Ribbon, two Bronze Stars, Arrowhead and Victory Ribbon. He died December 6, 1984.

★★★

TRAVIS S. HENRY was born June 28, 1920 at Clarksville,

Texas. His parents were Fred and Pearl Smith Henry, and he had a brother, Robert L. and two sisters, Francis Elizabeth and Mattie Louise. Travis and Jessie Marie Emery married and had a son, James Travis, and a daughter, Bonnie Kay.

Travis was a part of the Company I, 144th Infantry, 36th Division, entering the service on November 25, 1940 at Clarksville. His combat training was at Camp Bowie in Brownwood, Texas, and his administrative training was at Ft. Logan, Colorado. Travis transferred to the Air Force on July 25, 1941; attended administrative training school in Denver; and served as Administrative Specialist in the U.S. Air Force. He was discharged October 7, 1945 at Randolph AFB, San Antonio, Texas with the rank of Staff Sergeant and was awarded those medals given to the B17 Combat Group for service overseas from November 1943 to June 1945. He was called back into the Air Force during the Korean Conflict and served from August 17, 1950 until August 17, 1951. The Henrys now live in Winnsboro, Texas.

★★★

Obed P. and Claude L. Boze Coats lived in the Boxelder community and had six children: Onvie, Cecil, Sybil, Dorene, Marvin and Edward. They had two sons in the service during World War II.

I talked with **MARVIN COATS** at his home at Boxelder on November 13, 1999. He and Bobbie Jane Cooper were married forty-eight years when she died on September 7, 1999. He told me the following:

"When the National Guard was mobilized in 1939, I went into the Army for a year's training. This was the 142nd Infantry of the 36th Division. We took our basic training at Camp Bowie in Brownwood, Texas and our combat training at Big Sandy, Louisiana. Our knife, judo and swimming training was at Camp Blanding, Florida; our mountain training in Virginia and our snow and ice training in Massachusetts. In 1942 we went overseas to Africa and landed at Oran. We were thirteen days on the ship going over. Then I came back on a boat that brought prisoners of war, and we landed at Newport News, Virginia. I remember that one German sergeant said that he hoped he'd be put on a farm because in Germany before the war, he had been a farmer. I really don't know where they were sent. I was given a three day pass and decided that a 'one' in front of it would be better so I took a thirteen day pass instead and went home to see my folks.

Then it was back to Africa, and this time we landed at Casa Blanca. We rode in trucks across the desert. We went to Cork Forest and then to Oran. We left there and went across the Mediterranean Sea to take part in the invasion of Italy. We landed in Salerno, Italy. We took that with rifles cause we didn't have any artillery to amount to anything. Finally, one of our ships came in close to shore and unloaded on them. There were nineteen machine guns in one building that the ship leveled. That's where I was when I was wounded. I got hit with five machine gun slugs and three shrapnel. They took me back to Africa on a hospital ship, back to Oran again. I was in the hospital for eighteen months, and that included the time I spent convalescing.

I know you've heard a lot about 'Tokyo Rose'. Well, we had 'Sally the Slut'. When we landed in Africa, she welcomed us and called on us to lay down our arms. She said they had coffee and doughnuts for us. It was a pretty good radio program with American music. You know, the good bands like Tommy Dorsey, Benny Goodman and Harry James. The 36th Division had 36,000 men in it, and she announced that the men in the 36th had left in a jeep. Can you imagine that? Really, a lot of men had been lost, but there were still too many for a jeep.

My brother, Ed, and I met up several times overseas, one time in Rome. After eighteen months, I stayed over there and was assigned to Allied Military Government, which is really the Judge Advocate Department. I stayed with that for two years so with the time I was in battle, it was four years in all.

Company D of the 142nd had been together three or four years. After the 36th landed, they asked for volunteers, and we went 110% over strength. Lots of people call the invasion of France the first invasion in Europe, but really the invasion of Italy was first. What I can't really understand is the fact that they knew we were coming, but we got sent in anyway. The enemy was up on cliffs just waiting on our boys."

When Marvin was discharged, he received the Purple Heart, three Bronze Stars and the Expert Rifleman's Badge.

CHARLES E. (EDWARD) COATS married Lucille Whittle, and they live on their land east of Clarksville. He has two daughters, Pam and Susan. He related the following about his time in the service:

"I was drafted into military service on April 7, 1942. We left Market Square in Clarksville that morning before daylight and went to Tyler where we were sworn into service; took shots; and were given a physical. We spent most of the day there and then caught a bus for Camp Wolters in Mineral Wells. We went from there to Sheppard Field in Wichita Falls where we took our basic training. Going there meant that I had been chosen to go into the Air Force. They chose personnel to form a new air depot group, and I was assigned to Supply Squadron, 17th Air Depot Group. We were there about six weeks.

Next we went to Will Rogers Field in Oklahoma City where we were stationed in tents, called Tent City. After two months we moved to the new airport called Oklahoma City Air Depot in Midwest City. The name of this place was changed to Tinker Field after we left. We were the first ones to move into the new barracks after they were built there.

On October 27 we were loaded onto a troop train and rode day and night for two or three days going up to Chicago, into Canada and back to Staten Island in New York. On October 31, Halloween day, they played the ultimate trick on us. They carried us down to the dock and loaded us on a ship. The following morning when we got up and went out on deck, there was no land to be seen. We were in a huge convoy with battle ships all around. The next morning when we looked out, there were no other ships. We were traveling south; stopped in Rio de Janeiro to refuel; then traveled on around the south end of Africa to Bombay, India where we went inland to an English camp and stayed about a week. From there we went to Bombay and boarded an English ship to go up through the Red Sea into Egypt.

It was almost Christmas by this time, and we began to get letters and packages from home. It was good to hear from the family. The homemade cookies Mama sent were delicious even though they were just crumbs, and we had to eat them with a spoon.

We stayed in Egypt for about four or five months and then traveled by truck convoy to Tripoli to set up another supply depot. Then on to Tunis where we stayed more than a year receiving, storing and shipping supplies. Then the Air Force asked for volunteers to go to Oran to set up another depot. Since I knew my brother, Marvin, was there, I volunteered to go. I met him in the canteen in Oran, and we had several chances to visit before we parted ways again. Later the entire squadron moved to Oran where we stayed for more than a year.

Next we moved to Casa Blanca where we were when the war ended. Then we boarded another ship to cross the ocean and go home. Our ride back across the Atlantic took only seven days to the tune of *'Sentimental Journey'*. After almost three years overseas, I was ready to get back to home and family.

The ship that I went overseas on was built in Newport News, Virginia by the Newport News Shipbuilding and Drydock Company. It was launched on August 31, 1939 and entered service on August 22, 1940 as a luxury liner that was named *America*. In May 1941 she was called into dock, converted to a troop ship and renamed. She could carry a little over nine thousand people at a time and was the largest troopship in service during World War II. I was told that this ship traveled at a rate of thirteen knots per hour, and as it traveled, it zigzagged every few minutes so that a U-Boat could not draw a bead on it.

Even though I was in a foreign land where I could not speak their language, I was not even close to the front lines. I thank GOD that HE brought me through this turbulent time without a scratch. That was a time in my life when I was not doing very much to encourage HIM to watch over me.

Even though we have much wrong with our government and our country, it is by far the best place in the world to live. While over there, I talked to many people who would have given all they had just for a one-way ticket to America."

★★★

BILLIE S. CLACK was born July 15, 1923 in Detroit, Texas. His parents were Ben and Belle Lamb Clack, and there was another son, John, and three daughters, Bennie Bee, Ana Bel and Mary Jo. He married Ann Caine, and they had three children, Billy S., John C., and Marianne.

In 1943 he entered the Army Air Corps and was attached to the 398th Bomb Group in England. He was trained at radio and gunnery schools and became a ball turret gunner on a B17 bomber.

S/Sgt. Clack made thrity-five missions to German occupied countries. On November 2, 1944 the target was Luna Oil Refinery at Merseberg, Germany, This was touted as the largest air assault of the war with 1,500 4-engine bombers and 3,000 fighter escorts. He was there. Upon his discharge in 1945 at San Antonio, he was awarded the Air Medal with six Oak Leaf Clusters, Good Conduct Medal, Marksmanship Medal, ETO Medal, and Unit Citations.

★★★

HENRY LEE SUGGS, son of Henry Thomas (Boss) and Lora Lee Simmons Suggs, was born September 18, 1916 in Winfield, Texas. There were two daughters in the family, Virginia and Ruth. He married Wordner Brown, and they had one daughter, Barbara Ann.

Henry Lee enlisted in the Navy in July 1943 at Dallas and was a Seabee, serving as an equipment operator with the rank of Machinist Mate II. He served overseas on the Solomon Islands. His discharge was in November 1945 at Camp Wallace, Texas. Henry Lee died August 29, 1994, and Wordner lives in Dallas.

★★★

GEORGE MONROE (SKID) SKIDMORE, JR. was born December 14, 1918 in Red River County, Texas. His parents were George M., Sr. and Nelia Counts Skidmore. He had two sisters, Eileen and Elizabeth, and a brother, Harold. On December 24, 1937 he and Jonell Ragsdill married, and their children are Ronnie and Donna.

Skid entered the Navy on June 12, 1944 at Clarksville. At the time, the Skidmores lived next door to the Calvin Brannans. Both men knew they would be drafted, so they decided to volunteer and go in at the same time. As it turned out, the Skidmores were expecting their second child, Donna, who was late in coming so Calvin went into the Navy first. Skid's training was at Farigot, Idaho, Oxnard and San Nicholas Island, California. He wanted his family to join him so Jonell caught a train at Mineola, Texas going to El Paso. Her father took her and Ronnie, who was only five, and Donna only six months old, to the train. They were told that it was "standing room only", but Jonell insisted on going anyway. When she got on board, a serviceman gave her his seat. When the train arrived in Los Angeles, the conductor told the soldiers and sailors to help everyone with their luggage. Jonell was carrying Donna and dragging Ronnie so she appreciated one of the men taking her bags. Skid met them, and then she wondered how she would find her luggage. Sure enough, the serviceman had set the bags right beside them. Later, Bea Brannan and her two children, Mack and Jimmy, came out for a visit and found a place to stay. The Navy flew the sailors from San Nicholas Island to San Diego every sixteen days for a five day leave. Skid would hitchhike to Costa Mesa where his family was staying, and never had any trouble getting a ride. They prayed for "fog" because if it was foggy, he couldn't fly back to the island and sometimes got to stay ten to fifteen days.

Skid did not go overseas during his time of service and was discharged as a Seaman First Class on February 17, 1946 at San Pedro, California. He was at Gila Bend, Arizona when the war ended. The Skidmores returned to Clarksville, and Skid died August 13, 1994. Jonell remains in their home.

★★★

WILLIAM MACK RAGSDILL was born October 19, 1917, the son of Joe and Vera Veteto Ragsdill. He had a sister, Jonell, and a brother, Norris. He married Margaret Witmer, and they had two sons, Tommy and Bobby. After Margaret's death, he married Tommie Gehring. He died June 30, 1988. Before his death, he wrote "My Life in World War II" for his two sons, and it is quoted in part below:

". . . . Six months before entering the service, I went to work for Rapid City, Iowa Army Base in the finance department. The war continued to get worse, and I knew my time was coming up, and having some time in the Texas National Guard, I applied for Officers Candidate School but was declined because of my age, which was twenty-six years. I went ahead and enlisted in the Army and went to Ft. Riley, Kansas for induction in the service on December 13, 1943. Margaret and the boys rode the train with me to Ft. Leavenworth and then on to Clarksville. Next I went to Camp Fannin, Texas for basic training, sixteen long weeks in radio operator/cryptographer training. In April 1944 I was sent to Ft. Campbell, Kentucky and stayed there until D-Day. We were on bivouac June 6th and were ordered out of the field, packed and headed for Boston where we took a ship to Glasgow, Scotland. We landed there June 15 and trained in England in the Salisbury Plains.

After ten days, we went by ship to France, crossing the English Channel and landing on Omaha Beach. The ship was small, causing it to bounce around, and the waves were so high that we had to take rope ladders down side and then drop six to eight feet to landing barges. We were all scared, but we made it to the beach with nothing but sniper fire and a few planes strafing. I'll never forget the cliff we had to go up with full pack. We bivouacked near the beach and after two days loaded on coal cars for a train trip across France. We made a few stops, and I found a piece of plexiglas from the canopy of a downed fighter plane. On the stock of my M1 rifle, I cut out the heart shape and put Margaret's picture in it. It was with me until the day I got hit. . .

We entered Belgium before we crossed the Siegfried Line. By then I had joined the 3rd Armored Divison outside Germany as a replacement and was assigned to a mortar squad. I had never even fired a mortar, but I became a mortar gunner instead of a radio operator. My full squad consisted of 12 men, but never did we have more than 7 and sometime as few as 5. . . Our main purpose was to fight hard and push hard, take the town and hold it. . . From Aachen we fought our way further into Germany across the Siegfried Line. The fighting was as rough as it could be. . . After a few months I was moved out of the mortar squad and promoted to sergeant and squad leader for the headquarters squad. We would take three or four men and go through the German lines and report back to our command post the location of machine guns, artillery and observation posts. This was hard, and if you ever got caught, it was 'katy-bar-the-door'. . .

The armored infantry squad was made up and assigned to one tank. During street fighting there would be one tank on one side of the street and another on the other side. We would spot a machine gun or observation post and signal to the tank commander. Their cannon would be turned on it, and they would blow it out. We reached a little town called Giesh in late November. General Eisenhower came to see the new rocketlaunchers mounted on tanks and half-tracks, as this was the first time they were used. The main assault began on November 28, 1944, and after about 48 hours of constant rocket fire, we pushed out on our half-tracks with tanks following behind. For miles nothing was living. Cows, horses, people were dead. It was the most terrible thing I'd ever seen. We would fight for a town and then stay in it for a few days which gave us a dry place to sleep. The cooks would catch up with us, and we'd have a hot meal and not have to eat K-rations and C-rations. . .

On December 10, 1944 we started another push, reaching Obergiesh which is outside Giesh. . . All night long I felt that something was about to happen. The next morning we moved out across an open field. . . I gave my men the signal to spread out, and then I was hit. An anti-tank shell had shattered my left leg. . Every time I raised up to look for a medic, I would get hit again with machine gun fire. I held the pressure point to stop the bleeding and then released it, and this probably saved my life and kept me conscious. I took all my wound tablets, drank a canteen of water and decided to play dead. . . One of the men from Alabama that was always getting into trouble crawled, under fire, to get me out. . . His rifle jammed on him so I gave him mine, the one with Margaret's picture, and I don't know where it is now. . . By 0830 I was back at the aid station getting blood and waiting for a trip back to the hospital in Belgium. I arrived there December 13th, and after getting seven pints of blood, had surgery, was put into body and arm casts. . . They sent me to Paris for more surgery; then on an English hospital ship to Oxford, England. Our Christmas dinner aboard ship was boiled fish, cold potatoes and plum pudding. In England I had three more surgeries and then was shipped on the *Queen Mary* back to the states. . . In the five days crossing the Atlantic, my wounds were never redressed, and when I reached the Haleron General Hospital on Ellis Island, New York, my temperature was about 105 degrees. More surgery, and then on a hospital train to Longview, Texas. . I stayed there four months and then went to Temple, Texas for more surgery. . . In 1946 I was sent to a hospital in Springfield, Missouri for six months; then to an amputation center in Battle Creek, Michigan. . . On a leave home, I swam every day, and it helped the bone to knit. . . I was discharged after two years and seven months in army hospitals. . . We lived in Texarkana, and I was one of the first men hired by the Kiwanis Club 'Hire-a-Disabled-Vet' program when I went to work for Wooten's Dept. Store that later became Dillard's. . . In 1957 my leg got worse; there was more surgery; and a doctor told me that if I wanted to live, I'd better have my leg amputated. I agreed to this, and after about thirty operations, it was the best thing that happened, giving me a little relief. (When he was first injured, he was taking another man's place who had gone AWOL.)

During my service I was awarded the Combat Infantry Badge, Purple Heart, Bronze Star, European Theater Medal with two Battle Stars, Good Conduct Medal, and the World War II Victory Medal."

★★★

HUBERT JACOB FUNK was born October 15, 1914 in Clarksville at the Funk home place west of Clarksville. His parents were Cyrus H. and Elizabeth Inskeep Funk. He had a sister, Margaret, and a brother, Cyrus Funk, Jr. When he left school, Hubert joined the C.C.C. and worked in the Petrified Forest area of Arizona, making lodges with native rock. He was a member of the National Guard when it was activated and served in the Army on the west coast and in Florida where he was killed in an accident on June 19, 1943. Burial was made in the Clarksville Cemetery.

★★★

ROY RAINS, son of Sesil Roy and Mamie Nowell Rains, entered the Army in 1943, trained at Fort Knox, Kentucy, and served in Belgium and France as a T/Sgt. Roy was wounded in France in 1944 and died there in 1945.

★★★

ROBERT HOUSTON CANTERBURY was the son of Charles Culberson and Daisy Gentry Canterbury. He had a brother, Charles Morris, and four sisters, Minnie Lee, Virginia Ruth, Evelyn and Jean. He was married to Elizabeth A. Hicks. Robert entered the Army Air Corps in 1942 and trained at Wichita Falls, Texas. He served in Italy and was missing in action in 1945 and presumed dead in 1946. He was awarded the Air Medal with Oak Leaf Cluster, Presidential Citation and Good Conduct Medal.

★★★

JOHN THOMAS FELTS, JR. was the son of John Thomas, Sr. and Winifred Clark Felts. He had a sister, Marian Patricia. He entered the service as a U.S. Navy Reserve Aviation Cadet in 1942 at New Orleans. His training was in Athens, Georgia; Hollywood,

Florida; and San Diego. After attending Navigation School, he was commissioned as a 2nd Lieutenant in the U.S. Marine Corps Reserve and served in the Solomon Islands and the Asiatic-Pacific Theater. He was killed in action in 1943 when a plane he was in crashed at sea.

★★★

John K. and Mae Kelley Ford had eight children: John, Janice, Justine, Genieviene, Joe, Joyce, George, and Jean. Two of their sons were in the service during World War II.

An article in the *Bogata News* said: "Brothers serve together, separately—Seaman First Class **George D. Ford** and his brother, Pharmacist Mate First Class **Joe A. Ford** both served their country. Joe entered the service in 1942, and George in 1944. Joe was sent to Pearl Harbor, and two years later his brother, George, was sent there as well. From Pearl Harbor George went on to Guam, being discharged from the service in 1945, the same year that Joe also came home. In another war, Fireman Third Class Dom Buffo, son of Lela Buffo Ford served aboard the USS New Jersey during 1969-70."

Joe Ford was born July 17, 1920 in Bogata, Texas. He entered the Navy on April 29, 1942 at Dallas. He attended the USNH Corps School in San Diego. His discharge at Camp Wallace, Texas was on November 2, 1945 after thirty months sea duty. Joe married Lela McCullar. When I visited with the Fords in Bogata, he told me of an incident that happened in the spring of 1944 at Pearl Harbor when it was filled with ships ready to invade Saipan. It was on a Sunday afternoon, and there were five LST's, fully equipped and loaded with men, that blew up when a welder's torch caused a fire, starting a chain reaction. Over 1,000 men were killed.

George Ford was born May 28, 1926 in Bogata and married Ann Ford. He enlisted in the Navy on May 19, 1944 at Dallas and was discharged July 20, 1945 at Corona, California.

★★★

SAM K. HOCKER was born November 16, 1902 in Clarksville, Texas, the son of Sam T. and Emma Kneisley Hocker. His step-father was Dr. Nowlin Watson. He married Mary Ann Lennox, and they had one son, Sam Lennox Hocker. Sam volunteered in 1942 for the U.S. Navy and trained at the Naval Air Station at Quonset Point, Rhode Island. Lt. Hocker served at Espirito Santo in New Hebrides and Guadalcanal. He was Executive Officer of a carrier aircraft service unit. He was discharged in 1945 at Corpus Christi and was awarded the American Theater Ribbon, APO Ribbon, and Victory Medal He died February 25, 1959, and Mary Ann resides in Clarksville.

★★★

J. D. TACKETT was born March 19, 1925 at Broken Bow, Oklahoma, the son of Joseph William and Minnie Aaron Stafford Tackett. The other children in the family were Pearl, Eddie, Relis W., Eula, Mavis, and Winfred Paul and Winnie, twins who are deceased. J. D. married Dorothy Louise Kelsoe, and their children are Ginger Dell (deceased), Larry S., Rose Jeanette, James Dennis, and Michael L.

J. D. entered the Marine Corps on December 18, 1943 at the Marine Corps Base in San Diego. He was a Corporal in the 3rd Marine Division, 12th Artillery and trained at Camp Elliott, California to be a heavy truck driver and telephone man. He saw action at Iwo Jima, Volcano Islands, and Guam. He was in the Pacific Theater from June 1944 to February 1946. J. D. was discharged April 3, 1946 at San Diego. They reside in Clarksville, and we were neighbors of theirs for twenty years.

This is a note Dorothy wrote: "J. D. Tackett and Dorothy Kelsoe were married in Clarksville, Texas on November 2, 1946 by Mr. J. T. Claiborne. Martha Sue and her mother stood up with us. It was raining that night, and Martha Sue held an umbrella over my head when I was going to the car. One of my aunts said, 'I hope you don't shed as many tears as drops of rain fell.' We have had a good life together. We have eight grandchildren and four great-grandchildren."

★★★

Charlie Steele, Sr. and Ethyl Florence Beaty Steele had five children: Felix, Joseph, Edward, Bertha and Charlie Benjamin. Two of their sons were in World War II.

CHARLIE BENJAMIN STEELE was born March 3, 1912 at Clarksville, Texas. He married Gladys Whitten, and they had a son, James Arthur Steele. On December 21, 1941 Charlie was drafted into the Army and served in England loading bombs on airplanes.

He was a Private 1st Class, never in battle, and no information is known about any medals he might have received. He was discharged in 1945 and died December 25, 1987.

EDWARD ARTHUR STEELE was born March 25, 1916 in Clarksville. He enlisted in the Army in 1939 and served as a Medic who drove an ambulance to get the wounded off the battlefield. He was a Sergeant and was killed in action on Normandy Beach in July 1944. He received two Purple Hearts posthumously.

★★★

WILLIAM M. (BILL) McDONOUGH, the son of James Alvin and Lois Gray McDonough, was born August 8, 1925. He had a sister, Geraldine, who died at a young age. He married Pauline Bean on November 10, 1945, and they had a son, William M., Jr. (Butch) McDonough. Bill entered the service December 3, 1943 and was attached to the 95th Infantry Division. He served overseas in France and Germany and was wounded in the invasion of Germany on December 3, 1944. In March 1945 Bill was sent back to a hospital in El Paso. He was discharged March 6, 1946 and awarded the Purple Heart, Combat Infantry Badge, and a Bronze Star.

★★★

OSCAR MAURICE (BUD) FOWLER was born November 11, 1921 in Clarksville, the son of Oscar William and Lina Hays Fowler. He had three sisters, Bessie Marie, Mildred Louise, and Elizabeth Ruth, and one brother, Dewey Harvey. Bud enlisted in the Marine Corps in 1942 at Dallas and was attached to the 1st and 2nd Marine Divisions, 419th Platoon. His training was at San Diego. He was a PFC who served on the Solomon, Gilbert and Marianas Islands. He was killed in action June 17, 1944 on Saipan. He received the Purple Heart, Bronze Star, Pacific Campaign Medal, and Presidential Unit Citation.

★★★

JAMES A. SOWARD was born September 1, 1922 in the Lanes Chapel Community east of Clarksville in Red River County, Texas. His parents were Elbert B. and Kate J. Emery Soward, and he had one brother, Sam Soward. He married Joella King, and they had two sons, Larry R. and James B.

James entered the service in Clarksville on October 27, 1942 as a Private assigned to Company E, 382nd Infantry, 96th Division. His training, including basic, maueuvers, and amphibious, was in Oregon, Washington, and California. He advanced to Staff Sergeant as a squad leader of a rifle platoon.

James went overseas to the Philippines on October 20, 1944, but his time spent there was short because he was wounded on October 28, 1944. His division took part in the invasion of the island of Leyte. The Philippines fell to Japan early in 1942, and on March 11 General MacArthur left there as ordered by President Roosevelt. MacArthur returned as promised. He and his staff waded ashore at Tacloban about five hours after the first landing. The island of Luzon was invaded by the 6th Army on January 9, 1945. The troops that had surrendered on Corregidor and had been held prisoners in Manila were freed.

Because his wounds would not heal in that climate, James was one of the first taken back to Hawaii where he spent eighty days in the hospital. General Richardson, Central Pacific Base Commander, made the decision that anyone who spent more than sixty days in the hospital would be granted a furlough. While James was on furlough, the war ended in Europe. He was scheduled to go to Okinawa for the invasion of Japan April 1, 1945, but while he was waiting for his orders, he received a fifteen day extension on his furlough. He then went to Ft. Sam Houston and on to Camp Fannin in Tyler, Texas where he spent five months as a member of the Cadre, training infantry recruits.

His discharge on November 13, 1945 was based on the point system. He then returned to Red River County where he farmed and then worked at the Lone Star Ordinance Plant in Texarkana. In 1956 his family moved to Carrolton, Texas where he and his wife still reside, after retiring from Texas Instruments. James told me that he and his wife, Joella, both grew up during the Depression. He said, "We like the life we have now much better than then, the 'good old days' as some refer to them."

James was awarded an Expert Infantryman Badge, Combat Infantryman Badge, Purple Heart, Bronze Star, Unit Citation, WWII Medal, Philippine Liberation Medal with one Battle Star, Beachhead, American Campaign Medal, Asiatic Medal, and a Good Conduct Medal.

★★★

Martlin M. and Ella May Pratt Whitener had two sons in World War II. Their other children were Grady, Elma, and Jeanetta.

BILLY WAYNE WHITENER was born June 18, 1924 in Detroit, Texas. He married Margaret Kyle, and they had three daughters, Kathie, Sandra and Marla. He entered the Navy on Feburary 12, 1943 and was trained at the Fire Control Schools in San Diego and Washington, D. C. At the time of his discharge on March 1, 1946, he was a Fire Controlman, Second Class and was awarded the World War II Victory Medal, Purple Heart, American Campaign Medal and Asiatic-Pacific Campaign Medal. He died February 16, 1987.

MARSHALL THOMAS WHITENER was born January 27, 1916 at Post Oak, Texas on the family homestead and was raised in Detroit, Texas. He married Virginia C. Exparza, and they had five children: Regina T., Janice M., Stanley T., Marsha A. and Debra L. He died January 10, 1975.

His daughter, Marsha A. Whitener-Valdez wrote the following about her father: "Daddy wasn't your average soldier. He was what is called a 'Mustang Officer'. He entered the service as an enlisted man and retired as a Lt. Col. in 1963. (His last assignment was Squadron Commander of the 62nd Field Maintenance) He wore his hat in the familiar 'forty mission crush' but would never explain how he came to be able to wear it that way. He never liked to talk about his 'war stories' because they caused recurring nightmares. The stories he would tell were more humorous in nature. He didn't like to talk about or to even wear all of his medals—he said it was too much like 'bragging'.

I know he enlisted in the Air Corps sometime between 1939 and 1940. He was stationed at Lackland AFB in San Antonio when he met and married mother on 10-1-40. As with all active duty personnel, he reported to his unit when Pearl Harbor was attacked. He ws deployed to England and waited with the other troops. He landed in France on D-Day, although he claimed not to have been in the first wave of troops. He always laughed about 'following Patton' across Europe. . . While in Europe he took command of his battalion when his commanding officer ws incapacitated. He received the Bronze Star and a battle field commission to Captain. Once when he drank two beers (Daddy was never a drinker), he began to talk about the day he and his battalion liberated a concentration camp. He never finished the story and would refuse to answer any questions about the experience. He suffered nightmares because of it and we, his children, were not allowed to speak about our family's German heritage.

When Daddy enlisted, he was a Medic. When the Army/Air Corps split, he chose to go Air Force. It was then that he got into aircraft maintenance. He referred to B-52's as his 'babies' and once won an award for identifying a problem which was causing a rear engine to fall off in flight. He spent months sitting on the wings of the planes watching the engines rev until he noticed what was wrong—one screw, which was installed when the planes were built, was too small. . .

Daddy was a quiet man who was the epitome of national pride. To his dying day, he would stand at attention when he heard the National Anthem. Disrespect for the flag, for our country, for our leaders, was cause for 'court martial'. He instilled in all of us, his children, pride in country. His experiences taught us respect for others and the need for defense of human rights. He was a good man, whom I miss more than I could ever express in words."

★★★

MAURICE H. RANEY was born September 3, 1921 in Red River County. His parents were A. D. and Bertie May Rice Raney, and he had three sisters, Florance R., Mary, and Marjorie, and one brother, Gordon. He married Jeanetta Whitener, and they had two sons, Bruce and Travis

He entered the Army with Company I of the National Guard in 1940 and was trained in Texas, Louisiana, Florida and California. His overseas duty was in Africa and Italy, and he reached the rank of 2nd Lieutenant. At the time of his discharge in 1945 at Fort Bliss, Texas, he was awarded the Bronze Star, American Defense Medal and Good Conduct Medal.

★★★

ROY LEE HUTSON was born March 1, 1921 in the Shadowland Community. His parents were John Tim and Sally Runi Windham Hutson. He had two brothers, Tellas Andrew and Elbert

Ray, and one sister, Ruby Lois. He married Imogene Stephenson on October 5, 1945, and they have one daughter, Linda Bryson, and two grandchildren, Michelle and Scott. Since our visit at the Hutson home, Roy Lee died on May 3, 2000.

He was drafted and entered the service on October 1, 1942. As a Platoon Sergeant, he served in Company H of the 350th Infantry Regiment. They were called the "Blue Devils". His training was at Camp Wolters, Texas and Camp Polk, Louisiana, and he was the first draftee to go overseas from Lamar County. He was discharged on October 26, 1945 at Fort Sill, Oklahoma after serving in the Battle of the Bulge, Africa and Sicily. His discharge noted that he was a Heavy Mortar Crewman and had charge of a sixteen man heavy mortar section in an infantry heavy weapons company. He spent eighteen months overseas participating in the major European Campaigns. He was familiar with all basic infantry weapons, in their use and tactical employment. He was responsible for two 81mm mortar squads.

A school paper written by his granddaughter, Michelle Bryson, says in part the following: "Roy Lee Hutson departed the U.S. on December 6, 1943 and landed at Casa Blanca on December 15, 1943. They began fighting there and moved east through Algeria, to Tunisia and then up to Tunis. The division was then put on a boat to cross the channel to Trapani, Sicily, then to Messina, Sicily and on to Italy. They started out with about 2,000 men and wound up with only 250. Later on they went to Anzio where they had a hard battle, and then to Rome. Granddad was wounded in action by enemy mortar shell fragments in both thighs on the 17th of April in the Po Valley Region near Frozzona, Italy. He was taken to a hospital and released May 12, 1945 and returned to the U.S. At the time of his discharge he was awarded the Combat Infantryman Badge, Europen African Middle Eastern Theater Medal, Good Conduct Medal, Purple Heart and Purple Heart Cluster, Bronze Star with three Battle Stars, Unit Citation, Silver Star and five Battle Stars."

★★★

HERMAN LEE (PEPPER) MARTIN was born November 25, 1924 in Detroit, Texas, the son of Roscoe Alonzo and Effie Lillian Hastings Martin. He had a sister, Reba Aileen and a brother, William Weldon.

He enlisted in the service on March 23, 1943 at Camp Wolters, Texas. His combat training was in Casper, Wyoming, and his armament training was at Denver. He was attached to the 15th Air Force, 55th Wing, 485th Group, 829th AAF Bomb Squadron as a Nose Gunner on a B-24. His rank was Sergeant, and he served in the Mediterranean Area where he was killed in action on March 3, 1945. He was awarded the Air Medal and the Purple Heart.

A Paris News article dated July 8, 1993 entitled "PJC gets pieces of history" reads in part as follows: "A 1942 Paris Junior College letter jacket, earned by the late Herman L. (Pepper) Martin, has never been worn. Martin played on PJC's first state championship football team in 1942. He left for World War II immediately after the season was over and was later killed in battle in Italy. The jacket was apparently presented to his mother later in the year. It was presented to PJC by Martin's brother, Weldon Martin, of Paris who said the jacket was found in a cedar chest after their mother had passed away."

★★★

LONNIE LLOYD PETTY, son of C. C. and Mattie Dell Petty, married Dorotha Wilson of Bogata, Texas. Lonnie enlisted in the U.S. Army in the spring of 1943. He served in the 1st Army, 3rd Armored Spearhead Divison and participated in the Battle of Normandy and later in the Battle of the Bulge. Lonnie was awarded the Good Conduct Medal, Victory Medal, ETO Ribbon with five Battle Stars, and the Presidential Citation. He was discharged in November 1945. A note from his wife says that she and Lonnie were married 52 ½ years when he died May 3, 1998. They had a son, Wade, and a daughter, Margie. Lonnie was retired from LTV in Dallas after working for them for 38 years.

★★★

JAMES C. WILSON was the son of John N. and Bonnie Ragsdill Wilson. His brothers and sisters were Raymond, Leopal, Sarah Nell, Vera, Carmen and Dorotha. His sister, Dorotha Wilson Petty, sent me the following information about her brother:

"And now some information about my brother, J. C. Wilson, and his experiences as a Japanese POW during WWII. Jay was stationed in Tientsin, China in 1941. He was a young Marine, only 21 years old, and his outfit was assigned to the U. S. Embassy there.

While the Japanese were on their way to Pearl Harbor that fateful Sunday morning on December 7, 1941 to carry out their attack and destroy the U.S. Fleet, the Embassy was overrun, communication abilities destroyed, and personnel taken prisoner. Other foreign embassies suffered the same fate, but every other country demanded and got the return of their personnel to their respective countries. The U.S. never even requested our men's return. For many years now these ex-POW's have lobbied Washington for this oversight to be recognized and apologized for, but as yet this plea has fallen on deaf ears. J. C. Wilson and his military buddies spent over 3 ½ years in several Japanese prison camps.

They suffered many atrocities, beatings and starvation, beri-beri, extremely cold conditions in their harsh winters. They did fill huge wooden vats with scalding hot water once a month during winter for the prisoners to bathe together. This was an event they really looked forward to because it was the only time they could get really warm.

Jay began cutting two wisdom teeth and was in excruciating pain. The camp doctors held him down and extracted these teeth with no anesthesia. Jay was not bitter toward them about this because he said it was toward the end of the war and they had no anesthesia, not even for themselves. He also said he was thankful to get the wisdom teeth removed, at whatever cost.

Their meals consisted of mostly rice and green tea, and J. C. gave the green tea credit for saving their lives. They were allowed to drink all of it they wanted.

We were able to write postcards to him every now and then, and also the Red Cross sent us a list of things that the Japanese would allow us to send the prisoners every so often, things like a tooth brush, toothpaste and soap. We were so glad and rushed to send a box, but J. C. said he never got anything. I guess the Japanese enjoyed the Lifebouy Soap, razor blades, etc. and just laughed at us and the Red Cross.

World news was scarce in the camps, but new prisoners brought welcomed news about the U.S. from time to time that gave the prisoners hope. At last there was a rumor about an atomic bomb, and then one morning no one came to their barracks to wake them up to start their work detail. The Japanese military had evacuated all their men, and our men were just there alone, some so weak they couldn't stand.

Soon, they heard and then saw the beautiful American planes flying overhead, dropping leaflets announcing the end of the war and telling them to communicate as to how many men were in the camp. Two of the stronger prisoners climbed on top of a building and wrote '2,000', but it was interpreted as '200' so when the food was dropped, there was not nearly enough. J. C. and a dozen others formed a kind of martial law and took charge of the food, combining every single item in a big pot of soup. Everything went in together—tuna, salmon, spam, corn, beans, oatmeal, canned milk, chocolate, raisins. The men said it was the best soup they ever ate.

When they were finally airlifted to Guam to a hospital, J. C. weighed 78 pounds. He was not released to come home for several months, and when we finally did get to see him, he was thin but looked wonderful to us. Jay was able to put his war years behind him and to lead a full life, dying at age 71 on July 13, 1992, from diabetes and congenital heart failure. It was determined that his infirmities were attributed to his long incarceration and starvation at the hands of the Japanese military."

★★★

ROBERT LANE WHITEMAN was the son of C. L. and Gerthie Nance Whiteman. He had a brother, George. He and Carmen Wilson were married September 3, 1933 and had one son, James Robert (Butch). Robert entered the Navy in 1942 and was trained in San Diego. He was a MOMM 1/C who served on YMS 130 (Mine Sweeper) and in the U.S. He was discharged in 1945 and returned to Clarksville. He is deceased, and Carmen resides in Paris, Texas.

★★★

BEN BRYANT STOREY was born January 13, 1923 at English east of Clarksville, Texas. His parents were Joe and Bennie Bryant Storey, and he had four brothers, Quillard, Joe, Jr., Bobby Dean and Wayne, and one sister, Wanda. Ben married Doris A. Troxell August 3, 1948, and their children are Nancy, Byron, Ben Ray and Donna. Ben had this to say about his experiences:

"When World War II broke out on December 7, 1941, I was in Dallas going to business college. I came home to get ready to go to

Herman Lee Martin's plane crew (He is squatting on the left end of the front row.)

the army and worked on the roads at Red River Arsenal and at a plant in Oklahoma. I was called in the spring of 1943, and my training was at Camp Howze in Texas and in Louisiana. I went from there to Camp Shank, New York and left there on April 5 for England. From there we went to France on June 7, and I was wounded at the Battle of St. Lo on July 20, 1944. I was sent back to England. I went back to the front lines after eating Christmas dinner in Southern France. I was in the 9th Infantry Division, and we were the first to cross the Rhine River on a railroad bridge. I went back to Germany about six years ago. The bridge was gone, and a sign there read 'Where Two Great Armies Met.'

I served in the ETO and was awarded the EAME with four Bronze Stars, Distinguished Unit Badge, and Purple Heart. I was discharged October 25, 1945. I retired from 20 years in Civil Service and also from serving as County Commissioner for 14 years. My wife and I reside at English."

★★★

Walter Percy and Della Baird Bellotte had three sons serving in World War II. They also had two daughters, Lucille and Mary Lou, and two other sons, Guy and Edwin.

WALTER EARL BELLOTTE was born August 1, 1916 in Avery, Texas. He married Luncina Lee Tucker on December 14, 1938 and their children are Arville and R. V. Bellotte. He entered the Army in 1942 and trained at Ft. Lewis, Washington, Oregon, and San Pedro, California. A Pfc in the 151st Infantry, 38th Division, he served at Pearl Harbor, New Guinea and Luzon. In 1945 he was wounded on Luzon, and he was killed in action there on February 9, 1945. Pfc Bellotte was awarded the Purple Heart posthumously and a Battle Star for Volunteer Landing on Luzon and a Ribbon of Honor. His body was returned and burial was made at the Avery Cemetery in 1945.

LOUIS V. (VAUGHN) BELLOTTE married Lola Stinson, and they had one daughter. He entered the Navy in 1943 and trained in San Diego. He was a Seaman 1/C and served in Leyte, Okinawa, Iwo Jima, China and Alaska. In 1944 he was wounded in Leyte. He was awarded four Battle Stars and a Purple Heart. (Very little information could be found about him.)

TRAVIS H. BELLOTTE entered the Army in 1944 and

trained at Camp Hood, Texas and Camp Shelby, Mississippi. He was a Pfc in the Infantry and served in England, France, Holland and Germany where he was wounded in 1945. He received three campaign stars. (Very little information could be found about him.)

★★★

MELVIN F. ANDERSON, the son of Will E. and Martha J. Dixon Anderson, was born October 17, 1926 at Annona, Texas. The other children in the family were Willie, Ida, Flossie, Gladys and Edd. He married Ernestine Bellotte, and their children are Jerry, Allen and Karon. He enlisted in the Navy on August 3, 1944 at Dallas and went to the NTC in San Diego. He served as a MOMM 3/C on the USS Barnwell, APA 132 and was a part of Beach Battery B, Oceanside, California (amphibious training). His overseas duty was on Iwo Jima and Okinawa, and he was awarded two Battle Stars and an Asiatic-Pacific Campaign Ribbon. He was discharged March 12, 1946 at Norman, Oklahoma.

★★★

CHARLIE FRANK BELLOTTE, JR. was born September 20, 1925 at Avery, Texas. His parents were Charlie Frank, Sr. and Ocie Odell Chapman Bellotte. His sister was Neva Odell, and his brothers were Oswald and Robert. He enlisted in the Navy in December 1943 at Clarksville; took amphibious training; served as a Coxswain, Seaman 1/C, in the South Pacific, Marshall Islands. His discharge was in January 1946 at Norman, Oklahoma and he was awarded the Asiatic-Pacific Campaign Medal.

★★★

HAROLD L. TYNDELL, the son of Fred L. and Ruth Thames Tyndell, was born November 27, 1923 in Red River County, Texas. He had two brothers, Stanley and Wayne, who also served in World War II, and a sister, Carol. Harold married Martha Sue Roberts, and they had three sons, Terry, Russell and Timothy.

He enlisted in the Marines in 1942 at Dallas and trained in San Diego. He was attached to the lst Marine Divison as a Scout and served under General Sheppard and General Chesty Puller as a Pfc. His overseas duty was in the South Pacific, and he was wounded in action on Cape Gloucester in 1944. His discharge ws in 1944 at Mare Island,

California, and he received the Purple Heart and other medals. (While in the South Pacific, Harold accidentally met up with his brother, Stanley, who was also in the Marines.) Harold died February 15, 1987.

★★★

EDWARD GLENN DOZIER was born December 13, 1904, the son of Joe and Mandy Hightower Dozier. He had four sisters, Verna Fay, Mary, Sybil and Elizabeth. On November 15, 1931 he married Jessie Sale. He entered the Army Signal Corps on March 11, 1942 and was the first married man to leave Red River County for the service. For 2½ months he trained in Brownwood, Texas and Louisiana and then went overseas for 43 months to Italy and was in the Battle of the Bulge. His job was to fix telephone lines and work switchboards. Dozier was a barber and cut the officers' hair. While going over the ocean, he was very seasick. The ship carrying their supplies was destroyed. While in Europe, he ran into Gene Warthan several times. He was discharged in 1946 and came home to Red River County. He died October 15, 1996, and Jessie resides in their home in Clarksville.

★★★

THOMAS H. TANNER was born October 14, 1907 in Cooper, Texas, the son of A. D. and Margaret Hayes Tanner. He had a brother, Floyd, and two sisters, Ruby and Jo. He married Louise Frances Bull, and they had two children, Billie Joe and Margaret Lou. He enlisted in the Navy on April 24, 1944 at San Antonio and trained at the USNCH in Beaumont, California. As a PH 2/C he served with the SV V6 USNR at the US Naval Base #131 and US Fleet Hospital #105. His overseas duty was in the South Pacific, and he was awarded the World War II Victory Medal and Asiatic-Pacific Campaign Medal. He was discharged January 20, 1946 at Norman, Oklahoma. Mr. Tanner now lives in Tyler, Texas. (We will remember him as part owner of the Clarksville Pharmacy and as being Mrs. Morehead's brother.)

★★★

ELBERT S. EPPS was born August 7, 1909 at Rugby, Texas, the son of George W. and Eliza A. Blankingship Epps. He had one sister, Edna Jewel. He married Alva Angline Millaway, and they had one son, Darrell Elbert Epps. Elbert entered the service in Tyler, Texas on January 18, 1943 and was attached to the 860th Engineering (AVN) Bn as a Construction Machine Operator. His overseas duty was in the Philippines and New Guinea. His discharge was on December 20, 1945 at Ft. Sam Houston, Texas, and he received four Overseas Service Bars, Asiatic-Pacific Campaign Medal with two Bronze Stars, Philippine Liberation Ribbon with two Bronze Stars, Victory Ribbon, and Good Conduct Medal. He died March 8, 1982, and Alva lives in Clarksville.

★★★

JAMES R. BOLTON, the son of Francis Marion (Tom) and Rena Myrtle Woods Bolton, was born January 24, 1923 in Detroit, Texas. He had two brothers, Travis Corley and Thomas Paul, and two sisters, Betty Joe and Dorothy Marie. He was inducted into the service February 4, 1943 at Camp Fannin, Texas and his training was at Camp Howze, Texas and Camp Livingston, Louisiana. His rank was Corporal, and he served as an antitank gunner in France and the Rhineland. His discharge on January 21, 1946 was at Camp Fannin, and he was awarded the EAME Medal with two Bronze Stars, Victory Medal, Pacific Medal, Combat Infantryman Badge, Meritorious Unit Award, and ETO Medal.

★★★

THERON MILAM was born July 12, 1924 at the Midway Community east of Detroit, Texas, the son of Fred and Irene Patterson Milam. He had two sisters, Eva Dell and Billie, and one brother, Duane. He married Electra Flippo and they had three children, Ronnie, Vickie and Darlene. Theron entered the Navy on September 11, 1943 at Tyler, Texas. His training was at USNTC in Virginia as an Equipment Operator. He was a Machinist's Mate Third Class (CB) and served 22 months overseas in the Southeast Pacific. He was discharged at Camp Wolters, Texas on December 18, 1945 and received the Asiatic-Pacific Medal with one Battle Star. Theron also served in the Air Force Reserves as a sergeant and was called into active duty in March 1951. He served in Alaska and was discharged August 6, 1952. He died June 28, 1998.

★★★

NOEL F. MYERS, the son of Irenious C. and Ella Catherine Pappio Myers, was born August 19, 1921 at Superior, Wisconsin. He had a half-sister, Ione Jeunesse, and two half-brothers, Hilary and Wayne Jeunesse. He married Margie Hancock, and they had two daughters, Jackie and Lisa. Noel enlisted in the Navy on August 1, 1942 and served as a Naval Aviator; Patrol Plane Commander; Educational Officer, VPB203; Pilot's Certificate, Patrol Plane; Commander, Standard Inst. Card. He was a Lieutenant and received the Victory Ribbon, American Area Campaign Ribbon, European-African Area Campaign Ribbon, and a Personal Commendation from Admiral Ingram. He was discharged July 10, 1946 and reenlisted May 1, 1952 in the Naval Reserve, Aviator, Patrol Squadron 49, Bermuda. He was discharged again on May 1, 1954. Noel died April 10, 1971, and Margie resides in Bogata, Texas.

★★★

ROBERT SHIMPOCK was born January 22, 1913, in Hayworth, Oklahoma, the son of W. H. and Susie Tolison Shimpock. The other children in the family were Arthur, Alice, Mack, Willie and Vada. He married Dorothy Gaddis, and they had three children, Bruce, Rebecca and Timothy. Robert was drafted February 10, 1942 at Annona, Texas and was attached to the 963rd Bn. Field Artillery. His basic training was at Ft. Sill, Oklahoma, and he went to a cook and baker school at Ft. Bragg, North Carolina. He served as First Cook. Robert's group landed on Omaha Beach on June 9, 1944. He was in the Battle of St. Lo and the Battle of the Bulge. While in Frankfurt, Germany, he killed two deer for the men to eat. He said they looked more like goats. Robert said the happiest day of his life, while in Germany, was when the planes flew over dropping pamphlets saying 'The war is over.' They left Germany and rode a train to France where they stayed for six weeks. He landed in New York in September 1944. He was discharged at Tyler, Texas in October 1945 and received a Good Conduct Medal and five Battle Stars. Robert and Dorothy live in Annona.

★★★

HOUSTON LEE, the son of Jess and Janie Pryor Lee, was born in Red River County, Texas. He had three brothers, Afton, Edward and Leonard Joe. Houston and Ora Conyers were married

September 9, 1941. Houston entered the army in 1944; trained at Ft. McClellan, Alabama; and served in the ETO in northern France. After the war ended in Europe, he was returning to the states on the Queen Mary when news was received of Japan's surrender. Houston said that you could have heard a pin drop aboard the ship as the men heard the good news. He was discharged in 1946 and received an ETO Ribbon with one Battle Star, Good Conduct Medal, Victory Medal and ATO Ribbon. The Lees are retired and live in Clarksville.

★★★

George Henry and Eunice Lum Rhea had two sons in World War II. Their other children were Gladys, Onvie, Vivian, and Christine.

ALVIS LEE RHEA was born December 2, 1926 at Annona and raised at Boxelder. He married Mary Jo Smith on December 4, 1948, and they had three children, Charlotte, Linda and Rick. He went into the Navy on November 11, 1944 and trained at NTC, San Diego, California. He served as a Baker Third Class V6 USNR aboard the *USS LST 557, USS Sierra* (AP-18), and *USS LST* 1017. His discharge was on August 15, 1946, and he was awarded the Victory Medal and American Campaign Medal. He died February 1, 1999.

H.G. RHEA was born September 25, 1924 at Boxelder, Texas. He married Emma Jean Brookshire on December 14, 1947, and their children are Kathy and Harold. H. G. was inducted into the Army on December 30, 1944 and trained at Mineral Wells, Texas. He attained the rank of S/Sgt. and served in the Philippines and Japan. His discharge was on July 29, 1946. This is what he had to say: "I was working at the Red River Arsenal in Texarkana when God called me into HIS ministry. I left my job to go into full time ministry. For the past forty-eight years I have served in the ministry of the Gospel as a minister of God's Word. I have pastored charuches in several different states and have spent most of these years as a pastor of Southern Baptist Churches. I have retired from pastoring, but I am still preaching in supply and interim work. I reside in Texarkana, Arkansas."

★★★

KENNETH SMITH was born in Red River County, Texas,

and his parents were John and Maudie Blankenship Smith. He had seven brothers and sisters: Leonard, Lloyd, Edward, Weldon, Lizzie Lee, Mildred and Earlene. Kenneth and Adell Nunn Brown were married in 1974. Adell's first husband was Lennox Brown, and they had three daughters, Dorthy, Mary and Betty. Kenneth entered the Army October 12, 1942. He was in Headquarters Company, 383rd Infantry, 96th Division. His overseas duty was in the Philippines and Okinawa. He was discharged in 1945. He and Adell live east of Clarksville.

★★★

PFC GEORGE WILLARD BROWN entered the Marines in 1944. At that time he was working for Tommy Tucker, a farmer, in the Tucker Bottom near the Lennox Bottom south of Clarksville. He trained in Riverside, California and went overseas without having a furlough. He served on Iwo Jima and Okinawa where he was killed in action in 1945. The Purple Heart was awarded to him posthumously. He was the son of Johnny Brown.

★★★

William Henry and Katie Childress Alford had eight children: Coy, Travis, Hubert Pershing, Horace, Norris, Sybil, Lucille and Edith (Cook). Mr. Alford died at age 52. Mrs. Alford had four sons who served in World War II, and her fifth son would have served if he had not been too young.

COY ALFORD entered the Army in 1944. He served in England, France and Germany. At Marseilles, France he ran into Johnny Maxfield who was also from Clarksville. After he was discharged from the service in 1946, Coy was in a wreck and spent eighteen months in the VA Hospitals in Bonham and Houston, Texas. He was awarded the ETO Ribbon, Good Conduct Medal, Victory Medal, and one Battle Star.

TRAVIS ALFORD served in the Marines, and his overseas duty was in the Aleutian Islands where he was wounded. He died in 1985.

HORACE ALFORD entered the Army in 1942 and served in Australia and New Guinea. When a Japanese sniper in a tree above him came down on him with a bayonet, the field rations he was carrying saved his life. The others with him killed the Jap, and when going through his wallet they found a picture of his family. This made them all sad, but they had to kill him. Horace went on a volunteer mission, and when the ship let them off, they made their way to land and went through dense foliage where the Japanese were firing. When they went back, the crew on the boat threw ropes to two of them and pulled at high speed to save them. The Chaplain aboard the ship asked the two men if they were Christians. Horace said that he was, but the other man was not. When the man returned home, he became a Christian and let Horace know about it. Horace was awarded the PTO Ribbon with two Bronze Stars and a Good Conduct Medal. He was discharged in 1945.

HUBERT PERSHING ALFORD was already in the Navy when Pearl Harbor was attacked, as he had enlisted in 1940. He was at home on leave and got a call to get in uniform and come back to his duty station. He had served on the USS Rogers in the Atlantic. This time he shipped out from the Pacific Coast on the USS Coehann, a transport ship that took Marines to Guadalcanal. The ship was sunk in 1942, and he was only twenty-two years old when he died. Sarah Ragsdill with the Western Union in Clarksville delivered the telegram telling Mrs. Alford of her son's death. Sarah said it was the hardest thing she had ever done. Hubert was awarded the Purple Heart posthumously.

★★★

ALTON COOK was the son of John and Ora Christopher Cook. He had a sister, Lotene, and three brothers, Charles, Lewis, and Tommy who was killed in an airplane crash before the war started. Alton was a Staff Sergeant in the Army in World War II and was stationed in Maine. After he was discharged, he worked in the steel mines in Montana and then returned to Clarksville and worked for the Texas Highway Department until his retirement. He and Edith Alford married on June 7, 1953 and had one son, Tommy. Alton died May 8, 1994, and Edith lives in Clarksville.

★★★

Joe Thomas and Katie Halbrooks Conway had three sons who served in World War II. The other children in the family were Adell, Raliegh, Betty, Harold, and Robert, twin of Russell who died when he was only a year old.

JOE T. (J. T.) CONWAY was born December 20, 1915 in Deport, Texas. He married Marguerite Gray, and they had five children, Linda, Larry, Jerry, Karen and Bobby. J. T. entered the service on December 12, 1942 at Dallas and trained at Sheppard Field in Wichita Falls, Texas, New Jersey, Langley Field, Virginia, Florida and Bakersfield, California. He was a Staff Sergeant in the Army Air Corps who served as an airplane armored gunner attached to the 9th Radar Calibration Detachment. His overseas duty was in Hawaii and the Marshall Islands where he was wounded in 1944. J. T. was discharged February 14, 1945, at Ft. Sam Houston, Texas and was awarded the Good Conduct Medal, and Asiatic-Pacific Ribbon.

His son, Jerry, had this to say about his father: "J. T. Conway served in the Clarksville Unit of the National Guard from 9-11-35 to 11-13-37 and again from 1-17-40 to 6-3-40. He and my mother and Bob Isbell and Odessa Solomon were married in a double ceremony on 1-9-42, and J. T. and Bob enlisted in the Army Air Corps three days later. He was injured in an airplane crash on the Marshall Islands and was transferred back to Honolulu and later back to Brooke General Hospital at Ft. Sam Houston, Texas. After the war, J. T. came back to Red River County to do the only thing he knew how to do, which was farming. Due to his war injuries, for a few years he received a small monthly disability check from the government. It was later discontinued. I remember growing up being very much aware of the pain that he endured from those injuries and how it affected him while trying to farm and raise his family. Many years later, after we were all raised, he was finally put on 100% disability." (Both J. T. and Marguerite are deceased.)

ISAAC F. (IKE) CONWAY entered the Navy in 1944 and trained in Illinois and California. His overseas duty was in the Marshall Islands, Guam, Iwo Jima, and Japan. He was discharged in 1946 and awarded the American Theater Medal, AP Ribbon and 3rd Fleet Medal. He married Ella Jean Igo, and they had three children, Patsy, Ike, Jr., and Stacy.

RUSSELL M. CONWAY was born December 30, 1916 at Turner's Lake in Red River County, Texas. He married Jackie Martin and they had two children, David and Marizanna. He entered the service September 20, 1940 and took cook and baker training at Ft. Sam Houston and parachute training at Ft. Benning, Georgia. He was attached to the 513th Parachute Combat Infantry.

His overseas duty was in Belgium, France and Germany. He was discharged November 24, 1945 at Camp Fannin, Texas and was awarded the American Theater Campaign Medal, Meritorious Unit Award, EAME Campaign Medal with three Bronze Stars, WWII Victory Medal, Good Conduct Medal, Ardennes-Rhineland-Central Europe Medal, Presidential Citation, and American Defense Service Medal. He died in 1997.

His daughter, Marizanna Conway Underwood, had this to say, in part, about some stories her father told her: "My father, Russell M. Conway, was in the Army when the Japanese bombed Pearl Harbor. He was pulling guard duty on a railroad bridge somewhere in Washington State and was scheduled to have a two week leave. Needless to say, he did not take leave for a very long time. . .

Dad was in the National Guard several years before enlisting for active duty in the Army. He had trained as a cook so when the U.S. became involved in the war, he did not want to be a cook. The Army was asking for volunteers for a new type of Infantry group called the Airborne Infantry, so Daddy decided to join so he wouldn't have to peel any more potatoes. At Ft. Benning, Georgia he was trained to jump out of planes and also as an automotive mechanic. He shipped out in August 1944 to the European Theater with the 513rd Parachute Infantry which was part of the 101st Airborne Division. . .

He did not talk much about the war. I guess it was too horrible to talk about. His group served in France, Belgium and Germany. In France it was hard to find fresh water to drink so when they found empty champagne bottles, they hid them near towns with clean water, later to be filled. The language barrier was a problem because the French always wanted to fill the bottles with champagne or wine.

Dad was in the Battle of the Bulge in Bastogne, Belgium in December 1944. It was bitterly cold with snow waist deep and overcast skies the majority of the battle. They couldn't build fires to keep warm because the Germans were so near, and they didn't have hot meals or a warm place to sleep. They slept fully clothed in foxholes to keep warm and to be ready for battle at any time. They endured this for a week, and then one day Dad saw a chow wagon coming toward them on Christmas Day. He was so excited with thoughts of a hot cup of coffee and a warm meal, but then the chow wagon took a direct hit by German artillery. This was a terrible ordeal, and every Christmas Eve night while he was alive, he would always say, 'I can remember exactly where I was in '44.' He always had a drink that night to salute the memory of his friends who did not survive the battle...

Jerry Conway said that his favorite uncle, Russell, told him that from the time he started fighting in the Battle of the Bulge, he stayed out in the snow, day and night, for 28 days, except for one night spent in a farm house. They did not change clothes or take a bath during that entire time. To keep their feet from freezing, they cut up strips of a wool blanket to wrap around their feet and wore rubber galoshes over them. They went days with very little to eat.

★★★

OVAL H. POTTS was born November 14, 1922 in Clarksville, Texas, the son of Otis William and Mamie Pearl Howell Potts. His brothers and sisters were Otis William, Jr., Pauline, Ollie Jean, and Howell Vaughan. He married Helen Deviney, and they had seven children: Ronald Hugh, Paula Elaine, Jack Michael, Joseph William, Gary Carl, Linda Gail and Charles Anthony.

Oval enlisted in the Army on November 15, 1940 at Clarksville, and was a part of Company I, 144th Infantry Division until May of 1944. He was transferred then to Company G, 330rd Infantry, 83rd Division. He served as a machine gunner and was a Staff Sergeant. He was overseas in Normandy, France and Germany. He was wounded December 15, 1944 in Germany and hospitalized in France and England before being sent to Camp Carson, Colorado for treatment and rehabilitation. He was sent to Ft. Sam Houston, Texas in June 1945 for Military Police training, and he was a Military Police Officer in Texarkana, Arkansas until he was discharged September 27, 1945 at Camp Chaffee, Arkansas. He was awarded the Combat Infantry Medal, Purple Heart, WWII Victory Medal, American Campaign Medal, American Defense Service Medal, EAME Campaign Medal with three Bronze Stars, and a Medal for Normandy.

Oval's wife, Helen, told me that he was in a foxhole with another soldier who was killed. He had trench foot, and his nerves were bad after enduring the bitter cold and hard times while being overseas in the battlefields. She said that all our World War II veterans went through this, and the ones who made it home were very fortunate. (Oval and Helen reside north of Clarksville.)

★★★

Henry O. and Lucy Williams Eudy had two sons in the service during World War II. They also had two daughters, Callie and Mary Alice.

HOWARD EUDY was born October 23, 1919 in Clarksville, Texas. He married Louise Duke, and they had two sons, Don, and Mickey Hugh who died at six months of age. Howard entered the Army Air Corps in October 1942, and his basic training was at Sheppard Field, Texas. He was trained as a cook at Salt Lake City, and from there he went to Hays, Kansas and on to Salina, Kansas where Don was born. From Norfolk, Virginia he went to North Africa and India as a Corporal with the 20th Bomber Command. While in India, he received a three day pass and rode a train 75 miles to Calcutta. He remembered how crowded the train was, with people literally hanging on the top and sides. On the way back from overseas, they stopped in Bermuda to refuel and heard that the war in Europe was over. They went on to New York where there was a big crowd of people celebrating. Howard went from there to San Antonio and was given a ninety day furlough. He was discharged in November 1945 at Salt Lake City. He resides in Clarksville.

HUBERT PRESTON EUDY was born June 20, 1924 at Detroit, Texas. He was married to Joyce Herring and then to Ruby Brewer. His children were Phoebe Joyce, Mercedes Maurine, Lynn Howard, and Leland Hugh. Hubert entered the service in 1943 in Red River County and his training was in Kentucky and Pennsylvania. He was attached to the 33rd Armored Regiment, Spearhead Division as a Staff Sergeant. For five months he was a gunner on a tank, and then for twenty-four months, he served as a Technician 4th Class Tank Driver. His battle areas were Normandy, France, Rhineland, Germany and Central Europe. He was wounded two different times. His discharge was at Camp Fannin, Texas on November 20, 1945. He received a Good Conduct Medal, EAME Campaign Medal with four Bronze Stars, two Purple Hearts, and a WWII Victory Medal. Hubert died in Brawley, California on May 29, 1977.

His sister, Callie Eudy Finley, told me the following about her brother: "Mom and Dad received a letter dated July 23, 1944 saying that he had been on the front lines in Germany. Then on November 1, 1944 Hubert wrote saying that he was in the hospital because he had been wounded and almost lost his leg and foot. They censored his letters so much that mostly all Mother received was 'I'm doing fine; don't worry about me'. I ran across a letter they reevied from Lonnie Petty dated December 21, 1943 saying that he would be with Hubert for Christmas. He told us about his tank getting hit in Germany. They had to crawl out from the bottom and down the tracks of the tank. They went to a farm house, and the people hid them from the Germans. The Germans came and searched the house but didn't find them, which was a miracle. When he was in training, they were crawling under barbed wire when they came upon a snake. The soldier next to him raised up, and the gun fire cut him into. Hubert crawled out and reported what had happened, and they stopped the firing. He was in the hospital three different times, once with frost bitten feet, and the other times from being wounded. When he came home, his feet were still purple and there was lead in them. One time Mom and Dad didn't hear from him for a long time, and it was horrible. I thought Mom would lose her mind. When he came home, he was what they call 'shell shocked', and we had to be careful not to walk up behind him without him knowing we were there. We were living in the community of Brewster then, behind the school house. Several nights after he was home, he would wake up yelling, 'Take cover, take cover', and he would jump out of bed. He never liked to talk much about the war; he just seemed to want to forget it. I believe the war almost destroyed his life. I wish I could tell you more, but I was only eleven then. I don't remember anything good about it."

★★★

JOHN H. CHILDERS, M.D. was born May 21, 1923 in Bogata, Texas, the only child of John and Ruth Hancock Childers. He met Cristal Drake in Galveston, and after dating several months, they were married on March 2, 1946, the day he was graduated from Medical School (UTMB). On that day he was commissioned 1st Lieutenant in the Medical Corps. They had two children, John H., Jr. and Joan Carol.

Dr. Childers did his Internship and first year residency at the Santa Rosa Hospital in San Antonio. He was called in for active duty at Brooke General Hospital in San Antonio, and he continued pathology training there. His first assignment was Chief of

Pathology at Army-Navy General Hospital in Hot Springs, Arkansas. After serving there two years, he was sent to the 279th Station Hospital in Berlin, Germany where he stayed for about a year. This was during the blockade, and the airlift into Berlin brought supplies. He was discharged as a Captain in 1950. His death was on December 3, 1988, and he is buried in the family plot in the Bogata Cemetery. He loved Red River County.

His wife says: "When I met John, he was grieving over the death of his friend, Albert Broadfoot. He felt it was such a loss because he was outstanding in every way. When we visited Bogata in 1945, John took me to Bonham, Texas to meet the Broadfoot family. The visit brought closure, and John felt comforted in visiting with Albert's family."

★★★

An article from a Bonham newspaper reads as follows: "After riding through death in German skies and cabling his parents, Judge and Mrs. A. S. Broadfoot, Sr. that he had completed his required number of combat missions and was awaiting transportation home, **FIRST LT. ALBERT S. BROADFOOT, JR.**, 22, B-24 pilot, was killed in England March 13. He had received the Air Medal and five Oak Leaf Clusters and was serving as a check pilot at the time he was killed.

A graduate of Bonham High School and Paris Jr. College, he was a junior law student at the University of Texas when he was called to active duty with the air force in January 1943. (He and John Childers became good friends while they both were attending PJC.) . . .

In a recent letter to his parents he said: "I know what war costs; I have seen the toll paid in the sky. . . but I am not afraid." Besides his parents, he is survied by three sisters, Miss Jessie Butler Broadfoot, Miss Emma Gene Broadfoot, and Miss Alice Broadfoot, all students at Denton Teachers' College."

★★★

James Corley and Mollie Lucille Stephens Ward had two sons who served in World War II. Their other children were James Henry, Betty Jean, Virginia Ruth and Billy Sue.

SIMS CORLEY WARD was born October 24, 1921 in Red

River County, Texas. He entered the Army in 1939 and trained at Ft. Sam Houston and Camp Wolters, Texas; Massachusetts; and North Carolina. His overseas duty was in England, Africa, Sicily and France where he served as a PFC. He was wounded in France and died August 17, 1944. He was awarded the Purple Heart, Bronze Star, Infantry Badge, ETO Ribbon, Good Conduct Medal, and Pre-Pearl Harbor Ribbon.

GRADY S. (BUD) WARD was born January 4, 1923 in Red River County. He married Hazel Aliene Lawler on July 11, 1942, and they had two children, James Grady and Elaine. Bud enlisted in the Army Air Corps in the summer of 1942 and was trained in Florida, Missouri and California. He served as a Sergeant in England, France, Belgium and Germany and was assigned to the 22nd Mobile Repair and Reclamation Squadron of the 9th Air Force Service Command. His first assignment was in England where his unit assembled fighter aircraft, P5l's, P38's and P47's. The unit moved to France after the invasion of Europe and there they repaired or salvaged aircraft that had been downed by enemy action. The Unit received a Meritorius Conduct Award from the 9th Air Force for its operations in the European Theater. His discharge was in 1945, and he received the Good Conduct Medal, ETO Ribbon and Victory Ribbon. Bud died August 20, 1997, and Aliene is also deceased.

★★★

BURNY BUFORD BAIRETT was born September 24, 1912 in Royston in Fisher County, Texas. His parents were Sam Houston and Retta Mae Morgan Bairett. His brothers and sisters were Lillian, George Dee, Nola Mae, Vera, Faye, Frances, Mart, and Marie. He married Winnie King. Buford enlisted in the Navy on October 1, 1942 in Dallas. He was in the Seabees, V6 (CB) as a construction carpenter at the rank of Carpenter's Mate, First Class. His overseas duty was in the South Pacific. He was discharged September 8, 1945 at Camp Parks, California. He died May 28, 1970, and Winnie resides in Clarksville.

★★★

Henry Harvey and Elvira Levene Wright King had two sons in World War II. Their other children were Rufus, Mary, Winnie, Mabel, and Virgie.

SETH D. KING was born June 11, 1918, in Annona, Texas. He married Wilma C. Herdle, and they had two children, Wilma and Wayne H. Seth enlisted in the Navy in 1942 in Dallas and received his training at the University of Houston and Ward Island Navy Base in Corpus Christi. He was a Chief Petty Officer who served as a Radio Techician and Repairman. He served in the South Pacific on the aircraft carrier USS HANCOCK. He was discharged in 1945, and died December 17, 1979.

EARL LEE KING was born April 2, 1922 in Annona, Texas. He married Bobbye N. Dale, and they had two children, Richard Neil and Elizabeth. Earl enlisted in the Navy in 1943 at Little Rock, Arkansas. His training was at Michigan City, Indiana, the University of Houston, and Ward Island Navy Base in Corpus Christi. He was a First Class Petty Officer who served as a Radio Technician and Repairman in the United States. He was discharged in 1945 at Jacksonville, Florida. Earl and Bobbye reside in Clarksville.

★★★

RAYMOND E. BARRY, the son of Mr. and Mrs. J. H. Barry, was born in Clarksville, Texas on November 20, 1905. He married Winnie Lowe on October 20, 1945. They are both deceased. Raymond entered the Army on January 6, 1942 and trained at Ft. Leonardwood, Missouri. He was attached to the 3608th Quartermaster Truck Company as a TEC 5 and served overseas as a stevedore in Sicily, North Africa, Algeria-French Morocco, Tunisia, Naples-Foggia and Rome-Arno. He was discharged June 25, 1945 at Ft. Sam Houston, Texas and received the Good Conduct Medal, EAME Campaign Medal with four Bronze Stars, and the American Defense Service Medal.

★★★

Jim and Phoebe Ann Atterberry Herrington had two sons in World War II. The other children in the family were Cecil, Wayne, Lonnie, Ethel, Maggie, Ona, Bertha, Eula and Vera.

CLIFTON T. HERRINGTON was born October 24, 1922 in Clarksville, Texas. He married Wanda Duffie, and after her death he married Virginia Kiker. He was inducted into the Army at Tyler, Texas on December 21, 1942, and trained at Ft. Benning, Georgia and Ft. Ord, California. Clifton was a TEC 4 in the Infantry Headquarters of the 764th Amphibious Tractor Battalion and served as an auto mechanic. He was discharged February 22, 1946 at Camp Fannin, Texas after spending 38 months in the Army. He was awarded the Good Conduct Medal, American Theater Campaign Medal and WWII Victory Medal. He is deceased.

DONNIE D. HERRINGTON was born February 14, 1920 and had a twin brother, Lonnie, who died at age 17 from pneumonia. He married Mable Hand, and they had three children, Carol, Charles and Laura. Donnie entered the Army on February 10, 1942 at Ft. Sill, Oklahoma and trained at Camp Robinson, Arkansas. He served in Central Europe as a TEC 5 Supply Clerk in the 5th Grade Service Battery of the 373rd Field Artillery Battalion. He was discharged January 18, 1946 at Camp Fannin, Texas and was awarded the Good Conduct Medal, American Theater Campaign Medal, EAME Campaign Medal with one Bronze Star, and WWII Victory Medal. He is deceased.

★★★

GAYLORD HOWISON McCLUER, the son of Herman Charles and Elizabeth Howison McCluer, was born in Bogata, Texas on November 28, 1915. A graduate of the University of Texas at Austin, he volunteered for the service in 1942 and was commissioned an Ensign in the Navy. He trained at Pearl Harbor and served in the Pacific Theater of Operations. Gaylord was in the Battle for Peleiu Island and in the Battle of the Coral Sea, serving on the aircraft carrier *USS HORNET*. He survived its sinking in the Battle of the Santa Cruz Islands. Later he served on the battleship *USS Tennessee*. His discharge was in 1946, and he had attained the rank of Lieutenant (j.g.). He was awarded seven Battle Stars, the PTO Ribbon, and the Purple Heart. In November 1950 he married Eleanor Lamb in Austin, Texas, and their two sons are Gaylord L. and James H. Gaylord died July 27, 1973, and Eleanor resides in Bogata.

★★★

A short story, "Exploits of Alvis Jones at Sea—WWII", is quoted in part below. Time and space would not allow me to quote everything written by him.

"I, **ALVIS JONES**, was born of P. H. and Ada Kemp Jones into a family of one brother and one sister. Later another sister was born in September of 1923. Three months later my mother pased away and was buried in Snow Hill, Texas Community Cemetery. My father cared for us three older children, never remarrying...

In 1939 I entered the C.C.C. Camp located in Mesquite, Texas, serving there until June of 1940 when I was inducted into the Maritime Service School on Gallups Island in Boston for training in 'radio, wireless', and A. B. Seaman Facility in 1941, having graduated No. 8 in class of 32 as a radio operator.

In September 1941 I signed aboard an oil tanker of Esso in Bayonne, New Jersey as Radio and Communications Officer. This ship was plying the coastal waters from Galveston and Aruba to the refinery in Bayonne, New Jersey, loaded with crude oil. About the first of March 1942 I signed aboard the *Esso Bolivar*, a seized German tanker having been in New York Harbor when war was declared on Germany. This vessel had a complement of fifty crew and officers along with a Naval armed guard of eight men to operate the guns at the bow and stern as well as four 50-caliber machine guns amidship...

On the 8th of March 1942 we were enroute to Aruba with cargo of fresh water for the island, having passed between Cuba and Haiti at 2:30 A.M. An attack was launched by a German submarine upon our vessel, using four inch guns, 50-caliber machine guns using tracer bullets as well as pompons strafing our decks, life boats and rafts with damage to the stern deck, fire buring in the crews' quarters and deck cargo afire. Several shells were hitting around the Navigation Bridge and the top of the Radio Shack, resulting in concrete falling into the Radio Room. This shelling continued until about 4:00 A.M., and at this time a torpedo struck the ship between No. 6 and No. 7 starboard wing tanks, thus creating a hole approximately 20x20 feet above and below the water line. Fortunately, the tanks contained only fresh water, thereby not creating fires aboard and on the waters around her.

I sent out a SOS message of attack by wireless radio; then went to the bridge for instruction. Finding no one, I went to my quarters to don a morner life saving suit. This was made of rubberized fabric with a Mae West life belt built into it, including a shark repellant substance in it. I then went to the boat deck and saw the captain's body lying there. The ship was listing badly so I went to the off side from the submarine and jumped from the high side into the water. The deck cargo as well as the stern was ablaze. I determined that no one was in sight aboard and that the lifeboats and rafts were not in place because the crew had abandoned ship.

The submarine was still surfaced, using machine guns on the crew in the water and lifeboats. I swam away from the sub. The suit had filled with water making me lower in the water, up to my nose in fact, probably saving my life since I was not visible. A star shell from a naval vessel exploded above the scene, lighting up the area so the sub quickly submerged and left. An empty raft was spotted nearby, and as I swam to it, there were voices of crew members in the distance. As dawn came I could see a lifeboat low in the water with injured men aboard. This lifeboat had been machine gunned, making holes in it; so blood from the injured ones was seeping out, thus attracting sharks. They were swimming along side of me, but because of my suit, not attacking me.

A few hours later, about 11:00 A.M., March 8th, the forty-two survivors were picked up by the *USS ENDURANCE* and taken to Guantanamo Bay Naval Base in Cuba where the injured twenty men received medical attention. On May 9, 1942 fourteen men, including me, went abord the *Esso Bolivar* to bring her into port, accompanied by a Naval ship. I prepared the body of the captain for burial. When we boarded the ship, she was still burning in various areas of the aft quarters and storerooms and listing badly to the starboard. We did succeed in bringing her in under her own power. Eight men were lost in action, with four men buried ashore at Guantanamo Bay and the other four lost at sea to shell fire and the numerous sharks in the area. The ship received some repairs that allowed her to sail to Mobile, Alabama shipyard for further repairs.

This crew was awarded the Merchant Marine Combat Bar, having faced direct enemy action in a service of vital importance to the nation. In addition to this Bar, I also received the Mediterranean Middle East War Zone Bar, the Pacific War Zone Bar, and the Atlantic War Zone Bar...

Later Mrs. Hawkins Fudske, wife of the deceased Chief Mate, christened the 200th liberty ship named 'The Hawkins Fudske' at Baltimore, Maryland Bethlehem-Fairfield Shipyard Inc.

During my tenure of sea going, we ran coastwise from New York to Galveston and also to Aruba Curacao, South America. We were in numerous convoys to Scotland passing through the famous Loch Loman where the sea monster supposedly lives. It was here that we refueled the *Queen Elizabeth and Queen Mary* which had been refitted as troop carriers while we were on our way to Dublin to discharge remaining cargo. In 1944 the ship was transferred to the Pacific Ocean to supply the Naval fleets in that part of the war. . . When the war ended, we were south of Hawaii proceeding to San Diego where I was discharged from the Coast Guard and Merchant Marines on August 13, 1945. This ending my period of service, I went home!"

Alvis and Mary Elizabeth Skidmore were married December 23, 1944 and had two children, Reid and Lana Kay. The Jones reside in a retirement place, "The Harding Place" on the campus of Harding University in Searcy, Arkanas, and he says they are enjoying life tremendously and are very happy.

★★★

Will and Mattie Scarbrough Howland had two sons who served in World War II. Their other chldren were Willie, Roy, Floyd, John, Jimmy, Ludy, Maple, Jessie, Beaula, and Ernest.

HOYT H. HOWLAND was born October 12, 1917 in Red River County. He married Doris Faye Shoulders, and they had three children, Ann, Don and Terri. Hoyt entered the service in 1942 and trained at Ft. Knox, Kentucky as a cook. He was a T/4 and served in Hawaii. He was discharged in 1945 and awarded the Good Conduct Medal, ATO Ribbon, APO Ribbon, two Battle Stars and Victory Ribbon. He died September 18, 1993.

CECIL C. HOWLAND was born April 12, 1919 in Red River County. He entered the army in 1939 and trained at Ft. Sam Houston, Texas. He was a PFC and served in England and France where he was killed in action in 1944. He was awarded the Purple Heart, Good Conduct Medal, ATO Ribbon, ETO Ribbon and two Battle Stars.

★★★

W. A. (DUB) BUMGARNER, JR., the son of William Alvis, Sr. and Myrtle Thompson Bumgarner, was born February 9, 1923 in Annona, Texas. His brothers and sisters were Louise, Marie, Lillian, James and Bobby. He married Mary Jane Carlton, and they had two children, Bruce and Beverly. Dub was drafted on December 20,

1944 into the Army, Company B, 27th Infantry and trained in Texas a a cook. He was a Technician 4th Grade who served in the Philippines and Japan. He was discharged October 21, 1946 at Ft. Sam Houston, Texas and awarded the Good Conduct Medal, Asiatic-Pacific Theater Campaign Ribbon, Philippine Liberation Ribbon, Army Occupation Ribbon (Japan), Victory Ribbon and two Overseas Service Bars. After returning to Red River County, he was a rancher and served form 1965 to 1976 as County Commissioner for Precinct #3. Dub died August 28, 1990, and his wife is also deceased

★★★

W. L. DURRUM was born January 19, 1902 at Madras east of Clarksville, Texas, the only child of Dr. Will and Beulah Fulton Durrum. He married Carrie Marable. He enlisted in the Navy at Henderson, Texas and served as an Electrician, Chief Petty Officer, on a transport ship, the *USS CUSTER*. His date of discharge was August 30, 1945, and he died January 15, 1973. Mrs. Durrum resides in Clarksville.

★★★

JAMES W. (JIM) STEWART was born July 23, 1926, the son of Virgil A. and Effie Marie Green Stewart. Other children in the family were Ray, Lloyd, Jean and Brenda. He married Betty Gean Sutton, and they had three sons, James E., William W., and Charles. Jim died January 6, 2000 and is buried in Mt. Vernon, Texas City Cemetery. He served in the Navy (Submarine Service) from 1944-1946; attended Texas Technological College from 1946-1950 and graduated with a BSEE; served in the Regular US Army (Signal Corps) from 1950-1960; served in Korea 1951-1953, 2nd Infantry Division (awarded the Bronze Star); attended Harvard Business School 1954-1956 (MBA); served in the US Army Reserve 1960-1986 and retired as a Major. He worked for E-Systems 1963-1990 in electronics research. His wife resides in Mt. Vernon.

★★★

HAROLD BROWN, the only child of Will S. and Bert Parchman Brown, was born in Annona, Texas on April 22, 1916. He married Louise Grant, and they had one daughter, Carolyn Sue. He entered the service in Dallas on April 27, 1942 and was a part of Medical Detachment, 428th Armored Field Artillery Battalion as a Medical NCO, Staff Sergeant. He was discharged February 5, 1946 at Ft. Sam Houston, Texas and awarded the American Theater Campaign Medal, Asiatic-Pacific Campaign Medal, Philippine Liberation Medal, Victory Ribbon, one Service Stripe and one Overseas Service Stripe. He died May 12, 1993 and his wife resides in Annona.

Louise said this: "Most of Harold's training was in Texas, Gainesville, Mineral Wells, Abilene, Paris and Brownwood and also at Santa Barbara, California. From Brownwood he went to Hawaii and then on to the Philippines. He had a brother-in-law on another island so he asked the captain for a leave so he could go visit him. He caught a ride on a freighter. When he reached the island, he asked if they knew a Sgt. Lewis Grant. No one seemed to know him so Harold decided to catch the boat and go back. Before he reached the boat, someone called to him saying they knew him so they got to visit. When Harold returned, the captain told him he was surprised to see him because he never expected him to return."

★★★

HAROLD L. CHUMLEY was born May 31, 1923 on a farm in Detroit, Texas. His parents were Fred M. and Emily Neal Chumley, and the other children were John, Jeff, Grace and Tina. He married Judith E. Toney, and they had three children, Rex, Bruce and Chris. He entered the service on June 26, 1944 and was trained at the Navy Training Center in San Diego. He was attached to the 19th Marine Engineers, 25th, 23rd and 133rd Seabees and served in the South Pacific and Guam. His job was building and repairing hangers, quonset huts, airfields and "anything else that came along". He was a Carpenters Mate, 3rd Class and was discharged February 8, 1946 at Norman, Oklahoma, a little early because his mother and sister were dependent upon him.

★★★

H. G. WOOTTEN, JR. was born January 6, 1913 at Annona, Texas. His parents were Dr. Horace Greeley and Ruka Bishop Wootten, and he had one sister, Winnie Mattie. He entered the service in 1944 at Greenville, Texas and was attached to the 168th

Station Hospital in Ringwood, England as a Sergeant. This was a part of the 6th Field Hospital, 1st Platoon. He served there and in Kiska and Scotland. He was discharged in 1946 at Tyler, Texas. H. G. was a Pharmacist and died October 17, 1975.

★★★

CHARLES GRANT WALKER, the only child of Charles Thomas and Essie May Grant Walker, was born October 15, 1910, in Clarksville, Texas. He married Winnie Mattie Wootten, and they had two sons, Charles Greeley and James Wootten. Grant enlisted in the Navy at Tyler, Texas in May 1944 and trained in Gulfport, Mississippi; Syracuse, New York; Shoemaker, San Diego and San Francisco, California. He was a F 1/C aboard the *USS Cahaba*, and their job was to supply fuel to other ships at sea. He served in the Pacific Area, Victoria, and Hong Kong, China. His discharge was in January 1946 at Houston, Texas. He died March 23, 1979, and Winnie Mattie resides in Clarksville.

★★★

LOREN LEE BALLEW, JR. joined the Navy on September 5, 1941 at only seventeen years of age. He went to boot camp in San Diego and was sent from there to Alameda, California to enter Aviation Machinist Mate School. This course of study was completed on June 25, 1942, and he was sent to Pearl Harbor where he entered school for seven months. There he was promoted to AMM 2-C on May 1, 1943. He also completed a course of instruction at Kaneche Bay. Loren served in the South Pacific and was discharged July 1, 1947 at New Orleans. He was born October 21, 1922, and his parents were Loren, Sr. and Carrie Robinson Ballew. He has a brother, Bill. He married Evelyn (Mickey) Peterson, and their children are Duane, David, Janet and Paula. The Ballews reside in Clarksville, Texas.

★★★

Mr. and Mrs. J. L. Fowler of Clarksville, Texas had five sons and a daughter in World War II. I was unable to get any information on this, but I do want to name the Fowler children who served. They were: **A. D., ALVER J., GEORGE D., WILLIAM M., T. C., and JOSIE MAE.**

★★★

SAM McCONNELL was born June 30, 1926 in Red River County on the Hocker farm at Turner's Lake, southeast of Clarksville. His parents were Will and Annie Waddell McConnell, and he had ten brothers and sisters. He and Sammie McCasland were married in 1950 and had three children, Melanie, Ginger and Gary Sam. The McConnells reside in Bogata.

Sam graduated from high school in May 1944 and volunteered for the Navy in June. Since he was only seventeen years old, his parents had to give their permission for him to enlist. He told me that my father, Jim Claiborne, Justice of the Peace at that time, notarized the document that they signed.

Sam spent his eighteenth birthday in boot camp in San Diego along with his brother, Austin. (After this the two brothers went their separate ways.) Sam was in amphibious training at Coronado Island, California and then rode a troop train to Astoria, Oregon. The ship he was to serve on, the USS BOTTINEAU, was being built in Portland on the Columbia River, and when it was brought up the river, they were still welding on it. At Seattle the ship was loaded with ammunition—aerial torpedoes and bombs. A tug boat hit the propeller, about twenty feet in diameter, and this threw the ship out of balance. It limped down the coast to dry dock in Long Beach where a new propeller was installed. They were scheduled to be in the landing on Iwo Jima, but they missed that and went on to the Okinawa Campaign. While en route, the convoy which was made up of twenty-seven ships, was under attack by a submarine. Sam remembers the ship literally shaking from the depth charges. There was an oil slick in the water so it was assumed that the sub was destroyed.

The USS BOTTINEAU had a crew of 450 and could carry as many as 1,800 troops. They would be transported from the ship to shore in LCVP's (Landing Craft Vehicle Personnel). These carred thirty-two troops and had a crew of four—the coxswain who drove the craft, the motor man, and two gunners. Sam served as one of the gunners. The ship also had LCM's which could carry a tank ashore.

Troops were unloaded first from the ship in the morning, and then the equipment and supplies were taken ashore. The landing craft went right up on the beach as far as it could go; the front end was opened up; and the troops went right in. The next day many of the men who had been taken ashore were brought back to ship after being wounded. The critically wounded were taken to a hospital ship, and the others were put on a ship going to Guam. Many ships were anchored there at that time. Five Japanese suicide planes came in one day and hit the *USS NEW MEXICO*. The ship exploded but did not sink, and there were many killed and wounded. Those who had flash burns were in a terrible shape and would probably have been better off if they had been killed.

No one was killed aboard the *USS BOTTINEAU* so there was no burial at sea even though they had the equipment for this—the boards, weights and body bags. Five were wounded and received Purple Hearts. Sam was on sea duty for sixteen months. He was discharged in 1946 at Camp Wallace, Texas. He was awarded one Battle Star, ATO Ribbon, PTO Ribbon and a Victory Medal.

AUSTIN D. McCONNELL, brother of Sam, was born November 29, 1921. He entered the Navy in June 1944 at the same time that Sam did. As mentioned above, they took their basic training together but were then separated. Austin served in the Pacific Area, Okinawa, Philippines, China and Japan. He was awarded the Victory Medal, ATO Ribbon, and APO Ribbon with one Bronze Star. He was discharged in 1946. Austin married Evelyn Bartley, and they had one son, Austin Davis, Jr., and two daughters, Cammie and Marty. Austin died May 19, 1991.

★★★

CHESTER BERT (JACK) ATKINS was born July 12, 1918 in Montague County, Texas, the son of Phillip Sheridan and Jessie Myrtle Boyd Atkins. He had two brothers, Edward Boyd and Phillip Gordon, and four sisters, Oueida Merl, Vivian, Frances and Reba. Jack married Mary Virginia Hulen, and they had three sons, Dr. B. J. Atkins, J. B. Atkins, and E. L. Atkins.

Jack was drafted on June 20, 1944 and took his basic training at Ft. Bliss and Camp Maxey, Texas. He was an auto mechanic, TEC 5, and served in the European Theater of Operations. He was enroute to Japan when the war in Europe ended and was on furlough in Clarksville with his family when the war in Japan ended. He was placed in the antiaircraft at the beginning for training because of his knowledge of mechanics. His discharge was on

January 21, 1946 at Camp Shelby, Mississippi and he was awarded the ATO Medal, EAME Medal, Good Conduct Medal, WWII Victory Medal, and ribbons for battles and campaigns in Rhineland and Central Europe. Jack died December 21, 1995. Virginia resides in Clarksville.

★★★

Huey F. and Minnie Jumper Sheppard had six children: Zeno, Kenneth, Hughie A., Errel Lee, Tinnie, and Lula Mae. Three of their sons were in the service during World War II.

ZENO P. SHEPPARD and KENNETH EDGAR SHEPPARD, SR. married sisters, Mabel and Ella K. Storey. Zeno and Mabel had three sons, Storey, Jerry and Wayne. Kenneth and Ella had four children, Kenneth, Jr., Harold, Patsy and Karen Elaine.

Zeno entered the Army in 1944 and trained at Camp Abbot, Oregon and Ft. Lewis, Washington. He served in the USA and was discharged in 1945. For many years Zeno worked as the manager of the Northeast Texas Production Credit Association in Clarksville. He is deceased.

Kenneth was drafted into the service in 1944 when he was well into his thirties. It is thought that the U.S. had, by 1944, begun drafting older men into the Army because there was by then a shortage of younger men. Most of his Army acquaintances, as well as most of his commanding officers, were many years his junior.

Kenneth received basic training at Camp Wolters in Mineral Wells, Texas. In 1944 he shipped overseas and served in Belgium during the Battle of the Bulge. Mabel and Ella Storey Sheppard and their two sons, Kenneth, Jr. and Storey, lived together in a house due west of the Red River County Courthouse in 1944 and 1945. The boys often played around the courthouse lawn and were playing marbles when they saw Mr. Vaughan heading toward their house. He was delivering a telegram saying that Kenneth had been wounded, and his son remembers that it said, "wounds not threatening". (Information furnished by Dr. Kenneth E. Sheppard, Jr. and his wife, Sue Quarles Sheppard, now of Commerce, Texas)

Karen Elaine, Kenneth's daughter, remembers some things that her father told her. As he grew older, he became somewhat more willing to discuss his WWII experiences. And as he and his youngest child lived together, just the two of them, for a few years, she was often privileged to listen to him. He talked about the troops of the Allied Forces marching into Paris, France as a show of victory, and how he thought it was a most unwise action. During that march the upper stories of many buildings and towers were still held by Germans and Nazi sympathizers. From their vantage points, those snipers were able to "pick off" a large number of the Allied soldiers. Of one's chances of surviving the war in Europe, he often said, "I don't see how anyone ever got out of it alive." He felt that the ones who got out alive were just the lucky ones—that there was really nothing a soldier could do or no particular skill he could have to avoid danger. If a bullet "had your name on it, then the die had been cast." He and the others didn't feel like they were or wanted to be killers, but they all had to learn very quickly to do what they had to do without thinking about it. He was a foot soldier during his entire time of service. His first injury was when he received a head wound from an exploding shell. He was hospitalized and then sent back to the front lines. The second time he was wounded occurred before the Battle of the Bulge. He was hit with shrapnel in his hip and thigh, and the smaller pieces were never removed, causing him pain for the rest of his life.

He greatly admied U. S. Army General George Patton. He said that General Patton had the reputation among the soldiers that he would never point toward the enemy and say, "Go get them!" Instead he would say, "Follow Me, Men!" He would always be in the first tank to enter a battle. He was a good leader, one who cared for his soldiers. Kenneth said there was never a prettier sight to a foot soldier than to see those tanks rolling in to get between them and the enemy and protect them from enemy fire.

Kenneth was discharged in 1945 and awarded the ETO Medal with three Battle Stars, Purple Heart, and Combat Infantry Badge. He returned to Clarksville and later served for twenty-five years as the Red River County Clerk. He died in 1991.

ERREL LEE SHEPPARD, the youngest child in the Sheppard family, entered the Army Air Corps in 1942 and trained in Greenvile, Texas and Keesler Field, Mississippi. On a tragic note, Errel Lee had received his discharge and was on his way home to Clarksville when he was killed in an automobile accident in Oklahoma in 1945. It is difficult to imagine his mother's anguish when, as she awaited his homecoming, she received the terrible news of his death. The Sheppard family is very proud that, even though he was not killed in action during the war, his name is etched on the World War II Memorial on the lawn of the Red River County Courthouse in Clarksville. (information furnished by Karen Sheppard, Harold's wife)

★★★

E. G., Sr. and Emma Lee Jones Lum had two sons who served in World War II. Their other children were Brenos, Mavis and Audrey May.

E. G. LUM, JR. was born at Boxelder in Red River County, Texas on August 19, 1911. He volunteered for the service on February 27, 1942, and his training was in radio operation at the University of Georgia in Savannah. Training in maneuvers was in Louisiana. Before going overseas he was given a six day furnlough during which time he married Wanza Sue Brooks on August 19, 1942. Their children are Vincent, Eric and Annette.

As a part of the Army Signal Corps and serving as a Radio Section Chief under the 12th Air Support Command, E. G. went overseas in 1942. It was his job to furnish information for the aircraft. He landed at Fedilia, French Morocco in North Africa after riding to the North African Campaign on a troop carrier that was a converted banana boat. He participated in eight major battles while serving overseas for thirty-two months. From Africa he went to Gelo, Sicily for the D-Day Invasion; then to Salereno, Italy in the Italian Campaign; then to Rome; then to Southern France in the French Campaign; then across the Rhine River into Germany where he stayed until the war ended. He returned to the U.S. in July 1945 and was discharged at Brooke General Hospital in San Antonio. He was awarded eight Battle Stars and an Arrowhead Medal. He and his wife, both retired from many years in the education field, reside in Clarksville.

ALVIS MERLE LUM volunteered for the service at the same time as his older brother. Alvis was trained at Camp Wolters in Mineral Wells, Will Rogers Field in Oklahoma City, and at Hunter Field in Savannah, Georgia. He related to me that he saw smoke from burning ships that had been hit by German submarines in the Atlantic off our coast.

While serving in the States, he was in a Monitoring Unit at

Hollywood, Florida, monitoring German signals out of North Africa. He then was on the West Coast at Camp Pinedale in Fresno, California where he was in a unit that monitored the Japanese. Some of the operators there were sons of Japanese living in California who had been interred after Pearl Harbor. When he was only two days out in the Pacific Ocean going overseas, Germany surrendered. By way of Australia, he then went to Calcutta, India where his unit was on the edge of Burma. A couple of times he flew the hump over the Himalayas. On August 1, 1945 he was in China at the 14th Air Force Flying Tiger Base at Liuchow. A pilot came in from Tinian and told them to pack their bags because the war would soon be over. Sure enough, he was right because the Atomic Bomb was dropped. In a few days he hitchhiked back to India. Finally he was able to leave in January 1946 and arrived in the U.S. in February. He was discharged on February 12, 1946 after serving a little over four years. He was awarded the American Campaign Theater Medal, Asiatic-Pacific Campaign Medal with two Bronze Stars, Good Conduct Medal, and a Meritorious Unit Award. He and Geraldine Glenn were married and had two sons, Damon Neal and Don Rayburn. They reside in Cache, Oklahoma.

★★★

LAWRENCE M. VAUGHAN was born February 16, 1926 in Johntown, Texas, the son of George Avret and Mamie Elizabeth Hawkins Vaughan. The other children in the family were Jennings Harley, Kenneth Wayne, Avret Lynn, Mamie Eleanor, and Mary Ann. He married Helen Louise Watts, and they had three children, Steven Lawrence, Deborah Louise and Susan Ann. He entered the Navy on April 19, 1944 at Tyler, Texas and took his training at the USNTC in San Diego. He served as a radio operator, RM 2/C, aboard the USS APC 45 and the *USS General William Mitchell* in the Asiatic Pacific Theater. Upon his discharge on June 15, 1944 at the U.S. Naval Air Station in New Orleans, he was awarded one Battle Star.

His brother, **JENNINGS H. VAUGHAN**, entered the Army Air Corps in 1943 and trained at Sheppard Field, Texas. He was a Staff Sergeant who served in India and was awarded the American Theater Ribbon, APO Ribbon with two Battle Stars, Good Conduct Medal, Distinguished Unit Badge, Victory Ribbon and two Overseas

Bars. He was discharged in 1946. He married Pansy Alsobrook, and they had three children, David, Sarah Jane and Melissa.

★★★

CHARLES B. BREEDLOVE was born April 14, 1921 in Red River County, the son of John B. and Susie Ashford Breedlove. The family had nine children: Janetta, Mable, Ernest, Leroy, Lucille, Dorthy, Lula Lee, Charles and his twin Chester. Charles was drafted in 1942. He attained the rank of Staff Sergeant and made a career of the service, being discharged in 1962 at Topeka, Kansas. He now lives in Clarksville, Texas.

★★★

Johnny W. and Ruby Denison Ball had two sons who served in World War II. Their other children were Harry and Lucille.

JOHN D. BALL was born June 22, 1920 in Minter, Texas. He was married to Ruth Hulsey, and they had three children, Paul, Ruth Ann and John. An article entitled "From Horse Soldier to Foot Soldier" in the November 1999 issue of the *Bogata News* reads in parts as follows:

"On February 18, 1941 Carlys Denison, Martin Lawler and I volunteered for one year of selective service training. Five years later, I was home after a lifetime of a bumpy road. Carlys was assigned to the mail department, Martin to the fire department, and me to the 1st Cavalry, 91st Infantry, 705th Engineers. I was trained at Ft. Bliss, Texas. Basic training for six weeks at $21.00 a month, later a pay raise to $30.00.

Our quarters were tents with six men in each tent. The summer of 1941 was spent mostly in the desert east and north of El Paso. Later, Louisiana manervers for six weeks. It was estimated we rode those horses 5,000 miles that summer. Of course, much of that was walking and leading them. Much time was spent grooming our horses, polishing brass, shining boots and saddles. On one occasion we were to have a parade in El Paso. All horses in my troop were black, but some had white hooves. I had the job of putting stone black on those white hooves to make them all the same color. . . Sometime in late 1942 or early 1943 the Cavalry was dismounted and made an infantry unit, although it was still called the lst Cavalry Division as it is today. The summer of 1942 I was transferred to

Camp White, Oregon to help form the 91st Infantry Division. There we trained until 1943. . . then overseas to Oran, North Africa where we trained for landings. This training was meant to confuse Germany into thinking we were planning to invade Southern France. This was to take pressure off the Normandy landings. From Africa to Naples, Italy on a British ship; from Naples to Anzio. Our first bombing was in Naples and our first combat was north of Anzio.

I was there on the outskirts of Rome on June 4, 1944 when Rome was declared an open city. From Rome on north to the Po Valley of Italy. After losing more than half of our company of 250 men by death or wounds, the war in Italy was over. Yes, it was a long and bumpy road, but I had survived. I am so sorry that so many of my buddies did not. . . When you see someone who has the Combat Infantry Badge, you can say that he has been to 'Hell and Back'. That movie tells the story of Audie Murphy. It and 'Saving Private Ryan' came as close to the true story as any that I have seen, but it is impossible to put the whole story on film.

I was awarded the Combat Infantry Badge, Purple Heart, Bronze Star, European Campaign Medal, and Expert Rifleman Badge. Of these, the Infantry Badge is by far the most important to me because it represents the mud, rain, snow, heat and mountains that we had to overcome on our drive from Anzio to Northern Italy and a defeat of Hitler's best." T/Sgt. Ball was discharged on November 15, 1945 at Ft. Sam Houston, Texas. He resides in Paris, Texas. (A postcard sent to his parents stated there were 20,000 horses and men in the yard at Ft. Bliss, Texas in 1941.)

FRANK ELIHUE BALL, Colonel USA (retired) died December 18, 1999 in Reston, Virginia. The obituary in the *Bogata News* reads in part: He was born November 23, 1917 in Minter, Texas. . . After graduating from Texas A&M University in 1939, Colonel Ball began 32 successful years of active duty as a career officer in the U.S. Army. He served in the 2nd Division in Europe during World War II, participating in the invasion of Normandy at Omaha Beach and the Battle of the Bulge. . . (After many, many different and interesting assignments through the years, Col. Ball completed his career working in the Office of the Secretary of Defense.) He retired in March 1972. During his active duty years he was awarded the Silver Star, Legion of Merit with the Bronze Oak

Leaf Cluster, Bronze Star with Bronze Oak Leaf Cluster, Purple Heart, Combat Infantry Badge, Army Presidential Unit Citation, European Campaign Medal with five Stars, National Defense Service Medal, French Croix de Guerre, Belgian Fourragere, Korean Service Medal with one Bronze Service Star and one Silver Service Star, and the United Nations Service Medal.

He and his wife, the former Georgia Helen Whitney, formerly of Minter, were married fifty-seven years. Their children are Georgia Ann, Frank E. Ball, Jr., and David W. Col. Ball was interred at Arlington National Cemetery in Arlington, Virginia with full military honors.

★★★

GERALD DENTON ROBERTSON was born May 24, 1926, the son of Charles Lyon and Jessie Gertrude Young Robertson. There were eleven children in the family, eight boys and three girls. He married Dessie Mae Rogers, and they have three daughters, Sharon Elaine, Peggy Diane and Kitty Earlene. Gerald entered the Army on August 9, 1944 at Ft. Sill, Oklahoma and took his training at Mineral Wells, Texas. He was an Infantry Rifleman in the 17th Infantry Divsion. His overseas duty was in Southern France and Rhineland. He was discharged in January 1946 at Brooke General Hospital in San Antonio and received a Purple Heart, ETO Ribbon, Good Conduct Medal and Expert Rifleman Badge. Gerald and Dessie reside in Clarksville.

★★★

HAROLD HOLLOWAY, the son of O. S. and Fannie Reynolds Holloway, was born September 1, 1919 in Detroit, Texas. He had a brother, Walter, and a sister, Mary Kathryn. He married Mary Signor Ramsey, and their children are Sara Lou, Mary Ruth, John Ramsey, and Amy Jo. He enlisted in the Navy on March 17, 1944 at Oklahoma City. His training was: Aviation Radar Operator at Norman, Oklahoma; NST Combat Air Crewman Service; NRS Oklahoma City; NTS San Diego; Naftcen, Norman, Oklahoma; NAS Whidby Island, Washington; Hedron Fleet Air Wings 6. He was a S/2 C-AOM and served aboard the *USS Marka*, a destroyer tender. His wife said: "Harold worked for the government most of his working years. In the thirties, like most of the boys then, he did milking, worked in the cotton fields, delivered ice, and drove a truck. In 1939 he joined the C.C.C. and worked in New Mexico. In 1940 he went to work at Kelley Air Base in San Antonio and stayed with the air force until 1944 when he entered the Navy Air Foce. After his discharge, he went back to San Antonio, Wichita Falls and Big Springs until his retirement." He was awarded the Victory Ribbon and Asiatic-Pacific Ribbon. He died January 24, 1998.

★★★

CALVIN BRANNAN was born August 31, 1911 in Conway, Arkansas. His parents were John W. and Beulah Martin Brannan, and he had a brother, Martin, and three sisters, Flora, Ruby and Dorthy. He married Beatrice Cornett, and they had two sons, Mack and Jimmy. On May 12, 1944 Calvin enlisted in the Navy and was trained at San Diego as an Aviation Electrician's Mate. He was discharged at Norman, Oklahoma on January 3, 1946 and returned to Clarksville. Calvin retired with thirty-six years service as a lst Sergeant in the Texas National Guard. He died November 21, 1994, and his wife is also deceased.

★★★

JOHN OLEN RATER was born April 15, 1921 at Weatherford, Texas. His parents were James W. and Lottie Shaw Rater. His father later married Nanny Lou Broadway. His brothers and sisters were Jack W., James, George, Edgar, Arlene, Anita, and Myrtle. He married Ahmoy Rosson, and their sons are Robert John and Jack Rosson.

John enlisted in the Army in February 1941, at Clarksville, Texas. His training was at Camp Young, California, and he served in the 879th Ordinance under General George Patton. He was manager of the Post Exchange in the U.S. and then Staff Sergeant in charge of Company C in the Philippines. His company left Ft. Ord, California in December 1944 on the *USS Monticelleo*. They had Christmas dinner in Hawaii. His unit landed on Leyte Island in the Philippines three days before General MacArthur returned. Every day Tokyo Rose came on the radio with good music and told them that while they were away from home, their wives and sweethearts were out cheating on them. She said all sorts of things to lower their morale. There on Leyte he was wounded. His discharge was in

November 1946 at Ft. McArthur, California, and he was awarded the American Defense Medal, Philippie Liberation Medal with two Battle Stars, APO Ribbon, Good Conduct Medal, Victory Medal, and Meritorious Unit Award.

★★★

WILLIAM THOMAS AYDELOTT, the son of Claude Bennett and Fannie Rhea Aydelott, was born June 24, 1923 in Avery, Texas. He had four brothers, Curtis, Clovis, James (Dick), and J. B., and a sister, Christene. He married Jo Mac Mills, and they had four sons, Curtis, Jerry, Mark and Monty, and two daughters, Pam and Kala. On February 23, 1943 he was drafted at Tyler, Texas and served as a paratrooper in the 152nd Airborne Antiaircraft Artillery Battalion as a PFC. His overseas duty was in New Guinea, Southern Philippines and Luzon. He was discharged November 30, 1945 at Ft. Sam Houston, Texas and was awarded the Asiatic-Pacific Campaign Medal with three Bronze Stars and one Bronze Arrowhead, American Theater Campaign Medal, Philippine Liberation Ribbon with one Bronze Star, Good Conduct Medal, Victory Ribbon, and three Overseas Service Bars. He stayed in the Reserves from December 1, 1945 through November 30, 1948 and reenlisted during the Korean Conflict and served from February 23, 1950 through March 18, 1953. He died July 17, 1998.

★★★

Clarence Elmer and Minnie Amanda Suitor Gooding had three sons, Clarence Edward, Robert and Richard Morgan. Two of their sons were in the service during World War II.

CLARENCE EDWARD GOODING was born November 5, 1910 in Clarksville, Texas. After the death of his first wife, Harriet, he later married Eileen Haggerton. There was one son, Ronnie Gooding, M.D.

Clarence made a career of the Army and retired in 1965 at the rank of Colonel with thirty-six years military service. Col. Gooding enlisted at Ft. Logun, Colorado. He was commissioned a regular officer upon graduation from West Point in the Class of 1936. Part of his military education was at Stanford University. During World War II he commanded an Armored Unit in the Third Army Division in Europe. His last duty assignment was in St. Augustine,

Florida. He was awarded the Silver Star, Bronze Star with Oak Leaf Cluster, Purple Heart, EAME Campaign Medal, WWII Victory Medal, National Defense Service Medal and a number of decorations from foreign governments. He died March 26, 1981.

ROBERT GOODING was born August 26, 1914 in Clarksville, Texas. He married Frances Jean Bullington, who died in 1963. He later married Martha Grace Somerville. There are two sons, Robert Edward and William Carroll. Robert enlisted in the Army on February 22, 1943 and was trained at Ft. Benning, Georgia in an Infantry Officers Advanced Course. He was a Lieutenant and served as an Infantry Unit Commander 1542, later being promoted to Captain. Robert was overseas in the European Theater of Operations. He was discharged October 26, 1946 at O'Reilly General Hospital in Springfield, Missouri and was awarded the Purple Heart, ETO Medal with one Bronze Star, American Theater Ribbon, World War II Victory Medal, and American Defense Medal. Robert died November 14, 1977, and Martha Grace resides in Clarksville.

She related to me that Robert was struck by shell fragments on March 2, 1945 as his unit was in battle near Bonn, Germany. His men came together after the battle, and one soldier asked where the Lieutenant was. The soldier immediately started searching for Robert; found him severely wounded; and summoned the Medics, thus saving his Lieutenant's life. After being in the hospital in France and England, Robert was flown to the United States for further hospitalization. He said that one could not describe the emotions he experienced as the plane flew into New York and he saw the Statue of Liberty and knew that he was at home in America.

★★★

NANETTA P. MORRIS was born December 15, 1918 on the family farm west of Maroa, Illinois, a small rural town. Her parents were Frank H. and Nancy Parker Morris, and she had three brothers, Doyle, Lloyd and Max. Nan had the following to say:

"My parents purchased property east of Clarksville, Texas in 1917 and moved to Texas in 1919. My father died in 1922 in the old frame Clarksville hospital as a result of a ruptured appendix. When my oldest brother completed high school in 1924, the family moved back to Illinois to be near family. I attended grade school in Decatur and Urbana, Illinois. In 1932, Depression days, the Morris family returned to Texas where I enrolled in Clarksville High School, graduating in 1936. R. M. White was superintendent and also taught Latin. I attended Paris Junior College and Texas Technological College, and my first employment was as assistant dietician in a hospital in Pasadena, California.

After entry of the U.S. into World War II, I enlisted in the U.S. Navy as a WAVE for the duration of the war. Indoctrination of WAVES was at Hunter College in New York City. It was a long train trip across the U.S. because our train with several cars of enlisted WAVES was side-tracked many times for trains carrying drafted men and supplies to the West Coast. An aptitude test showed I knew what pliers, hammers and wrenches were, and the Navy determined I would be trained as a mechanic. I went to Norfolk Naval Air Station where I worked in a repair shop. My most scary remembrance was when I was required to sit in a cockpit of a Navy fighter plane, start the engine, and 'rev it up'. The roar of that huge engine and vibration of the plane were terrific, much more than any farm tractor!

Navy life was very regimented. We marched in platoons to eat, to work, and to pass inspections. Barracks life was quite an experience with very little privacy. Girls from all over the country were introduced and worked together. I have stayed in touch with four from Arizona, Missouri, Ohio and Pennsylvania whom I served with. A 48 hour pass away from the regimentation was a real treat. We saved our money and made side trips to Williamsburg, Virginia and Washington D. C.

After being discharged at the end of the war with two years and eight months service, I returned to the farm east of Clarksville. In less than a year I was employed at the Red River Army Plant near New Boston. I retired in 1974 and stayed at home with two brothers. Our mother died in 1964." (Nanetta and her brother, Doyle, remain on the farm today. Max, who lived with them, is dead, as is Lloyd who lived away.)

★★★

GEORGE MOORE was born May 31, 1926 in Dallas, Texas. His parents were Street and Carrie Leola Elder Moore, and he has one sister, Mary Virginia Bowers. George and Mary Bailey were married March 24, 1946 and have three daughters, Tessa, Vicky and Cherry. Mary and George are retired and reside in Paris, Texas. My husband and I visited with them in their home on January 24, 2000. George said:

"On July 1, 1943 when I was only seventeen years old, I volunteered for service in the Navy. I attended Officers' Training School in Monticello, Arkansas and had planned to be a pilot. After passing the flight training course in Pensacola, Florida, I was told that there would be a three month waiting period before assignment so I decided to volunteer for the Submarine Service. I took my training at the Submarine School in New London, Connecticut. Then I went to Pearl Harbor where I caught a sub tender and was part of a relief crew that repaired and restocked submarines while the regular crews rested after being at sea. In the middle of 1944 I was assigned to the *USS Segundo 398*, and I served on that submarine until my discharge on December 8, 1947. The skipper was Lt. Commander Morton H. Lytel. The war was not an old man's job, but rather the job of a young man who didn't take the time to think of the consequences and certainly didn't realize that he might be killed. There was a 27% loss of submarines and personnel during World War II, but this was kept quiet. Out of ten to twelve thousand men, 3,500 were lost.

Many subs in WWII were sent out after the Japanese tankers, the supply ships to Japan, because the idea was to keep the Japs from getting supplies in order to starve them out. Our subs sank 55% of the Japanese ships that were sunk, more than all the Navy combined. We were told to cut off the supply of oil and rubber to Japan. If there was a war ship and a tanker, the tanker was sunk first even though it would have been easier to sink the war ship. We were told to take the supply ships first, even though it was more dangerous.

The U.S. subs were 25 feet wide and 311 feet long. We were threatened many times by depth charges, but our sub was never damaged seriously. Mostly busted lights and minor leaks, but never any time did we feel, 'This is it'. If a depth charge came within 100 feet, it shook us up. At 50 feet, there would be minor damage; at 25 to 50 feet, severe damage. If it came as close as 25 feet, it was fatal.

We had really great food while at sea. Steak, shrimp, lobster. There was a cook from Waco, Texas named Newberry who made the best donuts. He told each of us we could have only two. There was no fresh milk or eggs, just the powdered kind. Of course, when we docked, we got enough fresh milk and eggs to do for about two weeks. Also, apples, oranges, tomatoes and lettuce. There was a large freezer on board to keep the food in, and the crew could eat any time they wanted to, if the food was there. In the regular Navy each man was fed for 87 cents a day, but in the Submarine Service, each man was allowed $1.50 each day. Lots of the men just lived on coffee. There would be cases of canned food like Spam, shrimp, lobster and juices.

At one time we had a man on the sub who had been a prisoner of the Japanese and had worked in the copper mines in Northern Japan. He had been a gunner's mate. He told of how the Japs had beaten them and made them work so hard. Then one day there were no guards, and they knew the war was over. He went back to a hospital in San Francisco, got a promotion and all the back pay he was due.

There were 65 men on the USS Segundo. During normal conditions, being on the sub was no different than sitting right here at home, except there were no windows. We had neon lights and air-conditioning that worked all right until it got real hot. Back then I was small enough to crawl into a crank case and work. We stayed out at sea six to eight weeks at a time and sometimes as much as ninety days on a long patrol. Several times sharks were caught and cooked for the crew. In port a boat picked up our laundry and brought it back in a couple of weeks. It cost about a dollar to have it done. Each man got to take two showers a week, using about three to five gallons of fresh water. The water was made in the engine room where a tank held as much as 2,000 gallons of sea water that had been distilled. They could do 50 to 100 gallons in an hour. We didn't shave every day while out at sea. Our trash was put in burlap bags with weights attached, and when we surfaced, it was dropped in the ocean. It had to sink so there would be no sign left of where we had been.

We were in a typhoon in 1945 while we were in a convoy going from Pearl Harbor to Guam. The waves were 40 to 50 feet tall. The cruiser *Pittsburg* had its bow torn off. The typhoon lasted about three days, and we had no warm food during that time, just sandwiches. I laid in my bunk while we rode it out. We had to stay up on the surface part of the time to charge our batteries; then we dropped 100 feet under the surface, and it would be smooth. Some of the men got really sick. The typhoon moved east, and we moved west about fifteen miles an hour.

During the war there were German subs off the east coast of the U.S. The Air Force had offered a bonus to anyone who sunk one of those subs. One day one of our planes was not up on recognition signals for that day (probably had changed at midnight), and they sank one of our own subs. Sixty-five men and a 12 million dollar sub. Of course, this was kept out of the newspapers.

I served as a Motor Machinist and also was the gun captain of a 40mm gun when we surfaced. When the men were up on the lookout post, two or three flying fish might come along and nearly knock them off. I still wake up at night sometime and think of diving procedures. We were at Guam when the war ended. Then we went to Northern China for about a year to teach them how to sink a sub. In 1972 the USS Segundo was sunk while being used for training." (George Moore received a War Patrol Medal, Submarine Qualification Medal, American Campaign Medal, Good Conduct Medal, Asiatic-Pacific Campaign Medal, and Meritorious Service Ribbon.)

★★★

BILLY JOE (BILL) CLARK was born in Ada, Oklahoma March 18, 1925 to Wimbly and Golda Finley Clark. He attended the University of Oklahoma at Norman during WWII, and before graduating he joined the Navy. He served with distinction aboard the battleship USS Indiana as a Lieutenant JG; participated in the Battle of Okinawa; and was among the first Americans to land at Tokyo after the war. He was always very proud that his ship transported American POW's home. After the war Bill returned to OU and received a degree in mechanical engineering and mathematics in 1947. After a couple of moves, he operated his own business, Clark Contractors, from 1955-58. When the Cold War was escalating, his company built missile silos in Florida to house some of America's nuclear arsenal. In the 1970's he went to work for Continental Mechanical Corp. and worked there until his retirement in 1985. He was in charge of all international contracts and was responsible for buildings in Saudi Arabia, Nigeria, Iran, Egypt and throughout Western Europe.

Bill married his first wife, Virginia Hill, after college. They had two children, Frederick Scott and Wimbly Wade. In 1957 Bill married Joyce Seaman, and they had one daughter, Lori Vanessa. Bill died November 17, 1999, and a military memorial was conducted under the Pavilion of the Bogata Cemetery in Bogata, Texas on November 21, 1999. This information was taken from the program that was handed out, and on the front was his picture and a poem that read: "Since thou canst no longer stay to cheer me with thy love, I hope to meet with thee again in your bright world above."

★★★

MELVIN MARX, JR. was born July 19, 1909 in New Orleans, the son of Melvin and Pearl Silberberg Marx. His brother was Jerrold Marx. Dr. Marx graduated from the University of Texas Medical Branch at Galveston in 1932. After internship at St. Louis, he practiced with the CCC. He married Frances Haberer, and they had two sons, Melvin Marx III and Stephen. In 1941 he entered the Army and became Head Surgeon of the Western Defense Command headquartered in San Franciso. While there he was the medical officer in charge of the Army section of the United Nations Conference on International Organization. Physicians under his command attended Joseph Stalin for a minor illness during that conference. Dr. Marx returned to Red River County in 1945 and was engaged in active practice until his death in 1975.

JERROLD MARX was born in Clarksville, Texas in 1913. He married Mildred Benton, and they had no children. He worked at Silberberg's store from 1934 until 1952, at which time he bought the store and changed the name to Marx's. During World War II Jerrold served in the Navy. Both he and Mildred are deceasesd.

★★★

On January 10, 2000, I talked with Herman Totty and his brother E. T. (Tom)Totty at their homes east of Annona, Texas. Three Totty brothers served in World War II including their younger brother, Charles Ottie Totty. Their parents were Winston and Dessie Garrison Totty, and besides these three brothers, there was another brother, J. D., and two sisters, Lorene and Nella Jane.

I first visited with **WINSTON HERMAN TOTTY** who was born February 15, 1918 in Hope, Arkansas. On April 30, 1938 he and Barbara Weemes were married, and their children are Russell Nolan, Glenda Sue, Curtis Herman and Larry Keith.

Herman was a sergeant in A Battery, 341st Artillery Battalion, 89th Division of the Army. He told me the following about his experiences: "I enlisted in the Army in Dallas on June 28, 1942. My brother, Tom, and I were working on the farm, and it rained that spring and we couldn't make a living. At that time the USA was losing on every front, so we thought it our duty to help out. (Both brothers and their wives already had two children and were expecting a third.)

We were sent to Mineral Wells where we spent two weeks. Then we were put on a troop train and traveled all that day and night, and the next morning the train stopped at Pueblo, Colorado where we were fed a good breakfast and told to take a break. We were loaded back on the troop train, and the soldier in charge of the train car I was on told us we didn't have far to go, that we were going to be stationed at Camp Carson, Colorado. Using the word 'we' or 'us' is referring to my brother, Tom, and me. We were put in a holding camp for two or three days, and then we were split up. Tom was sent to the Infantry, and I was sent to the Field Artillery, both stationed at Camp Carson.

The 89th Division was being activated, and we were the first group to get there. I was assigned to the Signal Communication because I had some experience in communication while I was in the C.C.C. in California where I was trained to wire poles and communicate. In about six weeks I was promoted to Corporal, and in about six weeks my Sergeant went AWOL, and I got his sergeant stripes. Then two others and myself were 'field chosen' for Officers Training School. After taking the IQ test, I was turned down due to math. I really loved the Army and the men I was over. The basic training we went through was real rough. We went to the firing range every week and ran the obstacle course every day. I had a real bad sinus infection, and they had me scheduled for surgery at Denver. A major in the hospital told me if he was me, he would turn it down. So on his advice I turned down surgery, and on June 1, 1943, I was told to turn in all my equipment because I was being transferred to a casualty company. I stayed there a few days and then was told to go to a certain place to be discharged. This was on June 22, 1943. I came home and went to work at Red River Arsenal at Texarkana."

*The crew of the submarine USS Segundo 398
(George More is on the top right with his hand on the barrel of the cannon.)*

My next visit was with **E. T. (TOM) TOTTY** who was born September 14, 1920 in Red River County. He and Lucille Weemes were married February 19, 1938, and their children are Irvin Wayne, Joyce, Nathan Ray, Sharon Gail, and two sets of twins, Don and Donald, and Harold and Darrell.

Tom enlisted on June 28, 1942 and was in the 89th Infantry Division of the Army serving as a Lineman, then a Section Chief, and then a Communications Chief. Tom had the following to say: "I was at Camp Wolters and then at Camp Carson, Colorado in the last part of 1943. Then I went to Louisiana for maneuvers and on to

A shark was on the menu for the crew aborad the USS Segundo.

California for training in the mountains. Next I went to North Carolina where a division was reactivated. I had been with a cadre division before that. We shipped out at Boston on January 10, 1944, to land in England. It took us ten days to get there, and many times we heard the depth charges fired at German subs. We didn't get to land there because there had been so much trouble with subs in the English Channel so we went on to a bombed out harbor in Le Harve, France. From there we went to an old German Airstrip named 'Lucky Stripe' and stayed to get our equipment. Next we went on to France, Belgium, Luxembourg, through the Siegfried

Line into Germany with Patton's Third Army. At the Rhine River crossing at St. Gorhousen, Germany we found a cave on the edge of the river. It was about a half mile under the mountain, and was full of wine kegs. Sometimes the snow was knee deep. We ate C-rations, some 'ten in one', a can with meals for ten soldiers for one day. There was also a hard chocolate which was supposesd to be one meal for a man. We always looked forward to getting mail, but it took a long time for it to catch up with us.

We lost lots of our men. The first casualty in our company happened in the first two or three hours we were there. A scout raised up to motion us to come and a bullet hit him in the back of the head. The first officer lost in combat was one of ours, a Capt. Edmonson, that was loved by everyone of us. If all commanders had been like Gen. George Patton, it would have been good because he believed in using anything at his disposal to win a battle. Rommel respected him, and Patton respected Rommel. The towns we went through had been destroyed by bombs.

We captured a concentration camp, and I'll never forget seeing a large pit at the end of one of the buildings. Peoples' bodies had been thrown in there, and there was a baby on top of one of the bodies. Then there were piles of bodies on the ground. There weren't many prisoners to liberate. The Germans had used machine guns on them cause they knew the US was coming. We had a field kitchen that stayed open all the time so our soldiers that were freed could eat any time they wanted to. We were on the edge of Czechoslovakia when the war ended. I was discharged at Camp Bowie, Texas on November 29, 1945 and was awarded a Combat Infantry Badge, Good Conduct Medal, two ETO Ribbons and Combat Medals. I wouldn't take anything for my overseas duty, but I sure wouldn't want to go through it again." (Since my interview with Tom, he has had a massive stroke.)

CHARLES OTTIE TOTTY was drafted in May after his eighteenth birthday on April 12, 1943. He was in the Infantry in a Half Track Division. He served under Gen. George Patton in the Battle of the Bulge and was wounded in Belgium. He was discharged in September 1945 and was married on October 6, 1945 to Auddie Hensley. They had three children, Charles Oliver, Billy Joe and Judy Carol. He died in July 1975.

GEORGE BOWER was born December 4, 1911 at Lydia

southeast of Clarksville, Texas. His parents were Charlie and Missie Rhea Bower. The other children were Stella, Mittie, Robert, Etta, Dollie, and Earlton who was kicked in the head by a mule and died at age fourteen. On May 24, 1941, he and Nella Jane Totty, only thirteen years of age, were married. They had a large family: Georgia Ann, Priscilla Faye, Charlie Winston, Sarah Jane, Rose Marie, William Dwayne, Brenda, Charlotte, Carol and George Barkley, Jr. George was drafted in December 1942 into the Army. He took his basic training at Connecicut and Camp Hood, Texas and then went overseas to the Philippines where he served on kitchen duty. After getting 'jungle rot' in his feet, he was sent back to Ft. Sam Houston where he was discharged in 1945.

★★★

DICK DeBERRY was born April 21, 1914 in Bogata, Texas. His parents were Clarence Charles and Genevieve Moseley DeBerry, and he had a sister, Mary Jane. He married Helen Maxton, and they had two daughters, Janet and Suan. Dick enlisted in the Navy in 1942 at Paris, Texas and received his training at San Francisco. He was a Chief Petty Officer who served on the USS Lawrence in the South Pacific. He was discharged in 1944 and died March 24, 1991.

JAMES WILFORD LOWRY, the son of William Kirb and Alma Ellen Smith Lowry, was born at Johntown, Texas on September 21, 1925. He had a sister, Bobbie Ruth. He married Mary Jane DeBerry, and they had one daughter, Alice Jane. He died Decemeber 31, 1994. His wife shared something that he wrote about his experiences in WWII, and it is quoted in part below:

"I joined the Navy in 1943 midway of my senior year of high school in Bogata. I went to San Diego for boot training, and then to Coronado Island. They placed me in the amphibious force which was ship-to-shore carrying of Marines during invasion. I went to Goat Island and boarded ship for overseas to New Hebrides Island. From there we went to the Solomon Islands to a little island named Talage off Guadalcanal. Then we were put aboard the *USS Zeilin* where I served as a Boatswain Mate the rest of the war.

The first invasion I made was at Tarawa, a small island in the South Pacific. The Japs were dug in there in concrete pill boxes, and it took us all day to get even one boat on the beach. We didn't put any Marines on the beach till late that afternoon. From there we went to the invasion of Guam. We stood by at Saipan and then came back to the states for repairs. I got to go home on leave after being away for a year. After I returned, we went back overseas and made invasions in the Philippines, Leyte and Luzon. As we left Luzon, we were out in the China Sea where kamikazes were so bad. They tried to fly their planes into our ships. One morning general quarters was sounded, and we shot one down before it got to us, but another one hit us along mid-ship. The ship had turned enough that it missed the smokestack. It blew a hole three decks down and took all the side out of the ship. Another plane was coming in, but two of our fighter planes shot it down, and that's what saved us. In this one attack we lost 38 men killed and over 20 wounded. When we got back to the islands, the hole in the side of the ship was patched while we were still under way. Welders were put over the side to patch the hole below the waterline and just above it with a piece of sheet meal. Then we returned again to the states to get repairs, and I got my second leave.

When we went back out, we made invasions at Iwo Jima and Okinawa. Then we went to New Caledonia and picked up troops there. Then back to the Marianas Islands where one of the greatest convoys was assembled, and we were told that we were going to hit Japan. We stayed there five days. The battleships, cruisers and aircraft carriers were already gone. We pulled anchor to leave for Japan, but we were given orders to go back to port. That afternoon we began to hear rumors that we had dropped an atomic bomb on Japan. The next day we were told that the second bomb had been dropped and that Japan had surrendered. They let us fly flares off the ship and shoot tracer shells. The whole sky was lit up.

Then we went to Korea and carried the occupational troops we had on the ship to occupy that part of the country that Japan was holding. We stayed there two weeks and then we went to Shanghai, China for six weeks. Our captain was going back to the States, and he came to Shanghai and picked up his boats, four of them, and brought us back with him. For a while after the war, we had what they called a shuttle cruise up and down the west coast because we picked up men at different places that had enough points to get out of the service. After about two months they brought our ship around to the east coast and decommissioned it. By that time we just had a skeleton crew. We came through the Panama Canal, up the east coast, and to Norolk. Our ship was put in 'mothballs', and all the crew was transferred off. My enlistment was up, and I came home—back to Bogata, Texas to live. I was discharged in 1946 at Norman, Oklahoma."

★★★

JOHN THOMAS McKENZIE was born October 2, 1902, in Red River County. His parents were David McAnally and Daisy I. Hughston McKenzie. He had two brothers, David and Travis, and two sisters, Eula and Patsy. He was married to Frances Lee, and his children were Carol McKenzie and Reagan, Donna and Gene Paul Skaggs. John Thomas was the great-grandson of Rev. John Witherspoon Pettigrew McKenzie, founder of McKenzie College in Red River County, and for whom the McKenzie Memorial United Methodist Church in Clarksville was named.

John Thomas' flying career began in 1922 when he took pilot training at Texarkana. He "barnstormed" for about ten years and then became an instructor at several different places. While serving as D.S. Control Officer for North American Aviation in Dallas, he learned of the Lend Lease Program and volunteered for that, thus becoming the first pilot to deliver a plane under that program. The delivery was made to Stockholm, Sweden.

John Thomas was employed with the Midwest Sector, Domestic Wing, Ferrying Command at Hensley Field in Grand Prairie, Texas but resigned effective June 10, 1942, to accept a commission as a 1st Lieutenant with the U.S Army Air Corps. He was a part of the 5th Group Ferrying Division Air Transport Command and was promoted to Captain on January 5, 1943. On February 17, 1946, he received an appointment to the Officer Reserve Corps as Major.

His job was to ferry P-51 type aircraft to the Eastern Seaboard. Also, the delivery of light aircraft was required for the new glider training program. John Thomas received too commendations for this service, and one of them reads in parts as follows: "This movement could not have been accomplished without the ability, industry, and loyalty of each pilot on this assignment. Your splended performance on this occasion is an important addition to the achievement of the Domestic Wing Ferrying Command."

He told that once while ferrying a plane, his instruments went out, and the sky was overcast. He was one of the original "seat of the pants and compass" pilots. Meanwhile, at the same time at his home in Clarksville, Texas, his mother felt a tug of her heartstrings, sensing it was her first born child in trouble. She got down on her knees and began praying for him. Back out over the ocean, the clouds began to roll away, and there was the bright Northern Star shining beautifully in the sky. John Thomas then knew the direction to fly and arrived safely at his destination.

He flew for Faucett Avaiation Company in Lima, Peru, first as a pilot and then as chief pilot from March 13, 1946 to May 16, 1949 and became the first person to fly over the Andes Mountains at night. His job was to fly a McDonald Douglas DC3 carrying passengers from Lima to Cousco, Peru. During one flight he lost an engine but managed to bring his plane in safely. He later learned that the natives had a funeral for him, thinking he would never make it back.

After leaving employment with Faucett on May 16, 1949, John Thomas came back to Red River County, started raising cattle and lived here until his death on April 2, 1972. He is buried in the historic McKenzie Cemetery west of Clarksville just down the road from where McKenzie College stood. He was still flying with friends at age 65 and even giving some advanced flying lessons.

★★★

John Lafayette and Bess Harvey Lawson had three sons who were in the service in World War II. Their other children were Olive Ruth, Tibitha Bess, John Harvey (a girl), Bryan Wayne, and Joyce Illene.

THOMAS LAFAYETTE LAWSON was born June 16, 1917 in Detroit, Texas. A "Memorial" in *Red River Recollections* reads as follows:

"Mr. and Mrs. J. L. Lawson of Detroit received a message from the War Department telling them their son, **THOMAS L. LAWSON**, who was a member of the 131st Field Artillery, 'The Lost Battalion' in Java, was a prisoner of the Japanese in Java. The last date they heard from him was Feb. 14, 1941, and last June they were notified that he was missing in action. Young Lawson completed two years service in the army; was trained at Camp Bowie in Brownwood, Texas, and was shipped from the West Coast October

20, 1941, for foreign service. The 'Lost Battalion' was composed chiefly of soldiers from West Texas, many of whom have not been heard from either directly or indirectly.

Thomas was reared at Detroit and had a great host of friends who rejoice to hear even indirectly and hope that the day will soon be here when **'The Lights Go On Again All Over the World'** and the boys are home again. Mr. and Mrs. Lawson received a letter advising that their son was officially dead. The letter read in part:

'You have been previously advised that your son was unaccounted for after the destruction at sea of a Japanese ship on which he was being transported while a prisoner of war. Information received from the Japanese Government through the International Red Cross is to the effect that the ship was sunk by submarine action on 20 June 1944 while transporting a group of prisoners, forty-three of whom were Americans, from Java to Japan. Thirteen of this group of forty-three survived and reached the Fukuoka prison camp in Japan. According to a report from the Japanese, all other Americans aboard were lost. . ."

Mr. and Mrs. Lawson received many letters from officers and men who were fellow prisoners with Thomas. They told of his unfailing good spirits and assistance he was willing to give. He was awarded the Purple Heart posthumously.

CHARLES TED LAWSON was born August 21, 1918 in Detroit, Texas. He married Nancy Jim Stiles and they had three sons, Ted Stiles, James Edward, and John Robert. Ted entered the Army Air Corps on August 27, 1942 in Dallas and was attached to the 2115th Aviation Service Unit as a Supply Technician 821 at the rank of Master Sergeant. He served in the Panama Canal Zone and was discharged January 24, 1946 at Camp Fannin, Texas. He was awarded the Good Conduct Medal, American Theater Campaign Medal and WWII Victory Medal. On January 25, 1946 Ted enlisted in the U.S. Air Force Reserve and was honorably discharged on January 12, 1949. He then reenlisted on January 13, 1949 and again was honorably discharged on January 12, 1953. Ted died July 13, 1971, and his wife, Jimmie, is also deceased.

ROGER S. LAWSON was born May 10, 1920 in Detroit, Texas. He married Roberta Mathis, and they had three children, Carolynn, Roger S. Jr., and Vivian Ann. In 1939 Roger joined the C.C.C. and helped build roads and scenic parks in Colorado.

Immediately after the attack on Pearl Harbor, he enlisted in the Navy. His basic training was at San Diego Naval Base where he was trained to be an antiaircraft gunner. When Roger finished his basic training, he was sent to Virginia Beach where he spent the remainder of the war as an antiaircraft instructor. He requested active duty numerous times. He was discharged in 1945 and came back to Texas. They made their home in Dallas where he worked for the *Dallas Times Herald* until repeated heart attacks forced his early retirement. Roger died November 14, 1971.

★★★

CHARLES COCO, the son of Joseph Gilmore and Mary Lenora Boudine Coco, was born in Louisiana and had five brothers and sisters: Viola, Helen Ethel, Joseph Nathan, Joseph Gilmore, Jr., and Henry. A newspaper article about him reads in part as follows: "36 years after gallant act, veteran receives Silver Star—As Nazi soldiers pummeled beleaguered American soliders during WWII, Sgt. Charles Coco defiantly held the line to save his comrades. He succeeded. Fifty-six years later, Uncle Sam, who asked Coco's generation to stop the Nazis, awarded the 87 year old Roseville resident the coveted Silver Star for 'gallantry in action against a hostile enemy'. The Silver Star is the nation's second highest military honor. The Medal of Honor is the highest.

No one knows for sure why he did not receive his Silver Star at that time. He had received two Purple Hearts for his feats during WWII. For many years Coco's military comrades and superior officers wrote letters to Rep John Doolittle urging him to right the wrong. On June 25 Doolittle mailed Coco the Silver Star. . . There was no explanation for why Coco received the important medal through the mail rather than normal protocol. . . Later Lt. Col. Terry Knight, a public affairs officer at the National Guard Headquarters in Sacramento, called the *Press Tribune* to say the post would provide the appropriate ceremony. . . It was November 7, 1943 when Coco and his platoon were fighting on the well known German Winter Line, south of Pazzelle, Italy. During the night, the soldiers divided to conquer the Nazi army from all sides, according to retired Lt. Col. W. E. Underwood, who served with Coco during the battle. He said, 'We attacked at night from the south while Coco's men attaacked on the right end of our line, swung around the nose of the hill, finding themselves between two hills with the enemy on both sides. Two officers and 12 men were killed, leaving Coco in command as sergeant. The rest of Coco's men had been wounded or captured. Sgt. Coco dragged his wounded men into a small farm house in the draw between the hills. Slain Nazi soldiers covered the floors.'

Coco said his heart sank when he saw the dead Nazi soldiers because he knew it meant their army would be there soon to claim their fallen soldiers... His worst fears materialized when the Nazis began an assault on the house. Coco said he and his men held the Germans back all day and well into the next night until they came at them with tanks and more infantry. He told his men to play dead. When the Germans took the farm house, they gathered their own, leaving what they thought were dead American soldiers. They lay still as Germans kicked them aside to get their own men. Coco had been shot in his arm and back... On Nov. 8 Sgt. Coco brought his wounded men off the hill through a mine field to the Battalion Aid Station... Coco finished the war serving in Africa and Italy. He says that when Uncle Sam asked for his help in 1941, he volunteered. He retired in 1961."

★★★

Marshall Rueban (Mack) McCain and his first wife, Emma Frances Young McCain, had the following children: Bonnie Bybee, two infants, Bernie Leak, James Calvin, Willie Margaret, Ruby Edwina, Marshall Young, Ballard Dinwiddie, Sara Emma Frances, and Janie Virginia. Three of their children served in World War II. After Emma's death in 1924, Mack married widow Lora E. Williams Stroud in 1933.

MARSHALL YOUNG (ROOSTER) McCAIN was born in 1916 and died in 1976. He was married to Peggy Simons, the mother of a son, Bernard Hunt, whose name was changed to Bernard Mc Cain after the marriage. He later married Mary Diana Dunning Aldridge, but had no children by either marriage. He entered the Army in 1943 and trained at Ft. Sill, Oklahoma. His overseas duty was in the Asiatic-Pacific Theater and in occupied Japan from April 1945 until his discharge in March 1953.

RUBY EDWINA McCAIN never married. She graduated from nursing school at Paris and entered the Army in July 1941. Edwina's places of service included New Guinea, occupied

Germany, the Philippines, Southwest Pacific, and New Zealand where she served as a nurse. She entered the service with the rank of 2nd Lieutenant. Edwina continued to serve her country when she was sent to the Korean Conflict as a nurse anesthetist. She was with an experimental MASH unit very near the front. After the Conflict was settled, she returned to Brooke General Hospital at San Antonio where she served the final years until her retirement with the rank of Major in 1962. Her time in foreign service totaled eight years, nine months, and twenty-seven days. When she retired, she returned to Clarksville to care for her father. She worked at area hospitals and also volunteered her time with the elderly. She was buried where the rest of her family had been buried at Stone's Chapel Cemetery at Cherry, north of Clarksville.

BALLARD D. McCAIN entered the Army in 1941 and trained in radio schools at Scott Field, Illinois, Keesler Field, Mississippi, Alabama, Arkansas and Texas. He was in Gander, Newfoundland when he was killed in action in 1943. Burial was made there, but after the war was over, his body was moved to Stone's Chapel Cemetery at Cherry where he was buried with full military honors. He was never married.

★★★

WILLIAM H. SMITH, son of Mr. and Mrs. Stan Smith, entered the Army in 1942 and trained at Camp Maxey, Texas and Camp Polk, Louisiana. He served in the ETO and was awarded the ETO Campaign Medal with five Battle Stars and Good Conduct Medal. He was discharged in 1945. He was married to Bernie Leak McCain. He is deceased, but Bernie resides in Clarksville.

★★★

Herschel M. and Lora E. Williams Stroud had four children: Hazel, Alden M., Arden, and Harlan J. Two sons served in World War I. (Very little is known of their time in the service.)

HARLAN A. STROUD entered the Army in 1937 and trained at Ft. Sill, Oklahoma, Camp Bowie and Camp Hood, Texas, and Ft. Bragg, North Carolina. He served overseas in Germany.

ALDEN M. STROUD also entered the Army in 1937 and trained at Ft. Sill and Chanute Field. His overseas duty was in the Caribbean.

★★★

GLENN ODELL WELCH was the son of Clyde (Bud) and Leola Faye Stroud Welch, and he had one brother, Billy Jo Kenneth (Chip) Welch. Glenn was born January 20, 1928, and died at Bath, New York in 1977. He married Nancy Carol Jamison, and they had seven children: Carolyn Joy, Lola Lorene, Susan Ann, Michael Glenn, Billie Kay, Jim Robert and Kimberly Faye. Glenn was later married to Donna Fellows. He enlisted in the Navy on October 24, 1945, at Paris, Texas and trained at San Diego and Jacksonville, Florida at Aviation Fundamentals and Target Aircraft Schools. He was discharged November 23, 1947.

★★★

MELVIN D. (BUD) EVERHART was born May 17, 1922 in Hymera, Indiana. His parents were Gilbert C. and Maudie A. Alsbrook Everhart. He had one sister, Opal M., and two brothers, Paul E. and Jack H. On July 6, 1944 he married Betty Bakke, and they have three children, Michaelynn D., Steven B., and Benson D. The Everharts are retired and make their home in Brookston, Texas.

Bud had the following to say about "How I met my spouse—On July 21, 1943, I was given my first liberty pass from Minneplis Naval Air Station when I was enduring Primary Flight Training. The first place I headed for was the USO Club. I had heard from some other cadets that there were three pretty girls singing there. From my vantage point at a far back table, I was sure that the most attractive of the two blondes and one redhead was singing direactly to me. After renditions of *God Bless America, Till We Meet Again, The White Cliffs of Dover*, etc., I made up my mind to become acquainted with that pretty miss. Sauntering over to her, I asked, 'Would you please dance with me?' Her reply was, 'I can't while on duty.' Deflated, but not discouraged, I immediately came back with, 'How about a date when you get off?' Again, 'No!'

After pushing this course of action on subsequent passes, I was finally accepted for a dance during intermission. Excited by the success, I then proceeded clumsily to step on the hem of her evening gown. After repairing the damaged shoulder strap, we did dance. The result was a lasting relationship. Upon my graduation from

John Thomas McKenzie with a group in Stockholm, Sweden.

Pensacola Naval Air Training Center as a 2nd Lieuteanant in the US Marine Corps, we were married on July 6, 1944."

Marine Fighting Squadron One-Two-Four (VMF-124)—This squadron was the first Marine unit to be equipped with Corsair fighters, and it scored seventy-eight official victories with this famous plane. The unit was organized on September 7, 1942, under the command of Capt. C. B. Brewer. The squadron arrived at Guadalcanal on February 11, 1943, aboard the *SS Lurline* and was in action there. The unit saw heavy action in the Solomons Campaign under the leadership of Capt. Brewer, Major W. H. Pace and Major

W. A. Millington. VMF-124 participated in the Russell Islands, New Georgia, and Veila Lavella operations and scored most of its victories during these actions. Major Millington led the unit back to the U.S. on October 13, 1943. After reorganization and retraining at Mojave, the squadron shipped to Pearl Harbor abord the *Ticonderoga* where it transferred to the carrier *Essex* on December 28, 1944. As a carrier based unit, it then participated in the Lingayen landings in the Philippines and conducted air strikes against Tokyo. During the spring of 1945 the unit operated in the Iwo Jima and Okinawa campaigns. Under the command of Major J. M. Johnson, the squadron returned to the U.S. once again in April 1945. After more training, it embarked for Ewa Marine Air Station near Pearl Harbor on September 2, 1945, V-J Day.

The F-4U Corsair World War II War Machine was built by the Chance-Vought Corp. It was the first fighter plane in WWII that could out perform the Japanese Mitsubishi (Zero). The Pratt and Whitney Radial 2000 horsepower engine provided the ncessary speed (450 knots) and weight carrying capability enabling it to fly with an armament of six fifty-caliber machine guns, rockets, and 500 pound bomb load. It was feared by the Japanese, who called it "Whistling Death", due to noise emitted on strafing runs by the oil cooler shutter, thus demoralizaing the enemy. It maintained an eleven to one victory ratio during the Pacific-Asiatic Campagin from 1942 to V-J Day in 1945. VMF 124 (Marine Fighting Squadron) was the first of twelve squadrons to use this plane in combat, racking up a victory of 78 enemy planes destroyed. Bud Everhart, after graduating from Pensacola Naval Aviation Training on June 20, 1944, flew the "Bent-Wing" 8,000 hours until his discharge on May 20, 1952.

A newspaper article said the following: "Airman changes services: Turns in stripes for bars—An Air Force Master Sergeant turned in his stripes for an Army Warrant Officer's bars Wednesday. Marion D. Everhart was discharged at the government's convenience. Then he immediately was sworn into the Army Reserve and called to active duty by Maj. Gen. Douglass Quandt, commander of the 16th Army Corps. Everhart left for Fort Carson, Colorado where he wil serve with the 5th Infantry Division as a helicopter pilot . . . Everhart had been in the Air Force ten years."

Bud Everhart retired June 30, 1970 after twenty-eight years of service as a Military Aviator, spanning the time from June 1, 1942 through June 30, 1970; flying 37,000 hours in 46 different types of aircraft, which include 561 combat missions during WWII, Korea and Vietnam. Awards earned were the Distinguised Flying Cross with "V" Device (Valor), eighteen Air Medals with "V", Navy and Marine Corps Medals, (These were awarded while participating in aerial flight), the Bronze Star with "V", two Purple Hearts, two National Defense Medals, eight Air Force Good Conduct Medals and four Longevity Service Awards; Combat Rediness; Combat Action, Navy 1944, Certificate of Recognition, Cold War 1945-1970, Expert Marksman, Meritorious Service and Army Commendation, Vietnam Service with seven stars, plus thirty-two other service and campaign awards and citations. (All of the information about Bud Everhart was contained in a scrapbook compiled by the Everharts. The first page was entitled, "The Path—Proverbs 3:5-6; The Way—Ephesians 4:4; For Life—II Timothy 3:12; From the Heart. (What a testimony!)

★★★

WILLIAM HOWARD KYLE was born September 21, 1911 at Brownwood, Texas. His parents were Benjamin Franklin and Florence Foster Kyle, and he had two sisters, Bessie and Mae, and a brother, Mack McKenzie. He married Vivian Irma Rinehart, and they had two children, Patsy Aylene and Ronald William.

Mr. Kyle enlisted in the Seabees in 1942 at Kermit, Texas. His training was at San Diego, and he was attached to the 52nd Battalion, Company D, N.E.T.C. He could not swim, but when they were on a ship, he was thrown in so it was "swim or drown" He tried, but it just wasn't working and after going under twice, he realized he was about to drown. Then another man jumped overboard and saved him. From then on he had to wear a life jacket twenty-four hours a day .

His company's job was to go to the islands in the Pacific to have camps ready for the army when they came. This was a very high security task. On one of these assignments, trenches had been dug to be used for look-out, and it was his watch. It was dark, but he could see in the distance a log that seemed to be moving toward the trench. He watched for a long time, and as it came closer, he prayed he would not have to fire on anyone because he believed in the Commandement, "Thou Shalt Not Kill". As the log came closer, the man sleeping beside him in the trench woke up, grabbed his gun and fired at what appeared to be a log but turned out to be the enemy. He thought his prayers were answered, and from then on he spent most of his time as a cook in the kitchen. His discharge in 1945 was at Pearl Harbor. He died July 30, 1982, and Vivian lives in Paris.

ALLEN HUMPHREYS McEWIN, the son of James Allen and Annie Mae Humphreys McEwin, was born September 20, 1923 in Paris, Texas. He had two sisters, Alice Marie and Elveyn, and a brother, James William. He married Patsy Aylene Kyle, and their chidlren are Ginger Shari, James Kyle, Dale Vayne and Darla Kay.

Allen enlisted in the Navy on January 20, 1943 and was trained at San Diego. He served on the deck force of the USS Feland, a troop transport, where he took care of cargo that came in and out and handled the Marine equipment. His overseas duty was in the South Pacific at Gilbert Island, Marshall Island, Pearl Harbor and Honolulu. He didn't see much action because he was on the ship most of the time. He said this: "It was a bad war. I left school to enlist because I wanted to serve my country. I didn't leave a wife or girl friend behind, and came home and married seven years later. We moved to Clarksville, Texas the summer of 1957, and I operated my own business, Quality Refrigeration, until my retirement in 1988." Allen was a B.M. 2/C and was awarded the Pacific Theater Medal with two Battle Stars and Good Conduct Medal. His discharge was on January 29, 1946 while at Pearl Harbor. He went from there to Norman, Oklahoma and then to San Francisco.

★★★

PEARIS C. ABERNATHY, the son of Charley Julian and Floita Rachel Phillips Abernathy, was born April 6, 1921 in the White Rock community in Red River County, Texas. He had two sisters, Mary Catherine and Dorthy May. He married Mary Hattie Webster, and they had two children, Robbie Marcell and Pearis C. Abernathy, Jr.

On July 24, 1942 at Tyler, Texas he entered the service. His basic training was at Camp Wolters, Texas, and he was trained as an airplane mechanic at Sheppard AFB in Wichita Falls, Texas. He took a special course in propeller training at Champaign, Illinois and became a propeller specialist and general airplane mechanic attached to the 107th Tactical Reconnaissance Squadron as a Staff Sergeant. He had this to say about his experiences in WWII:

"Thirty-six men from our outfit landed on D+4. We were on the end of a L.S.T. and landed on a bomb crater. We had to wait for high tide to float us off and then waited in the Channel for another low tide to land. We made it that time and walked all night with full pack. The next day we were lost, and a truck picked us up and carried us back to where we had landed. Just a short distance from there, the army engineers had dozed off an apple orchard and laid a runway with steel matting. We were to repair planes that were too damaged to fly back across the Channel to England for repairs. We took parts off the planes we couldn't repair and put them on planes less damaged and sent them back to England. Stayed there till the rest of our group came over, about a month. Then we supported General Patton's Third Army. Where he went, we went till the war was over. Lots of things to tell. Some good, some bad! I try to remember the good things and forget the rest. Doesn't work that way. Had millions of dollars worth of experience—wouldn't give a penny with a hole in it for that much more. I was one of the lucky ones. I never got wounded. I think things should be written down and kept for future generations, but they should be accurate. I am a history buff. I guess history was my favorite course in school. There are worlds of stories about the war that will die with us veterans."

S/Sgt. Abernathy was discharged September 24, 1945, at Ft. Sam Houston, Texas and was awarded the EAME Campaign Medal with six Bronze Stars, Good Conduct Medal, and Distinguished Unit Badge with one Oak Leaf Cluster. He served in Europe at Normandy, Northern France, Rhineland, and Ardennes.

★★★

HAROLD JAMES GARRETT was born January 7, 1919 in Red River County, Texas, the son of Samuel Knox and Ninny Era Stafford Garrett. He had four brothers and six sisters. He married Velma Moore, and they had two children, Sallie Elise and Stanley David.

On September 19, 1928 he enlisted in the Navy at Texarkana. He served as a Chief Petty Officer and was awarded the WWII Victory Medal, American Defense Fleet Medal, Good Conduct Medal, American-European Theater Medal, Asiatic-Pacific Theater

Medal, and African-Middle Eastern Theater Medal. After his discharge on August 15, 1958, he served in the Fleet Reserve for ten years. His final discharge was on December l, 1968. On a personal note, he was selected by COMSIXTHFLT in 1949 as one of five members of the Pistol Team to represent the Sixth Fleet in firing against the Marine Corps competion in Naples. He fired a score of 360 out of a possible 400. As the only representative from the Destroyer Force on the 6th Fleet Team in 1956, he won second place (silver medal) in the International Rifle and Revolver Match at Ricosal Naval Range on Malta. The American team won the contest for the second time. It is an annual event against the combined British Royal Navy and Marine Teams.

★★★

Lilbon Thomas and Sallie Elizabeth Buchanan Moore had two sons who served in World War II. There were six children in the family.

GEORGE LILBON MOORE was born May 3, 1927 in Avery, Texas. He married Patricia Jayne Reese, and they had two daughters and a son. On May 3, 1944, his seventeenth birthday, he enlisted in the Navy in Red River County. This was at the height of WWII. He served on a LST, landing troops on foreign soils. He served in the European and Mediterrean Theaters of operation and was in the Southern France invasion. Then he was sent to the Asiatic-Pacific Theater where they island hopped, preparing for the invasion of Japan. The atomic bombs dropped on Hiroshima and Nagasaki ended the war in September 1946. George came home and was discharged. He was awarded the WWII Victory Medal, American Defense Medal, Good Conduct Medal, American-European Theater Medal, Asiatic-Pacific Theater Medal, and African-Middle Eastern Theater Medal. He doesn't talk about his experiences during the war, although he had many.

THOMAS MARTIN MOORE was born March 30, 1921 in Avery, Texas. He married Hazel Marie Peek, and they had one daughter. He enlisted in the Army Air Corps as a cadet and received his wings with commision of 2nd Lieutenant in 1943. He served as a pilot and instrument instructor training cadets in piloting and instrument flying. He was discharged October 6, 1944 and later died in a mid-air collision near Rock Port, Texas.

★★★

JOHNNIE RUDOLPH KING was born September 2, 1921, near Boxelder, Texas. His parents were Iley Joel and Nellie Elizabeth Mace King. The other children were Berris, Dan, S. J., Milton Nuil (Bill), Henry Lane (Buck), and Robert Blanton (R. B.). On December 12, 1947, Johnnie and Wanda Marie Presley were married. They had one daughter, Kay, and a granddaughter, Misha Bethea.

On September 17, 1940, in his last year of school, Johnnie entered the Army for a three year enlistment.

He trained at Camp Shelby, Mississippi, Savannah, Georgia, Ft. Sam Houston, Texas and Camp Stoneman, California. He was attached to the 2nd Infantry as a Pvt and with the 193rd Ordnance Depot for overseas duty. Johnnie was on board ship on September 8, 1943 heading for the South Pacific on the day his three year enlistment was up. They landed in New Guinea on October 10, 1943, and served at Port Morsby, 'Death Valley'. From there they went to Nabzab, and in 1944 he was in the Dutch East Indies on Biak Island and Papa Lala Village. He spent two years, three months and three days in New Guineaa. On December 15, 1945 he received an honorable discharge as a T/Sgt at Ft. Bliss, Texas. He served his country five years, three months and eight days. He was awarded the Asisatic-Pacific Medal, American Theater Medal, American Defense Medal, Victory Medal and Good Conduct Medal.

His wife related the following that he had told her: "It took about four weeks on the ship to get to the South Pacific which was a long time for a bunch of sea sick soldiers. After a long stay in the jungles, Johnnie became ill with a fever. Of course, the climate was very hot since it was so near the equator. He was sent to the hospital where he spent many days, nearly dying. Then he went to Australia several times for R&R. When the Japanese strafed the area, they flew so low that their big white teeth could be seen as they laughed at the Americans. These were really tense moments as the planes circled around and around. A close call came one day while he was in his tent. He heard a large bomber fly over, and it crashed near the camp. They started running toward the crash sight when someone yelled and told them to get out of there because ther was a bomb on board. He turned and ran as fast as he could back to his tent. As he fell on his bunk, a large piece of red hot shrapnel fell on the bunk beside him. It barely missed him.

On Biak Island, a coral island 45 miles long and 22 miles wide north of Western New Guinea, the first thing they had to get used to was the blinding sunlight. It rained almost every day, and the humidity kept them soaking wet. The natives they saw were small people who saluted proudly the soldiers and were glad to eat their leftovers. It was a hard battle to win Biak. The 193rd Ordnance Depot Company was awarded the Meritorious Service Unit Plaque for superior performance of exceptionally difficult assignments. The activities of this unit contributed greatly to relieving the critical supply situation. The soldiers said, 'If nothing else has come from this little island in the Pacific, we can name one. Instead of my aching back, on this island, it is my aching Biak'.

Johnnie was happy to be back with his family after his discharge. In September 1947 he went to work at the Red River Arsenal in Texarkana in the Supply Division. When he was in the jungles of New Guinea, he experienced some close calls. At this time he began to call on God to spare his life, promising Him that he would live for Him and do whatever He called him to do. Johnnie kept his promise when in 1954 he was called into the ministry. On August 1, 1954 he was ordained as a Southern Baptist Minister at the Salem Baptist Church in Boxelder. His first pastorate was at the Lanes Chapel Baptist Church, and he pastored churches in Red River, Lamar, Bowie, Titus and Cass Counties. He preached his last message on July 11, 1993 at the Old Union Baptist Church in Simms, Texas. Johnnie left his earthly home suddenly for his heavenly home on July 15, 1993."

★★★

ORVAL FREDRICK COMBS, son of Mr. and Mrs. Ollie Combs, was born July 14, 1922 and reared in the Greenwood Community. He entered the service October 29, 1942 and married Faye Nell Crump when he came in on furlough July 1, 1943. Orval was in training about 21 months before going overseas. He served in Hawaii, Leyte and Okinawa. A newspaper article quoted a letter received by his wife:

"With deepest regret I write you of the death of your husband, Sgt. Orval F. Combs, which occurred in the vicinity of Kakazu, Okinawa Shina, on 9 April 1945.

While our company was attacking a heavily fortified enemy

position on Kakazu Ridge, heavy artillery and machine gune fire was encountered. One element of the company was completely isolated and later, all of its members were reported as missing in action. When our troops had forced the enemy to withdraw, the remains of the missing men, including Orval's, were recovered. An investigation revealed that all had lost their lives from enemy artillery and machine gun fire.

Orval was buried in the 96th Infantry Division Temporary Cemetery Number One, Okinawa Shima, Row No. 21, Grave No. 711. His burial was in accordance with the rites of his own faith, with full military honors in a quiet and peaceful setting.

It is regrettable that so fine a man as your husband should be called upon to make the supreme sacrifice. The knowledge that his sacrifice was not in vain, and that he died as he lived, with honor and courage, may assuage in some measure the pain of so great a loss; for I feel there is little I can say that would be of greater comfort. At the time of his death, Orval was courageously performing his duty as a squad leader. His devotion to duty, comradeship and gentlemanliness exemplified by his moral strength of character, made him an able and trustworthy leader. His loss is deeply felt by us, for we had worked together as a team both on the training field and on the field of battle. Orval will be remembered as an invaluable member of our company and as a close and cheerful friend. The officers and enlisted men of this company join in extending deepest sympathy to you in your bereavement. If at any time you feel that I can be of further assistance to you, please do not hesitate to call upon me. Most sincerely yours, Eric J. Newman, lst Lt., Infantry, Commanding"

★★★

An article in the *Bogata News* read: "John E. Coleman of Detroit, William J. Alexander of Talco, and Charlie Davidson, Jr. of Deport left for the service together. These three men took part in the D-Day Invasion in 1944. As evidenced by the grave markers, both Coleman and Alexander perished during the Invasion. Today, Coleman is buried in Detroit. Alexander is buried in the Normany Cemetery in France. Davidson lives in Deport with his wife, Joyce. In March of this year Davidson's step-son, Allen Williams, a Social Studies Instructor at Chisum High School, toured Normandy, France and took this picture of William Alexander's grave."

CHARLES E. DAVIDSON, JR. was born January 29, 1924 at Deport, Texas. His parents were Charles Edward and Lou E. Davis

Davidson. He had two sisters, Frances and Naomi, and a brother, J. L. He married Jo Nell Bell who is deceased, and later married Joyce McBrayer. He was drafted on July 8, 1943 at Tyler, Texas. His basic training in the Infantry was at Camp Wolters, Texas, and he was attached to the 29th Division, 175th Battalion, Company I from January 1944 to January 1946. He was a PFC and was discharged at Tyler and awarded the EAME Campaign Medal with four Bronze Stars, Good Conduct Medal, WWII Victory Medal, Bronze Arrowhead, and Expert Infantryman Badge. He took part in the Normandy Invasion and battle at St. Lo and then transferred to Headquarters Kitchen. His overseas duty was in Northern France, Normandy, Rhineland and Central Europe.

WILLIAM J. ALEXANDER, Pvt, 116th Infantry, 29th Divison, Texas died on June 13, 1944. This is on his marker in the cemetery in Normandy in France where he took part in the invasion. I have been unable to secure other information about him.

JOHN EDWIN COLEMAN enlisted in the Army in 1943 and took part in the Normandy Landing, during which he was killed. He was awarded the Purple Heart posthumously. Today he is buried in Detroit, Texas, and his veteran's marker reads: "John E. Coleman, Texas, Pvt 60 Inf 9 Inf Div, World War II, July 24, 1919— June 15, 1944".

PAUL COLEMAN, the brother of John Edwin Coleman, was born October 4, 1921 in Detroit, Texas. His parents were John and Bupha Wilson Coleman, and the other children in the family were Olive, Berniece and Billy. He married Virginia Lewis, and they had two sons, James Larry and Glen. Paul Coleman was drafted in August 1942 and was attached to the Anti-Tank Company, 128th Infantry, 32nd Division. He was discharged in November 1946 at San Antonio and received the Good Conduct Medal, Combat Infantry Badge with three Battle Stars and some other medals.

Paul Coleman said: "We had three months basic training at Camp Wolters and then went by train to Battle Creek, Michigan for two weeks. After that we boarded another train for Fort Meade, Maryland; stayed there two weeks; then had another train ride to San Francisco. There we boarded a ship for twenty-two days and nights to Sydney, Australia. We loaded on trucks to go to Brisbane, Australia where we joined the 32nd Division as replacements. The 32nd had been in battle in New Guinea where they lost over half their troops. After we joined them to bring the division back to full strength, we were sent back to New Guinea. After control of New Guinea, we moved on to Leyte in the Philippines. After control there, we moved on to Luzon, and that's where we were when the war ended. While overseas, I was promoted to Staff Sergeant and Platoon Leader. My uncle, Clarence Coleman, was killed in World War I; my brother, John Edwin Coleman was killed in World War II; and my son, James Larry Coleman was killed in Viet Nam on July 27, 1969. He had just turned nineteen years old on July 13. He had volunteered for the Marines."

★★★

Will and Willie Ann Moore Westfall of the Sherry Community southwest of Clarksville had two sons who served in World War II. The other children in the Westfall family were Luther, Ona, Lula and Lela.

OLEN FELIX (PAT) WESTFALL was born July 22, 1915. He joined the CCC in 1935 and remained in it through 1937. In 1943 Pat joined the Navy Seabees and trained in Williamsburg, Virginia and Gulfport, Missssippi. I talked with Pat on March 3, 2000, and he had the following to say about his experiences:

"The Seabees were a Construction Battalion for the 3rd Marine Division and also helped the Army's 14th Division. Two hundred ninety men left the States as maintenance men, and there were only one hundred thirty-nine men left when the war was over. The Seabees didn't fight unless we were attacked. The fighting men went in first; the Seabees went in second; and there might not be one hundred yards of beach secured at that time. We set up camp; maintained armor and ammunition; and did whatever was needed to be done.

My group left for overseas at Camp Holliday, a Marine camp in New Orleans. We crossed the Caribbean Sea, went through the Panama Canal to the Pacific Ocean. There was no convoy. We were on a troop ship that carried 5,000 men, not counting the crew. The ship zigzagged every seven minutes to avoid being attacked by a submarine. It took twenty-four days to reach Pearl Harbor where we saw the great destruction that had been done on December 7, 1941. From there we went to Guadalcanal for a couple of days; then to St. Isabella with the Marines. This was in the Russell Group in

THEY LEFT TOGETHER

JOHN E COLEMAN
TEXAS
PVT 60 INF 9 INF DIV
WORLD WAR II
JULY 24 1919   JUNE 15 1944

WILLIAM J. ALEXANDER
PVT 116 INF 29 DIV
TEXAS JUNE 13 1944

John E. Coleman of Detroit, William J. Alexander of Talco, and Charlie Davidson, Jr. of Deport left for the service together. These three men took part in the D-Day Invasion in 1944. As evidenced by the grave markers, both Coleman and Alexander perished during the Invasion.

Today, Coleman is buried in Detroit, Texas, Alexander is buried in the Normandy cemetery in France. Davidson lives in Deport with his wife, Joyce. In March of this year Davidson's step-son, Allen Williams, a Social Studies instructor at Chisum High School, toured Normandy, France and took this picture of William Alexander's grave.

A clipping from the Detroit News.

the Solomon Islands. The Japs had set up a partial landing strip. We finished it, and it was a good one. Instead of using cement, sand and gravel, we used cement and coral reef. There were eight to ten thousand Japs still on the island, and they were pushed into the hills. After some time, they finally surrendered. Our men stayed in pup tents during the day, but in trenches at night because that's when the Japs would attack the camp. There would be shells ankle deep in the camp and surrounding jungle the next morning. Next we went with the 3rd Marine Division to New Georgia Island where we didn't have too much trouble.

Just before the war was over, the Marine Commanding Officer called us together; told us we were in for extensive training; and that he hoped we could speak either Chinese or Japanese. At night we got to watch movies, and one night when the show was going on, the lights came on, and we were told the Japanese had surrendered. You've never heard such shouting. We were told to go to the cook shack and get a case of beer or cokes. From then on we maintained the island before going to New Hebrides in a three ship convoy across the Coral Seaa. This was a staging area, and we stayed there until we went home, about five months. I was put in charge of a shore patrol, twenty-eight men and ten jeeps. I remember the CO told us there would be a contest to see who could grow the best beard. I came in third with a handle bar mustache and a goatee.

In November there was a little trouble on the island so I took twelve men and we stopped it. There were five or six ships out in the harbor. I came home on the aircraft carrier *Casa Blanca*. They took the planes and gasoline off to make room for us. While we were on the Pacific, there was a really bad storm; waves twenty to thirty feet high. We were told not to stand out on the deck. One man was blown off the ship by the wind, and even though they searched, they never found the body. It took calling the roll three times before they found out who he was. He had been in the Army. We were three days out of San Francisco when this happened. There was burial at sea, but the coffin was empty.

We landed back in San Francisco at Thanksgiving time and went to Treasure Island, which was across the bay. The only clothes we had were Marine clothes so they issued us new ones. There was muster call every morning at 8:00 AM; then we were free to go to San Francisco. I stayed there eighteen days before starting for home on a train. I was discharged December 13, 1945 at Houston with the rank of Chief Machinist Mate. I had lost the hearing in one ear and had been hit in my right leg with shrapnel , but I felt very lucky to be alive. Pat and Betty Meredith were married July 1, 1950, and they have one daughter, Patsy. They are both retired and live in Clarksville.

CHARLEY M. WESTFALL entered the Army Air Corps in 1942. He received his training at Perrin Field and Pampa, Texas and Garden City, Kansas. He was born December 26, 1906 and because of his age was not sent overseas. He was "loaned out" and worked in an aluminum plant. He and Lynnie Hutchins were married in 1938. Charley died March 10, 2000, and his widow resides in Clarksville.

Ona Westfall Trussell and her husband, Noah, had four sons who were in the service. Ona and Noah are both deceased.

CLAUDE RAY TRUSSELL entered the Navy in 1942 and trained at Great Lakes, Illinois. He served in the Pacific and Atlantic operations and in Sicily. He was wounded in Italy in 1944 and awarded a Presidential Citation. He was discharged in 1945.

ROYCE W. TRUSSELL entered the Army in 1943 and trained

at Camp Haan, California. He served in Alaska and was wounded in 1944. He was awarded the Good Conduct Medal, American Defense Medal, APO and Victory Medals. He was discharged in 1946.

WALTER R. TRUSSELL entered the Army in 1945 and trained in Maryland. He married Margaret Newsom, and they are both deceased.

The fourth son of the Trussells, **MILLARD FELIX TRUSSELL**, joined the Navy in 1950.

★★★

ALTON CAMPBELL was born July 7, 1922 in Ardmore, Oklahoma. He was raised near DeKalb, Texas in a little community named Springhill. His parents were Thomas E. and Katie Porton Campbell. There were seven children in the family. Two sons, Alton and Alfred, were in the service during World War II. Alton and Jacqueline Crawford were married in 1975. They are retired and reside north of Clarskville near the location of the grocery store owned and operated by Jacqueline's father, B. F. Crawford, for many years.

When we visited with Alton, he told us the following about his experiences in World War II: "I enlisted in the Marine Corps on January 29, 1943, before my twenty-first birthday. My training was in San Diego, and I was a part of the 18th Antiaircraft Field Artillery which was attached to the 5th Amphibious Division. I went overseas on June 1, 1943. We boarded the *USS DONCASTER* in San Diego. The ship had been built by Kaiser-Frasier. It was a liberty ship run by the Army. A prop was lost off the ship; the convoy left us while we waited for the prop to be fixed. There was not much food on board, mostly split pea soup, and I lost twenty pounds. There were 5,000 Marines aboard. We were in Hawaii for a while and then went to Enewetak where the atomic bomb had been tested in the Pacific area. There was not a building or coconut tree still standing. We were there only about three weeks. Rockets shot the tops out of trees to take care of the snipers in them. Then it was on to Saipan and Tinian in the north Marianas Islands. Thirty-six months were spent on these islands. On Saipan 4,500 were lost, many of them my good friends.

The Seabees came in and built airstrips. This broke Japan

because it enabled the planes to go directly to Japan. That protected the B-29's from Japanese Zero fighters on Saipan. I remember when they were building the airports. Some boys were standing guard at an ammunition dump when the Japs shot into it and blew it up. We left those islands on board the ship in the harbor at Saipan with new gear and guns. We were given 120 mm guns instead of 90 mm ones. We had orders to sail into Tokyo Bay and to disembark on the peninsula instead of the mainland. On ship we were drilled for thirty to sixty days that even if we saw a child coming toward us after we landed, we weren't to hesitate to shoot because the Japs were so desperate at this point that the child would probably be booby trapped.

Word came from Harry S. Truman to hold up for a while because a new weapon was to be used. My division was scheduled to be the first to spearhead the invasion of the mainland of Japan. I believe that President Truman is the best President we've ever had and that he saved more lives than any other President in our history, even though many default him for ordering the Atomic Bomb to be dropped. I believe that not only did this save American lives, but even Japanese lives.

After the war ended and the peace treaty was signed, my division went back to Saigon. We were broken up into groups and sent to different places. I was in the group that went to Wake Island to get the remaining Japs off that island. When Japan first invaded Wake, the Marines put up a 'hell of a battle'. The Japs tied the Marines' hands behind them, bayoneted them, and put them in reefers (large iceboxes); and buried them.

The Japanese prisoners we took were forced to dig these reefers up, and I saw all of this. (With tears in his eyes, Alton said to me, 'Honey, I know what Hell on earth is'.)"

He was a Corporal and received the Asiatic-Pacific Campaign Medal with three Battle Stars. His Unit received a Presidential Citation for knocking down 65% of the Jap planes that came over the islands. Alton said, "I wouldn't take a fortune for what I've been through and learned in life but sure wouldn't give fifteen cents to go back. It tears me up to see young people who don't know what has been done for them and who take everything so for granted, not knowing what sacrifices have been made to make it like it is today." Alton came back to the States in June 1, 1946 and went home on furlough for thirty days. Then he went to Ferris Island, South

Carolina and had a good job in recruit distribution. There would be as many as eighteen to twenty-five recruits on a train to be taken to all different places. He finished his tour of duty and stayed in the Active Reserves for three years until April 1, 1950 when he got out because he did not want to go to Korea.

ALFRED CAMPBELL was born June 24, 1920. He was one of the first men drafted from Bowie County, Texas. He was assigned to the 44th Infantry Division and hauled gas for General George Patton. He was with the General when they burst through the Segfried Line. Fuel trucks were shot out from under him, making him have to jump for safety. He was overseas about three years.

★★★

J. C. SMITH was born July 1, 1921 in Red River County, Texas. His parents were Oscar and Norie Patton Smith, and he was one of ten children. He married Margaret Barton, and they have two children, Sherry and Donnie. The Smiths make their home in Bogata, Texas. He visited with us and said:

"I enlisted in the Army on June 22, 1942 and was sent to Camp Wallace, Texas. My basic training as a Medic was at Camp Barkley in Abilene, Texas. My job was to drive an ambulance to an aid station and back to the general hospital. From there I went by train to Ft. Lewis, Washington, Camp Pickett, Virginia, Ft. Dix, New Jersey, and New York. We boarded the USS MONTICELLO, an Italian luxury liner that had been in the harbor when the war started. It was converted to a troop carrier. The trip overseas was a rough one that lasted eight days. When we were at sea three days, we heard depth charges exploding. Later we learned that a ship had sunk with many lives lost. We were in a large convoy going to Africa where I served as a Medic. My outfit set up a hospital outside Algiers in a cork forest. Most all the patients went back to a town where hospitals had been set up in some buildings that had been schools. Then I became a part of the 53rd Amphibious, 3337th Ordinance Truck Company. My training for this was at Oran, Africa, and I drove a 2½ ton amphibious truck used for delivering supplies, equipment and personnel to the coast. This truck was called a "duck" because it ran on land or sea. It could land on the beach and keep going. Since there were no docks, the ships might be five miles out so those "ducks" would be used to go back and forth.

From Africa we participated in the invasion of Gelo, Sicily. We were fighting under General George Patton, and it took us about 28 days to take it. On our second trip into Sicily, the ship was out about three miles. The "duck" sank about 300 yards from shore. Luckily, we had on life preservers, and the tide took us in. Shells were hitting all around us, but this did keep the sharks away. Here we were attached to the 3rd Division. Then it was on to Italy with the 36th Division. We went through Italy, Southern France, and Belgium and then on to Germany. We took river crossing training before crossing the Rhine River. The Rhine was not as big as I thought it would be. After we crossed, we used pack saddles on mules to carry the big guns up in the mountains. We ate K-rations and C-rations and lots of times set them on the truck muffler to heat them. Our division did a lot. We were attached to Scottish and British outfits. After Patton went back to the U.S., we were under General Mark Clark. Everyone liked Patton, and when he slapped that boy, it was because the boy was shell shocked. We didn't make it to Berlin but did see Hitler's summer retreat. After the war ended, there were lots of German refugees that had to be sent back to replacement centers to be sorted out."

J. C. served in Algeria-French Morocco, Naples-Foggia, Normandy, Northern France, Rhineland, Ardennes, and Central Europe. He came back to the States on the *USS JOHN HOPKINS*, a liberty ship. It quit running twice before they landed in Baltimore, and a tug boat finally had to pull them in. He was discharged at the Separation Cengter, IGMR, Pennsylvania on October 8, 1945. He was awarded a Good Conduct Medal and European-African-Middle Eastern Service Medal with seven Bronze Stars.

★★★

NOEL N. MEADOWS was born November 23, 1918 in DeKalb, Texas. His parents were Leslie Oscar and Emma D. Pritchett Meadows. He had two sisters, Thelma Dorene who died in infancy, and Generia Maxine. His brothers were Leslie O. Jr. and Lareall Arthur who served thirty-two years in the Navy and received a concussion at Pearl Harbor. Noel and Emma Lou (Honey) Brem were married May 9, 1942. They had three children, Huey Pritchett, Anita Kay, and Andrea Lou.

Noel first enlisted in the C.C.C. at Arizona in 1937. He took

J. C. Smith and a buddy standing next to a Duck (code designation Dukw) which was an amphibious military vehicle used during World War II

his training for the Army, 9th Infantry Division, in San Antonio. He then served in the Army Air Corps and retired in 1959 as a Master Sergeant E8. He received the American Defense Medal, World War II Medal, American Campaign Medal, and others that have been misplaced. He died March 19, 1980 while serving as Mayor of Watauga, Texas. He served a total of 38 years in the Air Force and Civil Service, U.S.P.O.

★★★

Five sons of Ernest Jerome and Annie L. Faucett Williams were in the service in World War II. Their other children were St. Elmo, Lou Ellen, Edna Earl, Thelma Kate, Vashti Elaine, and Mamie.

CASEY WILLIAMS was born January 7, 1911 in Clarksville, Texas. He was married to Mildred McFarland Gouldsberry and later to Myrtle Cathy. Casey enlisted in the Army Air Corps on November 14, 1939 at Barksdale Field, Louisiana. He was attached to the 2811th Army Air Force Base Unit, and his training was in maintenance and quartermaster. He was a Tec 4, and his duties were in carpentry and maintenance. His overseas duty was in China, Egypt, Libya, Tunisia, Naples-Foggia, and Rome-Arno. He waas discharged July 6, 1945 at Ft. Sam Houston, Texas and was awarded the American Defense Service Medal, Good Conduct Medal, EAME Campaign Medal with four Bronze Stars, and Asiatic-Pacific Campaign Medal with one Bronze Star. Casey Williams died June 1, 1997.

RUSSELL A. WILLIAMS was born December 25, 1912 at Negley, Texas. He married Kathryn Louise Stokes, and they had two sons, David Arnold and Bruce Evan. Later he married Dorthea Moore Nellans. On July 24, 1936 he enlisted in the Army at Ft. Sam Houston, Texas and was attached to Company L of the 2nd Infantry Division. In 1939 he reenlisted in the Army Air Corps, which later became the U.S. Air Force, and served as a Master Sergeant. Russell was captured by the Japanese on April 9, 1942, while serving in the Philippines and survived the infamous Bataan Death March. He was a prisoner for forty-three months in Japan where he worked in a carbide factory. When he was liberated, he weighed eighty-two pounds. His normal weight had been 135. Sgt. Williams remained in the Air Force, making it his career and retired in June 1957 at Sheppard Air Force Base, Texas. He was awarded the American Defense Medal with one Star, American Theater Medal, APO Ribbon with two Stars, Philippine Defense Medal with one Star, Purple Heart, Silver Star with one Oak Leaf Cluster, and Distinguished Unit Badge. He died January 28, 1996.

ERNEST JUNIOR WILLIAMS was born September 11, 1919, at Negley. He married Beulah Belle Bradley, and they had one child, Rebecca Ann. He enlisted in the Army Air Corps in World War II on September 9, 1943, trained at several bases for his basic, flexible gunnery, navigation, and USAF air crew training. He was a

2nd Lieutenant, with no combat duty. His discharge was on October 18, 1945 at Chanute Air Force Base, Illinois. He was recalled April 11, 1951 during the Korean Conflict and served as a 1st Lieutenant in the 90th Bomb Squadron at Kunsan, Korea. Navigating an aircraft in combat and with general flying service, he flew full combat tour of duty over North Korea. His discharge from the Korean Conflict was on June 10, 1952 at Donaldson Air Force Base, South Carolina. He received the Korean Service Medal, Air Medal with two Oak Leaf Clusters, and Distinguished Flying Cross.

DAVID M. WILLIAMS was born January 15, 1924, at Negley. He enlisted January 25, 1942, in the U. S. Marine Corps and was attached to the 2nd Marine Corps Division. His training was at Camp Elliott in San Diego and Camp Pendleton at Oceanside, California. He was a PFC and served as a sharpshooter and signal man. His overseas duty was at Tarawa Atoll in the Gilbert Islands where he was killed in action November 20, 1943. (His sister, Mamie, made note that the battle for Tarawa Atoll was the bloodiest battle in the history of the Marine Corps and that he was the first man from Red River County killed in action.) He was awarded the Presidential Citation, Asiatic-Pacific Campaign Medal, Victory Medal WWII, and Purple Heart posthumously.

JOHN M. WILLIAMS was born May 7, 1926, at Negley. He married Juanita Moran, and they had three chidlren, Casey, Kevin and Karen. He enlisted in the Army on August 6, 1944, at Dallas. His basic training was at Camp Fannin at Tyler, Texas, and he was attached to the 71st Infantry Division during combat and the 9th Infantry Division for occupation duties. As a Staff Sergeant, he served in the radio message center and in telephone communications in the 60th Batallion of the 9th Infantry Division. His overseas duty was in the European Theater of Operations, and he was discharged July 3, 1946 at Ft. Sam Houston, Texas. He was awarded the Combat Infantry Badge and EAME Campaign Ribbon with two Battle Stars.

Mamie Williams was married to **CLYDE O. WINTERS**, and they had four children, Claude, Merry, Carole and David. Clyde's parents were Jim Enoch and Roxie Bybee Winters, and he was born June 17, 1924 at Reno in Lamar County, Texas. He had three brothers, Wallace, Cecil and Edward and a sister, Inez. All are deceased.

Clyde was raised at Kiomitia where he attended school and was in Detroit High School when he enlisted on August 29, 1942 in the Marine Corps. His training was at Camp Elliott in San Diego where he trained as a tank commander and driver and became a part of the lst Marine Division, lst Tank Battalion as a Sergeant. His overseas duty was in the South Pacific—New Guinea, Camp Glouster, Peleiu and Okinawa, and he was wounded three times. He was discharged November 9, 1945 at San Diego and received the Presidential Citation, Asiatic-Pacific Campaign Medal, and Purple Heart. He died November 19, 1996.

★★★

RUSSELL D. MOORE was born January 2, 1923 at Cuthand in Red River County, Texas. His parents were Albert P. and Eulla Bankston Moore. The other children in his family were Chalmer, Raymond, Nettie, Emmer, Leona, John, Ellis, Wade and Burl. He married Wilma L. Moore (a Moore married a Moore), and they had two daughters, Dorothy Louise and Sandra Sue. Russell volunteered for the Army at Tyler, Texas and trained to be a truck driver light 345 and qualified on November 4, 1943 for expert use of the carbine. He was a Pvt. in Battery B, 311th Field Artillery Battalion who served in Normandy, Ardennes, Northern France, Rhineland and Central Europe. His discharge was on December 26, 1945 at Ft. Sam Houston, Texas, and he was awarded the Victory Ribbon, American Theater Campaign Medal, three overseas service bars, one service stripe, Good Conduct Medal, and EAME Medal with five Bronze Stars. He died January 19, 1976.

ELLIS M. MOORE was born July 8, 1924 in Red River County. His parents were Albert P. and Della Butler Moore. (He and Russell were part of the same family.) He married Betty Rains, and they had two children, Linda Ann and Glenn. On July 13, 1943 Ellis volunteered for the Navy at Tyler, Texas. He trained at Corpus Christi, Texas and served as a Seaman lst Class aboard the heavy cruiser Augusta, a flag ship of President Harry Truman. His overseas duty was in the European Theater of Operations. He was discharged May 9, 1946 at Norman, Oklahoma and recevied the Victory Medal, American Campaign Medal, and European-African-Middle Eastern Campaign Medal. He related the following: "The most exciting story while in service was when we was coming from

France with a load of soldiers to the U.S. We got in a bad storm and struck a mine, blowing a big hole in the bow of the ship. The bulkhead of the ship was cracked; the ship was flooded with water; the Captain had ordered all crew to stand by to abandon ship. Then we got orders from Washington to turn back to Portsmouth, England and go in dry docks. This happened in February 1946."

★★★

FRANKIE B. PUCKETT was born two miles east of Annona on December 12, 1908. Her parents were Frank and Drilla Howard Carpenter Puckett. There were fifteen children in the family, and she was the fourteenth child born and is the only survivor. Miss Frankie is one of those I interviewed for my first book, and I quote in part what she said: "When the war started, I had worked at some different things, an insurance company in Dallas and a bank in Celeste... I was the only one who could go to the service so I decided to go. I applied for the Navy and the Army, and I was supposed to be in New Orleans on a Monday for the Navy and in Dallas on Monday for the Army. I stood in Gaines Drug Store and flipped a nickel to see which way I went, and it fell on Army. This is the truth. I went to Dallas and came home, and two weeks later they called me to come in.

I was one of the first ones to make officers' training. After I finished basic training, I was sent to Administrative School at Drake University, and from there we went to Fort Oglethorpe, Georgis to open a training center. I was called in one day to fill out some papers that had been sent from Washington. They didn't even know what they were for, and there were thirteen pages I had to fill out. I had to list all my brothers and sisters so they had to give me extra paper to list them on. Then I got orders to report to the overseas training center, and when I got there, there were twenty-four of us in all. We had come from different places in the U.S. . . . None of us knew what it was about because it was sort of 'hush hush'. We didn't take much training, and they shipped us out pretty quick to Fort Shanks, New York. We were there about forty-eight hours and then got on the Queen Elizabeth. We had to go up the Clyde River to Gurick, Scotland. They usually went in at Southhampton, but they had to do this to avoid the submarines. We landed there, and a colonel met us, and then we went to a camp in Scotland. The next day a man came out from London and told us we were in the O.S.S,

Officers Strategic Services, and that's why it was all so secret. That's the first intelligence outfit the U.S. had. We were there through the air raids and all that business, but you got used to it. I stayed in the service three years and then went right back to Washington D.C. doing the same job as I had done, only as a civilian. They sent me to Rome, and I was there when they passed the law creating the CIA, Central Intelligence Agency. . . I'm a charter member of the CIA. When I retired they gave me a plaque that reads 'CIA, United States of America, For Honorable Service, Frankie B. Puckett, 1947-1968.' This didn't count my army time or the time with the O.S.S., just the CIA time."[8]

Miss Frankie resides in Clarksville, Texas.

★★★

JOHN C. PORTERFIELD was born December 31, 1923, at Clarksville, Texas. His parents were Marvin and Hazel Metts Porterfield, and he had a sister, Frances, and twin brothers, Troy and Roy. After the war he married Mary Sue Coursey, and they had two children, Gary and Gail. John died April 9, 1981, and Mary Sue resides in Clarksville. John entered the Army on February 4, 1943, at Tyler, Texas. His training was at Ft. Knox, Kentucky and Indiantown Gap, Pennsylvania. He was a Corporal in the Infantry and served as a Light Truck Driver. His overseas duty was in England, France, Belgium and Germany. He was discharged December 3, 1945, at Camp Fannin, Texas and was awarded the EAME Campaign Medal with four Bronze Stars, Good Conduct Medal, and WWII Victory Medal.

★★★

John Wesley and Oma Cox Thompson of Clarksville had four sons in the service in World War II. Their other children were Muriel and Joyce.

CHARLES M. (MACK) THOMPSON entered the Army in 1940 and trained at Camp Bowie, Texas. He was discharged in 1944. He was married to Betty Emery. **JOHN A. (ALDO) THOMPSON** was married to Ruth Lawson. He served in the Army, but I was unable to find any information about him or his service.

RICHARD E. THOMPSON entered the Army in 1942, trained at Ft. Knox, Kentucky and was discharged in 1943.

JESSIE DEE THOMPSON volunteered for the Navy on March 13, 1940, and trained at San Diego. He was a Gunner's Mate on the *USS Essex* and participated in a number of major battles in the South Pacific. An article from the *Clarksville Times* reads in part: "The body of Jesse D. Thompson, Gunner's Mate, First Class, who lost his life in the South Pacific November 10, 1944, will arrive in Clarksville Friday evening at 6:15 from the Ft. Worth Quartermaster Depot. The funeral service will be conducted in the First Baptist Church at 3:30 Saturday afternoon by the pastor, the Rev. Claude Martin, assisted by the Rev. Richard Irvin, pastor of the Methodist Church. . . Jesse D. Thompson was born December 14, 1918, at Roxton, the son of Mr. and Mrs. J. W. Thompson. Other survivors are three brothers, R. E., John A. and Charles M. and two sisters, Mrs. June Meals and Mrs. Jack Lawson. He was married November 28, 1942 to Miss Gloria Turner, Bell Cross, North Carolina. His body, along with 202 other Texans, arrived in San Francisco March 21 on the U. S. Army Transport *Walter W. Schwenk* which sailed from Saipan February 26 with 3,175 bodies, stopping at Honolulu for an additional hundred."

A letter dated 5 July 1945 from Lt. Joseph S. McCauley, Catholic Chaplain aboard the *USS SAMARITAN (AH10)*, to Mrs. Thompson reads in part:

> "I received your letter inquiring of your dear son, Jesse. . . Jesse was aboard this hospital ship for several days and was under the care of some of our country's best physicians. However, it seemed that no human power could save him. Our dearest Lord wanted him for himself in Heaven. Jesse was certainly a perfect gentleman. While he was with us, we all learned to love him. He was so considerate of all who were attending him. It was my greatest pleasure to visit him several times a day. It is not my privilege to discuss his illness, but you may write to the Burea of Medicine and Surgery, U.S.N., Washington, D. C. Before he died, he asked me to baptize him. You may be sure that he is in Heaven and would not change places with any of us."

★★★

VERNON H. (BUD) JONES was born September 18, 1923, in Ft. Worth, Texas. His parents were Robert C. Sr. and Nollie Gaye Perkins Jones, and he had one brother, Robert C. Jones, Jr.

Vernon enlisted in the Army Air Corps on December 15, 1942,

and served in the Civilian Pilots Training (WTS) at Gainesville, Texas where he learned to fly Tandem Aeronca aircraft, better known as a two seater, tail dragger aircraft. This program was to train pilots for ferrying aircraft but was discontinued for men and turned over to WAFS. From there he went to Cadet Training at Texas Tech in Lubbock and then to Santa Ana, California for more training. After being diagnosed with night blindness, he was sent to radio school in Madison, Wisconsin and to Rantoul, Illiois for electronics training. Then to Boca Raton, Florida for radar training and on to Grand Island, Nebraska to train on the B29 bombing system using a new system called the APQ7 for pin point bombing for night bombing. There the 502nd Bomb Group of the 315th Bomb Wing was established in the 20th Air Force. This group was sent to Guam. Engine trouble developed on the B29 so they returned to Hawaii for repairs. Then they flew to Kwajalein and on to Guam. On July 4, 1945, he landed on the Northwest Strip of Guam which was in the process of being constructed by the Corps of Engineers. Guam served as a departure for the B29's to bomb the mainland of Japan. He served as a radar technician responsible for the mainteance of the radar systems on the aircraft. Numerous bombing flights were made to the Japanese mainland primarily targeting oil refineries. At the end of the war, 54 of his comrades had been killed in air crashes in the line of duty.

After the Japanese surrender, Vernon was transferred to the Air Inspectors Department on Guam and was over all radar and communications on the B29's. He served in this capacity until February 1946 when he returned on the *USS Amstead* to San Francisco and then went by train to Ft. Sam Hosuton, Texas to be discharged. He worked for General Dynamics Aircraft Corporation from 1949 until his retirement in 1979.

Vernon married Dora Rose on April 13, 1974, and they moved to Red River County in August 1980, purchasing the property of Robert and Anna Austin in the Mabry Community where Dora was born and raised. . . They now reside in Paris, Texas. He has three children, Vernon H. Jr., Pamela, and Charles Robert.

Vernon enjoys attending the annual reunion of the 315th Bomb Wing. During the 1999 meeting in Tucson, his grandson, Cory, flew to Guam on temporary duty 54 years after Vernon was there. He also had the opportunity to meet and talk with Gen. Paul

Tibbets who was the pilot of the B29, the *Enola Gay*, that dropped the first atomic bomb on Japan. Vernon has many good and sad recollections of his days in the Air Force. As many young men his age during this critical period of our country, he felt it was necessary to answer the call to fight for his country. And again like many, he was very happy to return home and start life over again. He was awarded the Good Conduct Medal, Presidential Citation, and Asiatic-Pacific Campaign Medal with two Bronze Stars.

★★★

Three Jamison brothers served during World War II. **CARROLL MOORE JAMISON** was born November 2, 1907, in Clarksville, Texas. His parents were David Carroll and Virgie Hopkins Jamison. He married Jessica Roberta Benningfield, and they had two children, Nancy Carol and John David. On May 1, 1944, he enlisted in the Navy; was trained at GM School in San Diego; and served as an instructor in the Antiaircraft Training Center. His rank was GM2C(T), and he was discharged December 8, 1945, at San Pedro, California and awarded the Victory Medal and ATO Medal. He died May 26, 1984, and his wife is also deceased.

FRANK HOPKINS JAMISON was born October 31, 1915, in Clarksville, the son of David Carroll and Virginia Ann Moore Jamison. He married Vera Christene Whitsell Southard, and their children are Damon L. Southard, Billy F., Barbara A. and Debra L. Jamison. Frank enlisted September 27, 1944, in Company I, 144th Infantry at Clarksville, Texas. He was trained in the Supply Quartermaster School at Camp Bowie, Texas and served as a Staff Sergeant as armory caretaker and antitank gun crewman. His overseas duty was in Rhineland, Ardennes and Central Europe. He was discharged at Ft. Sam Houston on August 12, 1945 and awarded the American Defense Service Medal, EAME Campaign Medal with three Bronze Stars and Good Conduct Medal. He died June 29, 1973.

JOSEPH DINWIDDIE JAMISON was born January 30, 1919, in Clarksville. His parents were David Carroll and Virginia Ann Moore Jamison. He married Elizabeth Cline, and they had two chidlren, John Patrick and Kimberely. He enlisted in the Marines April 1, 1942, while attending the University of Georgia at Athens, Georgia. His boot camp and officers school was at Quantico, Virginia; Camp Pendleton, California; and Auckland, New Zealand.

He was assigned to Company K, 3rd Battalion, 9th Marines and Headquarters Battalion, 3rd Marine Division. He served as a Weapons Patoon Leader in a rifle company and as Executive Officer in the Military Police Company of the 3rd Marine Division. He participated in three battles, Bougainville, Guam and Iwo Jima.

When he was discharged from active duty after WWII on December 31, 1945, he was a Captain. He received a Letter of Commendation, Presidential Unit Citation with gold star, Navy Unit Citation with gold star, American Theater of Operations Medal, Pacific Theater of Operations Medal with three Battle Stars, and a Good Conduct Medal. Remaining in the Marine Corps Reserves for 31 years, he retired as a Colonel on January 30, 1979.

★★★

ARLTON H. BROWER was born January 2, 1923, in Avery, Texas, the son of Chester Randolph and Amie Rosser Brower. There were twelve children born in this family. He and Elsie Marsh were married in 1949 and have one daughter, Vicki. The Browers live on land just down the road from where he was raised.

Arlton entered the service on Novebmer 5, 1942, and served as a Section Sergeant of a Heavy Mortar Platoon with Company D, 34th Infantry Division. His job was as a Scout, and his overseas duty was in New Guinea and the Philippines. When we visited with them he said: "I left from California for Hawaii and then went to Australia and on to New Guinea for our first combat. While we were in Hawaii, there was an inspection, and Eleanor Roosevelt came by to talk to us.

When we left the LCV after the end gate was down, since I was a Sgt., I was leading my troops out. A soldier in front of me stepped on a land mine, and his leg was blown off, and it flew back and hit me. We made 23 beachheads up and down New Guinea and the Philippines. We landed at Leyte, Luzon, Mindoro and Mindanao. At Luzon we went through the Zigzag Pass, and it was a tough battle. I was wounded on Mindanao on May 13, 1944. They took me to a medical tent, and one day a shell hit it, and the patient next to me was killed. We couldn't be moved, but the others had left for shelter. Then I went back to a hospital on Leyte and was there when the war ended.

When we were on Keli Ridge on Leyte Island in the

Philippines, we went from 800 men to 220 men. There were about 7,000 Japs surrounding the hill we were on. Planes were going over and dropping rations to us, and we were trying to catch them so they wouldn't roll down the hill to the Japs. One of those rations hit a good friend of mine, Capt. Campbell, and it broke his neck and killed him. I buried him myself right there. One time my uniform was so dirty that when I found some clean Japanese breeches, I put them on and wore them into camp. A soldier named 'Holly' told them not to shoot me because I was a Scout. Then he told me that Raymond Rosser had been killed. He was my cousin and from the same place I was from."

S/Sgt. Brower was discharged November 30, 1945. He received the Asiatic-Pacific Campaign Medal with two Bronze Stars and a Bronze Arrowhead, Philippine Liberation Ribbon, Good Conduct Medal, Purple Heart, Bronze Star, WWII Victory Medal, and Combat Infantryman Badge.

★★★

Taylor Franklin and Eva May Straub McCoy had five sons, Lewis Raymond, Hermon Wilson, John Douglas, Homer Franklin, and Jesse Willard. Four of their sons were in the service in World War II.

HERMON WILSON (MAC) McCOY was born May 1, 1914, in Clarksville, Texas. He married Mary Adele "Sitty" Keenan, and they had two children, Hermon Wilson, Jr. and Judith Ann. While attending Texas A&M College (now Texas A&M University), Hermon was appointed 1st Lieutenant in the U.S. Army. His training was at Texas A&M, Camp Breckenridge, Kentucky and Ft. Benning, Georgia. He was assigned to the 329th "Buckshot" Infantry Regiment, 83rd Division which was known as "The Thunderbolt". His overseas duty included landing on Omaha Beach in June 1944, Normandy, Battle of the Bulge and Battle of the Ardennes. He was wounded in action in January 1945 in the Battle of the Ardennes. As Company Commander, his Company L was the first of the 83rd Division to break through the German defense lines. He retired at the rank of Lieutenant Colonel in 1961 at Galveston, Texas. For his service during World War II, he had been awarded the Purple Heart, Silver Star, and ETO Medal with three Battle Stars.

JESSE WILLARD McCOY entered the Navy in 1939 and trained at Annapolis and New London, Connecticut. He was a Lieutenant Commander who served in the Pacific on the *USS NEW MEXICO* and *USS TEXAS*. He was awarded in all Pacific battle areas.

HOMER FRANKLIN McCOY entered the Navy in 1940 and trained in Maryland, Florida and Georgia. He was a Lieutenant Commander who served in the Atlantic, Pacific and Mediterranean areas. He was discharged in 1946.

JOHN DOUGLAS McCOY was born March 15, 1921, at Clarksville, Texas. He married Mildred Igo, and they had three children, Jane, Mary and Steven. He entered the Army Air Corps on November 22, 1940, trained as a Pilot P-38, and was attached as a Flight Officer to the 14th Fighter Group, 49th Squadron that participated in air combat with the Germans. He served in North Africa and Italy and was a prisoner of war of the Germans for two years. His discharge was on November 22, 1945, at San Antonio, and he was awarded the Air Medal and POW Medal. Quoted below in part is an interview that was conducted a while back about his imprisonment:

"The last mission I flew was over Rome, and the target was Orte, a marshalling yard. On August 29, 1943 I got hit by a Messerschmidt ME-109 while in formation... I looked up and my lights were on indicating my engines were overheating, and immediately I started losing power. The squadron just slipped away from me. I was at about 28-30,000 feet so I just peeled around and started home. Fire started burning in the left engine. I put it out, and the next thing the right engine began to burn. By that time I was down to about 4,000 and luckily the Germans hadn't followed me. I had gotten out to sea and decided I'd leave the plane.

I never thought that bailing out of a P-38 would be a difficult task... The hardest part is getting the body in a position to exit through the left opening while still controlling the plane. The floor was covered with hydraulic fluid, and it was almost impossible to get enough traction to rise up out of the seat. My only alternative was to turn loose of the wheel, grasp the sides of the left opening, and drag my body out of the plane. I landed about 80 miles off Rome in the sea... I had a dinghy, a seat-pack type, but as I was six feet one, I had to put mine on my back as I couldn't sit in the seat without my head hitting the canopy. I survived on what I had with me. I had about a pint of water in a survivor pack and one 'D' bar, a concentrated chocolate bar. That's all I had in the kit, and the dinghy was only about four feet long. The Mediterranean Sea got so rough the first night that waves washed in on me. I bailed out water all night and cut off a pice of my parachute to keep warm. I spent five days in the water before the Germans located me and picked me up. It was a freak thing that the merchant ship saw me. They wouldn't go out of their way to pick me up, but the next morning I heard a plane, a JU-88. That ship gave them my location, and they dropped a sea marker, waved at me and took off. Then the flying boat came and picked me up and carried me to a lake near Rome. At this point I didn't object to anyone picking me up.

I went from Rome to Frankfurt, Germany by train. I wound up in POW Camp Stalag Luft III. This was the only camp Air Force prisoners were being sent to at that time. The camp had up to 4,000 people at one time in my center compound. The camp was located in Sagan, Germany on the Oder River in the east side of Germany, almost into Poland or Czechoslovakia and south of Berlin. We were in barracks, and the food was the best they could provide. We survived off the Red Cross parcels that we got once a week, and we lived in groups of 8 to 10.

When the Germans started retreating, they moved us from Sagan to Mooseberg which is near Munich. That was in January 1945. When we made the march, we had about 25,000 men that were involved. For food it was whatever we carried with us as we just packed up and went. Some people would give us water, and if someone was sick, they'd be dropped off in towns we went through. Some couldn't take the weather. It was really cold, eight days of it. For clothes, what we had was what we wore. The German guards were just as cold and miserable as we were. We were out in the cold 12 days before we got into boxcars to go. We had to move that far to get to the train station. We were moved to a large camp, Stalag VII, where they had all kinds of people, not just Air Force. We were put in tents, and we had about ten enlisted men the Germans brought in so we could use them as orderlies. They liked being there with us and we played softball together. We had several people try to escape, but they always got caught. We got dysentery once, and I lost about fifty pounds. The Germans weren't very sanitary. They'd use human waste for fertilizer, and the water in the streams was polluted so you couldn't drink it.

As long as we behaved and followed orders, they were pretty

nice to us, but we didn't try and run over them. As to life in there, it was like 'Hogan's Heroes'. We had heard of all the atrocities, and when we went in, they had us all strip, took all our possessions, and told us to shower. Well, that's the way they killed a lot of Jews, so we were wondering what was going to happen. We took a shower; they sprayed us with DDT; and deloused us. That didn't last long because the barracks were full of fleas and lice and you couldn't hardly sleep. This went on from about February until the end of April 1945 when we got liberated.

Patton came on April 29 and liberated us. He was quite a colorful guy. I saw him. I have a lot of respect for him. Some people don't, but I think he was a great general. He did more good than you realize. He was tough, but that's the military. I made my trip back to the States and was discharged almost immediately. It took us 17 days to go over, zigzagging, and about 12 days to come back. I never had to go back to my unit. I had two or three months furlough built up, and by the time I took that and went down on R&R in Florida, V-E Day had already passed. As soon as V-J Day came, they let me out. I came back and went to the University of Texas. I thought I had enough military service, over five years.

I have no regrets; I think I am lucky. I don't have a mark on me from the war. I feel like life dealt me a fair and square deal. If I'd gotten back to my squadron some place, some how, the next time I might have gotten killed. I came damn close to it in the water."

★★★

JOHN QUICK was born November 25, 1913, the son of Gilbert P. and Rosa Roberts Quick. He had two brothers, Paul A. and Ira L., and a sister, Edith. He and Gillie Lee Woods were married February 10, 1940.

John entered the Navy in March 1944, took his boot camp training in California, and with no furlough was assigned to the *USS John D. Henley*. He was on the ship over twenty months and was discharged in 1945 and awarded the American Theater Ribbon, APO Medal with five Battle Stars, and Philippine Liberation Medal and one Star. John and Gillie made their home at Madras, where she still lives. He died July 16, 1996.

A letter dated December 13, 1945, from the Secretary of the Navy, Washington, reads:

"My dear Mr. Quick: I have addressed this letter to reach you after all the formalities of your separation from active service are completed. I have done so because, without fomality but as clearly as I know how to say it, I want the Navy's pride in you, which it is my privilege to express, to reach into your civil life and to remain with you always.

You have served in the greatest Navy in the world. It crushed two enemy fleets at once, receiving their surrenders only four months apart. It brought our land-based airpower within bombing range of the enemy, and set our ground armies on the beachheads of final victory. It performed the multitude of tasks necessary to support these military operations. No other Navy at any time has done so much. For your part in these achievements you deserve to be proud as long as you live. The Nation which you served at a time of crisis will remember you with gratitude. The best wishes of the Navy go with you into civilian life. Good luck!.

Sincerely yours,
James Forrestal"

Gillie Quick shared a Journal entitled "Homeward Bound" (Destroyer #553, Feb 1944–Sept 1945). I wish I could quote the entire Journal, but will quote in part as follows:

"The Cruise and Campaigns of the *John D. Henley*—Yard for yard, Iwo Jima was perhaps the most highly fortified island on the face of the earth. One of the tiny Volcano Islands, it literally bristled with heavy artillery, blockhouses, pillboxes and machine gun nests. Its countless caves formed a labyrinth of inter-connecting fortifications. Three airfields occupied the plateau tops. Lying directly in the path of the B-29 route to Tokyo, Jap held Iwo posed a constant threat to the strategic Marianas. It had to be taken.

We of the *HENLEY* are proud to have played a part in its conquest, a part which we believe was unsurpassed by any other destroyer. It was our most rugged and hazardous campaign. We take the liberty, therefore, of reviewing our part in this campaign. . . Iwo Jima, on the morning of February 16, 1945, was a cold silent little island. When we first saw it, it was a shadowy ghost shrouded in mist and partially obscured by a drizzling rain. It was D minus 3 Day and it didn't look tough—then. . . Around us loomed the reassuring outlines of powerful warships. . . No sound, no gunfire came from Mt. Suribachi, the extinct 600 foot volcano on Iwo's southern tip. There was no hint of the hell it harbored as we gazed at it early that first morning. . .

February 17th was D Minus 2 Day. At 0930 word came down over the speakers: 'All hands man your battle stations.' We were going in. Ahead of us mine sweepers swept slowly back and forth, their cutters searching for mine cables. Our job was a ticklish one. We were to cover the underwater demolition craft and swimmers while they searched the shallows close ashore off the eastern beaches for barriers to our invasion barges. Behind us, battleships and cruisers intensified their bombardment. The Japs sensed what was happening. . . they started a counter barrage. . . Several ships and LCI's took hits. . . Betweenn 1100 and noon, we were credited with a direct hit on a pillbox. . . Just before noon the *HENLEY* almost was put out of action as an LCI, her bridge smashed and out of control, bore down on us. . . Captain Smith slammed the engine telegraph to emergency speed. Word came down to 'Stand by for collision on the starboard side.' The Captain's maneuvers averted disaster. The LCI cleared our fantail by only ten yards. . . Around us ships were feeling the wrath of Jap shore guns. . . By noon we had closed to 1,200 yards to cover the swimmers, keeping up a withering, neutralizing fire on the beaches. At 1500 we were firing on Mt. Suribachi—'Hot Rocks'—to keep the enemy from wiping out the underwater teams as they began withdrawing. Then we retired, heading for the western beaches to cover demolition teams there. . .

We were on station at 1551, moving very slowly, often dead in the water. Kangobu Rock was taken under fire directly off shore where there were several emplacements, as well as the rugged, rock-studded terrain overlooking the beach where snipers and mortar teams lurked. As we fought at point blank range, the heavies kept up an intensive bombardment . . . Bombers worked methodically over the airfields, and fighters raked them with rockets and machine gun fire. We hit an ammunition dump. . . We retired at 1800. . . The night was uneventful. . . It was D minus 1 Day—the final day of preparation before invasion. Our role was a routine one—patrolling, screening the wagons and cruisers continuing their bombardment. . . At dusk the Japanese sent out a flight of suicide bombers. Several ships were damaged. . . All night we poured shells into the beach and airfields bright in the glare of star shells. Our mission was to keep the Japs from reorganizing their beach barrier defenses and planting new mines and udnerwater obstacles. . . We retired at 0615 in the morning.

D-Day, February 19th, found us tired, but morale was high. We'd come through three bombardments without a scratch. Some of the crew began referring to the ship as the 'Lucky Henley', a prophecy that time fulfilled. When dawn came, we found ourselves in the midst of a vast invasion armada of some 700 ships. . . Those who could were asleep when the loaded invasion barges headed for shore at 0900. Although the opposition to the 4th and 5th Marine Divisions was fanatic and losses heavy, the Leathernecks were soon able to secure enough of the eastern beaches to bring up tanks and heavy field pieces. Their radio reported the opposition fiercer than at Tarawa. . . Our final and most dramatic support operation began on the afternoon of the 21st when we relieved the *USS GREGORY* (DD802) on a fire support station. . . Later it was reported from the beach that nearly 800 dead Japs were counted there the following day. It was the first of two Banzai attacks the *HENLEY* was credited with thwarting. . .

Shortly after 0100 the fanatic Japs sprang a flanking counter attack on Marine lines attacking Mt. Suribachi. By 0340 we had closed to 1,500 yards and were pumping 5-inch and 40MM fire into Jap positions. . . 'Your shots are falling where we want them', the spotter reported. At about 1030, Old Glory fluttered in the breeze atop the battle scarred mountain.

The *HENLEY* was relieved at noon by the *USS HYMAN* (DD732) after 22 straight hours at General Quarters and was immediately assignesd to a radar picket station. . . It was later estimated that the *HENLEY* had poured more than a quarter million dollars worth of hot steel into sulphurous Iwo. Although the *HENLEY'S* part in the Iwo Jima campaign exposed her to many Jap guns at close range time and time again, she never was touched by enemy fire. The fighting efficiency resulted in a recommendation for the Silver Star for the Captain, Commander Charles H. Smith, USN, of Georgia. In his report summarizing the actions, Captain Smith wrote: 'All hands are deserving of special credit for the manner in which they performed their duties in action. Even after long hours at General Quarters, all hands were manning their stations with energy and enthusiasm and, as is evident by repeatead reports from the Shore Fire Control party and plane spotters, putting shots where they counted most.'

On the 23rd of February, the *HENLEY* was assigned to escort

496 ★ FOR LOVE OF COUNTRY THE PRICE OF FREEDOM

seven transports filled with garrison troops for Iwo. We returned on March 2nd and three days later left for Ulithi Atoll. Thus ended the *HENLEY'S* most spectacular role in her 18 months on the vast Pacific's fighting fronts.

The Journal ended with: "In Memoriam—Although these two we leave behind, In fathoms deep that shade the sun, We'll meet again some other time, When life's long voyage is done.—Jacob Joseph Rosenberg and Kenneth Dowd Russell". (Tragedy overtook the *HENLEY* on the morning of January 9th. An after stanchion supporting a life line broke as they leaned against it, and two men, Jacob J. Rosenberg, EM3c, of Boston, Massachusetts, and Kenneth D. Russell, Flc, of Spartansburg, South Carolina, plunged overboard. During the rescue effort, the motor whale boat had to be cast loose when the hoisting padeye snapped as it was being lowered. Four men and an officer were thrown into the water, but as they had life jackets on, were soon rescued by PC 1079. Although a thorough search was made, we were unable to locate the two men. These were to be the only casualties the *HENLEY* was to experience although nine more months of fighting and voyaging still lay ahead.

Ribbons and Battle Stars Earned by the
SS JOHN D. HENLEY (DD 553)
I. American Theater Service Ribbon—Feb. 2, 1944–April 13, 1944
II. Asiatic-Pacific Area Service Ribbon—April 12, 1944–September 1945
BATTLE STARS
1. Marianas Operation—10 June 1944–August 1944
2. Western Caroline Islands Operation—6 Sept. 1944–October 1944
3. Leyte Operation—10 Oct. 1944–25 Nov. 1944
4. Iwo Jima Operation—15 Feb. 1945–7 March 1945
5. Okinawa Operation—24 March 1945–27 June 1945
III. Philippine Liberation Ribbon—17 Oct. 1944–20 Oct. 1944
1. Bronze Star—19 Nov. 1944–25 Nov. 1944

★★★

Henry C. and Rosa Lee Hart Somerville had ten children: Paul Hart, who died at birth, Henry Lee, John, Margaret, Ann, Mary, Rose, Martha Grace, Lucy and Rae Jeanne. Their two sons were both in the service in World War II.

HENRY LEE SOMERVILLE was not drafted but enlisted in

the Army in January 1942. His training was at Ft. Sill, Oklahoma and Ft. Sam Houston, Texas. From there he went to Kelly Field into flying but was taken out of that because of his physical exam. He became a Second Lieutenant in the Army Air Corps in June 1942 with his service mostly in Air Transport Command. In October 1945 he was a "high point man" and left the Air Corps as Captain with promotion to Major by mail and returned home. In February 1951 he was recalled and went to Japan and Korea and other places in Asia. From there he went to Research and Development Command in Baltimore, Maryland and then to Air Force assignment as Associate Professor, Air Force ROTC, at Texas A&M in College Station. There were other assignments, including special duty in Saudi Arabia. He was in New Mexico with Atlas-F Intercontinental Ballistic Missiles when he retired at his own request as Lieutenant Colonel on February 29, 1964. Henry Lee was married to Margaret Alsip, and they had three children, George, Mary and Richard. He later married Emily Moore, and they have two daughters, Kathleen and Jeanie. Henry Lee and Emily reside in Paris, Texas.

JOHN WILLIAM SOMERVILLE entered the Navy in 1944 after graduating from Bogata High School. He completed his basic training at San Diego, and was sent to Hawaii for amphibious training. He served aboard the troop transport, *USS RUTLAND*, as part of the landing crews in the invasions of Okinawa and Iwo Jima. Once when he was on a landing craft carrying troops to shore on Iwo Jima, it was shot out from under them, and they were picked up by another craft in the area. When John was discharged in 1946 from service in World War II, he received the APO Medal with two Battle Stars and a Philippine Liberation Medal. John was also called back into service during the Korean Conflict. He and his brother, Henry Lee, were in Tokyo at the same time and got to visit with each other. John married Elza Connie Anderson, and they have two children, Tim and Pam. John and Connie reside in the country west of Clarksville.

★★★

An article written by Wanda Bray entitled "Veteran Returns to Scene of Bloodiest WWII Battles" in the May 27, 1999 editiion of the *Clarksville Times* reads in part:

"On September 20, 1998, a Clarksville resident made a long awaited trip back to Europe. Back to the scene of one of the toughest, bloodiest battles of World War II. A battle in which he participated, along with other soldiers of the 602nd Tank Destroyer Battalion. **DEWEY WILBURN** and his old Army buddy, **RAYMOND YOUNG** of Michigan, returned to the site where they and their battalion fought at the Battle of the Bulge. They returned to that infamous place to remember and to honor their fallen friends and comrades. And to celebrate what they accomplished there—fighting the Germans through Belgium and Luxembourg and into Germany. 'We pushed them before us until we were just 45 miles from Berlin when the war was over', Wilburn said with pride, recalling his wartime experiences. . . Together, the two Army veterans visited a Third Army Cemetery in Hamm, Luxembourg. 'It's the cemetery where General George Patton is buried', Wilburn said. 'He didn't die during the war, but he was killed in an auto accident in Germany. It was his wish that his body be buried with those of the men he commanded in the Third Army who died in the fearsome battles that ended the war against the Germans.' (General Patton was killed December 21, 1945.)

'The cemetery is filled with row after row of crosses where American GI's are buried, and the citizens have erected huge memorials everywhere in Western Europe—near the Ardennes Mountains, at the site of the Malmedy Massacre near Malmedy, at Bastogne, Belgium. The people there have not forgotten that terrible war or the part the American military played in winning it. Of course, the battles were fought on their soil, right at their doorsteps and sometimes in their homes. And they know it was fought to save them from Nazi tyranny. So they remember and are grateful.'

Dewey Wilburn joined the Army Setpember 29, 1940 before Pearl Harbor but had a long four year wait before being shipped out to the European Theater. . . On August 24, 1944 the battalion finally forded the English Channel and landed on Omaha Beach 45 days after Patton's 3rd Armored Division. . . The 602nd Tank Destroyer fought the Germans through Belgium and Luxembourg while attached to the 11th Armored Division, 17th Airborne Division, 101st Airborne Division, and the 87th Infantry Division. . .

Wilburn was a Communication Sergeant through most of the war. . . Of his experiences during World War II, he said there are some memories he never wants to forget. 'Like the friends I made. We were a close knit bunch. We had to be. We depended on each other. Sometimes our lives depended on our buddies. If I had to do it all over again, I'd do it all the same because it was my duty as an American.' (Dewey is retired from Texas Power & Light Company. He and his wife, Lavenia, reside in Clarksville. He has two sons, Chesley and Roy.)

Parts from a "Day to Day Unit Journal, 24 August 1941 to 9 May 1945" are quoted below:

"This book is dedicated to those men who have made its successful conclusion possible. Our first thought is of our comrades, our fellow soldiers, who have fallen along the way never to rise again but never to be forgotten either. Let there never again be a world conflict so these men shall not have died in vain. . . Our second thought is of those who started on this long journey with us or joined us on the way but who due to illness or wounds sustained, left us before our task was completed. Let their wounds bear further testimony that a free country will fight whenever necessary to retain that freedom. Such is the birthright of a true democracy. Our last thought is of those still remaining. They have seen the end and see a bright future ahead with this war behind them. Some may return to civilian life, to those let us offer our congratulations and say 'Good, you deserve it'. Others may continue on in this battle against greed, brutality, aggression and every good thing all Christians abide by in the daily conduct of their lives. Let these men be guided by the powers above and let them go on and defeat our Japanese enemy with the same courage and determination that has characterized their actions in this campaign.

It will be noted that at one time (with the exception of one day) this organization spent 131 days 'on the line' without rest or any relief. . . May 9—Today is proclaimed as V-E Day since officially all resistance is supposed to have ceased at 0001 this morning. There were no celebrations. Things were as usual. Deep in the hearts of us who had spent many long hard bitter months for the cause of freedom, there was a feeling of relief and thanksgiving that the war was over here in Europe. Most of us spent a quiet day remembering, wishing and hoping. It had not been easy, and our comrades and brothers in arms, less fortunate than us would have liked to have been with us today. The score is before us, 'Two Down and One to Go'."

★★★

CHARLES THOMAS WRIGHT was born April 24, 1922, in Caviness, Texas, the son of Charles Ernest and Minnie Pearl Holding Wright. He had two sisters, Lillian and Betty Ruth. He was drafted on December 15, 1942, at Paris, Texas and trained at Camp Howze, Texas and Camp Claiborne, Louisiana as a part of Combat Infantry. He was assigned to the 335th Infantry Division, Company L, as a Corporal.

At church on June 27, 1945, he told of some of his experiences in World War II, and this is quoted in part:

"We left Newport News, Virginia on March 24, and after we'd been at sea a while, we ran into some rough water... We had an Easter Service on the deck and passed through the Rock of Gibraltor. Then on the 11th we were attacked by German planes. We shot down two, but two got away. The Navy Escort picked up two of the German survivors. The next stop was Sicily, and on April 18 we landed in Naples, Italy. We got on a train and rode about 50 miles to a training camp and stayed there a month before we went to the front. The Germans bombed us one night, but they missed their target and didn't kill any GI's. I left the training camp on May 21 and went to the front for the first time. The big push on Rome was on July 5. We took Rome, came back and got a pass to Rome. St. Peter's Cathedral was the most beautiful building I was ever in...

We were called up to the front one night. We knew it was suicide, but it was an order and we had to go. We had to go 500 yards behind the German lines to take our objective. It was high ground, and to get up there we started up single file. They let us get almost to our objective when they started firing on us. That cut 34 of us off from the Regiment, and we had no help from the line, right or left. They pinned us down—machine gun fire coming from all directions. We fought them until we ran out of ammunition. Then they came at us with bayonets. We decided it was best to give up, and the Germans recognized our surrender and stopped firing. They lined us up and marched us back and questioned some of us. We were taken on back further into Italy to a camp that stayed lit up all night. The allies would bomb it, but they never hit the buildings. Then they took us inside Germany. In Munich we worked on the railroad in rain or snow. Worked there about a month; then I was sent to N. Stalag 7-B. There I worked for a month putting away potatoes—200 box cars of potatoes. Then I worked in a rock quarry at another location. We didn't have any socks to wear—just our shoes. Had plenty of clothing but just no socks. We cut pieces out of our underwear for socks. Then I worked in a woodwork shop, and I liked that pretty good. Next we dug air raid shelters. . . I felt my faith was steadfast and I felt the presence of God. Because of this song, *God Will Take Care of You*, and the people back home praying for me day by day, I really believe with my whole heart that was what brought me back. That song kept going over in my mind. *God Will Take Care of You*, and He did.

One bomb fell 30 yards from where I was, and a lot were injured. That was my closest call. The Germans couldn't give us anything but a slice of bread a day, potato or barley soup. They depended on the Red Cross to feed us, and they did a wonderful job. Since we were in Southern Germany near Switzerland, we got our packageas regularly. . . I lost quite a bit of weight when I worked in the rock quarry 12 hours a day—before sun up and after sunset—seven days a week with a day off a month.

I was working in Augsburg, and they marched us all out the 24th of April. They were taking us to the Alps which was about 50 miles away to turn us over to the SS, the worst of Hitler's picked men. . . The American planes would come down so they could radio General Patton where we were—our position—and he drove 100 miles to cut us off before we got to the Alps. We were liberated on the 27th. . . It was still snowing. . . The next day was pretty and we took off to an airport, and I rode in my first plane. . . We flew up to Reims, France to a camp where we got cleaned up. They gave us shots, fed us good and looked us over. Then we flew to La Harve. The boat finally got there, and it took us 27 days going but only 5 days coming back. Got off the boat at New York. The Red Cross was there with coffee, milk and doughnuts. It was really good to be back in the U.S. I phoned Mother and talked to her. It was really wonderful."

He was discharged November 30, 1945, at Ft. Meade, Maryland and was awared the Combat Infantryman Badge, Sharpshooter Rifle Badge, Good Conduct Medal, American Theater Service Ribbon, European-African-Middle Eastern Service Ribbon, WWII Victory Ribbon, Expert Bar Rifle Medal, and Italy-European Theater Ribbon.

★★★

JAMES ARCHIE UPCHURCH was born May 25, 1920, at Clarksville, Texas. His parents were William Franklin, Sr. and Amelia Rives Bachman Upchurch. He has one brother, William Franklin Upchurch, Jr.

Archie enlisted in the Navy September 26, 1944, and received his training at San Diego. He was a Seaman lst Class assigned to the aircraft carrier *Bunker Hill* (CV-17). His duty assignment was to operate motion picture equipment for fleet commanders. This was to enable them to plan appropriate strategy for US forces by reviewing film taken of enemy positions. In addition, the equipment was run so that members of the crew could watch movies from home. Archie's assignment mixed buisness (the war) with recreation (for the crew members during their off duty hours).

On the morning of May 11, 1945, while supporting the Okinawa Invasion, *Bunker Hill* was hit and severely damaged by two suicide planes. Gasoline fires flamed up, and several explosions took place. The ship suffered the loss of 346 men killed, 43 missing, and 264 wounded. Although badly crippled, she managed to return to her home port in Bremerton, Washington via Pearl Harbor. Although the entire ship was endangered by fire and smoke, Archie escaped serious injury. At the time of the strike, he had gone from his duty post on an errand to the ship post office, an area which escaped the worst of the destruction. He was assigned to other ships during the remainder of the war and was discharged from the Navy on February 23, 1946 in Norman, Oklahoma. He was awarded the WWII Victory Medal, American Campaign Medal, and Asiatic-Pacific Campaign Medal with two Bronze Stars. He married Margaret Hilliard Simmons, and they have two children, James Archie, Jr. and Paula. They moved to Greenville, Texas. Archie retired from E-Systems in 1984 after 32 years of service.

BUNKER HILL (CV-17) was launched 7 December 1942, by Bethlehem Steel of Quincey, Mass; sponsored by Mrs. Donald Boynton; and commissioned 24 May 1943, Captain J. J. Ballentine in command. Bunker Hill reported to the Pacific in the fall of 1943 and participated in many carrier operations... On 19 June 1944 during the opening phases of the Battle of the Philippine Sea, there was damage when an enemy near miss scattered shrapnel fragments across the ship.

Lest We Forget ★ 503

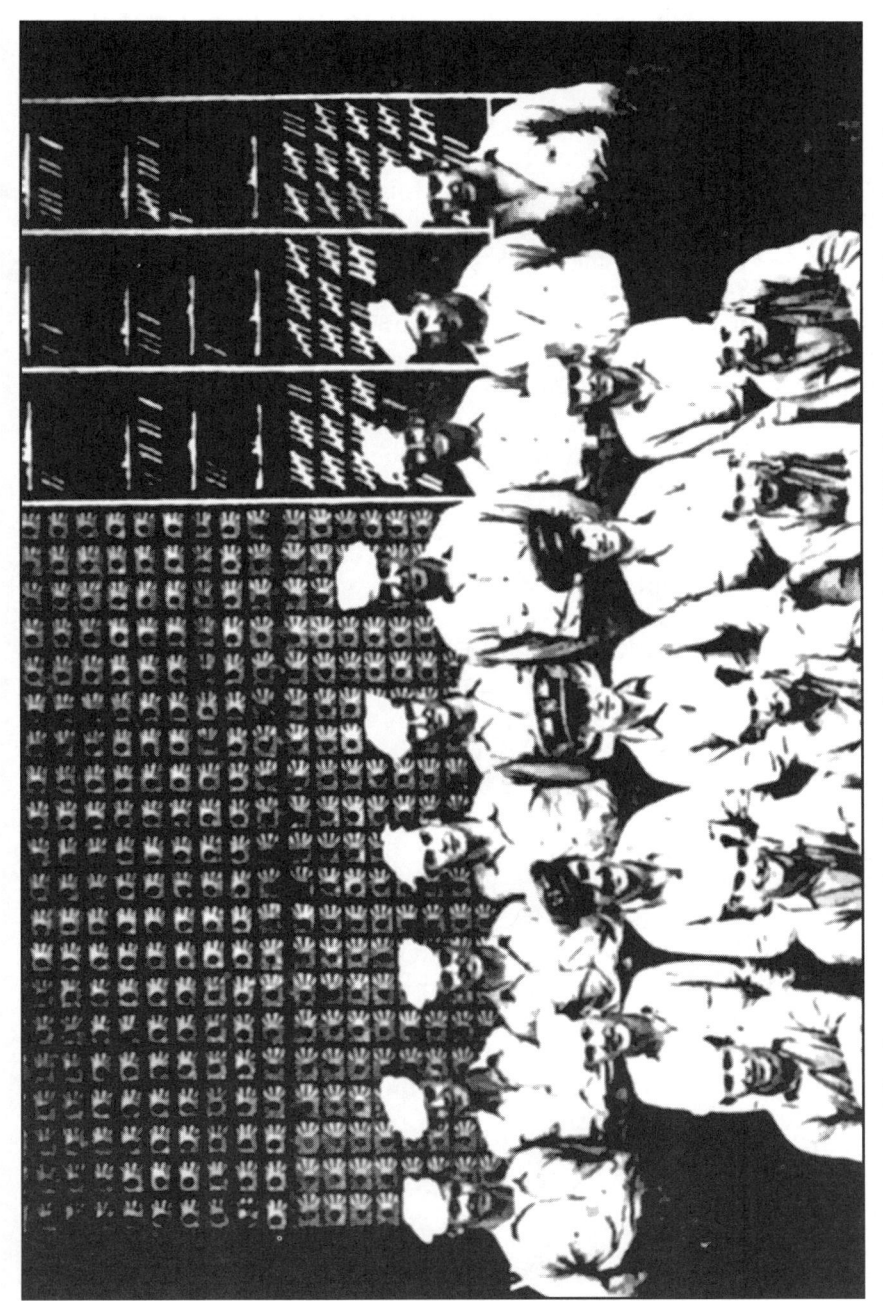

Crew of the Photo Division aboard the Aircraft Carrier Bunker Hill. (Archie Upchurch is on the back row, fourth from the left. In the background is a board containing the "kills" credited to this carrier)

Two men were killed and over 80 wounded. She continued to do battle, and her planes aided in sinking one Japanese carrier and destroying part of the 476 Japanese aircraft that were downed. During September she participated in the Western Caroline Islands operations and then launched strikes at Okinawa, Luzon and Formosa until November. On November 6 she retired from the forward area and steamed to Bremerton, Washington for a period of yard availability. She returned to the war front 24 January 1945. . . (The incident that happened on May 11, 1945, has already been covered above.) In September she reported for duty with the "Magic Carpet" fleet, returning veterans from the Pacific until January 1946 when she was ordered to Bremerton for inactivation. She was placed out of commission in reserve there 9 January 1947. *Bunker Hill* received the Presidential Unit Citation for the period 11 November 1943 to 11 May 1945. In addition, she received 11 Battle Stars for her World War II service.[9]

★★★

Jesse and Zelphrea Cherry Anderson of Bagwell, Texas had five sons in the service during World War II.

They also had four daughters, Willie May, Bessie, Odessa and Elza Connie. I was told by Connie that they watched for the mail to come every day, hoping to hear from their sons, but dreading to go to the mailbox for fear that there might be bad news. She also told me that her parents both had gray hair practically over night when all five of their sons were overseas in combat areas at the same time. Only two of their sons suffered any injuries, and the Andersons thought this was truly a blessing. Joe and Tom (Herman T.) are the only two of the five who are still living.

ROBERT F. ANDERSON entered the Army Air Corps in 1942 and trained at Atlantic City with additional training in New Orleans. He was sent to the European Theater and served in Italy. He was a T/Sgt and was discharged in 1945. He was awarded the ATO Medal, EAME Ribbon with one Bronze Star and Good Conduct Medal. He married Nancy Council.

JOE W. ANDERSON entered the Navy in 1944 and trained at Farragut, Idaho. He served in the South Pacific as a Seaman 1/C. Upon his discharge in 1946 he was awarded the APO Medal with two Battle Stars, ATO Medal, and Philippine Liberation Medal with one Battle Star.

HERMAN T. ANDERSON entered the Army in 1943 and trained at Camp Buster and Ft. Bragg, North Carolina. As a Corporal he served in the European Theater of Operations. While in Normandy his feet froze, but the doctors were able to save them. He was discharged in 1945 and awarded the Good Conduct Medal, ATO Medal, ETO Medal with five Battle Stars and Victory Medal.

WILLIAM F. ANDERSON entered the Army Air Corps in 1942 and trained at Sheppard Field, Colorado Springs, and Barksdale Field, Louisiana. As a Corporal he served in the South Pacific and Philippines. He was discharged in 1945 and awarded the Philippine Liberation Ribbon, APO Medal, ATO Medal, Good Conduct Medal and Victory Medal. He received a leg injury when a sniper bullet hit the tire on a supply truck he was driving, causing the truck to overturn.

JAMES J. ANDERSON entered the Army in 1940 and trained at Camp Bowie, Texas. He was a member of Company I, 144th Infantry, which was made up of many men from Red River County. His overseas duty was in New Guinea, Biak and the Philippines. While in the Philippines, he and his brother, William F., were within fifty feet of each other, but neither one knew about it until after the war. He was a T/Sgt. and was discharged in 1946 and awarded the APO Medal, Philippine Liberation Medal with 2 Battle Stars, and the Purple Heart. He was wounded in the hand and arm in 1945 when a land mine exploded in the Philippines.

He was married to Gertie Elson.

★★★

Seymour and Lizzie Bell Peek had three sons in the service during World War II. Their other children were Janet, Mary Holly, Mobelia, Barney Bell, and Thomas Ray.

ALTON BLAIN (TEBO) PEEK was born November 25, 1921, at Boxelder, Texas. He married Hazel Lucille Nicks, and they had two children, Jamie and Alton Douglas. Tebo volunteered for the Army in 1942 at Clarksville, Texas. He was trained as a Gunner 864 at Camp Haan, California and served as a Technical Sergeant in England, France, Belgium, Luxembourg and Germany. He was in the Battle of the Bulge. Jamie remembers him saying that it was so cold in Germany that they had to crank the half tracks every twenty minutes or so to keep them from freezing to the ground. He had frostbite on

Alton Blain (Tebo) Peek was welcomed in Germany by a young girl with flowers.

his fingers and toes, and during the winter when it was cold, they turned white for as long as he lived. Tebo was discharged December 4, 1945 at Camp Fannin, Texas and returned to Boxelder. He was awarded the Good Conduct Medal, EAME Ribbon with five Battle Stars, Victory Medal and ATO Ribbon. Tebo died July 8, 1988.

RUSSELL LEE PEEK was born at Boxelder. He married Dorothy Walters, and they had two children, Linda and Bruce. He entered the Naval Air Corps in 1940 and trained at Pensacola, Florida, graduating as an Instructor. He served in Guam as

Operations Officer and flew with some of the "Baa Baa Black Sheep". He was a Lieutenant Commander and was discharged in 1946 at Treasure Island, California.

LONNIE HASKELL PEEK was born at Boxelder. He married Vivian (Jack) Rhea and they had no children. Haskell volunteered for the Army and trained at Ft. Sill, Oklahoma and Ft. Bliss, Texas. He was attached to the 572nd Antiaircraft Artillery Battalion and served overseas in the European Theater at Rhineland, Ardennes and Central Europe. He was a Chief Warrant Officer and sometimes helped as a Chaplain. His discharge was in 1946 at Camp Fannin, Texas, and he was awarded the EAME Medal with three Battle Stars, ATO Medal, and Victory Medal. Haskell died May 11, 1998.

★★★

OMA LEE PEEK was born September 20, 1924 at Boxelder, Texas. He was the grandson of Mr. and Mrs. David A. Peek. He enlisted in the Marines in 1943 and was trained as a Rifleman at San Diego. His overseas duty as a Corporal was in the South Pacific on Guam, Iwo Jima and the Marshall Islands. He was wounded twice, on Guam and on Iwo Jima. He was discharged September 4, 1945 at Portsmouth, Virginia and awarded the Purple Heart with Gold Star, Good Conduct Medal, and other medals. Lee volunteered for service during the Korean Conflict. I was told that when some American troops were trapped behind enemy lines, he parachuted in and led the group to safety.

★★★

JAMES ROSS GOODE was born August 23, 1925, at Madras, a small community northeast of Clarksville, Texas. His parents were Robert E. and Beatrice Bliss Williamson Goode. His brothers are Billy Ray, Robert E. (Mickey), Carroll Glynn, and Gerald Franklin. He married Jolace Ferrell Burrow, and their children are Michael Richard and Debra Renee.

On January 8, 1944, James Ross joined the Navy at Tyler, Texas. His training was in California at San Diego, Coronado, Morro Bay and San Bruno. He became a Coxswain (driver) on a L.C.V.P. (landing craft boat) and was assigned to Standard Landing Craft Unit #40. His overseas duty was in the Philippines, Okinawa and Ryukyu Islands. His discharge was at Camp Wallace, Texas on

May 6, 1946, and he was awarded the Philippine Liberation Medal with one Battle Star, Asiatic-Pacific Theater Medal with one Battle Star, American Campaign Medal, and Expert Rifleman Badge. He had the following to say about his experiences during World War II:

"On June 8, 1944, my group arrived at Morro Bay, California and formed Standard Landing Craft Unit #40. Allan Irvin, from Tyrone, Pennsylvania, and I were assigned to the same boat, and we remained together throughout the remainder of the war until he went home under the point system. We trained there on landing craft boats and went aboard A.P.A. 200, a new ship, on January 4, 1945, and left for Hawaii. During gunnery practice, the five inch gun on the stern caused a seam to split, causing us to have several feet of water in the bilges. We were put off on a base as we started in the channel leading to Pearl Harbor, and we were there about three weeks. Then half of my unit went aboard L.S.T. 575, and we headed to the Philippines. The top speed of the L.S.T. was 12 or 14 knots, a knot being 1.15 miles an hour. We felt like we were on a 'slow boat to China'. We were the only ship, and one day out in the middle of the ocean, they let the ramp down and let everyone go swimming who wanted to. I decided the water was too deep and there might be a hungry shark around so didn't go in. A couple of times a destroyer caught up with us, threw a line over and sent us our mail and picked up our outgoing mail.

We sighted the Marshall Islands on February 7 and two days later went in close to Kwajalein where we anchored for two nights. Then on to the Caroline Islands, Palau Island, and Leyte Bay. While there two of the boys went swimming and got caught in an undertow and drowned. We worked off the supply ship Dixie, delivering supplies to other ships. I was on the island two or three hours which turned out to be the only time I was on land between January 28 and June 15. We left Leyte on March 18 and joined a convoy of all types of landing craft vessels headed for the Ryukyu Islands of Japan. We knew that wouldn't be a 'picnic' because we had a destroyer escort. On March 26, 1945, the battle was going full force. Our planes were going in firing rockets into the mountains. Several of our ships were hit by kamikazes, including the cruiser Indianapolis. The Japs had spotters on the islands that used short-wave radios to let their command know where the ships were. The islands were close together, and we moved into a good sized bay between two of them. A boat came along side ours with about 20 or 25 boys in it. When I looked down into the boat, I was shocked because they were covered in blood. They were just sitting there and didn't seem to be aware of anything. I later heard that some of them had parts of their arms, hands and feet blown off when their ship had been hit by a kamikaze plane.

The islands broke down the wind and waves and provided a good place for other ships to come in and anchor—to rest, make repairs, or just to get in off the ocean. We had collected enough boats to supply our unit, and when a ship needed a boat, they contacted us and one of our boats was sent out to work for them. We worked for several ships that had been hit by a suicide plane. One or two still had bodies trapped in flooded compartments. Irvin and I started working at night. They mounted a small motor on the back deck of our boat and loaded two 55 gallon barrels of oil into the tank deck. We would be assigned to a ship to lay smoke for each night. We would go to the ship late in the evening, tie to the boom, and wait for the air raid warning to sound. Then we moved up wind of the ship; Irvin would start the little motor and it drew oil out of the barrels through a hose, burned it and made a terrible smoke. We tried to cover the ship with the smoke so the plane couldn't see it. We also had smoke pots about two gallons in size, and they were filled with solid material that would burn. They floated so we could set them in the water, light them like candles, and they would make lots of smoke. One night between raids we returned to our supply ship for more pots, and as we returned, someone took a shot at us, just barely missing us. Sometimes when all the ships started firing, there were so many tracers going up that it was almost like a fireworks celebration, only more so.

Later we were sent to lay smoke for a ship all the way at the south end of the big island where we had never worked before. It was raining and the wind was strong when we tied our boat to a line let down from the stern of the ship. About midnight we got permission to go back to our ship. Irvin was on the front with a two cell flashlight and I got down close to the steering wheel to see the compass. We knew we must not run upon any of the ships along the way or they might shoot at us; that there was a large reef ahead that would tear the bottom out of our boat; and that if we went three fourths of a mile too far, we would be out in the ocean. Several times when it seemed that we had gone far enough and I had an urge to turn left, a small voice said, 'Not yet'. It was really hard to keep going, and then after we went about a half mile, Irvin said, 'Here's our ship.' We had gotten there just like we would have on a bright, sunny day. There is no doubt in my mind but that the Angel of the Lord had brought us safely to our ship. Praise the Lord!

On June 15, 1945, we went to Buckner Bay at Okinawa. We left the L.S.T. and joined the other half of our unit on White Beach II. We had not heard from them since we left Hawaii, and the bad news was that they made the invasion on April 1, 1945, and several of the boys had been killed. A suicide plane had hit the ship they were on. Several had been blown off the ship into the ocean but were able to swim back. There we worked for ships that came in for a while, and then they started us running a taxi boat through the bay to pick up sailors that wanted to come ashore.

In July we were assigned permanent duty to the USS HAMUEL, A.D. 200. They furnished our food and a place to sleep so we didn't have to go back to our base at night. The first part of August the bay began to fill up with ships, and by the middle of the month there were hundreds of ships there. We knew we must be getting ready to invade mainland Japan and that we would be in on it, helping to land soldiers, equipment and supplies. We weren't looking forward to it, for sure. They they dropped the atomic bombs, and that ended it.

In September we had a bad typhoon, and another one in October. Many of the ships that were still in the bay were blown aground. Some were badly damaged and they and their cargo were blown up. On December 8, 1945, we went off permanent assignment to the USS HAMUEL which soon left the bay. Then there wasn't much to do. The A.P.A. 200 that we left the States on came into the bay, and some of our boys went on board to visit the crew. That evening a suicide plane hit it, killing quite a few. After Irvin left, I took off a few days and went over to Naha, the capital. There was not a building standing. On March 22, 1946, I went to Brown Beach and on April 15 went aboard the USS Glenn and left Okinawa for the States. On May 6, I received my discharge at Camp Wallace, Texas and headed for home."

James Ross was awarded the Philippine Liberation Medal with one Battle Star; Asiatic-Pacific Theater Medal with one Battle Star;

American Campaign Medal, and Expert Rifleman Badge. He related that Buckner Bay was named for General Buckner who was killed in that invasion. When he signed a register on Brown Island at a recreation building, Cap Lee from Clarksville had signed on the page ahead of him. When James Ross got back to Clarksville, Cap had already been killed in a car wreck. Also, while at Buckner Bay he saw John Quick, Selby Pace and Charles Tipping, all from this area.

★★★

JESSE LAWRENCE SHELBY was born June 28, 1923, at Tuggle Springs in the northern part of Red River County, Texas. His parents were William Thomas and Nannie Jean Patton Shelby. He had one brother, J. W. (Billy), and five half-brothers and sisters, all Shelbys: Asa, Travis, Archie, Pat and Alice. On September 7, 1946, he and Glyn Juanita Ray were married in Clarksville by Rev. Claude J. Snowden, pastor of the First Christian Church. They had four daughters, Barbara, Jo Ann, Glenda Sue, and Phyllis Kay. Jesse entered the service on January 28, 1943, and was discharged on November 13, 1945. He was awarded five Bronze Stars, Good Conduct Medal, World War II Victory Medal, as well as others. Jesse died April 29, 1999, and Glyn resides in Wills Point, Texas.

An article from the *Edgewood Enterprise* by Glenda Lee, Editor, dated June 2, 1994 reads in part:

"Jesse Shelby remembers with vivid detail D-Day, June 6, 1944. The biggest event of World War II, the day Allied troops invaded Europe. It was also the largest military invasion that has ever occurred. Shelby, 70, was born in Red River County where he lived until he recevied his 'personal invitation' from the U.S. Army. He signed up to work on tank destroyers, but the Army had other ideas. Shelby was assigned to the 146th Combat Engineers, Company C.

He was stationed at Camp Swift near Austin and then moved on to Camp Miles Standish in Boston. A short time later, he was sent to England where he trained for combat. He embarked on his journey to Normandy Beach unaware of the terror and chaos he would witness once he arrived. Crossing the English Channel, Shelby's craft swamped. The men had to be transferred to a smaller craft, drenched and seasick. He was part of the first wave to hit Normandy Beach on D-Day. According to historical documents, the first men to land on the beach at 6:30 poured into waist-deep water under some of the heaviest enemy fire ever known. Shelby was twenty years old at the time.

'It was bad; if anyone says they weren't scared, I'd say they were lying. Men were falling all around us. . The military figured 95 per cent casualties during the first wave, but we made it out losing only 60 per cent.' Several of the men that perished on Normandy beach were in Shelby's company. 'We started out together at Camp Swift; they were mostly Southern boys', he said.

As a combat engineer, Shelby was responsible for blowing up the obstacles. He carried 40 pounds of explosvies on his body. Although he was equipped with a M-1 rifle, he wasn't allowed to use it. 'Our job was to blow up obstacles, not to fight back,' he said. His company was assigned a section of beach to clear. They were told to blow up obstacles and mines. . . He recalled the horror of seeing the bodies of soldiers stacked in piles on the beach."

Carroll F. Guidry of Gretna, Louisiana, historian for the reunions held by the surviving members of the 146th Engineer Combat Battalion, furnished this information: The 146th Engineer Combat Battalion was one of the most decorated army units in WWII. It received the Distinguished Unit Citation, and an Arrowhead for D-Day. Besides 64 Bronze Stars, 23 Silver Stars, and 11 Distinguished Service Crosses; Captain Sam Ball, Company A Commander, received the Distinguished Service Order of the British Empire which was pinned on by General Bernard Law Montgomery. The Battalion also received the French Croix de Guerre and 5 campaign stars. Captain Arthur Hill, H&S Company, recevied the Military Medal of the Czechoslovakian Republic for his work after V.E. Day. Company A received a second Distinguished Unit Citation for their heroics near Monschau during the Bulge. Along with the 99th Division, the 99th Norwegian-American Separate Infantry Battalion, and the 38th Cavalry, they helped anchor the northern shoulder near Monschau against several determined German attacks.

For two days in November, A and C Companies, acting as Infantry, relieved a regiment of the 28th (Bloody Bucket) Infantry Division at Vossenack. There it was being overrun by strong German counter attacks. This was in the Huertgen Forest near the Roer River dams, whose capture was deemed critical in our drive to the Rhine. The 28th Division General stated, "Without the 146th Engineers, this Infantry would have been overrun, and the town would have been lost to the Germans." A captured German officer said about the same: "We would have recaptured Vossenack if those damned engineers in heep boots (hip boots) had not been brought into the battle."

★★★

KEENER BRYAN MARSH was born July 18, 1913, in Annona, Texas. His parents were Marlin Austin and Lydia Francis (Fannie) Hearne Marsh. He had two half-brothers, Edward Mercer Marsh and Robert Marsh; a brother, William A. and three sisters, Maggie Lee, Lula, and Ruby. He married Lavada Parker, and they had two children, Sandra Kay and Buddy. Keener died September 8, 1979 and burial was made at the Garland Cemetery in Annona. He enlisted in the Army in 1934 and served in the Cavalry and Infantry. He was discharged at the rank of Staff Sergeant in 1945 and received the Purple Heart and other Medals. His niece, Bonnie Sturgeon, gave me the following information about her uncle:

"Uncle Keener was captured when Corregidor fell. He was wounded three days before being captured (shot in the left knee). When captured, he was placed in a compound hospital. He did get some medicine, but not what he really needed for full recovery. However, he would not have gotten that much, but the Japanese officer in charge of his bay slipped him medicine as he could. The officer was schooled in San Francisco, spoke English, and knew American customs well. On partial recovery Keener was sent to work in the fields with other prisoners. The Japanese overseers taunted the prisoners any way they could—just to get them to beg for mercy. And if they did beg, they ran the risk of being stabbed or slashed with bayonets. This was at the Bilibid prison camp.

One day while the group (platoon) was bending over, one or more Japanese officers walked up behind them and slashed their legs, sometimes to the bone. Keener told us he just raised up and looked the officer straight in the eyes, which normally was not allowed. The officer just looked at him and laughed like a hyena and went on down the line of prisoners. Because the main meal for the prisoners was rice and not very much of that, Keener developed beriberi and was sent back to sick bay where he was able to stay mostly for the rest of his time.

Keener told us that they were all called out to an open space and told at gun point to dig their own graves. No one knew who, or if all would be killed. If anyone uttered a word of any kind, they were shot that instant. There was a set of identical twins in the group. When all had finished digging their graves, everyone was ordered to stand at the foot of the open grave. Completely at random, the Japanese went down and shot prisoners, skipping some. Kenner was skipped over, but one of the identical twins was shot. Keener said any of the men would have given their life instead, but no one could say a word. The ones left had to cover the ones killed.

This was not all the suffering of the men. They were on almost starvation diets. When the natives would throw bread or any kind of meats (including dogs) over the fence, they risked being caught and fastened to a post just outside the compound. The Japanese then killed them for the prisoners to see. They were killed either by torture or starvation, or both. Because Keener was allowed to help in sick bay, he was able to get some food and medicine slipped to him.

When he was liberated, he weighed 86 pounds. On landing in the U.S., he was sent to Brooke General Hospital for recovery. After being checked over, he was allowed to come back to Annona because his Dad was dying. My Grandpa lived only a few days after Keener got home. After the funeral, Keener had to return to the hospital to complete his rehabilitation. He told my mother, Maggie Lee Marsh Lumpkin, many things about the atrocities they all suffrered. He couldn't talk about their hardships until he wrestled with the memories."

★★★

PAUL GARMON was born August 4, 1917 in Mt. Pleasant, Texas, the first child of Joseph Haden and Birdie Etta Tate Garmon. The other children in the family are William Morris (Buddy), Charlene, Mary Lou, and James Haden (Pete).

Paul went to work for the W.P.A. in the spring of 1935 when he decided he could no longer afford to go to school. At that time he also signed up for the C.C.C. and worked for them on soil conservation projects. Paul feels that the C.C.C. was the government project that did the best job in rebuilding and turning our country around. He also thinks that the practices started by President Roosevelt were the first in the history of our nation that raised our standing of living.

On August 22, 1935, he boarded the train for Bowie, Arizona where it was 110 degrees. Pat Westfall, Allen McGuire, Louie O'Dell, Bennie Burns, William Austin, and P. D. Weaver were some of the boys in the group with him. Paul stayed out there until July 20, 1936, when he came home and picked cotton for two months. Then on September 17, 1936, he joined the Army. The Army was paying $19.25 a month. In the C.C.C. he was given room and board, $5.00 a month spending money, and sent $25.00 to his parents each month. He trained at Ft. Sill, Oklahoma, Camp Hood and Camp Bowie in Texas, and Ft. Jackson, South Carolina. In 1943 he was wounded by a muzzle explosion of an artillery piece while in South Carolina. A piece of steel went into his left ear, completely destroying the ear drum. After spending about seven months in and out of the hospital, he was retired from the service. Paul resides in Longview, Texas.

★★★

Thomas Fletcher and Florence Johnston Harmening had two sons in the service during WWII. They also had three daughters, Lucilla, Dorothy, and Dixie Dimple.

ROYCE HARMENING was born June 19, 1917. He entered the Army in 1945 and trained at Camp Hood, Texas and Camp Pickett, Virginia. Very little is known about his time in the service, and he died in 1979.

OLIVER P. HARMENING was born April 5, 1919. He married Ruth Wood, and they had one son, Anson Boyd Harmening. He entered the Army on July 11, 1941. A certificate was given to him from the School for Bakers and Cooks at Camp Grant, Illinois on October 9, 1941. On October 28, 1942, he was appointed to Staff Sergeant in the Medical Department as X-Ray Technician, Grade IV from the station hospital at Ft. Frances E. Warren, Wyoming. From D-Day to V-Day, he was attached to the 42nd Field Hospital, Second Platoon in the European Theater of Operations. Upon his discharge in 1945, he was awarded the ETO Medal with five Battle Stars, Bronze Star, and American Defense Medal. He died January 7, 1987, and Ruth lives in their home at Manchester. She shared the history of the 42nd Field Hospital, Second Platoon, and I quote in part below:

"The Field Hospital is a mobile 400 bed organization consisting of a Headquarters and three Hospitalization Platoons, each capable of operating independent of the others. The Field Hospital, by virtue of its ingenious design, has proved itself a versatile unit in warfar, performing a great variety of missions in the different theaters of war. History will reveal that the SECOND PLATOON, 42nd FIELD HOSPITAL not only upheld the reputation of versatility, but established an enviable record in the European Theater of Operations during the Normandy, Northern France, Ardennes, Rhineland, and Central Germany campaigns.

Activated at Camp Carson, Colorado, 15 July 1943, . . . we sailed on 26 Feb for England to become an organic part of First United States Army and spearhead the Army medical troops in the greatest military undertaking in history—the invasion of France. There were the days at Bromyard, England—of training and raining, of dancing, of struggling to gather essential equipment in preparation for D-Day. The middle of May found the 42nd already at the marshalling area on the coast of Wales. This life was not a happy one, an area of foxholes and pail latrines, of long lean chow lines, of road marches, of delayed incoming mail. . .

June 3rd—The Second Platoon, back on the *SUSAN B. ANTHONY*, their old love, the worthy ship on which we had originally crossed the Atlantic. Briefing, good chow, calm waters, proud men, all scheduled to land on D + 1, and set up the first hospital for the invasion. We landed, and we're wearing the coveted Arrowhead insignia now as a sole reward, but we almost didn't land. June 7th about 0750 it happened, just prior to debarkation. . . The *SUSAN B* struck two mines that lifted her clear out of the water. We dropped all personal equipment and fled to our stations on deck to prepare to abandon ship. The Second Platoon was dispersed into four different rescue vessels and our ship went down, to rise no more, the end of her gallant and enviable record. We landed D + 1 as scheduled—one party marched six miles direct into mortar fire and was forced to retreat; another party dodged strafing planes all night on the beach; a third sweated out some dive bomb attacks on their Liberty ship at anchor off the beach. June 8th—all dispersed parties of the Second Platoon reunited—one man still missing. The Second reinforced the 261st Medical Battalion on the beach and watched their own equipment arriving piece by piece. . .

On June 9th (D + 3) the Second Platoon set up its 200 bed

installation in suppoert of all VII Corps troops. This was the first hospital, per se, erected on Utah Beach and was located near the vicinity of St. Come D'Mont. June 10th—battle casualties arriving by the hundreds beginning at 0600. Personnel of Headquarters and the lst and 3rd Platoons pitched in to help during the rush. In 24 hours equipment of the lst Platoon was attached to the original installation to meet the demands for expansion, and later a platoon of the 45th Field Hospital was erected on an adjacent field. A fierce week! Over 1100 casualties admitted, cleared or operated; working days 24—36 hours long, sleeping nights only 3 and 4 hours—the sky a spectacle of hell, the air an echo of weird noises. . .

June 20th—The march began to St. Saveur Vicompte with the 9th Division. Here we sat between two fronts until Cherbourg fell. Lt. Col. Lahourcade, our present CO, joined us at this spot. July 5th—to Carentan with the 83rd Division. . . The 4th Division later joined us here, for 146 admissions and loss of a kitchen tent by artillery fire. . . We followed the 9th Division on to Percy on 2 Aug and then to Beauvain . . . by this time the great St Lo breakthrough was history, and we had taken an active part.

August 30th—The Second Platoon saw Paris with champagne, billowing skirts and bicycles. . . The Eifel Tower and Notre Dame Cathedral were visited in masse. Driving north on 5 Sep in support of the entire V Corps, we admitted 776 casualties within the next 2 weeks at Laon; over half of them within 24 hours. . .

All personnel were called upon to work day and night, without sleep, until the war moved on and gave us a needed break. October 5th—After a lengthy bivouac in the ankle-deep mud of Belgium, we joined the 4th Division again at Heppenback. . . Then a new move to St. Vith, and here we had our first taste of 'Buzz Bombs'—not nice. . . Nov lst—The rat race began; the platoon moved into its first building at Walferdangen, Luxembourg in support of the 83rd Division again. This was our first heat, electric lights and hot baths. After only 48 hours we followed them out into the mud and sleet at Frisange and back to tents again. On Nov 10th back to Bettemburg into a convent the Nazis had used as a Hitler Youth School. On the 15th we returned to Luxembourg and settled down in winter quarters where the 4th replaced the 83rd. We had many air raids and alarms, and these were followed by the Ardennes Counter Offensive. . . From there to Fischbach and our next bivouac was in

Bastogne until Feb 15th. We moved forward to Bleialf, our first stop in Germany, then to Prum on 5 March. We operated a German Hospital March 11—19. March 20th we took a long trip to Kaiserlslautern with the 80th Division. There we had 67 casualties. . . We journeyed by autobahn across the Rhine to central Germany on 7th April. We were at Eschwege and Meerane and on 27th April at Ingolstadt on the Danube River until V-E Day, May 7. Following termination of the war the platoon moved into the shadows of Hitler's Stadia in Nurnberg to function as a Ramp Hospital for Prisoner Stalag XIII-D.

Total statistics from D + 1 to VE Day—31 moves by motor company—2547 combat admissions. The platoon was fortunate in many respects, losing only 3 members through illness: T/3 Emil Aralle, PFC Raymon Bonnell, and Pvt. Clarence Devinney. . . The Unit has earned 5 battle stars, the Arrowhead, 3 overseas service bars to date, and several individual Bronze Star Awards are on the way. . . Her history, perhaps has not all been written yet, but a proud chapter has, and existing here on these pages it will likewise linger in the memories of each and every member of the gallant SECOND PLATOON, 42nd FIELD HOSPITAL. Good luck, Bon Chance, Auf Wiedersehen, and thanks to a swell bunch of people."

★★★

WARREN H. LOVE, Commander, USN (Ret), was born July 27, 1923, in St. Paul, Minnesota, the son of Robert and Margaret S. Rochette Love. He had one brother, **LESLIE R. LOVE,** Sgt. US Marines, who was killed by sniper bullet on the island of Rendova in the Philippines in 1944. Warren and Merle L. Yelvington were married July 27, 1944 in Klamath Falls, Oregon and have three children: Lawrence L. Love, M.D., Randal T. Love, and Janis K. Love Wagner.

In 1942 Warren enlisted as a Naval Aviation Cadet in Minneapolis. He went through civilian pilot training at the Univeristy of Minnesota and was sent to Iowa City for pre-flight training. His primary training was in Livermore, California, and he received his Navy Wings at the Naval Air Station at Corpus Christi, Texas. His Operational Training in dive bombers was at Daytona Beach, Florida where he met his wife, Merle.

Warren retired July 1, 1967, as a Commander USN and was

awarded the Distinguished Flying Cross, three Air Medals, American Area Ribbon, Philippine Liberation Ribbon, and four various Area Ribbons. He shared some writings about his war experiences and they are quoted in part below:

"After the battle of Daytona Beach, we were sent to Chicago where we qualified for carrier landings on the *USS WOLVERINE*, a converted river boat with a huge paddle wheel on the stern. Five arrested landings were required to qualify for the next stage, that being getting your butt shot off in the Pacific. Next step was San Diego where we were put in a pool of aviators awaiting assignment to a permanent squadron. We subsequently went to the Naval Air Station at Seattle where we commissioned a new squadron, Composite Squadron Ninety-nine (VC-99) on 22 March 1944. This was a fighter/bomber squadron equipped with Gruman F4F/FM-2 aircraft for the fighter pilots, of which I was a member, and Gruman TBF/TBM torpedo bombers for the bomber jockeys.

On January 7, 1945, VC-99 was embarked aboard the *USS BOUGAINVILLE*, a jeep carrier. Destination: Pearl Harbor, Honolulu, Hawaii. After one night in Pearl Harbor, the squadron was

The field hospital to which Pete Harmening was attached (This was the forerunner of the future "Mobile Army Surgical hospital (MASH) of the Korean War.)

flown to NAS Kahului on the island of Maui where we spent three months in further training. During our carrier qualification training, we operated off numerous carriers: *USS TAKANIS BAY; USS SHIPLEY BAY; USS TRIPOLI*; and the *USS FANSHAW BAY.*

On April 9, 1945, VC-99 departed the Hawaiian area on board His Majesty's Ship HMS Tracker, a British aircraft carrier. After eleven days the squadron disembarked on the island of Saipan where we spent ten very hot days. During that stay, I was able to fly to Guam to visit my brother's grave. He had been killed by a sniper bullet on Rendova Island a few months earlier. On April 30, 1945, VC-99 was embarked on its mother carrier, the *USS HOGGATT BAY* at Tanapag Harbor, Saipan. The training was over, and the real stuff commenced.

After a short stop at Ulithi and a couple of trips to MogMog Island, the ship joined other carriers, and with the flag of Rear Admiral Harold M. Martin, commenced operations against the Japanese in the vicinity of Okinawa Gunto, and Sakishima Gunto in the Ryukyu Islands Group. From 14 May 1945 to 24 June 1945, VC-99 pilots flew 1327 sorties, dropped 140 tons of bombs, and expended over 1000 five-inch rockets on enemy airfields, fortifications, and other installations.

One of the highlights of this 'paid for cruise' occurred during a strike on an airfield on the island of Myako Shima. We came in at about 20,000 feet, dove to the airstrip and unloaded our five-inch rockets. As I started to pull up, there was some fool trying to take the runway, no doubt with the idea of spoiling our fun. I donated about ten seconds worth of 50 caliber rounds into his fuel tank and spoiled his whole day. (The question is asked many times, 'How many enemy did you kill?' At the time when we would return to the carrier, we would brag to each other and to the debriefing officer about the number we had 'splattered' that day. It is difficult to explain these days, but the mood then was to kill anything that moved or looked like it was going to. I made many trips back to Japan during my Navy career and made many Japanese friends. It is difficult to explain even to myself the mechanics of the transition process from war time to present. You wonder how you could measure your successes by the number you killed.)

As I pulled out and started to climb, there was a bang and a feeling that I had flown into a brick wall. About ten seconds later my engine quit. I hit the primer and got a restart, but it didn't last long. I found that if I held the primer down, the engine would run for a few seconds, then flood and quit. If I let up on the primer, the engine would catch and run for a few seconds. With my wingman doing the navigating, we made it back 75 miles to the formation. After one pass over the carrier, I was informed that they could not take the aircraft aboard in its present condition. I ditched the aircraft ahead of the lead destroyer, got out of the bird and waited for pickupk by the destroyer. I spent the night on the destroyer and was sent back in a basket on a high line to the carrier.

Being shot down by enemy AA ground fire was a noteworthy event, but not the most prominent one during this deployment. In July 1945 I was returning from a four hour combat air patrol (CAP) when, on final approach for recovery, my propeller started to go into high pitch. This was a fairly common problem with the old Curtis Electric prop. In full high pitch, the aircraft will not stay in the air. When I got a frantic wave off from the landing signal officer, I jammed the throttle forward to get clear of the ship. I cleared the ship, but the maneuver caused the aircraft to snap roll and spin in. After hitting the water straight in, the aircraft remained afloat about fifteen seconds. My memory is foggy as to how I exited the plane, but pictures taken from the carrier deck showed that I exited the same way I did when I was shot down. I had learned from the first ditching to wear my shoulder harness and lap belt very tight, and this undoubtedly saved me from serious injury. Again, I was picked up by one of the screen destroyers, and again transferred from ship to ship on a high line. I came out with a dislocated shoulder and multiple contusions. It was the practice for the Scheduling Officer to come to sick bay and inquire about the injured pilot's condition. He asked, 'Can I put him on tomorrow's flight schedule?' It took a few days.

On July 26 orders were received to proceed to Adak, Aleutian Islands, via Ulithi and Aniwetok to join the 4th Fleet. The operation for which the *HOGGATT BAY* was scheduled was cancelled due to the Japanese surrender. We were ordered to proceed immediately to Japan. As carrier flagship, we flew cover for the Naval force that entered Nutsu Wan and for the ceremony that was held in the harbor of the Ominato Naval Base, Japan. During flights over Japan, we located several prisoner of war camps and participated in supply drops consisting of food, newspapers, magazines, and medical supplies for the prisoners. By this time the prison gates were open, and the guards were nowhere to be seen. We would fill fuel wing tanks with articles and drop them in the prison yards. It was quite a sight to see all the American POW's running around the yard waving at us. After a ten month 'expense paid Pacific cruise' covering 60,000 miles, VC-99 headed homeward."

★★★

George Calvin and Sophie M. Horne Walker had two sons in the service in World War II. Their other children are Ruth, Bobby Joe (who served in the Korean Conflict), Wilburn and Eva Kate.

ALFORD WALKER was born June 16, 1921. He married Dorothy Rosser, and they had three children, Janie Beth, Larry Jim, and Michael. Alford enlisted in the Army Air Corps on September 8, 1942. His training was at Barksdale Air Field in Shreveport, Louisiana and later in San Antonio. He was stationed at Love Field in Greenville, Texas for most of the war but later went to Biloxi, Mississippi and then to San Antonio for a few months. He went to Kessler Field, Mississippi on November 13, 1945, for AP and Engineer Mechanical training. Alford was discharged at the rank of Sergeant at Barksdale Air Field on December 11, 1945. He received the American Theater Ribbon, Good Conduct Medal and Victory Medal. Alford died August 4, 1997, and Dorothy resides in their home at DeKalb, Texas.

LEE VOYD WALKER was born June 18, 1923 at Dalby Springs, Texas. He married Doris Evelyn Tutt, and they had three children, James Doyle, Dwight Lee, and Virginia Gail. On December 2, 1942 he entered the Army and was trained at Camp Fannin, Texas as a Glider Mechanic. He was a part of the 50th Troop Carrier Squadron and at times rode gliders into battle. His overseas duty was in Sicily, Naples, Rome, Normandy, Northern France, Rhineland, Central Europe, Foggia-Italy, and Africa. While in Sicily, he became very ill and was rushed to a field hospital where it was found that his appendix had ruptured. His family remembers that their mother sensed something was wrong and prayed all day. Lee Voyd was discharged at the rank of Sergeant on October 5, 1945 and was awarded the Good Conduct Medal, American Theater Campaign Medal, European-African Medal, Eastern Campaign Medal with seven Bronze Stars, and Distinguished Unit Badge with one Oak Leaf Cluster. Lee Voyd died July 1, 1976, and Doris resides in DeKalb, Texas.

★★★

Ernest Gay and George Lottie Burkett Rosser had two sons who served during World War II. Their other children were Gladys, Hobert, Syble, and Dorothy.

HUBERT ROSSER was a First Sergeant in the Medical Corps and came home from the war physically unscathed but mentally scarred and saddened from the death of his younger brother. The younger brother, **RAYMOND ROSSER**, was in the Battle of Leyte Gulf. General Douglas MacArthur's forces had invaded Leyte in mid-October, and after fighting by land, sea and air, the conquest of Leyte was complete on Christmas Day 1944. Raymond was killed in December by a shot from a Japanese sniper. His memorial is in the West Bowie Cemetery in Bowie County, Texas, and Hubert Rosser is also buried there. Raymond was married to I. V. Carr, and there were no children.

The Rosser family lived in West Bowie, a small community between Avery and DeKalb, Texas. Besides their son, Raymond, who was killed in action, two other young men from West Bowie, **NOBLE TUCKER** and **RAYMOND BROWN**, were also killed. The young men were all good friends.

★★★

J. T. EASON was born near Ivanhoe in Fannin County, Texas on July 29, 1918. His parents were John Thomas and Mary Palestine Tucker Eason, and he had two younger sisters, Lois Emiline and Cleoria Magdaline. He lived most of his life in Fannin County but moved to Clarksville in 1986. His daughter, Karen Kay Sheppard and her husband, Harold, live at Dimple, north of Clarksville. His other child Cheryl Beth Adkins lives in Irving, Texas. On August 16, 1987, he married Wilma Smith Mayes, and they live east of Bogata.

Karen had this to say: "Daddy's memory of the World War II years has been astounding to me. I have heard other people express the same thing about their relatives. Perhaps these men were 'hyper-alert' during those times and under great stress. Perhaps their heightened awareness of events as they happened is what etched those memories so deeply."

During 1939 J. T. was in the Civilian Conservation Corps in

Mesa Verde, Colorado. While there he filled out all the papers to register for the draft and passed his physical examination. He thinks this registration process was then required of all American men of age 18 or older. In May of 1940, back in Fannin County, he was drafted into the U.S. Army. He completed his training at Fort Leonardwood, Missouri and was then sent to Fort Ord near San Francisco. He was scheduled to ship out to the Philippines on December 8, 1941. After Pearl Harbor was attacked by Japan on December 7th, his troop ship's orders were changed. His ship was immediately sent to Honolulu, Hawaii. It took about twelve days to make the trip. When he arrived, he witnessed the terrible devastation of what was left of Pearl Harbor. He was 23 years old then; even now he admits that he was scared to death at what he saw. J. T. remembers that first ocean voyage very well because for the first several days on the huge ship, he was terribly seasick. He was stationed on an Army base in Hawaii for two years as a member of the 47th Engineers Unit.

He was injured twice during WWII. Both injuries occured while he was in Hawaii. Although neither of his injuries were life threatening, both required hospitalization. The first injury took place when his Unit was building an airport. He was unloading building materials from the back of a big truck, and the driver suddenly made the truck lurch forward and then slammed on the brakes. J. T.'s right index finger was caught under some lumber, causing a bone to be broken and a cut. A Hawaiian doctor stitched up the cut but did not set the bone. Later an Army Surgeon had to rebreak the bone and set it. One day while he was stacking dynamite, he dropped a whole case on his right foot. His big toe was broken, and he was put in the Army hospital. While there, his entire Unit, the 47th Engineers, was shipped from Hawaii to Saipan. When he was released from the hospital, he was assigned to another outfit and never saw any of his buddies again.

His new outfit was sent on a troop ship from Hawaii to Okinawa, the scene of terrible conflict between the Allies and the Japanese. The worst of this was over before they arrived. He was then sent from Okinawa to a small island at its north tip called Ieshema. J. T. says, "Thank the Lord, I never saw battle, but I was in a great many air raids by the Japanese. I remember watching tracer bullets flying through the night skies. I never witnessed any casualties, but there were some deaths in my units, mostly from various illnesses."

He was stationed at Ieshema for only about a month and was then flown back to Okinawa. From there he was shipped back to a seaport on the coast of California. The return voyage was a nightmare. It took about three long weeks. While they were still on the dock at Okinawa loading the ship, a bad typhoon hit the island. Huge waves crashed over the ship, and it began to take on water. They all had to work hard for many hours to get the water pumped out. All the GI's had to eat during the entire trip were stale chocolate bars and C-Rations.

J. T. was then stationed in San Antonio and while on a three day pass he and his first wife, Alberta Ileene, were married. He was discharged from the Army in November of 1945 after serving for over five years. He returned to Fannin County where he lived, worked and raised his family. He says this: "I had a rough time, but if I needed to, I would do it all over again."

During his youth, J. T. worked for Sam Rayburn, a United States Congressman and later Speaker of the House of Representatives for many years. Mr. Sam owned a large amount of land in Bonham. Then in the early 1950's construction was begun there on the Veterans' Administration Hospital. This was probably due to the influence of Sam Rayburn. J. T. got a job in construction, and when the hospital opened in 1953, he got a job and stayed there for thirty years until he retired.

Karen told this about Mr. Sam, and even though it happened in the 1960's, I feel that it should be included in my book. She said: "I was a sophomore in high school when Mr. Sam died November 16, 1961. Four American Presidents attended his funeral on November 18, 1961: President Harry S. Truman, President Dwight D. Eisenhower, President John F. Kennedy, and then Vice President Lyndon B. Johnson. His funeral was held at the First Baptist Church in Bonham, the only place that was large enough to hold all the dignataries and all the common people who attended.

Most of the dignataries flew into Perrin Air Force Base at Sherman, Texas and were then flown into Bonham in Army helicopters. The small Bonham Airport could not handle all that so the helicopters landed at the Bonham Golf Club. Black limousines were brought in from Dallas to transport the people from there to the church.

Mother, Cheryl and I saw all four Presidents. Both Kennedy

and Johnson left their Secret Service escorts behind, walked over to the crowd of people who had gathered at the Golf Club, and began shaking hands. Eisenhower waved to everyone, but Truman was not there since he didn't fly in. He came part of the way by train and the rest of the way by automobile. We did not go to the funeral, but watched it on television.

There is a very famous photograph of the four American Presidents sitting together on the front pew of the First Baptist Church of Bonham. This photograph is prominently displayed in the Sam Rayburn Library. We recently discovered this photograph in a new restaurant in Plano, 'Love and War in Texas'. The owners say this photograph is the most prized piece in their extensive collection of Texas memorabilia."

★★★

KIRK NORVEL ICENHOWER was born on December 21, 1921. His parents were Luther C. and Lee Bell Guest Icenhower, and he had two brothers, Junior and Charles, and a sister, Kathalee. Kirk married Ann Alsobrook, and they had four sons, Ken, Billy, Joel and Ronnie. Kirk was in the Army Air Corps during World War II. A diary kept by the Pilot of the plane that Kirk served on is quoted in part below:

"There is no real reason for starting this book on April 6, 1945, but it seems like a good idea just now... Have been here at Clovis Army Air Base since the 22nd of February... We have our entire crew and about forty-six hours in the B-29 as of present.

> Airplane Commander—Raymond E. Shumway originally from Oregon but living in Minneapolis
> Pilot—me, George S. Lomas
> Bombadier—Henry Goldstein from Los Angeles, California
> Navigator—James E. Brechtbill from Los Angeles
> Radar—Richard Meriam from Massachusetts
> Engineer—Kirk Icenhower from Texas
> Radio Operator—Sam C. Kidd from Michigan
> C.F.C.—Harold Winberg from Minneapolis
> Left Gunner—Frand Blackett from Nevada
> Right Gunner—Warren Bartlett from Rochester, New York
> Tail Gunner—Yearby Ashby from Indiana

Friday 27 July—This was to be our most difficult mission... We had run into trouble on our last four msisions and got around to completing only one. Old 'Jonah' was lying in wait for us... Everything went OK, and we took up our heading from Iwo for Yawata where we were to lay our mines. About five mintues after land fall, we lost our oil pressure on No. 1 engine... We cirlcled right and made a run and layed them in the inland sea in a small bay on the left side going in. We took up a heading for Iwo and slowly headed out to sea. We wanted to shake the spinning prop and didn't have long to wait. It got white hot and pieces of metal started flying out. I went back and opened the hatch door and kidded 'Ike' about bailing out. About that time one came loose and hit No. 2. The whole plane shuddered and seemed to stop for a minute in mid-air. I had gone back to my seat when flames started from No. 2. I got up to take a look and the whole left wing appeared to be in flames. Ray had tried to feather two, but the prop was gone. Ike used the fire extinguishers, but they were of no use at all. Evidently the prop had knocked a hole in one of the gas tanks. I checked with Ray, and he gave the order to bail out so I put the nose gear down and Goldy opened the bomb bays. They didn't come open except for a few inches. The electrical system had gone out. I told Goldy and Ike to bail out, but they didn't seem to want to go so I went by them and bailed out.

Sat. 28 July—It was about 1:30 in the morning when we bailed out and my chute opened with a snap. The plane seemed to be heading toward me when it exploded. I hit the water; my 'Mae West' wouldn't work so I went to work on my dingy. I climbed aboard my raft and realized my shoulder was dislocated. Before I could get out any flares, a P-47 flew over at about 5000 feet and came back over again in about 15 minutes headed back toward Iwo.

Sun. 29 July—I heard a plane and before I realized what was happening, a B-29 dipped over me at less than 100 feet. Then I saw something I don't think I'll ever forget as long as I live. At first I thought it was a destroyer bearing down on me, but as it came closer, I could see it was a submarine. As it got closer, someone on the deck tossed a line to me from the bow. The next thing I knew, I was sitting on the deck. Jim was already on board. Icenhower came aboard next; then Shumway and Kidd; then Bartlett and Winberg. No one else turned up although they searched until darkness took over. Jim and Ike had been all by themselves as I was.

Our second day aboard we rode out a typhoon, 200 feet below the surface, and it was plenty rough down there. We got news of the first atomic bomb being dropped on Hiroshima and of the peace talks. On the night of 9 August we were transferred from the *USS WHALE* to the *USS BLACK FISH* in a rubber boat and made our return trip to Guam in about four and a half days. It was made entirely on the surface except for a few dives. They had a total of 23 air crew members on board."

A letter written by the Airplane Commander, Raymond E. Shumway, to his family on August 8, 1945, while aboard the *USS WHALE* is quoted in part. Reading this shows just how horrible it was to bail out of a burning plane and be out in the ocean on a raft, waiting to be rescued.

"Please excuse my delay in writing. I went down and have been on this boat since the 29th—went down on the 27th. I'm in good health and did not get hurt at all. . .My parachute worked fine and I got my one man life raft inflated without any trouble when I hit the water. I heard a man yelling and I went over to pick up my radio man—he didn't have a raft and was drowning when I got there. . . In about 30 minutes I had three sharks circling my raft. Sgt. Kidd, luckily was unconscious. I got out my 45 automatic and fired it near the sharks and scared them away. Shortly, I had 5 more sharks around my raft. One came so close I could have put my hand on his dorsal fin that was sticking out of the water. This shark made a quick turn and came in on Sgt. Kidd's feet. I fired not a foot from his feet and not six inches from the shark's nose. He turned and left. I fired 16 shots at sharks that first night. In the morning Sgt. Kidd came to, and we found he could turn over and sit in front of me tobaggon style with his feet in. It was very cramped for both of us.

Some Navy fighters flew over and I sent a flare up, but they didn't see it. The wind came up and we were in for some rough seas. Sgt. Kidd told me that he was unable to send our distress message so no one knew what had happened or where they should start looking for us. The second night it was very stormy. One high wave knocked us over, and it took us some time to get back on again. About noon two B-29's flew over and I sent a smoke signal up to them. They saw it! They came over us, took pictures of us, and then dropped us a large life raft and some supplies. We got within ten feet of the raft but couldn't catch it. We received nothing they dropped to us, but we knew they had our position and that we would be picked up.

Very late in the afternoon another B-29 came over and we signaled it. they led the boat to the resuce. Frankly, I cried when I saw we would not have to spend another night at sea. We could not walk when we got aboard. We had been in the water for 42 hours—sitting in water up to our waists and not being able to move our legs. . . Four of our eleven men are still missing. Life aboard this boat is good." (Although this letter was not written by Kirk Icenhower, it is evident that he went through the same experiences while in a raft on the ocean waiting to be rescued. I feel sure that he never forgot this.)

Summary

It has been a year since my first interview with a World War II veteran. There have been many trips, many visits, many calls to secure the information for this book. Without the help of my husband, Robert, I could not have done it. Many times veterans would speak to him, more at ease with a man, perhaps, than a woman as they recalled their war experiences. His being in the service during the Berlin and Cuban Crises and spending many years in the National Guard and Army Reserves enabled him to help me with the military parts of the interviews as I transcribed my notes or tapes.

 Scrapbooks belonging to Mary McAllister, Ben Bowers, and Bessie W. Strickland of Clarksville and Lawrence Wood of the Rugby Community have been so much help. Mr. Wood's sister, Elsie Wood Alsobrook, kept his scrapbook during World War II. Mary McAllister's nephew, John Thomas Lamb, and his wife, Lorraine, put together five scrapbooks for her from things that she had saved from the war years. People have shared newspaper clippings, photographs, correspondence, and military histories. Some information came from the Internet, and as with my other book, the Red River County Public Library was a source of much I needed in writing. Gavin Watson's personal collection of books about World War II were a "gold mine" of information. These books were donated to the Library, after Gavin and Martene both died, by her brother, C. B. Holland.

 When I grew up in the small town of Clarksville in Northeast

Texas, patriotism was something we were taught about at home, at school and at church. The Pledge of Allegiance began our school day, and patriotic songs were a part of our curriculum as well as the history of how our great Nation came to be. World War II was a vital part of our lives, even though we were not quite old enough to realize the intensity of it. When peace finally came, it was wonderful to see those who had been in the service return home. It was sad though to see those families who had lost loved ones in the war.

Several veterans of World War II have died, even since I interviewed them. It is my sincere hope that "For Love of Country—The Price of Freedom" will preserve the memories of those who sacrificed so much through the years to preserve the freedoms of the United States of America.

GOD BLESS AMERICA!

Endnotes

Chapter 1: Early Beginnings
1. Emma Guest Bourne, "A Pioneer Farmer's Daughter of Red River Valley Northeast Texas", The Story Book Press, Copyright 1950 (book belongs to Martha Wood, Bogata, Texas)
2. Van Craddock, "Family Left Mark on Early East Texas", Longview News Daily, 1999 (Albert H. Latimer is his great-great uncle.)
3. From personal files of Sharon Stephens Black, Paris, Texas (Jacob Blanton was her great-great grandfather.)
4. Victor Cox, "How Bogata Got Its Name", Bogtata News, 11-18-99
5. From personal files of Virginia Rose Bowers, Clarksville, Texas
6. Newspaper article from personal files of Jo Miller, Avery, Texas
7. The *Clarksville Times*, 10-28-1924

Chapter 2: Gray and Blue—Some Who Served
1. T. R. Fehrenbach, "Lone Star—A History of Texas and the Texans", American Legacy Press, New York, copyright 1983, pages 350, 354-356
2. Note from personal files of Edna Joiner Weston, Harleton, Texas
3. From personal files of Mary Jane Lowry, Blossom, Texas
4. From diary of Joseph Henry Harris, Oakbowery, Alabama (used with permission of Jim Harris)
5. From personal files of Mary Jane Lowry, Blossom, Texas

Chapter 3: World War I—The War to End All Wars
1. "Ballard's Book of the Great War", published by James F. Ballard,

St. Louis USA (from personal files of Mr. and Mrs. Delma Gibbs, Detroit, Texas])
2. Issued by the Commission on Training Camp activities of the Army & Navy Departments, price 25 cents, to those in the service 15 cents, Washington Government Printing Office 1917 (from personal files of Mr. and Mrs. Charles Shelton, Clarksville, Texas)
3. From personal files of Venita Jo Gibbs Oldfield, Detroit, Texas
4. From personal files of Nellie Pratt Abney, Arlington, Texas
5. From personal files of Juavanee Carpenter, daughter of Oma Day Daniell, Deport, Texas
6. From personal files of Mr. and Mrs. Billy Bob Hill, Clarksville, Texas
7. From personal files of Mr. and Mrs. M. D. Everhart, Brookston, Texas
8. From personal files of Mary Jane Lowry, Blossom, Texas
9. From personal files of Mr. and Mrs. Gene Simmons, Annona, Texas
10. From personal files of Pauline Glenn, Longview, Texas
11. "In Flanders Field"—"The Making of the Poem" by Rob Ruggenberg—from the Internet (shared by Sharon Stephens Black, Paris, Texas)

Chapter 4: Hard Times
1. "Texas—The Story of the Lone Star State", a school history by George C. Hester, A.M., L.L.D., W. C. Nunn, PhD, Rose Mary Henson, A.M., Henry Holt & Co., copyright 1948, pages 326-327
2. ibid, page 327

Chapter 5: Day of Infamy—December 7, 1941
1. "Pearl Harbor—The Way It Was—December 7, 1941", Text by Scott C. S. Stone, An Island Heritage Book, Second Edition 1980, Copyright 1977, Island Heritage Limited, Foreword
2. "Day of Infamy" by Walter Lord, copyright 1957, In Canada, George J. McLeod, Ltd., Foreword and pages 214-218
3. "Attack on Pearl Harbor" by Robert Parkinson, G. P. Putnam's Sons, N.Y. 1973
4. "Pearl Harbor—The Way It Was—December 7, 1941 (same as above), pages 5-48 in part

Chapter 6: The War Years in Europe
1. "The Military History of WWII: Volume 1, European Land Battles 1939-1943" by Trevor Nevitt Dupuy, Col., U.S. Army, Ret., Franklin Watts Inc., 575 Lexington Avenue, New York 22, copyright 1962 (from personal collection of Gavin Watson,

Jr., Clarksville, Texas, donated to Red River County Public Library)
2. ibid, except Volume 2
3. Cornelius Ryan, "The Longest Day, June 6, 1944", Simon & Schuster, New York 1959, Foreword
4. Same as footnote #1 and #2
5. American Heroes, 9th Division, "They Broke the Rhine Line", story by Don Wharton, Drawings by Robert Frankenberg, 50th in Look's American Series" (from personal files of Ben Bowers, Clarksville, Texas)
6. Same as footnote #1 and #2, pages 72, 78
7. Newspaper clipping, "Berlin Falls to Russians; Million Troops Surrender"—name of paper and date unknown
8. Newspaper clipping, Deport, Lamar County, Texas (date unknown)

Chapter 7: The War Years in the Pacific
1. The Military History of WWII: Volume 9, "Asiatic Land Battles: Japanese Ambitions in the Pacific" by Trevor Nevitt Dupuy, Col. U.S. Army, Ret, Franklin Watts, Inc., 575 Lexington Avenue, New York 22, copyright 1963 (from personal collection of Gavin Watson, Jr. donated to the Red River County Public Library, Clarksville, Texas)
2. "The 4th Marine Division in WWII, Edited by Carl W. Proehl, Infantry Journal Press, Washington, copyright 1946 (from personal files of Bill White, Bogata, Texas)

Chapter 9: The Forties
1. *Clarksville Times*, 8-2-77, "Taxis"
2. Post card from the files of Mr. and Mrs. Charles Shelton, Clarksville, Texas
3. "A Camera Trip Through Camp Maxey, A Picture Book of the Camp and Its Activities, prepared and printed in Gravure by the Ullman Co., Brooklyn, N.Y. with courtesy and cooperation of the Camp Maxey Public Relations Office (no date)— Paris Public Library
4. "Prisoner of War", Paris News, 10-19-87, by Betty Hensley, News Staff Writer
5. "Rosie the Riveter, We Can Do It!", Dallas Morning News, 12-29-99, by Paula Watson, Staff Writer

Chapter 10: In the Line of Duty
1. "America Remembers—The Purple Heart Tribute" presented by the Armed Forces Commemorative Society (from the personal files of Mr. and Mrs. M. D. Everhart, Brookston, Texas)

2. CMOH Society, copyright 1997, last updated 13 October 1999, Sherry Russell (used with their permission)
3. Letter, page 174, "101 Famous Poems", Revised Edition with a Prose Supplement, copyright 1926, R. J. Cook, 301 South Wabash Avenue, Chicago
4. Poem by Father Denis Edward O'Brien, USMC
5. Prayer from the scrapbook of Ben Bowers, Clarksville, Texas, author unknown
6. "Heroism" (from the personal files of Mr. and Mrs. M. D. Everhart, Brookston, Texas)
7. "Fly Your Flag", Dallas Morning News, 11-11-1999
8. "Jimmy Doolittle: In Love With the Wild Blue Yonder", The Bridgebuster, The Men of the 5th Bomb Wing, Vol. II. No. 1, June 1980 (from the personal files of Billie Bishop, Bogata, Texas)

Chapter 11: Lest We Forget
1. "America the Beautiful", from the Baptist Hymnal, words by Katharine Lee Bates, Music by Samuel A. Ward
2. "Tragedies of American War"—(from the personal files of Naomi Davis, Clarksville, Texas)
3. Newspaper article on Co I, 144th Infantry Division, *Clarksville Times*, no date (from the personal files of Naomi Davis, Clarksville, Texas)
4. "4th Marine Division WWII", Edited by Carl W. Proehl, lst Edition 1946, Infantry Journal Press, Washington, D.C. (from personal files of Bill White, Bogata, Texas)
5. "Remembrance—The 57th Bomb Wing" (from the personal files of Billie Bishop, Bogata, Texas)
6. Red River Recollections, published by Red River County Historical Society, 1986, page 255
7. Paul Davis Marable, Jr., "Two Hundred Fifty-five Days", Texian Press, copyright 1971
8. Gateway to Texas—History of Red River County" by Martha Sue Stroud, pages 360-3
9. Bunker Hill (from personal files of Rev. William Upchurch)

Index

Abernathy, Charley Julian, 465
  Dorthy May, 465
  Floita Rachel Phillips, 465
  Joyce, 257
  Mary Catherine, 465
  Mrs. Emmons, 166
  Murel, 258
  Pearis C., 102, 465
  Pearis C., Jr., 465
  Raleigh, 258
  Robbie Marcell, 465
  Roy A., 158, 257
  Thelma, 257
  Viola Cowell, 257
  Wallace, 158, 257
  Will, 257
Abney, Ed, 384
  John Edward, 384
  John Orval, 384
  Rosa Lee Crow, 384
  Rose Marie, 384
  Thomas Harvey, 384
  William Osco, 384
Ada, Donna, 362
  Gerry, 362
  John F., 362
  Robert L., 362
  Verna Owens, 362
Adams, 37
  Allen, 66
  Bess, 66
  Beulah, 66
  Charles, 66
  Dora, 249
  Doris Lucille, 66
  Ella, 66
  Gladys, 70
  Grace Coker, 66
  James Millican, 66
  James Monroe, 66
  Joe, 66
  Mary Jim, 66
  Norah, 66
  Sallie, 66
Adkins, Cheryl Beth, 523
  Wm., 47
Admiralty Island, 147, 162, 363, 388
Afrika Korps, 186
Aikin, Bobby, 246
  Dorthey, 246
  Erbie George Jr., 246
  Erbie George, Sr., 246
  Floy Mae, 246
Aikin Grove Cemetery, 345
Aikin, J. C., 246
  Lee, 45
  Lilous Melton, 246
Alabama, 49th Infantry Regiment, 26; Home Guard State Militia, 34
Albritton, Toby, 258
Aldridge, Mary Diana Dunning, 459
Aleutian Island, 128, 142, 143, 415; Aleutians, 234, 309
Alexander, J. D., 280
  William J., 470, 471
Alford, Coy, 415
  Edith (Cook), 415, 416
  Horace, 415
  Hubert, 212
  Hubert Pershing, 415, 416
  Katie Childress, 415
  Lucille, 415
  Norris, 415
  Sybil, 415
  Travis, 415
  William Henry, 415
Allen, Ada Fulton, 84
  Alice Joyce Fowler, 362
  Bonnie Dickson, 270
  Charles Tanner, 162, 212
  Ed, 48
  General, 76
  James William, 270
  Johnson William, 84
  Linda, 271
  Lou Ann, 271
  Mary Ruth Summers, 317
  Mr. and Mrs. Charles, 162
  Nell Dickson, 271
  Paul F., 317
  Paula Dianne, 317
  Sally, 84
  Samuel W. Jr., 84, 317
  Samuel W., Sr., 84, 317
  Seth Dinwiddie, 84
  Thomas, 7
  Thomas Early, 270
  Tommy, 196
  Vade, 212
  William C., 37
Allison's 23rd Tex. Cavalry, 25
Allred, Govener James V., 60, 97
Alsip, Margaret, 497
Alsobrook, Elsie Wood, 157, 240
  Pansy, 438
American 9th Armored Division, 135; Expeditionary Force, 53, 68, 45, 69; First Army, 130, 132; Pacific Fleet, 137; Rangers, 150; Seventh Army, 133,

134; Third Army, 132; VI Corps, 133
Anderson, Allen, 410
  Bea, 84
  Bessie, 504
  Dolly, 84
  Dora, 84
  Edd, 84, 410
  Elza Connie, 497, 504
  Flossie, 84, 410
  Gen. John B., 186
  General, 379, 380
  Gladys, 84, 410
  Herman T., 505
  Ida, 84, 410
  James J., 505
  Jerry, 410
  Jesse, 504
  Jim, 158
  Joe, 84
  Joe W., 504
  John E., 84
  Karon, 410
  Lilly Dunsthun, 84
  Martha J. Dixon, 410
  Melvin, 84
  Melvin F., 410
  Merta, 84
  Odessa, 504
  Oscar, 84
  Robert F., 504
  Will, 71
  Will E., 84, 410
  William F., 505
  Willie, 84, 410
  Willie May, 504
  Zelphrea Cherry Anderson, 504
Anderson's Brigade, 37
Andersonville, 26
Annin, Col. Robert O., 186
Antone, Haywood, 157
Anzio, 207, 348, 404, 439; Anzio Beachhead, Italy, 366
Appomattox Court House, 35
Archer, Jonathan, 256
Ardennes, 256, 306, 340, 341, 357, 376, 466, 478, 482, 487, 507, 516, 517; Campaign, 288; Mountains, 498
Argonne Forest, 70, 71, 244, 302, 343; Forest Battle, 55; Woods, 44, 84
Arkansas, Territorial Legislature, 4

Arlington National Cemetery, 440
Armistice, 3, 44, 57; Day, 60, 208, 214
Army of Northern Virginia, 35
Army's 7th Infantry Division, 145
Arnold, Kelley, 234
Ashby, Yearby, 526
Atkins, Chester Bert (Jack), 433
  Dr B. J., 433
  E. L., 433
  Edward Boyd, 433
  Frances, 433
  J. B., 433
  Jessie Myrtle Boyd, 433
  Oueida Merl, 433
  Philip Gordon, 433
  Phillip Sheridan, 433
  Reba, 433
  Vivian, 433
Aubrey, Matt, 37
Auburn University, 35
Austin, Anna, 486
  Charles Robert, 486
  Jess, 47
  Pamela, 486
  Robert, 486
  Stephen F., 118
  Texas, 6, 65, 425
  Vernon H. Jr., 486
  William, 515
Auxiliary Remount Depot # 328, 84
Avalon, 118, 197; Avalon Theater, 65, 116, 117, 192, 338
Aydelott, Christene, 442
  Claude Beentt, 442
  Clovis, 442
  Curtis, 442
  Fannie Rhea, 442
  J. B., 442
  James (Dick), 442
  Jerry, 442
  Kala, 442
  Mark, 442
  Monty, 442
  Pam, 442
  William Thomas, 442
"Baa Baa Black Sheep," 507
Bachman, Fred, 48
  Henry, 48
Back-Break Hill, 298
Bagwell, Bill, 11
Bailey, Anna Marie, 248
  B. G., 248

Benjamin Garvie, 248
Blanchard S., 248
Eugie Elizabeth Tomlinson, 248
Herman C., 248
Hoyle Dean, 332
John David, 248
John H., 248
Larry Wayne, 248
M. Mozelle, 327
Mr. & Mrs. J. B., 168
Sherry, 248
T/Sgt. James Curlee, 167
Tyrus Reginald, 248
Baird, Ava, 378
  Burvell, 378
  Eula Lumpkin, 378
  Harriet Jean, 378
  Iris, 378
  J. V., 378
  John, 378
  Katherine, 378
  Leon, 378
  Naomi, 288
  Rickey, 378
  Rodger, 378
  Sharon, 378
  Virginia, 378
Bairett, Burny Buford, 423
  Faye, 423
  Frances, 423
  George Dee, 423
  Lillian, 423
  Marie, 423
  Mart, 423
  Nola Mae, 423
  Retta Mae Morgan, 423
  Sam Houston, 423
  Vera, 423
Baker, Alvin Bosley, 266
  Charles, 47
  Col, 335
  Dr., 24
  J.H.P., 22
  Mary Alice McLean, 266
  Mrs. J. H. P., 22
Bakke, Betty, 461
Ball, Captain Sam, 512
  David W. Col., 440
  Frank E. Jr., 440
  Frank Elihue, 439
  Georgia Ann, 440
  Harry, 438
  John, 438
  John D., 102, 438
  Johnny W., 102, 438
  Lucille, 438
  Paul, 438
  Ruby Denison, 103, 438

Ruth Ann, 438
Ballard, Alvin Glenn, 75
Ballentine, Captain J. J., 502
Ballew, Bill, 431
  Carrie Robinson, 431
  David, 431
  Duane, 431
  Janet, 431
  Loren Lee Jr., 431
  Loren, Sr., 431
  Paula, 431
Banks, Janie Prentice, 318
Barkley, Alben, 108
Barksdale Air Base, 315
Barlett, Velma, 312
Barnes, Mrs. Alvin, 165
Barnett, Christine, 281
  Howard P., 158
Barnoth, Alexander, 191
Barry, Mr. and Mrs. J. H., 424
  Raymond E., 424
Bartlett, Annie, 312
  Beulah, 312
  Cpl. Lewis, 158
  Geoffrey Winfred, 67
  James, 312
  James F., 312
  Lewis E., 312
  Mary Frances Eve Cagle, 312
  Ona, 312
  Verna, 312
  Warren, 526
  William, 312
Bartley, Andrew Jenkins, Sr., 293
  Clara, 75
  Dan, 293
  Deloyce, 293
  Evelyn, 433
  Gayla, 293
  Jr., Andrew J., (A. J.), 293
  Marcedis, 293
  Myrtle, 293
Barton, Billy, 157
  Henry, 193
  Ida Mae, 387
  Margaret, 162, 477
Baryms, Willie Mae, 71
Bataan, 140, 141, 224, 225, 227, 305; Death March, 166, 171, 224, 227, 305, 480; March, 225
Bates, 'Speedy', 95
Batson, Mrs., 26
Battle for Peleiu Island, 425
Battle of Anzio, 310, 311, 312; Bataan, 140, 127; Corinth, 28;

Corregidor, 150; 34;
Leyte, 150, 523;
Midway, 350;
Murfreesboro, 40;
Normandy, 405; Savo Island, 144; St. Lo, 409, 413; the Ardennes, 489; the Argonne Forest, 66; the Bulge, 135, 243, 244, 245, 320, 323, 338, 357, 404, 405, 411, 413, 418, 419, 434, 435, 439, 452, 489, 498, 505; the Coral Sea, 143, 425; the Marne, France, 57; the Philippine Sea, 502; Verdun, 53; Row, 105
Battleship Arizona, 108; California, 110; Colorado, 115; Maryland, 110; Missouri, 156; Nevada, 110; Oklahoma, 108; Pennsylvania, 110; Row, 110, 111; Tennessee, 110; West Virginia, 110
Baxter, Lydia M., 379
Beadle, Lela Mae, 16
Bean, Arley, 359
  Bobby, 359
  Cadmus, 271
  Cecil, 359
  Clyde, 157, 276
  Clyde Robert, 271
  Eddie, 359
  Eva Blankenship, 271
  George Mac, 359
  Hazel, 357, 359
  Larry, 359
  Louise, 271
  Martha Clyde, 271
  Mary Beth, 271
  Mary Reep, 100
  Pauline, 359, 400
  Sarah, 359
  Sheree, 271
  Velma Blankenship, 359
Bearden, Cecil Albert, 82
  Clyde, 82
  Garland A., 83
  Hobert Albert, 83
  Napoleon Bonaparte, 82
  Sue Nell, 83
Beasley, Mildrid, 363
Becknell, Captain William, 5
Bedford County Tennessee, 24
Bedoin, Willie, 244
Beecher, Gordon, 208

Beeson, Capt. William E., 30
Begemann, Dr. Rosemary, 68
Bell, Bill, 96
  Mrs. John Lee, 160
  Norma Jean, 294
Bellar, Mary Ann, 5
Belleau Woods, 57
Bellotte, Arville, 409
  Charlie Frank Jr., 410
  Charlie Frank, Sr., 410
  Della Baird, 409
  Edwin, 409
  Ernestine, 410
  Guy, 409
  Louis V. (Vaughn), 409
  Lucille, 409
  Mary Lou, 409
  Neva Odell, 410
  Ocie Odell Chapman, 410
  Oswald, 410
  R. V., 409
  Robert, 410
  Travis H., 409
  Walter E., 212
  Walter Earl, 409
  Walter Percy, 409
Bellows Field, 113
Benningfield, Irene, 289
  James T., 158
  Jessica Roberta, 487
  Marie, 345
  Wendel, 158
Benton, Mary Frances, 325
  Mildred, 448
Berlin, Irving, 214
Bethlehem Steel, 502
Bethlehem-Fairfield Shipyard, Inc, 427
Bettes, Betty Lou, 382
  Bill, 382
  Billy, 382
  Bobby, 384
  Della Craigo, 382
  Jim, 382
  Patsy, 384
  Pvt. Bill, 159
  Tommy, 382
  W. P., 382
  Walter L., 382, 384
  William C. (Bill), 382
Beville, J. C., 197
Bilibid prison camp, 513
Birge, George A., 49
Bishop, Billie, 346, 348
  Dixie Horner, 347
  Edna, 347
  Jay, 337
  Judith Ellen, 337
  Kathy Ann, 337

Margaret, 337
Melanie, 347, 348
Mrs. Rom, 80
Pene, 347
Robert, 346, 347, 348
Roma, 347
Romulus, 347
Sharon Kay, 337
USAF, (ret) Major Pene, 348
Vicky May, 337
W. R., 347
William H., 212
William Horner (Bill), 347, 349
Bismarck Archipelago, 270, 312, 316, 384
Bisset, Major General Stephen, 56
Bivin, Capt. John M., 9
Bivins, Atha, 85
Bixby, Mrs., 204
Black Brothers Co., 100, 182; Hawk Division, 307, 365
Black, Byron Sr., 253
Ervin, 32
Sharon Stephens, 6, 22, 24
Blackett, Frand, 526
Blackmon Pharmacy, 191, 199
Blair, Cassie Estilene, 259
Cassie Murphy, 259
Elizabeth, 260
Forrest H., 259
Forrest H., Jr., 260
Gail, 261
Gerry, 261
Juanell, 260
Mary, 260
Melvin, 261
Mrs. Robert, 165
Weslie Geraldine, 259
Blanc Mont Ridge, 69
Bland, Annie Laurie Moore, 55
Bruce Sr., 45, 55
Dolly Roberson, 354
J. N., 55
Jr., Bruce M., 55, 354
Marguerite, 55, 354
Blanton Creek, Cemetery, 24, 25, 26, 27, 377; Creek School, 5
Blanton, Jacob, 5
Julia Ann, 25
Bledsoe, Edna Veach, 259
George, 259
John E., 158
Lucy Wood, 259

Magaline, 259
Thomas C., 259
Walter, 259
Weldon, 259
Blossom Prairie, 3
Blue Devils, 216, 404; Ridge Path, 274
Bodwell, Grant, 48
Bogata, Cemetery, 165, 422, 448; High School, 160, 162, 497; Methodist, Church, 12; News, 13, 29, 157, 181; Rodeo, 198; School, 27
Bogota, Columbia, 6
Bolch, Lydia, 71
Bolton, Betty Joe, 412
Dorothy Marie, 412
Francis Marion (Tom), 412
James R., 412
Mary Christine, 376
Rena Myrtle Woods, 412
Ted, 95, Ted, 96
Thomas Paul, 412
Travis Corley, 412
Bone, Bobby Gene, 377
Elizabeth Claire, 377
Helen Ethel Coco, 377
Martha Jo, 377
Rachel Leigh, 377
William B., 377
William J., 377
Bonnell, Raymon, 518
Booker, Luther, 47
Booth, Captain, 283, 284
Boots and Wings, 164
Bourne, Emma Guest, 1
Bower, Brenda, 453
Carol, 453
Charlie, 453
Charlie Winston, 453
Charlotte, 453
Dollie, 453
Earlton, 453
Etta, 453
George, 452
George Barkley, Jr., 453
Georgia Ann, 453
Missie Rhea, 453
Mittie, 453
Priscilla Faye, 453
Robert, 453
Rose Marie, 453
Sarah Jane, 453
Stella, 453
William Dwayne, 453
Bowers, Beal V. Sr., 242
Ben, 157, 158, 207, 242
David, 242

Deborah, 242
Ella Mae Proctor, 242
Eugene, 37
Hoyt, 65
Inez, 242
Jack, 242
James Hoyt, 65
Jr., Beal Vinson, 245
Robert, 242
Robert Lawson, 245
Sgt. Woodrow, 210
Stephen Beal, 245
Veda, 242, 304
Virginia Rose, 31
Woodrow, 245
Bowie, Jr., J. B., 212
Boxelder Cemetery, 55, 67, 212
Boynton, Mrs. Donald, 502
Brackett, George, 245
Bradford, Argent, 49
James Cope, 31
Mrs. J. C., 33
Nancy (Nannie) Culpepper, 31
Bradley, Beulah Belle, 480
General Omar, 130, 132, 135, 256
Brandon, Vera, 336
Brannan, Bea,. 394
Beulah Martin, 441
Calvin, 393, 441
Charles Calvin, 165
Dorthy, 441
Flora, 441
Jimmy, 394, 441
John W., 441
Mack, 394, 441
Martin, 441
Ruby, 441
Branson, Grady Austin, 212
Brantley, Pauline, 241
Brasenose College, Oxford University, England, 204
Braswell, Rachel Clark, 362
Bratton, Jake, 47
Brechtbill, James E., 526
Breedlove, Charles, 438
Chester, 438
Dorthy, 438
Ernest, 438
Janetta, 438
John B., 438
Leroy, 438
Lucille, 438
Lula Lee, 438
Mable, 438
Susie Ashford, 438

Brem, Carey, 67
　Ellen Ballard, 67
　George B., 27
　James Albert, 67
Brenner Line, 348
Brewer, Capt. C. B., 462
　Ruby, 420
Brewer Hotel, 199
Bridges, Samp, 47
British 6th Airborne
　　Division, 130; Guyana,
　　248; Royal Air Force,
　　126; Royal Navy, 125,
　　127; Second Army, 130
Brittany American Cemetery,
　　304
Broadfoot, Albert, 422
　First Lt. Albert S. Jr., 422
　Judge and Mrs. A. S. Sr.,
　　422
　Miss Alice, 422
　Miss Emma Gene, 422
　Miss Jessie Butler, 422
Broadway, Nanny Lou, 441
Brooke General Army
　　Hospital, 257, 421, 460,
　　514
Brooks, Billy Eugene, 166
　Dr., 17
　James Howard, 166
　Mr. and Mrs. J. B., 166
　Raymond Benjamin, 166
Brookshire, Emma Jean, 414
Brookston, Texas, 461
Brower, Amie Rosser, 488
　Arlton H., 488
　Chester Randolph, 488
　Vicki, 488
Brown, Adell Nunn, 415
　Anzett, 47, 48
　Beach, 510
　Bert Parchman, 429
　Betty, 415
　Carolyn Sue, 429
　Dorothy, 415
　Frances, 83
　George W., 212
　Harold, 429
　Jesse, 85
　Johnny, 415
　Lennox, 415
　Louise, 316
　Mary, 415
　PFC George Willard, 415
　Raymond, 523
　Will S., 429
　Wordner, 393
Brummett, Lenard R., 268
Bryant, Jeff, 314

Bryson, Linda, 404
　Michelle, 404
　Mr R. H., 160
　Mrs. R. H., 160
　Scott, 404
Buchanan, Joe, 212
　Sallie Elizabeth, 84
Buchannan, Sgt. Joe, 164
Buckner Bay, 282, 510, 511
Buckner, General, 155, 282,
　　284, 511
　Lieutenant General Simon
　　B. Jr., 153
Buffo, Dom, 398
　Lela, 398
Bull, Louise Frances, 411
Bullington's Drug Store, 158,
　　199
Bullington, Frances Jean, 443
Bumgarner, Beverly, 428
　Bobby, 428
　Bruce, 428
　James, 428
　Lillian, 428
　Louise, 428
　Marie, 428
　Myrtle Thompson, 428
　W. A. (Dub), Jr., 428
　William Alvis Sr., 428
Bunch, June, 366
Bunker Hill (CV-17), 502
Burgess, David, 194
　Elaine, 199
　Forrest, 199
　Jim, 194
Burkhead, William, 37
Burks, Colonel John C., 40
Burma, 128, 142, 318, 437;
　　Burma-China Road, 257
Burns, Bennie, 515
Burrow, Jolace Ferrell, 507
Bush, Gov. George W., 210
Butts, Blaine, 275
　Deborah, 275
　Dr. T. R., 275
　Eulalia, 275
　Howell, 275
　Lela, 275
　Lydia Wycough, 275
　Paul Bradley, 275
　Paul H., 275
　Turner C., 275
Byers, Dillard, 381
　Dora, 382
　Etta Young, 381
　Frank, 382
　Gary Allen, 382
　J. L., 382
　Mae, 382

　Marvin, 382
　Mildred, 382
　Ruby, 382
　Ruth, 382
　Valton, 381
Bynum, Donald Rains, 158
C.C.C., , 331, 365, 397, 426,
　　441, 449, 448, 457, 472,
　　478, 514, 515
Cab Wolf, 354
Caddo Lake, 12
Cagle, Adelbert R., 212
　John, 304
　Ray, 158
　Sidney, 158
　Sidney, 372
　Vida, 17
Cain, Vella L. (Flaxie), 324
Caine, Ann, 392
Caldwell, Jasper Clinton, 212
Calhoun, Jessie, 100
Camp Adair, Oregon, 357,
　　369; Barkeley, 160, 260,
　　354; Beale, California,
　　369; Benjamin, 30;
　　Bowie, 48, 56, 67, 71,
　　84, 85, 231; Butner,
　　North Carolina, 266;
　　Carson, Colorado, 269,
　　419, 449; Chaffee,
　　Arkansas, 257, 419;
　　Claiborne, Lousiana,
　　322; Cody, N. M., 47,
　　50; Cook, California,
　　250; Coxcomb,
　　California, 342;
　　Crowder, Missouri, 264,
　　363; Detroit, 169;
　　Edwards,
　　Massachusetts, Camp
　　Gordon, Georgia, 240;
　　Elliot, California, 399;
　　Fannin, 216, 245, 246,
　　264, 522; George
　　Washington, 339;
　　Glouster, 482; Gordon
　　Georgia, 376; Grant,
　　Illinois, 354, 515
　　Gruber, 188; Hann,
　　California, 306, 339;
　　Holliday, 472; Hood,
　　Texas, 257, 320, 344,
　　356, 410; Hospitality,
　　31; Howze, 239, 320,
　　322, 345, 409; John C.
　　Burks, 40; Kilmer, New
　　Jersey, 243, 322, 324;
　　Limburg, 45;
　　Livingston, Louisiana,

239; Logan, Texas, 81; Mabry, 65; Mackall, North Carolina, 360; Maxey, 116, 186, 187, 191, 247, 259, 280, 324; McCoy, Wisconsin, 254; Merritt, New Jersey, 70; Mills, New York, 68, 71; O'Donnell, 359; Peary, Virginia, 303; Pendleton, 294; Pickett, Virginia, 339; Pike, Arkansas, 85; Pinedale, 437; Polk, Louisiana, 168, 243, 324, 342, 259, 260; Roberts, California, 316 Robinson, Arkansas, 336; Rucker, Alabama, 342, 366; San Luis, Obispo, California, 354; Shank, New York, 379, 409; Shelby, Mississippi, 344, 410, 434, 468; Stanley, 183; Stoneman, California, 468; Toccoa, 360; Travis, Texas, 48, 61, 65, 71, 82; Wallace, Texas, 361, 398; White, Oregon, 289; Wolters, 77, 260, 268, 288, 322, 339, 346, 361, 405; Young, California, 441
Campbell, Alfred, 475, 477
 Alton, 475
 Capt., 489
 Jacqueline Crawford, 475
 Katie Porton, 475
 Thomas E., 475
Canterbury, Charles Culberson, 397
 Charles Morris, 397
 Daisy Gentry, 397
 Evelyn, 397
 Jean, 397
 Minnie Lee, 397
 Robert Houston, 212, 397
 Virginia Ruth, 397
Cantrell, Nellie Gertrude, 363
Captain Smith, 494
Carlton, Ben, 75
 Bert H., 75
 Claude, 75
 Cora, 75
 Emma Martin Rains, 75
 Frances, 75
 Mary Jane, 75, 428
 Nola, 75
 Thomas, 75

Carney, Joan, 362
Caroline Islands, 285, 496, 508
Carpenter, Belle, 82
 Cynthia, 82
 Doshie, 63
 Homer Roy, 82
 John Franklin, 82
 Kate, 82
 Nancy Jane, 63
 Ola, 82
 Oran Gerald, 82
 Orlean Glazner, 82
 Sam H., 82
Carr, I. V., 523
Carsee, William M., 49
Carter, Verna, 82
Cass, Mr., 192
 Peggy, 353
Casten, Henry, 187
 Werner, 188
Castleman, Janice Mauldin, 27
 Martha Tennison, 27
 William, 27
 Thomas John, 27
Cathy, Myrtle, 480
Caviness, F. P., 48
 Odis W., 48
Chalons Sur Marne, 275
Chamberlain, Prime Minister Neville, 123, 125
Chambers, Claude, 244
Chaney, Elizabeth, 31
 Garrison, 31
 James M., 31
 William H., 31
Chanute Air Force Base, Illinois, 318, 341, 481
Charles, Clarence, 10
Charlie-Dog Ridge, 300
Cheatham, 337
Cherokee Nation, 36
Chesshire, Thelma Lorene, 371
Cheyne, Amos Dean, 71, 371
 Athalanda Furr, 71
 Betty, 371
 Bobbie, 371
 Brenda Gail, 371
 Bruce, 371
 Charles Oscar, 371
 Clyde, 71
 Connie, 371
 Dee, 71
 Donna, 371
 Effie, 71
 Hattie, 71
 James Howard, 371

Janice, 371
Jimmy Ray, 371
Joe Don, 71, 370
John Ray, 71, 371
Johny, 71
Josiah S., 71
Kevin, 371
Lanelle, 371
Lonie, 71
Louise, 71
Lydia Myrtle Boch, 370
Melinda, 371
Mollie, 71
O. T., 71
Oscar, 71
Oscar C., 370
Oscar Terry, 371
Randy, 371
Terris Glen, 371
Will, 71
Chickamauga, 30
Chickamauga Park, 32
Childers, Joan Carol, 421
 John H. Jr., 421
 M.D., John H., 421, 422
 Ruth Hancock, 421
Chiles, Maudie Mae, 371
Choctaw Nation, 22
Christian Church, 244
Chumley, Bruce, 430
 Chris, 430
 Emily Neal, 430
 Fred M., 430
 Grace, 430
 Harold L., 430
 Jeff, 430
 John, 430
 Rex, 430
 Tina, 430
Church of Jesus Christ of Latter Day Saints, 6, 327
Churchill, Prime Minister Winston, 119, 123, 125, 126, 128, 129, 142, 329
CIA, 484
Civil War, v, 4, 6, 9, 21, 24, 30, 31, 34, 36, 63, 80, 202, 202, 203
Civilian Conservation Corps, 523
Clack, Ana Bel, 293, 392
 Belle Lamb, 392
 Ben, 392
 Bennie Bee, 392
 Billy S., 392
 John C., 392
 Marianne, 392
 Mary Jo, 392

INDEX ★ 543

Claiborne, Jim, 103, 193, 194, 196, 261, 399, 432
   Lee Ivy, 103, 193
Clark, Alice Vaughan, 264
   Billy Joe (Bill), 447
   Frederick Scott, 448
   General Mark, 348, 478
   Golda Finley, 447
   Lori Vanessa, 448
   Wimbly, 447
   Wimbly Wade, 448
   Winifred, 85
Clarksville Cemetery, 29, 91; High School, 16, 171, 224, 239, 262, 337, 382, 444; Mounted Reserves, 27; Pharmacy, 157, 199, 219, 411; Standard, 30; Telephone Exchange, 48
Clay, Sr., Henry, 253
Cleaver, Wilma J., 360
Clement, Ezra, 171
   Julia, 171
Clements, "Clemo", 262
Clovis Army Air Base, 526
Coast Guard, 166, 202, 378
Coats, Cecil, 389
   Charles E. (Edward), 390
   Claude L. Boze, 389
   Dorene, 389
   Edward, 389
   Marvin, 389, 392
   Obed P., 389
   Onvie, 389
   Pam, 391
   Susan, 391
   Sybil, 389
Cobb, Claressa J., 337
Coca Cola Plant, 100
CoCo, Charles, 458
   Helen Ethel, 458
   Henry, 458
   Joseph Gilmore, 458
   Joseph Gilmore, Jr., 458
   Joseph Nathan, 458
   Mary Lenora Boudine, 458
   Viola, 458
Coffman, A. J., 37
   Andrew Jackson, 36
   David Micheral, 10
   Jacob, 11
   Jacob Warren, 36
   James, 11
   Martha Jane, 11, 12
   Lovell, 11, 12, 36
   M. T., 158, 212
   Pvt. Henderson, 159
   William, 37
   William Washington, 36

Cole, William, 5
Coleman, Ben, 47
   Berniece, 471
   Billy, 471
   Bupha Wilson, 471
   Clarence, 48, 66, 472
   Cleffie, 48
   Glen, 471
   James Larry, 471, 472
   John, 471
   John E., 212, 470
   John Edwin, 471, 472
   Olive, 471
   Paul, 66, 471
   Stroud R., 212
   Virginia Lewis, 471
Collins, Amos, 358
   Catherine, 358
   Debra Jean, 358
   Earnestine, 358
   Ernest Sutton, 159
   Henry, 358
   Howard, 358
   Ida Bell, 358
   James Lawrence, 358
   James Mick, 358
   Josephine, 61
   Nadra June, 358
   Norman, 358
   Ples, 358
   Ples Ricky, 358
   William Howard, 358
Coltharp, Glenn, 199
Coltharp twins, 196
Combs, Mr. and Mrs. Ollie, 469
   Orval Fredrick, 469
Como, Perry, 196
Company of Grenadiers, 27
Compton, Col. K. K., 335
Confederate, 21; Confederate Army, 5, 41; Hospital, v, 22; Monument, 40, 117, 118; Reunion, 37; Reunion grounds, 189
Congressman Wright Patman, 83
Conine, Faye 305
Connell, Buddy, 182
CONUS, 183, 270
Conway, Adell, 416
   Amanda, 93
   Arkansas, 441
   Betty, 416
   Bobby, 417
   David, 417
   Harold, 416
   Hattie, 93
   Ike Jr., 417

   Isaac F., 164, 417
   J. T., 94, 95, 318, 417
   Jerry, 93, 417, 418
   Joe, 93
   Joe Thomas, 416
   Karen, 417
   Katie Halbrooks, 416
   Larry, 417
   Linda, 417
   Marizanna, 417
   Mr. and Mrs. Joe Thomas, 164
   Patsy, 417
   Raliegh, 416
   Robert, 94, 416
   Russell, 94, 95, 416, 417, 418
   Stacy, 417
   William, 93
   Ora, 413
Cook, Alton, 416
   Charles, 416
   Elbert M., 48
   George B., 47
   John, 416
   Lewis, 416
   Lotene, 416
   Ora Christopher, 416
   Tommy, 416
Cooper, Bobbie Jane, 389
Coral Sea, 474; Battle, 369
Corbell, Annie Ruby Stevens, 319
   Billie, 319
   Carol, 319
   Charles R., 319
   Christine, 319
   Dorthy, 319
   Nina, 319
   Peggy, 319
   Ray, 319
   Tommie, 319
   William J. (Dude), Jr., 319
   William J., Sr., 319
Cork Forest, 390
Cornett, Beatrice, 441
   Harve, 304
   Jayne, 63
   Mr. and Mrs. A. J., 168
   Myrtle, 63
   Pvt. Travis, 168
   Sgt. Edgar R., 168
Cornetts, 96
Corregidor, 140, 141, 166, 224, 225, 305, 401, 513
Cotter, Chaplain, 187
Cotton, Charles W., 212
Couch, Arvil Lee, 341
   Dorothy, 341

Helen, 341
Herman, 341
Ira, 341
Judy, 341
Kenneth, 341
Mattie, 341
Mildred, 341
Noman, 341
Nonar, 341
Rickey, 341
Ruby, 341
Shirley, 341
Coulter, Nikki Jamal, 337
Council, Nancy, 504
Counts, Louis, 45
County Poor Farm, 18
Coursey, Mary Sue, 484
Court House, 66, 194, 195, 212
Cozort, Bobby, 246, 246
Coba, 246
James, 246
John, 246
Madeline, 246
Maj. (Retired), William M., 247
Maud Bannister, 246
Pvt. Bobby J., 247
Tom, 246
Virginia, 246
William (Maxie), 246
Crader, Clark, 251
Crater, John, 182
Crawford, B. F., 475
Creager, Paul, 190
Crenshaw, Etta, 75
Gertrude, 75
Henry, 75
John William, 75
Leatha, 75
Lettie, 75
Mark, 75
Mary Jane Stevens, 75
Patria, 75
Seaborn, 75
Thomas, 75
Willie, 75
Criner, John, 37
Critchlow, Arthur, 245
Crittenden, Thomas, 85
Cross, Albert Atlas, 376
Ida Frances Altom, 376
Marcell Atlas, 376
Margaret, 339
Rodney Gene, 376
Ronnie Marcell, 376
Winnie Bee, 384
Crow, Allie, 199
Cruces, A. L., 17

Cruisers, Detroit, 110; Helena, 110; Honolulu, 110; New Orleans, 110; Phoenix, 110; Raleigh, 110; San Francisco, 110; Stl Louis, 110
Crump, Faye Nellie, 469
Cuff, Ward, 105
Culpepper, Billy, 33
C. C., 33
Capos Conley "Chip", 33
Charles Capers, 34
County, Virginia, 29
Dan, 33
Elias Daniel, 34
Francis Marion, 34
John Jefferson, 34
John Malcolm, 31, 32, 34, 35
Private William Araspes, 35
Pvt. John M., 33
Robert Jefferson, 34, 35
Thomas, 33
William Araspes, 34
William Henry, 34
William Washington, 34, 35
Cunningham, 277
Cunningham, Barbara, 65
J. B., 267
D-Day, 130, 134, 172, 174, 246, 259, 275, 339, 511, 516
Dachau, 382; Concentration Camp, 383
Daladier, Premier Edouard, 123
Dalby, Captain Benjamin Bullock, 24
Green D., 24
Lucinda (Davis), 24
Warren K., 24
Dale, Bobbye N., 424
Darnell, Willie, 48
Davidson, Charles Edward, 470
Charles Jr., 470
Frances, 471
J. L., 471
Jo Nell Bell, 471
Joyce, 470
Joyce McBrayer, 471
Lou E. Davis, 470
Naomi, 471
Davis, Albert Houston, 291
Alva Mae, 291
Carl Ray, 292
Carolyn Fay, 292
James Houston, 292
Jefferson, 21

John D., 68
Marcell, 291
Margaret Marie, 292
Mary Gladys, 66, 68
Matt, 18
Mrs. Joe, 17
Naomi Mauldin, 229
Pearl Estella, 68
Vessie Lerner Jones, 291
William Jasper, 291
Dawson, Doris, 303
Eunice, 81
Day, Anna, 53
Callie, 51
Caroline, 51
Eddie M., 51
Guy Even, 51
Jessie H., 51
John Wesley, 51
Lester G., 53
Margie, 53
Mary Frances, 51
Murta, 51
Oma, 51
Opal, 51
Ora V., 51
Pvt. Guy E., 53
Ruby, 51
William Steven, 51
Dead Man's Gulch, 298
Deakons, C. L., 17
Dean, Amanda Clem Huddleston, 327
Edwin E., 327
James E., 327
James L., 327
John A., 327
John Robert, 327
Kelley Ruth, 327
M. Lynette, 327
Melba, 327
Deaver, Mack, 37
DeBerry, Alan, 57
Albert S., 57
Alice Jane Gaines, 57
Clarence, 57
Clarence Charles, 453
Dick, 10, 57, 453
Genevieve Moseley, 10, 453
Gordon, 57
Henry, 57
Henry Drew, 12
Janet, 453
Luther, 57
Martin Luther, 12, 57
Marvin W., 57
Mary Jane, 453
Minnie, 57
Paul H., 57

Susan, 453
Thomas A., 57
Thomas Arthur, 60
DeMorse, Col. Charles., 178
DeMorse House, 199
Dempsey, General Sir Miles, 130
Denison, Carlys, 438
Denny, Buford E., 212
Denton Hardware, 16
Denton, Calvin, 17
  John Carlton Woodson, 16
  Laura Mae, 17
  Lynn, 17
  Mason, 17
  Ray, 17
  Rozelle, 17
  Sarah Elizabeth (Perry), 17
Denton's Teachers College, 422
Depression, 15, 90, 91, 92, 95, 100, 229, 280, 401, 444
Derryberry, Lt. Miss Jewell, 158
Destroyer, Cassin, 113; Curtiss, 112; Downes, 113; Henley, 112; Monaghan, 112; Neosho, 113; Shaw, 113; Tangiers, 112; Ward, 114
DeShazer, Betty, 360
  Billy, 360
Deveraux, Major James P. S., 138
Deviney, Helen, 419
Devinney, Clarence, 518
Dickerson, Dorothy, 353
  Ernestine, 388
  Geraldine, 353
  Jimmie Lee, 353
  Louie, 353
  Maggie Gray Ricks, 353
Dickson, 10
  Bonnie, 7
  Clyde Johnson, 7
  Frank, 7
  John B. 7
Dickey's, John, Company of Scouts, 26
Dill, Doc, 118
Dillard, Lt. Col. Miles, 30
Dillow, Mary Fuller, 338
Dingee, Major G. S., 182
Dingee packing plant, 177
Dinwiddie, Addie, 199
  Ballard, 47
  Captain C. R., 234
  Miss Addie, 195
  Roy, 118

197
Dixon, Martha J., 84
Dodd, Birty Lee Holliway, 97, 253
Cora, 13
Danise Ann, 254
David, 98
David Hiram, 253
H. C., 19
Henry, 97
Henry Clay III, 254
Herschel, 13
Hiram Cornelius Franklin, 13
Dodd, Jr., Henry Clay (Jack), 13, 96, 97, 253
Kristy Lynn, 254
Martha (Dutch), 13
Mary Lee, 98, 253
Stephen, 48
Dolan, Patrick, 22
Dombrowski, Bombadier Lt., 351
Donaldson Air Force Base, South Carolina, 481
Doolittle, Jimmy, 209
  Rep John, 458
Dorsey, Tommy, 196, 390
Douglas, Alton, 505
  Jamie, 505
Dowdal, James F. (Dowdell), 31
Dowdell, Colonel James, 34
Dozier, Edward Glenn, 411
  Elizabeth, 411
  Joe, 411
  Mandy Hightower, 411
  Mary, 411
  Sybil, 411
  Verna Fay, 411
Dragon Teeth, 269
Drake, Cristal, 421
Drug Store News, 157
Dudley, Alice, 309
  Lucy Ann Haley, 309
  Reuben, 309
  Wanda, 371
Duffie, Wanda, 424
Duke, Louise, 420
Dunne, Lois, 264
Durham Station, North Carolina, 35
Durrum, Beulah Fulton, 429
  Dr. Will, 429
  W. L., 429
Dycus, Sgt. Morris, 158
Dyer, Fred, 348
Dysart, Parson, 23
'E. Petty', 381

Earley, Arvelee, 249
  Brent, 250
  Carolyn, 250, 249
  Charles, E., 250
  Keith Stanley, 249
  Larry, 250
  Mary Virginia Holley, 249
  Pam, 249
  Robert, 249
  Roger, 249
  Steve, 249
  Thomas N., 249
  Vernon, 249, 253
  Winnie Dodd, 249
Early Birds Radio Show, Dallas, 198
Eason, Alberta Ileene, 525
  Cleoria Magdaline, 523
  J. T., 523
  John Thomas, 523
  Lois Emiline, 523
  Mary Palestine Tucker, 523
East Carolina Teachers College, 280
East Ward School, 200
Edmonson, Alma Lee, 388
  Capt., 453
Edrington, Ima, 18
Edwards, Eula M., 353
  Lt. Ben F., 168
  Mr. and Mrs. Frank, 168
Eichelberger, Lietenant General Robert L., 143
Eiffel Tower, 255, 517
8th Brigade, 36
80th Infantry Division, 275
84th Division, 170; Infantry, 324
86th Division, 338; Infantry Division, 307
88th 'Blue Devil' Infantry Division, 161, 216; Rangers, 320
829th AAF Bomb Squadron, 405
Eighth Army, 150
Eiler, Franklin, 158
Eisenhower, Dwight D., 107
  General, 129, 130, 134, 135, 136, 255
  Mrs., 108
  President, 203, 525
Ella Stafford, 289
Ellett, W. A., 5
Ellicombe, Captain Robert, 41
Elliot, Dr., 23
Elliott, Bill, 117
Ellis Island, New York, 396

Elmwood Cemetery, 36
Elson, Gertie, 505
Elysian Garden Club, 159
Emery, Aaron Lewis, 346
　Ardell D., 346
　Betty, 484
　Bruce, 346
　Jessie Marie, 389
　Leonard, 45
　Marna Bowman, 346
　Romie Tolison, 346
　Sgt. Darcus W., 158
Enola Gay, 294, 487
Enox, Willie T., 212
Enterprise, 109, 114, 115
Epps, Darrell Elbert, 412
　Edna Jewel, 411
　Elbert S., 411
　Eliza A. Blankingship Epps, 411
　George W., 411
Eric Bollman's Store, 199
Ervin, Arthur B., 212
Escort Carrier Hoggatt Bay, 258; Cavalry, 27
Esso Bolivar, 426, 427
Ester, Mary, 9
Eudy, Callie, 420
　Don, 420
　Henry O., 420
　Howard, 420
　Hubert Preston, 420
　Leland Hugh, 420
　Lucy Williams, 420
　Lynn Howard, 420
　Mary Alice, 420
　Mercedes Maurine, 420
　Mickey Hugh, 420
　Phoebe Joyce, 420
European Theater, 443, 505
Evans, Geneva, 332
Everhart, Benson D., 461
　Gilbert C., 461
　Jack H., 461
　Marion D. (Bud), 461, 463
　Maudie A. Alsbrook, 461
　Michaelynn D., 461
　Opal M., 461
　Paul E., 461
　Steven B., 461
Evetts, Clinton, 196
　Curtis, 196, 198
Exparza, Virginia C., 402
Exum, Bob, 322
　Carol, 321
　Gail, 322
　James Byron, 321
　Leon Conine, 321
　Nelson, 322

　Rickey, 322
　Sharon, 322
　Tom, 199, 321
　Tommie, 321
　Weldon, 322
Exums, 96
Fairfield Air Force Base, 313
Fairview Cemetery, 65, 268
Faith O'Clyde Harbor, 339
Farley, Belle San, 304
　Bert Tate, 304
　Doris, 304
　Emma, 304
　Florence, 304
　Hershel, 304
　Mamie, 304
　Marjorie, 304
　Rachel, 304
　Tom, 304
　Wayman, 304
Farnady, Frank, 330
Farrier, B., 197
　Isobel, 157
Farris, Ice, 11
　Isham, 5
Faucett, Bennie W., 212
Feeley, Lt. E. G., 333, 335
Fellows, Donna, 461
Felts, Almyra Pirkey, 85
　John T. Jr., 85, 212, 380, 397
　Jonn T., Jr. Auxiliary # 45, 16
　John T. Sr., 85, 211, 397
　Marian Patricia, 85, 157, 397
　Thomas Franklin, 85
　Winifred Clark Felts, 397
Ferguson, Dane, 341
　Louise, 341
Field, Shelly Storey, 355
5th Arkansas Infantry, 25; Engineers, 55
50th Illinois Volunteers Infantry, 28
513rd Parachute Infantry, 418
Fifth Amphibious Corps, 172; Engineers, 80;
　Fleet, 146, 153
'Fifty Two-Twenty Club,' 191
Fighting Two, 173
Finley, Callie Eudy, 420
　David, 360
　Imogene, 360, 361
　James, 360
　John, 360
　Oneida Taylor, 360
　William F., 360
　William L., 360

1st and 6th Marine Divisions, 154
1st Field Artillery Brigade, 86; Marine Division, 144; MS Artillery, C.S.A., 26; Virginia Regiment, 27
First Baptist Church, 66, 485; in Clarksville, Texas, 7; in Bonham, 525
First Canadian contingent, 86
First Christian Church, 511; of Clarksville, 304
First Methodist Church, Paris, Texas, 185
First Presbyterian Church, 16
Firth of Clyde, Scotland, 383
Fisher, Allen, 72
　Bernard Francis, 202
　Bill, 72
　Thomas C., 72
　Tommy, 72
Flanagan, H. C., 285
　Hugh, 285
　Nettie Smith, 285
　Patsy, 285
　Regenia, 285
　Velma, 285
Flippo, Electra, 412
Floyd, Amos, 254
　Darwin, 254
　Florence Stout, 254
　James Dean, 254
　Jan, 254
　Joan, 254
　John C., 254
　John D., 254
　Leslie, 45
　Mack, 254
　Paul, 254
Fly, Letha Jo, 194
Flying Tiger Base, Liuchow, 437
Fobbs (Forbes) Cemetery, 5
Fodge, Mary Aline, 317
Fogelman, Earldene, 254
Fogleman, Mary, 261
Fooks, John, 358
Ford, Ann, 398
　G. W., 27
　Genieviene, 398
　George, 398
　George D., 398
　Janice, 398
　Jean, 398
　Joe, 27, 67, 398
　John, 398
　John K. 398
　Joyce, 398

INDEX ★ 547

Justine, 398
Mae Kelley, 398
Martha Ramage, 27
Susan Maxine (Mackie Mae), 55
Forester, Mr. and Mrs. John, 165
Robert, 165
Sgt. William H. (Bill), 165, 213
Forrestal, James, 493
Fort Benning, Georgia, 229, 234, 271, 317, 325, 328, 342, 360, 417, 418; Bliss, Texas, 245, 292; Chaffee, Arkansas, 346; Dix, New Jersey, 84, 260, 339; Frances E. Warren, 224; Hood, Texas, 271, 285, 317, 353; Knox, Kentucky, 168, 243, 282, 327, 331, 397; Leonardwood, Missouri, 524; Lewis, Washington, 232, 250, 282, 289, 369; Logan, Colorado, 364; McArthur, California, 442; McClellan, Alabama, 317, 414; Meade, Maryland, 471; Ord, California, 219, 239, 240, 285, 316, 360, 365; Riley, Kansas, 243, 305, 394; Robinson, Arkansas, 292; Sam Houston, 53, 107, 241, 254, 256, 285, 312, 322, 339, 341, 357, 369, 401, 417, 453; Shanks, New York, 483; Sill, Oklahoma, 165, 242, 285, 289, 309, 347, 354, 413; Smith, Arkansas, 336, 353; Towson, Oklahoma, 318; Vaux, 44; Warren, Wyoming, 306; William McKinley, 171, 358; Wolters, Texas, 293, 333
Foster, Anna, 366
Bobby Neal, 366
Carl, 366
Dale, 366, 366
Dennis Kevin, 366
Donald Casey, 366
Donna Jean, 366
Eddie Dale, 366
Elmo Kidd, 366

Geary, 366
Jo Ann McDonald, 68
Juanita, 366
Kenneth, 366
Kidd, 366
Lorena A., 370
Lucien Paul, 366
Myrtle Casey, 366
Richard, 366
Ronald, 366
Susan Marie, 366
Teresa, 366
Vickie, 366
Virginia, 366
Foster Field, 347
4th Marine Division, 145; Marines, 226
14th Machine Gun Battalion, 53
40th and 8th, 72
42nd Bomb Group, 312; Field Hospital, 515; Rainbow Division, 57
43rd Infantry Division, 165
44th Regiment, 51
47th Artillery, 84; Infantry, 277
446th Antiaircraft Artillery Battalion, 306
464th Motor Transportation Company, 61
Fourth Division, 299; Marine Division, 294, 296, 303
Fowler, A. D., 431
Alver J., 431
Bessie Marie, 400
Dewey Harvey, 400
Elizabeth Ruth, 400
Essien, 47
George D., 431
Josie Mae, 431
Lina Hays, 400
Mildred Louise, 400
Mr. and Mrs. J. L., 431
Oscar M., 213
Oscar Maurice (Bud), 400
Oscar William, 400
T. C., 431
Thomas, 325
William M., 431
Franklin, Berniece (Billy), 347
Frederick, Hubert, 47
Freeman, John T., 213
French 2nd Armored Division, 132; Frigate Sound, 220
French, Gloria Ann, 254
Fryar, Donald, 199

Thomas Jefferson, 37
Fuchida, Commander Mitsuo, 109
Fudske, Mrs. Hawkins, 427
Fukuoka Prison Camp, 457
Fuller, Everett, 324
Fulton, Eliza, 27
William, 37
Funk, Cyrus H., 397
Cyrus Jr., 397
Elizabeth Inskeep, 397
Hubert J., 213
Hubert Jacob, 397
Margaret, 397
Gable, Jr., Arthur, 213
Gaddis, Austin, 71
Gaddis, Bell Peek, 71
Billy, 71
Cary, 71
Doris, 71
Dorothy, 413
E. G., 71
Eula, 71
Henery, 71
John, 71
Patsy, 71
Raymond, 71
Gaines, Alice Jane, 12, 29
Artie, 29
Bob, 37
Col. Thomas W., 12, 27, 28, 29
Eliza, 29
Thomas, Jr., 29
W. A., 37
Gaines Drug Store, 483
Gallender, Leoran Chester, 213
Gamble, George, 180
Garland Cemetery, 55, 513
Garmon, Birdie Etta Tate, 514
Charlene, 514
James Haden (Pete), 514
Joseph Haden, 514
Mary Lou, 514
Paul, 514
William Morris (Buddy), 514
Garner, George W., 47
John Nance, 3
Garrett, Benjamin A., 270
Harold James, 466
Ninny Era Stafford, 466
Rufus E., 213
Sallie Elise, 466
Samuel Knox, 466
Stanley David, 466
Garson, Greer, 191

Gate City Medical College, in Texarkana, 26
Gathings, Adam, 378
Geary, Doris Rae, 313
   Inis Caviness, 313
   Raymond, 313
Geer, G. W., 324
   Jim, 195
Geers, Paul, 310, 311
Gehring, Tommie, 394
Geiger, Major General Roy S., 146, 154
General Hasbrook, 343
   John R. Hodge's XXIV Army Corps, 154
   Krueger's Sixth Army, 150
   Smith's V Marine Amphibious Corps, 145
George, Harry D., 351
Gettysburg, 80
Ghormley, Admiral, 143, 144
   Vice Admiral Robert L., 142, 143, 144
GI Bill, 191
Gibbs, Delma, 49
   Fannie Miller Thompson, 49
   Jakie, 49
   James Preston, 49
   Joe, 85
   Joe and Argent Bradford, 51
   Joseph Melvin, 49
   Lovice, 49
   Margie, 49
   Moses Calvin, 49
   Nora, 49
   Paul, 49
   Rosa, 49
   Silas, 49
   Sue, 75
   Venita Jo, 49
Gibson, Babe, 96
Giddens, Homer A., 158
   William Albert, 213
Gilbert, Anne, 72
   Betty Jo, 327
   Cathy, 327
   Hattie Pritchett, 327
   John, 327, 332
   Joseph, 327
   Leiron, 72
   Margaret Pauline, 72
   Mrs. William, 72
   Neal, 327
   Paul, 72
   Rev. William, 72
   Susan, 327
   Winfred, 72, 75

Gilbert Island, 145, 173, 220, 465, 481
Gilliam Cemetery, 67, 212; Horace Greeley, 89
Gist, William James, 213
Glenn, Abigile Ellen Tillory, 81
   Charles O. (Oscar), 81
   David H., 81
   Geraldine, 81, 437
   Johnnie, 72
   Mary Elizabeth, 81, 381
Glenview Naval Air Station, 249
Glover, Joe, 333
   Margaree, 333
Goebbels, Paul Josef, 136
Goering, Hermann, 188
Goings, Hattie, 53
Gold Beach, 130
Goldstein, Henry, 526
Gonzales, Scott, 51
Goode, Beatrice Bliss Williamson, 507
   Billy Ray, 507
   Carroll Glynn, 507
   Debra Renee, 507
   Gerald Franklin, 507
   James Ross, 507
   Michael Richard, 507
   Robert E. (Mickey), 507
   Robert E., 507
Gooding, Clarence Edward, 442
   Harriet, 442
   Minni Amanda Suitor, 442
   Richard Morgan, 442
   Robert, 442, 443
   Robert Edward, 443
   Ronnie, M.D., 442
   William Carroll, 443
Goodman, Benny, 390
   Bonnie Jo, 61, 380
   Charles Leslie, 60
   Dick, 380
   Ellis, 45, 61, 324
   Faye, 101
   Fred, 18
   Fred Lee, 60
   James Dale, 61
   James Ellis, 61, 380
   John, 101
   John Purvie, 61, 101, 324
   John Robert, 60
   Josephine Collins, 380
   Kelsey, 92, 101, 189
   Lucina Evaline Barmore, 60, 61
   M. T., 18

   Martin T., 61
   Mary Evelyn, 61, 380
   Mary Payne, 380
   Mrs. J. P. (Ruby), 91
   Ollen Ellis, 60, 380
   Robert Ervin, 60
   Sena Etta, 61
   William Jesse, 61
Gould's 23rd Texas Cavalry, 9
Gouldsberry, Mildred McFarland, 480
Grady, Wm. M., 47
Graham, Preacher, 37, 66, 195, 199
Grant, Dowdy, 316
   Jonathan Bryant, 317
   Lewis Bryant, 316
   Louise, 429
   May Bryant, 316
   Sgt. Lewis, 430
   Ulysses S., 35, 28
   William, 316
Gray, Luther L., 158
   Marguerite, 318, 417
   Mary, 264
   Mose, 47
   Robt., 47
Grayson, Dr., 99
   Miriam, 293
Great Depression, 88, 89, 96
Great Locomotive Chase, The, 202
Green, Alec, 31
   Berdie Buena Gregg, 315
   Carl, 315
   Clarence Otho, 315
   Cpl. Floyd, 159
   Cpl. Nowlin, 158
   Floyd, 372
   Hollister S., 315
   Loyd Ray, 315
   Willa Mae, 316
Griffin, Alex, 48
   Billy Pat, 315
   Sgt. A. N., 158
Grimes, Charlie T., 81
   James Augustus, 81
   Sam H., 81
   Senator James W., 202
   Tennessee Lucille Fisher, 81
Grubbs, Tho., 24
Guadalcanal, 144, 207, 296, 363, 416, 453, 462, 472
Guam, 137, 138, 146, 147, 151, 221, 289, 296, 299, 386, 398, 399, 417, 433, 446, 447, 454, 486, 488, 506, 507, 520

Guantanamo Bay Naval Base, 427
Guards, Rosalie, 25
Guarke, Floyd, 47
Guest, Isaac, 2
  John Martin, 3
Guest's Prairie, 3, 8
Guidry, Carroll F., 512
Guinn, Lou Ella, 309
Guinndolyn Lane, 309
Gullion, Charlie Senter, 281
  Christine Barnett, 312
  Elic, 281
  Fieldon, 281
  George R.(Dick), 281
  James Paul, 213
  James Richard, 281
  John, 281
  Nannie Ruth, 307
  Rena, 281
  Susie Kate, 281
  Tammie Jean, 281
Gunther, Hugh Michael Sharpe, 247
Guthrie, Alice, 306
Haberer, Frances, 448
Haggerton, Eileen, 442
Halbrooks, Katie, 93
Hale, Guy, 37
  Jr, Charlie F., 158
Hall, Catherine, 387
  Curtis Doward, 387
  Edith Emery, 281
  Garlin, 387
  Grace, 387
  Juanita, 281
  Patricia, 387
  Sidney, 281
  Virgie Cox, 387
Halsey, 208, 209
  Admiral, 109
Halsey's Third Fleet, Admiral, 149
Hamilton Air Force Base, 313
Hamilton, LeRoy, 158
Hamm, Shirley Sloan, 318
Hampton, Principal Charles G., 351
Hancock, Margie, 413
Hand, Mable, 425
Haralson, Elizabeth, 34
Harcrow, J. R., 324
Hardman, Mary Jo, 92, 93
Hargus, Alfred Pete, 325
  Doris M., 325
  Edna Edwards, 325
  Jennie C. Toney, 325
  Norris L., 213, 325
Harmening, Anson Boyd, 515

Dixie Dimple, 515
Dorothy, 515
Florence Johnston, 515
Lucilla, 515
Oliver P., 515
Pete, 519
Royce, 515
Thomas Fletcher, 515
Harris, Doug, 330
  Fred, 47
  Jane, 351
  Joseph Henry, 35
Haskins, Kenneth, 82
Hasting's Service Station and Garage, 17
Hastings, Cassandra (Raulston), 25
  Effie Lillian, 65
  Gilbert, 17
  William H. , 5
  William Henry, 25
Hatcher, Dixon, 262
Hatton, Lt. Bill, 335
Hawkins, Cleo, 379
  Earl, 379
  Etta, 379
  Eugenia Kay, 379
  Horace E. (Gene), 379
  Irene, 379
  Isabel, 379
  Lilie May, 379
  Mammie, 379
  Mary Jane Askins, 379
  Roger G., 379
  William John, 379
Hawkins Fudske, The, 427
Hayes, Berl Swancy, 258
  Billy Wayne, 258
  Dorothy Jo, 258
  Edna Sewell, 258
  Effie, 258
  Gavin Edward, 258
  James Earnest, 258
  Jennie Mae Cherry, 258
  Kenneth, 258
  Lorene Screws, 258
  Louise, 258
  Lucille, 258
  Margaret, 258
  Muriel, 258
  Nella Park, 258
  S/2 C James Marvin, 258
  Willie, 258
Hays, Billy, 196
  Gabby, 117
  Walker, 196
Hefflefinger, James, 5
Heidelberg, 323
Hemingway, James, 388

Norman, 158
Henderson Field, 144
Henderson, John M., 213
  Watha Jo (Stroud), 194
Henry, Bonnie Kay, 389
  Ernest Franklin, 266
  Francis Elizabeth, 389
  Fred, 389
  James Travis, 389
  Mattie Jane, 266
  Mattie Louise, 389
  Mrs. Effie, 18, 192
  Nannie Baker, 266
  Pearl Smith, 389
  Robert L., 389
  Samuel Franklin, 266
  Travis, 158
  Travis S., 388
Hensley, 452; Hensley Field, 455
Herdle, Wilma C., 424
Herrignton, Phoebe Ann Atterberry, 424
Herring, Joyce, 420
Herrington, Bertha, 424
  Carol, 425
  Cecil, 424
  Charles, 425
  Clifton T., 424
  Donnie D., 425
  Ethel, 424
  Eula, 424
  Jim, 424
  Laura, 425
  Lonnie, 424, 425
  Maggie, 424
  Ona, 424
  Vera, 424
  Wayne, 424
Heston's Drug Store, 326
Hewitt, American Vice-Admiral Henry K., 133
Hickam Field, 111
Hickman, Tom, 19
Hicks, Elizabeth A., 397
Higgins boat, 172
Higgins, Fred, 103
  Gerald D., 158
Hill, Audrey Lee, 53
  Billy Bob, 53
  Captain Arthur, 512
  George Eugene, 53
  Jessie P., 53
  Martha A. Fletcher, 53
  Martha Jane, 53, 384
  Mrs. G. F., 33
  Neva Jo, 53
  Robert Jessie, 53
  Verdun, 53

Virginia, 448
Wilma Earl, 53
Hindenburg Line, 69
Hiroshima, 109, 156, 252, 379, 467, 528
Hitler, 123, 124, 125, 126, 127, 128, 131, 134, 207, 255, 289, 383, 478, 500; Adolf, 122, 136, 231; Youth School, 517; Stadia, 518
Hoald, Thomas Dwight, 158
Hocker, Emma Kneisley, 398
   Sam K., 381, 398
   Sam Lennox, 398
   Sam T., 398
Hodges, Lieutenant General Courtney H., 132, 321
Hoffman, Helen, 355
   Sonja Alexander, 280
'Hogan's Heroes,' 492
Holder, Lucy Bell, 13
Holland, Martene, 286
   Mrs. M. A., 159
Holley, Britt Alan, 339
   Charles, 338
   Charles M., 338
   Charles T. (Skeet), 338
   Dorothy, 338
   Hugh (Bud), 338
   James B. (Ballard), 338, 339
   Jim, 253
   Johnny, 338
   Kathy, 338
   Mary Virginia, 253
   Phyllis Carol, 339
   Rosa Sinclair, 253
   Rosie McGill, 338
Hollingsworth, Lindo, 191
   R. B., 48
Holloway, Amy Jo, 440
   Clyde Burett, 318
   Fannie Reynolds, 440
   Harold, 440
   Hubert Harmon, 318
   John Ramsey, 440
   Kathryn, 440
   Lloyd, 372
   Lloyd L., 213, 318
   Mary Jane Taylor, 318
   Mary Ruth, 440
   Miss Dean, 182
   O. S., 440
   Opal Etheline, 318
   Sara Lou, 440
   Walter, 440
   William Foster, 318
   Willie Mildred, 318
Holster, Jake, 345, 381

Homma, Lieutenant General Masaharu, 139, 141, 142
Hooker, Iva Lassiter, 7
Hooser, Dan, 242
   Helen, 242
   Henry, 196
   J. C., 242
   Jesse C., 242
   Joe J. (Jodie), 213, 242
   Lela, 242
   Lillie, 242
   Mable, 242
   Mary Williams, 242
   Melvin, 242
   Omie, 242
   Ramah, 242
Hoover, Onus, 95
   President Herbert, 88
Horn, Dorothy Nell, 248
   Howard, 315
Horne, James, 167
   Lawrence, 167
   Lt. Paul E., 167
   Mary Alice, 167
   Mr. and Mrs. Will C., 167
   Ruth, 167
   S/Sgt. Frank F., 167
Houston, Cap, 47
Howard, Cathryn, 11
Howison, Capt. Jack, 168
   Edna, 5
   Graham, 362
   John M., 77, 361, 362
   John Neil, 362
   Marha Lynne, 362
   Mr. and Mrs. J. W., 168
   Neil M., 80
   Raviah Sullivan, 362
   Stephen Carney, 362
   Virginia, 80, 347
   William Clatterbuck "Buck", 80
Howland, Ann, 428
   Beaula, 428
   Cecil C., 213, 428
   Don, 428
   Ernest, 428
   Floyd, 428
   Hoyt H., 428
   Jessie, 428
   Jimmy, 428
   John, 428
   Ludy, 428
   Maple, 428
   Mattie Scarbrough, 428
   Roy, 428
   Terri, 428
   Will, 428
   Willie, 428

Hubbard, J. M., 37
Huddleston, Betty, 307
Hughes, Rev. J. S., 33
Hughston, Ross, 159
   Sam, 80
Hulen, John Wallace, 213, 320, 344
   Rena Gladys Moore, 342, 344
   Robert Allen (Slim), 193, 342, 344
   Robert C. (Bob), 342, 344
   Sally, 342, 344
Hulsey, Ruth, 438
Hume, Bessie Burtrude Galbreath, 277
   Erbert, 277
   Frank, 277
   Ina, 277
   Lleen, 277
   Maurine, 277
   Milan, 277
   Milow, 277, 279
   Nonie, 277
   Thelma, 277
   Weldon, 277, 279
Humphrey, Johnnie Lee, 359
   Louis, 77
   Mack, 198
   Ouida Westbrook, 376
   Sammy, 168, 369
   W. V., 334
   William, 93
   Wilma Tucker, 357
Humphries, William, 27
Huneke, Kathryn, 221
Hunt Family, 194
   Annie Malinda, 62
   Bernard, 459
   Betty Ann, 194
   Cleophas Daniel, 62
   Cpl. Edward F., 61
   Cynthia, 194
   Henry Dudley, 62
   Jesse May, 62
   John Paul, 194
   John Vasco, 62
   Lela Ethel, 62
   Oliver Randall, 62
   Richard, 350
   S. H., 61
   Samuel Buford, 62
   Samuel Hinson, 61
   Sudie Florence, 62
   Susan Caroline McLeroy, 62
   Thomas George, 62
Hunter College, New York City, 444

Index ★ 551

Hutchins, Lynnie, 474
Hutchinson, Lou, 234
  Louise Ward, 94, 234
  Thomas S., 186, 234
  Tommy, 234
Hutson, Elbert Ray, 403
  John Tim, 403
  Mr John T., 161
  Mrs. John T., 161
  Roy Lee, 161, 403
  Ruby Lois, 404
  Sally Runi Windham, 403
  Tellas Andrew, 403
Icenhower, Ann Alsobrook, 526
  Billy, 526
  Charles, 526
  Joel, 526
  Junior, 526
  Kathalee, 526
  Ken, 526
  Kirk, 526, 528
  Kirk Norvel, 526
  Lee Bell Guest, 526
  Luther C., 526
  Ronnie, 526
Igo, Ella Jean, 417
  Harry, 158
  Mildred, 490
Imposter's Hill, 298
influenza, 3, 49
Ink Spots, 196
Irvin, Allan, 508
  Rev. Richard, 485, 346
  Leslie, 277
Irwin, Assistant Surgeon Bernard, 202
Isbell, Annie Halbrooks, 317
  Bob, 417
Isbell Frances, 171
  George, 83, 170,
  Gerald, 83, 170, 213
  Gilbert, 317
  Jim, 83
  John, 83
  John, Jr., 317, 318
  Louraine, 83
  Mary Susan Westbrook, 83
  Pauline, 317
  Robert Carroll, Jr., 83
  Sam, 83
  Thurman Robert (Bob), 317
  Virginia, 317
  Will, 83
Ivy, E. Q., 19
  Maud, 83
  Sarah Lee, 261
  Willie, 261

Iwo Jima, 151, 152, 172, 173, 192, 234, 284, 295, 296, 299, 302, 399, 409, 410, 415, 417, 454, 488, 493, 496, 497, 507
Jackson, Coreene Askins, 387
  Curtis, 213
  David Richard, 387
  H. D., 326, 368
  John H., 387
  Lemuel, 9
  Mattie, 368
  Maude Ruth, 387
  Richard, 221
  Tennessee, 332
  Will, 47
  William Richard, 387
Jakes's Creek School, 92
James, Harry, 390
Jamison, Barbara A., 487
  Billy F., 487
  Captain, 25
  Carroll Moore, 487
  David Carroll, 487
  Debra L., 487
  Elizabeth Cline, 487
  Frank Hopkins, 487
  J. K. P., 25, 37
  John David, 487
  John Patrick, 487
  Joseph Dinwiddie, 487
  Kimberely, 487
  Nancy, 182, 461, 487
  Vera Christene Whitsell Southard, 487
  Virgie Hopkins, 487
  Virginia Ann Moore, 487
Japanese Empire, 155; Fleet, 115
Jefferies, Ann, 117
Jeunesse, Hilary, 413
  Ione, 413
  Wayne, 413
Johnson, Ada Hall, 371
  Bert T., 371
  Buster, 371
  Carl Wright, 47
  Col., 27, 335
  Cpl. Martin (Buddy), 166
  Diane, 371
  Donald, 371
  Fred, 158
  Hiram, 108
  J. Haskell, 182
  John A., 185
  Johnny, 371
  Kay, 371
  Leonard, 198
  Major J. M., 463

  Martin L., 213
  Vice President Lyndon B., 525
Johnston, 22
Johnston, General Joseph E., 35
Jolley, J. T., 270
Jolley's Funeral Home, 270
Jones, Ada Kemp, 425
  Alvis, 425
  Arvel, 94
  Charles David, 213
  Dr., 13
  Henry, 47
  John Paul, 332
  Lomax W., 213
  Major General Albert M., 140
  Mrs. Clara M., 164
  Nollie Gaye Perkins, 485
  P. H., 425
  Pauline, 83
  Pvt. Bobby D., 164
  Robert C. Jones, Jr., 485
  Robert C. Sr., 485
  Ruby N., 309
  V. D., 17
  Vernon H. (Bud), 485
  Will, 47
Jonesborough, 11
Jordan Bus Lines, 194
Joyner, Alvin, 221
  Alvin D. (Durwood), 158, 221, 223, 228
  Betty Crabtree, 221
  David, 221
  Diane, 227
  General Stevenson, 83
  Janet, 227
  Lena, 221, 223
  Myrtle, 224
  Neil, 221
  Rev. A. C., 84
  Robert Ray, 221
Juno Beach, 130
Kaiser, 74
Kaiser's Cleaners, 267
Kakazu, Okinawa, 469; Ridge, 470
Kamikaze, 150, 153, 154, 252, 270, 509
Kane, Col., 335
Keenan, Mary Adele "Sitty", 489
Keesler Field in Mississippi, 313
Keisser, Arkansas, 257
Keli Ridge, 488
Kelley Air Base, 441

Kelsoe, Betty Metts, 241
  Dorothy Louise, 399
Kennedy, Charles L., 213
  President John F., 525
Kern, Jerome, 196
Kidd, Sam C., 526
  Sgt., 528
King, Berris, 468
  Carla Miller, 321
  Commander, 224
  Dan, 468
  Earl Lee, 424
  Elizabeth, 424
  Elvira Levene Wright, 423
  Henry Harvey, 423
  Henry Lane (Buck), 468
  Joel, 468
  Joella, 400
  Johnnie Rudolph, 468
  Johnny, 314
  Jr., Otis, 158
  Kay, 468
  Mabel, 423
  Major General Edward P., 141
  Mary, 423
  Milton Nuil (Bill), 468
  Nellie Elizabeth Mace, 468
  Richard Neil, 424
  Robert Blanton (R. B.), 468
  Rufus, 423
  S. J., 468
  Seth,D., 424
  Virgie, 100, 423
  Wayne H., 424
  Willie, 423
  Wilma, 424
  Wilson, 304
  Winnie, 100, 423
Kinkaid, Admiral Thomas C., 145
Kinkaid's Seventh Fleet, Admiral Thomas C., 149
Kirby, Jerome, 47
Kirker, Virginia, 424
Kirkland, Mary, 289
Kiwanai's Club, 396; Minstrels, 198
Knight, Lt. Col. Terry, 458
Korea, 207, 270, 282, 283, 327, 337, 356, 385, 429, 454, 464, 477, 497
Korean Conflict, 338, 355, 389, 460, 481, 497, 507, 522; War, 202, 270
Kostelantez, Andre, 196
Kougphmann, 10

Ku Klux Klan, 26
Kunkel, Lucille, 94
  , Martha Ann, 378
Kyle, Benjamin Franklin, 464
  Bessie, 464
  Florence Foster, 464
  Mack McKenzie, 464
  Mae, 464
  Margaret, 402
  Patsy Aylene, 464
  Ronald William, 464
  William Howard, 464
Lackland AFB, 402
Lahourcade, Lt. Col., 517
Lamarr, Hedy, 159
Lamb, Elenor, 425
  John Thomas, 241
  Lorraine, 241
  Mary Lucille, 240
Landers, Martha Louise, 377
Lanes Chapel Baptist Church, 469; Cemetery, 229
Langley Field, Virginia, 383
Langston, Sherrie, 279
Lanza, Mario, 196
Lassister, Emily Jane, 8
  Sgt. Hskell R., 160
Lassiter, Mr. Bryan, 160
  Mrs. Bryan, 160
Laster, John A., 357
Latimer, Albert, 4
  Big Dan, 37
  Fulton, 45
  Henry Russell, 4
  James Wellington, 4
  James, 4
  Lt., 174
  Lt. John D., 173
Lawler, Hazel Aliene, 423
  Martin, 438
Lawson, Bess Harvey, 456
  Bryan Wayne, 456
  Carolynn, 457
  Charles Ted, 457
  Christine, 309
  James Edward, 457
  John, 456
  John Harvey, 456
  John Robert, 457
  Joyce Illene, 456
  Mrs. J. H., 174
  Mrs. Jack, 485
  Olive Ruth, 456
  Roger S., 457
  Roger S. Jr., 457
  Ted Stiles, 457
  Thomas L., 213
  Thomas Lafayette, 456
  Tibitha Bess, 456

Vivian Ann, 457
League of Nations, 123
Leavelle, Hasseltine (Tiny), 326
Lee, Afton, 413
  Cap, 511
  Cornelia Ann, 388
  Edward, 413
  Gene, 189
  General, 24
  Harrison, 83, 388
  Houston, 413
  Isaac, 23
  Janie Pryor, 413
  Jess, 413
  Leonard Joe, 413
  Pauline Jones, 388
  Robert E., 22, 35
  William C., 83, 388
  William Charles Jr., 388
Lemon, Curtis, 196
Lennox, Bagby, 101
  Mary Ann, 398
Leverett, Ben, 303
  Joe, 303
  John Waymon, 303
  Rena Bell Hollman, 303
  Woodrow Wilson, 212, 303
Lewis, Betty Lou, 372
  Dr., 98, 99, 100
  Lloyd, 158
Leyte, 149, 162, 245, 258, 314, 356, 385, 401, 409, 454, 472, 488, 496, 508; Island, 285, 314, 441
'Liberty Ship', 361, 362
Liggett, General, 76
Likins, Bill, 346
Lincoln, Abraham, 21, 22, 24, 202, 204
Linton, Chester, 193
Lions Club, 85
Loch Loman, 428
Lochards Mission, Creek Nation, 36
Lodge, Cabot, 107
Loftin, James Robert, 212
Logan, Ulestus, 47
Lomas, George S., 526
Lombardy, 348
Lone Star Ammunition Ordinance, 266, 268;
Long, Mrs. John B., 162
  Mrs. Stella, 162
  Pfc. John B., 162
Look, C. S., 36
  Dr. E. S., 36
Lookout Mountain, 32
Lost Battalion, The, 456

Love, Alan, 71, 100
  Debra, 381
  Ed King, 66
  Furd, 70
  Furd Hinton, Jr., 71
  Laura Viola Bagwell, 381
  Lawrence L. M.D., 518
  Leslie R., 518
  Linda, 71
  Margaret S. Rochette, 518
  Melissa, 381
  Pearl Reed, 71
  Randal T., 518
  Robert, 518
  Roger Maurice, 381
  Sam, 66
  Warren H., 518
  Will, 17
  Willie Hubbard, 381
'Love and War in Texas', 526
Love Field, 313; Dallas, 318
Lovell, Dirl Randolph, 365
  Dorthy Louise, 365
  Elizabeth, 10
  James Delbert, 365
  James Edward 365
  Johnnie L., 212
  Johnny Lory, 365
  Leta Mae Brotherton, 365
  Madge Catherine Josephine, 365
  Mildred Agnes, 365
  Myrtle, 365
  William Albert, 365
Lowe, Hugh, 95
  Winnie, 424
Lowery, Becky, 99
  Joe, 77
  Nettie, 77
Lowery Field, 313; Air Force Base, 271;
Lowry, Alice Jane, 453
  Alma Ellen Smith, 453
  Bobbie Ruth, 453
  James Wilford, 453
  Mary Jane DeBerry, 10, 28, 184, 453
  William Kirb, 453
Lubbock, Governor Francis R., 21
'Lucky Stripe', 451
Ludendorff Bridge, 135
Luftwaffee, 127, 207
Lum, Alvis Merle, 436
  Annette, 436
  Audrey May, 436
  Brenos, 72, 436
  Damon Neal, 437
  Don Rayburn, 437

E. G. Sr., 71, 436
  Emma Lee Jones, 436
  Eric, 436
  Mavis, 436
  Vincent, 436
  Wanza Sue Brooks, 436
Lumpkin, Maggie Lee Marsh, 514
  Tirza Quintilla, 24
Luna Oil Refinery, 393
Lynch, Aubrey, 326
  Bill (Eulis Oren), 326
  Gary, 326
  Lois, 326
  Mae Jewel, 326
  Mattie, 326
  Pauline, 326
  Sam, 326
Lytel, Lt. Commander Morton H., 445
M-Stammlager PID, 170
Mabry, William L., 6, 7
MacArthur, General, 139, 140, 142, 143, 147, 148, 149, 150, 155, 156, 205, 224, 225, 241, 401, 441, 523
MacGrain, Lt. Col. Donald, 341
Mackie, John, 202
Madras, Cemetery, 15; Cemetery Society, 16
Maginot Line, 275
Malmedy Massacre, 498
Manchester, Cemetery, 66
Manila, 140, 141, 150, 162, 167, 173, 226, 256, 401; Bay, 140, 141
Mann, Edna, 17
Marable, Allen Corley, 372
  Amy Margaret, 372
  Ben, 47
  Betty Sue, 372
  Bubba, 119
  Carrie, 429
  Cathy Ann, 372
  Dorothy Ann, 371
  Linda Ruth, 372
  Marilyn, 372
  Maude Dorothy Cook, 371
  Mr. and Mrs. Paul D., 166
  Paul, 324
  Paul D. III, 372
  Paul Davis, Jr., 119, 166, 372
  Paul Davis, Sr., 371
  Robert Lewis, 372
Marcell, Robbie, 465
Mare Island, 45, 410

Marianas, 145, 147, 166, 172, 220, 294, 299, 496;
  Islands, 146, 151, 248, 298, 454, 475
Marks, Margaret, 25
Marne Battle, 43
Maroney, Mr. and Mrs. O. M., 164
Maroney, Pvt. Curtis E., 164
Marsh, Buddy, 513
  Edward Mercer, 513
  Elsie, 488
  Keener Bryan, 513
  Lavada Parker, 513
  Lula, 513
  Lydia Francis (Fannie) Hearne, 513
  Maggie Lee, 513
  Marlin Austin, 513
  Robert, 513
  Ruby, 513
  Sandra Kay, 513
  William A., 513
Marshall, General George C., 108, 148
Marshall Islands, 138, 163, 166, 172, 220, 294, 297, 298, 410, 417, 417, 417, 465, 507, 508
Marshalls, 145, 161, 296
Martin, Amanda F. Morris, 65
  Charles Proctor, 65
  Charlie, 65
  Dot, 47
  Edna, 65
  Effie Lillian Hastings, 404
  Grace, 65
  Helen, 65
  Herman L. (Pepper), 65, 212, 404, 405, 408
  Ida, 65
  Jackie, 417
  Jullian Russell, 65
  Louise, 65
  Rear Admiral Harold M. Martin, 520
  Reba Aileen, 65, 404
  Rev. Claude, 367, 485
  Roscoe Alonzo, 65, 404
  Weldon, 405
  William Allen, 65
  William Weldon, 65, 404
Marx, Dr., 198
  Jerrold, 448
  Melvin, 448
  Melvin III, 448
  Melvin, Jr., 448
  Pearl Silberberg, 448
  Stephen, 448

Mason, Thos., 47
Mathis, Charlie, 199
  George E., 212
  Roberta, 457
Maui, 294, 295, 296, 299, 301, 520
Mauldin, Betty J., 229
  Billie, 229
  Donnie G., 229
  Ensign Vivian, 164
  Lois M., 212, 228, 234
  Lt. Travis L., 158
  Mr. and Mrs. W. E., 164
  Myrtle Cagle, 229
  Naomi, 229
  Nora, 63
  Peggy, 234
  Sandra, 234
  Travis L. (T. L.), 229, 234
Maxey, Col. Sam Bell, 30
  General Sam Bell, 186
Maxfield, Johnny, 415
Maxton, Helen, 453
May, Ella Mae Todd, 342
Mayes, Dorothy, 173
  Margie Williams, 29
  Mr. and Mrs. Archie, 173
  T/Sgt. Leon, 172
  Wilma Smith, 523
Maynard, Hafford, 93
  Willie, 93
Mayo's College, 81
Mays, Willie, 212
McAdams, Joseph B., 182
McAlexander, General, 76
McAllister, J. O. (Bud), 240
  James Lindsay, 240
  Lindsay, 157, 162, 164, 210, 211, 368
  Mary, 211
  Missura Cornett, 240
McAnear, Jane, 5
McCain, Ballard D., 212, 460
  Ballard Dinwiddie, 459
  Bernard, 459
  Bernie Leak, 459, 460
  Bonnie Bybee, 459
  Dr. Clifford, 47
  Emma Frances Young, 459
  James Calvin, 459
  Janie Virginia, 459
  Marshall Rueban (Mack), 459
  Marshall Young (Rooster), 459
  Ruby Edwina, 459
  Sara Emma Frances, 459
  Willie Margaret, 459
McCartney, 386

Phil, 385
McCarver, Giles, 336
  Giles Richard (Dick), 336
  James Edward, 336
  Pearl Giles, 336
McCasland, Sammie, 432
McCauley, Lt. Joseph S., 485
McClanahans, 96
McClinton's Furniture Store, 101
McCluer, Elizabeth Howison, 425
  Gaylord Howison, 425
  Gaylord L., 425
  Herman Charles, 425
  James H., 425
McClure, Nellie Marie, 316
McConnell, Annie Waddell, 432
  Austin D., 433
  Austin Davis Jr., 433
  Cammie, 433
  Gary Sam, 432
  Ginger, 432
  Marty, 433
  Melanie, 432
  Sam, 432
  Will, 432
McCoy, 304
  Charley, 17
  Eva May Straub, 489
  Hermon Wilson (Mac), 489
  Hermon Wilson, Jr., 489
  Homer Franklin, 490
  Jane, 490
  Jesse Willard, 490
  John Douglas, 490
  Judith Ann, 489
  Lewis Raymond, 489
  Lt. Willard, 159
  Mary, 490
  Molly, 17
  Steven, 490
  Taylor, 195
  Taylor Franklin, 489
  Worth, 17
McCracken, Sue, 82
McCrae, John, 85, 86
McCrary, Floyd, 47
McCullar, Lela, 398
McCulloch Greenhouse, 159
McCullouch, J. Ritchie, 378
  J. Ritchie III, 379
  James R. Jr., 378
  Martha Ann, 379
  Ruth Ellis Reed, 378
McDaniel, Chester, 199

McDavid, Elizabeth J. (Betty), 248
McDonough, Geraldine, 400
  James Alvin, 400
  Lois Gray, 400
  William M. (Bill), 400
  William M. (Butch) Jr., 400
McDuffie, Betty, 313
  Dorrace, 313, 336
  Edna, 313
  Hoyt, 313
  Hubbard, 313
  Jack Russell, 313
  Janie Maud Lanier, 313
  Willard Bruce, 313
  Woodrow, 313
McEwin, Alice Marie, 465
  Allen Humphreys, 465
  Annie Mae Humphreys, 465
  Dale Vayne, 465
  Darla Kay, 465
  Evelyn, 465
  Ginger Shari, 465
  James Allen, 465
  James Kyle, 465
  James William, 465
  Patsy Aylene, 465
McGill, Martha Jane, 364
McGuire, Allen, 515
  Dorthy, 256
  Malcolm, 158
McKenzie, Carol, 455
  Daisy I. Hughston, 455
  David, 455
  David McAnally, 455
  Eula, 455
  Frances Lee, 455
  John Thomas, 189, 455, 461
  Patsy, 455
  Rev. John Witherspoon Pettigrew, 455
  Travis, 455
McKenzie Cemetery, 456;
  College, 455, 456;
  Institute, 24; Memorial United Methodist Church, Clarksville, 286, 346455
McKinley, Fred, 351
  William, 3
McKinley Junior High, 350, 351
McKinney, Scott, 17
McLaughlin, Alvin Joseph, 364
  Charlene, 364
  Effie, 364

Florence, 364
James H., 364
Janell, 364
Joseph Hugh, 363
Laura, 364
Lorena, 364
Mabel, 364
Martin, 364
Myron Daniel, 364
Rebekah Mae Near, 363
Vivian, 364
McMahan, Mr., 197
McNary, Charles, 108
Meadows, Andrea Lou, 478
  Anita Kay, 478
  Emma D. Pritchett, 478
  Emma Lou (Honey) Brem, 478
  Generia Maxine, 478
  Huey Pritchett, 478
  Lareall Arthur, 478
  Leslie O. Jr., 478
  Leslie Oscar, 478
  Noel N., 478
  Thelma Dorene, 478
Meals, June, 485
  Ralph, 315
Means, Don, 193, 194
  Doris, 193
  Jerry, 193, 194
  Jimmie, 193, 194
  Pauline O'Donnell, 193
Medal of Honor, 202
Medford, Brose, 251
  Elmer, 47
Meeks, Minnie, 322
Meets, A. J., 158
Melton, Evelyn, 369
  Virginia, 234
Merchant Marines, 369
Meriam, Richard, 526
Metts, Betty, 241
  Bonnie, 241
  Ethel, 241
  Haywood, 241
  Hazel, 241
  Hershel, 241
  John T. (Pete), 241
  Johnie, 241
  Linda, 241
  Lizzie Thacker, 241
  Margaret, 241
  Pauline, 241
  Pearl, 241
  Robert H., 241
  Shirley, 241
Meuse-Argonne, 69;
  Campaign, 85
Mexican War, 4, 8, 27, 29

Middleton, Scott, 47
Milam, Billie, 412
  Buane, 412
  Darlene, 412
  Eva Dell, 412
  Fred, 412
  Irene Patterson, 412
  Ronnie, 412
  Theron, 412
  Vickie, 412
Milan, Frank, 159
Millaway, Alva Angline, 411
Miller, Beryl Jean Legate, 321
  Earl, 321
  Edward, 321
  Herbert R. (Hub), 320
  James, 321
  Margaret Eva McAnear, 321
  Randy, 321
  Rufus E., 321
  Tom, 100
  Wayne D., 212
Millington, W. A., 463
Mills, Jo Mac, 442
Mims, Robt., 47
Mindanao, 141, 149, 149, 258, 488
Minelayer, Oglala, 111
Mindoro, 245, 488
Minneapolis Naval Air Station, 461
Minter, Mrs. Ed, 33
  Mureline, 371
Mission Theaters, 65
Missouri, 44, 22, 221, 315
Mitchell, Ada Bell Douglas, 366
  Albert, 367, 369
  Beulah, 367
  Clyde, 367
  Douglas, 366, 369
  Edith, 367
  Essye, 367
  Francis Marion, 366
  James, 367
  Jim, 369
  Lilly Mae, 367
  Maude, 367
  Nola, 367
  Opal, 367
  Sheryl, 367
Montgomery, British General Sir Bernard L., 130, 328, 332, 512
Moore, Albert P., 482
  Bennie Jean, 358
  Betty Rains, 482
  Binney, 182

Burl, 482
Carrie Leola Elder, 444
Chalmer, 482
Charley, 17
Cherry, 445
Cpl. Ona H., 159
Della Butler, 482
Dorothy Louise, 482
Ellis M., 482
Emily, 497
Emmer, 482
Eulla Bankston, 482
George,
George Lilbon, 467
Glenn, 482
James Leroy, 84
John, 482
Leona, 482
Lilbon Thomas, 84, 467
Linda Ann, 482
Margaret Annie McConville, 84
Mary Bailey, 444
Mary Sue, 246
Mary Virginia, 245
Mary Virginia Bowers, 444
Mrs. Margaret, 164
Nettie, 482
Pfc. William D., 164
Ray, 47
Raymond, 482
Russ, 37
Russell D., 482
Sallie Elizabeth Buchanan, 467
Sandra Sue, 482
Street, 444
Tessa, 445
Thomas M., 212
Thomas Martin, 467
Velma, 466
Vicky, 445
Wade, 482
Wilma L., 482
Moore's Variety Store, 17
Moran, Juanita, 481
More, George, 450
Morehead, F. M., 157, 324
  Mrs., 411
Morgan, Claudia, 306
  Dr., 23
  Lucinda C., 27
Morris, Bobby, 198
  Carl L., 212
  Doyle, 443
  Frank H., 443
  Lloyd, 443
  Max, 443
  Nancy Parker, 443

Nanetta P., 443
Mount Suribachi, 152, 235, 300, 494
Mullins, Emma Estell Kerbow, 387
　Lala, 388
　Ruth, 388
　W. N., 387
　William Ralph, 387
Munro, Douglas, 202
Munson, Russell W., 315
Murphy, Audie, 210, 439
　Chuck, 192
　Elizabeth, 357
Murrie, Chas., 45
Mussolini, 124, 125, 126, 128
　Prime Minister Benito, 123
Myers, Ella Catherine Pappio, 413
　Irenious C., 413
　Jackie, 413
　Lisa, 413
　Noel F., 413
N. Stalag 7-B, 500
Nagasaki, 109, 156, 208, 252, 379, 467
Nailling, Ben, 171
　Lee, 171
　Novelle, 171
　Ollie, 171
Nameless Crag, 298
Nance, Audrey 355
　Bill, 158
　Elbert, 354
　Eva, 354
　Leola, 354
　Ola Bramlett, 354
　Richard Earl, 354
　Roy, 45
　Sidney R., 354
Nance Bus Lines, 194
Newman, Eric J., 1st Lt., 470
Newport News Shipbuilding and Drydock Company, 392
Newsom, Margaret, 475
Nicar O Nickel Company, 379
Nicks, Hazel Lucille, 505
　Nancy A., 25
　Robert Anderson (R. A.), 24, 25
Nimitz, Admiral, 142, 145, 146, 149, 151, 152, 153, 155, 208, 209
9th Armored Division, 206, 243; Infantry Division, 409; Regiment, 30;

Texas Cavalry, 36; Texas Infantry, 36
90th Division, 319
91st Infantry Division, 439
95th Infantry Division, 400
96th Division Cemetery, 282; Infantry Division Temporary Cemetery Number One, Okinawa Shima, Row No. 21, Grave N. 711, 470; Infantry Division, 289
Nix, Clarence L., 337
　Clarence L., Jr., 337
　Joyce Lynne, 337
　Willie Lee Johnson, 337
"No Man's Land", 44
Noe, Robert L., 212
Noels, Joe, 47
Norfolk, Naval Air Station, 444
Normandy, 129, 130, 131, 132, 135, 174, 207, 242, 256, 256, 260, 269, 306, 324, 328, 340, 357, 376, 419, 420, 439, 466, 471, 478, 482, 489, 505, 516, 522; American Cemetery & Memorial, St. Laurent, France, 242; Beach, 257, 260, 400, 511; Cemetery, France, 470
Norris House, 66
Norris, Louie, 116
Northern Standard, 178
Notre Dame Cathedral, 517
Nowell, Ora Mae, 57
O'Daniel, W. Lee, 97
O'Dell, Louie, 515
O'Dells, 96
O'Donnell, Betty, 249
　Billy, 249
　Donald Ray, 249
　Emma Lou Moore, 249
　Gaston, 249
　Gordon, 249
　Hugh, 249
　Hugh Albert (Bill), 249
　Hugh Wesley, 249
　Jack, 116, 261
　Kathleen, 261
　Lee Ivy, 261
　Margaret, 261, 338
　Marlin, 249
　Mary, 83, 171, 261
　Michael Pat, 262
　Pat, 116, 261, 262
　Pauline, 261

Reba, 249
Sr., John, 261
Teresa, 249
Thelma, 249
Oakdale Cemetery, 25
Obravatz, Machine Gunner Sgt., 351
Okinawa, 153, 154, 155, 209, 245, 254, 282, 283, 284, 285, 290, 291, 296, 314, 315, 356, 369, 401, 409, 410, 415, 432, 433, 447, 454, 463, 482, 496, 497, 502, 504, 507, 510, 524, 525
Old Glory, 207, 298, 300, 495
Old Jonesboro, 2
Old Starksville, 8
Old Union Baptist Church in Simms, Texas, 469
Oldfield, Venita Jo Gibbs, 31, 32
Oliver, Willie, 212
Omaha Beach, 130, 131, 207, 256, 323, 379, 383, 395, 413, 439, 489; Normandy, 340; France, 275
113th Infantry, 65
133rd Seabees, 430
144th Infantry, 82, 229
145th Infantry, 292
146th Engineer Combat Battalion, 512
151st Machine Gun Battalion, 57
152nd Airborne Antiaircraft Artillery Battalion, 442
165th Depot Brigade, 57, 65, 82, 84
Operation ANVIL, 133; COBRA, 131; Flintlock, 298, 297; OVERLORD, 129, 130, 131
Oriental Laundry, 267
Orphan Train, 83, 171
Osmena, President Sergio, 149
Owens, Ballard, 199
　Francis Ann, 26
Pace, Shelby, 511
　W. H., 462
Pacific Fleet, 110, 115, 137, 166
Palmer, Frieda Kishner, 327
　Lieut. Col. C. H., 186
　Veda Lorene, 371
　Wallace, 194

INDEX ★ 557

Papagos, General, 127
Paradise, Jim, 17
Parker, Cpl. James, 47
  Joe D., 212
  Jr., Pvt. Leo L., 164
  Mrs. L. L., 164
  Newt, 17
Parks, Chester, 336
  Christine, 336
  Doris M., 325
  Gladys Hazel Greer, 336
  James C., 336
  James Michel, 336
  Mary Jane, 336
  Tommie Joe, 336
Parris, Carl, 356
  Carl David, 356
  Lula McDaniels, 356
  N. J., 356
  Steve, 356
  Tom, 356
Parrott, Jacob, 202
Patch, Lieutenant General
    Alexander M., 133
Patman, Wright, 63
Patterson, Jack, 47
  Joyce, 246
Patton, Gen. George, 133,
    134, 231, 229, 255, 271,
    321, 325, 331, 328, 379,
    380, 382, 388, 402, 435,
    441, 452, 466, 477, 478,
    492, 498
  Norie, 81
Patton's Third Army, 132,
    134
Payne, Dr. Ross, 25, 198, 199
  Matthew, 25
Pearl Harbor, 105, 107, 109,
    110, 111, 114, 115, 116,
    117, 118, 120, 128, 137,
    138, 149, 162, 163, 168,
    173, 188, 208, 209, 220,
    221, 224, 226, 232, 235,
    254, 270, 285, 287, 297,
    299, 303, 305, 368, 398,
    402, 406, 409, 416, 418,
    425, 431, 437, 445, 446,
    458, 463, 465, 472, 478,
    498, 502, 508, 519, 524
Pecan Bayou, 5; Plant, 100;
    Shelling Plant, 253
Peck, Gregory, 192
Peek, "June Bug", 219
  Alicia Kay, 309
  Alton Blain (Tebo), 505,
    506
  Barney Bell, 505
  Billy, 216

Bruce, 506
Carolyn, 216
Dan M., 309
Dick, E. M., Jr., 309
Dillard, 309
Dudley, 309
Earl, 385
Ernest Morton, 309
Ervin, 385
Ethyl, 215
Eudora, 215
Geraldine, 216
Harrold B., 309
Haskell, 158
Hazel Marie, 467
Janet, 505
Johnnie Bell, 216
Jr., R. H., 215
Lallie, 216, 385
Linda, 506
Lizzie Bell, 505
Lonnie Haskell, 507
Louis, 386
Louis E., 212, 385
Margie, 385
Marvin, 215
Mary Holly, 505
Mellie Knight, 385
Mobelia, 505
Mr. and Mrs. David A., 507
Oma Lee, 507
Otis, 215
Pearlene, 309
R. L. (Raymond Leon),
    309
Rufus Henry, 215
Russell Lee, 506
Seymour, 505
Sula Pearl Strout, 309
Suzanne, 309
Thomas Ray, 505
Wayne, 215
Wylie Tom, 385
Penn, William, 10
Penny, Floyd, 337
  James T. (Jay), 337
  May Godwin, 337
Perkins, Ann Katherine
    (Kitty), 264
  Gordon, 264
  James Herbert, 264
  Sarah Katherine Jones, 264
  Tom, 314
Pershing, General John J., 69,
    76
Petersburg, 80
Peterson, Evelyn (Mickey),
    431
Pettit, Pfc. Norvill, 160

Petty, C. C., 405
  Earl, 381
  Lonnie, 421
  Lonnie Lloyd, 405
  Margie, 405
  Mattie Dell, 405
  Wade, 405
  Wilson Dorotha, 405
Philippine, Commonwealth,
    138, 139, 149, 166;
    Scouts, 139; Scouts 26th
    Cavalry Regiment, 140
Philley, Mr. and Mrs. J. N.,
    170
  Mrs. J. E., 170
  Pvt. Larry E., 170
Phillips, Cecil, 158
Phillips, Earline, 388
  Edwin, 388
  Eugene, 388
  Felix G., 388
  Floyce, 388
  Haskell, 388
  Larry, 388
  Morris S., 388
  Rubye, 388
  Stephen, 388
  Willie A. Stuart, 388
Pine Forest Cemetery, 33
Pirtle, Ab, 48
Pledge of Allegiance, 116, 118
Poison Ridge, 298
Polland, Gene, 366
Pope's Grocery Store, 91
Port Darwin, 141; Hudson,
    26; Moresby, 143, 367,
    468; Odessa, 375;
    Orchard, Washington,
    355; Said, Egypt, 375,
    376;
Porterfield, Frances, 484
  Gail, 484
  Gary, 484
  H. S., 357
  Harold, 357
  Hazel Metts, 484
  Irene Williams, 357
  John C., 484
  Linda Sue, 357
  Marvin, 484
  Michael Ray (Mickey), 357
  Roy, 484
  Troy, 484
Poss, A. R., 18
Post Oak ridge, 23
Potsdam Declaration, 155
Potsdam Proclamation, 156
Potts, Charles Anthony, 419
  Gary Carl, 419

Howell Vaughan, 419
Jack Michael, 419
Joseph William, 419
Linda Gail, 419
Mamie Pearl Howell, 419
Ollie Jean, 419
Otis William, 419
Otis William Jr., 419
Oval H., 419
Paula Elaine, 419
Pauline, 419
Ronald Hugh, 419
POW Camp Stalag Luft III, 491
Pratt, Acha, 51
 Allie Balma, 51
 Angella, 51
 Arden Leroy, 384
 Arlen Leroy, 51
 Dorothy Marie, 51, 384
 Ella Mae, 51
 Emmitt Noel, 51
 Eva Onella, 51
 James Earl, 51
 James Leroy, 384
 John Harvey, 51, 85, 384
 John Leonard, "Len", 51
 Joseph Crosley, 51
 L. T., 51
 Louise Elizabeth, 51
 Mirty Mae Swint, 51, 384
 Nellie Ruth, 51, 384
 Sarah Incy "Sally" McWilliams, 51
 Sidney John Harvey, 51, 384
 Zelma Lee, 51
Prentiss, Woodard, 368
Presley, Wanda Marie, 468
 Will, 45
Preston, Captain James P., 27
Prisoner Stalag XIII-D, 518
Proctor, Allen B., 158
 Mr. and Mrs. Ed, 162
Proctor, Frances, 65
Pryor, Ed, 192
 Helen, 192
Puckett, 66
Puckett, Drilla Howard Carpenter, 483
 Frank, 483
 Frankie B., 483
 Nancy Ann, 25
Puller, General Chesty, 410
Purple Heart, 56, 57, 161, 164, 166, 170, 171, 201
Pyle, Ernie, 282, 283, 284
Pyles, Bonnie Lee, 241
Quakers, 10

Quandt, Maj. Gen. Douglass, 463
Quarles, Aubrey, 199
 Dorothy Blanch, 322
 Garland Eugene, 322
 Mrs. Lee, 164
 Rachel Smith, 322
 Thelma, 322
 Thurman, 322
 Tommie Marie Exum, 322
 William Richard (Billy), 322
 William Richard (Dick), 322
Queen Elizabeth, 383, 428, 483
Queen Mary, 243, 339, 343, 367, 375, 396, 414, 428
Quezon, President, 139, 149
Quick, Edith, 492
 Gilbert, 492
 Gillie, 493
 Hazel, 356
 Ira L., 492
 John, 492, 511
 Paul A., 492
 Rosa Roberts, 492
Radar Hill, 298
Radney, John, 32
Ragsdill, Bobby, 394
 Joe, 394
 Jonell, 393, 394
 Norris, 394
 Sarah, 416
 Tommy, 394
 Vera Veteto, 394
 William Mack, 394
Rain, Baily, 197
Rainey, John, 92
Rains, Adlia E., 378
 Archie, E., 378
 Bailey, 168
 Barbara E., 378
 Effie, 77
 Etta M. Crenshaw, 378
 Mamie Nowell, 397
 Pvt. Bernard, 168
 Roy S., 212, 397
 Sesil Roy, 397
 Teresa A., 378
Ralston, Lt. Wilson, 158
Ramsey, Mary Signor, 440
Raney, A. D., 403
 Bertie May Rice, 403
 Bruce, 403
 Florence R, 403
 Gordon, 403
 Maurice H., 403
 Travis, 403

Rater, Anita, 441
 Arlene, 441
 Edgar, 441
 George, 441
 Jack Rossen, 441
 Jack W., 441
 James, 441
 James W., 441
 John Olen, 441
 Lottie Shaw, 441
 Myrtle, 441
 Robert John, 441
Raulston, Aubrey, 16
 Beth, 16
 Cassandra, 25
 Rozelle Denton, 16
Rawleigh, Lawrence, 212
Ray, Howard K., 234
 Rev. Carroll B., 157
Rayburn, Sam, 108, 189, 525, 526
Reconstruction Period, 6
Red Cross, 78, 159, 170, 176, 184, 218, 226, 270, 274, 278, 279, 373, 374, 406, 457, 491, 500
Red River Arsenal, 15, 77, 182, 183, 197, 261, 266, 409, 414, 444, 449, 469
 County Court House, 211, 434, 436
 County Jail, 15
 County Rodeo Association, 158
 National Bank, 19, 199
Reed, Dr. C. B., 198, 252, 324, 354
 Ida Mae, 83
 Lewis, 71
Reep, Mary, 271
Reese, Patricia Jayne, 467
Reeves, Mozelle, 308
 Walter Lee, 57
Reid, Clifford F., 212
Remagen, 135; Bridge, 244
Remount Cavalry, 81
Repair Ship Vestal, 110
Republic of Texas, 5
Reston, Virginia, 439
Rhea, Alvis Lee, 414
 Charlotte, 414
 Christine, 414
 Eudora, 216
 Eunice Lum, 414
 George Henry, 414
 Gladys, 414
 H. G., 414
 Harold, 414
 Kathy, 414

Linda, 414
Onvie, 414
Rick, 414
Vivian (Jack), 507
Vivian, 414
Rhodes, Alice, 354
   Alma Mae Ray, 353
   Carole Lynne, 354
   Charles Reynolds, 354
   Pat, 47
   Rhonda Lucille, 354
   W. D. (Dub), 353
   Walter Harvey, 353
Rice, Anna Virginia, 65
   Bill, 308
   Cynthia, 308
   Lane, 308
   Mozelle Reeves, 57
   Nancy, 308
   Ora Mae Nowell, 308
   Robert Lane, 57, 308
   Ruth Ann, 308
   Walter, 308
   Walter Lane, 57
   Walter Samuel, 57, 308
   William C. (Billy), 57, 308
Richardson, General, 401
   James, 5
Richie, Jan Welch, 305
Ricks, A. J., 356
   Cornilia, 356
   Dennis K., 356
   Eddie, 356
   L. V., 356
   Maggie, 356
   Malisa Dixon, 356
   Odell, 356
   Odessa, 356
   Pauline, 356
   Richard, 356
   Ruby, 356
   Tom, 356
   Will, 356
   William C., 356
Riddle, Theodore R., 212
Ridley, Harold S., 213
Ridlon, Capt. Walter J., 301
Riggs, Bruce, 329
Rinehart, Vivian Irma, 464
Ringwall, Lucy, 26
RKO Pathe, 118
Roach, Dr. Harley D., 48, 98, 99, 164, 262, 264
   Frances, 262, 264
   Lt. (jg) Thomas Donald, 164, 212, 262, 264, 263
   Mrs. Florence Grant, 164, 262, 264
   Mrs. H. D., 164

Roberson, Dollie, 55
Roberts, Archie G., 212
   Carl, 198
   Ethel, 47, 48
   Fred, 56
   Howard, 45
   Martha, 240
   Martha Sue, 410
   Nancy, 356
   Virginia, 275
Robertson, Charles Lyon, 440
   Dessie Mae Rogers, 440
   Dorothy, 369
   Gerald Denton, 440
   Jessie Gertrude Young, 440
   Johnny, 12
   Kitty Earlene, 440
   Peggy Diane, 440
   Sharon Elaine, 440
Robins, John, 11
Roddy, Gen., 27
Rodgers, Dorothy, 172
   Joe, 171
   Leo, 171
   Othelo Arnold, 171
Rodzinski, Arthur, 106
Rogers, John K., 5
   Miss Vera, 195
   T/Sgt. James Cecil, 174
Roi, 294; Island, 220, 294, 302, 296, 297
Rommel, 128, 131334, 452
Roosevelt, Eleanor, 180, 488
   Jimmy, 106
   President, 89, 98, 106, 107, 108, 117, 119, 128, 129, 139, 141, 142, 149, 180, 247, 401
Rose, Dan, 65
   Dora, 65, 486
   Kenneth, 65
   Leonard, 65
   Virginia, 65, 242
   Willard Mabry, 65
Roseberry, Bennie, 370
   Carol, 370
   Charles I., 370
   Charley, 370
   Cora, 370
   Edna, 370
   Elton M., 370
   Grace, 370
   James, 370
   Kelly, 370
   Larry, 370
   Melba, 370
   Nora, 370
   Richard, 370
   Susan Octavia Peyton, 370

   Wanda, 370
Rosenberg, Joseph, 496
Rosie, the Riveter, 188, 294, 348
Rosmarino River, 231
Ross, Gertrude, 82
Rosser, Dorothy, 522, 523
   Ernest Gay, 523
   George Lottie Burkett, 523
   Gladys, 523
   Hobert, 523
   Hubert, 523
   Raymond, 489, 523
   Syble, 523
Rosson, Ahmoy, 63, 441
   Frances C., 271
   May, 63
Rotary Club, 180
Royal Air Force, 127
Rozell, Neil, 264
   William, 264
Ruby Dycus, 345
Rush, John, 17
Russel Exchange Bank of Annona, 45
Russell, Kenneth Dowd, 496
   Leon, 219
Ruth McCulloch Guild, 16
Saipan, 146, 147, 151, 161, 172, 248, 289, 294, 295, 296, 298, 299, 302, 314, 400, 454, 475, 476, 485, 520, 524
Sale, Jessie, 411
Salem Baptist Church at Boxelder, 469
'Sally the Slut', 390
San Diego, Naval Air Station, 223, 458
Sargent, Homer, 199
Sauls, Alvin, 259, 323
   Alvin A., 324
   Bill, 322
   Frankie Lee, 322
   Grace, 322
   James, 322
   John, 324
   Mattie V. Kelley, 322
   Patti, 324
   Paula, 322
   Robert L., 322
   Roy, 324
   Roy James, 322
   Royia, 322
Savanah Cemetery, 385
"Saving Private Ryan", 383, 439
Sawers, Robert W., 308
Sawyer, 2nd Lt. Louis V., 169

560 ★ FOR LOVE OF COUNTRY THE PRICE OF FREEDOM

Mr. and Mrs. G. A., 169
Schofield Barracks, 111, 282
Schooler, T. P., 22
Schultz, Orlene, 327
Scott, Forrest Milton, 49
  Fred F., 213
Screws, Era, 365
  Hellen Esper Nash, 365
  John Henry, 365
  Lorene, 365
  Lorraine, 365
  Rachael, 365
  Raymond Roland, 365
  Raynard, 365
  Roland, 365
  William Thad, 365
Seabee, 220, 295, 393, 464, 472, 475
Seaman, Joyce, 448
2nd and 4th Marine divisions, 146
2nd Arkansas Infantry, 34; Infantry Division, 254; Marine Division, 145, 154; U.S. Cavalry Regiment, 305
7th Infantry Division, 145
17th Tank Bn., 168
76th Infantry Division's 304th Regiment, 169
77th Division, 154; Field Artillery Regiment, 71; Infantry Division, 146, 154
734th AAF Bomb Squadron, 247
Shackelford, Elwin, 45
Shackelford's Greenhouse, 159
Shadid, Alvin Eugene, 357
  David, 357
  Deana, 357
  Elizabeth, 357
  Ethel Straub, 357
  Glen, 357
  John, 357
  Kathryn, 357
Sharpe, Clara Martin, 247
  George M., 247
  Hugh M., 213
  Jack M., 248
  Jack M. Jr., 248
  Linda, 248
  Nancy, 247
  S/Sgt. Hugh M., 247
Shelby, 22
  Alice, 511
  Archie, 511
  Asa, 511

Barbara, 511
General Joseph O., 22
Glenda Lee, 511
Glenda Sue, 511
Glyn Juanita Ray, 511
J. W. (Billy), 511
Jesse Lawrence, 511
Jo Ann, 511
Nannie Jean Patton, 511
Pat, 511
Phyllis Kay, 511
Travis, 511
William Thomas, 511
Shelton, Mr. and Mrs. Charles, 179, 178
Shenandoah, 19
Sheppard, Dr. Kenneth E. Jr., 434
  Errel Lee, 213, 434, 435
  General, 410
  Harold, 434, 523
  Huey F., 434
  Hughie A., 434
  Jerry, 434
  Karen Elaine, 434
  Karen Kay, 523
  Kenneth, 434
  Kenneth, Jr., 434
  Lula Mae, 434
  Minnie Jumper, 434
  Patsy, 434
  Storey, 434
  Sue Quarles, 434
  Tinnie, 434
  Wayne, 434
  Zeno, 434
Sheppard Air Force Base, 293; Field, 333, 383; Field, Texas, 275; Field, Wichita Falls, Texas, 367
Sherman, General William Tecumseh, 12, 22, 35
Shiloh, 36; Cumberland Presbyterian Church, 4, 14; TN, 26
Shimpock, Alice, 413
  Arthur, 413
  Bruce, 413
  Mack, 413
  Rebecca, 413
  Robert, 413
  Susie Tolison, 413
  Timothy, 413
  Vada, 413
  W. H., 413
  Willie, 413
Shirley, Dowdy Buel, 213
Shirleys, 96
Shoffner, Bryan, 45

Short, Captain, 227
Shoulders, Carnell, 268
  Doris, 268
  Doris Faye, 428
  Elmer, 268
  Elmer Junior, 268
  John, 268
  Joyce, 268
  Jr., Elmer, 213
  Rena Spangler, 268
Shumway, Raymond E., 526, 528
Siegfried, 269; Line, 133, 135, 170, 275, 395, 451, 477
Signal Corps, 161
Silberberg's Store, 100
Simmons, David Vasco, 270
  Eugene Crockett, 270
  Gene, 61
  Hiram Chessie, 61, 269
  J. W., 17
  James, 315
  James Archie, Jr., 502
  James Hiram, 270
  John William, 270
  Margaret Hilliard, 502
  Margaret Sue, 269
  Marvin Neil, 270
  Mr. and Mrs. Gene, 269
  Paula, 502
  Peggy, 459
  Robert Samuel, 270
  Sudie Florence Hunt, 269
  Thomas Newton, 270
Sims, Capt. M. L., 9
  David L., 332
  Deborah, 332
  Frank, 47
  Gibson F., 60, 332
  Leland A., 60, 332
  Mary Bennet, 60, 332
  Robert A., 332
  Robert Earl, 60, 332
Sisco, Lavyn Wright, 31, 32
Sivley, John, 37, 314
  Moorman, 47
  Mr. & Mrs. B. S., 47
6th Armored Division, 170; Infantry Division, 337
16th U. S. Infantry, 7
63rd, U.S. Army Reserve Command, 56
64th Infantry, 71
68th Armored Division, 245
69th Infantry Battalion, 344; Infantry Division, 320
602nd Tank Destroyer Battalion, 498
Skaggs, Donna, 455

Gene Paul, 455
Reagan, 455
Skidmore, Donna, 393
  Eileen, 393
  Elizabeth, 393
  George M., Sr., 393
  George Monroe (Skid) Jr., 393
  Harold, 393
  Lana Kay, 428
  Mary Elizabeth, 428
  Nelia Counts, 393
  Reid, 428
  Ronnie, 393
Slaton, Pete, 213
Smiley, Belle, 13
  Mary, 13
Smith, Barbara G., 360
  Commander Charles H., 495
  Donnie, 477
  Dorothy, 360
  Earlene, 415
  Edward, 415
  General, 152
  George L., 360
  George R., 360
  George R. Jr., 360
  Gloria, 382
  Guy, 81
  Ida, 341
  J. C., 81, 477, 479
  John, 415
  Kate, 214
  Kenneth, 414
  Leonard, 415
  Lieutenant General H. M., 146
  Lizzie Lee, 415
  Lloyd, 415
  Lucy I., 312
  Major General William R., 69
  Margaret, 366
  Margaret Hayes, 258
  Mary Jo, 414
  Mary Lynn, 82
  Mary Modesta, 16
  Maudie Blankenship, 415
  Mildred, 415
  Mr. and Mrs. Stan, 460
  Nora Henson, 81
  Norie Patton, 477
  Oscar, 81, 477
  Peral Gray, 360
  Sherry, 477
  Van, 81
  Virginia Ruth, 82
  Walter, 85
  Wayne, 196
  Weldon, 415
  William Claude, 81, 82
  William H., 460
  William Morgan, 81
Smokey Hill Air Base, 333, 334
Snow Hill, Texas Community Cemetery, 426
Snowden, Rev. Claude J., 511
Solomon, Odessa, 318, 417
  Ethyleene, 250
Solomon Islands, 128, 142, 143, 263, 264, 285, 292, 380, 384, 393 398, 453, 473; Gilbert and Marianas Islands, 400
Solomons, 144, 306, 363, 462
Somerville, Ann, 496
  George, 497
  Henry C., 496
  Henry Lee, 310, 496
  Jeanie, 497
  John, 496
  John William, 497
  Kathleen, 497
  Lucy, 496
  Margaret, 496
  Martha Grace, 443, 496
  Mary, 496, 497
  Pam, 497
  Paul Hart, 496
  Rae Jeanne, 496
  Richard, 497
  Rosa Lee Hart, 496
  Rosalie, 312
  Rose, 496
  Tim, 497
Sothern, Ann, 159
South African War, 86; Pacific, 270, 504, 505; Philippines, 361
Southard, Damon L., 487
Soward, Elbert B., 400
  James A., 400
  James B., 400
  Kate J. Emery, 400
  Larry R., 400
  Morris, 158
  Sam, 400
  Sgt. Joe P., 158
Spangler, George, 94
Sparks, Ann Marable (Priest), 117
Spivak, Charlie, 330
"Splivens Boys", 60
Spruance, Admiral Raymond, 146, 153
SS John D. Henley, 112, 493, 495, 496; Lurline, 462; Troops, 382
Stafford, Billy, 285
  Ollie, 289
Stalag 7A, 320; 9B Prison Camp, 162; Luft I at Barth, 362; VII, 491
Stalin, Joseph, 124, 329, 448
Stalls, Mr. W. D., 75
  Mrs. W. D., 75
Stalls, Sergeant Felix, 75, 77
Stanley, S. B., 19
  Col. W. A., 36
Stewart, 19
Stanton, Valeria, 227
Star Spangled Banner, 207
Stark, Admiral, 108
State Theatre, 338
Statue of Liberty, 51, 256, 324, 443
Steamship Lusitania, 42, 43
Stearman, Belinda, 288
  Florene Hare, 288
  Glenna, 288
  Horace, 288
  Larry E., 288
  Marie, 288
  Marvin Elliam, 288
  Ruby, 288
  Willie Jackson, 288
  Willie Lee, 288
Steele, Bertha, 399
  Charlie Benjamin, 399
  Charlie Sr., 399
  Edward, 399
  Edward A., 213
  Edward Arthur, 400
  Ethyl Florence Beaty, 399
  Felix, 399
  James Arthur, 399
  Joseph, 399
Stemmons, Lt. L. S., 336
Stephens, Alta Hastings, 377
  Christine, 384
  Dr. Willis Walter, 26
  Elbert, 377
  Gilbert, 377
  Nicholas and Mary, 26
  Rex, 377
  Sarah E., 31
  Scynthia C., 26
  W. E., 213
  W.E., (Dub), 377
  Will Ed, 377
  William, 377
  Willis Commodore (Dr. W. C. Stephens), 25
Stephenson, A. D., 292
  D'Ann, 293

Dessie A., 293
Imogene, 404
Mabel Bogard, 293
Mark, 293
Stephen Zachary, 293
Sterling, Caraway, 47
Rufus, 293
Steuben, Inez, 366
Steward, Frank, 47
Stewart, Brenda, 429
Charles, 429
Effie Marie Green, 429
James E., 429
James W. (Jim), 429
Jean, 429
Lloyd, 429
Ray, 429
Virgil A., 429
William W., 429
Stidham, Anna Lee Motes, 55
Dean, 55
Dr. Joseph, 55
Gaylord, 55
Gerald Dean, 281
Harold Earl, 281
Horace, 55
Joe, 55
Joe Willis, 281
Mackie Ford, 281
Marilyn Ann, 281
Pearl, 55
R. W. Jr., 55
R. W., Sr., 55, 281
Reese, 55
Stidham, Robert Sidney, 281
Stiles Drug Store, 158, 191
Stiles, Jimmie, 157
Nancy Jim, 457
Stillwell, Jess, 47
Stinson, Lola, 409
Stokes, Kathryn Louise, 480
Stone's Chapel Cemetery at Cherry, 460
Storey, Ben Bryant, 407
Ben Ray, 407
Bennie Bryant, 407
Bobby Dean, 407
Byron, 407
Clara Reeder, 355
Donna, 407
Ella K., 434
Joe, 407
Joe, Jr., 407
Mabel, 434
Margie, 316
Nancy, 407
Quillard, 407
Steve, 355
Wanda, 407

Wayne, 407
Stout, Henry, 5
Strain, Hazel, 369
Strait of Dover, 126
Strickland, Bessie Whiteman, 14, 16, 37, 157
Frances Ann, 15
James Allen (Tobe), 15, 324
James Allen, Jr., 15
Wayne Dickson, 15
Stringer, Helen, 387
Stroud, Alden M., 460
Arden, 460
Harlan J., 460
Hazel, 460
Herschel M., 460
James R., 213
Lora E. Williams, 459, 460
Mr and Mrs. Lonnie, 161
Sgt. J. R., 161
Stroupe, Frances Marie, 292
Submarine Service, 445
Suggs, Barbara Ann, 393
Henry Lee, 393
Henry Thomas (Boss), 393
Lora Lee Simmons, 393
Ruth, 332, 393
Virginia, 262, 393
Summers, Bill, 363
Carrie Mae King, 363
Harold, 363
Haskell H., 387
Ivy, 387
Jimmy R., 387
John Robert, 363
Mary Ruth, 84
Nancy, 363
Ruth, 387
Vestel Clem, 387
W. H., 387
Wilbert, 387
William, 387
Susan B. Anthony, 516
Sutton, Betty Gean, 429
Sweeney, Warren, 106
Swint, Mirty Mae, 51
Sword Beach, 130
T/3 Emil Aralle, 518
Tackett, Eddie, 399
Eula, 399
Ginger Dell, 399
J. D., 399
James Dennis, 399
Joseph William, 399
Larry S., 399
Mavis, 399
Michael L., 399
Minnie Aaron Stafford, 399

Pearl, 399
Relis W., 399
Rose Jeanette, 399
Winifred Paul, 399
Winnie, 399
Tanner, A. D., 411
Billie Joe, 411
Floyd, 411
Jo, 411
Margaret Hayes, 411
Margaret Lou, 411
Ruby, 411
T. H., 157
Thomas H., 411
Taps, 41
Tate, Augustus Columbus (A. C.), 26
Taylor, Bill, 55
Bobbie M., 158
Gen. Zacharia, 7
Teenor, A. H., 25
Templeton, Rev. S. W., 14
Terry, Berry, 49
Franklin William, 27
Texas & Pacific Railroad Depot, 18; Centennial Marker, 3; Declaration of Independence, 4; Legislature, 6; Revolution, 5; Salvage Committee, 182; Turkey Week, 60; War with Mexico, 11
Thames, Albert Roy, 48
Thedford, Jr., Marine Sgt. Vernon, 172
III Amphibious Corps, 146; Marine Amphibious Corps, 154
Third Army Cemetery in Hamm, Luxembourg, 498; Infantry Division, 211
3rd Armored Division, 395; East Tennessee Cavalry, 27; Marine Division, 147
13th Machine Gun Battalion, 53
30th Infantry Division, 229
32nd Cavalry from Texas, 31
36th Division, 57, 66, 69; , 312, 303
37th Alabama, 34, 35
Thirty-seventh Alabama, 31, 34
Thomas, Betty, 347
Donald, 161
Elmer, 108

Herman G., 213
Julian, 161
Lula, 160
S/Sgt. James Wallace, 160
W. I., 160
Wallace, 213
Walton, 47
Thompson, Berry (Chut), 293
  Charles M. (Mack), 484
  Charles M., 158, 485
  Dee, 158
  Dora, 333
  Effie, 66, 293
  Eli, 49
  Fynus, 68
  Gratie, 293
  Jessie D., 213
  Jessie Dee, 485
  John A. (Aldo), 484, 485
  John Wesley, 484
  Joyce, 484
  Mary Jane Ward Geer, 68
  Mendia, 49
  Mr. and Mrs. J. W., 485
  Muriel, 484
  Oma Cox, 484
  R. E., 485
  Richard E., 484
  Ruth Lawson, 484
  Wendell, 158
  William Henry, 68
Thornton, Kenneth, 162
  Mr. and Mrs. Joe, 162
  Paul, 162
  Pfc. Vernon A., 162
  Vernon A., 213
329th "Buckshot" Infantry Regiment, 489
344th Field Artillery, 84
345th Mg Bn, 63
359th Infantry, 53, 61, 76
Tiller, Bettye Joyce, 240
Timberlake, Brig. Gen. E. W., 339
Tinian, 147, 151, 172, 294, 299, 302, 437, 475
Tipping, Charles, 511
Titanic, 3
Tokyo, Rose, 390, 441
'Tom's Toasted Peanuts', 271
Toney, Judith E., 430
Totty, Billy Joe, 452
  Charles Oliver, 452
  Charles Ottie, 448, 452
  Curtis Herman, 449
  Darrell, 450
  Dessie Garrison, 448
  Don, 450

Donald, 450
E. T. (Tom), 450
Glenda Sue, 449
Harold, 450
Irvin Wayne, 450
J. D., 448
Joyce, 450
Judy Carol, 452
Larry Keith, 449
Lorene, 448
Nathan Ray, 450
Nella Jane, 448, 453
Russell Nolan, 449
Sharon Gail, 450
Winston Herman, 448
Townes, 96
  Dorothy Jo Hayes, 258
  Winifred, 258
Trilling, Harry, 103
Trimble, Hannah Tippin, 66
'Tropic Lightning Division', 239
Troxell, Doris A., 407
Truman, President Harry S., 136, 281, 282, 329, 476, 482, 525
Truscott, Major General Lucian K., 133, 134
Trussell, Claude Ray, 474
  Millard Felix, 475
  Noah, 474
  Ona Westfall, 474
  Royce W., 474
  Walter R., 475
Tucker Dovie, 378
  Lucina Lee, 409
  Noble, 523
  Tommy, 415
Tuggle Vivian L., 378
Tull, Boyce, 307
  Florence Wood, 307
  Jack, 307
  Jasper Bruce, 213, 307
  Joyce, 307
  Robert H., 307
Turk, J. W., 17
Turkey Knob, 300, 301
Turner, Admiral, 146
  Gloria, 485
  Vice Admiral, 153
Tutt, Doris Evelyn, 522
25th Infantry Division, 239
27th Regt. of TX Calvary, 25
28th (Bloody Bucket) Infantry Division, Vosenack, 512; USN Const. Battalion, 246
Tyer, Mrs. R. L., 173
Tyndell, Carol, 410

Cpl. Stanley G., 158
Fred L., 410
Harold L., 410
Russell, 410
Ruth Thames, 410
Stanley, 410
Terry, 410
Timothy, 410
Wayne, 410
U. S. Navy, 15; Coast Guard, 337, 355; Military Cemetery, No.1, St. Mere, Eglise, France, 318;
U.S.O., 116, 118, 461
U.S.S. Cascade, 304; Princeton, 162
Uncle Sam, 250, 458
Underwood, A. C. (Allen Clark) Sr., 63
  A. C. (Blue), 63, 220
  Billy, 63, 220, 221, 222
  Cecil (Aubrey), 63
  Frank, 63
  Kathy, 221
  Lt. Col. W. E., 458
  Mae (Grant), 63
  Marizanna Conway, 418
  Nancy, 221
  Nora Gail, 220
  Nora Johnson, 220
  Nora Mauldin, 220
  Oscar (Oss), 63
  Thomas Allen (Tommy), 63, 220, 221, 222
  Uta, 63
Union County, North Carolina, 31
United States, 88. 122, 128; Maritime Service, 371
Upchurch, Amelia Rives Bachman, 502
  Archie, 503
  James Archie, 502
  William Franklin Jr., 502
  William Franklin, Sr., 502
USS Bogue, 220; Rockbridge, 371; Amstead, 486; Appalachian, 379; Bainbridge, 248; Barnwell, 410; Black Fish, 528; Bottineau, 432, 433; Bougainville, 519; Cahaba, 431; Coehann, 416; Columbia, 307; Custer, 429; Doncaster, 475; Endurance, 427; Essex, 485; Fanshaw Bay, 520;

Feland, 465; General Waggle, 270; General William Mitchell, 437; Glen, 510; Gloucester, 337; Gregory (DD802), 495; Hamuel, A.D. 200, 510; Hancock, 424; Hoggatt Bay, 520; Hornet, 425; Hyman, 495; John D. Henley, 492; John Hopkins, 478; Klamath, 355; Lawrence, 453; Marka, 440; Matanikau, 220; Minneapolis, 254; Missouri, 283; Monticello, 441, 477; New Jersey, 398; New Mexico, 433, 490; Patrol Frigate Sandusky, 355; Rogers, 416; Rutland, 497; Samaritan, 485; Sea Cardinal, 249; Segundo 398, 445; Segundo, 446, 447, 450, 451; Shipley Bay, 520; Sierra, 414; Takanis Bay, 520; Tennessee, 425; Texas, 490; Tripoli, 520; Whale, 528; Wolverine, 519; Zeilin, 453
- Ussery, Barbara, 353
  - Bobbye Jean, 83, 353
  - Ira DeWitt, 83, 353
  - Ira Dickson (Dick), 83, 116, 353
  - Joseph Lane, 83
  - Marian, 353
  - Martha Idella Russell May, 83
  - Maud Ivy, 353
  - Paul Wade, 83
  - Reubon Jerome, 83
  - Richard, 353
- Utah Beach, 130, 131, 517
- V Marine Amphibious Corps, 146
- V-E Day, 307, 492, 499
- V-J Day, 492
- Vancill, Earl, 256
  - Frank, 256
  - Geraldine, 256
  - Horace, 256
  - Jack, 256
  - Louise, 256
  - Martha, 256
  - Mary Bennett, 256
  - Nellie, 256
- VanDeaver, Clovis T., 164

Mr. and Mrs. T. M., 164
Vandegrift, Major General Alexander A., 144
Vandenburg, Arthur, 107
Vandyke, L.D., 27
Varley, Bernard, 94
  Betty, 256
  Byron, 364
  Clarence, 364
  Earl Watson, 364
  Edward, 364
  Emma, 364
  Erma Dell, 256
  James, 364
  Johnnie, 364
  Kenneth, 256
  Malcom T., 364
  Mrs. Esther, 195
  Paula, 364
  Rebecca Mae Jones, 364
Vaughan, Adeliade Luella Holden, 266
  Alice Jane, 264
  Alice Verna, 266
  Avret Lynn, 437
  David, 438
  Deborah Louise, 437
  George Avret, 437
  Helen, 266
  Helen Nan, 266
  II, Vernon Vincent, 267
  James, 266
  James Baker, 267
  James W. (Buddy), 380
  Jennings H., 437
  Jennings Harley, 437
  Kathleen Luella, 266
  Kenneth Wayne, 437
  Lawrence M., 437
  Mamie Elanor, 437
  Mamie Elizabeth Hawkins, 437
  Mary, 266
  Mary Ann, 437
  Melissa, 438
  Michael Joseph, 267
  Pamela Rena Ilene, 267
  Patrick Henry, 266
  Sarah Jane, 438
  Shane, 268
  Steven Lawrence, 437
  Susan Ann, 437
  Vernon Vincent, 264
  Victoria, 267
  William, 266
VC War, 258
Verdun, 43, 44, 69, 76
Versailles peace conference, 81

Vickers, Arthur L., 307
  Arthur Lee, 305
  Arthur Lee, Jr., 307
  Billy Joe, 305
  Blanche Robison, 305
  Carolyn, 306
  Enie Morgan, 341
  Faye, 305
  H. W., 341
  Harold Franklin, 305
  Henry Wyatt, 341
  James Monroe, 305
  Jerrel D., 306
  Jerry Dale, 306
  Jim, 305
  Jimmy Glenn, 305
  John Ray, 306
  John Ray, Jr., 306
  Jonnie, 341
  Kenneth, 341
  Linda Sue, 306
  Louis Dean, 306
  Marie, 306
  Mark, 341
  Mowery Wayne, 341
  Pat, 341
  Paula, 307
  Thelma, 341
Vicksburg, 26, 31, 32, 35
'Victory Garden', 189
Volcano Islands, 399, 493
Von Kluge, Field Marshal Gunther, 132
W. W. Bullington, 158; Stephens & Son, 17
W.P.A., 514
Waco, Texas, 445
Waggoner, Martha Elizabeth, 27
Wagner, Janis K. Love, 518
Wainwright, Major General Jonathan Mayhew, 140, 141, 142, 224, 305
Wake, 137, 386, 476; Island, 115, 138, 148, 220, 476
Waldrep, Burnell, 325
  Joanne, 325
  Laurie, 325
  M. E. (Marvis Edmund), 325
  Mary McSwain, 325
  Neal, 325
  Norma, 325
  Richard E. (Dick), 325
  Rufus, 325
Walker, Alford, 522
  Annie Edwards, 307
  Bobby Joe, 522
  Charles Grant, 431

Charles Greenley, 431
Charles Thomas, 431
Dr. Mary, 203
Dwight Lee, 522
Elizabeth, 307
Essie May Grant, 431
Eva Kate, 522
George Calvin, 522
James Doyle, 522
James Wootten, 431
Janie Beth, 522
Larry Jim, 522
Lee Voyd, 522
Margaret, 72
McKinley, 47
Michael, 522
Nelson, 45
Robert, 307
Ruth, 522
Sophie M. Horne, 522
Thomas Robert, 307
Virginia Gail, 522
Wilburn, 522
Will, 307
Wallace, Audrey, 310
  Donnie Jane Watkins, 310
  Emmett, 310
  Ernest, 310
  Glenna, 63
  Harold, 95
  Ilie, 310
  Joshua Bartley, 63
  Lela, 310
  Louella F. Goodman, 63
  M. K., Jr., 310
  Mac Grady Rudolph (Ruda), 63
  Mary Florence, 310
  Michael Kelly, 310
  Nellie, 310
  Virdie, 310
  William S., 63
  Zelma, 63
Walter W. Schwenk, 485
Walters, Dorothy, 506
Walton, Pvt. Carroll, L., 160
War Between the States, 9
Ward, 114
  Arden, 341
  Betty Jean, 422
  Billy Sue, 422
  Charley, 360
  Chas., 47
  Corley, 360
  Darrell S., 341
  Edith, 360
  Elaine, 423
  Elgin, 341
  Elizabeth, 360

  Fay, 341
  Grady, S. (Bud), 423
  James Corley, 422
  James Grady, 423
  James Henry, 360, 422
  Jett, 360
  Jewel, 341
  John, 48
  Maud Lou Butts, 341
  Minnie, 360
  Mollie Lucille Stephens, 422
  Myrtle, 360
  Nola Etta Winders, 360
  Ramah, 356
  Robert Andrew, 341
  Robert, Jr., 341
  S., 37
  Sims Corley, 213, 422
  Virginia Ruth, 422
Warner, Dixie, 75
Warren, Ben, 48
  Lowery C., 213
Warrick, Betty, 169
Warthan, Gene, 411
Washington, George, 118, 201, 205
  Sonny, 196
Watkins, Marvin C., 213
Watson, Alice Watson, 356
  Dr. Gavin, 285
  Dr. Nowlin, 398
  Emma McClinton, 286
  Gavin Jr., 285
  James Harold, 356
  Jim, 356
  Margaret, 321
  Miss Ella, 195
  Remah, 360
Watts, Helen Louise, 437
Wayne, John, 194
Weatherly, Charles Edwin, 72
  Clyde, 72
Weaver, Alan, 289
  Billy T., 289
  Dave, 289
  David J., 289, 380
  Jessie, 289
  Keith, 289
  Kirk, 289
  Linda Carol, 289
  Lisa, 289
  Miss Elizabeth, 159
  Miss Ellis, 159
  Mrs. John, 159
  P. D., 515
  Sheriff Will, 15
Webb boy, 198
Webster, Mary Hattie, 465

Weemes, Barbara, 363, 449
  Bessie, 363
  Essie, 363
  George Washington, 363
  Henry Curtis, 363
  James David, 363
  John Bernard, 363
  John Henry, 363
  Joseph Rodger, 363
  Lucille, 363, 450
  Margaret Joan, 363
  Martha Ann Elizabeth Williams, 363
  Ora, 363
  Richard Ray, 363
Welch, Billie Kay, 461
  Billy Jo Kenneth (Chip), 461
  Carolyn Joy, 461
  Clyde (Bud), 461
  Glenn Odell, 460
  Jim Robert, 461
  Kimberly Faye, 461
  Leola Faye Stroud, 461
  Lola Lorene, 461
  Michael Glenn, 461
  Mr. and Mrs. J. W., 305
  Orvil, 305
  Susan Ann, 461
Wells, George, 348
  Navy Secretary Gideon, 202
Wendel, 275
Wendover Field, Utah, 275
Weser River, 340
West Bowie Cemetery in Bowie County, Texas, 523
West, Forrest, 158
  Forrest R., 213
  Jerry, 194
  Peyton, 47, 118
West Point, 205, 442
Westbrook, 94
  Berta Mae, 369
  Boyd, 376
  Clyde W., 369
  Don, 369
  Donald, 376
  Earl H., 376
  Elbert, 376
  Esker, 376
  Gladys, 369
  Hesta Lee, 369
  Inez, 367, 368
  James R. (Robert), 369
  James Robert (Jimmy), 369
  Johnny, 369
  Kathy, 369

Marcia, 369
Marleah, 369
Maurice G., 369
Ollie Campbell, 369
Sam, 369
Sam H., 376
Westfall, Betty Meredith, 474
　Charley M., 474
　Lela, 472
　Luther, 472
　Olen Felix (Pat), 94, 515, 472
　Ona, 472
　Will, 472
　Willie Ann Moore, 472
Wharton, Sgt. Charles, 158
Wheeler, Burton, 107
White, Bertie Rowden, 294
　Billy G. (Bill), 55, 56, 294
　John A., 45
　John C., 342
　Luther, 55, 161, 294
　Mr. and Mrs. Rufus, 165
　Mrs. Luther, 161
　Pfc. Billy Gene, 161
　R. M., 444
　Ronnie, 294
　Sgt. Eugene M., 165
　Shirley, 56, 294
Whiteman, Bessie Maye, 15
　C. L., 407
　Charles Davis (Pete), 15
　Dora Francis McGill, 345
　Forest Dickson (Dick), 15
　George, 407
　Gerthie Nance, 407
　Hub (Herbert Loman), 345
　James Robert (Butch), 407
　Jim, 345
　Johnny, 15
　Justus, 37
　Kate, 345
　Mackey Donnelly (Joe), 15
　Mary LaNell ("Red"), 342, 345
　Otic, 15
　Raymond (Bud) and Emmie Rebecca Allen, 14
　Raymond Howard, 15
　Robert Lane, 407
　Sis, 345
　Squire Loman (Babe), 345
　William Allen (Doc), 15
　Winfred, 345
Whitener, Bill Wayne, 402
　Debra L., 402
　Ella May Pratt, 402
　Elma, 402
　Grady, 402
　Janice M., 402
　Jeanetta, 402, 403
　Kathie, 402
　Marla, 402
　Marsha A., 402
　Marshall Thomas, 402
　Martlin M., 402
　Regina T., 402
　Sandra, 402
　Stanley T., 402
Whitener-Valez, Marsha A, 402
Whitfield's 1st TX Legion, 5, 9, 25
Whitley, Bonnie, 285
　Georgia Helen, 440
Whitten, Gladys, 399
Whittle, Lucille, 390
Wilburn, Chesley, 499
　Dewey, 498
　Joe E., 385
　Lavenia, 499
　Roy, 499
Wilcox, Margaret (Marty) Davis, 291
'Wild Bill Elliot', 191
Wilhite, Carolyn Ruth, 354
Wilkinson, Alli Pearl, 332
　Charles W., 332
　Charley, 332
　Dan Mabry, 332
　Dora, 332
　Mamie Pearla Wright, 332
　Margaree, 332
　Marvin Lynn, 332
　Stanley, 332
　Thomas Paul, 332
Williams, Annie L. Faucett, 480
　Bruce Evan, 480
　Carrie Frances, 303
　Casey, 480, 481
　Charlie, 357
　Christopher, 29
　David Arnold, 480
　David M., 213, 481
　Dorthea Moore Nellans, 480
　Doug, 303
　Edna Earl, 480
　Elizabeth Rebecca Evans, 29, 30
　Ernest Jerome, 480
　Ernest Junior, 480
　Gippie Bruton, 303
　I. N., Sr., 30
　John, 202
　John E., 30
　John M., 481
　Karen, 481
　Kevin, 481
　Lou Ellen, 480
　Lucille, 303
　Mamie, 480, 481
　Nathan Avant Evans, 31
　Rebecca Ann, 480
　Robert, 202
　Russell A., 480
　St. Elmo, 480
　Thelma Kate, 480
　Tom B. (Bruton), 303
　Vashti Elain, 480
　Will, 303
Wilson, Bonnie Ragsdill, 405
　Carmen, 405, 407
　Christine, 321
　Dan, 47
　Dorotha, 405
　Dr. S. W., 11
　J. C., 406
　James C., 405
　John N., 405
　Leopal, 405
　Mrs. Woodrow, 108
　President Woodrow, 42, 57, 81
　Raymond 405
　Ruby, 72
　Sarah Nell, 405
　Thomas Woodrow, 303
　Vera, 405
Winberg, Harold, 526
Winninger, Richard, 186
"Winter Line", 129
Winters, Carole, 481
　Cecil, 481
　Claude, 481
　Clyde O., 481
　David, 481
　Edward, 481
　Inez, 481
　Jim Enoch, 481
　Merry, 481
　Roxie Bybee, 481
　Wallace, 481
Wisconsin, 245, 330
Wisinger, Joyce Abernathy, 257
Withers, Col. William P., 169
Witmer, Ernest, Sr., 224
　Max, 159, 234
　Margaret, 394
　Myrtle, 227
Wolf, Barbara Cunningham, 338
　Cab Lee, 338
　Cab Newman, 65, 197, 338

Carroll Manly, 338
Dana Jo, 338
Elvis Newman, 65
Furman Lee, 65, 117, 159, 338
Laurie Ellen, 338
Lula Virginia Stone, 65
Wood, Carl, 240
  Col, 335
  Douglas, 240
  Elsie, 240
  Emma Grant, 240
  Frances, 240
  Gus, 47
  Lawrence, 157, 240
  Paul, 240
  Ruth, 515
Woods, Gillie Lee, 492
Woodson, Ora Lee, 356
Woolen, Major Tom G., 76
Wooley, Bonnie Dixie Gray, 361
  Francis Marion, 361
  Frank Dixon, 361
  James Harold, 361
  Mamie Estelle, 361
  Mildred Alice, 372
  Robert Carey, 361
  William Marion, 361

Wootten, Dr. Horace Greenley, 430
  H. G., Jr., 430
  Ruka Bishop, 430
  Winnie Mattie, 430, 431
World War I, v, 14, 42, 45, 49, 51, 53, 55, 56, 57, 60, 61, 63, 65, 66, 70, 75, 80, 122, 125, 208, 294, 472
World War II, v, vi, 15, 72, 77, 89, 96, 472
Wortham, Alton, 331
WPA (Works Project Administration), 101, 177
Wren, Allie Maud Gaines, 357
  Mack, 357
  Richard Dean (Dick), 357
  Thomas, 357
Wright, Ann, 289
  Betty Ruth, 500
  Bettye, 240
  Billy Dale (Frog), 240
  Charles Ernest, 500
  Charles Thomas, 500
  Dimple, 239
  Dr. J. L., 159, 198, 354
  George W., 5

  Henry, 363
  J. D., 213, 363
  J. W., 363
  James Robert, 239
  Jim, 239
  Jim Bob, 240
  Lee, 363
  Lillian, 500
  Mary (Lizzie) Grimes, 363
  Minnie Pearl Holding, 500
  Pete, 158
  Ruby, 239
  Sallie Johnson, 239
  Seena, 363
  Steve, 47
  Wilmer Lee, 364
Wynn, Lawana, 382
Yamamoto, Admiral Isoroku, 143
Yancey, Leola, 53
Yeley, Lewis, 162
Yellow Cab Company, 180
Yelvington, Merle, 518
  Warren, 518
Young, Emmett, 17
  Raymond, 498
Young's Regiment, 36
Zigzag Pass, 488